WITH NATIONWIDE MEMBER SUPPORT F
SIONALS, PARENTS, AND CHILD DEVELOPMEN
FIRST! HA   Y'S MOST
HIGHLY   IS WHAT
THE EX

"We   t work
you h

"A ni   when
they

"The   ting an
effect

                                       earch,

"Thar   rce of
good,   can sit
and v   ting to
shoot

"I am   worthwhile   ive to
the d   r."

The New York Times

COALITION
FOR QUALITY
CHILDREN'S
MEDIA

APPROVED BY
KIDS FIRST!®

GUIDE TO

The Best Children's Videos

Foreword by LeVar Burton
Preface by Linda Ellerbee

POCKET BOOKS
New York   London   Toronto   Sydney   Singapore

An *Original* Publication of POCKET BOOKS

 POCKET BOOKS, a division of Simon & Schuster Inc.
1230 Avenue of the Americas, New York, NY 10020

Commentaries and film listings copyright © 1999 by The New York Times Video and CD-ROM entries copyright © 1999 by Coalition for Quality Children's Media

ISBN: 0-671-03669-6

First Pocket Books trade paperback printing November 1999

10   9   8   7   6   5   4   3   2   1

POCKET and colophon are registered trademarks of Simon & Schuster Inc.

Cover design and photo by Anna Dorfman

Printed in the U.S.A.

Contents

Part III
Family Films for Teenagers

Foreword

by LeVar Burton

I am a child of the television age, and for the record, let me say: I love TV. I love to watch television, and for the past twenty years of my life I have loved making television as well. My affection for TV extends well beyond my appreciation of it as an art form. I truly believe that in extending it to every corner of our country we have created in television the most powerful tool ever imagined for promoting growth and change in our society.

Television offers us a unique opportunity to entertain ourselves, to travel vicariously, to inform ourselves about what's happening "out there" and to meet amazing folks from all parts of the globe. Most importantly, though, I think of the opportunity that television offers to lift ourselves up and light the way for each other. Like so many others, I am acutely aware that much of what currently goes out over the airways in the form of children's programming does little in the way of enlightenment. Because of the enormous influence this medium wields in our lives, it is critical that we remain vigilant about the kinds of television we allow our children to consume. If not us, who?

One of the most common fantasies parents have is finding the quintessential manual for raising children. This is not that book by any means, nor does it pretend to be. But when it comes to harnessing the power television has over our children, this is a remarkable tool for every family that wants the best for its kids. I recommend this book because the programs featured here are inspiring, interesting and fun. You'll find stories that motivate kids, encourage friendship and promote a strong sense of self—stories that explore real kid problems and offer real kid solutions, and stories that reinforce the value of community in our lives.

From my experience working in the entertainment industry, I've found that there *are* people who care about making quality programming for children. This guide may not be the fantasy manual that we're all looking for, but it will help you find wonderful programs for your children that might have otherwise gone undiscovered. Use it . . . and enjoy.

LeVar Burton is the host and executive producer of Reading Rainbow. He is an actor, director, and children's advocate.

Preface

by Linda Ellerbee

Children are constant reminders of what makes us inherently human. They begin life as outsiders, and most of what they learn is drawn from their experiences with the people, places and events in the world around them. What causes children to interact with others in certain ways? How do different situations influence their attitudes and viewpoints? Their experiences and the quality of the interaction will, to a large degree, determine who they become as adults.

As adults and parents, we are constantly making choices about our children's lives The most difficult aspect of this process is to discern what choices have the best impact. There are almost as many opinions about child-rearing as there are child development specialists. But the best expert for any child is his or her own, well-informed parent. Here is a book that makes parents better informed about children's media. It addresses parents' concerns while keeping in mind the stake of children. The information contained here comes not just from experts, but from an array of adults and kids of diverse backgrounds. We know that we can serve children best when their learning experiences are engaging, challenging, and offer inspiration and hope.

Parents, it's our turn. We all complain about what's on TV. Now we can make it more useful by selecting the best and tuning out the rest!

Linda Ellerbee is executive producer and host of Nick News.

A Note to the Reader

At first glance, the suggestion that *The Times* create an all-inclusive guide to help parents choose good videos for their children seemed useful but daunting, and not quite feasible. Though the newspaper reviews and reports extensively on television as a leading industry in the thriving business of popular culture, the staff is not organized to systematically watch and evaluate thousands of videos, nor do we have a rating system that awards stars to movies, plays, or television programs.

Nevertheless, the idea for a regularly updated *Times*-sponsored guide to children's videos that would be complete, entertaining, and enlightening remained a tempting project. For one thing, no such book existed in the marketplace, as far as we could tell. Also, the idea seemed appropriate to *The Times* as an institution that consistently seeks to do well by doing good. The collaboration with the Coalition for Quality Children's Media was the welcome solution. KIDS FIRST! is independent, professional and non-profit, and for almost a decade has led the way in monitoring and evaluating the best in kids' videos. This joint effort relies on the Coalition's experts, including kids themselves, to compile and comment on the videos judged good enough for inclusion in these pages, along with special reports by four *Times* writers. A list of 500 feature films that the entire family can enjoy was selected by Peter Nichols, who writes the Home Video column for the paper.

The yearlong partnership in preparing this book has been thoroughly congenial and professional. At the same time, our contributions are independently our own. Although neither party sought nor gave explicit cross-endorsement to the contents, we preserved the mutual respect with which we undertook the book. We hope you agree that the result is worthwhile and interesting.

Mitchel Levitas
Editorial Director, The New York Times
Book Development

Introduction

A reporter recently asked me, "Is it the media industry's responsibility to deliver programming for children that is not only devoid of violence but that perpetuates positive values and role models?" I suggested that it has a responsibility to not simply make a profit, but to behave in a socially responsible fashion by promoting programs with pro-social values. I've listened to many media executives rationalize their highly violent children's programming by exclaiming, "We're only giving people what they want!" However, it's not popularity that supports media violence but global marketing strategies. Most people prefer to watch TV programs without violence. The time to behave responsibly is now, not some time in the distant future. In the words of the Reverend Martin Luther King, "We must use time creatively . . . and forever realize that the time is always ripe to do right."

What's In This Book?

This book is for people who are seeking out the good, the better, and the best media for their children. Parents who have made a conscious decision to be more selective about what their children watch are then faced with the predicament of trying to locate the good stuff. This book is the comprehensive guide they need, reviewing all the best children's videotapes and CD-ROMs available, with chapter introductions by leading media and child development specialists.

What makes this project unique is the contribution of KIDS FIRST! — an initiative of the Coalition for Quality Children's Media (CQCM). CQCM is a national not-for-profit organization that evaluates and rates children's media, using a volunteer jury of over 300 adult professionals (child development specialists, child media specialists, librarians, and teachers) and more than three thousand kids of diverse cultural, ethnic, socioeconomic, and geographic backgrounds. Our jury system, compiled with well-defined criteria and evaluation tools, provides both a quantitative and qualitative score that gives parents extensive information, enabling them to make informed program choices.

This is not broccoli TV. Not only is every title adult-approved but it's also kid-tested! At the bare minimum, to be endorsed every title must meet or exceed our baseline criteria:

- no gratuitous violence or sexual behavior
- no physical or verbal abuse
- no racial, gender, cultural, or religious bias
- no condescension toward children
- no unsafe behavior

Beyond that, for a program to be endorsed, kids must tell us that they like the program, would watch it again, or would share it with a friend.

How to Use This Book

Not all children's programs are appropriate for all children. Because the needs of a two-year-old are quite different from those of a twelve-year-old, or even a six- or seven-year-old, we have taken great care to screen the programs with different groups of children to determine the most appropriate age for each title. Accordingly, the chapters are designated for specific age groups, i.e., Infant/Toddler, Preschool, Early Elementary, etc. Each chapter is then subdivided into appropriate subject categories, including Educational/Instructional, Family, Foreign Language, etc. Because some titles overlap age groups, they will be listed with a full review only once, in the chapter designated for the youngest age, and then cross-referenced in the chapter designated for the older age.

Each review includes a brief summary of the program, the producer or supplier's name, the manufacturer's suggested retail price, the best age fit (as tested with our focus groups) and feedback from both adult evaluators and child jurors that explain, among other things, why kids enjoyed it. Each title is rated with one, two, or three stars. The three stars constitute our "All-Star" rating: these titles have received the highest ratings by both adult and child jurors. They are outstanding and appeal to a broad audience. Two stars indicate good, but not exceptional quality. One star also indicates good quality but the video or CD-ROM may appeal only to a special audience. The jurors' summary supports the rationale for each rating. Appendices are also included for easy reference to special interest titles, i.e., videos targeted especially for girls or boys, multicultural titles, titles that offer positive means of conflict resolution, etc.

Where to Find These Titles

Before setting you loose to read this book, here are a few final suggestions to help you. Most titles in this book that come from mainstream companies, including MGM, Sony, Twentieth Century Fox, Warner, Universal, and Disney, will be available wherever videos are sold or rented. Titles from independent producers will be more difficult to find; specialty stores, both retail and online, will be your best bet. KIDS FIRST! works closely with Reel.com, which has agreed to make as many titles available on its Web site as possible *(www.reel.com)*. I also recommend that you check the Coalition's Web site *(www.cqcm.org)* which, though it doesn't sell the titles, offers links to many other sites that do. Another good reason to visit our Web site is to get new endorsements that are added once or twice a month.

Happy hunting! And remember how important this is. It's not just about children, media, and marketing. It's about serving our children's future.

Ranny Levy
President
KIDS FIRST!/Coalition for Quality Children's Media

Acknowledgments

Many people have contributed to the making of this book: from our wonderfully dedicated staff to the producers of the programs, to our editors at *The New York Times* and Pocket Books. The most important contributions come from the KIDS FIRST! jury, the 3300 adults and children from all over the United States who volunteer their itme and expertise. I'd like to personally acknowledge my children. Samsunshine and Alanna Nevada Levy, who have truly made KIDS FIRST! a vital part of my life and who both have contributed untold hours to this book. Victoria Jewett, Maggie Konzen, Jane Morelli Johnson, Margie Sarrao, and Stephanie Wilson are all CQCM staffers who have worked tirelessly as juror coordinators and editors; without them this book would not exist. The Coalition for Quality Children's Media's National Board members and trustees who provide the guidance and support to keep this organization going, day in and day out, are without a doubt some of the most important contributors, especially Bill Weinrod, Gay Dillingham, Dr. Irving Lazar, Katie Peters, Shannon Gilligan, George Cowan, Suzy Pines, and our trustees. Last, it has been an extreme pleasure to work closely with Mike Levitas at *The New York Times*. Mike, who participated far beyond what we expected from an editor, is now without a doubt the single best-informed editor in the world on the subject of children's media.

—*Ranny Levy*

PART I

Reports From the Field

1

TV for Girls

Jan Benzel

My daughter Julia quickly discovered a great advantage of learning to read: it allowed her to decipher the television schedule.

Let me stop right here and say for the record that I began parenthood as one of those sanctimonious mothers whose personal goal it was to lower the national TV-watching average among children—now something like three hours a day—by turning in a paltry few hours a week for our family. We'd finger-paint! Bake! Read the classics! Go camping!

I soon realized there were big problems with that approach. First, as the parent who walked into a room and turned the TV off, I was very unpopular.

Second, TV—and video—have some practical applications from a parent's point of view: Appeasing children left under protest with a new babysitter. Distracting children while parents gobble down dinner. Allowing an exhausted parent to take a Saturday afternoon nap (for this, *Mary Poppins*, at 139 spellbinding minutes, is recommended). And sometimes kids, like adults, just need to escape, cool out, calm down, be entertained.

Then there's the peer-pressure argument. Other kids watch TV. I still remember my own childhood indignity of not knowing the ins and outs of *Batman* when other third-graders were dissecting the previous night's episode over their peanut-butter-and-jelly sandwiches. Did I want my daughters to grow up feeling geeky?

Lastly, I didn't enjoy the role of hypocrite. I like TV myself. *Batman* notwithstanding, I watched television, as much as my parents would

JAN BENZEL, Former television editor at *The Times*, is deputy editor of the paper's Travel section.

allow, and I turned out okay. It's a huge force in American culture. To forbid TV watching in a household is something like ignoring a two-ton elephant sitting in the middle of your living room. Better to approach it with intelligence and care. The forbidden becomes all the more desirable. Fortunately, there's more good programming than ever for children, and it can open up all sorts of windows on the world.

There's public television's rich lineup, from *Sesame Street* through *Bill Nye the Science Guy*; Nickelodeon's Nick Jr.; Steven Spielberg's *Tiny Toon Adventures,* new animation in the classic mode set to vintage rock and roll or symphonic music, with layers of humor to reward different ages; the Disney Channel (despite its endless self-promotions); the nature shows on the Discovery Channel. And once in a while, the networks offer an appealing show, although they've seen their Saturday morning stronghold slip away as Fox, WB, and the cable channels gather steam.

But I still feel some consternation, even when we've narrowed the choice of programs to the best among the flowering proliferation of shows.

When Julia, who is six years old, reads the TV listings, excitedly perusing the possibilities for her precious hour of screen time (not on school nights, reminds her Sanctimonious Mom), these are the names she sees: *Winnie the Pooh, Arthur, Rocko's Modern Life, Doug, Charlie Brown, Barney* (anathema to anyone over three), and *Wishbone.* Not so different from what I saw when I devoured *TV Guide,* that bible to the first generation of TV kids: *Popeye, Rocky and Bullwinkle, Daffy Duck, Mickey Mouse, Casper the Friendly Ghost, Dennis the Menace,* and *Leave it to Beaver.* Then and now, it's a boys' club.

Yes, an occasional female character appears on some of these programs, but almost always she's Olive Oyl to Popeye, Lucy to Charlie Brown. Females get second billing if they have a part at all. What's most distressing to me is how early the models emerge. Even in television for the youngest children, from the most enlightened programmers, females have yet to gain a substantial foothold. The creators of *Sesame Street,* that bastion of diversity, scratched their heads long and hard over creating a female Muppet. Their attempts, including Prairie Dawn, have been feeble at best and never captured the writers' and viewers' imagination the way Elmo, Cookie Monster, Ernie, and Bert have. Why is it that in thirty years, only one girl Muppet, Miss Piggy, made it? At least in the 1950's we had Lassie.

Julia and her sister, Rebecca, who is eight, soak up the subtleties and puzzle over what girls are "supposed" to do when they grow up. Boys absorb the messages too: Girls aren't important, and they don't get to do the fun stuff. Who would you rather be, Jasmine or Aladdin?

In the throes of establishing their elementary school identities, my girls and their friends favor the pithy slogan "Girls rule, boys drool." But there's cognitive dissonance. Their parents and teachers tell them they can do anything they put their minds to. It's true that more of their mothers have careers these days, but what they see still doesn't match what we tell them. We have Madeleine Albright and Janet Reno, but Bill Clinton is in charge. Tom Cruise makes upwards of $20 million a picture; female leads command only a quarter of that. There's a professional women's basketball league, but try to find news of the players on the sports pages. Women's soccer has only just burst upon the scene. The world has changed, but not that much, little girls. Minorities are even less visible than females. It's clear where the power lies.

The primary role of pop culture is not, of course, to be an agent of change. It's a mirror, driven by the demands of its viewers. The reason most often cited for the male dominance on children's television is marketing related: conventional wisdom holds that girls will watch shows about boys, but boys will not watch programs about girls. Throw in a token pink Power Ranger, and girls will tune in. Mark Johnson, who produced the independent film *A Little Princess,* based on the children's novel by Frances Hodgson Burnett, is still chagrined that although the beautiful, literate movie received critical accolades, it flopped at the box office. "Boys just couldn't bring themselves to say to their friends on the playground: 'Hey, I saw this great movie, *A Little Princess,*'" he said.

By the time boys get to elementary school, the barrier between the sexes has already been established and is only fortified by the images delivered by the culture. The relentless barrage of commercials, on the networks and most cable channels alike, is the most pointed source of gender distinction: girls are fed pink everything, from baby dolls to nail polish to Barbie CD-ROMs; boys get action figures, which mostly seem to come in putrid shades of green. Neither stereotype holds much appeal.

But there are some challenges to the status quo. The expansion of the television universe—along with the increasing number of women (and fathers of daughters) among television's creative ranks—has altered the balance a bit in the last five years. Among the legions of superheroes and boy-centric series, a few females have achieved star billing, especially at off times and in corners of TV that don't depend so much on mass audiences. Many are based on books or otherwise established creations, and there are at least one or two for each age range. Nickelodeon has had hits with *Clarissa Explains It All* and *The Secret World of Alex Mack,* both live-action series, now in reruns, that appeal to preteen-agers. The main character in the animated *Wild Thornberrys* is Eliza, the level-headed daughter of a nature-show host, who travels the world with her family in a van. Girls can have superpowers too: the fourteen-year-old Alex uses hers to help her navigate the shoals of adolescence. For the preschool set, there's *Allegra's Window,* which addresses the big hurdles of early childhood like surviving the chicken pox, and the new *Maisy,* an animated series for preschoolers, about the capers of a high-spirited mouse and her friends. HBO has *Little Lulu, Pippi Longstocking,* and two new series: *Dear America,* based on Scholastic books that convey history through the eyes of fictional girls and *Happily Ever After,* fairy tales retold with a feminist twist. Disney offers *The Little Mermaid, Madeline, Katie and Orbie,* and *The Baby-Sitters Club.*

Disney, the granddaddy of them all when it comes to entertaining children and now the behemoth of the huge and lucrative children's video market, has had a franchise on female characters, about which much controversy has raged. Movies like *Snow White* and *Sleeping Beauty* have drawn Bronx cheers from revisionists and feminists for their female-in-distress-awaiting-their-someday-prince themes. Although a prince of some description is still always in the wings, some of Disney's more recent movies, including *Beauty and the Beast, Pocahontas,* and *Mulan* have bona fide heroines who see far more action than their predecessors. Ariel, the Little Mermaid, is among them and continues her underwater adventures in the animated series.

"Girls like adventures as much as boys," Madeline tells Lord Cucuface in *The New Adventures of Madeline.* Based on the characters from Ludwig Bemelman's books written in the 1930s, the story has been updated. "Children live in a world they don't control, and power is a compelling concept," said Robby London, an executive at DIC Entertainment, which produced the series. "It always has been for boys, and now power is starting to appeal to girls, too." Magical powers are a big draw: Rebecca's must viewing now includes *Sabrina, the Teenage Witch* on ABC (*Two of a Kind,* starring Ashley and Mary Kate, the ever-popular Olson twins, is a close second). Sabrina lives with her mother, aunt, and a wisecracking black cat, and spends her time getting in and out of hot water casting spells on her classmates.

Most heartening to me are the shows where boys and girls mix it up, like HBO's *Little Lulu,* based on Marjorie Buell's 1930s comic strip. "Girls can do everything boys can," Lulu says. "Actually, girls can do everything better than boys. Climb trees, catch fish, throw snowballs. Girls can even eat more grilled cheese sandwiches than boys if they feel like it. Girls are so much better than boys in every way. They just don't go round bragging about it." Ronald Weinberg, executive producer of the series, warmed to Lulu because, he said, she's a free-thinking young woman with a clear idea of where she's going and how she's going to get there. "She's a strong little girl you would like a lot," he said, but added that the series, like the comic strip, would have "as much boy stuff as girl stuff." "Lulu is the star the way Murphy Brown or Lucy were the stars, but she's part of a gang of kids," he added.

Karen Jaffe, the executive director of Kidsnet, a clearinghouse for information about children's television and radio, said children's shows with elements of action, power, or cleverness appeal to both sexes. "Kids like to watch other kids who stay one step ahead of the grown-ups," she said. "If a character is cool, it doesn't seem to matter whether it's a boy or a girl."

Shows like *Arthur, Rugrats,* and *Doug* are also in that mold, and the girl characters—Arthur's friend Francine and little sister D.W., and Doug's friend Patti Mayonnaise—are often brainy, plucky types. More important, both boys and girls are also pains in the neck, conceited, anxious, athletic, thoughtful, and everything in between. In the adult-role-model department, there is Ms. Frizzle, the wacky science teacher who takes her class on unusual field trips in *The Magic School Bus* on public television, videos, and CD-ROMs. Lily Tomlin is the voice of Ms. Frizzle, trilling Socratic questions to her charges as they spin in their rattletrap school bus through the solar system, the human body, or anyplace else where they might learn something.

With the potential for more and more channels has come the inevitable news of plans for gender-segregated programming. Fox, who brought the world Mighty Morphin Power Rangers, will splinter its children's programming into a Girlz Channel and a Boyz Channel. Heads are wagging at the prospect of the gender stereotyping, in both programming and commercials, which will probably ensue, at least on those two channels.

I'm not too alarmed. Television these days involves choice, and in children's programming, more choice is a good thing, for girls and boys. I sat and watched my classmates play Little League games. My daughters play soccer, basketball, and softball in leagues of their own. So they'll have a channel of their own. It's far better than being invisible.

2

Congress and TV: Living With the Law

Lawrie Mifflin

When producers claimed, with straight faces, that a cartoon series like *The Jetsons* was educational because it taught about life in the twenty-first century, something had to be done.

The 1990 federal law requiring broadcast TV stations to offer more educational programming for children had no teeth, and the response to it had been a minimal, if not mocking, adherence. So in August 1996, overruling objections about the danger of quotas, the Federal Communications Commission strengthened the law with a new regulation: Stations must provide at least three hours a week of programs with significant educational content.

Since then, first-rate television shows for children have sprouted all over the dial—but not necessarily where Congress intended. More often than not, the best children's programs are on cable networks, which are not subject to the federal educational rule, or on public television, which has been providing them anyway, rule or no rule. The commercial broadcast networks, which are regulated because they get their free licenses from the federal government in exchange for meeting some public-interest obligations, have mostly struggled to keep up—particularly with PBS and the children's cable network, Nickelodeon. Only recently, on February 2, 1999, Nickelodeon, in partnership with Children's Television Workshop, created an all-educational channel called Noggin, where quality shows like

LAWRIE MIFFLIN covers television news for *The Times*.

8

Ghostwriter, originally created for PBS, use reading and writing lessons in an entertaining, detective-story format. Nickelodeon itself, now available in about seventy-four million of the nation's nearly 100 million homes, has added two British shows based on the lauded children's books *Maisey* and *Kipper*. And the Disney Channel, also on cable, has a preschool time block with shows emphasizing creative play, including *Bear in the Big Blue House*, *PB&J Otter*, and *Rolie Polie Olie*.

Indeed, most of the high-quality educational fare, whether it teaches social lessons or reading, writing, and 'rithmetic, is for preschool and early-elementary-school children, most of whom have not yet learned to equate learning with eating spinach. *Teletubbies,* on PBS, speaks in "bye-byes" and "uh-ohs" to children too young to talk. *Blue's Clues,* a popular show for preschoolers on Nickelodeon, presents the same installment Monday through Friday for a week because repetition is an important tool for early learners. *Sesame Street, Mister Rogers' Neighborhood, Arthur,* and *Wishbone* on PBS still offer quality episodes each weekday, as does the network's newer series *Noddy,* about a toys-and-notions shop where children explore imaginative worlds and toys come to life when the adults aren't looking. PBS has also started a new animal education series for younger children called *Zoboomafoo,* produced and hosted by the Kratt Brothers, whose original animal-adventure show, *Kratts' Creatures,* appeals to older children.

While PBS and Nickelodeon have been upgrading their children's line-ups, some commercial broadcast stations have dutifully produced programs that were educational but so dull or patronizing that no self-respecting child would voluntarily watch them. Others have grudgingly met the letter of the federal regulation, but hardly its spirit. The Fox network, for example, gives its affiliated stations five half-hours a week of reruns of *The Magic School Bus,* a much-praised PBS show, but schedules them in the early morning or early afternoon on weekdays, leaving the competitive Saturday-morning hours—traditionally the most lucrative in children's television—free for action-adventure attractions like *Spider-Man, Godzilla,* or the latest version of the karate-kicking *Power Rangers*. Likewise, the WB network shunts its history-based animated show, *Warner Bros. Hysteria,* into early-morning time slots on weekdays, leaving most of Saturday morning to more popular show like *Pokémon* and *Batman Beyond*.

Only ABC, most analysts and critics agree, has responded successfully to the three-hour rule for broadcasters, perhaps not coincidentally because its corporate parent is the Walt Disney Company, with its enormous financial stake in family entertainment. ABC's *One Saturday Morning* aims at being a kind of cool video hangout for children from two to eleven. Both a concept and an address, the programming block centers around a computer-animated building inhabited by zany characters who invite children inside for the day's fun. The two-hour period includes three half-hour shows: *Recess, Pepper Ann,* and *Doug* (born on Nickelodeon but moved to ABC when Disney bought its creator's company). The block's remaining half-hour is filled with brief segments, called interstitials, that are also educational, like *Schoolhouse Rock* or *How Things Work.*

"ABC went out on a limb and tried a new approach to packaging educational programming for kids with *One Saturday Morning,* and it's a rip-roaring success," said Susan Ness, the lone FCC commissioner left from the group that passed the 1996 regulation. "They've packaged it in a way that kids will sit through the whole two-hour block, and they're getting tremendous ratings. We hoped someone could show that programming could be educational and entertaining at the same time, and this is."

ABC has two other half-hour educational programs: *Squigglevision,* formerly called *Science Court,* features the voice of the comedian Paula Poundstone as the judge who presides over humorous "cases" involving scientific judgments or discoveries. The other is *101 Dalmatians,* with story lines generated by the producers of *Doug* that place the Disney-animated puppies in social-learning situations.

How does a movie-based cartoon manage to count as educational? "Some criticize these kind of shows, saying they only deal with emotional problems or social issues and there isn't enough classroom-type programming, but we didn't require it be classroom-type programming," said Commissioner Ness. "Children can benefit tremendously from working through social issues with characters on shows they like."

Indeed, NBC meets the federal requirement by weaving lessons about self-esteem, peer pressure, alcohol abuse, and the like into high-school soap operas like *Hang Time* or *Saved by the Bell,* specifically addressing young teens.

CBS has tried two radically different approaches. In the fall of 1997, the first season the three-hour rule was in effect, the network tried to offer something different from the cartoon-based schedules of its rivals, with *Sports Illustrated for Kids* and a children's version of *Wheel of Fortune.* CBS stations lost half their children's audience that year, partly because the network has the oldest average audience for any network and had no place to promote its new children's shows. Now CBS offers its stations three hours of cartoons with social and emotional lessons blended into them.

For school-age children, though, Nickelodeon is just about the only network providing shows with both educational value and audience appeal. These include the animated *Hey Arnold!* and *The Wild Thornberrys,* and three live-action series in which young people cope with social and emotional problems: *The Secret World of Alex Mack, The Journey of Allen Strange* (which deals with divorce, among other issues), and *The Mystery Files of Shelby Woo.*

On both cable and broadcast networks, there is more children's programming on more stations than ever before — the Discovery Channel has a three-hour programming block called *Discovery Kids* every Sunday and also produces a Discovery Kids Channel, HBO has added an HBO Family Channel with children's program in the daytime and family films at night, and the Fox Family Channel plans spin-offs (the Boyz Channel and the Girlz Channel). Although educational programming has increased proportionately, there is also still plenty of what Peggy Charren, the doyenne of the crusade to improve children's television, would call "schlock."

"I never thought this rule would happen and then everything for kids would be breathtaking," said Ms. Charren, who started her crusade more than a quarter-century ago, and then led the mid-1990s lobbying effort for the three-hour rule. "There are more opportunities now for children's shows that aren't junk," she added. "It doesn't mean there isn't still junk out there. But that's true in the library, too; there are junk books for children as well as wonderful books. That's life in a democracy."

But Ms. Charren also believes that the FCC rule, if it failed to generate oodles of high-quality shows, at least stopped the marketplace from eliminating those programs. "In an unregulated world, there's always movement to serve the bottom line instead of to serve the audience," she said. "Other institutions have to help keep choices alive. The press helps, the government helps, nonprofit institutions help."

And Alice Cahn, the former head of children's programming for PBS, who now works for Children's Television Workshop, noted another benefit. "I think the whole debate over the three-hour rule, the very public debate it spurred, has made parents more aware of what's out there," she said. "And that makes them, as consumers, slightly more demanding of broadcasters and cablecasters, which is good."

3

Teletubbies

By Sarah Lyall

No one knew quite what to make of *Teletubbies* when it bounced onto British television screens in 1997, billed as the country's first program to be created specifically for children as young as a year old. The Tubbies themselves—four brightly colored creatures shaped like bowling pins, with round faces and ears as big as saucers—were unquestionably weird, with their strange, alienoid antennas, and television-set tummies. They didn't speak proper English, but used a language of their own that was admittedly low on articles, pronouns, and verbs. They didn't seem to do much besides jump up and down and have rudimentary conversations in strange toddler-speak. Plus, who wanted to admit to letting their one-year-old watch television?

But *Teletubbies* has proved to be one of the world's most popular programs for children, touching off a marketing juggernaut that has, inevitably, branched out into a whole new industry of more than one thousand spin-off products, from stuffed Tubbies to Tubby books and videos to Tubby sheets and pillowcases. At the same time, parents have generally come to appreciate the Teletubbies' peculiar appeal, in part because their childrens' love of the characters—pink Po, purple Tinky-Winky, yellow Laa-Laa, and green Dipsy—seems so genuine and visceral. Here is a show made especially for very young children, using images, words, and activities that they might be likely to understand. It is, the program makers say, not for older children who are ready to learn and might watch something like *Barney* or *Sesame Street*, but for their tiny brothers and sisters—children who are said to be "ready to be ready" to learn.

SARAH LYALL is a correspondent in the London bureau of *The Times*.

"The premise of the show is that it's about the celebration of play," says Kenn Viselman, president and chief executive of the Itsy Bitsy Entertainment Company, which markets the program in North and South America. "What we try to do is get the children engaged, give them really funny bits, and while they're engaged, we can challenge them, give them questions and raise their curiosity and get them to take risks."

Teletubbies was created by Anne Wood, a Briton who has been making childrens' television for more than fifteen years through her production company, Ragdoll Productions, and by Andrew Davenport, a former actor in *Tots TV*, one of Ms. Wood's programs, and now a scriptwriter. In her early sixties, the press-shy Ms. Wood is known for her uncanny ability to plumb children's psyches and create the sort of programs they clamor to watch. "This is the culmination of twenty-five years of work with children for Ann," Mr. Viselman says of *Teletubbies*, which was based on exhaustive observations of hundreds of preschool children at play. "All the things she's learned about children and the way they think and play and respond are based went into the creation of the series," he adds.

The action takes place in a simple spot "over the hills and far away" called Teletubbyland, which is designed to be technologically advanced in a non-threatening way and is described by the program makers as the place where television was invented. Teletubbyland is populated by the four Tubbies, who sleep under Mylar-style blankets in an underground warren with their friend Noo-Noo, a conscientious vacuum cleaner, and assorted flowers and rabbits who live outside. The whole thing is presided over by a friendly yellow sun with the face and goofy laugh of a baby, but there is no authority figure—no Mister Rogers or Barney—to keep everyone in line. Anarchy often reigns, and the ruling principle is affection—one of the Tubbies' favorite activities is a group hug in which they proclaim that they love each other very much.

Occasionally, the televisions on the Tubbies' stomachs begin to glow brightly, and the action shifts to show real-live children doing things like milking cows or baking cookies. When the segment is finished, the Tubbies jump up and down, shouting "again," and the segment is repeated all over again, a feature that tends to delight toddlers as much as it infuriates their adult supervisors. The Tubbies don't do much—a whole half-hour show might be devoted to their efforts to find a couple of missing objects, for instance—but that is just the point. "A chair shows up in Teletubbyland and they say, 'What's that?'" explained Mr. Viselman. "We're trying to get children to use their limited vocabulary and take a risk and say, 'It's a chair.' We'll go through it seventy-five times, at a pace they can follow, and the last time they'll say it—'It's a chair!' "

Teletubbies may look simple, but each episode costs hundreds of thousands of dollars to make, in part because of the sophisticated visual effects required, and in part because the actors—small people dressed in enormous, unwieldy suits without much breathing room—can keep their heavy heads on and remain in costume for only about forty seconds at a time. But the costs are more than offset by the tremendous success of the series, which now appears in more than forty countries around the world. Most of the action is dubbed in various languages, but, increasingly, the "television" segments involving real children are filmed using children from each country, speaking their native languages.

According to various estimates, *Teletubbies* is now watched by some fourteen million children in the United States, where it appears on PBS stations. But without advertising revenue, the money comes from the merchandising. The astonishing range of Teletubby products are expected to generate some $2 billion in revenue in the United States this year. Royalties are generally split between PBS, Itsy Bitsy, and Ragdoll. Although Ragdoll went heavily into debt to make the series in the first place, "they're way past the point of breaking even," says Mr. Viselman, and so is Itsy Bitsy.

One of the biggest initial objections to the Teletubbies had to do with their language, which is not exactly correct English. But the program makers are quick to point out that young toddlers don't speak correct English, either, but rather come up with creative variations of what they hear from grown-ups. That's what the Teletubbies do, too, repeating the words of the narrator, the unseen voice of adult authority, in unequivocal toddler-speak. Thus, if the narrator says, "Tinky-Winky has a lovely song in his bag," Tinky-Winky will say, "Lovely song in bag." The Tubbies don't say "hello," but rather something that sounds more like "eh-oh." When they discuss their second-favorite food, Tubby Custard, it comes out as "Tubby Tustard."

Michael Cohen, a developmental psychologist and a principal at ARC Consulting in New York, says that the fuss about language is misplaced. "If this was the only language the kids were exposed to for twenty-four hours a day, seven days a week, then we should be concerned," he says. "But to watch some imaginary characters, who are clearly seen as peers, speak a peer language which they're all exposed to, is fine. What *Teletubbies* presents is an imaginative world that meets children at their level. It's a one-year-old's world, with color, sounds, language, pacing, and magic."

The more serious question is a philosophical one. Should one-year-olds be watching television at all? The answer seems to be no, they shouldn't— but they do nonetheless.

"I understand that criticism," Mr. Viselman says. "But many parents and caregivers have been using TV as wallpaper—they've needed half an hour and put the kids in front of the televison. The shows weren't age-appropriate, and this gives them something that is age-appropriate. It gives them an opportunity to let their children watch and to not feel guilty. We've never suggested to people, 'Hey, put your kids in front of the television,' but we've given them something to show if they do."

Some adults, of course, tend to read more into *Teletubbies* than the program makers intended. The show has been attacked for being frivolous, for presenting children with dumbed-down television, and for failing to have a moral center. And last February, the Reverend Jerry Falwell, once the head of the now-defunct Moral Majority, announced in the *National Liberty Journal*, which he edits and publishes, that Tinky-Winky was definitely gay and definitely a bad influence on the future youth of America.

In an article entitled "Parents Alert: Tinky-Winky Comes Out of the Closet," the magazine argued that Tinky-Winky is suspect because he is purple, the color of the gay pride movement, and has an antenna shaped like a triangle, another gay symbol. Not only that, but Tinky-Winky's handbag, described as a "magic bag" by the program makers, was said to be a woman's purse and thus a dangerous prop. "As a Christian, I feel that role modeling the gay lifestyle is damaging to the moral lives of children," Falwell wrote.

Is Tinky-Winky gay? Of course not, said Steve Rice, a spokesman for Itsy Bitsy, and it's ridiculous to even think about it. "The fact that he carries a magic bag doesn't make him gay," Mr. Rice says. "It's a children's show. To think we would be putting sexual innuendo in a children's show is kind of outlandish." As it happens, the fuss had a happy effect, from the company's point of view: it increased sympathy for Tinky-Winky and caused a small increase in the sale of Tinky-Winky products.

4

Reinventing Children's Television Workshop

Anita Gates

Sesame Street looks different these days. Big Bird and Snuffleupagus have been known to spend considerable time figuring out what to do when they both want to use the red crayon. (Take turns.) Big Bird and Baby Bear have had to learn to wait patiently—although they can't keep themselves from asking—"When? When? When?"—while the grown-ups write and rehearse a special play. And Elmo, possibly the most enthusiastic Muppet on the planet, has his own daily fifteen-minute segment, "Elmo's World." It includes visits with Elmo's goldfish, Dorothy, and regular features like Mr. Noodle (a comically inept adult played by Bill Irwin), fantasy super-niche television (the Eating Channel, the Book Channel, the Jacket Channel) and Ask a Baby. Elmo also sings a song about the topic of the day; "The Jacket Song," for instance, goes "Jacket, jacket, jacket, jacket, jacket, jacket, jacket, jacket, jacket."

Children's Television Workshop, which created *Sesame Street* and has produced the series since its beginning, in 1969, has always looked ahead. So it's no surprise that at the turn of the millennium its empire has come to include C.T.W. Online, CD-ROM's, and a cable television venture (Nog-

ANITA GATES is television editor of the Arts and Leisure section of *The Times*.

16

gin, a channel owned by C.T.W. and Nickelodeon, which will run shows from both partners' television libraries). In addition to *Sesame Street,* Children's Television Workshop has *Big Bag,* a weekly series for preschoolers on the Cartoon Network; *Dragon Tales,* an animated fantasy adventure series on PBS (premiere date: fall 1999); a feature film, *The Adventures of Elmo in Grouchland;* five monthly magazines; a book publishing division that has produced more than six hundred titles; broadcasts of *Sesame Street* in 140 countries; nineteen *Sesame Street* co-productions, in countries from Brazil (*Vila Sesame*) to Kuwait (*Iftah Ya Simsim*), and more than ten thousand licensed Children's Television Workshop items, from toys and games to clothing. Something has to help pay for all those dancing numerals and letters.

"There are challenges ahead for everyone in children's media in trying to adapt to changes in technology," says Gary Knell, the organization's executive vice president for operations, "making sure you are understanding those technologies and providing quality content in those new formats."

"You can now tickle Elmo online" at www.sesamestreet.com, he adds. (Asked what made Elmo such a big Muppet star, Mr. Knell departed from his serious corporate tone for a moment, saying: "He's furry, he's red, and he giggles. And he likes being tickled. So what's not to like?")

But the greatest change, the true reinvention of Children's Television Workshop, is not so much in new media or global expansion but in what producers and executives call the curriculum. The company began as an experiment, one modest PBS television show to see if the medium was capable of helping children learn, and there is always new research about how to do that best.

"We reinvent *Sesame Street* every year," says Alice Cahn, C.T.W.'s group president for television, film, and video. "The changes that are made in the show are based on research about how children and adults use television."

So what have they learned lately? In the 1998–99 season, says Ms. Cahn, levels of repetition were increased and the filmed segments became shorter.

"A key factor has been moving from a magazine-variety format to a more linear storytelling series," she adds. "What we learned is that children are looking for a linear story that's told in a more cohesive format." In one show, for instance, Big Bird spends the entire hour looking for a working toaster so he can have Granny Bird's special birdseed bread, toasted, for breakfast.

The preference for linear stories in recent research may be because "children at a younger age are watching dramatic television in greater proportion than they were," Ms. Cahn suggests.

The other most visible change is the new emphasis on social skills and emotions. *Sesame Street* is still brought to you by a particular letter and a particular number each day and there is a lot of counting, but more and more there are segments about sharing, delayed gratification, tolerating frustration and the like.

"The affective side of *Sesame Street* is as important as the teaching of cognitive skills," says Milton Chen, executive director of the George Lucas Educational Foundation in Marin County, Calif., and a former C.T.W. research director. "We didn't say, 'That's the squishy side, let's not talk about it.'"

Even grief has been part of the *Sesame Street* curriculum, Mr. Chen points out. After Will Lee, the actor who played Mr. Hooper, the show's lovable neighborhood grocer, died in 1982 at the age of seventy-four, the series devoted an episode to his memory. It included an explanation of the irreversibility of death to Big Bird, who was upset about Mr. Hooper's absence.

"He's got to come back," said Big Bird, the eight-foot-tall yellow-feathered Muppet who reflects a six-year-old's abilities and concerns. "Who's going to take care of the store? Who's going to make me birdseed milkshakes and tell me stories?"

The character David, played by Northern J. Calloway, reassured Big Bird. "I'll make you birdseed milkshakes, and we'll all tell you stories and make sure you're O.K."

This episode, like many of Children's Television Workshop's work, was helpful for parents, too. "It gave them a vocabulary for talking about death with their kids," Mr. Chen said.

Social and emotional skills seem to be the focus of *Big Bag*, too. In an early episode, a segment explained the meaning of the phrase "join the club" and taught that people don't have to like all the same things to be friends. It also suggested that children try to think of other viewpoints and tastes simply as different, not weird. The only trace of cognitive teaching in *Big Bag* is the use of occasional Spanish, mixed with English ("Tuna fish, my favorita!," "Mira! Look at that!").

A *Big Bag* video with a use-your-imagination theme includes a Troubles the Cat cartoon that teaches about empathy and promises. In the cartoon, May Linn is jumping rope with Sally, but while Sally is inside, getting some juice, other friends pass by and May Linn goes skating with them instead. Later, when Troubles uses his "troublescope" (young viewers are encouraged to make their own, using a cardboard paper-towel tube), which reveals how people are really feeling, to observe Sally's hurt, May Linn changes her mind.

The *Big Bag* videos follow the lead of *Sesame Street* by continuing one long story throughout the hour. In the case of the imagination video, children are listening to a story about pirates, when the adult reading the story discovers the last pages of the book are missing—so the children will have to imagine the rest themselves. They use a blanket for their ship's sail, a frying pan as a steering wheel, and the shape of open salad tongs is the X that marks the spot for buried treasure.

There is welcome silliness in the series and the videos as well. The show's host is a dog with a tuft of green and yellow hair who wears socks on both his floppy ears. There are cartoons about Slim Pig (who is, in fact, so thin that he's two-dimensional), Koki (who appears to be part of a blended family of ducks, chickens, and roosters), and Samuel and Nina (blue dog, gray chipmunk).

The newest Children's Television Workshop television series, *Dragon Tales*, may look like a half-hour of pure fantasy, but there's a social or emotional skills lesson around every corner.

Yes, the dragons on the playroom wallpaper do come to life in a magical swirl of sparkles, and transport little Emmy and Max to Dragonland. And from there they visit Rainbow River (with water of many colors), the Forest of Darkness (which includes a star tree that lights up) and the Cloud Playground. But all the characters have qualities and personality traits that lend themselves to learning. Even the dragons.

Emmy is an enthusiastic, adventure-loving six-year-old girl whose favorite word is "definitely." Her four-year-old brother, Max, is a rambunctious mischief maker determined to keep up with his older sister, no matter how hard that is.

Cassie, a small pink dragon with lemon-yellow wings, scales, and belly, is sweet, compassionate, and shy. Ord is a big blue dragon with celery-green accents and a huge appetite, who despite his size has a lot of fears (insects, thunderstorms, the dark) to overcome. Zak (green) and Wheezie (purple) are a two-headed dragon with polar-opposite personalities and tastes (imagine Felix Unger and Dharma Finkelstein), but they're learning to appreciate each other's differences. Quetzal, who is from Mexico, is the wise old dragon teacher, the show's adult figure.

Each episode is centered on one character's challenges. What *Dragon Tales* is meant to do, says Nina Elias Bamberger, an executive producer of the series, is to encourage children "to take chances, to try things—and to keep trying, that's a big message."

The lessons are also that there are many ways to approach experiences and learn from them and that partial success is fine. In an episode about Cassie's first sleepover, for instance, she manages "a half sleepover," staying until it's time for bed. "It's not all-or-nothing," Ms. Bamberger stresses.

"The child can say to himself or herself, 'I'm a little better. Next time maybe I'll be a little less afraid.'"

But everything doesn't have to be a profound emotional lesson. In the middle of each show, there's an original song, which little viewers are encouraged to sing along with. "It's kind of the time for the kids to take a break," says Ms. Bamberger, "and shake and wiggle and jump around." Which is very important, too.

PART II

KIDS FIRST!
Video
Reviews

5

Infants and Toddlers
(Ages 0 – 4)

Introduction: Dr. Irving Lazar

It was inevitable that the video industry would turn its attention to infants. Video has become the baby-sitting tool of choice for many parents and child-care providers. Be aware that while some videos for infants and toddlers are worthwhile, some should be avoided.

By the age of four, most kids can differentiate between reality and make-believe. They have an adequate repertoire of words and experiences to place a pictorial story in its context. They are able to turn off the TV or VCR and walk away. Infants are quite different. Current estimates are that only about fifteen percent of the brain is "hardwired" at birth. Whatever learning has taken place before birth simply addresses physical survival. What the baby experiences in the first two years of its life directly affects how its brain files, stores, and recovers information.

Here's how it works: When the baby encounters a multisensory experience, its brain files the visual elements in one place, the auditory components somewhere else, and the other sensory inputs in still other places of the brain. These elements are connected to each other by nerve cells. The more senses that are excited by an event, the richer the network of cells that store that event. The wider the network, the more pathways are created for the baby to recall with, making it more likely the baby will re-

IRVING LAZAR, Professor Emeritus of Human Ecology, Cornell University, is a member of the external faculty at the Santa Fe Institute. He has conducted large-scale research demonstrating the long-term positive effects of infant and preschool educational services.

late the event to other events. How experiences are filed, how they relate to future experiences, and how they are available for recall are determined to a large degree by what happens in the first year of life when the brain's filing system is being constructed. This means that the more multisensory an experience is, the more widely it is filed and the more readily it will be recalled.

What kinds of multisensory experiences are we talking about? Listening to Bach or Mozart or the Beatles from a recording stimulates only one sense—hearing. It does not promote a complex filing system. Watching a video stimulates sight and sound. Its influence is greater but hardly the best. What is the richest experience? The perfect one is a mother breast-feeding her baby. Touch, taste, smell, motion, hearing, sight, and pressure are all combined into a single multisensory pleasurable experience.

Babies need human contact. They learn from complex human interaction in settings that offer rich stimuli for all the senses. Rich does not mean overwhelming; it means complex and interrelational. A mother (or father or caregiver) can increase the sensory impact of a video by holding the baby while talking, dancing, or singing along.

Recently, I have seen videos supposedly made for babies and toddlers that simply show lots of pictures of babies. Because an infant cannot interact with the pictured babies, he or she soon becomes bored. This may later discourage social interactions with real babies. Other videos attempt to teach infants vocabulary unsuitable for this age. These programs are not educational in any real sense and may have a negative effect if they are used as substitutes for interactions with real people or doing real things.

However, if parents or caregivers are willing to watch videos with their infants or toddlers and engage in play with them, they can increase both the child's pleasure and learning. Some videos aimed at babies and parents can be useful. For example, a video title you'll find in this chapter, *So Smart!,* is designed to give a parent or caregiver audiovisual tools for playing with a baby. Using simple moving designs accompanied by gentle music, it provides instructions for playing with an infant, giving the infant stimuli at a comfortable pace, and responding to the baby's limited attention span.

Educational/Instructional

*** BABY LET'S PLAY: Takes toddlers on a ride aboard a diesel engine; shows children in a gym daring to swing twenty feet in the air; jumping; climbing with balls, parachutes, and bubbles. Original music. Adult Juror Comments: Delightful music, charming children. Well paced, interesting, good flow between activities and images. Good modeling for mothers and care-givers. Kid Juror Comments: Combination of music and children at play is excellent, good attention grabber. Kids asked to see it again immediately. All seemed to enjoy it, although it may be too long for one sitting. Age: 6 months–3; Length: 30 min.; Suggested Retail Price: $12.95, LITTLE ONES' PRODUCTIONS

*** BABY'S FIRST IMPRESSIONS, VOL. 1: SHAPES: Takes an infant's view of four basic geometric shapes and uses a cinematic approach to find those basic shapes in everyday items familiar to an infant or toddler. Adult Juror Comments: Diverting and attractive. Good pace. Beautifully done. Keeps their interest. Lends itself to ooh's and ah's. Variety of "shape" movement on-screen is visually stimulating. Adults were riveted! Kid Juror Comments: Youngest children watched as they were playing. Held attention of two- and three-year-olds. Older kids retained learning best. Age: 0–2; Length: 32 min; Suggested Retail Price: $14.95, SMALL FRY PRODUCTIONS

*** BABY'S FIRST IMPRESSIONS, VOL. 2: COLORS: Takes an infant's view of colors. Uses a cinematic approach to find colors in common items an infant or toddler is familiar with to reinforce the educational impact. Adult Juror Comments: Eye-catching. Shows wonderful variety of images, music, and children. Quick pace and content keeps infants attention. Helps teach colors in different settings. A definite favorite, kids will watch it! Kid Juror Comments: One fourteen-month-old actually watched for five to eight minutes, intrigued by the colors. Four- and five-year-olds followed along exceptionally well. "I liked everything. I felt like I was inside the video." Age: 1–4; Length: 32 min.; Suggested Retail Price: $14.95, SMALL FRY PRODUCTIONS

*** BABY'S FIRST IMPRESSIONS, VOL. 5: OPPOSITES; see p. 41

** BABY'S FIRST IMPRESSIONS, VOL. 6: ANIMALS; see p. 41

*** BABY'S FIRST IMPRESSIONS, VOL. 7: SOUNDS: Open your children's ears to the world out there. Video is designed to sharpen listening skills and develop cognitive abilities through games such as guessing what sounds are. Sounds are accompanied by imaginative visuals. Adult Juror Comments: Here's a different type of video for preschoolers. The clear sounds and color appeal to the youngest toddler. Older kids enjoy guessing the sounds. Helps children identify sounds around them through a collection of common items. Kid Juror Comments: Kids responded to the different sounds. They enjoyed trying to figure out which phone sounded familiar. The barnyard animals made the children laugh. Then they imitated their sounds. Learned some new words and enjoyed the scenes of friendship. Age: 1–3; Length: 32min.; Suggested Retail Price: $14.95, SMALL FRY PRODUCTIONS

** BABY'S FIRST IMPRESSIONS, VOL. 9: **HEAD TO TOE**; see p. 41

** IN THEIR FAVORITE PLACES (BABIES AT PLAY): Toddlers enjoy watching young children visit the zoo, toy store, grandma's house, and other great places. Adult Juror Comments: Good at showing parents participating in activities. Use of single words is instructive but not obtrusive. Choices of favorite places are universal: merry-go-round, ice cream parlor, etc. Shows beautiful variety of children. Kid Juror Comments: An interesting video for children to observe parent/child interactions. Kids loved the fair and climber parts. One five-year-old made a toy store afterwards. Kids found the sound track difficult to sing along with. Age: 1–3; Length: 39 min.; Suggested Retail Price: $12.98, WARNER HOME VIDEO

* IT'S POTTY TIME (THE DUKE FAMILY SERIES): Makes toilet training something it's never been: FUN. Demonstrates ideal behaviors portrayed by boys and girls attending a birthday party. Uses songs to capture and keep children's attention. Adult Juror Comments: Simple, straightforward handling of the subject matter that has a creative slant. An entertaining approach to potty etiquette. The sing-along is effective; the Raggedy Ann story was a good addition. At times, it talks down to children and is too silly. Kid Juror Comments: Kids age two related to it best. It's not appropriate for children much older or younger. Age: 2–5; Length: 30 min.; Suggested Retail Price: $14.98, LEARNING THROUGH ENTERTAINMENT, INC.

* IT'S SLEEPY TIME (THE DUKE FAMILY SERIES): Created to help parents and their children establish bedtime routines. Designed for repeat viewing to absorb ideal bedtime habits. The parents' guide gives a variety of views concerning sleeping problems. Adult Juror Comments: Good for parents to view together with their children. Offers useful tips and pleasing songs. It does promote the separation approach, keeping children out of parents' beds whatever the situation and portrays a middle-class lifestyle. Most appropriate for parents if it fits within their value structure. Kid Juror Comments: Okay but didn't stay with it. It's best viewed with parents. Children thought the songs were "bossy." "It made me think about being nice." Age: 2–6; Length: 30 min.; Suggested Retail Price: $14.98, LEARNING THROUGH ENTERTAINMENT, INC.

** SEE IT! SAY IT! SING IT! PLAY IT!; see p. 49

*** SO SMART!: An infant stimulation video that uses images based on research related to babies' visual and auditory preferences and early cognitive development. Beautifully animated in black and white and complementary colors. Set to classical music. Adult Juror Comments: High quality, excellent visual and aural training for infants. Beautiful music. Carefully instructs parents on proper use. One Adult Juror said, "If accompanied by an adult, it's the only infant video I'd recommend." Kid Juror Comments: Excellent timing, very stimulating for infants. "Even my toddler sat and watched and told his baby sister what he saw on the screen." Age: 6 months–3; Length: 30 min.; Suggested Retail Price: $14.95, THE BABY SCHOOL COMPANY

*** SO SMART! VOL. 2: ALL ABOUT SHAPES: Exposes babies to geometric shapes and objects through clever transformations of Cecil Circle, Suzie Square, and Traci Triangle. Words appear on-screen, creating a new way for parents to read to their toddlers. Adult Juror Comments: Good introduction which explains how to use the video, recommend interaction with adult. Wonderful classical music, bright colors, and movement suitable for infants. "I thought this would be boring, but it captivated all the kids for a long time!" Kid Juror Comments: Adults were amazed at how long it actually engaged babies from three to fifteen months. The older ones watched for twenty-five minutes. Even the shyest said the name of a letter or object out loud. Toddlers and preschoolers chatted and talked among themselves. Age: 6 months–3; Length: 30 min.; Suggested Retail Price: $14.95, THE BABY SCHOOL COMPANY

*** SO SMART! VOL. 3: ALL ABOUT LETTERS: Exposes babies to the shapes and forms of each letter of the alphabet. Older children begin to see the relationship between letters, words, and images. Parents can teach their child as each letter forms in a creative way. Adult Juror Comments: Letters displayed familiarly, individually, and in the usual order. Excellent sound, animation, and editing. Simplicity appeals to young children; even zero to two can benefit. Kid Juror Comments: Potential for learning beyond what the video actually presents. Parents could play memory games with kids. Children loved the "walking" shapes. Kids smiled and talked back to the video throughout the screening. Some got up and danced to music. Age: 1–3; Length: 30 min.; Suggested Retail Price: $14.95, THE BABY SCHOOL COMPANY

** TODDLER TAKES (TODDLERS AT PLAY): Features dozens of children in natural settings delighting in their own achievement, falling down and bouncing back, learning to take turns at play, venting anger, sharing, and overcoming fears. Adult Juror Comments: Nice shots of toddlers being toddlers. Very appealing to children and adults. Entertaining, soothing, fun and visually well done. Good discussion of toddler issues: anger, sharing, and talking. Little diversity is shown. Kid Juror Comments: Kids tuned in. The lack of excessive verbiage was appreciated by the children. The children responded by laughing and interacting with one another. Age: 1–5; Length: 25 min.; Suggested Retail Price: $12.95, TOW TRUCK PRODUCTIONS, INC.

** TODDLER TREASURY, A: Developed by the creator of Nickelodeon and Pinwheel for children under the age of three. Animated songs, stories, rhythms, and rhymes invite participation and creative play. Adult Juror Comments: Charming collection of nursery rhymes and tunes. Enjoyable, clear images; simple, familiar songs; suitable pacing. Good repeat viewing value. "The kids had more fun watching this program than I had expected." Kid Juror Comments: Children thoroughly enjoyed it and were actively involved and engaged in the songs and pictures. Good music choices—kids loved the familiar songs. Even a seven-month-old watched. Age: 1–3; Length: 18 min.; Suggested Retail Price: $14.95, PARAGON MEDIA

** UNDER A BLUE, BLUE SKY (BABIES AT PLAY): Explores the park, some puppies, a carnival, and other sunny places. Shows real toddlers in live-action segments. Adult Juror Comments: Good child-centered activities for this age. Nice ending segment on nap and sleep. Great for modeling play. Key words on screen are lost on younger preschoolers. Limited cultural diversity shown. Kid Juror Comments: Captured children's attention and left room for questions. Kids liked the songs and responded well to the activities. Comments and narration are age-appropriate. Series title, "Babies at Play" is misleading. Kids shown are toddlers, not babies. Age: 1–3; Length: 38 min.; Suggested Retail Price: $12.98, WARNER HOME VIDEO

Family

** BABY BACH: A whimsical music video that introduces infants and toddlers to Bach and classical music. Based on research in the area of music therapy and its positive effect on physical health and intelligence. Adult Juror Comments: Wholesome and aesthetically beautiful. Steady flow of music and objects but somewhat slow. Though production well done, a little choppy and fragmented. Some toys used were too sophisticated for baby to understand. Lacks cultural diversity. Kid Juror Comments: Liked the interaction with the puppets and the visuals of the young children. They identified several objects and would identify what they were doing. Good to break up into sections. Babies lost interest after a while. Age: 0–2; Length: 30 min.; Suggested Retail Price: $15.95, THE BABY EINSTEIN COMPANY

** BABY EINSTEIN: Addresses the theory that children exposed to different languages in the first year find it easier to learn foreign tongues later on. Stresses the alphabet, counting, and nursery rhymes. Uses real-world objects and phrases in foreign languages. Adult Juror Comments: Large pictures, colorful, gentle voices. Exposure to multi-ethnic sounds. A little slow-moving and choppy at times. Some visual scenes did not match the audio content. "I'd like to know how different languages at such short length help little ones." Kid Juror Comments: Babies enjoyed seeing familiar objects; some sat for at least half an hour. Some kids got very bored. Kids responded best to the English-language sections. Age: 0–2; Length: 30 min.; Suggested Retail Price: $15.95, THE BABY EINSTEIN COMPANY

* BABY FACES THE VIDEO (BABY FACES): Shows 30 minutes of toddlers and children. Comes with an audio cassette with twenty nursery rhymes. Adult Juror Comments: Simple production with appealing photography and a variety of music. Suggests opportunities for adult/toddler interaction. Babies enjoy looking at other babies' faces. Although this has no value in terms of child development, it is entertaining. Kid Juror Comments: Most babies loved watching the other babies. The songs are appealing but overall the video is long, slow and non-engaging because it lacks structure. Age: 0–3; Length: 30 min.; Suggested Retail Price: $12.99, BRENTWOOD HOME VIDEO

*** BABY MOZART: Infants and toddlers will view a parade of colorful objects, the sorts of items parents and children can name aloud. The simple visuals are accompanied by the music of Mozart in arrangements and instrumentation designed to appeal to youthful ears. Adult Juror Comments: The toys, movements of objects and animals are captivating. Creative use of objects draws attention to the wonderful music of Mozart. Very age-appropriate. "The breaks between sections give children a chance to rest their eyes before the next picture." Kid Juror Comments: Lots of laughter. Children seemed more attentive to Mozart and requested replays. "I know that song!" At the end of the tape children requested more "dance" music. Age:

0–2; Length: 30 min.; Suggested Retail Price: $15.95, THE BABY EINSTEIN COMPANY

** GOOD MORNING, GOOD NIGHT: A DAY ON THE FARM (BO PEEP): Enjoy a day on the farm. Wake up with a little child and watch how all the farm animals get up. Everyone has something to eat. Then it's time to play. Did you know that pigs play ball? After all the fun, it's time to sleep. Accompanied by folk songs. Adult Juror Comments: Gentle and positive, though some camera work is overexposed or underexposed. Shows good clips of farm animal behavior. Simple production, with upbeat music and a slow pace. Helpful resources are included—a songbook and recommended activities. Kid Juror Comments: Children moved along to the music, though some thought it was boring. They liked seeing the muddy pig and the boy feeding the dog. The younger kids pointed out which animals they recognized and compared them to others they had seen. Age: 1–3; Length: 17 min.; Suggested Retail Price: $14.95, BO PEEP PRODUCTIONS, INC.

*** TELETUBBIES: DANCE WITH THE TELETUBBIES: A charming video about movement and play. As children interact with this video, they will clap their hands, stomp their feet, and wiggle their toes one at a time. Adult Juror Comments: Colorful, sweet, fun, childlike, well produced. Predictable and consistent, which is age-appropriate for young children. Structured to encourage child's participation (dancing and singing). Great modeling of sharing and taking turns. Little diversity. Kid Juror Comments: Appealing. Younger children responded enthusiastically to music: clapping, dancing, squealing with laughter. At the end one child shouted, "More!" An older child commented—"If babies want to watch TV, Teletubbies is the best." Age: 1–3; Length: 60 min.; Suggested Retail Price: $14.95, WARNER BROS. FAMILY ENTERTAINMENT

*** TELETUBBIES: HERE COME THE TELETUBBIES: The series was created to enhance a child's early development and creativity. When the wind blows, a magic windmill brings pictures from far away and the Teletubbies are joined to the world of real children celebrating the joy of play! Adult Juror Comments: Cute, endearing characters; simple story lines; well presented. Age-appropriate use of predictions, math concepts, recall, and identification. Story lines are very simple and perfect for preschoolers. Music is catchy. Kid Juror Comments: Captivating. Kids wanted to watch it again. Viewers were enticed to pay attention by guessing what was going to happen next. Kids were fascinated; some vocalized, laughed, pointed, and mimicked. "I loved everything." Age: 1–3; Length: 60 min.; Suggested Retail Price: $14.95, WARNER BROS. FAMILY ENTERTAINMENT

** ZEEZEL THE ZOWIE ZOON IN THE COLOR CHASE; see p. 90

Music

** **BABY SONGS: BABY ROCK:** Kids dance to rock and roll favorites. Ten song-filled, toe-tapping vignettes include: Fats Domino's "I'm Walkin," Little Eva's "Locomotion," "Woolly Bully," and "Twist & Shout." Adult Juror Comments: Great tunes. Children enjoyed participating. Works best when viewed in segments. Appropriate use of language. Some safety concerns on this title, i.e., a child jumping on a bed near a window. Kid Juror Comments: Very colorful. Children enjoyed the character Baby Rock. Not all children liked the rock and roll music. Age: 1–5; Length: 30 min.; Suggested Retail Price: $12.98, ANCHOR BAY ENTERTAINMENT

*** **BABY SONGS: BABY SONGS:** Playfully portrays familiar themes for little people learning about the big world. Adult Juror Comments: Great tape. Invites child/parent participation. Excellent photography. Zeroes in on what's important to children. Encourages joining in normal, natural activities by providing good examples. The cartoons shown before each song are particularly enjoyable. Kid Juror Comments: Children became very interested and engaged. They related to activities in the video: sleeping through the night, using the potty, security blankets, etc. Kids swayed to music, imitated the action, and identified with subject matter and characters. Age: 1–5; Length: 30 min.; Suggested Retail Price: $12.98, ANCHOR BAY ENTERTAINMENT

*** **BABY SONGS: BABY SONGS GOOD NIGHT:** Contains ten original songs by Hap Palmer with live-action toddler shots. Lullabies and gentle songs designed to appeal to toddlers and parents. Adult Juror Comments: Super, well produced. Sweet and calming, well paced. Appropriate mix of fantasy and reality from dancing bears to real children playing with dolls. Age-appropriate images shown, such as sleeping, playing with parents, parents leaving and returning. Kid Juror Comments: Three- and four-year-olds sang and danced to the songs. Even two- and four-month-olds watched for 15 minutes. All enjoyed the on-screen babies. One three-year-old wanted to watch it again immediately. Age: 6 months–5; Length: 30 min.; Suggested Retail Price: $12.98, ANCHOR BAY ENTERTAINMENT

*** BABY SONGS: EVEN MORE BABY SONGS: These Hap Palmer songs celebrate a child's everyday world, from getting up, eating and dressing, to everyone's favorite activity—playing. Adult Juror Comments: Very clever and lively, shows nice range of images, animation, live action, and graphics. Each song is introduced by engaging animation. One could view one segment at a time. Best for three-, four- and five-year-olds. Kid Juror Comments: Very appealing . Music is fast but it keeps their attention. Children giggled at teddy bear. Age: 1–5; Length: 32 min.; Suggested Retail Price: $12.98, ANCHOR BAY ENTERTAINMENT

*** BABY SONGS: HAP PALMER'S FOLLOW ALONG SONGS: Imaginative, wonderful, joyful songs by Hap Palmer that invite kids to clap their hands, stamp their feet, dance, and act out the lyrics. Introduces colors, the alphabet, and shows how to make musical instruments from ordinary things like bottle caps. Adult Juror Comments: Creatively inviting. Movement included children, held their attention. Music is great and lots of fun! Encourages participation even without guidance. Suggests activities and good songs to sing. Kid Juror Comments: Actively involved. Those familiar with the music were enthralled. Kids enjoyed acting like "monsters," tapping sticks, and clapping. Age: 1–5; Length: 30 min.; Suggested Retail Price: $12.95, ANCHOR BAY ENTERTAINMENT

** BABY SONGS: JOHN LITHGOW'S KID-SIZE CONCERT: John Lithgow, with his infectious good humor, performs favorite children's songs, inviting the audience to sing along. From "She'll Be Coming 'Round the Mountain" to the story of "The Runaway Pancake," Lithgow delights with whimsy and song. Adult Juror Comments: Gentle and loving, Lithgow's a natural for kid songs. He's quiet, subtle, and relaxed. Child centered, child sensitive. Induces kids to sing along. Kid Juror Comments: Excellent choice of songs— toe-tappers and hand-clappers—and they come alive. Age: 2–8; Length: 32 min.; Suggested Retail Price: $12.98, ANCHOR BAY ENTERTAINMENT

*** BABY SONGS: MORE BABY SONGS: Continues the energy of the original hit, "Baby Songs," with more playful songs. Adult Juror Comments: Great songs and lovely images of kids engaged in a variety of activities. Material is intelligent and sweet. The witch segment is not age-appropriate. Kid Juror Comments: Fun! Kids liked this and enjoyed repeated viewings, except for witch segment. Kids danced and attempted to sing along. Age: 1–5; Length: 30 min.; Suggested Retail Price: $12.98, ANCHOR BAY ENTERTAINMENT

** **BABY SONGS: SUPER BABY SONGS:** From the creators of "Baby Songs" with irresistible sing-along songs from Hap Palmer, this upbeat collection contains such titles as "When Daddy was a Little Boy," "Chomping Gum," "Hurry Up Blues," and "When Things Don't Go Your Way." Adult Juror Comments: Entertaining and well produced. Great introductory song. Includes some nice role reversals and wonderful songs. Has some inappropriate behavior models for toddlers, balanced diversity. It's more for toddlers than "babies." Kid Juror Comments: The music was lovely: They tapped and sang along. A little long for attention span of youngest kids. The claymation section (animation done with clay figures) moves pretty fast. Age: 3–7; Length: 30 min.; Suggested Retail Price: $12.98, ANCHOR BAY ENTERTAINMENT

** **BEDTIME (STORIES TO REMEMBER);** see p. 102

* **INFANTASTIC LULLABYES:** Presents ways to communicate, educate, and entertain. Shapes, primary colors, animals, and easily recognizable objects are animated and set to familiar nursery songs, including "Row Your Boat" and "Rock-A-Bye." Adult Juror Comments: Beautiful images, visually appealing, and a good music score make this an overall favorite. Useful for learning and entertaining. Jurors recommended using the program in small segments and encouraged active participation with parent or caregiver. Kid Juror Comments: Some kids liked this a lot, while others were so-so. The music captured their attention. This was an overall favorite with youngest children. They loved singing along. Age: 1–3; Length: 25 min.; Suggested Retail Price: $14.98, V.I.E.W. VIDEO

** **ON A FUN RAINY DAY (BABIES AT PLAY):** Come in from splashing to enjoy a dressy tea party, baking cookies, fuzzy friends, and more. Shows real babies and toddlers at play. Adult Juror Comments: Well paced, good interpretation of music and images. Well produced. Perfect for age group. Kids are natural and appealing. Activities selected are age-appropriate. Good diversity shown. A little too long. Kid Juror Comments: "Cute babies." They loved the songs and the colorful images and clapped their hands while they watched. Stimulated discussion afterwards from older kids. Age: 1–3; Length: 37 min.; Suggested Retail Price: $12.98, WARNER HOME VIDEO

** **SINGING TIME (STORIES TO REMEMBER);** see p. 107

*** **STORYTIME (STORIES TO REMEMBER);** see p. 108

Nature

** MEET YOUR ANIMAL FRIENDS; see p. 117

Special Interest

* BEACH, THE (ELBEE'S BABIES PLAYING SERIES): A non-scripted, non-narrative action-oriented production showing babies between infancy and four years. Outdoor activities are filmed with natural sounds and music. It is simple and fun, showing contentment and joy. Adult Juror Comments: Good baby shots of kids walking, eating, and playing. Shows happy, positive emotions. Scenes of babies putting sandy things into their mouths models poor behavior. Not much diversity. Jurors objected to the description on the box calling the tape a "baby-sitter." Kid Juror Comments: Evoked some interest but not a great deal. They wandered in and out while viewing, which is a natural response for this age. Kids asked why there was only music, no talking. Program could be used to prepare for or reminisce about a trip to the beach. Age: 0–3; Length: 30 min.; Suggested Retail Price: $14.95, ELBEE PRODUCTIONS

* BOULDER & MAUI BABIES (ELBEE'S BABIES PLAYING SERIES): A non-scripted, non-narrative, action-oriented production featuring infants and toddlers to age four. Outdoor activities are filmed with natural sounds and music. It is simple and fun. Adult Juror Comments: Shows affection in a calming way. Learning to play with puppies and kittens is good modeling behavior for this age. The content is mostly soothing music set to visuals. Not much educational or developmental value. Kid Juror Comments: Okay. Limited interest to babies—does not hold their interest for long. Toddlers wandered in and out of the room. Some ignored it completely. This could be useful for quiet time/nap/bedtime. Age: 0–2; Length: 30 min.; Suggested Retail Price: $14.95, ELBEE PRODUCTIONS

* HI DADDY!: Captures the magic created when dads play with their babies. Babies will hear familiar tunes accompanied by bright learning blocks, and watch laughing faces similar to their own play, smile, and tumble with their fathers. Adult Juror Comments: Dads who watched this were amused but not eager to watch again. Songs were familiar. Shows good racial diversity and a pleasant interaction between parent and child. Poor production quality and nothing to hold a baby's attention. Kid Juror Comments: Even older children were delighted to see the

daddies for short periods of time. Initially there was a lot of pointing and bouncing to the music, but overall they were easily bored. The children enjoyed the music and laughed at times. Age: 0–2; Length: 30 min.; Suggested Retail Price: $12.95, ELC PRODUCTIONS, LLC

** LET'S DANCE ON THE FARM: Visits the "Adventure Farm" and introduces preschoolers to farm animals through song and dance. Adult Juror Comments: Simple production. Contains good content on natural world. Used by parents and children together, it maximizes the opportunity for children to play along. Kid Juror Comments: Okay. Two's and three's loved it and tried their hardest to move along with it. Even crawlers enjoyed moving to it. Age: 1–4; Length: 30 min.; Suggested Retail Price: $14.95, DANCE ADVENTURE ENTERTAINMENT CO.

* PLAYGROUND, THE (ELBEE'S BABIES PLAYING SERIES): Babies from infancy to age four engaged in outdoor activities with natural sounds and music. It is a simple production showing happy, healthy, active babies. Adult Juror Comments: The behaviors modeled are positive. Good diversity. Adult interaction could elicit more responses. Although babies like watching babies, it is live babies that interest them. This is not harmful but has little developmental value. Kid Juror Comments: The music is nice, but overall this has limited appeal. Pace too slow for most. Some kids watched briefly and walked away. If not shown all at once, it's good for a brief diversion. Age: 0–2; Length: 30 min.; Suggested Retail Price: $14.95, ELBEE PRODUCTIONS

** RHYMIN' TIME (STORIES TO REMEMBER); see p. 126

6

Preschool

(Ages 2–5)

Introduction: Dr. Bettye Caldwell

My tennis club has a wonderful child-care center in full view of the courts. As an inveterate (and professional) child-watcher, I never pass it without pausing to look at the children and their play-school equipment: climbing bars, a maze appropriate for preschoolers, various hoops and balls of all sizes, a seesaw, and even a small merry-go-round. Mounted on one wall is—you guessed it—a television-VCR set. Whenever I walk by, it's always turned on. Of the approximately twenty children in the play school, almost fifteen are watching whatever is on the monitor. The maze is empty, unused, just like all the other equipment. If I spot one brave little soul wandering around with a ball in hand, that is unusual.

The message is clear: The power of our television screens is so great that it can nullify the best designed, most attractive play equipment available—the kind that children used to pine for and which can still provide important benefits. Preschoolers need to exercise their muscles as much as their mothers and fathers do on the tennis court! They need to be involved in active, not passive, learning most of the time.

Because the "moving picture," throbbing with compelling images and attractive sound and color, dominates today's pop culture, we cannot be

DR. BETTYE CALDWELL is a professor of pediatrics and child development and education at the University of Arkansas Children's Hospital. A former president of the National Association for the Education of Young Children, Dr. Caldwell has published more than two hundred articles and received many awards, including the 1990 National Governors Association Distinguished Citizen Award.

indifferent to what our children observe. Note that I didn't write "watch," the verb we generally use when talking about television and videos. For children do much more than watch: they listen, they process images and sounds; they respond with body movements and emotional and verbal expressions. And they absorb and retain for a long time these impressions that profoundly influence their developing brains, their interests, and their emerging values.

Children don't have to *learn* to receive television and video messages the way they must *learn* to read and write. There is no television code to crack in order to comprehend and remember what appears on the screen, no motor movements to be mastered. If children are born with the usual complement of sensory receivers—good eyes and ears—and brains capable of making connections between these sensory systems, they are able to "receive" television and video shortly after birth. This built-in receptivity demands that parents and other adults who supplement parental care with children's media be acutely sensitive to the format and content of the programs their young children observe. This kind of adult awareness requires vigilance; they need to "screen" what their young children will see on the small screen as carefully as they screen books and other experiences they want their children either to encounter or to avoid.

So much for playing defense. Playing offense multiplies the benefits. When parents watch a video or a program on television, or play with a CD-ROM together with their child, the benefits are tremendous. Let's be honest. Videos, TV, or CD-ROMs can be a godsend when we are trying to prepare dinner, make an important telephone call, or have an intimate adult conversation. At such times, a wisely selected program can give you just the break you need. But be sure you also take the time to watch programs with your child as often as you can. Not only does that give parent and child an opportunity for emotional closeness and perhaps physical contact, it also communicates to the child your conviction that his or her interests are valid. Moreover, it naturally opens the door to something as simple as further conversation—the questions and answers and comments that are a vital part of growing up, discovering ideas, and exploring new worlds.

The Coalition for Quality Children's Media has provided a wonderful set of tools for parents of preschoolers and for early-child-care professionals. This chapter offers an invaluable guide to videos and CD-ROMs appropriate for preschoolers. Preschool children themselves have found the selections entertaining. The evaluations don't tell parents what to do or buy or how many hours to allow for television; they simply give accurate and informative guidelines that enable parents to make their own good choices. And good choices are what we all want to make—and what our children need from us.

Educational/Instructional

* 1, 2, 3 COME COUNT WITH ME: Counting Cat introduces the world of numbers. Children can sing and play along with parachuting kangaroos, buzzing bees, and purple porcupines while learning to count. Adult Juror Comments: The presentation and content are suitable to make learning pleasant. Provides counting exercises with unusual objects, using questionable techniques. Repetitive. May be more effective when viewed in segments. The "real" face inserted seems strange. Kid Juror Comments: Just okay. They lost interest by number five, although counted straight through. Only some stayed for the entire program. A little too long for one sitting. Age: 2–6; Length: 22 min.; Suggested Retail Price: $29.95, KIDEO PRODUCTIONS, INC.

** 1, 2, 3 COUNT WITH ME (SESAME STREET): Ernie, Elmo, and The Count make learning numbers and counting a musical treat. Ernie shows everyone just how useful learning to count can be. Stars the Muppets. Musical numbers include: "Count With Me," "Seven Goldfish," and "Counting Vacation." Adult Juror Comments: Excellent techniques for teaching numbers. It's fun, musical, and has lots of repetition. Appeals to adults and children. Well-produced, high-quality sound and visuals. Kid Juror Comments: Reinforces counting. One four-and-a-half-year-old practiced her numerical skills after watching. Two hyperactive kids sat and watched the whole program. "I really like Elmo." Age: 2–5; Length: 30 min.; Suggested Retail Price: $12.98, SONY WONDER/CTW

** ABC'S & SUCH (RUSTY & ROSY): Teaches names, shapes, and sounds of letters. Contains different versions of the "ABC Song." An animation sequence for each letter forms its shape with objects or animals. Adult Juror Comments: Educational and fun. Good reinforcement. Encourages participation. Good music. Moves a little slowly at times. Uses rote method of learning. Kid Juror Comments: Good for three- to five-year-olds. Has lots of repetition and is easy to understand. Interaction required of kids is well done. Age: 2–6; Length: 35 min.; Suggested Retail Price: $24.95, WATERFORD INSTITUTE

** ALL ABOARD FOR BED (THE BIG COMFY COUCH): Climb on the Big Comfy Couch with Loonette and Molly. Teaches preschoolers imaginative ways that make the dark not so scary. Includes "The Flashlight Dance," "The Sweet Dream Train," and "Fuzzy and Wuzzy," the couch dustbunnies. Adult Juror Comments: Encourages imaginative play. Presents ideas children can relate to in regard to sleep issues and fears. Mollie is endearing, but Loonette is offensively cute. Kid Juror Comments: A hit. They liked the song "In the Dark." "That's pretty weird that you can go inside a couch. How does she do that?" "I'd watch it a thousand times." Age: 2–5; Length: 25 min.; Suggested Retail Price: $14.99, TIME-LIFE VIDEO & TELEVISION

** **ALL ABOUT ABC'S:** Children will have fun learning the alphabet as they take a magic carpet ride with their new friends, Letter Lizard and Magic Man, on an animated adventure to Alphabet Land. Adult Juror Comments: Simple animation. Sometimes words don't match action and are beyond a preschooler's comprehension. Video is broken into segments so viewing time is shortened. Young kids will enjoy the first segment, older kids the second segment. Repetitive. Kid Juror Comments: Kept the attention of four- and five-year-olds. Some children had difficulty with the cute phrases and alliteration. Age: 3–6; Length: 30 min.; Suggested Retail Price: $6.99, UNITED AMERICAN VIDEO CORP.

*** **ALPHABET GAME, THE (MY SESAME STREET HOME VIDEO):** Sunny Friendly is the host of a new game show with prizes and surprises. The contestants are Big Bird, Gary Grouch, and Dimples the Dog. The object of the game is to be the first to find something that starts with the letter of the alphabet shown. Adult Juror Comments: Visually appealing, silly game show format. Funny puppets, lively songs, guest appearances by Kermit, Grover, Cookie Monster, Oscar, and Big Bird. Sesame Street follows through with humor and lots of color. Kid Juror Comments: "I liked it very much." "I liked the talking 'S,' he was funny." "I like watching for the letters." "I know my ABC's." Kids sang the Alphabet Song after watching the video. Age: 3–5; Length: 30 min.; Suggested Retail Price: $12.98, SONY WONDER/CTW

* **ALPHABET SOUP (LOOK & LEARN):** This sing-along uses flying pictures and flipping words to help reinforce and retain the alphabet. Jaunty rhymes, spirited music, and charming pictures. Adult Juror Comments: Helpful for children who are learning the alphabet. Some words too difficult for audience. Stretches learning in a positive way. Simple production. Starts slow with lots of verbal information, making this best viewed in segments. Kid Juror Comments: A little slow-moving, especially at the beginning. Some kids asked to see it again. Others said they sang the ABC song "wrong." Content suitable for elementary age. Age: 3–6; Length: 30 min.; Suggested Retail Price: $14.98, V.I.E.W. VIDEO

* **ALPHABETLAND (REDBOOK LEARNING ADVENTURES):** The magic power of letters and words through songs and games. Includes other lessons about

patience, friendship, and imagination. Adult Juror Comments: Reinforces learning alphabet. Songs are creative and catchy. Program links letters to words. Gets off to a slow start and the presentation is jumbled. It's hard for kids to gather the material. Kid Juror Comments: Kids listened as soon as the music started. Story line is a little difficult and complicated to follow. They didn't understand references in the songs. Some older children sang the ABC song afterwards. Age: 2–6; Length: 30 min.; Suggested Retail Price: $12.98, VIDEO TREASURES, INC.

*** ALPHABET ZOO, THE: Teaches the alphabet through bright, interactive songs and colorful scenes of animals in their natural habitat. Teaches letter recognition with visuals and sounds. Adult Juror Comments: Multi-sensory with interesting animals. Good repetition and content. Excellent suggestions for parents/caregivers that reinforce the lessons. Attractive settings, good pacing. Almost interactive because it stimulates participation. Kid Juror Comments: They sounded out the letters, made animal sounds, and learned a lot about the animals after repeated viewings. One of the best alphabet tapes, great for zoo trips. Age: 3–7; Length: 25 min.; Suggested Retail Price: $14.95, DOLPHIN COMMUNICATIONS

*** BABY LET'S PLAY; see p. 24

*** BABY'S FIRST IMPRESSIONS, VOL. 2: COLORS; see p. 25

** BABY'S FIRST IMPRESSIONS, VOL. 3: LETTERS: Takes an infant's view of the alphabet and uses a cinematic approach to find letters in common everyday items that an infant or toddler is familiar with. Adult Juror Comments: Nice. Beautiful, colorful images and music. Adults found it a little repetitive and thought the fast pace somewhat difficult to follow. "Animated flashcards." Develops a knowledge of letters and colors at a young age. Kid Juror Comments: Three- to five-year-olds followed along best, recognizing letters and objects. Younger children watched in segments. Age: 2–5; Length: 32 min.; Suggested Retail Price: $14.95, SMALL FRY PRODUCTIONS

** BABY'S FIRST IMPRESSIONS, VOL. 4: NUMBERS: Helps preschoolers learn their numbers by using object association and repetition. Adult Juror Comments: Good diversity. Good pacing for the count-and-answer segment. Helps motivate children to learn how to count. Kid Juror Comments: Fine. Children enjoyed the objects selected for counting. Children who are speaking benefit most from this video. Age: 2–5; Length: 32 min.; Suggested Retail Price: $14.95, SMALL FRY PRODUCTIONS

*** **BABY'S FIRST IMPRESSIONS, VOL. 5: OPPOSITES:** Inspires and challenges creative kids' minds. Interesting visuals to show differences like up/down, left/right, hot/cold. Adult Juror Comments: Insight into difficult concepts using repetition to reinforce learning. Minimal comprehension for under age two. Beautiful visuals, music, and voices. Culturally diverse, good aspects for ESL preschool learning. Kid Juror Comments: Children watched enthusiastically, repeating opposite words and sharing gestures as well as their own opposite words. Viewing this program calmed children. "My infant loved it." Age: 1–5; Length: 32 min.; Suggested Retail Price: $14.95, SMALL FRY PRODUCTIONS

** **BABY'S FIRST IMPRESSIONS, VOL. 6: ANIMALS:** Shows all types of animals, even some insects, interacting with children. Names of animals are spelled on the screen, and each section has a recap learning period. Adult Juror Comments: Good pace, visually captivating, excellent diversity. Invites involvement with animal costumes and sounds. Reinforces concepts and stimulates responses. Some words difficult for audience. Educational value is more applicable to over-twos. Kid Juror Comments: Evoked questions about animal facts. Even the older kids learned something new, like how fast an emu can run. Good link to familiar songs. Infants and 18-month-olds loved it! A little long, but can be viewed in segments. Age: 1–5; Length: 32 min.; Suggested Retail Price: $14.95, SMALL FRY PRODUCTIONS

*** **BABY'S FIRST IMPRESSIONS, VOL. 7: SOUNDS;** see p. 25

** **BABY'S FIRST IMPRESSIONS, VOL. 8: SEASONS:** Teaches the differences between the four seasons: fresh winter snow, spring flowers, summer sunshine, and fall colors. Many holidays are explained so the child can learn connections between holidays and seasons. Adult Juror Comments: Colorful but very slow pace. Depicts children in the garden, at the beach, other playful activities. Not much diversity in discussing traditional Christian Easter, Thanksgiving, and Christmas. Kid Juror Comments: Enthusiastic. Children were moving around and pretending to smell the flowers along with the on-screen kids. They liked seeing the different seasons. "We could grow flowers." "There is no snow here, we could make sand angels instead." Age: 2–5; Length: 32 min.; Suggested Retail Price: $14.95, SMALL FRY PRODUCTIONS

** **BABY'S FIRST IMPRESSIONS, VOL. 9: HEAD TO TOE:** Teaches how to make learning connections as on-screen children demonstrate how a hand can do many things, like hold, touch, or clap. Encourages children to be interactive. Exercise demonstrations included. Adult Juror Comments: Looks great. Shows realistic pictures of children and their body parts. Very clear images and simple music. May help kids identify their own body parts and develop a sense of self. Repetition becomes a little annoying after a while. Kid Juror Comments: Children enjoyed finding their body parts and following along with what they saw. Good exercises. Some kids lost interest and wandered off. "I liked the sit-ups." "I liked the jumping jacks." Age: 1–4; Length: 32 min.; Suggested Retail Price: $14.95, SMALL FRY PRODUCTIONS

** BIRTHDAY! PARTY (PROFESSOR IRIS): The Professor Iris series is a part of "Ready, Set, Learn!" programming. Developed especially for preschoolers, it's a unique blend of education and entertainment. Adult Juror Comments: Terrific puppets. Information rich but not very well integrated for comprehension. Most appropriate for older preschoolers. Rather long, best viewed in segments. Kid Juror Comments: Four-year-olds stayed with it the most, asked questions and would watch it again. Children sang along, swaying back and forth and clapping to the music. Balloon section was popular. Age: 2–6; Length: 40 min.; Suggested Retail Price: $12.95, DISCOVERY COMMUNICATIONS

* BUSY DAY, A (LIL' IGUANA): A busy day at Lil' Iguana's house means making huge bubbles, unpacking special delivery boxes, cleaning out the refrigerator, deciding whether to put jelly doughnuts on pizza, and figuring out a mixed-up story, not necessarily in that order. Adult Juror Comments: Well produced. Quirky subject matter. The timing is too fast for significant audience participation. The characters and stories are appealing, but some content is slow and uneven. Seems a little forced and stilted. Kid Juror Comments: They liked learning bubble making, inventing the pizza, and the "day at the beach" sections best. Kids liked using "yum" and "yuck" as descriptors. Some children really responded to the iguanas. "The adults taught us good things about fresh food." Age: 3–5; Length: 30 min.; Suggested Retail Price: $12.95, WABU-TV 68

*** CIRCUS OF COLORS AND SHAPES, THE: Energetic music videos, a magic show, and clown antics teach children primary and secondary colors and basic shapes. Adult Juror Comments: Good pace, sequencing, and humor. Straightforward information for learning names of colors and shapes while encouraging creative activities. Additional parent follow-up activities are outstanding. Kid Juror Comments: Absorbing. Afterwards, they pointed out shapes around them. They touched the screen during the shapes quiz. Some kids requested watching the video every day for a week, so they could memorize the songs and point out the shapes! Age: 2–5; Length: 22 min.; Suggested Retail Price: $14.95, DOLPHIN COMMUNICATIONS

** CLEARED FOR TAKEOFF (FRED LEVINE'S ORIGINAL): Follow a family through Chicago's O'Hare International airport as a pilot shows them the control tower, baggage handling, takeoffs, and landings of giant jets. Adult Juror Comments: Interesting production, well paced, with realistic photography and an extensive vocabulary. Nice music. Appropriate for age group. They will relate to the story line. Some found the plane information insufficient. Kid Juror Comments: They wanted to know more. One child didn't realize that planes take off and land; she thought they just flew around. Children were disappointed when the video didn't show the final destination (Grandma in her house). Age: 2–5; Length: 30 min.; Suggested Retail Price: $14.95, FRED LEVINE PRODUCTIONS, INC.

*** CLIFFORD'S FUN WITH LETTERS: Developed by early childhood specialists, gives children new tools for learning to read. The circus is in town, but Emily, Elizabeth, and Clifford have no money for tickets. A message service seems like a great moneymaking idea but... Adult Juror Comments: Creates good learning opportunities. Word-shape song is more appropriate for 5–6 year olds. The activity booklet is a good resource for using message writing as an introduction to learning letter concepts. Kid Juror Comments: Very attentive and comfortable with Clifford. Helpful to have Clifford read aloud the words and phrases as he sees them. Age: 3–7; Length: 27 min.; Suggested Retail Price: $12.98, ARTISAN/FAMILY HOME ENTERTAINMENT

*** CLIFFORD'S FUN WITH NUMBERS: With Emily, Elizabeth, and Clifford— her big red dog—this episode teaches number recognition and mathematical vocabulary. An activity booklet gives parents or teachers additional content. Adult Juror Comments: High-quality production, brings characters to life for active viewing. Teaches kindness to animals. Children learn basic concept of number recognition. Kid Juror Comments: Attentive and interacted with the tape, counting out loud and anticipating each segment. Older kids taught younger ones. Kids asked to see it repeatedly. Age: 3–7; Length: 27 min.; Suggested Retail Price: $12.98, ARTISAN/FAMILY HOME ENTERTAINMENT

*** CLIFFORD'S FUN WITH OPPOSITES: Teaches the concept of opposites and relationships: The longest and shortest, the curliest and the straightest, the wildest and the tamest—there's something for everyone at the craziest pet show ever! Adult Juror Comments: Activity book that accompanies the video is excellent. Concept of opposites is a difficult one to get across, but this does a pretty good job. Some adults felt it was not dynamic viewing material, but found that kids enjoyed it more than they expected. Kid Juror Comments: Captivating. Children responded to scenes in the film out loud; only a couple got antsy toward the end. Age: 3–7; Length: 28 min.; Suggested Retail Price: $12.98, ARTISAN/FAMILY HOME ENTERTAINMENT

*** CLIFFORD'S FUN WITH RHYMES: Rhyming is a trick poor Clifford can't lick. Gives the child new tools for expanding vocabulary. Through rhymes, riddles, and songs, children develop listening skills essential to reading—and while having fun. Adult Juror Comments: Story line and vocabulary are challenging for three- and four-year-olds and simple for older kids. Reflects today's fun with use of music. Because it is book-based, video has potential to stimulate interest in literature and reading. Kid Juror Comments: Clifford knows best. They participated in rhyming and liked the story because it teaches friendship and cooperation. One group went on to read many Clifford books and had a Clifford Birthday Party. Children wanted to watch this over and over. Age: 3–7; Length: 27 min.; Suggested Retail Price: $12.98, ARTISAN/FAMILY HOME ENTERTAINMENT

** CLIFFORD'S FUN WITH SHAPES: The town carnival is in full swing, and Emily and Elizabeth take the lead in the scavenger hunt with the help of Clifford. Teaches identification and differentiation of various shapes and colors. Adult Juror Comments: Good quality animation—kids who enjoy the books will enjoy this a great deal. Contains introduction to early math concepts. Songs are nicely done. Lacks cultural diversity. Kid Juror Comments: Good interaction in identifying colors and shapes, but found it the least engaging of all the Clifford tapes. Age: 3–7; Length: 27 min.; Suggested Retail Price: $12.98, ARTISAN/FAMILY HOME ENTERTAINMENT

*** DO THE ALPHABET (SESAME STREET'S KIDS' GUIDE TO LIFE): Get ready to sing, dance, and laugh all the way from A to Z! It's 26 times the fun when you learn the alphabet with Big Bird and friends! Adult Juror Comments: Learning in the best of Sesame Street tradition. Great combination of children and characters. "Alphabet Blues" is really cute. The alphabet support group is clever. Kid Juror Comments: A winner! They cheered when Baby Bear got to "Z." An eight-year-old said, "I wish they had invented great alphabet songs like this when I was a kid." Age: 2–5; Length: 45 min.; Suggested Retail Price: $12.98, SONY WONDER/CTW

*** DOING THINGS—EATING, WASHING, IN MOTION (LIVE ACTION VIDEO): Compares children and animals engaged in everyday activities of eating, washing and playing. Non-narrated with musical accompaniment. Adult Juror Comments: Delightful! Good production, fun to watch. What a beautiful variety of children, the diversity is really a treasure! Kids enjoy watching animals and people do the same things. Kid Juror Comments: "That's awesome." "That was fun." The two's were ready to see it again right away. Age: 2–5; Length: 27 min.; Suggested Retail Price: $14.95, BO PEEP PRODUCTIONS, INC.

* EXPLORING COLORS & SHAPES OF THE DEEP BLUE SEA (REDBOOK LEARNING ADVENTURES): Fluffy Duffy and his friends are off on their greatest adventure yet: a voyage beneath the sea, where they learn all about colors and shapes. Adult Juror Comments: A meaningful video. The actors did a good job, but the story line seems contrived. The story and jokes are given more emphasis than teaching shapes and colors. Simple production, developmentally appropriate. Kid Juror Comments: Funny characters. Story line is a little over the heads of the younger ones, yet the educational goals are geared for younger ones. Age: 2–5; Length: 30 min.; Suggested Retail Price: $12.98, VIDEO TREASURES, INC.

* FIRE AND RESCUE (FRED LEVINE'S ORIGINAL): A behind-the-scenes look at the life of firefighters, from the training academy to the firehouse. Provides fire safety tips. Adult Juror Comments: Stimulating for older children. Good introduction to fire safety, equipment, and procedures. Inspires admiration for firefighters. Toddler appearing to play near burning building evoked safety concerns. Recommend adult facilitation. Kid Juror Comments: Attentive. Good for fire department field trips. Boys were most interested. Some parts are very scary for this age. Age: 2–5; Length: 30 min.; Suggested Retail Price: $14.95, FRED LEVINE PRODUCTIONS, INC.

* GERM BUSTERS, THE (CHILD SAFETY SERIES): The Germ Busters are coming, so prepare yourself. Clean up, wash your hands, flush, brush your teeth, and take your time doing it all. These are lessons children learn, featuring Kemi and Zemi from Nickelodeon's Roundhouse. Adult Juror Comments: Gets across valuable information on basic hygiene. Good ethnic mix. Kids liked the Germ Buster dance. Promotes bathing every day. A little intrusive, some strange interaction. Kid Juror Comments: Mixed reaction. Some thought it was okay, some parts boring. "I liked it a lot because we learned how to take care of our body," one five-year-old said. After watching the entire video, kids got up to wash their hands. Age: 3–6; Length: 30 min.; Suggested Retail Price: $19.95, KIDSAFETY OF AMERICA

* HELLO NUMBERS (LOOK & LEARN): Interactive games, sing- and count-along, teach children to count from one through 100. Adult Juror Comments: Educational and interesting. Repetition and encouragement are from robot host. Simple production proves that kids don't need high-tech presentation to learn educational concepts and be entertained. Some Jurors objected to using war toys as counting objects. Kid Juror Comments: Cute. Children participated by singing and following instructions such as touch your nose. The counting by 10's was too fast to follow. Liked the music. Too slow for some children. Age: 2–5; Length: 30 min.; Suggested Retail Price: $14.98, V.I.E.W. VIDEO

** HEY! THAT'S MY HAY: Geraldine, a talking cow, is eager to demonstrate how hay is made on her farm, and other things about farm life. Peter, the farmer, shows farm machinery and the tractors and horses that pull them. Adult Juror Comments: Though some segments were fascinating, program is too dry and long. Using a talking cow as a teacher is a cute idea, but the explanations are way beyond the child's comprehension. Humor is effective. Spurs interest in caring for animals. Kid Juror Comments: They liked the animals but got tired of all the machinery. Lots of questions, such as "Where do the animals go in the winter?" "The talking cow was fun to watch and listen to." "We liked seeing hay being made." Age: 3–6; Length: 30 min.; Suggested Retail Price: $12.95, FARMER SMALL PRODUCTIONS

** IN THEIR FAVORITE PLACES (Babies at Play); see p. 26

*** LEARNING TO SHARE (SESAME STREET'S KIDS' GUIDE TO LIFE): Special program featuring Katie Couric helps make growing up a lot more fun and gives parents tips for teaching kids to share. Adult Juror Comments: Demonstrates good conflict-resolution strategy in very real situations, including a child in a wheelchair. Elmo is perfect character to take on the "it's mine" attitude. Kid Juror Comments: All the children loved the characters and story. "You learn special rules in this tape." Kids wanted to know why Elmo wouldn't share. "I danced along for a minute, a couple times." Age: 2–5; Length: 45 min.; Suggested Retail Price: $12.98, SONY WONDER/CTW

* LET'S TRY SHARING (THE BIG COMFY COUCH): A cozy place for sharing lots of love. Loonette and Molly learn how sharing makes others feel good, even though it's sometimes hard. They also discover all the fun things fingers can do, like pointing, tickling, and tying ribbons! Adult Juror Comments: Putting stuff away under couch cushions is hardly what most families mean by tidying up. Lead character is a bit ambiguous. Is she a child or adult? Kid Juror Comments: Loonette was very mean to Molly.

Later she told Molly she was sorry. "We liked when they played with their hands and sang 'the itsy, bitsy spider song.' " "We'd like to learn more finger songs." Age: 3–5; Length: 30 min.; Suggested Retail Price: $14.99, TIME-LIFE KIDS

* LOVE (NEW ZOO REVIEW): Freddie discovers that love is giving, so he sells his beloved record player to buy a community swing that everyone loves to use. Featured songs: "I Love Most Everyone and Everything," "L.O.V.E.," and "A Little Love." Adult Juror Comments: Slow-moving, but animals are cute and colorful. "Made in 1971 and looks it." It's a little condescending. Women are shown in stereotypical roles. Some songs are lip-synched and awkwardly integrated into rest of show. Kid Juror Comments: "Boring." "Silly." "I liked how they danced." Kids liked the messages about learning to be nice and share. For the most part, they enjoyed the singing and the characters. "The hippo sang bad." Age: 3–5; Length: 25 min.; Suggested Retail Price: $9.95, BLACKBOARD ENTERTAINMENT

*** MORE PRESCHOOL POWER: Preschool-age "teachers" show how to tie shoes, brush teeth, make fruit salad, and play with shadow puppets. Packed with songs, music, jokes, and tongue twisters. Adult Juror Comments: This is a great child-centered tape. Excellent choice of activities, well produced. Segments are the perfect length for this age. Kid Juror Comments: Fabulous. Kids loved watching others their own age, dancing, playing, and being nice to one another. Good diversity and lovely songs—interacted throughout and afterwards talked about brushing teeth and the shadow finger animals they made. Age: 2–5; Length: 30 min.; Suggested Retail Price: $14.95, CONCEPT ASSOCIATES

** MY ALPHABET: Teaches letter and word recognition while introducing characters Alexander G. Bear and a cast of others who explore the alphabet together. Adult Juror Comments: Straightforward, pleasant learning. Fine premise for letter recognition as reinforcement; rote knowledge is not as important during the preschool years as is active exploration. Contains some static images. Kid Juror Comments: Children liked singing the songs afterward. They recognized the letters and responded by thinking up other words. Some chose to watch this based on the box cover. Age: 2–5; Length: 22 min.; Suggested Retail Price: $34.95, KIDEO PRODUCTIONS, INC.

** NUMBERS EXPRESS, THE: A friendly engineer on a turn-of-the-century steam engine introduces numbers, number relationships, and counting with catchy songs and games. Adult Juror Comments: The train ride is fun. Too many types of enumeration are mixed together. Introduces counting, sorting, sequencing. Encourages parent involvement. Good length, but not a lot of trains. Kid Juror Comments: Very nice, especially for the younger ones who enjoyed the songs and counting along. Age: 2–5; Length: 24 min.; Suggested Retail Price: $14.95, DOLPHIN COMMUNICATIONS

** OUR WORLD OF WHEELS: Designed to teach early skills in visual tracking, shape recognition, pre-reading readiness, sight and sound association. Portrays different vehicles in motion, such as fire engines, trains, motorcycles, police cars, and airplanes. Adult Juror Comments: Simple and fascinating. Lots to watch for. Authentic sounds are good. Good video for language development, recognition, and labeling of objects. The lack of narration makes this a good teaching tool without any interruption. Kid Juror Comments: Interesting sounds and vehicles. They relaxed on the floor and discussed what they recognized as it came on the screen. Children seemed to like the "realness" of the video. Age: 2–5; Length: 25 min.; Suggested Retail Price: $9.95, TOP SHELF PRODUCTIONS

*** PRESCHOOL POWER: JACKET FLIPS & OTHER TIPS: How to button, buckle, zip, wash hands, put on jackets, tidy rooms, make snacks, and pour without spilling a drop. Featuring the proven methods of Maria Montessori. Preschoolers will learn the lasting gift of self-reliance. Adult Juror Comments: A great musical series. Activities are age-appropriate, well executed, and fun. Very child-centered and well produced. "It's great to see what kids are capable of doing, because parents sometimes forget." Kid Juror Comments: They immediately imitate the behaviors they see on-screen, and ask questions about what the kids were doing. Age: 2–5; Length: 30 min.; Suggested Retail Price: $14.95, CONCEPT ASSOCIATES

***PRESCHOOL POWER #3: Preschoolers learn to do things for themselves: putting on gloves, making a paper fan, sweeping up spills, making French bread, blowing giant bubbles, setting up dominoes. Imagination and cooperation are emphasized. Adult Juror Comments: Great series with Montessori-designed activities in a music video format. Well produced, good diversity. Kid Juror Comments: Tops! KIDS FIRST! has put the videos into waiting rooms of health clinics, where the staff and clients enjoy them equally. Age: 2–5; Length: 30 min.; Suggested Retail Price: $14.95, CONCEPT ASSOCIATES

** PRIVACY PLEASE (THE BIG COMFY COUCH): Sometimes we all need some time alone. Preschoolers learn valuable lessons about quiet time and friendship. Includes physical activities, songs, and stories. Adult Juror Comments:

"It was entertaining yet gentle." The theme of Loonette and her doll encourages young children to express their feelings. Lacks multi-cultural diversity. Kid Juror Comments: "I laughed." "It made me think about my other friends at my school." "It made me want to play the violin." "Sometimes you need privacy." Age: 2–5; Length: 25 min.; Suggested Retail Price: $14.99, TIME-LIFE VIDEO & TELEVISION

** RICHARD SCARRY'S BEST ABC VIDEO EVER!: Huckle Cat and his classmates present the alphabet in 26 charming stories. Adult Juror Comments: Great ABC video, but shows little cultural diversity in the voices. Characters are appealing. Some Jurors don't like using it with children under four, since they may not understand the relationship between a letter symbol and a sound. Kid Juror Comments: Excellent. They laughed at the jokes, called out each other's names when their letter came up. Works well with the Scarry books. Age: 2–6; Length: 30 min.; Suggested Retail Price: $9.98, RANDOM HOUSE HOME VIDEO

*** RICHARD SCARRY'S BEST COUNTING VIDEO EVER!: Children will love helping Lily Bunny count from one to 20. On her counting adventure, she meets Lowly Worm, Wrong-Way Roger, Bananas Gorilla, and other Richard Scarry characters who help her find funny things to count. Adult Juror Comments: Good animation, dialogue, songs. Promotes learning in a pleasant way. Perhaps a little too long for youngest kids—good to break it up into segments. Kid Juror Comments: Kids love Richard Scarry. They relate well to the animal characters. Some older kids requested it again. Age: 2–6; Length: 30 min.; Suggested Retail Price: $9.98, RANDOM HOUSE HOME VIDEO

** SEE IT! SAY IT! SING IT! PLAY IT! (PRIMALUX VIDEO EDUCATIONAL SERIES): Teaches word association, object recognition, and counting through familiar images and the sounds they make. Includes counting games and songs such as the "ABC's," "Ten Little Fingers," and "Itsy Bitsy Spider." Adult Juror Comments: Entertaining and encourages basic reading readiness. Good use of different ways to learn: music, words, visuals. Concrete examples. Kid Juror Comments: Appealing across the board. From one-year-olds to the "just-turned-four" kids, especially the boys. Children sang along with the songs. "I liked that the kids were funny." Age: 1–6; Length: 25 min.; Suggested Retail Price: $14.95, PRIMALUX VIDEO

*** SO SMART!; see p. 27

*** SO SMART! VOL. 2: ALL ABOUT SHAPES; see p. 27

*** SO SMART! VOL. 3: ALL ABOUT LETTERS; see p. 27

* SOUNDS OF LETTERS (READING LESSON): How do the letters of the alphabet sound? Animated characters help the child take the first steps into the world of reading. Adult Juror Comments: Sounds and visuals are effective and appropriate for introducing the alphabet, but rather dry and slow-moving. Presents the alphabet, simply. Kid Juror Comments: For children who do not know their alphabet, this tape will have the appeal of repeat playing. Older children who know their ABC's will be less interested. Age: 2–5; Length: 32 min.; Suggested Retail Price: $29.00, ATTAINMENT COMPANY, INC.

** SPACE CADETS (PROFESSOR IRIS): Professor Iris rockets off into space to get a better look at the moon, the earth and sky, and, of course, space! The view is magnificent from Professor Iris' rocket ship classroom. Adult Juror Comments: Good production, excellent colors, and humor. Strongest virtue: the way it conveys information. Difficult to follow because the production attempts to cover too many topics. As a result, it's too long for the audience. Kid Juror Comments: Boys seemed to like it best. They thought it was too long to view all in one sitting. Age: 2–6; Length: 40 min.; Suggested Retail Price: $12.95, DISCOVERY COMMUNICATIONS

** TODDLER TREASURY, A; see p. 28

**TRACTORS, COMBINES AND THINGS ON THE GROW: Food doesn't magically appear on grocery shelves. Explores "where food comes from" as narrators pursue the trail from food production to processing and distribution. Adult Juror Comments: Quality of production works for a child's perspective. Children are terrific narrators. From planting to touring the bakery where the flour is made into bread—it's all there. A look at why farmers work so hard. A little long for this audience. Kid Juror Comments: Favorite segments: time-lapse photography of plant growth, watching closeups of the big machines in action. Older kids enjoyed this best. Age: 2–8; Length: 30 min.; Suggested Retail Price: $19.95, JUST OUR SIZE VIDEOS

*** TRUE FRIENDS (THE ALL NEW CAPTAIN KANGAROO): Joey gets a pet turtle and thoughtlessly builds a house for it using the Captain's hat. He learns to be more responsible. Joey tells a fib about messing up the Captain's garden and learns the importance of telling the truth. Adult Juror Comments: Appealing, gentle, nice atmosphere. "Children are so captivated that it's a pleasure to view with them." Good variety of reality and fantasy. Positive and respectful of the way kids think. Language play is fun. Great blending of characters and media. Kid Juror Comments: Enthralling. A two-year-old boy stated, "I LOVE Captain Kangaroo." "Why is he a Captain?" Kids liked Mr. Moose's jokes. Age: 2–11; Length: 54 min.; Suggested Retail Price: $12.98, TWENTIETH CENTURY FOX HOME ENTERTAINMENT

** UNDER A BLUE, BLUE SKY (BABIES AT PLAY); see p. 28

** WHEN IT'S WINTER (THE BIG COMFY COUCH): Loonette the clown and her best friend, Molly, discover fun ways to warm up on cold winter days. Features the "10-second tidy," storytelling, and lots of pretending. Adult Juror Comments: Children will relate to the clown's experiences and the whimsical couch. Making winter indoors was an interesting concept, particularly for those who have never experienced winter. Kid Juror Comments: "I liked it because it was funny." "It made me feel cold and warm at the same time." "I knew that Molly was thinking about snow, even if she didn't talk." "I would like to try knitting." Age: 2–5; Length: 25 min.; Suggested Retail Price: $14.99, TIME-LIFE VIDEO & TELEVISION

* YOU CAN'T WIN 'EM ALL (HUGGABLE CLUB, THE): Being a good sport is the focus of this music-packed video. Do your best, play by the rules, play it safe, learn to share. Kids will learn they can't always be the winners. Adult Juror Comments: Very sweet, with good discussions about playing fair. Demonstrates positive social behaviors. Some parts moved slowly. Actors were stiff, artificial, and empathizing with them was difficult. Lively songs. Kid Juror Comments: Music had children moving in their seats. Some were singing the songs long after the tape had ended, but some children had lost interest. "I'm thinking about the different characters and the poor sport, Sally." Age: 2–5; Length: 27 min.; Suggested Retail Price: $12.98, HUGGABUG PRODUCTIONS

CD-ROMs

** A TO ZAP!: Teaches letters and words. Explores concepts such as over and under or quick versus slow. Offers 26 different activities. Adult Juror Comments: Easy to use. Fun, interactive approach. Good characters. Kids liked the orchestra at the beginning and the variety of activities. It does require small-muscle coordination, making it somewhat difficult for the youngest users. Kid Juror Comments: Really nice, especially the orchestra section at the beginning and the various activities throughout. Kids said they would play it at least once or twice. Age: 3–7; Suggested Retail Price: $14.95, SUNBURST COMMUNICATIONS, INC.

** ALPHABET ADVENTURE WITH DIGBY AND LYDIA (LEARNING LADDER): Teaches the alphabet through storytelling, music and animation. Using Quicktime movies, songs, and interactive tests, kids find hidden letters, learn word association and the alphabet. Rewards spelling, reading, and perception. Adult Juror Comments: Simple presentation. Great characters, good developmental level. Comes with good adult handbook. Voice-overs are respectful, instructive, and reassuring. "Click and point friendly." Minimal choice of levels. Kid Juror Comments: Story held interest of five- and six-year-olds; three- and four-year-olds liked the games. Unless computer literate, help is needed to find fully utilize the program. Kids liked the lively music and printing out the awards. Age: 3–5; Suggested Retail Price: $34.95, PANASONIC INTERACTIVE MEDIA

** ARTHUR'S READING RACE: Takes children on a walk around town with Arthur and his little sister D.W. Children are encouraged to learn words throughout the story and through three additional activities. Adult Juror Comments: Slick, high-quality production. Excellent graphics, fun games. Develops word recognition, increases vocabulary, reading comprehension, computer literacy. "Great early-learning title." Jurors thought Arthur and D.W. were at times rude to each other. Kid Juror Comments: Kids enjoyed playing the 'let me write' games, because they make nonsense sentences. They also like the clickable window, ice cream section and enjoyed playing it with their friends. Works best in a situation where kids can play repeatedly. Age: 3–6; Suggested Retail Price: $29.95, THE LEARNING COMPANY

** BABES IN TOYLAND: AN INTERACTIVE ADVENTURE; see p. 144

*** DISNEY'S READY FOR MATH WITH POOH (DISNEY'S LEARNING SERIES): In the heart of the 100 Acre Wood, math is an adventure. Pooh and friends guide children through activities that reinforce beginning math skills. Fun rewards are used to build their own gardens. Counting, sorting, adding, and subtracting are covered. Adult Juror Comments: Excellent production quality. Quite creative and fun to do. Adorable use of characters in imaginative setting. Reinforces problem solving, critical thinking, and visual-motor skills. Holds place when play is interrupted. Kid Juror Comments: Very easy for child to operate. Kids loved this. Easy to use without much assistance. "The characters were awfully polite to each other." "Rabbit wasn't so grumpy today." Praises the children—definitely a confidence booster. Age: 3–7; Suggested Retail Price: $39.99, DISNEY INTERACTIVE

*** DISNEY'S READY TO READ WITH POOH: Pooh and friends guide children through activities that stimulate imagination and reinforce critical skills.

Offers lots of surprises as kids learn to read through play and collecting fun rewards. Includes alphabet, phonics, spelling, and rhyming. Adult Juror Comments: Adorable. Excellent graphics, good variety of characters, imaginative setting, flows easily. Reinforces pre-writing skills. Sometimes difficult. A loving, polite group of animals help provide good role models for self-esteem and friendship. Kid Juror Comments: "It's magic." Characters and music help hold kids' interest. They can navigate without much help. Kids wanted to play over and over again. They stayed in at lunch, recess and after school to play. Age: 3–7; Suggested Retail Price: $39.99, DISNEY INTERACTIVE

*** DR. SEUSS KINDERGARTEN: Offers a year's worth of math, reading, and other essential kindergarten skills. Gerald McGrew is building a zoo in Seussville. As children help him find exotic animals, they learn math and reading skills. Moral: Kids who laugh more, learn more. Adult Juror Comments: Superb. Fantasyland draws child in, offers breaks and playtime. Learn, participate, watch, listen, and sing along. Gets progressively harder. "I wish all CD-ROMs were as entertaining, educational and engaging." Creative, well planned. Kid Juror Comments: Kids loved this. They enjoyed checking their progress throughout the game. They didn't want to stop playing and were inspired to read the books. "Dr. Seuss put me in the mood to do math." "It's like solving a puzzle. I felt good when I got it right." Age: 3–7; Suggested Retail Price: $19.99, BRODERBUND SOFTWARE

*** DR. SEUSS PRESCHOOL: Pairs learning activities with a guided adventure. Offers a year's worth of important preschool skills. While helping baby Elma Sue look for her mother, Horton the faithful elephant leads children on a delightful learning adventure. Adult Juror Comments: Appealing. Keeps with the spirit of Dr. Seuss' stories with classic characters, great content, and good reinforcement for number, letter, and color recognition. Appropriately challenging. "I have played many kids' CD-ROMs, and this is one of the best." Kid Juror Comments: Definitely a hit. A three-year-old could do it with little assistance. "The kids were spellbound from the beginning." Children remained involved with the characters and enjoyed learning material. Great value for home learning. Age: 3–5; Suggested Retail Price: $19.99, BRODERBUND SOFTWARE (CD-ROM)

* DR. SEUSS'S ABC: The magic of Dr. Seuss' books comes to life in this introduction to reading. Adult Juror Comments: Very cute and a pleasure to play. Requires high-level vocabulary for alphabet learning. Has limited educational value. Jurors weren't crazy about the "alphabet" programming, but using the Dr. Seuss characters, a perennial favorite, made it palatable.

Kid Juror Comments: Some children adored it, particularly those who are Seuss fans. Humor is catchy. Did not hold most children's interest through to the end. Age: 2–5; Suggested Retail Price: $29.95, THE LEARNING COMPANY

** FISHER-PRICE READY FOR SCHOOL-TODDLER: Join the Little People characters on a magical journey of learning and discovery created just for toddlers. Disk One includes 20 activities, carefully planned to help toddlers discover the world around them. Disc Two is a parenting guide. Adult Juror Comments: Positive, clear linear presentation, child-centered, encourages self-esteem. Variety of music, cultures, and experiences. The animated flashcards and worksheets offer minimal educational fare. Information on nutrition and breastfeeding are excellent. Kid Juror Comments: Quite enchanting. Wanted to play again. Easy, though a child still needs adult help. Has two levels of difficulty. Requires direct parent involvement. Age: 3–6; Suggested Retail Price: $20.00, KNOWLEDGE ADVENTURE

** FISHER-PRICE TIME TO PLAY PET SHOP: Children are invited to run their very own pet shop, selecting cute dogs, cats, fish, reptiles, hamsters, bunnies, and other critters. Six activities allow them to care for, groom, and feed the animals. Offers a unique experience each time they play. Adult Juror Comments: Good combination of cute animals and catchy songs. Easy installation. Reinforces the need to take care of pets, introduces various types of pets and encourages decision-making. Mouse response is overly sensitive. Program overuses the phrase "real good." Kid Juror Comments: Riveting for younger children. Preschoolers wanted to play this over and over. Instructions are very clear. Kids enjoyed the selection of items they can print. They came away with a renewed interest in taking care of animals. It was a favorite. Age: 3–6; Suggested Retail Price: $20.00, KNOWLEDGE ADVENTURE

*** JUMPSTART KINDERGARTEN: Children explore an interactive kindergarten classroom where fun, music, and games are the rewards for curiosity. This new version of the original classic has updated graphics and animation, new phonics activities, a printable workbook, and more. Adult Juror Comments: Nice mix of content for developing critical thinking, interpersonal behaviors, visual-motor skills, and problem solving. Well organized, clearly presented, motivating, and easy to use. Facilitates learning in an entertaining manner. Kid Juror Comments: Fun and interesting. Kids like the coloring book activity. All the children enjoyed it. Good kindergarten program, covers variety of material. Age: 4–6; Suggested Retail Price: $30.00, KNOWLEDGE ADVENTURE

*** JUMPSTART KINDERGARTEN READING: A grade-based reading program that gives kindergartners an early start in their reading efforts by teaching ten fundamental reading concepts and reinforcing these concepts with extended activities in printable color and write pages. Adults Juror Comments: Great songs, engaging games, enticing rewards. Gives gentle suggestions to try different sections. Contains a bonus section for adults that enables them to check each child's progress. Kid Juror Comments: Good variety of activities, music and graphics, but kids found that sometimes the program requested things they didn't know, such as "What is a vowel?" Age: 4–6; Suggested Retail Price: $33.00, KNOWLEDGE ADVENTURE

*** JUMPSTART PRESCHOOL: Join animal pals as they explore a colorful classroom of ten interactive play areas covering more than twenty preschool skills such as colors, shapes, letters, numbers, pre-reading, music, and listening. Adult Juror Comments: Easy to install, excellent levels of difficulty. Much better than the previous version, better graphics, lots of positive feedback, one click to move, low frustration factor. "Assesses difficulty and moves it up, but parent can also choose levels." Kid Juror Comments: "I loved it." Gave children confidence for activities at their own levels. Instills pride in personal achievement. Age: 2–5; Suggested Retail Price: $20.00, KNOWLEDGE ADVENTURE

*** JUMPSTART SPANISH: Designed for preschool kids when they're most receptive to learning and retaining a new language. Kids explore ten activities that introduce more than two hundred words and conversational phrases, providing a solid bilingual foundation. Adult Juror Comments: Stimulates language development. Audio is awesome, satisfying, and gratifying—everything a learning program should be. Easy to install and use. Kid Juror Comments: Great. "Let's do this again." Kids were so occupied with the activities they didn't realize they were learning how to say words in Spanish. Couldn't wait to take turns. A little frustrating for some. Age: 3–6; Suggested Retail Price: $30.00, KNOWLEDGE ADVENTURE

** LET'S GO READ! AN ISLAND ADVENTURE: Develops reading, comprehension, and vocabulary skills while interacting with friendly characters and a colorful environment. Multileveled activities with interactive books allow children to choose the ending they prefer. Adult Juror Comments: Reinforces and encourages fundamental reading, thinking skills, and cooperative behavior. Develops beginning reading skills and other fundamental skills such as matching and discrimination. Does not allow the player to bypass certain tasks. Kid Juror Comments: Mixed reaction. Kids enjoyed how the characters encouraged each other. "If I learn to read, you can too." But parts were frustrating. Technically difficult. Child cannot bypass certain tasks, must complete before he moves on. Too slow for kids who are readers. Age: 3–6; Suggested Retail Price: $44.95, EDMARK

** MAGIC LETTER FACTORY, THE: A challenging romp through an introduction to reading. Brimming with interactive pre-reading adventures and Hap Palmer songs and videos. Includes four Hap Palmer alphabet songs that can be played on any CD player. Adult Juror Comments: Very cute but a little slow. Best for pre-readers developing early reading skills. Pace good for this audience. Voices are irritating and a little hard to understand. Kid Juror Comments: Most children found transition difficult and slow. One two-year-old loved it. Challenging content for three-year-olds, while some fours and fives were eager to demonstrate the parts they liked best. Age: 2–5; Suggested Retail Price: $49.95, EDUCATIONAL ACTIVITIES, INC.

*** MICROSOFT ACTIMATES EARLY LEARNING SYSTEM: The system captivates children with fun, educational activities using preschooler character, Barney, as a 16-inch plush toy, accompanied with software and videos. Adult Juror Comments: Potential as a teaching tool is fantastic. Respectful of children and diversity, paced well. A gentle, non-threatening appeal, large vocabulary, and responds to signals by external media. "This doll has endless possibilities." Kid Juror Comments: "My son enjoyed the Barney doll by itself and was fascinated with the interactivity between the video and CD-ROM. It increased his computer skills." When the doll is not receiving any stimuli, it announces it's "tired" and turns itself off. Age: 3–7; Suggested Retail Price: $99.99, MICROSOFT

** MICROSOFT MY PERSONAL TUTOR: A comprehensive learning solution for families with children ages three to seven. Contains hundreds of activities, games, tutorials, and songs that encourage confidence, exploration, and a love of learning. Adult Juror Comments: Well designed with a variety of information. Good graphics with clear and vivid colors. User-friendly, good pace, age-appropriate vocabulary. Levels of difficulty are gradual enough for child to be successful. There are "no wrong answers." Kid Juror Comments: Most children liked this program and asked to play it again. Five-year-olds could navigate on their own with occasional help. Kids really enjoyed the graphics. Age: 3–7; Suggested Retail Price: $54.95, MICROSOFT/SHANDWICK

*** MILLIE AND BAILEY KINDERGARTEN (MILLIE AND BAILEY EARLY LEARNING): Features well-structured activities designed to build a solid foundation in basic skills that support a child through kindergarten and beyond. Covers math, reading, language arts, science, problem solving, and critical thinking. Adult Juror Comments: Excellent, very appealing. Works smoothly and mistakes are handled thoughtfully. The "discovery mode" is particularly good, stimulating exploration. Promotes critical thinking and problem solving skills. Little diversity. Kid Juror Comments: Children learn while they're having fun. They enjoyed the question-and-answer section best. Younger children may need adult help. Encourages kids' self-esteem. Rewards correct answers, gently corrects errors. Kids learn from their mistakes. Age: 3–6; Suggested Retail Price: $29.95, EDMARK

*** NICK JR. PLAY MATH; see p. 150

** PHONICS ADVENTURE WITH SING-ALONG SAM (LEARNING LADDER): Animated program teaches basic phonic skills with fifteen tunes and twelve sequenced lessons. Teaches letter and sound recognition, consonant and vowel blends, and simple sentence structure. At the end, child's name is included in the "Hall of Fame." Adult Juror Comments: Good tool that develops early reading skills. Wonderful for beginners. Some thought it dragged a bit. Feedback doesn't emphasize the positive. Easy to install. Kid Juror Comments: Good program. Most kids enjoyed it. Those who didn't, at first, were later drawn into playing with the game. Age: 4–6; Suggested Retail Price: $34.95, PANASONIC INTERACTIVE MEDIA

** POUND PUPPIES INTERACTIVE STORYBOOK & ACTIVITY CENTER: The player becomes the star. After a puppy is adopted from the pound, the puppy follows the child throughout the story. Teaches basic reading skills at multiple skill levels. Includes a paint program. Adult Juror Comments: Stimulates awareness about pets and veterinarians. Challenging game levels. Great coloring book, entertaining story. Good for inexperienced users. Some feedback is lost on non-readers. Contains some gender stereotyping. Doesn't hold child's place. Kid Juror Comments: They liked seeing their names in the story. The puzzles, picking the puppy, painting with the rainbow, and the puppy theme were favorite parts. Pre-readers found it difficult. Girls enjoyed it best. Some kids were quickly bored. Age: 3–6; Suggested Retail Price: $19.95, EL-KO INTERACTIVE, INC.

** SESAME STREET: GET SET TO LEARN: Integrates preschool skills that develop critical thinking and problem-solving skills. Features more than 25 essential skills, 20 activity combinations and four skill levels. Skill levels adjust, based on child's progress. Adult Juror Comments: Nice reinforcements, ties in with well-known Sesame Street characters. Scored high with kids. Overly chatty characters slow down child's pace, however. Kid Juror Comments: Big Bird's counting was the best part, and the size game the least liked. Kids didn't have adequate time to answer question and complete the task before the characters interrupted them. Age: 4–6; Suggested Retail Price: $39.95, THE LEARNING COMPANY

*** SHEILA RAE THE BRAVE: A sing-along adventure in an interactive storybook based on the children's book by the Caldecott Award–winning author Kevin Henkes. Adult Juror Comments: "Makes a good book even better!" Songs are ideal. Female role model is excellent. Shows respect for family members. Instructions are clear, though adults experienced some technical problems in the map section. Kid Juror Comments: Big hit when a favorite book comes to life. Taps into three- and four-year-old humor. Kids stuck with it through to the end and played it again right away. Loved the music. Age: 2–7; Suggested Retail Price: $40.00, THE LEARNING COMPANY

*** WINNIE THE POOH AND THE HONEY TREE (DISNEY'S ANIMATED STORY-BOOK): Read, sing, and play along with Winnie the Pooh. A friendly bear and a familiar story offer a jump into Pooh's world for exciting adventures. Pooh, Piglet, Tigger, and the gang make reading lively and fun. Adult Juror Comments: Makes an excellent first CD-ROM for children. It is well organized, easy to use, and encourages independence. Familiarity with characters and art add to its appeal. Content and material are age-appropriate though they lack depth. Kid Juror Comments: Kids enjoyed the characters. They liked hearing the book in Spanish as well as English. Games section is perfect for preschoolers. Kids weren't interested in playing the storybook section more than once, even though it could enhance their skills. Age: 2–6; Suggested Retail Price: $29.95, DISNEY INTERACTIVE

Family

** AND BABY MAKES FOUR (THE HUGGABUG CLUB): Maria is concerned about the new baby coming into her family. The Buggsters learn how special it is to be a brother or a sister and the importance of families. Adult Juror Comments: Helps children cope with becoming an older brother or sister. Entertaining costumes and music. Some vocabulary is beyond comprehension of preschoolers. Some segments overly focus on negative aspects of the new baby such as crying and funny smells. Kid Juror Comments: Children responded by talking about their siblings and families, and some even drew pictures of their families. "I want my mom to have a baby." "I liked the baby songs." Age: 2–6; Length: 30 min.; Suggested Retail Price: $10.95, HUG-GABUG PRODUCTIONS

** ALL ABOARD FOR SHARING (BARNEY & FRIENDS COLLECTION): BJ, Baby Bop, and the children are left a host of surprises by trains passing through the playground. Barney, however, must wait for his surprise. Finally, it arrives: Stella the Storyteller recounting the story of "The Little Engine That Could." Adult Juror Comments: Nice imaginative play sequences have a sharing theme, although the sharing theme doesn't come across as well as expected. Adults thought the children in video are too perfect and not real enough. Kid Juror Comments: Barney is lovable in every form. Most of the child jurors sing and dance along. Some children were uncomfortable with "feeling" songs. Younger kids enjoy it most. Age: 2–5; Length: 30 min.; Suggested Retail Price: $14.95, LYRICK STUDIOS

*** ALLEGRA'S CHRISTMAS (ALLEGRA'S WINDOW): Allegra learns the true meaning of Christmas giving when she finds out that one of Santa's helpers expects to spend Christmas alone. Allegra to the rescue! Adult Juror Comments: Colorful characters. Engaging, thoughtful story. Wonderfully instructive in showing how to be happy about simple things. Good message about giving. Good color and amusing puppets. Appropriate language. Pace/visuals at times too fast. Kid Juror Comments: A nice Christmas message for kids. Prompted discussion among kids afterwards. Allegra is very lovable! The children sang along and laughed and talked about what they saw. Some dialogue scenes are somewhat long. Age: 2–7; Length: 47 min.; Suggested Retail Price: $9.95, PARAMOUNT HOME VIDEO

*** ANIMAL ALPHABET: From a skittish armadillo to a playful zebra, Animal Alphabet provides preschooler with an exciting way to learn the ABC's. Lively footage of 26 exotic animals help illustrate each letter. Each animal has its own toe-tapping song. Adult Juror Comments: Well done, bright. and fast-paced. Teaches new animal names as well as the letters. Exceptional educational value. Kids learn through songs and repetition. Older kids will continue to enjoy the animals even after they've learned their ABC's. Kid Juror Comments: Seeing a wide variety of animals was wonderful. Kids learned their names and songs to go with them. They danced, sang, and asked for the animal names to be repeated for the animals they were unfamiliar with. "You shouldn't eat butterflies!" Age: 2–5; Length: 44 min.; Suggested Retail Price: $12.99, TIME-LIFE KIDS

** AT THE AIRPORT; see p. 157

** BANANAS IN PAJAMAS: SHOW BUSINESS: The Bananas have a cold and are miserable so the Teddies put on a show, which is a disaster. The Bananas laugh so much at the show that they feel better. Adult Juror Comments: It's nice to know that cute videos can be produced with simple props and backgrounds. The short stories held the children's attention. Not enough assets for an all-star. Kid Juror Comments: Seeing the cover, one five-year-old commented, "Oh good, I really like these." Some kids found it boring and too light. They relate to the hiccup story. Age: 2–5; Length: 25 min.; Suggested Retail Price: $12.95, POLYGRAM VIDEO

*** BARNEY GOES TO SCHOOL: Barney joins the Backyard Gang at school for finger-painting and to learn numbers, letters, colors, and shapes. Barney discovers why the children love to go to school. Adult Juror Comments: Quality production. Songs, fantasies, and school lessons are fun, hands-on, and well presented. Promotes learning at school. Introduces water and pretend play. The patriotism is a little overdone and conformist. Kid Juror Comments: They smiled and danced to the music. Responded well to the combination of learning and fun. Age: 2–5; Length: 30 min.; Suggested Retail Price: $14.95, LYRICK STUDIOS

*** BARNEY IN CONCERT: Barney and the Backyard Gang hold a live musical extravaganza at the Majestic Theater in Dallas. Features traditional songs that encourage interaction and audience participation. Introduces Baby Bop, a forever two-year-old. Adult Juror Comments: Enjoyable for intended audience. Songs and skits encourage participation. Shots of the audience are delightful. Kid Juror Comments: "My two-year-olds really enjoyed this tape. They were dancing, clapping, and screaming." It held their interest. Age: 2–5; Length: 45 min.; Suggested Retail Price: $14.95, LYRICK STUDIOS

*** BARNEY LIVE! IN NEW YORK CITY: Barney appears on stage in New York for an imaginative and lively musical extravaganza. Barney, Baby Bop, and BJ teach the importance of having friends and sharing. Adult Juror Comments: Even Barney critics enjoyed this show. Nice awareness of gender roles (example: changing song that includes both mom and dad). It's entertaining for young and old to sing childhood songs with Barney and friends. Audience shots show good diversity. Kid Juror Comments: Smash success. Children got up and danced, sang along. Kids were entranced, particularly younger ones. Barney makes them feel good. "Winkster is a fun character." Some wanted to watch it again. Age: 2–5; Length: 75 min.; Suggested Retail Price: $19.99, LYRICK STUDIOS

** BARNEY RHYMES WITH MOTHER GOOSE: A bookworm has eaten the pages of Mother Goose's book. Barney and friends help Mother Goose remember her favorite nursery rhymes. Features songs, dances, puzzles, and puppets. Adult Juror Comments: Barney is child-centered, caring, and encouraging. This tape comes with an activity guide recommending follow-up activities to reinforce message. Adults found inadequacies in the forced puppetry, heavy-handed diversity, and lack of musicality. Kid Juror Comments: Younger kids loved it and wanted to watch it again. Some found it too long for one sitting and were easily distracted. Kids sang and danced along. They discovered Mother Goose rhymes are fun to say but thought that "Barney was not real." Age: 2–5; Length: 30 min.; Suggested Retail Price: $14.95, LYRICK STUDIOS

*** BARNEY SAFETY: Makes it fun to learn safety lessons. Attached to special market sleeves is a free 24–page safety guide developed by the Johns Hopkins School of Public Health. Adult Juror Comments: Good production, culturally diverse, clear messages, and accurate information. Though adults find Barney corny and boring, they believe it's good for kids. Helps enhance children's sense of self-esteem. Demonstrates love and friendship. Kid Juror Comments: Great! Barney is always a hit. Children immediately identify with character. Kids loved this and watched it again the next morning. Provoked discussion about disabilities. Age: 2–7; Length: 45 min.; Suggested Retail Price: $14.95, LYRICK STUDIOS

*** BARNEY'S ADVENTURE BUS: Bus driver Barney takes the gang to some favorite imaginary destinations—a castle where Brett can rule; Barney's Purple Pepperoni Pizzeria; a rootin', tootin' ride into the Wild West; and a stop at the circus—all filled with fun and music. Adult Juror Comments: While tries to appeal to older audience is more suitable for preschoolers. Emphasis on careers encourages kids to think about their future. Well produced. Pace is too fast at times. Sets are unoriginal; messages a little simplistic. Good diversity. Kid Juror Comments: Great! Preschoolers recognize and enjoy Barney and the other characters. They loved the music and fantasy parts, especially making pizza, the tightrope scene and "all the adventures." It's a little on the long side, best viewed in segments. Age: 2–5; Length: 50 min.; Suggested Retail Price: $14.95, LYRICK STUDIOS

*** BARNEY'S BEST MANNERS: Barney and friends picnic and have a bubble splash party with Baby Bop. Songs reinforce saying "please" and "thank you," taking turns, opening and closing doors for friends. Adult Juror Comments: Offers exceptional reinforcements for using good manners. Relative naturalness of children is appealing. Activity guide offers appropriate, engaging suggestions. Pacing is a little slow. Overall feeling is positive. Kid Juror Comments: Two levels of satisfaction: Terrific or super-terrific. Enjoyed the songs that reinforce politeness, and imitated such behavior afterwards. All the kids enjoyed the bubble scene. Age: 2–5; Length: 30 min.; Suggested Retail Price: $14.95, LYRICK STUDIOS

***BARNEY'S BIG SURPRISE:** Barney the Dinosaur is planning a Super-Dee-Duper surprise party for BJ, and it's going to be a musical extravaganza with Professor Tinkerputt, Mother Goose, and others. Includes "Barney Is a Dinosaur," "If You're Happy and You Know It," and other songs. Adult Juror Comments: Lively, entertaining combination of old and new songs. Enthusiasm is contagious. Mother Goose section explains what rhyming is. Even the kids who thought they'd outgrown Barney enjoyed the video. Kid Juror Comments: Children broke out into smiles and giggles. "If kids like Barney, they will like this." "The Humpty Dumpty rhyme part was my favorite." Stimulated questions about acting, theater, and production. Kids wanted to perform with Barney. Age: 2–5; Length: 78 min.; Suggested Retail Price: $19.99, LYRICK STUDIOS

*** BARNEY'S BIRTHDAY:** For Barney's birthday, his friends throw the best party ever. Introduces birthday customs from other parts of the world. Adult Juror Comments: A pleasant, happy experience. Birthdays always appeal to kids. Portrays cooperation, creativity, and making your own party materials. Shows social skills representing different cultures. Kid Juror Comments: Love that Barney, especially the girls. They sang along and asked to see it again. Every child spoke about their own birthdays—what they would do and who they would invite. Age: 2–5; Length: 30 min.; Suggested Retail Price: $14.95, LYRICK STUDIOS

* BARNEY'S CAMPFIRE SING-ALONG:** The children meet all sorts of woodland creatures, study the stars, learn forest safety lessons, and discover the delights of using their imagination. Adult Juror Comments: The content, songs, and concepts are more suitable to school-age children than the preschool audience Barney attracts. The studio forest set looks phony. The solutions to problems are too easy, kids are not encouraged to find solutions. Adults objected to the Barney doll advertisement and thought the program was too long for the intended audience. Kid Juror Comments: This Barney seems a little long. Children always like singing along to the familiar songs. Age: 2–5; Length: 40 min.; Suggested Retail Price: $14.95, LYRICK STUDIOS

*** BARNEY'S GOOD DAY GOOD NIGHT: It's a warm, sunny day, and Barney and his friends are soaking up some wonderful fun. When Robert wishes that just once he could stay up all night long, Barney uses his special "Night Timer" to create "night" during the day. Adult Juror Comments: Cheerful, with limited adult appeal. Well produced, colorful, nice songs. A pleasant look at the simpler side of day and night—wind, crickets, and fireflies. Barney gives children lots of praise for their thoughts and ideas. Kid Juror Comments: Liked the music and the songs. "There were silly parts like the moon getting dressed up." "Everyone was nice." "Learned some new flower names." Twos and threes like this best. Even a one-year-old watched, clapped, and laughed along with Barney. Age: 2–5; Length: 50 min.; Suggested Retail Price: $14.95, LYRICK STUDIOS

*** BARNEY'S HALLOWEEN PARTY: Barney and his friends decorate the school gym for a party. BJ and Baby Bop prepare their costumes for a night of trick-or-treating. Although the trick-or-treaters come up empty-handed, their friends have goodies and friendship to share. Adult Juror Comments: Wow, a Halloween theme without the scariness. Colorful, good special effects, cheerful music encourages cooperation, good manners, and diversity. Well produced with an overall good feeling that encourages participation but doesn't challenge kids. Kid Juror Comments: Appealing, especially Barney's teal-and-purple pumpkin. "It had lots of funny parts." "It showed how to dance and sing." "They were having so much fun." A boy who said he hated Barney before watched the whole video and enjoyed it. Age: 2–5; Length: 50 min.; Suggested Retail Price: $14.95, LYRICK STUDIOS

* BARNEY'S HOME SWEET HOME: There's no place like home. Barney's friends discover that there are many kinds of homes in the world, for animals as well as for people. Adult Juror Comments: Good tips for parents. Adult intervention helps expand on concepts in video. "A bit didactic. Barney is stiff and artificial-looking. Character interaction is too contrived. Children in video overact." Kid Juror Comments: Enthusiasm wavered throughout; didn't hold their attention. Age: 2–5; Length: 30 min.; Suggested Retail Price: $14.95, LYRICK STUDIOS

*** BARNEY'S MAGICAL MUSICAL ADVENTURE: A great adventure to a real castle. On the way, the troupe travels through a magical forest and discovers Twynkle the Elf. Adult Juror Comments: Different themes and the music make this very appealing. Has good learning potential and age-appropriate language. Nice diversity. Kid Juror Comments: Totally absorbed. Watched intently and asked to see it over and over. "Magical Barney" had kids glued to their seats and promoted further discussion of Barney's adventure, as well as spontaneous clapping. Age: 2–5; Length: 40 min.; Suggested Retail Price: $14.95, LYRICK STUDIOS

*** BARNEY'S MUSICAL SCRAPBOOK: Remember when Barney and his friends sailed to Coco Island? Or when the wind came along and blew BJ's hat away? Aaaah, the memories. One look through Barney's scrapbook and you'll be reminded of some of the best Barney moments ever. Adult Juror Comments: Appealing and educational stories motivate parent and child to sing, dance, and play together. Vivid colors, friendly characters, multicultural, entertaining with lots of love, laughter, and lessons about respect and feelings. Kid Juror Comments: Great! Children don't just sit and watch, they get up and dance, sing, and clap. It prepares them for reading by teaching pre-reading skills using songs and language. "Let's do what they are doing. It's fun and has silly parts." Age: 2–5; Length: 50 min.; Suggested Retail Price: $14.95, LYRICK STUDIOS

*** BARNEY: CAMP WANNA RUNNA ROUND: After a forest ranger visits the school, Jake decides he wants to be a ranger when he grows up. There's only one problem, he's never been in a real forest. With a little imagination and some help from Barney, Jake soon learns about the outdoors. Adult Juror Comments: Appeals to a large audience. Encourages children to use their imagination and be respectful of others. Well produced. Bravo for putting promos at end of the show and not at the beginning. Good safety and environmental lessons. Kid Juror Comments: Excited by singing the songs and doing the exercises afterwards. Watched it twice. Prompted discussion about their camping experiences. Kids liked watching the child actors. Age: 2–5; Length: 50 min.; Suggested Retail Price: $14.95, LYRICK STUDIOS

*** BARNEY: IN OUTER SPACE: It's a Super-Dee-Duper surprise when Barney and the children in the Astronomy Club look through their telescope and see someone staring right back at them! Adult Juror Comments: Cheerful, with limited adult appeal. The astronaut and history about NASA was interesting. Explains the difference between being in space and on earth. Instills pride in living on earth and offers good conservation messages. Kid Juror Comments: Kids liked the the astronomy lessons and seeing the telescope. "The stuff about space was really good." "I'd like to go into space like those kids did." "My little brother would sing with them, maybe even dance." Age: 2–5; Length: 50 min.; Suggested Retail Price: $14.95, LYRICK STUDIOS

*** BARNEY: IT'S TIME FOR COUNTING: When Stella the Storyteller loses the numbers from her magic clock it's up to Barney and his friends to help her find them. Their number search leads them straight to the library for some good old-fashioned storytelling fun. Adult Juror Comments: Thoroughly enjoyable. Humor is age-appropriate, shows good diversity, story moves well. Emphasizes importance of books and the library. "Barney is great at teaching social skills such as self-esteem." Kid Juror Comments: Children readily participated. Enjoyed finding the numbers, going on the treasure hunt. "He makes learning easy and makes me feel good." Kids wished they could play in the on-screen tree house. Twos and threes liked it best. Age: 2–5; Length: 30 min.; Suggested Retail Price: $14.95, LYRICK STUDIO

*** BEAR IN THE BIG BLUE HOUSE, VOL. 1: Bear tours the Big Blue House, introduces his friends, and together they point out their favorite things about each room. After all, "Home is where your favorite stuff is." Adult Juror Comments: Excellent, engaging production down to the most minute details. Colorful characters. Presentation taps into kids' natural curiosity about other people's homes. Offers many opportunities for learning new words through songs and language. Kid Juror Comments: Very interested in discussing different types of houses. Liked the idea of creating their own pretend spaces. "Can we visit Bear's house?" "Can we play mail carrier?" "We want to write a letter." Age: 2–5; Length: 50 min.; Suggested Retail Price: $9.95, JIM HENSON COMPANY

*** BEAR IN THE BIG BLUE HOUSE, VOL. 2: Bear and his friends explore friendship and what it means to be someone's friend. Ojo learns to make new friends while still keeping all the old friends. Adult Juror Comments: Delightful. "Combines high-quality production and cuddle-cute characters with solid educational values. Shows children how to care for one another and demonstrates kindness." Adults found characters to be loud and obnoxious. Kid Juror Comments: Great. "The bear and his friends are very kind to each other." "We like the puppets." "The bear is big but friendly." Older kids didn't like the screechy voices. Younger ones weren't bothered by them. Most were familiar with the characters. Age: 2–5; Length: 50 min.; Suggested Retail Price: $9.95, JIM HENSON COMPANY

*** BEAR IN THE BIG BLUE HOUSE, VOL. 3: Bear demonstrates different dances such as the Bear Cha-Cha-Cha, a jig, and a waltz. Bear teaches Tutter to dance because, after all, everybody can dance, even a little mouse. Adult Juror Comments: Tunes into child's world with a variety of colorful puppet characters who speak directly to the children and review the material. Excellent role models. Introduces new words, many opportunities for learning. Kid Juror Comments: Music is a big attraction. Kids clapped and danced along. "Tutter is my friend." "I could watch this every day." "I want to dance like Bear." "We like the puppets." Older children sang the goodbye song. Age: 2–5; Length: 50 min.; Suggested Retail Price: $9.95, JIM HENSON COMPANY

*** **BEAR IN THE BIG BLUE HOUSE, VOL. 4:** Bear has a case of the sniffles, and he's taking some quiet time. Everyone is helping to make him feel better, and with all the help Bear will be back on his feet in no time. Adult Juror Comments: Characters are friendly and sincere. Plots are simple and well paced. Shows self-respect and compassion. Colorful production without being garish. Careful listening is required to develop language and problem-solving skills. Kid Juror Comments: Appealing. Humor perfectly suited to children's sensibilities. Variety of characters and expressive features make them attractive but not cutesy. "I could watch this every day." Age: 2–5; Length: 50 min.; Suggested Retail Price: $9.95, JIM HENSON COMPANY

*** **BEDTIME STORIES:** Timeless stories promise only the sweetest of dreams. These eight beautifully animated films are in the tradition of childhood fa-vorites. Adult Juror Comments: Charming, lovely stories with real child-hood bedtime rituals and issues. Comforting and fun to watch. Well illustrated and colored. Wonderful pace. "This is one of the best videos for young children I have seen." Kid Juror Comments: Attentive, calm, and smiling. Asked to see it again and again. "Everyone was very interested in commenting on their own bedtime rituals and feelings." "I like this one." "It's pretty." Age: 2–5; Length: 44 min.; Suggested Retail Price: $12.99, TIME-LIFE KIDS

** **BERENSTAIN BEARS, VOL. 2:** Contains three episodes, "The Berenstain Bears and the Truth," "The Berenstain Bears Save the Bees," and "The Berenstain Bears in the Forbidden Cave." Adult Juror Comments: Stories are great, with just enough conflict to provide interest but not enough to distress a toddler. Characters are easy to identify with, though the father is often presented as foolish, and the production is attractive, simple, and re-assuring. Kid Juror Comments: Related easily to the message: Telling the truth is always better than lying. "I liked the characters." "It was fun to watch." "How did they get the flowers to eat the bees?" "They argued a lot but in the end they got along." Age: 3–6; Length: 36 min.; Suggested Retail Price: $9.95, COLUMBIA TRI-STAR

** **BERENSTAIN BEARS, VOL. 3:** Contains three episodes: "The Berenstain Bears Learn About Strangers," "The Berenstain Bears and the Disappearing Honey," and "The Berenstain Bears and the Substitute Teacher." Adult Juror Comments: The characters are endearing. Story lines address appropriate issues such as strangers in the house. Some stereotyping, i.e., Mama Bear always defers to Papa Bear. Third story has some offensive behavior that goes unrecognized. Kid Juror Comments: Attentive. They recognized the characters and their traits from the books and asked to watch it again. "I liked Sister Bear." "I think everyone except bullies will want to watch this tape." Age: 2–5; Length: 36 min.; Suggested Retail Price: $9.95, COLUMBIA TRI-STAR

*** BEST OF ELMO, THE: Elmo presents his greatest hits, from "Happy Tapping" to "Elmo's Song." Whether he's dancing onstage with Herry and Prairie Dawn, explaining heavy and light to Telly, or singing along with Ernie, Elmo makes you smile. Whoopi Goldberg makes a guest appearance. Adult Juror Comments: Excellent, really holds kids' attention. Perhaps a little long for youngest kids but can be viewed in segments. Kid Juror Comments: Fast pace. Kids love Elmo for his childlike qualities and enjoy singing along with him. Kids were attentive; they particularly enjoyed the music. Age: 2–5; Length: 29 min.; Suggested Retail Price: $12.98, SONY WONDER/CTW

** BEST OF KERMIT ON SESAME STREET (SESAME STREET): Kermit the Frog has been named "Frog of the Year." It couldn't have happened to a nicer amphibian. Kermit's old pal Grover is on hand to host a special tribute to Kermit's most memorable moments on Sesame Street. Adult Juror Comments: Kermit is everyone's favorite. Exciting, bouncy, a little too chaotic at times. Encourages discovery, fosters learning, offers variety of musical styles, diversity, and silly humor. Front-loaded with commercials and inappropriate physical behavior. Kid Juror Comments: "It was fun." Kids were upset that Grover hit the pigs to get rid of them. "I'd like to talk to Kermit." "I liked the ABC song the best." Some children found the pace too slow and lost interest. Kids enjoy the familiar Sesame Street characters. Age: 2–5; Length: 30 min.; Suggested Retail Price: $12.98, SONY WONDER

*** BIRTHDAY STORIES: Captivating stories celebrate the wonder and anticipation of every child's birthday. These seven beautifully animated films are in the tradition of childhood classics. Adult Juror Comments: Visually interesting, great graphics. Offers a lot for kids. "I loved the stories. The colors, music, and voices were calming." English accents were fine, but kids will not understand some English words. Addresses social values such as sharing. Kid Juror Comments: Enjoyed what they saw and talked about the program afterward. "Can we have a birthday party?" "I learned how to share and help each other." "I want it to be my birthday." Age: 2–8; Length: 44 min.; Suggested Retail Price: $12.99, TIME-LIFE KIDS

* BLINKY BILL'S FIRE BRIGADE: When a brush fire almost destroys the new school, Blinky and his gang set up the town's first fire brigade. Their first emergency call saves Blinky Bill. Adult Juror Comments: Children's actions are positive, but Blinky's troublemaking is negative behavior. Story is poorly constructed. Too many things happening all at once. Has some name-calling. It's interesting to watch the Australian cartoon animals. Kid Juror Comments: Some children recently had contact with people involved in a real fire and became very animated in discussing fires afterwards. Age: 3–6; Length: 30 min.; Suggested Retail Price: $12.99, TRIMARK ENTER-TAINMENT

*** BOY & HIS CAR, A; see p. 160

* CAT'S MEOW, THE: Shows sixty minutes of pampered cats and kittens at play. Adult Juror Comments: Simple and entertaining but somewhat repetitive and long. It may make a child want a cat without encouraging discussion of animal needs. Little to learn but enjoyable to watch. Kid Juror Comments: "It's cute, but has too many cats." After a while kids got bored watching it. The only ones who stayed with it were those with cats at home. Age: 3–6; Length: 60 min.; Suggested Retail Price: $12.99, BRENTWOOD HOME VIDEO

*** DANCE ALONG WITH THE DAISE FAMILY (GULLAH GULLAH ISLAND); see p. 167

** DIG HOLE, BUILD HOUSE (REAL WORLD VIDEO); see p. 168

** ELMO SAYS BOO! (SESAME STREET): Elmo drops by the Count's castle to stir up some scary fun ! Lots of jokes, songs and spooky surprises—even a visit from Julia Roberts as everybody's favorite furry red monster in the first-ever Sesame Street Halloween special. Adult Juror Comments: Excellent graphics, good jokes, and riddles to engage everybody. Content is age-appropriate. Counting with the Count is well done. Kids enjoyed going inside his house. A little spooky for littlest ones. Some found the "baby talk" disturbing. Repetition is used well. Kid Juror Comments: "It was just a little scary." Kids liked the songs, jokes and Elmo—a perennial favorite. Afterwards, kids pointed out the bones in their own skeletons. Age: 2–5; Length: 30 min.; Suggested Retail Price: $12.98, SONY WONDER/CTW

** **ELMO'S SING-ALONG GUESSING GAME:** Elmo hosts Sesame Street's wackiest TV game show. Guess the answer to Elmo's questions with the help of some sing-along video clues. Features favorite songs like Big Bird's "My Best Friend," Kermit's "I Love my Elbows," and more. Adult Juror Comments: Scored high with adults. Themes of cooperation and friendship are excellent. Has good diversity and mix of age groups. Beginning is a little confusing. Kid Juror Comments: Okay. Thrilled to see their favorite Sesame Street characters. Story line a little difficult for younger kids to follow. Age: 2–5; Length: 30 min.; Suggested Retail Price: $12.98, SONY WONDER/CTW

* **EMILY AND HAPPINESS (A CREATIVE IMAGINATION SERIES):** Emily and her father make up stories together. In this story, Emily and her dog, Oscar, see a strange sparkling in the night sky, and wonder if it is happiness. It evokes a quest to discover what is happiness. Adult Juror Comments: Subject and characters are interesting to this age group. Each character is unique and interesting. The idea of a child spending time with a parent, making up stories, is commendable. Too bad it's slow-moving with poor sound quality. Little diversity. Kid Juror Comments: Kids thought it moved slowly but liked the stories. "I like that they're nice to each other." "It got me interested in drawing pictures." Age: 2–5; Length: 30 min.; Suggested Retail Price: $12.95, INTERAMA, INC.

* **EMILY AND HER FRIENDS:** Two animated stories from Finland. In one, twin brothers receive a new bathtub boat they must share. In the other, Emily lives in the middle of an apple tree forest in which the trees are mysteriously disappearing. Adult Juror Comments: Uniquely introduces environmental awareness and encourages imaginative thinking, listening skills. Portrays good parent/child relationship. Slow pace, simple animation, poor sound quality. Connection between lake pollution and dirty bathwater is unclear. Kid Juror Comments: Inspired by family interaction: father and daughter making up stories together. Seven- to eight-year-olds created their own stories afterwards. Stimulated a discussion about conservation. Three- and four-year-olds liked the bathtub boat. Age: 3–6; Length: 30 min.; Suggested Retail Price: $12.95, INTERAMA, INC.

*** **FAMILIES ARE SPECIAL:** Barney and his friends celebrate and explore the uniqueness of individual families. Ella Jenkins makes a guest appearance. Adult Juror Comments: Entertaining, invites participation, nice songs. Subject is treated well, although all the families are two-parent families. Positive lyrics value uniqueness and encourage self-esteem. Ella Jenkins is a fabulous addition. Kid Juror Comments: Good stuff. Kids sang and danced along, especially with Ella Jenkins and the "Boppity Bop" song. Good pace for two- to five-year-olds. Stimulated discussion about twins. Age: 2–5; Length: 30 min.; Suggested Retail Price: $14.95, LYRICK STUDIOS

*** FAMILY TALES (MAURICE SENDAK'S LITTLE BEAR): Contains four episodes addressing family relationships based on books by Else Holmelund Minarik, illustrated by Maurice Sendak. Little Bear's adventures on an overnight camping trip, a surprise breakfast, and assurance from the howling wind. Adult Juror Comments: Very enjoyable and positive. Deals with emotions and behavior in clear, concrete ways. Great quality and appropriate for age group. Promotes further inquiry. Resolutions of problems are clever and insightful while conveying a feeling of warmth. Kid Juror Comments: Funny. It also made them think and explore feelings. They were intrigued by the production. "How did they get the characters to walk?" "I like this movie!" "We like all of the movies of Little Bear!" Age: 2–6; Length: 34 min.; Suggested Retail Price: $9.95, PARAMOUNT HOME VIDEO

** FINGERMOUSE, YOFFY AND FRIENDS; see p. 170

** FIRE TRUCKS IN ACTION: Fire trucks and firefighters in action on the job. Demonstrates how equipment works and includes safety rules for children. Appropriate for home or school. Adult Juror Comments: Well done and informative. Great question/answer format. The accident scene may be a little scary. Lacks cultural diversity and female firefighters. Some kids were glued to the program for the entire time. Kid Juror Comments: Absorbing, especially while watching the firefighters at work. Surprisingly, one child who has serious fears of fire loved it. "They showed stop, drop and roll." Good job! Age: 2–5; Length: 25 min.; Suggested Retail Price: $14.95, HIGH PROFILES

** FISHY TALE, A (MUMFIE): Mumfie, an elephant, and his best friend, Scarecrow, win a goldfish at the local fair. Sadly, they learn they can't keep it, set out to find the perfect home for it, and end up helping others along the way. Adult Juror Comments: Cute, friendly, good animation. Appropriate content about sharing, cooperating, families, and caring for animals. Approaches emotional aspects of issues. "Why is the cloud sad?" Humor is more suited to adults than kids. Refers to past shows. Kid Juror Comments: Fun, good music. Kids enjoyed the friendship theme and related to the characters. They asked why an elephant, pig, and scarecrow would be friends. Despite the title only the first story is about a fish. They kept asking to see the fishy video. Age: 2–5; Length: 45 min.; Suggested Retail Price: $12.98, BMG VIDEO

*** FLIPPER; see p. 171

** FREEDOM ROCKS (THE ADVENTURES OF ELMER & FRIENDS): Celebrates nature's wisdom with original songs, and a special guest, Joanne Shenandoah of the Iroquois Nation. Live-action musical adventure rewards children of all ages with a delightful journey. Adult Juror Comments: Discusses equality, acceptance, and purpose. Fosters insightful thoughts on Native American traditions. A cheerful production with scenic shots of animals, fun songs, respectful behavior. Mixed race, culture, and gender. Contains Christian overtones. Kid Juror Comments: Understood the humor. Younger kids enjoyed dancing to the songs and music. "I like the forest part. The puppets and the different animals are great. We liked learning about how Native American sports compare to our sports." Age: 3–6; Length: 30 min.; Suggested Retail Price: $14.95, FEATHERWIND PRODUCTIONS

** GOOD ADVICE, CAPTAIN! (THE ALL-NEW CAPTAIN KANGAROO): Unsuccessful at building his new Billiwompis machine without following the directions, Joey learns the value of following directions. He also learns the value of safety rules after skateboarding inside the Treasure House and getting hurt. Adult Juror Comments: Good messages, songs. Sets are fanciful and colorful. Very age-appropriate. Lots of action and variety, yet all focused on topic. Just enough silliness to hold interest. Teaches difference between fantasy and reality. Little diversity. Kid Juror Comments: Valued the pleasant attitudes of the characters and puppets. "I learned to help each other and follow directions." "Next time we make a cake we should follow the directions." They enjoyed singing along and watching the animals. Age: 2–5; Length: 54 min.; Suggested Retail Price: $12.98, TWENTIETH CENTURY FOX HOME ENTERTAINMENT

** GOOD MORNING, GOOD NIGHT: A DAY ON THE FARM; see p. 30

* GRUMPY TREE, THE: Animated story about a tree that never wants to share. The tree is unkind to everyone and never realizes how lonely he is. When he's attacked by termites, the kindness of the forest animals helps him discover the meaning of true friendship. Adult Juror Comments: Teaches friendship and idea of working together. Starts slowly but picks up later. Addresses issues of personal competence, forgiveness, sharing, and friendship. Tree is a little too aggressively grumpy. The presenter's guide is excellent. Kid Juror Comments: Well worth watching despite slow beginning. Stimulated a discussion about friendship afterwards. "The drawings are pretty." "It made me think about being grumpy." Age: 2–6; Length: 13 min.; Suggested Retail Price: $9.95, PAULINE BOOKS AND MEDIA

* HAPPY NESS, VOL II: Join the McJoy children—Halsey, Haden, and Hanna—as they discover the magical land of Happy Ness, which dwells far beneath the infamous Loch Ness. With their Scottish guide, Sir Prize, they meet the most lovable monsters of all time. Adult Juror Comments: Has upbeat, clear format most suitable for younger children. Too long for one sitting. Tends to offer simple solutions to improbable situations. Kid Juror Comments: Stayed with it, though it was a little scary at times. They related to "darkness" and "happiness." Some found it extremely slow-moving; others watched quietly and attentively. Some requested to see it again right away. Age: 2–5; Length: 95 min.; Suggested Retail Price: $19.95, JUST FOR KIDS/CELEBRITY HOME VIDEO

** IMAGINE WITH US (BIG BAG): Molly is reading a great story about pirates, but the last few pages of the book are missing! What do you do when you don't know the ending of a story? How about using your imagination to discover a treasure? Adult Juror Comments: Appealing colors and graphics. Very good animated children's drawings. Stretches the imagination. Good multicultural friendships demonstrated. Shows sharing, cooperation, and problem-solving. Kid Juror Comments: Enjoyed making up the endings to finish the stories. It was slightly difficult to follow. May be best viewed in segments. Best for ages three and up. Age: 3–5; Length: 60 min.; Suggested Retail Price: $12.95, WARNER BROS. FAMILY ENTERTAINMENT

** JAY JAY'S FIRST FLIGHT (THE ADVENTURES OF JAY JAY THE JET PLANE): Join Jay Jay and friends on an aerial adventure on which they overcome fears, use their imaginations, follow the rules, and never give up. Adult Juror Comments: Good format with four stories, best viewed in segments. Good story lines and characters with expressive personalities. Children relate to the humor and other emotions. The ideas for discussion at the end of each segment are helpful and appropriate. Kid Juror Comments: Children relate to the characters, especially the planes. Kids laughed out loud at the funny parts, although some younger kids lost attention. It's better for them to watch individual stories separately. Age: 2–5; Length: 30 min.; Suggested Retail Price: $12.95, KIDQUEST

* JUNGLE JAMBOREE: Combines a playful mix of puppets, costumed characters, and live-action performers to create a show full of song and education. Adult Juror Comments: Pace is somewhat slow, but catchy tunes contain good messages that promote a good sense of self-awareness and offer safety concepts. Content is age-appropriate. Segment about strangers gives kids mixed messages about trusting strangers. Kid Juror Comments: Video okay but not the songs. Set and characters appealed to kids. Discussion followed about being nice and being mean. Age: 2–5; Length: 138 min.; Suggested Retail Price: $19.95, JUST FOR KIDS/CELEBRITY HOME VIDEO

*** LAND BEFORE TIME VI: SECRET OF SAURUS ROCK, THE; see p. 179

* LET'S DO IT! (PROFESSOR IRIS): Professor Iris plays host for an afternoon of fun with games, dancing and sports. Adult Juror Comments: Kids responded to the music but lost interest when the subject became too difficult. Information is interesting but is not presented clearly. It's too long for this age; best viewed in segments with activities in between. Kid Juror Comments: Two- and three-year-olds danced along, the four-year-olds stayed with the whole program, laughing at visual jokes, answering questions. Age: 3–6; Length: 40 min.; Suggested Retail Price: $12.95, DISCOVERY COMMUNICATIONS

*** LET'S GO FLY A KITE (MUMFIE): Mumfie and Scarecrow are having a tough time flying their special homemade kite, when suddenly the kite gets tangled in the tree. They learn a valuable lesson. Adult Juror Comments: Pleasant with a touch of reality in a lighthearted way. Mumfie shows empathy, is respectful and cooperative. Teaches kindness and concern for a diversity of individuals. They enjoy their adventures. Vocabulary is a little sophisticated. Kid Juror Comments: Splendid musical interludes, and noticed how kindly the characters treated each other. They loved the flying piggy with the squeaky voice. Even two-year-olds were toe-tapping to the songs. Age: 2–5; Length: 45 min.; Suggested Retail Price: $12.98, BMG VIDEO

* MAGICAL WORLD OF TRAINS, THE (TRAIN ADVENTURE FOR KIDS): The magical engineer Smoky Jones examines trains both big and small. From passenger to freight, engine to caboose, Smoky shares the excitement of railroading. Adult Juror Comments: Appealing to children. Encourages creativity, exploration, and imagination. Relates experiences with explanations of safety issues. Good format and music. Concern about "strangers" and kids going places with them. Kid Juror Comments: Okay. Age: 2–10; Length: 30 min.; Suggested Retail Price: $12.95, GOLDHIL HOME MEDIA

** MAKING NEW FRIENDS (BARNEY & FRIENDS COLLECTION): Children learn that making new friends and attending a new school can be fun. Adult Juror Comments: Contains good topics related to friendship, old friends, new friends, and a new school. Language concepts are clear, simple, and entertaining. Kid Juror Comments: Most children can relate to having new friends at school. This is a popular topic. Barney fans loved this and were excited just to see Barney on the screen. Age: 2–5; Length: 30 min.; Suggested Retail Price: $14.95, LYRICK STUDIOS

*** MAMA, DO YOU LOVE ME? (DOORS OF WONDER): In a distant northern land, a little Inuit girl asks, "Mama, do you love me?" The answer makes for a charming tale about affection, adventure, and wonder in this original and imaginative animated adaptation of the award-winning children's book. Adult Juror Comments: A lovely story about relationships that easily leads to discussions about Alaska, the Inuit people, and family. Video expands on the theme of the book, making it even more enjoyable. Excellent portrayal of Eskimos and their respect for animals. Kid Juror Comments: "It was great." "I want to know more about Alaska and sled dogs." "I thought about love and how I treat people." "Mother showed she really loved her daughter even when she was mad." Age: 3–8; Length: 30 min.; Suggested Retail Price: $12.98, SONY WONDER

** ME AND MY TUGBOAT: A little boy loses his model tugboat in a creek and dreams about a colorful adventure on a real tugboat. Warm and humorous, with fascinating people and awesome machines. It's about children's dreams that DO come true. Adult Juror Comments: Captain Bob's acting seemed so real! The comparison to Christopher Columbus was distracting. Not a lot going on, better for kids interested in boats. Pleasant background music. Kid Juror Comments: The calypso-style music went over fine. Didn't understand the Columbus comparison. Definitely for younger children; older kids felt talked down to. Age: 2–8; Length: 34 min.; Suggested Retail Price: $19.95, TONY ARZT SUPREME VIDEO WORKS FAMILY FLICKS

** MRN: CIRCUS FUN (MISTER ROGERS' NEIGHBORHOOD): The circus is fascinating, full of interesting people with unusual talents. Mister Rogers and Lady Aberlin go backstage to visit performers and learn how much practice it takes to be a performer. Adult Juror Comments: Imaginative, informative, realistic presentation. A variety of characters and locations. Circuses can be fun, but scary too. The animals were fascinating, although the caged tigers stimulated discussion about the treatment of circus animals. Kid Juror Comments: Children enjoyed it and wanted to do face-painting. They liked the way Nancy's friends helped her feel better about herself. Age: 3–6; Length: 28 min.; Suggested Retail Price: $9.98, FAMILY COMMUNICATIONS

*** MRN: GOING TO SCHOOL (MISTER ROGERS' NEIGHBORHOOD): Children often wonder what school will be like for the very first time or starting a new school year. Mister Rogers takes a ride on a real school bus and helps children realize that there are many caring teachers who will help them learn. Adult Juror Comments: Enjoyable. By the end of the tape even adults sang along. Structure helps explain what happens in school and then shows what it's like to actually ride a bus. Emphasizes the importance of caring, and teaches children not to be afraid. Great music. Kid Juror Comments: Children got excited about going to school. Loved the puppets, sang along with the songs and moved to the music. They wanted to ride a school bus. Particularly helpful to kids who are just starting kindergarten. Age: 2–5; Length: 28 min.; Suggested Retail Price: $9.98, FAMILY COMMUNICA-TIONS

*** MRN: KINDNESS (MISTER ROGERS' NEIGHBORHOOD): Being kind means responding to the needs of others. Mister Rogers helps children know that when they are kind to others, they'll discover something worthwhile about themselves. Adult Juror Comments: Engaging, entertaining, and educa-tional. Simple, comfortable, welcoming. Reinforces importance of teachers. Discusses need to practice (music, for example) every day. Adult discussion helps to reinforce concepts. Kid Juror Comments: Children wanted to learn more about the accordion and the trolley. They liked the music and songs, and clapped along with the rhythm band. Too slow at times. "I like Mister Rogers, he is very nice." Age: 2–5; Length: 28 min.; Suggested Retail Price: $9.98, FAMILY COMMUNICATIONS

*** MRN: LEARNING IS EVERYWHERE: (MISTER ROGERS' NEIGHBORHOOD): Mister Rogers helps children know that the world is full of lots of things to wonder about and that learning is everywhere when we're with people who care about us. Adult Juror Comments: Gentle but funny. The songs and music are slow and comforting. Mister Rogers asks lots of questions, talks about things he's doing, and is very conscious about demonstrating how both sexes—and all ethnic groups—can do everything. Kid Juror Comments: "I like Mister Rogers because he does nice things." "I want to find out about everything in this video." "It was too short." Most impor-tantly, the show encourages young children to explore and learn about their environment and broaden their horizons. Age: 2–5; Length: 28 min.; Suggested Retail Price: $9.98, FAMILY COMMUNICATIONS

***MRN: MUSIC AND FEELINGS (MISTER ROGERS' NEIGHBORHOOD): Cele-brates the many ways music touches our lives. Visits with cellist Yo-Yo Ma and folk singer Ella Jenkins. Explores how bass violins are made. Adult Juror Comments: Informative, delightful, moving, at times slow. Mister Rogers excels in his child-centered approach. Contains a lot of information useful for music classes. Ella Jenkins is great! Kid Juror Comments: Exciting, especially making the violin. Stimulated lively discussion and interest in music as a follow-up activity. Children hummed along with the pitch pipe and liked the song "Head and Shoulders." Age: 2–7; Length: 65 min.; Suggested Retail Price: $12.95, FAMILY COMMUNICATIONS

*** MRN: OUR EARTH: CLEAN AND GREEN (MISTER ROGERS' NEIGHBORHOOD):

Mister Rogers helps children appreciate the wonderful beauty of our world. There's a visit from a real live goat and some ideas for making playthings from things that might have been thrown away. Adult Juror Comments: "Mister Rogers can do no wrong in my book." Subject of recycling is great. A little slow at times. Creates parent/child craft activities using simple things found at home such as a shoebox. Teaches that everything has a purpose. Kid Juror Comments: Very attentive, especially enjoyed seeing the goats. "I liked the shoebox being turned into a train." "Can we do that?" "I want to make puppets too." "Will we see the two puppets he made again?" Age: 2–5; Length: 28 min.; Suggested Retail Price: $9.98, FAMILY COMMUNICATIONS

*** MRN: THE DOCTOR, YOUR FRIEND (MISTER ROGERS' NEIGHBORHOOD):

Children can better manage difficult experiences such as going to the doctor when they know what to expect. Mister Rogers visits a pediatrician during a young girl's routine checkup and lets children know that doctors care about them. Adult Juror Comments: Good cultural diversity. "Mister Rogers' warmth makes you feel like you're watching a friend." Briefly mentions private areas of the body and what to do if touched there. Kid Juror Comments: Elicited comments from the children about their experience with doctors. Most of the children watched closely but some didn't. The big favorite was Mister Rogers himself. A little slow-paced but compelling. "How can I be a doctor?" Age: 3–5; Length: 28 min.; Suggested Retail Price: $9.98, FAMILY COMMUNICATIONS

*** MRN: WHAT ABOUT LOVE? (MISTER ROGERS' NEIGHBORHOOD): Love is

never easy to understand, especially when people who love each other get angry. Program helps appreciate love and other feelings that accompany it. "It's the people we love the most who can make us the gladdest and maddest." Adult Juror Comments: It's thought-provoking, with simple, easy-to-understand style and a clear and compassionate tone. Provides a supportive emotional video environment for kids. Very age-appropriate. Mister Rogers speaks slowly and clearly. Presentation allows time to stop and reflect. Kid Juror Comments: Appealed to older four- and five-year-olds. They responded best when questioned by an adult about the content.

One child said, "I like everything Mister. Rogers does." Age: 2–7; Length: 51 min.; Suggested Retail Price: $12.95, FAMILY COMMUNICATIONS

* MY PARTY WITH BARNEY: A personalized video that features the child of your choice starring Barney and Friends in his or her video about a birthday party. Barney says the child's name and appears onscreen along with Barney, BJ, and Baby Bop. Lots of songs and animation. Adult Juror Comments: Music and visuals foster positive self-concept and social skills. Personalization feature a real plus. Contains cheerful, catchy rhyming music, good visuals, and good animation. Overall, however, the production is very choppy. Kid Juror Comments: The music motivated them to get up and dance. One song says "You can tie your shoes," but most this age can't, and they noticed it. Competitive games are portrayed, which are inappropriate for this age. Age: 3–5; Length: 18 min.; Suggested Retail Price: $34.95, KIDEO PRODUCTIONS, INC.

** OLD OSCAR LEADS THE PARADE AND OTHER STORIES (ADVENTURES OF JAY JAY THE JET PLANE): Model airplanes come to life in the storybook land of Tarrytown. In four short stories, Jay Jay discovers why it's always best to be "True Blue." Teaches respect for others. Adult Juror Comments: Addresses important social issues in ways that children can understand. "Presents idea that everyone is equally important and you don't always have to win first place." Could be more diverse about culture, race, and gender. Kid Juror Comments: Thoroughly enjoyable. They found the plane characters were entertaining. "Jay Jay told a fib and he was blue. He should have told the truth first." Age: 2–5; Length: 35 min.; Suggested Retail Price: $12.95, KIDQUEST

* OPERATION: SECRET BIRTHDAY SURPRISE (THE ADVENTURES OF TIMMY THE TOOTH); see p. 184

** PAPER BAG PLAYERS ON TOP OF SPAGHETTI, THE: Laugh, dance, and sing along with the Paper Bag Players in their first video. A runaway meatball, a heroic plumber, and a dreamy postman play parts in the stories, plays, and songs that make up this fabulously silly show. Adult Juror Comments: Entertaining stories that address issues such as sharing and making up for wrongdoing. Uses theatrical structure to present eight different skits but it's a little too simple for today's child. Why do plays seem to lose their luster when videotaped? Kid Juror Comments: Laughed loud and often. Liked the content but most were unimpressed by the delivery. Only one group did not respond positively. "It was funny." "I like singing." "My friends would love

this." Age: 3–7; Length: 57 min.; Suggested Retail Price: $15.00, THE
PAPER BAG PLAYERS

** PET FORGETTERS CURE, THE / NEVER-WANT-TO-GO-TO-BEDDERS CURE; see
p. 185

** PIRATE ISLAND; see p. 186

** PLAY ALONG WITH ALLEGRA AND FRIENDS (ALLEGRA'S WINDOW): Stand up
and join the fun as the Hummingbird Gang offers nine get-up-and-sing
numbers. Adult Juror Comments: Lively! Sets and characters are appealing. Allegra is very pleasant. Transitions are well timed and entertaining.
Nice diversity. Appropriate characterization of competitive game behavior.
Music also is age-appropriate. A little overstimulating and visually cluttered. Kid Juror Comments: "Good singing." Enjoyed the mix of people and
characters. They liked the flying horse, the sharing, the flashback effect, and
thought there were some good ideas. They noticed that the cat always
wanted to win. Age: 2–5; Length: 29 min.; Suggested Retail Price: $9.95,
PARAMOUNT HOME VIDEO

** PLAY ALONG WITH BINYAH AND FRIENDS (GULLAH GULLAH ISLAND): Teaches
about a variety of different games: pretend, clapping games, team sports.
Includes "I Love a Haircut," a barbershop sextet that makes Simeon's first
haircut memorable. Adult Juror Comments: Offers role models from multicultural age groups, preschoolers to seniors. Emphasizes positive ways to
deal with mistakes: "continue practicing and try your best." Games invite
audience participation. Binyah's voice is hard to understand. Kid Juror
Comments: Three- to six-year-old kids loved the songs, games, and Binyah
character, though they thought the kids weren't really singing along in the
video. Age: 2–6; Length: 30 min.; Suggested Retail Price: $12.98, PARA-
MOUNT HOME VIDEO

*** QUIET TIME (SESAME STREET): Big Bird's not sure what to do when his
Granny Bird tells him it's quiet time. Fortunately, Oscar, Telly, Rosita, and
his other Sesame Street friends have plenty of great ideas, like reading stories and playing quiet games. Features Daphne Rubin-Vega. Adult Juror
Comments: Great subject. Adults love Sesame Street, too. Perfect four- to
five-year-old humor. Excellent choice of vocabulary level, selected experiences, activity breaks, and music. Interracial mix of kids. One adult felt it
was "too loud to be a quiet-time video." Kid Juror Comments: Endearing

and fun. "It was silly." Kids liked suggested activities: touching tongues to nose and balancing spoons. Kids offered their ideas about appropriate quiet-time activities. Age: 2–5; Length: 30 min.; Suggested Retail Price: $12.98, SONY WONDER/CTW

* RAGGEDY ANN & ANDY: THE MABBIT ADVENTURE; see p. 186

* RAGGEDY ANN & ANDY: THE PIXLING ADVENTURE: Raggedy Dog finds a baby in a basket. The baby is Prince Luke, heir to the Pixling throne. To be crowned, he must reach the Pixling Castle by nightfall. Adult Juror Comments: Contains a scary stalker, inappropriate language, and baby's crying is constant and irritating. It's intense and frightening to young viewers. Little diversity. Shows teamwork, humor, adventure, suspense, and resolution. Kid Juror Comments: Kids asked why the baby was always crying. Younger viewers had a hard time understanding the finer points of the story line. "Grouchy bear is mean, but sometimes he does help." Age: 3–7; Length: 28 min.; Suggested Retail Price: $9.98, TWENTIETH CENTURY FOX HOME ENTERTAINMENT

*** ROCK DREAMS (THE PUZZLE PLACE): Puppet-kids learn to solve life's little problems. Native American figure Red Thunder shows how music can help harmonize your life. Adult Juror Comments: Attractive characters, cooperation, and problem-solving. Excellent puppetry and real people playing instruments. Social issues are seldom portrayed as insightfully as this. Adults loved the Boys Choir of Harlem. Best viewed in segments. Kid Juror Comments: Really liked singing along. "This is really good at showing people from different places," one six-year-old commented. Children played their own instruments afterward. Age: 2–7; Length: 55 min.; Suggested Retail Price: $9.98, SONY WONDER

** ROCK WITH BARNEY: Barney joins the Backyard Gang on a happy adventure to a movie studio. A protect-our-earth theme encourages children to sing and play along. Adult Juror Comments: Good values. Songs have appealing ideas and concepts. Ecology content depicted on cover is deceptive since it is not a strong theme in the video. Parents feel Barney is foolish, and the child actors seem too old and unnatural for the targeted age group. Kid Juror Comments: Captivated by the music and dancing. They clapped and swayed, especially the girls. Children like Barney for his soft, appealing, comfortable look and his behavior, which seems to honor them. And they love Baby Bop! Age: 2–5; Length: 30 min.; Suggested Retail Price: $14.95, LYRICK STUDIOS

** RUPERT: "Rupert the Bear" has been Britain's most beloved comic strip since 1920. Video contains twelve delightful stories featuring Rupert and his friends Bill Badger, Tiger-Lily, and Jack Frost. Adult Juror Comments: Not full animation, but nicely illustrated. May have too little action for kids today. Appealing and friendly characters. Charming rendition of storybook style. Likely to encourage reading of similar stories. The rhyming is fun. Kid Juror Comments: "That was a great one." "I liked the magic ball." Narration was too fast for kids to understand, maybe a little too long. Age: 2–5; Length: 57 min.; Suggested Retail Price: $9.98, TWENTIETH CENTURY FOX HOME ENTERTAINMENT

** RUPERT AND THE RUNAWAY DRAGON: Join Rupert and his friends Bill Badger, Tiger-Lily, and Jack Frost on an enchanted journey in this tape containing seven stories. Rupert the Bear has been Britain's favorite comic strip for almost eighty years! Adult Juror Comments: Entertaining and unusual stories, but not full animation. "This video is like reading stories from a book." Narration was read too fast. Length of episodes and video well done. Kid Juror Comments: Children enjoyed the video for the first twenty minutes then became restless. "Rupert is nice." "He plays with friends." "Who is Rupert?" Kids had a hard time keeping up with the narrator. Age: 2–5; Length: 36 min.; Suggested Retail Price: $9.98, TWENTIETH CENTURY FOX HOME ENTERTAINMENT

** SEE WHAT I CAN DO (GREGORY AND ME): The viewer becomes the star of the show. Gregory Gopher—inventor, explorer, adventurer—leads him or her on many adventures, discovering new ideas for projects, travels, shows, and parties. Adult Juror Comments: Well paced, though the "personalized" segments are primitive. Encouragement messages are clearly presented, focusing on thinking through problems. Characters are polite. Contains some gender stereotyping and is crammed full of commercials. Kid Juror Comments: "They watched, got up and down, and followed the character's actions." Music is "hummable." Good mixture of real and pretend. "The bird yells a lot!" Children wanted to be included in the tape. Age: 2–5; Length: 25 min.; Suggested Retail Price: $34.95, KIDEO PRODUCTIONS, INC.

*** SESAME STREET CELEBRATES AROUND THE WORLD: Everyone on Sesame Street is staying up late for a monster New Year's Eve party! Features festivities in Mexico, Japan, Portugal, Israel, Norway, and Germany. Adult Juror Comments: Excellent. Good multiculturalism in a mix of live action, animation and "street scenes." Music is pleasant. Contains creative activities such as making a pinata. A little long, it's best viewed in segments. Kid Juror Comments: Possible confusion over the production techniques, although in general it was well received. Best used in segments rather than as a whole. Age: 2–5; Length: 60 min.; Suggested Retail Price: $9.98, SONY WONDER/CTW

*** SESAME STREET VISITS THE FIREHOUSE: When Oscar's trash-can barbecue gets a little too smoky, the Sesame Street gang gets a visit from some firefighters who invite them back to the firehouse for a tour. Big Bird, Elmo, and Gordon learn all about fighting fires. Adult Juror Comments: Informative, full of safety tips and great learning potential. Kids see the equipment, are exposed to procedures, noises and terminology. Closed-captioned for hearing-impaired. Kid Juror Comments: Children love to laugh at Elmo's antics. Really held their attention and stimulated continued play with firefighter props. Interacted with the dialogue in the video. "We need to have a fire drill." A little scary for younger ones. Age: 2–5; Length: 30 min.; Suggested Retail Price: $9.98, SONY WONDER/CTW

*** SESAME STREET'S 25TH BIRTHDAY: A MUSICAL CELEBRATION: An hourlong collection of favorite Sesame Street songs, such as "C is for Cookie," "Bein' Green," "Monster in the Mirror." Ernie sings a medley of Duckie songs, and Big Bird lead a rousing finale of "Sing." Adult Juror Comments: Lively, contains lots of songs and shows excellent cultural diversity. Wonderfully ethnic! Great for active parent/teacher involvement: dancing, singalong, creative movement. Long and best viewed in segments. Kid Juror Comments: Children clapped and danced, loved the singing and music—especially the African songs and singers. Age: 2–5; Length: 60 min.; Suggested Retail Price: $12.98, SONY WONDER/CTW

*** SESAME STREET: KIDS' FAVORITE SONGS: Elmo is getting ready for his Top Ten Countdown on the radio, and everyone on Sesame Street wants him to play their favorite songs! But with so many great songs to choose from, how will Elmo pick which ones to play? Adult Juror Comments: A lighthearted video, fun for parents and kids alike. "Not only did the video play music that kids liked but they learned to count, too!" Upbeat, lively singalongs. "Watching with a child is a great excuse to act like a kid." Kid Juror Comments: Great enthusiasm. Sang loudly to all of the songs and frequently giggled. "I know all the songs so I can sing EVERYTHING!" "I want a radio that plays all these songs." Had the kids counting along. "Let's do our ABC's." Age: 2–5; Length: 30 min.; Suggested Retail Price: $12.98, SONY WONDER/CTW

*** SESAME STREET: LET'S EAT: Grover the waiter has a new job working at Planet Storybook. When his favorite customer comes in, Grover becomes a monster with a mission—to introduce this picky eater to all the fabulous foods that he could be enjoying. Adult Juror Comments: Funny, witty characters, charming story line, attractive multi-faceted presentation. An entertaining, well-made, colorful, and culturally diverse show. All complex ideas and words are explained in a kid-friendly manner. Great cultural diversity. Kid Juror Comments: Kids were riveted throughout the entire program. "Yes, we would watch it again because it is so funny." "It taught us about vegetables. We didn't know there were so many." Children sang and danced. "I don't like broccoli." Age: 2–5; Length: 30 min.; Suggested Retail Price: $12.98, SONY WONDER/CTW

*** SESAME STREET: THE ALPHABET JUNGLE GAME: Elmo, Zoe, and Telly explore the Alphabet Jungle, where letters grow on trees. Every letter from A to Y leads them on an animated adventure, but Zoe's favorite letter is missing. What will happen if Zoe can't find the letter Z? Adult Juror Comments: Imaginative, interesting, invites participation. "Fun to watch with my grandchild." Rhythmic pace, eye-catching, too. Occasionally inconsistent: skipped definitions for letters Q, R, S, and V. Kid Juror Comments: Fabulous, especially the ending, in which they had to find what started with "Z." "The alphabet party was fun." They recognized lots of words and wanted to see it again. "I love Elmo and Zoe." Age: 2–5; Length: 30 min.; Suggested Retail Price: $12.98, SONY WONDER/CTW

*** SESAME STREET: THE GREAT NUMBERS GAME: With a push of the start button, Elmo and friends find themselves transported to a magical forest filled with hidden numbers. Each one they find leads them to one of Sesame Street's classic counting cartoons, but will they make it to number 20? Adult Juror Comments: Cute characters, engaging video clips, and lively colors. Made by people who truly understand kids. Emphasizes how numbers are sequential. Discussion of time, using clocks and days of the week. Kid Juror Comments: "I would like everyone to like it." "Number 14 is my favorite!" "I'd like more videos about numbers." Children asked to see it again, immediately after first viewing. Age: 2–5; Length: 30 min.; Suggested Retail Price: $12.98, SONY WONDER/CTW

*** SHARE WITH US (BIG BAG): Molli and Chelli learn to share crayons. Chelli's not sure he wants to share, so it's up to the viewer to convince him that it's the right thing to do. Invites the viewer to find out how great it feels to help a friend. Adult Juror Comments: Very cute, likable characters. Nice mix of animation and puppets, imaginary and real-life characters, with catchy music and wonderful songs. Subject is age-appropriate. Many ethnic groups are positively represented. Excellent at showing difficulty of sharing. Kid Juror Comments: Promotes friendship between people, characters, and animals of all genders, races, shapes, and sizes. Reinforces feelings and emotions respectfully. Gives the viewer a sense of control. "My friends would like everything about this video." Age: 2–5; Length: 60 min.; Suggested Retail Price: $12.95, WARNER BROS. FAMILY ENTERTAINMENT

*** SHARING IS CARING (THE ALL NEW CAPTAIN KANGAROO): Two stories: In the first one, Bunny wins a prize and hoards his prize carrots. He ends up learning the importance of sharing. In the second, Moose, Bunny, and Joey learn to take turns, listen to each other, and create music as a band. Adult Juror Comments: Attractive, interesting, and helpful themes—taking turns and sharing. Respectful of other people and animals. Good variety of characters. Concepts may be difficult for children under three. Reinforces idea that learning can be fun. Kid Juror Comments: Appealing and repeatable. Kids especially liked the live animal segments. Also liked the Captain. He laughs a lot instead of getting angry. Good environmental awareness. Age: 2–5; Length: 54 min.; Suggested Retail Price: $12.98, TWENTIETH CENTURY FOX HOME ENTERTAINMENT

** SIMON THE LAMB (PRECIOUS MOMENTS); see p. 189

*** SMALL IS BEAUTIFUL (ALLEGRA'S WINDOW): Everyone tells Allegra that she's too little to share her brother's toys or to help in the diner. She finds a tiny key that solves big problems. Adult Juror Comments: Good multicultural, intergenerational characters. Fine topic, positive adult behavior, nice visuals, and interactive design to demonstrate key concepts. Incorporates reading skills. Kid Juror Comments: Easily related to the human-like puppets. More appropriate for the five- and six-year-olds. Age: 4–6; Length: 28 min.; Suggested Retail Price: $9.95, PARAMOUNT HOME VIDEO

** SUE'S BIRTHDAY ADVENTURE (GRANDPA'S MAGIC SHOEBOX): Barely out of the egg, Sue the Alligator sings instead of hisses—unheard-of for an alligator. Exiled from her jungle home, Sue rises to fame and stardom as a singer. Adult Juror Comments: Good production quality, simple story. Jurors enjoyed the message about Sue's struggle to fulfill her dream to become a singer. It teaches kids to believe in themselves. Story is somewhat long for younger children and too simple for older kids. Kid Juror Comments: The story provoked questions from the kids about the characters' motives/actions. "Paper trees are easy to make and the puppets are cool." Age: 3–7; Length: 44 min.; Suggested Retail Price: $12.95, BARRY SIMON PRODUCTIONS

* TALE OF THE BUNNY PICNIC: Bean Bunny learns that he is worthwhile even though he seems too insignificant to be of much help to anyone. Adult Juror Comments: Engaging characters and story. Younger kids will enjoy the puppets but have difficulty comprehending the moral of the story. Long, slow-moving, audio poor, some inappropriate language. Toddlers won't understand the farmer's cruelty to the dog. Kid Juror Comments: Farmer's bad language is excessive and bothersome to preschoolers. They enjoyed the bunnies and the songs. Kids sang along and clapped. "It was funny when the bunnies scared the dog." Age: 2–5; Length: 51 min.; Suggested Retail Price: $9.95, JIM HENSON COMPANY

*** TELETUBBIES: DANCE WITH THE TELETUBBIES; see p. 30

*** TELETUBBIES: HERE COME THE TELETUBBIES; see p. 30

** TEO: Teo is a redheaded, restless, curious, kind, and good-natured four-year-old. In his company, the viewer is introduced to various situations and characters related to family, friends, and animals. Adult Juror Comments: A simple, well-paced production with good music, artwork, and age-appropriate vocabulary. What two- to five-year-old doesn't relate to a walk to the park? Lacks diversity in characters and shows some gender stereotypes. Reinforces safety issues. Kid Juror Comments: Stimulated discussion about parks and family outings. Children liked the simple music and presentation. They commented on the English accents. The program is short and left kids wanting to see more. "The mommy and daddy are nice." Age: 2–5; Length: 30 min.; Suggested Retail Price: $14.95, B.R.B. INTERNACIONAL, S.A.

** THEODORE HELPS A FRIEND (THEODORE TUGBOAT): Boats take on character and names in these stories that tell how Northumberland, the Sleepy Submarine, makes himself surprisingly scarce when another boat visits the big harbor. Bedford Buoy puzzles everyone when he wants to leave the harbor. Adult Juror Comments: Characters and stories teach good value lessons about respect while building good vocabulary. Social interactions are well done, if long-winded: helping others, keeping friends, dealing with conflict. Little diversity. Kid Juror Comments: Boys really enjoyed the boats. Children were particularly interested in the submarines. They sang along and wanted to play in the water afterwards. Vocabulary is sometimes too advanced for this age. They liked the different characters. Age: 3–6; Length: 43 min.; Suggested Retail Price: $12.95, WARNER BROS. FAMILY ENTERTAINMENT

** THEODORE'S FRIENDLY ADVENTURES (THEODORE TUGBOAT): A new visitor arrives with a big cargo and a bad attitude. Theodore must get the ship in shape. A cove seems like good place to hide until the coast guard ship sounds the alarm. Hank goes looking for a sunken ship and discovers how to be liked. Adult Juror Comments: Children identify with the characters' problems, prompting a good discussion on cooperation and problem-solving. Contains fine themes, good voices, personalities. Boats are appealing, with large eyes, happy faces, and color contrast. Adults liked the anthology format. Kid Juror Comments: Compelling stories and characters, although the kids were bothered by the story about poor listening ears and bad behavior. Children could relate to the feelings and emotions of Theodore and his friends. Though it's slow, they wanted to watch it again. Age: 2–5; Length: 43 min.; Suggested Retail Price: $12.95, WARNER BROS. FAMILY ENTERTAINMENT

** THOMAS THE TANK: BETTER LATE THAN NEVER; see p. 192

** THOMAS THE TANK: DAISY AND OTHER STORIES; see p. 192

** THOMAS THE TANK: JAMES GOES BUZZ BUZZ; see p. 192

** THOMAS THE TANK: JAMES LEARNS A LESSON; see p. 193

** THOMAS THE TANK: PERCY'S GHOSTLY TRICK; see p. 193

*** THOMAS THE TANK: THOMAS AND HIS FRIENDS GET ALONG; see p. 193

** THOMAS THE TANK: THOMAS BREAKS THE RULES; see p. 194

** THOMAS THE TANK: THOMAS GETS BUMPED; see p. 194

** THOMAS THE TANK: THOMAS GETS TRICKED AND OTHER STORIES; see p. 194

** THOMAS THE TANK: THOMAS' CHRISTMAS PARTY; see p. 195

** THOMAS THE TANK: THOMAS, PERCY & THE DRAGON; see p. 195

** THOMAS THE TANK: TRUST THOMAS; see p. 195

*** TOM SAWYER; see p. 197

*** TOTS TV: TILLY'S MAGIC FLUTE: In a secret magical cottage in the woods live the Tots—Tom, Tiny. and Spanish-speaking Tilly. In this episode, the tots go on an adventure, see a musical instrument constructed out of wood and listen to Tilly play her magic flute. Adult Juror Comments: Lively and engaging with cute and diverse characters. Production uses puppets and live action to address a musical theme. Shows curiosity as positive, respect for others, the importance of friends, and a love for nature. Reinforces art appreciation. Kid Juror Comments: Happily lapped up every bit of information and asked lots of questions about the instruments. The music was catchy and inspired them to dance. They wanted to play with musical instruments afterwards. "This is one of my favorites." Age: 2–5; Length: 31 min.; Suggested Retail Price: $12.95, ITSY BITSY ENTERTAINMENT COMPANY

*** TOTS TV: THE TOTS AND THE GREAT BIG LIGHT: Find out what happens when the Tots go on a seashore adventure and discover a lighthouse. Listen as Tilly tells the Tots about three mischievous elves. And laugh at Tom's silly new game. Adult Juror Comments: Great puppetry. Characters are lovable and cute. An excellent opportunity to learn respect for different cultures and languages, including an introduction to Spanish. Good-quality production. Colors, animation, and detail all excellent. Kid Juror Comments: Children were deeply engaged, enjoyed the songs, and loved learning Spanish. Prompted good discussion about the fear of thunder and how to handle it. They wanted to share the themes of friendship. Age: 2–5; Length: 31 min.; Suggested Retail Price: $12.95, ITSY BITSY ENTERTAINMENT COMPANY

*** TOTS TV: THE TOTS AND THE LOVELY BUBBLY SURPRISE: Tiny's Bolsa Magica (magic bag) contains a gift for the giraffe. Discover who can build the tallest Tot's Tower. Smile as Tilly, Tom, and Tiny discover the magic of bubble making. Adult Juror Comments: Interesting and humorous. Tots' antics bring back childhood memories. Reinforces positive themes that children recognize, such as respect, sharing, and playing with others. Colors are warm and realistic, voices are gentle. Lots of diversity. Kid Juror Comments: All thumbs up! Children talked about bubbles, blew bubbles, and stacked towers all the next day. Lots of conversation about what they could use for bubbles and safe things to stack. "I have never seen a giraffe." Age: 2–5; Length: 35 min.; Suggested Retail Price: $12.95, ITSY BITSY ENTERTAINMENT COMPANY

*** TOTS TV: THE TOTS FIND A TREASURE MAP: In a secret magical cottage live the Tots—Tom, Tiny, and Spanish-speaking Tilly. Finding lost things is the Tots' specialty. In doing so, they reunite a lost girl with her mom, track down Donkey when he gets loose, and find a secret map. Adult Juror Comments: Main characters are quite entertaining. They sang, gardened, and played together, imparting a feeling of warmth and concern for one another. Good insight into getting lost, doing business, and problem-solving. Good introduction to Spanish. Kid Juror Comments: Glued to the screen when the child got lost in the grocery store. "How do they know what Tilly is saying?" (Tilly speaks Spanish only.) "I know they are good friends because they help each other." Repeatable. Age: 2–5; Length: 31 min.; Suggested Retail Price: $12.95, ITSY BITSY ENTERTAINMENT COMPANY

*** TOTS TV: THE TOTS, THE MOON, & THE HAPPY HOUSE: Three characters live in a magical cottage. A mixture of live action and puppetry. One tot, Tilly, speaks only Spanish. Adult Juror Comments: It's delightful, with cute characters, good production values and well-paced story. Excellent way to introduce Spanish and keep children interested. Very positive. Portrays cooperative family relationships, care, and respect for living things. Kid Juror Comments: Wonderful! Cute! Kids were mesmerized. Liked the fantasy world and the kittens. They enjoyed the different languages. "I learned how to say uno, dos, tres which means 1, 2, 3." "I liked the Spanish. I tried to learn some words." Age: 2–5; Length: 31 min.; Suggested Retail Price: $12.98, ITSY BITSY ENTERTAINMENT

** TRACY'S HANDY HIDEOUT & THREE OTHER STORIES (ADVENTURES OF JAY JAY THE JET PLANE): Contains three stories addressing the importance of taking care of the things you love, how teamwork works in a stormy situation, and how sharing can solve problems. All this plus a magical flight through the clouds. Adult Juror Comments: Simple production, somewhat repetitive with appealing characters and worthy story lines addressing ecology, friendships, and elders. Lacks diversity. Kid Juror Comments: Kids liked the stories, which are short and easy to follow. Children related to the different plane characters. Some disliked the "scary" faces, others noticed that they were all "smiling." Two- and three-year-olds liked it best. Age: 2–5; Length: 32 min.; Suggested Retail Price: $12.95, KIDQUEST

*** VEGGIE TALES: ARE YOU MY NEIGHBOR?: Loving thy neighbor is the theme, featuring two funny stories that help kids understand and celebrate the many differences that make people unique. First, a Dr. Seussian retelling of the Good Samaritan; second is a Star Trek spoof. Adult Juror Comments: A well-animated, comical program. Promotes kindness and understanding differences. Christian overtones, not overly religious, just solid positive values. "Made me smile." "Tunes are catchy, colors are vivid, and use of spaceships and faraway lands attracts all ages." Kid Juror Comments: Liked the characters. They thought it was fun to dance and sing along. "They were talking nicely and being nice, I like that." "I liked the tomatoes and spaceships and how they made them fly." "What a fun video!" Age: 2–8; Length: 30 min.; Suggested Retail Price: $12.99, BIG IDEA PRODUCTIONS

** VEGGIE TALES: MADAME BLUEBERRY: A very blue berry delivers a message about thankfulness. Madame Blueberry has everything she needs, but she's not satisfied. She and her friends learn that "being greedy makes you grumpy, but a thankful heart is a happy heart." Adult Juror Comments: Excellent production: music is catchy, animation is flawless, has brilliant colors, and is very imaginative. Humorously teaches a lesson about greed and thankfulness. Helps kids explore their emotions. Unfortunately, it contains unnecessary racial stereotyping. Kid Juror Comments: Learned that you don't need a whole lot of stuff to be happy. They were amused when Madam Blueberry bought so many things that her house crashed. They noticed stereotypical representations of people of different cultures. Loved the humor and the music. Age: 3–8; Length: 30 min.; Suggested Retail Price: $12.99, BIG IDEA PRODUCTIONS

** VEGGIE TALES: RACK, SHACK & BENNY: Kids learn to resist peer pressure in an engaging way. Even when they get permission to eat as many chocolate bunnies as they want, Rack, Shack, and Benny remember what their parents taught them. They do what's right even when their friends don't. Adult Juror Comments: The veggies have individual characteristics, a sense of humor and wit, moral development, and they're lively and personable. Shows excellent examples of peer pressure and positive gender portrayals. The content respects kids' thinking. Some stereotypes. Also contains Christian overtones. Kid Juror Comments: Children loved the perfectly silly songs, singing, and dancing at the end. It simplifies some big issues for kids. "I liked how the girl carrot saved her friends and God put the fire out in the furnace." Kids learned why "sissy" is a mean word. Age: 3–8; Length: 30 min.; Suggested Retail Price: $12.99, BIG IDEA PRODUCTIONS

*** WAITING FOR GRANDMA (ALLEGRA'S WINDOW): Allegra can't seem to wait for anything. It's even harder knowing that today is the day of the "Hummingbird Alley Holiday Happy Hoopla" and the day her grandma is coming to visit. Adult Juror Comments: Puppets are wonderful! A great tribute to grandmas everywhere with positive messages of cooperation, helping others, family tradition, memories. "This is one swinging, modern grandma!" Emotional themes are explored thoughtfully. "A feel-good program." Kid Juror Comments: A sweet and lively story about grandmothers and grandchildren. Kids admired the characters and related well to them. "This

movie's about waiting and Christmas celebrations. I just loved Grandma."
Age: 2–5; Length: 30 min.; Suggested Retail Price: $12.98, PARAMOUNT
HOME VIDEO

* WE CAN GET ALONG (TREASURE ATTIC): Children discover the secrets to
building lasting friendships. Promotes the idea that there is no need to compare, each of us is very needed and special. The song "Little Things" shows
how even small deeds of kindness can reap big results. Adult Juror Comments: Teaches the importance of trying hard and appreciating differences.
Live action mixed with animation offers good messages divided into short
segments, making it a little choppy. Addresses new neighbors and self-
acceptance. Excessively sweet. Kid Juror Comments: Children continued
to draw the flowers and trees from this video afterwards. Five-year-old girls
enjoyed watching it a second time. Their favorite parts were seeing the kitten rescued and the art lesson. Age: 3–7; Length: 25 min.; Suggested Retail
Price: $14.95, FAMILY CARE FOUNDATION

*** WHICH WAY WEATHER? (LIVE ACTION VIDEO): A group of children explore
seasonal weather conditions and related activities, from puddle stomping
to ice-skating. Includes a songbook. Adult Juror Comments: Wonderful,
child-centered, hands-on. Good for stimulating thinking and imagination.
Makes weather exciting, gives kids good ideas and concepts. A multicultural mix of children. Kid Juror Comments: The children on screen were
very attractive. Prompted discussion about what they had done or wanted
to do like the kids in the video. Stimulated interest about the weather. Age:
2–5; Length: 30 min.; Suggested Retail Price: $14.95, BO PEEP PRODUC-
TIONS, INC.

** WIDE AWAKE AT EUREEKA'S CASTLE (EUREEKA'S CASTLE): The sun's gone
down but Batly and Magellan don't want to go to bed—ever again! Who
wins the contest to stay awake as Eureeka guides the viewer on a tour of the
castle? Adult Juror Comments: Colorful, cute, and fast-moving. Creative
ways to combat anti-bedtime behavior. Promotes respect and cooperation.
Deals with "night noises." A little overdone with outrageous and "loud"
characters. Front-loaded with commercials which adults found objectionable. Kid Juror Comments: Older kids thought it was for younger kids but
watched and laughed anyway. Young kids enjoyed it a lot and asked to see
it again. Children wanted to sing along with the songs but just couldn't make
it. Suggested Retail Price: $12.98, PARAMOUNT HOME VIDEO

** WUBBULOUS WORLD OF DR. SEUSS: The "Wubbulous World of Dr. Seuss"
takes place in the wildly decorated house of the Cat in the Hat, where the

colorful cast of characters has a good time while learning how to face daily dilemmas. Adult Juror Comments: Well produced. Characters are true to the spirit of the original. Adults enjoyed the animation and rhymes. Enriches children's imaginations through creative play. The mini-stories, running one after another, make it hard to follow the story. Kid Juror Comments: Mixed response. Some sang along with the opening song, and others thought it was slow and boring. "We could be friends with these cats." "I wish I had a wubblouscope and could see magical things, too." Age: 2–5; Length: 50 min.; Suggested Retail Price: $12.95, JIM HENSON COMPANY

ZEEZEL THE ZOWIE ZOON IN THE COLOR CHASE: Laugh at the frolics of Zeezel the Zowie Zoon as he sets out to find his missing colors on an imaginative chase. Live action with vivid animation and original songs. Adult Juror Comments: It's a simple, age-appropriate production with good animation. The characters solve the dilemma together. Zeezel well represented diversity. Some segments are repetitive or inconsistent in teaching colors. Kid Juror Comments: Cheerful participation. Answered the main character's questions, sang along, and loved the different colors. Younger kids enjoyed it best. Has a good female role model. Age: 1–5; Length: 30 min.; Suggested Retail Price $12.95

Fairy Tales, Literature, Myth

ADVENTURES OF CURIOUS GEORGE; see p. 205

*** ARTHUR'S BABY (ARTHUR):** Arthur is not sure he's ready for a new baby in the house. As the months fly by, Arthur imagines how his life is about to change—and it isn't a pretty picture. When the baby arrives, it seems as if she doesn't like Arthur very much—or does she? Adult Juror Comments: Excellent production, good content. Deals with jealousy, anxiety, and safety. Insightful and well paced. The section with opinions by "real" children is excellent. Useful for families expecting a new baby. Kid Juror Comments: "My kids laughed so much it made me laugh." Kids with siblings really responded well. One five-year-old said, "Everything they say is very, very true!" Stories capture kids' thoughts and feelings. The characters respected each other. Age: 2–7; Length: 30 min.; Suggested Retail Price: $12.98, SONY WONDER/CTW

ARTHUR'S LOST LIBRARY BOOK; see p. 207

** **ARTHUR'S TEACHER TROUBLES (ARTHUR):** Arthur's biggest fear has come true: Mr. Ratburn is his third-grade teacher. The man is rumored to eat nails for breakfast, to turn into a vampire at night, and give homework every day! Adult Juror Comments: Good subject matter about misconceptions—handled well, good content. Some vocabulary not age-appropriate. Kid Juror Comments: Enjoyed it, especially the child comments between the programs. The three-year-olds didn't understand the concept of false impressions. They like the fact that the characters are all different animals. Age: 3–6; Length: 30 min.; Suggested Retail Price: $12.98, SONY WONDER

** **CHILDREN'S STORIES FROM AFRICA—VOL. 1;** see p. 211

** **CORDUROY AND OTHER BEAR STORIES (CHILDREN'S CIRCLE);** see p. 212

*** **DAISY HEAD MAYZIE BY DR. SEUSS:** Mayzie McGrew wakes up to find a daisy sprouting from her head. Faced with ridicule, she acquires the hard-won knowledge that love is more important than fame and glory. Adult Juror Comments: Colorful, fun, rhyming, great music, with a moral—the kids sing along. Brings an adventurous old-fashioned Dr. Seuss story to life. Some adults didn't quite understand the point. Kid Juror Comments: Fascinated. They joined in with the chant, "Daisy Head Mayzie" and were singing the song all day. Age: 2–9; Length: 23 min.; Suggested Retail Price: $12.95, WARNER HOME VIDEO

** **DR. DESOTO AND OTHER STORIES (CHILDREN'S CIRCLE);** see p. 212

*** **FRANKLIN PLAYS THE GAME;** see p. 171

*** **HAROLD AND THE PURPLE CRAYON (CHILDREN'S CIRCLE);** see p. 215

** **HERE COMES THE CAT! AND OTHER CAT STORIES (CHILDREN'S CIRCLE);** see p. 215

** **IT ZWIBBLE: EARTHDAY BIRTHDAY;** see p. 216

** **JOEY RUNS AWAY AND OTHER STORIES (CHILDREN'S CIRCLE);** see p. 217

*** **LINNEA IN MONET'S GARDEN;** see p. 218

** **LITTLE ENGINE THAT COULD, THE:** This beloved children's story is retold this time as an animated feature. Adult Juror Comments: Nice adaptation. Simple production. The female character is determined, confident, and presents a positive message for girls. Lesson is portrayed without much imagination and by stereotypical characters, perhaps to make the point clear. Kid Juror Comments: A winner. Most are familiar with the story and love seeing it come to life. They giggled and listened. Age: 3–6; Length: 30 min.; Suggested Retail Price: $12.98, UNIVERSAL STUDIOS HOME VIDEO

*** LOST & FOUND (JANE HISSEY'S OLD BEAR STORIES): Join Old Bear and his friends in a bit of mystery and intrigue as they band together in some puzzling situations. Based on the classic "Old Bear" storybooks by Jane Hissey. Includes "Little Bear Lost," "Little Bear's Trousers," and "Jigsaw." Adult Juror Comments: Engaging, with clever, appropriate humor and images. Stop-motion animation works well. Discusses trust and the harmony of working together, as well as respect for adults. Accurately paced and simple, yet very engaging. Some vocabulary is too advanced for audience. Kid Juror Comments: Calming yet captivating. Children enjoyed the stories, loved the puppets and the jigsaw puzzle. "My two-year-old watched it two times, start to finish! He giggled at the silly parts." Age: 2–6; Length: 30 min.; Suggested Retail Price: $9.98, SONY WONDER

** MADELINE'S RESCUE; see p. 219

*** MAX'S CHOCOLATE CHICKEN: The Easter Bunny is watching to see if Max will play by the rules when he and his sister compete for the chocolate chicken. Directed by Michael Sporn. Includes three more book-based titles: "Each Peach Pear Plum," "Picnic," and "The Circus Baby." Adult Juror Comments: "Thumbs up." Wonderful, lovely, engaging video based on award-winning children's literature. Inspired kids to seek out these books. Animation is touching. Kid Juror Comments: Big success. Kids relate to animal themes and were taken by the characters. They liked the lead story and "Picnic" best, but truly enjoyed the whole program. Age: 2–7; Length: 36 min.; Suggested Retail Price: $14.95, CHILDREN'S CIRCLE HOME VIDEO

*** MEET LITTLE BEAR (MAURICE SENDAK'S LITTLE BEAR): One of the most cherished characters in all of children's literature, Little Bear, comes to life in these four stories full of warmth, humor, and mischief. Includes "What Will Little Bear Wear?," "Hide and Seek," and "Little Bear Goes to the Moon." Adult Juror Comments: Characters are charming, delightful, and pleasant to watch. Story line is easy to follow. The language is simple and age-appropriate. Reinforces good behaviors and emotions of preschoolers. Encourages adults to hug children. Stores are true to the book. Kid Juror Comments: Terrific reception. Related to such activities as playing in the snow, fishing, and pretend play. Many children recognized the story. "The baby bear was cuddly." They liked the fish soup story best. Age: 2–5; Length: 34 min.; Suggested Retail Price: $9.95, PARAMOUNT HOME VIDEO

** ONCE UPON A DINOSAUR; see p. 222

** RAINBOW FISH (DOORS OF WONDER): With his coat of sparkling scales he was the most beautiful fish in the sea. He was so proud that his selfishness left him feeling very alone. But as he is about to discover, the best feeling of all comes from sharing the things you care about most! Adult Juror Comments: Good message about teamwork and sharing. Production features colorful special effects. Some messages are too mature for this age group and they are not adequately resolved. Kid Juror Comments: A keeper! Three-year-olds were very responsive. They loved the fish and the story. "I'm glad rainbow fish learned how to make friends." Age: 3–6; Length: 30 min.; Suggested Retail Price: $12.98, SONY WONDER

*** RICHARD SCARRY'S BEST BUSY PEOPLE VIDEO EVER!: All the Richard Scarry Busytown characters take turns answering every child's favorite question: "What do you want to be when you grow up?" Shows children what it's like to be a farmer, a firefighter, a teacher, or a truck driver. Original music. Adult Juror Comments: Fun, book-based title. Shows better cultural and gender roles than the original books do. Music is catchy, easy to learn. Exceptional use of language. Promotes children's interest in literature. Kid Juror Comments: Fast-moving, holds children's interest. Kids wanted to view it again. Identified with the characters and sang along. Generated discussion on what boys and girls wanted to be when they grew up. Age: 2–6; Length: 30 min.; Suggested Retail Price: $9.98, RANDOM HOUSE HOME VIDEO

** RICHARD SCARRY'S BEST SILLY STORIES AND SONGS VIDEO EVER!; see p. 225

** RICHARD SCARRY'S BEST SING-ALONG MOTHER GOOSE VIDEO EVER!; see p. 226

*** ROSIE'S WALK & OTHER STORIES (CHILDREN'S CIRCLE): "Rosie's Walk" stars an overeager fox and the hen he is stalking. Includes: "Charlie Needs a Cloak" by Tomie de Paola, "The Story about Ping," and "The Beast of Monsieur Racine." Adult Juror Comments: Wonderful stories, great music that fits the mood of the stories. Good choices for discussion starters. The "Ping" story may work better for older children; younger ones didn't like the animation on this story. Kid Juror Comments: A hit, especially among the younger ones. Elicits participation. "I like Rosie a lot." Age: 2–8; Length: 32 min.; Suggested Retail Price: $14.95, CHILDREN'S CIRCLE HOME VIDEO

** **STORY OF JOSEPH AND HIS BROTHERS, THE:** Joseph's jealous brothers throw him down a well. He is captured and taken to Egypt, where he becomes a favorite with the Pharaoh and finds himself sitting in judgment over his brothers. He must choose between vengeance and divine forgiveness. Adult Juror Comments: Appealing, with good handling of sibling rivalry, jealousy, spirituality, and lying. Egyptian symbols are instructive. Story is harsh for this age, promoting faith without enriching the themes. Christian overtones are prominent. Kid Juror Comments: Good songs and characters, particularly the four-year-olds. Whether or not children learn lasting lessons about lying or rivalry is questionable. Some scenes are scary for younger kids. Age: 3–6; Length: 30 min.; Suggested Retail Price: $12.98, SONY WONDER

** **TALE OF PETER RABBIT, THE;** see p. 231

** **THREE LITTLE PIGS, THE (TODDLER TALES):** Designed for use by parents as well as kids. By incorporating toddler issues such as learning to "use your words," children enact the traditional story with a toddler twist. Adult Juror Comments: It's enjoyable to see a child-acted play. Shows many positive behaviors such as sharing, working together, taking turns, using words to solve problems and communicate feelings. Low production level, poor sound, entire program is shot in a backyard. Kid Juror Comments: Kids enjoyed this. Humor is just right for this audience. "I liked it when the first pig built her house." "Why were all the pigs girls?" Kids dressed up and began role-playing afterwards. Age: 2–5; Length: 20 min.; Suggested Retail Price: $14.95, TODDLER TALES

** **WHEN NINO FLEW:** Inspired by Mayan legends. Maria flies on her winged burro to get a feather from the old serpent of the mountain to cure her sick baby brother. Their flight includes many adventures, an epic battle, and triumphant return. Tale demonstrates love, selflessness, and courage. Adult Juror Comments: Simple production demonstrates bravery, sibling love, and positive values. Gives the sense that anything is possible. Features a female heroine and narrator. Touching story is good foundation for discussion. Simple, childlike illustrations give it a "real" quality. Kid Juror Comments: Very well appreciated. Kids liked the dragon and the sense of danger without being scary. An Ojibwa girl who is very proud of her cultural heritage thought this was a great film and was inspired to create a film of her own. Age: 3–7; Length: 25 min.; Suggested Retail Price: $14.95, WEST HILL PRESS

* **WINNIE THE POOH:** Contains four of the famous A.A. Milne stories animated in the original animation style. Adult Juror Comments: Faithful to the book, characters encourage acceptance and diversity. Adults enjoyed the illustrations, but the "original" animation style did not appeal to children who are familiar with the more current film version of Pooh. Kid Juror Comments: Though children liked the stories, the British accent was difficult for preschoolers to understand. They thought it had too much talking. Age: 2–5; Length: 57 min.; Suggested Retail Price: $14.98, TWENTIETH CENTURY FOX HOME ENTERTAINMENT—CBS/FOX

*** **WINTER TALES (MAURICE SENDAK'S LITTLE BEAR):** Join Sendak's beloved Little Bear and a menagerie of friends in a frosty, glistening winter wonderland in these four snowy tales. Adult Juror Comments: It's playful, well paced, and kindhearted. Main character is funny, curious, and endearing. Beautifully produced. Emphasis is on family and traditions. Motivates interest in using a compass and introduces new vocabulary. Good seasonal entertainment. Kid Juror Comments: Lots of questions about the snow. "My two- and four-year-olds have been playing the story of the winter tree, ring around the rosy, and making snow angels." Good discussion starter about what to do with grumpy behavior. Age: 2–7; Length: 32 min.; Suggested Retail Price: $9.95, PARAMOUNT HOME VIDEO

Foreign Language

** EL BARCO MAGICO; see p. 237

*** **ERES TU MI MAMA? (ARE YOU MY MOTHER?):** Spanish adaption of P.D. Eastman's classic about a baby bird who sets out to find his mother, asking everyone he meets along the way "Are you my mother?" Adult Juror Comments: Good video to show to young children who are learning their first words. A great tool to integrate a group of multicultural kids. Adults used the books as a follow-up to the video. Can be used to teach Spanish to very young children. Kid Juror Comments: Mostly silly, but fun. Bilingual children adored it, and Spanish-speaking children also enjoyed it tremendously. English-speaking children were interested but had to work hard to understand. Overall, it's a winner. Age: 2–6; Length: 30 min.; Suggested Retail Price: $9.98, RANDOM HOUSE HOME VIDEO

* PROFESSOR PARROT SPEAKS SPANISH LEARNING SYSTEM: Teaches Spanish by having children sing, dance, and play games. Introduces 150 Spanish words. Includes a 30-minute video, a parent/caregiver guide, and an audio cassette of sing-along songs. Adult Juror Comments: It's a crisp, clear production with good introductory teaching techniques. Characters are visually appealing and likeable. The short songs make learning Spanish fun for children. Requires repeat viewings to benefit from the Spanish lessons. Kid Juror Comments: Learned some Spanish phrases, loved the songs and the puppets. Younger kids danced and sang along. The Goldilocks story was difficult for kids to understand. Age: 3–5; Length: 30 min.; Suggested Retail Price: $19.95, SOUND BEGINNINGS

Holiday

** BEAR WHO SLEPT THROUGH CHRISTMAS, THE; see p. 239

** CHANUKA AT BUBBE'S; see p. 240

** CHRISTMAS ADVENTURE, THE (THE ADVENTURES OF RAGGEDY ANN AND ANDY): Everybody's favorite rag dolls discover someone has stolen Santa's reindeer, his sleigh, and all the children's toys! By following clues, Raggedy Ann and Andy meet their old friends and discover who's behind the Christmas-napping. Adult Juror Comments: Children enjoy stories about Christmas. And this one presents a dramatic situation with a satisfying resolution. Displays good teamwork. Teaches children to think and care about others. Adults disliked some of the aggressive language and behavior shown. Kid Juror Comments: Generated lots of comments about Christmas, reinforces the myth of Santa. Most of the children watched the entire video. "It's a good show. I like the camel. But they can't really fly, only reindeer can." Age: 3–7; Length: 25 min.; Suggested Retail Price: $9.98, TWENTIETH CENTURY FOX HOME ENTERTAINMENT

*** CHRISTMAS EVE ON SESAME STREET: As everyone is getting ready for Christmas on Sesame Street, Oscar asks a disturbing question, "How does Santa, who is built like a dump truck, get down those skinny chimneys?" While solving the riddle they discover the true meaning of Christmas. Adult Juror Comments: A lovely Christmas story with nice focus on giving. Sign language portion is a pleasant addition. Some parts are a little slow. One scene in which Oscar flies out of the skating rink and falls down a stairwell is unnecessary and unsafe. Kid Juror Comments: Great ice skating. Very attentive, enjoyed the singing. It's a little long for younger children. Good to show it in segments. They sing "Feliz Navidad." Age: 2–5; Length: 60 min.; Suggested Retail Price: $12.98, SONY WONDER/CTW

*** CHRISTMAS PRESENTS (OLD BEAR STORIES): Three lighthearted holiday tales starring a cast of whimsically animated playroom toys brought to life through animation. Based on the books by Jane Hissey. Adult Juror Comments: Characters are appealing, simple, inventive, and creative. They show concern, sharing, and friendship. Enjoyable mix of animation and real environments. Artfully understated. Contains lovely noncommercial Christmas message: "Sharing is the true meaning of giving." Kid Juror Comments: The old-fashioned quality was wonderful, and the children requested several reruns. They wanted to hold stuffed bears while they watched. One seven-year-old said it gave her ideas of things to make. Age: 2–5; Length: 32 min.; Suggested Retail Price: $14.95, SONY WONDER

* CHRISTMAS TREE TRAIN, THE (CHUCKLEWOOD CRITTERS): Buttons and Rusty accidentally board the Christmas Tree Train on a delivery run to the big city. A wise owl befriends them, telling them all about the city, and Santa comes to their rescue. Adult Juror Comments: Old-fashioned style of animation has marginal entertainment value. Adults didn't find any special qualities in this program. The cubs' mischievous nature creates situations that are alarming but not addressed. Kid Juror Comments: The Christmas theme spurred an animated discussion about Santa, what the kids wanted for Christmas, and getting lost from one's parents. Age: 3–6; Length: 25 min.; Suggested Retail Price: $9.98, UNAPIX/MIRAMAR

*** COUNTRY MOUSE AND THE CITY MOUSE, A CHRISTMAS STORY, THE: When Emily, the country mouse, visits her worldly cousin, Alexander, for the holidays, they discover the true meaning of Christmas—love and family. Based on an Aesop's fable. Animation by Michael Sporn. Voices by Crystal Gayle and John Lithgow. Adult Juror Comments: Good, consistent, understandable story line. Strong in showing values of friendship, relationship, non-materialism, respect for differences. Appeals more to younger kids, although the older kids enjoyed it as well. Kid Juror Comments: "Excellent, great, really good, funny, super-cute—we liked it a lot!" Kids had sympathy for the mouse lost in New York City and delighted over the "welcome home Christmas gifts." Age: 2–6; Length: 25 min.; Suggested Retail Price: $9.95, RANDOM HOUSE HOME VIDEO

** FIRST EASTER EGG, THE: Easter-theme animated tale of a bunny named "One" who searches for a gift for his mother and starts a worldwide tradition! Adult Juror Comments: Simple story with cute animation, vivid colors, cheerful music, and a mix of familiar characters. The message is a playful explanation of the Easter egg's origin. Some language is grammatically incorrect, and characters at times make fun of one another. Kid Juror Comments: The Easter theme was appealing. "The chickens were silly and the pigs were really silly." Some liked the bunny, others thought his speech was too babyish. He was polite, though. Age: 2–5; Length: 30 min.; Suggested Retail Price: $9.99, ANCHOR BAY ENTERTAINMENT

* HE AIN'T SCARY, HE'S OUR BROTHER (CASPER): Casper refuses to go spooking with the other ghosts, planning instead to trick-or-treat dressed as a real boy. Adult Juror Comments: The moral of the story teaches that ghosts can't hurt you. Vocabulary level is uneven. The "ghosts" have poor enunciation. The resolution of the story is not quite credible. Kid Juror Comments: Casper can't miss, especially the music and songs. Four-year-olds were interested, threes wandered around. Even the two-year-olds watched for a while. Age: 3–6; Length: 25 min.; Suggested Retail Price: $9.98, WARNER HOME VIDEO

* NIGHT BEFORE CHRISTMAS, THE (ENCHANTED TALES): Magic tale about a young orphan boy and his cat who discover a miracle on Christmas Eve. Adult Juror Comments: Not very believable, odd mixture of songs and music. Addresses sharing, giving, and caring. Uses "Nutcracker" soundtrack in a peculiar way. The mouse character is appealing. Animation is average, Some characters are mean. Kid Juror Comments: Mixed reaction. Some didn't really pay attention to the story, while others enjoyed it. Provoked discussions about sharing, giving, and caring. Age: 5–8; Length: 48 min.; Suggested Retail Price: $9.98, SONY WONDER

** NODDY GIVES A BIRTHDAY PARTY: To earn money for a birthday present for Big Ears, Noddy takes a delivery job and gets all mixed up. Meanwhile, the cake he made burns to a crisp. Mrs. Tessie Bear saves the day with a new cake! Includes two additional episodes. Adult Juror Comments: Well produced, teaches kindness and handling life when things aren't perfect. Outstanding production with good diversity. Noddy is constantly getting himself out of messes. Characters' inappropriate and at-times-rude behavior goes uncorrected, but it's not a major issue. Kid Juror Comments: Noddy amused the kids by flying around or singing songs. Enjoyed the story, especially the two-year-olds. All wanted to watch it again. "It seemed real because they used toys." Kids noticed the respect shown at times. Age: 2–5; Length: 30 min.; Suggested Retail Price: $12.95, POLYGRAM VIDEO

*** SHARON, LOIS & BRAM: CANDLES, SNOW & MISTLETOE: An original musical fantasy that combines the familiar warmth, wit and magic of Sharon, Lois and Bram with the hijinks of their adorable pal, Elephant. Full of new songs as well as familiar classics, while discovering the true meaning of Christmas. Adult Juror Comments: "Bigger than life" characters are very entertaining. Well produced, entertaining. The holiday season comes across with song and movement. Kid Juror Comments: Enjoyed the songs and sang along, but also thought it moves a little slowly and is a little long. Best viewed in segments. Age: 2–6; Length: 50 min.; Suggested Retail Price: $9.98, VIDEO TREASURES, INC.

* TALES & TUNES: CHRISTMAS TALES & TUNES: The creators of "Baby Songs" presents a holiday assortment of Christmas stories and songs for young viewers. Video disc jockey K.J. narrates. Adult Juror Comments: Nice mix of animation and live action. The puppet story promotes values of friendship and giving. It's very silly and somewhat fragmented. Talks down to kids at times and has some name-calling. Kid Juror Comments: Songs are catchy. Kids sang along the first time they viewed it. Gets off to a slow start but then captures their attention. Children thought it was a bit jumbled, though. Age: 2–6; Length: 30 min.; Suggested Retail Price: $12.98, VIDEO TREASURES, INC.

** TALES & TUNES: HANUKKAH TALES & TUNES: The creators of "Baby Songs" present an assortment of Hanukkah stories and songs, hosted by video disc jockey K. J. Adult Juror Comments: This video is well done and conveys important information in an interesting and exciting way. The music and dance numbers with children are appealing. Production quality is low and slow-paced. Kid Juror Comments: The children liked to watch the kids in the video dancing. They got up and joined in! Kids liked all of the Hanukkah music and learning about the holiday. Age: 5–8; Length: 30 min.; Suggested Retail Price: $12.98, VIDEO TREASURES, INC.

** THUMPKIN AND THE EASTER BUNNIES: The colorful tale of Johnny's discovery of the Easter egg's secret and the first Easter egg hunt. Adult Juror Comments: A good story accompanied by nice music. Great to show along with egg-dyeing. Some thought it was a little too cute and slow-paced. Kid Juror Comments: Absorbing and instructive. Kids wrote Easter stories for several days after watching program. They asked when the Easter Bunny would arrive. Age: 3–6; Length: 29 min.; Suggested Retail Price: $12.98, ARTISAN/FAMILY HOME ENTERTAINMENT

* TURKEY CAPER, THE (CHUCKLEWOOD CRITTERS); see p. 246

* 'TWAS THE DAY BEFORE CHRISTMAS (CHUCKLEWOOD CRITTERS): Buttons and Rusty prepare for the gala Christmas celebration by gathering ornaments and other goodies from the forest. There's a monster lurking in Chucklewood, which the cubs learn is imaginary. Adult Juror Comments: Although the cubs' mischief-making goes unnoticed, there is positive content. The animals work together for the good of the whole group. Enforces the joy of celebrating Christmas without the emphasis on presents. Too much emphasis on monsters. Kid Juror Comments: Motivated questions from the kids about the characters and their actions. It's long for the intended age group. Most kids were not interested in seeing it a second time. Age: 3–6; Length: 25 min.; Suggested Retail Price: $9.98, UNAPIX/MIRAMAR

** VEGGIE TALES: THE TOY THAT SAVED CHRISTMAS: It looks like the worst Christmas ever, until brave little Buzz-Saw Louie doll takes matters into his own hands. Teaches children that anyone can have Christmas, but it's more important to understand Christmas. Adult Juror Comments: Offers easy-to-understand Christian message about the meaning of Christmas (giving). Lessons employ positive role models. Encourages problem-solving. Animation is unique and inviting. Contains some stereotyping. Kid Juror Comments: Sang along with the songs and found the animation inviting. "At first I was sad when I thought Christmas would be ruined, but then I was happy when the penguins and the toy saved Christmas." "I liked the song about 'It's okay to be different.'" Age: 3–8; Length: 30 min.; Suggested Retail Price: $12.98, BIG IDEA PRODUCTIONS

How-To

** ART PARTY (PROFESSOR IRIS): Professor Iris, in search of artistic inspiration, mixes up a rainbow of colors, discovers shapes, and creates a masterpiece. Adult Juror Comments: Lovable puppets, stimulating. Kids respond to the music by dancing and enjoy recognizing familiar shapes. A tool for seeing and creating, it emphasizes seeing art in everyday life. Perhaps doesn't encourage creativity as much as copying a model. Kid Juror Comments: Very nice. They moved around with the music and enjoyed recognizing the shapes and colors. "This is great!" Contains too much information for preschoolers to absorb all at once. Age: 2–5; Length: 40 min.; Suggested Retail Price: $12.95, DISCOVERY COMMUNICATIONS

** BREADTIME TALES; see p. 248

** I CAN BUILD! (CAN TOO!): Children embark on a real-life adventure designing and building a dream playhouse. Time-lapse action and whimsical 3–D animation demonstrate the logistics of building. Adult Juror Comments: Shows parents and kids working together (multiple ages/skills). Talks directly to kids. Computer graphics were popular and helpful in illustrating the building process: how everything comes together from start to finish. Music is repetitive. Kid Juror Comments: Great to discover that they could be a part of a building project. Sparked interest in building. Provoked lots of conversation about making things. "I'm going to draw a picture, so that I can make a castle too." Age: 2–8; Length: 25 min.; Suggested Retail Price: $14.95, CAN TOO! TAPES/BELLMAN GIRLS, L.L.C.

* ANOTHER GREAT DAY FOR SINGING, WITH JAMES DURST: Features fourteen melodic songs—many familiar—performed with guitar accompaniment. Several are enhanced with digital effects, including duets with guests "Eb and Flo" and an introduction to the orchestra with "Old King Cole." Adult Juror Comments: Light, catchy, lively American folk songs. Encourages imagination. Simple, clear presentation. Durst has a soothing voice and friendly appearance. Lyrics are easily repeated. Best viewed in two sessions or for quiet time. Format is a bit dull. Kid Juror Comments: While this engaged some children, others were bored. "There weren't a lot of songs with pictures." Some kids readily sang along, laughed and participated with hand gestures. Overall, it was too long to hold their interest throughout. Age: 3–7; Length: 37 min.; Suggested Retail Price: $12.98, SIDEWALK PRODUCTIONS

Music

** BABY SONGS: BABY ROCK; see p. 31

*** BABY SONGS: BABY SONGS; see p. 31

*** BABY SONGS: EVEN MORE BABY SONGS; see p. 32

*** BABY SONGS: HAP PALMER'S FOLLOW ALONG SONGS; see p. 32

** BABY SONGS: JOHN LITHGOW'S KID-SIZE CONCERT; see p. 32

*** BABY SONGS: MORE BABY SONGS; see p. 32

** BABY SONGS: SUPER BABY SONGS; see p. 33

** BEDTIME (STORIES TO REMEMBER): Judy Collins invites young viewers on a gentle journey into dreamland with a collection of best-loved lullabies: "Hush Little Baby," "Lullaby and Good Night," and "The Land of Nod." Adapted from Kay Chorao's "The Baby's Bedtime Book." Adult Juror Comments: Parents who are Judy Collins fans are thrilled to share this charming production with their kids. Moves from fast-paced songs to slow, sleepy ones. Kid Juror Comments: It works. One adult juror commented, "My six-month baby went to sleep with it right away." Age: 1–5; Length: 26 min.; Suggested Retail Price: $9.95, LIGHTYEAR ENTERTAINMENT

*** CONCERT IN ANGEL-LAND: Children take a magic journey to Angel-Land, where song and dance abound. Whimsical angels and children from many cultures sing along with recording artists Megon McDonough and Victor Cockburn. Adult Juror Comments: Teaches respect through simple songs, stories, and games. Presented at a child's level, it simplifies ideas that reassure young children. Simple production, showing the diversity of children's artwork. Kid Juror Comments: Fabulous music, great storytelling. One leader had to sneak the tape away after viewing. Children were totally engaged by the material and the angels. Age: 2–8; Length: 25 min.; Suggested Retail Price: $10.95, MVP HOME ENTERTAINMENT, INC.

** FINGERPLAYS AND FOOTPLAYS: Focuses on activities that develop coordination, concentration, and listening skills. Everything can be performed while standing, seated in a chair, or with legs crossed on the floor. Adult Juror Comments: Basic production values, repetitive. Songs and characters are simple and easy to follow. Good balance of kids, adults, and pictures. Ideal for preschoolers, who pick up the tunes quickly. Nice diversity. Clear instructions. Kid Juror Comments: Danced along and did movements. Some fingerplays were familiar. Older kids suggested it for their younger brothers and sisters. Age: 2–5; Length: 30 min.; Suggested Retail Price: $19.95, EDUCATIONAL ACTIVITIES, INC.

* FRIENDS (THE PARABLES OF PETER RABBIT): The adventure of a lifetime begins when four unsuspecting children stumble upon the burrow of Peter Rabbit. Based on the parable of the Good Samaritan and what it means to be a friend. Adult Juror Comments: Friendship concepts presented within Christian framework. Though not overstated, presents God and the Bible

throughout. Good child acting, catchy music but really corny! Kid Juror Comments: Remained interested, though they didn't like the lip singing. They did like seeing the girl teaching the boy to play catch. Kids thought it was too long, but enjoyed the message: "Friends are *really* important." Age: 3–6; Length: 30 min.; Suggested Retail Price: $14.95, BRENTWOOD MUSIC

** GREAT DAY FOR SINGING, A: A colorful sing-along introducing twenty-five well known nursery rhymes and children's songs in a relaxed setting. Features James Durst on acoustic guitar in studio and on a 19th-century working farm with kids and barnyard animals. Adult Juror Comments: Pleasant songs and varied backgrounds with appeal for both boys and girls. Good transitions between songs showing the title and the children's art work depicting that title. Good sound quality. No multicultural children or songs. Kid Juror Comments: Kids enjoyed the singing and the music. The simplicity inspires imagination and conversation, some dancing. "I liked the spider song." "I didn't want it to end." Started a discussion about farm animals. Age: 2–5; Length: 30 min.; Suggested Retail Price: $12.95, SIDEWALK PRODUCTIONS

** I DIG DIRT; see p. 253

*** JOE SCRUGGS IN CONCERT; see p. 253

** JOE'S FIRST VIDEO; see p. 254

** IN SEARCH OF THE LOST NOTE: A missing musical note leaves Lil' Iguana and Buk feeling unharmonious. After making a homemade musical instrument and forming an impromptu conga band, Lil' Iguana and friends try adding a quarter-note to end their rendition of "The Silly Song" on key. Adult Juror Comments: The live segments are well done. Encourages cognitive and intellectual skills. Provides an introduction to musical elements—notes, tunes, instruments, rhythm, and melody at a basic level. Entertaining for preschoolers. Kid Juror Comments: Mixed reaction. Some children attentive, while others walked away. The kids who attend music lessons enjoyed it the most. Liked the art project that showed them how to make a tambourine. Age: 3–5; Length: 25 min.; Suggested Retail Price: $12.95, WABU-TV 68, BOSTON

* INFANTASTIC LULLABYES; see p. 33

** JUNGLE JAMBOREE SING-A-LONG: Hosted by Gus the gorilla. Features an array of other jungle animals and their human friends, Pancho and Denise.

Kids can discover something about themselves by singing these songs of self-awareness. Adult Juror Comments: Fun, engaging, lively songs have potential for further discussion about self-awareness. Some skits had positive messages, though lack transitions that further explain subject matter. Cluttered sets, distracting method to prompt the audience to sing. Kid Juror Comments: Some children danced to the music, joined in with the singing, but by and large the reaction was mixed. Some kids loved watching it repeatedly, others were less responsive and didn't pay much attention. Age: 2–5; Length: 35 min.; Suggested Retail Price: $9.95, JUST FOR KIDS/CELEBRITY HOME VIDEO

** KIDS MAKE MUSIC: Full of activities: singing, dancing, rhyming, and clapping. Orff Schulwerk's approach to music education directs children's natural instincts into an active process, teaching music by making music. Adult Juror Comments: A good teaching video with many examples of music activities. Encourages active participation, creativity, and self-expression. If possible, have musical instruments available for kids' use. Simplified for those with no musical background. Kid Juror Comments: Young children (ages three to four) loved this approach. Inspires an interest in musical instruments. Age: 2–5; Length: 45 min.; Suggested Retail Price: $14.95, MUSIC RHAPSODY

** KIDSONGS: MEET THE BIGGLES: Invites viewers to join in the fun as Billy and Ruby Biggle use their special powers to take their friends, the Kidsongs Kids, to magical Biggleland for a musical adventure. Adult Juror Comments: This program has a selection of good songs sung competently, though uninspiringly, by a group of relentlessly cheerful children and puppets in relentlessly cheerful settings. The performers cheerfully dance, in a prepubescent jubilation. Exhausting. Kid Juror Comments: Songs are enjoyable, kids sang and danced along. Kids pointed out that all the kids on-screen looked like they were from middle- to upper-class families with nice clothes, rooms full of tapes, big houses. Little diversity there. They liked the songs. Age: 2–5; Length: 30 min.; Suggested Retail Price: $12.98, SONY WONDER

* LET'S SING (SING ALONG WITH JOHN LANGSTAFF): Invites children to clap, move, and sing with master music educator and Pied Piper John Langstaff. Designed for children to watch alone or in groups. Adult Juror Comments: Good content. Easy to learn but challenging at the same time. Format could become boring if watched all in one sitting. Jurors found it useful to view in segments. Excellent diversity, songs from different regions. Kid Juror Comments: Best when shown in segments. Some songs were difficult for

children to hear, follow, and sing along. Age: 3–5; Length: 45 min.; Suggested Retail Price: $19.95, LANGSTAFF VIDEO PROJECT

* **LITTLE MUSIC MAKERS BAND:** Combines music and movement while introducing children to rhythm instruments. Teaches through traditional songs with creative new arrangements. Adult Juror Comments: Colorful environment for introducing music. On-screen children are not engaged. Instruments used are well selected. Demonstrates cooperation. Lacks diversity. Kid Juror Comments: Not much of a grabber. Motivated physical activity from some kids—swinging, tapping, and playing their own instruments—but it did not hold the attention of all. Age: 2–5; Length: 26 min.; Suggested Retail Price: $9.95, B & D ENTERPRISES

** **MONKEY MOVES;** see p. 254

** **MOVE LIKE THE ANIMALS;** see p. 254

** **MUSIC MANIA (PROFESSOR IRIS):** A musical medley of classroom antics. Professor Iris is tuning up the classroom orchestra for music, song, and dance with a symphony of musical instruments from around the world. Adult Juror Comments: Adults thought this was too long and lacked variation. Best to view in three segments according to how the tape is divided. Kid Juror Comments: Older kids, three to five, got more out of this program than did the two-year-olds. They thought it was a little slow compared to the music they're accustomed to hearing. Age: 2–6; Length: 40 min.; Suggested Retail Price: $12.95, DISCOVERY COMMUNICATIONS

*** **MRN: MUSICAL STORIES (MISTER ROGERS' NEIGHBORHOOD):** Two musical, whimsical adventures dealing with themes important to children. In one, a cow learns to feel good about who he is. The other celebrates a family reunion. Adult Juror Comments: Meaningful messages for children. Mister Rogers offers quality entertainment without a lot of flash. Pace is good for this age, encourages children to engage in the material. It's long. Jurors viewed individual stories separately. Kid Juror Comments: Scored high. Kept their attention and led to discussion afterward. Age: 2–7; Length: 59 min.; Suggested Retail Price: $12.95, FAMILY COMMUNICATIONS

* **NURSERY SONGS & RHYMES (RUSTY & ROSY):** A collection of twenty-six favorite nursery rhymes, songs and chants teach many vital pre-reading concepts. Reinforces learning letters, names, shapes, and sounds. Adult Juror Comments: Good for reinforcement, as secondary to active learning. Somewhat static, music more lively than pictures. Kid Juror Comments: Children

liked this better than adults. Held their attention. Helpful for early readers to have the words on the screen. Kids sang along. Age: 2–6; Length: 37 min.; Suggested Retail Price: $24.95, WATERFORD INSTITUTE

** ON A FUN RAINY DAY (BABIES AT PLAY); see p. 33

*** RICHARD SCARRY'S BEST LEARNING SONGS VIDEO EVER!: Huckle Cat and friends put on a backyard show full of songs and surprises. Characters from Busytown sing about letters, shapes and numbers. Adult Juror Comments: Cheerful preschool activity. Nice incorporation of known subjects with new materials. Easy to absorb information, songs, and characters. Very effective teaching tool to learn shapes and the alphabet. Stimulates interest in the Scarry books. Kid Juror Comments: Charming. The songs and characters went over big. "My son was riveted to the screen and identified letters and objects." All of the children asked to watch it again. Age: 2–6; Length: 30 min.; Suggested Retail Price: $9.98, RANDOM HOUSE HOME VIDEO

*** SHARON, LOIS & BRAM: ONE ELEPHANT WENT OUT TO PLAY: Children of all ages sing with the trio, lighting up their eyes with pleasure. Adult Juror Comments: Excellent. It's full of life and good spirits; playful, cheerful, and active. Appealing audio: great music, good variety of songs. Fabulous program. Unfortunately, box cover lacks appeal. The breaks between segments create sudden stops that disrupt continuity. Kid Juror Comments: Enthusiastic response. Enjoyed the familiar songs, especially the four- and five-year-olds. They sang along with most songs. Age: 2–6; Length: 60 min.; Suggested Retail Price: $9.98, VIDEO TREASURES, INC.

* SHARON, LOIS & BRAM: SING A TO Z: Sharon, Lois, and Bram, along with their fuzzy elephant friend, sing and dance, teaching every letter of the alphabet. Adult Juror Comments: Entertaining introduction of the alphabet with many familiar songs. Some adults felt this was very entertaining; others said it was a little monotonous. Kid Juror Comments: Okay. It was a little hard for them to follow which letter they were on. Long, best viewed in segments. Age: 2–5; Length: 50 min.; Suggested Retail Price: $9.98, VIDEO TREASURES, INC.

*** SING ALONG WITH BINYAH BINYAH (GULLAH GULLAH ISLAND): Contains eleven popular songs, including "Eensy Weensy Spider," "B-I-N-G-O," and "Loop De Loop." Adult Juror Comments: Familiar songs for children are presented in an entertaining, compassionate way. Great cultural mix, good movement activities, and appropriate pace encourage interactive viewing. Kid Juror Comments: A winner! They sang along and wanted to watch again. Great interactions from kids. Age: 3–6; Length: 30 min.; Suggested Retail Price: $12.98, PARAMOUNT HOME VIDEO

*** SING ALONG WITH EUREEKA (EUREEKA'S CASTLE): A special collection of eleven favorite songs from the television series "Eureeka's Castle." Adult Juror Comments: Lively, colorful, funny puppets—a fun fantasy with lots of musical variety. Kid Juror Comments: Enraptured. They were singing along, tapping their feet, and bopping their heads. Wanted to watch again. Age: 2–5; Length: 30 min.; Suggested Retail Price: $9.95, PARAMOUNT HOME VIDEO

** SING ME A STORY: RABBI JOE BLACK IN CONCERT: Rabbi Joe Black in concert explores stories and songs from the Jewish tradition, such as looking for the afikoman, and lighting the Chanukah menorah. Original and favorite songs celebrate and entertain at the same time. Adult Juror Comments: Great songs. Lots of toe tapping, humming, and singing along. Special appeal to Jewish kids. A great way to expose non-Jewish children to this culture. "Definite educational value. Mr. Black is a good performer, he appeals to children." Kid Juror Comments: A hard time understanding the unfamiliar words. Would work best with activity book or lesson. "Our two-year-olds hung in there for the entire 45 minutes!" Age: 2–8; Length: 45 min.; Suggested Retail Price: $15.95, LANITUNES

*** SING YOURSELF SILLIER AT THE MOVIES (SESAME STREET): Hosts Telly and Oscar review the silliest movies you've ever seen, with the silliest songs you've ever heard! Will these daffy ditties rate a "wow" or a "phooey"? They can't seem to agree. Contains "Eight Balls of Fur," "Hey Diddle Diddle," and more. Adult Juror Comments: Good catchy songs from Sesame Street. Clever production techniques. Artistic excellence, great humor, engages children and adults. Good for parent/child interaction and critical thinking skills. May stimulate dramatic play. Kid Juror Comments: Sang and danced to the songs. Liked Telly and Oscar as the hosts. Kids familiar with Sesame Street identify readily with it. Age: 2–5; Length: 30 min.; Suggested Retail Price: $12.98, SONY WONDER/CTW

** SINGING TIME (STORIES TO REMEMBER): Judy Collins sings the beloved poetry of Robert Browning, Emily Dickinson, Gertrude Stein, and others. Music by award-winning composer Ernest Troost. Animation by Sesame Street's Daniel Ivanick. Based on Kay Chorao's "The Baby's Good Morning Book." Adult Juror Comments: What a delightful way to introduce young children to classic poetry! Showing children the book along with the video is a good idea. Kid Juror Comments: Enjoyable. Younger ones tend to watch in segments rather than all in one sitting. Age: 1–5; Length: 25 min.; Suggested Retail Price: $9.95, LIGHTYEAR ENTERTAINMENT

*** SOMETHING SPECIAL: Fast-moving animation, expressive children, and colorful art bring these Hap Palmer favorites to life. Selections from the popular Walter and Sally albums help students increase vocabulary while having fun. Adult Juror Comments: Promotes good self-image while stimulating creative responses in children to interpret music and dance in their own way. Helps develop gross-motor skills and following directions. Culturally diverse. Kid Juror Comments: Great fun to dance and sing along! It's silly and made them feel happy. Shows lots of different people, including good cartoon monsters. "I can pretend to do things like throw a rope and ride a horse." "It's fun and you can dance to it." Age: 2–6; Length: 25 min.; Suggested Retail Price: $19.95, EDUCATIONAL ACTIVITIES, INC.

** STELLA AND THE STAR-TONES: Living among the stars in the night sky, Stella and her cast of whimsical constellations come alive as you play their music. Contains twenty-one illustrated screens with animated characters, each with an original musical score, from blues to jazz to polka. Adult Juror Comments: Great learning tool with lots of variety. Introduces musical awareness by giving children free rein to create their own concerts. Provides positive and encouraging support. Simple and fun. Lacks levels of ability. Kid Juror Comments: Captivating and easy to use. Nothing you do on the computer is wrong in this program. Kids enjoyed creating their own songs. Younger kids were dancing in their seats. Appeals most to kids interested in music. Comes with a star poster. Age: 2–5; Suggested Retail Price: $25.00, BOHEM INTERACTIVE (CD-ROM)

*** STEPPING OUT WITH HAP PALMER: Hap Palmer is an innovator in using music and movement to teach basic skills: shapes, days of the week, counting, and movement. Encourages the use of imagination. His music has been widely used in schools and day-care centers for over 20 years. Adult Juror Comments: Palmer's songs suit child's developmental level perfectly. Activities are fun, varied, and easy to sing. Number learning is incidental and very well integrated. Shows excellent representation of handicapped kids and diverse cultures. Kid Juror Comments: Enthusiastic, especially the music and movement. One kids' jury commented, "We didn't watch it— we did it!" Age: 2–6; Length: 30 min.; Suggested Retail Price: $19.95, EDUCATIONAL ACTIVITIES, INC.

*** STORYTIME (STORIES TO REMEMBER): Legendary singer-songwriter Arlo Guthrie brings his whimsical wit and music to storytelling: "The Three Little Pigs," "Henny Penny," and "Little Red Riding Hood." Animation by Michael Sporn. Adapted from Kay Chorao's "The Baby's Story Book." Adult Juror Comments: Fun and funny. Arlo Guthrie fans were delighted and anxious to share it with their kids. Kid Juror Comments: Kids get a kick out of Guthrie's manner and loved seeing and hearing their favorite stories. Age: 1–5; Length: 26 min.; Suggested Retail Price: $9.95, LIGHTYEAR ENTERTAINMENT

*** STORYTIME SING ALONG (ALLEGRA'S WINDOW): Poco wants Allegra and Lindi to read him a story, but they don't know how to read yet. Instead, they tell stories and draw pictures of their friends. By the end, they've created a beautiful book of their own. Adult Juror Comments: Contains easy-to-follow, colorful, catchy tunes. Prompts creativity; making up new words to songs, expression through music. Teaches reflection and storytelling through pictures. Kid Juror Comments: Three- and four-year-olds particularly enjoyed it. Children wanted to sing the songs afterwards and asked to hear specific selections. Age: 2–5; Length: 30 min.; Suggested Retail Price: $12.98, PARAMOUNT HOME VIDEO

** TALES & TUNES: ORIGINAL TALES & TUNES: A collection of whimsical stories and music for young children guided by a spunky little character named K.J. Contemporary tales and upbeat tunes are combined with live action, animation and puppetry. Adult Juror Comments: Funny. Adults liked the overall content. Kids were interested in the "William Small" section, to see how the picture would develop. In one section, children behave in an adult fashion. In another, mothers are stereotyped. Kid Juror Comments: Enjoyed observing other children, particularly the "silliness." They followed along with everything, enjoyed singing, and joined in. Too long for younger kids without breaking it up; older ones loved it. Age: 2–8; Length: 30 min.; Suggested Retail Price: $12.98, VIDEO TREASURES, INC.

** TALES & TUNES: SILLY TALES & TUNES: From the creators of "Babysongs" comes this assortment of comical stories and sing-along songs. Video disc jockey K.J. hosts this collection of rib-tickling tales, kooky cartoons, laugh-packed tunes, and non-stop fun. Adult Juror Comments: Nice variety of elements to keep young viewers interested: animation, live action, jokes, stories, songs. Some cultural stereotyping and not such good role models—i.e., high heels on monkey bars. Kid Juror Comments: Very nice, especially the music and sing-along songs. "I want to see that one again." Age-appropriateness changes, humor and content best suited for older kids. Age: 2–8; Length: 30 min.; Suggested Retail Price: $12.98, VIDEO TREASURES, INC.

* TALES & TUNES: SPOOKY TALES & TUNES; see p. 257

** TICKLE TUNE TYPHOON: LET'S BE FRIENDS; see p. 258

* TUBBY THE TUBA: Tubby is a member of a great orchestra, but he's unhappy with his monotonous "oompah" sound and envious of the other instruments. Tubby leaves the orchestra in search of a tuneful melody, and his wanderings bring success, failure, and heartbreak. Adult Juror Comments: A sweet, classic story. Tuneful but not stellar music. Fairly old-fashioned and slow-moving for today's audience. Kid Juror Comments: Okay. They especially liked the elephant dance scene. The beginning is a little sad. Age: 3–7; Length: 81 min.; Suggested Retail Price: $12.98, SONY WONDER

** VEGGIE TALES: SILLY SING-ALONG 2: THE END OF SILLINESS?: A fast-paced sing-along collection that finds Larry the Cucumber drowning his sorrows in the ice cream parlor. Features songs from the Veggie Tales Series and asks the question "Is this the end of silliness?" Adult Juror Comments: Definitely silly, colorful, and bright. The humor, fast music, and funny characters are age-appropriate and enjoyable. "I loved watching the children watch it." The rapid speech is difficult to follow. Relates slightly to Bible stories. Kid Juror Comments: Stellar. The children laughed and sang along. "If you don't watch this kind of movie, your heart will be broken." Some kids wanted to watch it again, tomorrow. Age: 3–7; Length: 30 min.; Suggested Retail Price: $12.99, BIG IDEA

** WEE SING FAVORITES: ANIMAL SONGS: Wee Sing characters Singaling and Warbly guide the audience through an assortment of fifteen favorite animal songs, including "Mary Had a Little Lamb" and "Eensy Weensy Spider." Adult Juror Comments: Material drawn from previous productions still works. Demonstrates minimal cultural diversity and is very fast-paced. Simple production works for this age group. Characters are appealing, animation is eye-catching. Gives good points for discussion. Kid Juror Comments: A hit! Good length that readily engaged their attention. Kids hummed along to their old favorites. They loved the animals and costumes. Age: 2–5; Length: 33 min.; Suggested Retail Price: $9.98, UNIVERSAL STUDIOS HOME VIDEO

** WEE SING IN SILLYVILLE: Songs, dances, and an uplifting story show that the world is a better place when people of all colors (blue, green, and purple) live together in happiness. Adult Juror Comments: Magical, full of fun, silly, colorful. Addresses discrimination and cooperation. Little diversity. Children love the silly creatures as they work to become friends again. Humorous music. Kid Juror Comments: Enjoyable. Kids participated by singing and dancing along. Program is long for this age, good to watch in segments to enjoy the whole thing. Age: 2–8; Length: 60 min.; Suggested Retail Price: $12.98, UNIVERSAL STUDIOS HOME VIDEO

** WEE SING IN THE BIG ROCK CANDY MOUNTAINS: A zany romp in a land of food and fun teaches children about the importance of friendship, recycling, and nutrition. Adult Juror Comments: Very cute, lively, colorful. Addresses excluding others and cooperation. Morals, riddles, and humor are for older children. Honesty, good eating habits, and imagination are emphasized. Little cultural diversity. Kid Juror Comments: Thoroughly enjoyable, with lots of laughter. Participated by singing, dancing, and clapping. A bit long for this age, best viewed in segments. Age: 2–8; Length: 60 min.; Suggested Retail Price: $12.98, UNIVERSAL STUDIOS HOME VIDEO

** WEE SING IN THE MARVELOUS MUSICAL MANSION: Sing and dance with Alex, Kelly, and Benji. Solve a baffling mystery while learning about music, self-esteem, and friendship. Adult Juror Comments: Good production, great learning potential. Incorporates musical knowledge into story: scales, names of notes, instrument names. Wonderful incorporation of musical knowledge into informative story content. Little diversity. Kid Juror Comments: Wonderful. Great story and music. Kids joined in singing and dancing. Held kids' attention all the way. Stimulated discussion. "I wish I could watch it a hundred times." Song booklet a plus. Age: 2–8; Length: 60 min.; Suggested Retail Price: $12.98, UNIVERSAL STUDIOS HOME VIDEO

***WEE SING THE BEST CHRISTMAS EVER!: The Smith family travels to Santa's workshop to help solve an elfin problem and sees that challenges can be overcome with the help of friends. Adult Juror Comments: Great holiday viewing. Entertaining, magical, and fun. Good ethnic diversity. Addresses maintaining friendships, respect, honesty, and manners. Kid Juror Comments: Lots of laughter. Sang along, danced, and clapped their hands. Age: 2–8; Length: 60 min.; Suggested Retail Price: $12.98, UNIVERSAL STUDIOS HOME VIDEO

** WEE SING TOGETHER: Join Sally for her birthday party and celebrate the fun of music and the joy of friendship. Adult Juror Comments: Acknowledges valid feelings. Adults find these to be okay and too long for one sitting. Kid Juror Comments: Good, especially the familiar songs. Kept their attention and they danced while watching. Age: 2–8; Length: 60 min.; Suggested Retail Price: $12.98, UNIVERSAL STUDIOS HOME VIDEO

*** **WEE SING TRAIN, THE:** Takes children on singing and dancing adventures through the old West, a fairy-tale castle, and other exciting lands. Imagine playing with a toy train and suddenly becoming a passenger! This can only happen in the land of make-believe. Adult Juror Comments: Children's voices are particularly enjoyable. Fun and silly. Some cultural diversity. Kid Juror Comments: Exceptional. All age groups were very attentive, best with twos and threes. Enjoyed the story, music, and singing along. Lots of fun and just enough silliness. Age: 2–8; Length: 60 min.; Suggested Retail Price: $12.98, UNIVERSAL STUDIOS HOME VIDEO

** **WEE SING UNDER THE SEA:** Takes children to a place they've never been— under the sea. Sing, dance, and swim along with the wet and wonderful characters. Experience the beauty and splendor of the world beneath the waves. Adult Juror Comments: Musical score is lively and suitable, but adults felt it was overly didactic in addressing the audience. Very little is creative or original. The exotic starfish puppet is campy but amusing. Kid Juror Comments: Pretty good. Best were the puppets. One boy, quite young, liked the big clam. Kids' jury was looking for more from the characters, wanted to know more about what is under the sea. A bit long. Age: 2–9; Length: 60 min.; Suggested Retail Price: $12.98, UNIVERSAL STUDIOS HOME VIDEO

** **WEE SING: CLASSIC SONGS FOR KIDS:** Introduces WeeSing characters Singaling and Warbly. Features a compilation of favorite traditional songs from the Wee Sing collection, including "Row, Row, Row Your Boat" and "Home on the Range." Adult Juror Comments: Lovely, simple, well staged production which emphasizes cooperation children understand. Structure is a little unorganized and presentations seem a little artificial. Music does make children want to sing along. Kid Juror Comments: It didn't take long for them to join in. Some kids absolutely loved singing the songs. Several wanted to see it again. Age: 2–6; Length: 31 min.; Suggested Retail Price: $9.98, UNIVERSAL STUDIOS HOME VIDEO

** **WEE SING: GRANDPA'S MAGICAL TOYS:** Join Peter and his friends on their visit to the world's most wonderful grandpa and discover how important it is to be young at heart. Adult Juror Comments: Invites participation through familiar songs, different dance steps, movement songs, and partner hand-clapping games. Good values. Little diversity. Kid Juror Comments: Sang and danced with the video. They noticed that all the adults were Caucasian and there was only one black child. Too long for one sitting. Age: 2–8; Length: 60 min.; Suggested Retail Price: $12.98, UNIVERSAL STUDIOS HOME VIDEO

** **WEE SING: KING COLE'S PARTY:** At a royal, rollicking party for Old King Cole, children realize that the most precious gifts of all aren't jewels or gold, but ones that come from the heart. Adult Juror Comments: Imaginative and entertaining. Links familiar nursery rhymes. Effective plot, good message about non-materialism. Vocabulary is sometimes beyond level of audience. Little diversity shown. Kid Juror Comments: Okay, but it was too long for the younger ones. Kids noticed that all the people on screen were Caucasian. Age: 2–8; Length: 60 min.; Suggested Retail Price: $12.98, UNIVERSAL STUDIOS HOME VIDEO

*** **WEESINGDOM—THE LAND OF MUSIC AND FUN:** Enter a tuneful new land of enormous family appeal. Combining classic and original songs, a festive story, and a cast of favorite sing-along friends, this Wee Sing volume captivates young imaginations from the first note. Adult Juror Comments: Cute story, cute characters, a lot of fun. It models cooperation; eye-catching and personable characters. Addresses making mistakes such as forgetting words to a song, but learning to have fun anyway. "Wee sing tapes are like old friends." Kid Juror Comments: Even non-English-speaking children were mesmerized. Has great familiar old songs and fun new ones. A little long for some kids, but all ages danced along. Age: 2–5; Length: 64 min.; Suggested Retail Price: $12.98, UNIVERSAL STUDIOS HOME VIDEO

** **YODEL-AY-HEE-HOO! (CATHY AND MARCY'S SONG SHOP):** Cathy and Marcy lead children and adults in singing, signing, dancing, and yodeling. Filled with uncommon instruments and vocal styles. Adult Juror Comments: Enjoyable. Great music, great social behavior modeling, rich in diversity, lots of interactive shots. Hosts are very genuine. Invites participation. Kid Juror Comments: Favorites: storytelling, sign language, and everyone tried to sing along. Kids liked hearing familiar songs. Age: 2–8; Length: 30 min.; Suggested Retail Price: $14.95, COMMUNITY MUSIC, INC.

Nature

* **ANIMAL ANTICS (PROFESSOR IRIS):** Professor Iris, on safari with his camera and binoculars, is on the lookout for elephants, monkeys, and other jungle animals. Adult Juror Comments: Nice information, very entertaining, although it offers little insight into the world of animals. Good pacing, best viewed in segments. Reinforces African and female stereotypes. Kid Juror Comments: "My two-and-a-half-year-old enjoyed it very much, but I don't know that he'll watch it again." Good for kids who like animals. Often, the

Professor Iris characters are just goofing around. Age: 2–5; Length: 40 min.; Suggested Retail Price: $12.95, DISCOVERY COMMUNICATIONS

** AT THE ZOO: Toe-tapping, hand-clapping songs about monkeys, elephants, giraffes, zebras, meerkats, aardvarks, sea lions, polar bears, and dolphins. Adult Juror Comments: Good content. Interesting footage of animals at the zoo. The learning potential is high, especially when used with other materials or experiences. Kid Juror Comments: Really good. Talked about the animals afterwards and danced to the songs, including the three-year-olds. Repeat viewings would be needed in order for children to learn songs. Age: 3–8; Length: 25 min.; Suggested Retail Price: $14.95, GOLDSHOLL: LEARNING VIDEOS

** AT THE ZOO: 2 (PICTURE THIS! SING-A-LONG): An exciting, educational, fun-filled visit to the zoo, with original songs and interesting animals, starring: bears, otters, piglets, gorillas, woodpeckers, kangaroos, reptiles, ibex, water loving animals, and the rainforest. Adult Juror Comments: Delightful. Interesting selection of animals. Songs are fun, children could pick them up after just a few viewings. Stimulates further inquiry, some advanced language. "Ties animals to habitats very well, emphasizing the beauty of nature." Kid Juror Comments: Lots of toe-tapping and head-bobbing to the fun songs that kids picked up right away. "Let's go on a field trip to the zoo." Children wanted to see it again. Led to a discussion about animals. Age: 2–7; Length: 30 min.; Suggested Retail Price: $14.95, GOLDSHOLL: LEARNING VIDEOS

** ANIMAL QUEST (ADVENTURES WITH BAACO): Baaco, a friendly visitor from the planet Baacia, magically transports Mr. Dean and his science class to the international zoo, where they learn about animals from around the world. Eet-oot, earthlings! Adult Juror Comments: Good information with simple, lively music. The review at the end was helpful. Dancing segments were an unnecessary interruption. Kid Juror Comments: Much to the adults' surprise, children enjoyed integrating the dancing and singing with a trip to the zoo. They were interested to learn about the animal facts. Age: 2–8; Length: 32 min.; Suggested Retail Price: $14.95, KIDS TREK PRODUCTIONS

*** ANIMALS & ME: EATING AT THE ZOO; see p. 261

*** BEAR CUBS, BABY DUCKS, AND KOOKY KOOKABURRAS (GEOKIDS); see p. 261

* BEARS EVERYWHERE (ANIMAL CRACKER): Seeing a bear cub in the woods, a young boy dreams of playing with him on the playground. Filled with bear

facts and lively music. Adult Juror Comments: Well done, entertaining with excellent storytelling. Good music and images. Great footage of bears, multiculturally sensitive. Safety issues not addressed. Children are shown playing with wild bears. Interjecting Spanish words was good addition. Kid Juror Comments: Captivated by the bear stories. They enjoyed the multicultural information and storytelling. Motivated discussion about bears, fishing and animal safety. Age: 3–7; Length: 30 min.; Suggested Retail Price: $14.95, CARTER PRODUCTIONS

*** BUGS DON'T BUG US! (LIVE ACTION VIDEO): A fascinating look at children observing insects, spiders, and other common invertebrates in a friendly, amusing way. Observes detailed motions and eating habits of these creatures. Adult Juror Comments: "One of the best." Has superb cinematography and nice musical choices. Sequence with butterflies is excellent. Shows good ethnic diversity among children, who act naturally and are a pleasure to watch. Excellent resource; good repeat viewing value. Kid Juror Comments: "It was great." Kids were active, commenting, and questioning. They responded by going on a bug hunt. Naturally educational, kids asked to see it again. Age: 2–5; Length: 35 min.; Suggested Retail Price: $14.95, BO PEEP PRODUCTIONS, INC.

** CAMOUFLAGE, CUTTLEFISH, AND CHAMELEONS CHANGING COLOR (GEOKIDS): Looks at nature's camouflaged animals, including three-toed sloths, arctic foxes, hermit crabs, and octopuses. Bobby and Sunny discover that chameleons like Uncle Balzac can change color with their mood. Adult Juror Comments: Good resource. Great teaching supplement for animal theme. Shows good examples of natural camouflage. Some felt that this imposes adult ideas on children watching. Kid Juror Comments: Very informational; children interested in finding the camouflaged animals. Held most kids' attention. The "Mood" song dragged a bit. Age: 2–10; Length: 40 min.; Suggested Retail Price: $14.95, NATIONAL GEOGRAPHIC/WARNER HOME VIDEO

*** CHOMPING ON BUGS, SWIMMING SEA SLUGS AND STUFF THAT MAKES ANIMALS SPECIAL (GEOKIDS): With the help of Uncle Balzac de Chameleon, Sunny and Bobby learn about the special traits of chameleons, turtles, cheetahs, zebras, and other animals. Each puppet character is based on a real animal, created by Hank Saroyan. Adult Juror Comments: Excellent editing and music. Good pace. Includes learning components of alphabet, number recognition, and tolerance for different living situations. Information and presentation are suitable for younger kids, sophisticated enough for older kids. Kid Juror Comments: Watching the animals was terrific. Different voices held their attention. A little too long for one sitting, especially for younger ones. "The animal acrobat section is great!" Age: 2–10; Length: 35 min.; Suggested Retail Price: $14.95, NATIONAL GEOGRAPHIC/WARNER HOME VIDEO

** CREEPY CRITTERS (PROFESSOR IRIS): Snakes, bats, bugs, and bees are some of the creatures that come out to play when Professor Iris investigates his attic. Don't be afraid, they're all quite friendly and fascinating, as the Professor will show you. Adult Juror Comments: Good program. Promotes comparisons in thinking on children's part. Kid Juror Comments: The songs and the humor were nice. They discussed many of the concepts and facts afterwards. Age: 2–6; Length: 40 min.; Suggested Retail Price: $12.95, DISCOVERY COMMUNICATIONS

* EARTH DAZE (PROFESSOR IRIS): On Earth Day, Professor Iris discovers how precious and beautiful our planet is. Adult Juror Comments: Good introduction to the natural world. Stimulating, with appealing characters—a little difficult for preschoolers in language and ideas. Original songs are "upbeat." Appropriate language used to deliver important environmental messages. Best shown in segments. Kid Juror Comments: Interesting and fun. Some wanted to play it regularly. Some kids lost interest in one sitting. Older kids paid attention to the ideas. Age: 2–5; Length: 40 min.; Suggested Retail Price: $12.95, DISCOVERY COMMUNICATIONS

** FIRST LOOK AT MAMMALS, A: When most people think of mammals they think of dogs, cats, or horses. Nevertheless, beavers, otters, whales, dolphins, and bats are mammals too. Explores the common characteristics of mammals whether they live on land, in water, or fly through the air. Adult Juror Comments: Good content. It's most suitable for library collections. Format is good for learning but it's visually flat (most shots are stationary), quality appears old, lacks action. Kid Juror Comments: Well-focused, good length. Some giggled at nursing animals. Most suitable for one-time viewing. Not highly entertaining. Age: 2–5; Length: 13 min.; Suggested Retail Price: $29.95, AIMS MULTIMEDIA

** FLYING, TRYING, AND HONKING AROUND (GEOKIDS); see p. 265

** IF WE COULD TALK TO THE ANIMALS (KIDSONGS): Features live performances and original arrangements by the Kidsongs Kids. Children learn about many different animals and enjoy singing along with the kids as they talk with a cast of animal friends. Adult Juror Comments: Entertaining and lively. Nice outdoor production, with changing scenery, several adult characters, a good mix of cute kids, fun songs, and real animals. Has learning potential to discuss different habitats, encourages physical participation. Kid Juror Comments: A good time was had by all. Sparked interest in a discussion of animals and a trip to the zoo. The "Monkeys Jumping of the Bed" song was a hit. One child sang straight through nap time. "I just love those songs." Age: 3–7; Length: 30 min.; Suggested Retail Price: $12.99, TYCO TOYS

** JUNGLE ANIMALS (SEE HOW THEY GROW); see p. 266

** LET'S EXPLORE . . . FURRY, FISHY, FEATHERY FRIENDS: Seven-year-old Mekenzie showcases frogs, birds, snakes, rabbits, lizards, and more: what they eat; how they sleep; and other behaviors. Adult Juror Comments: Great introduction to the world of pets—both usual and unusual. Main character is appealing. It's very informational but brings up some safety issues. Kid Juror Comments: Wonderful. Discussed proper names for animals and which ones bite. Some kids didn't like how the animals were picked up and hugged. Beware: Children might want a pet after watching this video. Age: 2–8; Length: 30 min.; Suggested Retail Price: $14.95, BRAUN FILM AND VIDEO, INC.

** MEET YOUR ANIMAL FRIENDS: Lynn Redgrave hosts this wonderful visit with baby animals, to the delight on infants and toddlers who giggle with glee at the funny antics of sheep, deer, horses, dogs, and other species. Adult Juror Comments: Kid Juror Comments: "I loved the kittens, they're so cute. I liked watching the funny things that the animals do. Rheas are funny-looking birds." Inspired the kids to want to go to the zoo. Age: 1–6; Length: 54 min.; Suggested Retail Price: $14.95, JSK ENTERPRISES

* MOMMY, GIMME A DRINKA WATER: Child's point of view portrayed in songs, words, and pictures. Stars Didi Conn and Stacy Jones of "Shining Time Station." Adult Juror Comments: Good theme, fun presentation. Beautiful inclusion of senior citizens. Didi Conn is believably childlike. Songs are hard to follow. Objection to the "Don't tickle me" song: children should be respected and listened to. Little cultural diversity. Kid Juror Comments: Okay. Liked the songs, although some of the words were hard to follow. Favorites: "Playing on the See-Saw" and "I'm Hiding." Age: 3–6; Length: 35 min.; Suggested Retail Price: $14.95, WHITE STAR VIDEO

*MORE ZOOFARI!: Sir Arthur Blowhard and his assistant, Smythe, head out on an adventure, visiting different members of the animal kingdom on an exciting "zoofari." Adult Juror Comments: Has excellent production quality. Informative and factual—good introduction to animal study. Lacks human diversity. Pace is slow and difficult to follow. "Wacky tour guides are a fun approach." Kid Juror Comments: Nothing special. "It's like visiting the zoo, only the animals are close-up instead of far away." Stimulated discussion afterwards, especially with kids interested in animals. Age: 4–6; Length: 30 min.; Suggested Retail Price: $14.95, WHITE TREE PICTURES, INC.

* MY AMAZING ANIMAL ADVENTURE (GREGORY AND ME): Your child is the star of the show in this combination of live-action, puppets, and animation. Your child travels the world with Gregory, visiting animals big and small, returning with a big surprise. Adult Juror Comments: Good information, fun antics, and factual tidbits. Parts are not suitable for non-readers. Notion of personalized video is appealing—good idea for families. Humor and vocabulary are not always age-appropriate. Kid Juror Comments: Features kids' favorite animals, sparked some toe-tapping. Children enjoyed it but not many wanted to watch again. Gregory and his sidekicks were a big hit! Age: 2–5; Length: 25 min.; Suggested Retail Price: $34.95, KIDEO PRODUCTIONS, INC.

** SEA ANIMALS (SEE HOW THEY GROW); see p. 268

*** TADPOLES, DRAGONFLIES, AND THE CATERPILLAR'S BIG CHANGE (GEOKIDS): A pod hanging from a branch is a sort of sleeping bag, where a caterpillar becomes a butterfly in a big change called "metamorphosis." Curiosity leads an exploration of other big-change artists. Adult Juror Comments: A beautifully photographed nature discovery, it gives child a good picture of the environment. "It's the best nature series I've seen." Kid Juror Comments: It all was great, from the music to the movement of the plants. They thought it was fast-paced and packed full of information about growth and development. Age: 2–10; Length: 40 min.; Suggested Retail Price: $14.95, NATIONAL GEOGRAPHIC/WARNER HOME VIDEO

* ZOOFARI!; see p. 271

Special Interest

* BIG BOATS, LI'L BOATS; see p. 274

*** BIG TRAINS, LITTLE TRAINS: An interesting, amusing look at trains of all sizes, from toy trains to an incredible miniature backyard railroad with tunnels, bridges, and a cliff-top ocean view. Includes a giant outdoor model run by remote control. Adult Juror Comments: Trains are a favorite topic with children. Content is self-contained, with good, accurate information. Great resource tool. "I loved the two child hosts!" Shows little diversity. Kid Juror Comments: Little boys particularly enjoyed this one. Children under four years of age did not stay with it. "I love trains, I want to play trains." Age: 2–8; Length: 27 min.; Suggested Retail Price: $14.95, SANDBOX HOME VIDEOS

** CLASSIC NURSERY RHYMES: Offers a collection of nursery rhymes produced with original musical arrangements and captivating computer-animated visuals appealing to children and adults. Adult Juror Comments: Visually interesting and original, but at times the visuals seem poorly integrated with the story. The three-dimensional presentation tends to be more important than the nursery rhymes and images. Pacing is too fast at times. Kid Juror Comments: High-scoring appeal. Some characters will be scary for sensitive viewers. Age: 3–6; Length: 32 min.; Suggested Retail Price: $14.95, M3D INC.

** COWBOYS . . . ON THE JOB: Features live action, real cowboys, a Montana ranch, roundup, and everyday chores set to foot-stompin' cowboy songs by "Riders in the Sky." Adult Juror Comments: In-depth presentation of the cowboy's job. Kids liked the fast-motion segments. Great music. Scenes of calves are being roped and branded made some viewers uncomfortable. Female participation is minimal. Fun music. Kid Juror Comments: Smashing. "It's a big job to be a cowboy. See how much work a ranch can be." Children clapped and danced along with the music. Boys loved the big machines, tractors and ranch kids. Girls thought the roping and branding was cruel. Age: 2–10; Length: 30 min.; Suggested Retail Price: $19.95, ON THE JOB PRODUCTIONS

* DAYCARE LIVE!: Features a "live" day at day care. Viewers are invited to participate in a typical day that includes arrival, mealtimes, singing, structured play, swimming, nap-time, and a birthday celebration. Adult Juror Comments: This is a good model for day-care providers, with entertainment, as developmental activities. Jurors objected to use of balloons, popcorn as a snack, and multiple use of the wading pool. Kid Juror Comments: Fun! Twos and threes liked it best. They smiled, sang, clapped, and giggled. "I liked the children walking around barefoot on the cushioned floor." Age: 2–5; Length: 39 min.; Suggested Retail Price: $9.99, MOTHER'S HELPER INC.

* DR. BIP'S NEW BABY TIPS: Dr. Bip, an animated character, explains to young children what to expect when Mommy and Daddy bring home a new baby. Addresses the emotional aspects and some practical, commonsense tips for kids. Adult Juror Comments: Deals with jealousy, responsibility, and safety. May motivate questioning by siblings. Bip is appealing to some, but many found his rhyming annoying. The language used is not always age-appropriate. Stereotypical gender representations, lacks diversity. Kid Juror Comments: Appeals to those who are expecting a brother or sister. Kids remembered the safety tips: "Never let go and never pick up the baby without an adult. It's slippery." Kids didn't care for the rhyming, and content was sometimes missed due to the rhyming. Age: 3–6; Length: 14 min.; Suggested Retail Price: $14.95, KIDZ-MED, INC.

*** FRANKLIN AND THE SECRET CLUB: When Porcupine, jealous of Franklin's popularity, creates a secret club for the sole purpose of keeping him out, Franklin teaches her the true meaning of friendship. Adult Juror Comments: Content is refreshingly meaningful. Issues of friendship, belonging, honesty are dealt with appropriately and relevantly in situations common to preschoolers—teasing, exclusion, sharing. High learning potential. Kid Juror Comments: Captivating. They wanted to see it again immediately. Kids seem sensitive to Franklin's feelings. "We could watch it together and laugh." "Made me think about being nice." Age: 2–5; Length: 25 min.; Suggested Retail Price: $12.95, POLYGRAM VIDEO

** GRANDPA WORKED ON THE RAILROAD: Combines songs and activities easy for young children to learn. Includes demonstrations of actual steam trains. Teaches some basic skills that grown-ups use at work: teamwork, communication, and working with machines. Adult Juror Comments: Trains seem to have an eternal appeal, and this story is engaging. Very informative though somewhat hokey. Would be effective as part of a unit. Kid Juror Comments: Absorbing. Prompted lots of discussion about trains. Some information is too technical for three-to-five age group. Age: 2–8; Length: 30 min.; Suggested Retail Price: $14.95, PHOENIX MEDIA

** HEAVY EQUIPMENT OPERATOR (WHAT DO YOU WANT TO BE WHEN YOU GROW UP?): Spotlights construction workers working with big machinery. Features bulldozers, ringer cranes, scrapers, excavators, and backhoes moving mountains of earth and lifting tons of steel. Adult Juror Comments: Fascinating footage, especially for the little ones. Safety tips are good. Kid Juror Comments: Enthusiastically watched the machines work and the explanations of how they work. The young boy's excitement captured the viewer's interest as well. Prompted a discussion on safety issues and the heavy equipment kids are familiar with or have seen. Age: 2–8; Length: 30 min.; Suggested Retail Price: $14.95, BIG KIDS PRODUCTIONS, INC.

** HERE WE GO VOL 1: Take an action-packed voyage on some of the most exciting vehicles ever, capturing a child's fascination with such diverse conveyances as steam locomotives, ocean liners, fire engines, blimps, and more. Narrated by Lynn Redgrave. Adult Juror Comments: Great exploration of various modes of travel, from helicopters to bulldozers to hovercrafts. Gives very child-centered explanations of how the vehicles work. Kid Juror Comments: They were fascinated by the amphibious hovercraft. "It looks like a spaceship. I wonder how many cars it holds." Age: 2–5; Length: 32 min.; Suggested Retail Price: $14.95, JSK ENTERPRISES

** HERE WE GO VOL2: This show takes children on a musical adventure on different modes of transportation, such as helicopters, bulldozers, dump trucks, bicycles, fire engines, and an aerial tramway. Narrated by Lynn Redgrave. Adult Juror Comments: Excellent production, showing various modes of travel from double-decker buses in London to a cruise ship, a hydrofoil, and a fire truck. Kid Juror Comments: "Where's London? Can we go there? I want to ride a double-decker bus." Kids loved the swimming pool on the cruise ship. Kids thought some of the British terminology was funny and noticed that they didn't lock up their bikes. Age: 2–5; Length: 34 min.; Suggested Retail Price: $14.95, JSK ENTERPRISES

** HERE WE GO AGAIN: Hosted by Lynn Redgrave, this program takes youngsters on close inspections of vehicles such as tow trucks and jets, police cars and trolleys, subways and construction cranes. Adult Juror Comments: Shows a wide variety of vehicles and situations, from tow trucks to the Concorde to a cable car to boats of various sizes. Second-guesses kids' questions with informative narrative. Kid Juror Comments: It made kids want to travel somewhere so they could ride on a plane or a cable car. "It's too long for me. I can't watch it all at once." "Ooh, I want to live on a barge." Age: 2–5; Length: 60 min.; Suggested Retail Price: $14.95, JSK ENTERPRISES

** HEY, WHAT ABOUT ME: A warm, straight-forward talk to preschoolers about adjusting to new siblings. Teaches games, lullabies, and rhymes. Adult Juror Comments: Addresses sibling rivalry in a fun way. Great for showing kids they have a role to play when the new baby comes. Shows other kids helping with the baby, singing to him, playing with him, being quiet when he is sleeping. Kid Juror Comments: Related to the subject matter quite well. "The girl was mad because there was a new baby coming." "I learned to be nice to babies and to rock them." "I sing to my brother." Age: 2–6; Length: 30 min.; Suggested Retail Price: $14.95, KIDVIDZ

** HOUSE CONSTRUCTION AHEAD (WHEN I GET BIG): Shows house construction, from site-clearing and excavation to blasting at rock quarries. Also, harvesting timber and a visit to the sawmill. Adult Juror Comments: Informative. Nice camera work, with many close-ups. Illustrates parallels between kids' play and house construction. Lacks diversity and solid safety guidelines. Kid Juror Comments: The language is too advanced for preschoolers. Kids didn't understand sections. Stimulated kids' thinking about houses and how they're built. The backward explosions were a big hit with the boys. "It made me think about how many parts go into a house." Age: 3–6; Length: 30 min.; Suggested Retail Price: $14.95, FRED LEVINE PRODUCTIONS

* HOW TO BE A BALLERINA: Most little girls dream of becoming a ballerina. Their dreams are encouraged in this informative program that demonstrates some simple but beautiful ballet movements that can be learned at home. Adult Juror Comments: Well done visually and organizationally. Instructional value most appropriate for six- and seven-year-olds. Instructor is stern but reassuring. Introduces children to idea that dance requires discipline and practice. Kid Juror Comments: The girls were crazy about the video, dancing and hopping around afterwards, as a result of viewing the tape. Boys were not as engaged, no boys in the video. May be too long for children under four. "My friends who study ballet would like this." Age: 3–7; Length: 40 min.; Suggested Retail Price: $9.98, SONY WONDER

* IT'S POTTY TIME; see p. 261

* IT'S SLEEPY TIME; see p. 261

* IT'S TOOL TIME FOR KIDS: Meet the tool-truck man, the lawnmower lady, and fix-it pros. Hosted by a four-year-old tool lover, features household and construction tools. Adult Juror Comments: Gamely, Mom tries out heavy equipment. Camera style is jerky, with strange camera angles. "Great to see the mother handling tools. That four-year-old host makes the tape." Brought up concern over safety issues and wearing goggles. Kid Juror Comments: Mixed reactions. Some kids loved it, but others thought it was so-so. Boys liked it best. One, whose father is a machinist, wanted to take it home because it reminded him of building together. Age: 3–6; Length: 21 min.; Suggested Retail Price: $12.95, A KID AT HEART PRODUCTIONS, INC.

** **KIDS LOVE THE CIRCUS:** Elephants help put up the tent at the old-fashioned Clyde Beatty-Cole Bros. Circus. Children take center stage and imagine themselves taming lions and walking the high wire at the backyard circus. Adult Juror Comments: A wonderful, catchy musical extravaganza! Encourages children to use their imagination for a backyard circus and offers behind-the-scene information. Encourages creativity. Kid Juror Comments: Terrific, especially seeing how to stage a circus and the old circus footage. The songs held the children's interest. "I'm going to try to balance on the floor just like they did." Age: 2–8; Length: 40 min.; Suggested Retail Price: $14.95, ACORN MEDIA PUBLISHING, INC.

** **KIDS LOVE TRAINS;** see p. 279

* **KIDS ON THE BLOCK (EARLY LEARNING SERIES):** The "Kids on the Block" puppets bring 20 years of experience in teaching children about disabilities and differences. Includes important lessons on aggression, compassion, and perseverance for young audiences. Includes suggested follow-up activities. Adult Juror Comments: Offers positive examples of good social skills and concrete ideas for dealing with anger. Excellent diversity but low production values. Prompts good discussion. Messages sometimes unclear. Slow pace. Kid Juror Comments: Mixed reactions. Enjoyed the characters, although their attention drifted. Information was good, but messages were a little bit unclear to young children. Age: 3–5; Length: 30 min.; Suggested Retail Price: $39.95, THE KIDS ON THE BLOCK, INC.

** **LET'S CREATE FOR PRESCHOOLERS:** An opportunity to introduce preschoolers to the world of art. Teaches about colors and shapes while working on six projects. Adult Juror Comments: Clever instructional ideas for parents or caregivers who want to enrich child's artistic abilities by engaging in art activities. Jurors objected to the product-versus-process focus. Makes a good instructional tool for parents and teachers. Kid Juror Comments: Mixed reactions. Best shown in segments. Some kids objected to doing exactly what the instructor did and wanted more creative freedom. Age: 2–5; Length: 45 min.; Suggested Retail Price: $24.95, LET'S CREATE, INC.

** **LET'S DANCE ON THE FARM;** see p. 35

** **LET'S GO TO THE FARM:** Mac Parker spends a year as the hired man on a Vermont family farm. Learns how cows are milked, crops are planted and harvested, maple syrup is made, and hay is baled. Adult Juror Comments: Introduces young children to farming, depicting activities in different seasons. Full of information and requires an informed adult to assist in discussions of material. Best viewed in segments. Kid Juror Comments: City kids were very interested in this video, because they're not familiar with farm life. They found it fascinating. Age: 2–5; Length: 60 min.; Suggested Retail Price: $14.95, VERMONT STORY WORKS

* LOOK WHAT HAPPENS . . . AT THE CAR WASH: Shows in detail exactly how the car wash works, from start to finish. Teaches key words through soapy action and clean fun. Adult Juror Comments: Entertaining and silly; interesting comparison between hand washing and a car wash. Kid Juror Comments: Loved the humor, but overall not particularly appealing. Children got a kick out of the reverse segment and watching the police car get washed. They weren't interested in watching it again. Too long, and they lost interest. Age: 3–6; Length: 25 min.; Suggested Retail Price: $19.95, INFORMEDIA

* MAX AND FELIX; see p. 281

** MIGHTY CONSTRUCTION MACHINES: Puts you in the operator's seat of some powerful, earth-shaking construction machines. Diverse musical interludes, realistic sound effects, awe-inspiring power of machines-at-work, delightful surprises in an interactive format. Adult Juror Comments: Creative video techniques. Good demonstrations, replicates hands-on learning. Visually appealing. Provides insight for curious minds into different types of equipment. Excellent multi-ethnic and gender roles portrayed. Music works well with video. Kid Juror Comments: Involving. They wanted to draw the machines. They liked the women truck drivers and the teenage female narrator. "Look, he's pushing over a mountain!" "I've been on a backhoe before." "My little brother would like this." Age: 3–6; Length: 33 min.; Suggested Retail Price: $14.99, BANG ZOOM! ENTERTAINMENT

** MISS CHRISTY'S DANCE ADVENTURE: As an introduction for younger children, it teaches the basics of ballet, tap, and jazz through visualization and association. Adult Juror Comments: Encourages interest in dance and use of imagination. A pleasant way to learn some dance steps. Children pictured dancing were appealing and "real." Miss Christy shows love and respect for the students. Best used in addition to a dance class. Kid Juror Comments: Fabulous. Preschoolers went crazy over this video! Children got up to join in the dancing. Some kids had a hard time following the steps. "One tape to surely show again." Age: 2–5; Length: 35 min.; Suggested Retail Price: $12.98, PPI ENTERTAINMENT GROUP

*** MOVING MACHINES (LIVE ACTION VIDEO): Close-up views of bulldozers, backhoes, cranes, and other heavy equipment in action. Playing with similar toys helps children identify with the action. Adult Juror Comments: Well presented, informative. Shows kids' perspective and interaction with machines. Good gender-role models and cooperative teamwork. The juxtaposition of real machines and children's replicas is well done. The activity book makes a nice addition. Kid Juror Comments: Realistically cute. Captured their attention, intrigued and delighted. Boys watched the entire program, girls' attention wandered. Age: 2–5; Length: 25 min.; Suggested Retail Price: $14.95, BO PEEP PRODUCTIONS, INC.

* MR. TIBBS & THE GREAT PET SEARCH: Invites children on an adventure in search of the perfect pet. Travels to a farm, the jungle, and the ocean. Adult Juror Comments: Cute animal story. Concept of including a child in the video is clever, but the image gets tiresome. May be a nice touch for families. The rhyming narration works well. Kid Juror Comments: Okay but wanted to see the image of the child move. Two-year-olds enjoyed the whole video. Afterwards, kids drew pictures of animals with their own photo included. Kids showed little interest in watching again. Age: 2–6; Length: 22 min.; Suggested Retail Price: $34.95, KIDEO PRODUCTIONS, INC.

*** MRN: WHEN PARENTS ARE AWAY (MISTER ROGERS' NEIGHBORHOOD): Helps deal with the anxieties that arise when parents are away. Visits a child-care center and a graham cracker factory while addressing lots of feelings about being apart. Adult Juror Comments: Great content and subject. Well paced. Mister Rogers relates to children most effectively. He is clear, takes his time, and treats subject in a sensitive way. Kid Juror Comments: Top marks. Prompted discussion later. "I get scared, but I like my babysitter." It's a little long for this audience, best viewed in segments. Age: 2–7; Length: 66 min.; Suggested Retail Price: $12.95, FAMILY COMMUNICATIONS, INC.

* MY BODY ME! (PROFESSOR IRIS): Professor Iris teaches preschoolers about their hair, eyes, voice, and other senses. Adult Juror Comments: Good subject matter but adults felt too much was going on simultaneously. The content is good and the music is memorable, but the production looks unprofessional. The puppets are creative yet unattractive. Learning concepts are lost. Kid Juror Comments: Not bad, but not great. Some sang the songs and asked to see it again or listen to the tape. Other kids did not stay with it. It's too long for this age. "The characters look crazy." Age: 2–5; Length: 40 min.; Suggested Retail Price: $12.95, DISCOVERY COMMUNICATIONS

*** NEW BABY IN MY HOUSE, A (MY SESAME STREET HOME VIDEO): Mrs. Snuffleupagus reads her children a fairy tale about a prince who feels neglected when his baby sister arrives. It helps Snuffy realize that even though he's not the only child anymore, everyone still loves him just the same. Adult Juror Comments: Deals with an issue that is meaningful to children—sibling rivalry. Humorous, thought-provoking. Presents the same theme in several ways as a story within a story. Has a good mix of animation and live action, with lively, simple songs. Kid Juror Comments: Funny, loved the upbeat songs. Message is delightful and authentic. Children with special needs are included. "My brother gets on my nerves too." A little advanced for two-year-olds. Age: 2–5; Length: 30 min.; Suggested Retail Price: $9.98, SONY WONDER/CTW

** POLKAROO'S BIRTHDAY PARTY (POLKA DOT DOOR): Celebrate Polkaroo's birthday. Join the preparation, hanging decorations, wrapping gifts, and waiting for the surprise birthday guest to appear. Adult Juror Comments: Very engaging theme. Mother Goose songs were clever. Nice ethnic and gender mix of adults, but not of children. Has qualities that engage the audience in asking questions. Features children's artwork. Too long, without strong thematic glue. Kid Juror Comments: Nice enough. Kids liked sharing their own birthday traditions during and after video. Too long for most two-year-olds; four- and five-year-olds imitated the video afterwards. Age: 2–5; Length: 60 min.; Suggested Retail Price: $14.95, SUPERIOR PROMOTIONS, INC.

* RAILROADERS (WHAT DO YOU WANT TO BE WHEN YOU GROW UP?): Conductors, engineers, and workers teach all about steam, freight, and passenger trains. Learn about engines, boxcars, flat cars, hoppers, and tankers, working on the railroad every step of the way. Adult Juror Comments: Has fascinating footage of train movies. Great music, excellent for train presentations. Jurors felt the acting was not respectful to children and promoted some stereotyping. Kid Juror Comments: Scored well. Ready to go on a train ride. A great subject for little ones. Age: 3–6; Length: 30 min.; Suggested Retail Price: $14.95, BIG KIDS PRODUCTIONS, INC.

** RHYMIN' TIME (STORIES TO REMEMBER): Mother Goose, welcome to the '90s. Phylicia Rashad, star of *The Cosby Show,* sings a collection of great nursery rhymes. Animation based on Kay Chorao's "The Baby's Lap Book," music by composer Jason Miles. Adult Juror Comments: This book-based title can be complimented by sharing the book with your child as well as the video. Book/video exposure like this encourages reading. Kid Juror Comments: Good to hear their favorite nursery rhymes, especially "This Little

Pig," "Old King Cole," "Humpty Dumpty," and "Twinkle, Twinkle Little Star." "I liked the constellations that the stars made." "All the music was my favorite." Age: 1–5; Length: 26 min.; Suggested Retail Price: $9.95, LIGHTYEAR ENTERTAINMENT

** RICHARD SCARRY: THE BEST BIRTHDAY PARTY EVER: There's a birthday disaster in Busytown: Kenny and Lynnie are going to throw birthday parties on the same day. Their friends plan to get everyone into the same room so it's a big surprise. Lynnie and Kenny end up having the best birthday ever. Adult Juror Comments: Excellent. The characters seem "human" and come to life. Plot stimulates creative interpretations and problem-solving. Sharing qualities are displayed. Suggests good follow-up activities. Kid Juror Comments: Interested, attentive, and enjoyed the film. They love Richard Scarry books, were inspired to read more. "I like thinking about the animals in the story and how real animals solve problems. I laughed when he borrowed the bulldozer." Age: 2–5; Length: 25 min.; Suggested Retail Price: $9.95, POLYGRAM VIDEO

** ROAD CONSTRUCTION AHEAD (FRED LEVINE'S ORIGINAL): Shows every step in a road construction project, from surveyors staking out the job site to blasting rock to the first car traveling down the finished highway. Adult Juror Comments: Good overview of large pieces of machinery. Nice cuts to children playing with toy trucks. Background music a little overpowering at points. Good safety tips. Little diversity, no female role models. Kid Juror Comments: Most kids enjoyed watching, especially the boys ,who were captivated throughout viewing this program. Favorite part: the explosives. Age: 2–5; Length: 30 min.; Suggested Retail Price: $14.95, FRED LEVINE PRODUCTIONS, INC.

*** SAMMY AND OTHER SONGS FROM GETTING TO KNOW MYSELF; see p. 283

** SIGN SONGS; see p. 283

** SIGN-ME-A-STORY; see p. 284

** SOUNDS AROUND (LIVE ACTION VIDEO): Explores sounds made by toys, machines, animals, people, and musical instruments. Varied children listen to and imitate these sounds. Helps understand differences and similarities. Adult Juror Comments: Great, lots of information. The real animal sounds contrast with sounds that adults usually attribute to animals. Offers a variety of mechanical and natural sounds. Lends itself to active viewing. You can extend the activities beyond the video. Kid Juror Comments: Very appealing, especially seeing the animals and hearing the sounds they make. They danced to the music and recognized each sound. Lots of information. Kids request this one repeatedly, enjoyed it every time. Age: 2–5; Length: 28 min.; Suggested Retail Price: $14.95, BO PEEP PRODUCTIONS, INC.

* TELLING THE TRUTH (SESAME STREET: KIDS' GUIDE TO LIFE): Telly learns that even when you mean to tell the truth, a little lie can balloon into a big problem. He learns a lesson after he lies to impress his friends by telling them his uncle (Dennis Quaid) is a ringmaster at the circus. Adult Juror Comments: Age-appropriate subject. Opens up many opportunities for discussion about "telling the truth." High-quality sound and visuals. Good for day care or families. "There's lots to talk about in this video." Kid Juror Comments: Initial enthusiasm dissipated. Action was too slow for younger kids. Older ones stayed with it better. Needs an adult facilitator to work well. Age: 2–5; Length: 30 min.; Suggested Retail Price: $12.98, SONY WONDER/CTW

** THERE GOES A BULLDOZER; see p. 285

** THERE GOES A FIRE TRUCK; see p. 285

* THOSE DOGGONE DOGS AND PUPPIES: Introduces perky young puppies at play, and carefree canines. Adult Juror Comments: Cute but extremely long. Lacks substance, depth and has virtually no learning benefits. Photos fit the musical selections. "I love dogs but had a hard time attending sixty minutes." Kid Juror Comments: Okay, but a little redundant. Cute dogs overall, but too long. Beware: may inspire children to want a dog. Age: 3–6; Length: 60 min.; Suggested Retail Price: $12.99, BRENTWOOD HOME VIDEO

*** TOOL POWER: Here's a play-along for children who love tools, music, magic and adventure. Packaged with a tool set. Adult Juror Comments: Well-paced and entertaining, it teaches things kids enjoy. Tasteful contemporary music: rap, rock, and gospel. Combines reality, dreams, magic, and the work involved. Good safety messages, multicultural diversity. Kid Juror Comments: Excellent. Teaches how to make things they like. Kids enjoyed watching something be created. Age: 3–7; Length: 30 min.; Suggested Retail Price: $19.95, COOKOO PRODUCTIONS

** VRRROOOMMM-FARMING FOR KIDS: Look, listen, and learn how the food we eat is grown. Explores how modern farm equipment is used in food production. Tractors, combines, and cultivators are shown from planting to harvesting. Adult Juror Comments: Good visuals—shows equipment kids don't often see unless they live on a farm. Low-budget production, inexperienced narrator, but offers interesting perspective on farming. Family picnic segment was great. Kid Juror Comments: "City kids" wanted to know more about how everything on a farm works—how plants grow and what the farm machinery does. Some terminology is too advanced for younger children. Age: 5–8; Length: 30 min.; Suggested Retail Price: $19.95, RAINBOW COMMUNICATIONS

** WACKY DOGS: A hilarious and educational journey into the fascinating world of dogs. See fifty-one breeds of adorable canines doing funny, unusual, and often amazing things. Adult Juror Comments: Entertaining and very cute. Gives good pointers on taking care of one's pet. "I loved it!" Has a lot of information about dogs, but the information is not reinforced. The dialogue gives personality to the animals. The kid hosts were good. Kid Juror Comments: Depends on the child. Those with dogs enjoyed it best and wanted to watch it repeatedly. Those who don't have dogs didn't understand the humor. "I thought the dogs were funny." Age: 2–10; Length: 33 min.; Suggested Retail Price: $9.95, CLOVERNOOK COMMUNICATIONS

** WALK, RIDE, FLY (PICTURE THIS SING-A-LONG): Explores many unusual and everyday forms of transportation: hot-air balloons, airplanes, space shuttles, windsurfing, wheels, and even feet! Filled with exciting visuals and original toe-tapping, hand-clapping music and lyrics. Adult Juror Comments: Music is easy to sing, keeps a momentum, and the camera works effectively for subject matter. Shows a wide variety of vehicles. Adults felt that it lacked a theme and had mediocre music. Kid Juror Comments: Entertaining. Useful introduction about these familiar and appealing objects in children's lives. Younger ones watched on-and-off. They liked the balloon section as well as the feet, wheels, and trucks. Age: 2–9; Length: 30 min.; Suggested Retail Price: $14.95, GOLDSHOLL: LEARNING VIDEOS

* WE'RE GOIN' TO THE FARM WITH FARMER DAN: Farmer Dan and his friends journey to a farm full of animals and music. The animals get fed, the cows herded, and the hay baled. Adult Juror Comments: Presents good information about farms. Music is catchy. Farmer Dan seems artificial and has minimal interaction with kids. Video seems patched together, but it's fun. Little diversity. Kid Juror Comments: Identifying the animals was fun. They did not respond well to Farmer Dan. Kids tapped their feet to the music. Interest recaptured when the farm footage reappears. Age: 3–5; Length: 30 min.; Suggested Retail Price: $19.95, SHORT STUFF ENTERTAINMENT, INC.

** WHERE THE GARBAGE GOES (WHEN I GET BIG): Children see how the operations of the haulers, grinders, dozers, loaders, and compactors used at a state-of-the-art waste-handling facility. Shows how materials are sorted, crushed, and compacted. Explains why recycling is so important. Adult Juror Comments: Typical of this genre of videos, "the fascination of big machines." The production values are suited to the audience, but it has no story line or depth. Provides a good introduction to environmental and recycling issues in a realistic presentation. Kid Juror Comments: Large machines keep kids interested, but they would rarely watch it a second or third time. Boys responded best. Kids asked questions, enjoyed the music. They lost interest in non-narrative parts. Kids spotted recycling truck next time they saw it. Age: 3–6; Length: 30 min.; Suggested Retail Price: $14.95, FRED LEVINE PRODUCTIONS, INC.

** WHISTLEPUNKS & SILVERPICKERS; see p. 288

*** YOGA KIDS: Adventuresome yoga activity for children, introduces safe and simple movements which are imaginative and fun. Children learn balance and coordination as they stretch like dogs, roar like lions, and stand like flamingos. Adult Juror Comments: Excellent! Nice explanation and illustration of movements. Engaging and child-centered, it values imagination, good health, and self-esteem. Generates interest in enriching a child's life, stimulates creativity, language, and cognitive development. Kid Juror Comments: Works best with younger kids, relaxing for quiet time. Even shy children joined in. "It was neat to try to be the animals." "I learned new ways to exercise. We decided to watch this once a week as a class." Age: 3–6; Length: 30 min.; Suggested Retail Price: $9.98, LIVING ARTS

7

Elementary

(Ages 5-8)

Five-year-olds vary in their understanding of how their favorite TV shows are delivered. They understand that Barney and Mister Rogers aren't actually inside the TV set, but when questioned further, it is clear that they are not certain about what's real and what's not in the videos and CD-ROMs that they watch. Programs that can create anxieties about injury or abandonment are frightening to most of them, sometimes producing nightmares. While they are less frightened by a scary story than when they were four, five-year-olds benefit from the reassurance of a happy ending. They may experience some fear during the program, but by the story's ending they feel a sense of accomplishment and bravery for having stuck with it. Videos and CD-ROMs that celebrate friendship, independence, and exploration offer hope and reassurance to this age group.

School forces kindergartners to do things on their own and to be accountable for their own actions. Themes on independence that also meet a child's need for security are appealing to this age group. Many of the video and CD-ROM titles in this chapter feature stories about characters who undertake a journey and return home feeling ever-so-proud of their accomplishments. At this age children adore stories about characters who, like themselves, are members of a family and are learning about friendship, problem-solving, and conflict resolution.

MARTHA DEWING is the publisher of *Children's Video Report*, has a B.S. in education from New York University and a M.A. in educational media and interactive technology from Harvard University.

For five-year-olds, school is also about learning and work. You will find a variety of programs here with familiar characters that challenge and engage while reinforcing important academic principles—such as *Captain Kangaroo: Life's First Lessons* and *Disney's Animated Storybook, Mulan*. The appropriateness of the educational content is an important component in the evaluation process for the Coalition for Quality Children's Media. However, not every title you'll find here offers educational value. Some are just plain fun, like *Dennis the Menace Strikes Again*. And even when the titles score high on entertainment, they show respect for others, feature a variety of cultures, and avoid promoting stereotypes.

In first grade, children are learning to read and appreciate a good story. This chapter includes beautiful adaptations of favorite books, classic mythology, and folk tales—such as *The Snow Queen* and *Ivan and His Magic Pony*—as well as superb live-action documentaries, such as *The Big Park*. The fact that a child is just learning to read does not mean that he or she cannot follow a complex story line. Children this age can readily identify with many of the selections here that offer challenging characters and situations—such as *The Land Before Time VI: The Secret of Saurus Rock*.

Six- and seven-year-olds are gaining in physical competence and developing gross motor skills as well as an interest in games, rules, sports, and hobbies. Programs such as *You Can Ride a Horse, Nutcracker on Ice,* and *New Soccer for Fun and Skills* enhance their new skills in ballet, baseball, soccer, and horseback riding, and introduce these children to the rigors and romance of their newfound interests.

By second grade, children often think they are old enough to watch the more sophisticated programming that their older siblings are enjoying. They are savvy to the ways of school and are developing interests of their own, separate from their families. Although they appear independent, many would benefit from programs such as *Sometimes I Wonder* or *The Morris Brothers Live in Concert* that offer them comfort and hope as they struggle with such issues as sibling rivalry, peer pressure, death, and divorce.

Third graders are generally grounded in what's real and what's not. Although these eight-year-olds know when the story is just a story, they are still interested in knowing whether it's based on fact or fantasy. Children are extremely curious about the world outside their own community. Videos and CD-ROMs that tap into their love of animals, the natural world, and the environment reinforce their innate curiosity, broaden their knowledge, and allow them to explore new information at their own pace. Some excellent choices for this age group include *Babe, Balto, Buddy, Ferngully 2: The Magical Rescue,* and *Lassie Come Home*.

Educational/Instructional

* 1,2,3 COME COUNT WITH ME; see p. 38

** ABC'S & SUCH; see p. 38

** ALLIGATOR TALE, AN (THE AMAZING VOYAGES OF NICCI PIPER): Two young explorers and a cast of puppets go on an adventure to Alligator Island. After one of the crew gets into trouble with an alligator, the others travel to Gatorland to learn all they can from a specialist. Adult Juror Comments: This video incorporates factual material into the story, providing good background and resource material about alligators. Reading ability is necessary. Shows good diversity and a female role model. Jurors were bothered by the kids traveling without their parents' permission. Kid Juror Comments: They watched it again and again. It provoked questions. Liked the fact that it shows respect. "It's sort of fake but still fun." Some thought that Captain Crab was rude. "It would be cool to live on an island." Age: 5–7; Length: 32 min.; Suggested Retail Price: $14.95, NEW DISCOVERIES, INC.

* ALPHABET SOUP; see p. 39

* ALPHABET TRAIN, THE: From A to Z, children learn vocabulary and phonics skills while exploring aspects of real trains and concepts such as in and out, over and under, teamwork, off and on. Adult Juror Comments: Concepts are too advanced for two-year-olds, yet the production is too slow for older kids. Has lovely scenery and great footage of trains. Language is not age-appropriate. Limited appeal, no story line, too boring for younger kids. Kid Juror Comments: Boys liked it better than girls. "I like trains." Older children need more of a story to hold their attention. Age: 4–7; Length: 60 min.; Suggested Retail Price: $19.95, SUPERIOR PROMOTIONS/ HOME VIDEO, INC.

* ALPHABETLAND; see p. 39

*** ALPHABET ZOO, THE; see p. 40

* BIG CABLE BRIDGES: Have you ever wondered how cable-stayed bridges are built? Young hosts examine the action-packed construction that creates impressive structures such as the Sunshine Skyway Bridge in Tampa, Florida. Adult Juror Comments: Offers a good look at a subject kids are curious about, and addresses the technical components of bridge-building.

The female engineer-narrator is a bit stilted. Shows little gender diversity. Kid Juror Comments: Very excited. Boys delighted at seeing the big machines and the computer segment. They thought the helmets looked phony. Five-year-olds got a little restless at the end. Age: 5–8; Length: 30 min.; Suggested Retail Price: $19.95, SEGMENTS OF KNOWLEDGE, INC.

** BIRTHDAY! PARTY (PROFESSOR IRIS); see p. 42

* CHICKEN FAT AND THE YOUTH FITNESS VIDEO: Children's exercise video based on the song written by Meredith Willson (composer of *The Music Man*) for President Kennedy's Council for Physical Fitness. Adult Juror Comments: Repetitious. Exercises are taught to accompany one song, "Chicken Fat." Format is military-style and adult-directed. Instructions are clear but outdated. Shows good cultural diversity. Kid Juror Comments: Kids were slow at responding. Kids in general like exercising to music, but they disliked the name of this tape and the theme song. Age: 5–10; Length: 23 min.; Suggested Retail Price: $14.95, CHICKEN FAT ENTERPRISES

*** CLIFFORD'S FUN WITH LETTERS; see p. 43

*** CLIFFORD'S FUN WITH NUMBERS; see p. 43

*** CLIFFORD'S FUN WITH OPPOSITES; see p. 43

*** CLIFFORD'S FUN WITH RHYMES; see p. 44

** CLIFFORD'S FUN WITH SHAPES; see p. 44

** COOPERATIVE GROUP GAMES; see p. 292

* DIGGING FOR DINOSAURS: Professor Fossilworth, a rather unconventional scientist, searches for fossils that give more clues about what happened to dinosaurs. This program offers information about different types of dinosaurs and shows what they looked like. Adult Juror Comments: The live scenes with the kids are well done. The information is sometimes suitable for younger kids, sometimes older. The content is a bit weak. It's a good introduction to general vocabulary concepts about dinosaurs. Shows little diversity. Kid Juror Comments: Inspired to dig afterwards but they definitely thought the program didn't teach them enough. The humor is perfect for this age group. "It was fun. The guy was goofy and the dog is great!" Kids found some parts too slow and a bit dry. Age: 5–10; Length: 35 min.; Suggested Retail Price: $14.95, DOLPHIN COMMUNICATIONS

** **EI EI YOGA:** Provides children with a balanced and enjoyable practice session, combining twenty-five yoga postures to create strength, balance, flexibility, and stamina. Designed to get everybody off the couch and moving. Encourages children and adults to sing, dance, and play. Adult Juror Comments: Gives clear, accurate instructions in a very child-appropriate presentation. Shows a variety of poses, all taught by children of diverse cultures. We recommend that an adult assist at least in the initial viewings of this program. Kid Juror Comments: Enjoyed finding a new way to exercise, stretch, and relax. Some language too difficult. Kids participated readily and wanted to know more about movement. They liked the songs. Age: 5–8; Length: 38 min.; Suggested Retail Price: $14.95, MYSTIC FIRE VIDEO

*** **FAMILIES OF JAPAN (FAMILIES OF THE WORLD):** Spend a day with Seichi and Ayako's farm and city families, and take in Sports Day, a silent piano, feeding chickens, grocery shopping, an engagement ceremony, rice planting, and calligraphy. How are kids in Japan similar or different from us? Adult Juror Comments: Well-paced, educational presentation. Shows the respect Japanese children have toward one another and their high regard for education and self-responsibility. Children exploring geography and other cultures will find this particularly interesting. Kid Juror Comments: Welcomed learning that Japanese children play the same things they do, such as tug of war, basketball, and tennis. They noticed that they have more letters to learn. They particularly enjoyed seeing Sports Day, sumo wrestlers, and a day in school. Age: 5–10; Length: 29 min.; Suggested Retail Price: $29.95, ARDEN MEDIA RESOURCES

*** **FAMILIES OF SWEDEN (FAMILIES OF THE WORLD):** Evelina and Matthew take you through a day in their lives—a birthday party, computer games, history class, pony ride, feeding ducks, swimming lesson, and eating moose steak. An intriguing introduction to another culture. Adult Juror Comments: Good for discussion about other lands, traditions, and family backgrounds. Shows both boy's and girl's perspective. Children's opinions are recognized and their needs are respected. Raises environmental awareness. Slow-moving, but a good educational program. Kid Juror Comments: Enjoyed comparing their experiences to those of the Swedish children. Intrigued by the Swedish kids taking off their shoes when they come into a house, and learning that their favorite stories are enjoyed by the Swedish kids as well. Age: 5–10; Length: 29 min.; Suggested Retail Price: $29.95, ARDEN MEDIA RESOURCES

* **FIT FOR A KING: THE SMART KID'S GUIDE TO FOOD & FUN:** Teaches the basics of good nutrition: how nutrition and physical activity go hand-in-hand,

how adding grains, vegetables, and fruits to your diet decreases fat, and how healthy eating can mean discovering new foods. Adult Juror Comments: Gives good information. Good diversity. Production is somewhat flat and didactic. Best used in a classroom setting. Some kids will already know most of the information. Kid Juror Comments: A good introduction to nutrition for children, though it's not particularly entertaining. "It was just right. I think it has special virtues." Many children liked the use of the fairy tale. Age: 5–10; Length: 9 min.; Suggested Retail Price: $19.95, AMERICAN ACADEMY OF PEDIATRICS

* FREDDY'S SCHOOL OF FISH: Hosted by an animated fish named Freddy, the video covers the basics of fishing from rod-and-reel operation and casting to tying knots, boat terminology, and safety. Adult Juror Comments: Good information for a child interested in fishing (and for adults, too). Little cultural diversity. Kid Juror Comments: eight- to twelve-year-olds enjoyed this best. One six-year-old said, "(I) felt wonderful fishing." It could be scary for younger kids. One child commented, "I didn't like the fish with sharp teeth." Age: 6–12; Length: 40 min.; Suggested Retail Price: $19.95, JUST FISH IT, INC.

**HAPPY AND HEALTHY (TREASURE ATTIC): Teaches how to cope with sickness and encourages good habits in health and nutrition, as well as a healthy positive attitude. Mr. Protein and company spring to life in the "Nutrition Song," which also encourages good eating habits. Adult Juror Comments: Entertaining format that encourages healthy exercising and taking care of oneself. Cute production, though it does have some lip-sync problems and primitive sets. Good diversity and deals well with health-related situations. Kid Juror Comments: Appealing. "This would be a good movie for our PE teacher to show us." Kids enjoyed the music but sometimes it was difficult for them to understand the words to the songs. Age: 4–7; Length: 25 min.; Suggested Retail Price: $14.95, FAMILY CARE FOUNDATION

** HEY! THAT'S MY HAY; see p. 46

* HOSPITAL TRIP WITH DR. BIP, A: Dr. Bip, an animated character, guides a child through a true-to-life visit to the hospital for an operation. Dr. Bip explains pre-operative and post-operative routines with bouncy rhymes and light music. Adult Juror Comments: The simple messages work well. Showing actual hospital equipment is useful. Good for preparing kids for a hospital visit although the language is too advanced. It's also somewhat misleading, promoting the idea that "everything's going to be fine, it won't hurt." Kid Juror Comments: Helpful in telling them what to expect when you visit the doctor or hospital. They liked the doctors and nurses, but some didn't care for the cartoon character Dr. Bip. The program brought up a lot of questions afterwards. Age: 4–7; Length: 12 min.; Suggested Retail Price: $14.95, KIDZ-MED, INC.

** HOW MUCH IS A MILLION? (READING RAINBOW); see p. 292

* IMPORTANCE OF TREES: Describes how trees grow and their benefits to the environment—as a source of material, food, oxygen, and air-conditioning. Illustrates the role of trees in fighting pollution, preventing soil erosion and more. Adult Juror Comments: An important and current topic. Production value is low, and child actors slightly amateurish. Some film clips were dated, but text flows well. Shows great shots of different cultures with trees. Creates awareness of the need to care for our trees. Kid Juror Comments: Hard to get kids interested initially; once they started, it captured their attention, particularly for saving trees. Pictures were blurry at times and sound difficult to hear. Kids thought music was corny. They learned a lot about trees, though. Age: 6–10; Length: 30 min.; Suggested Retail Price: $59.95, FILMUS/THE KIDS SHOP

*** JET PILOT; see p. 293

* KEEPING KIDS SAFE! A GUIDE FOR KIDS AND THEIR FAMILIES (THE PERSONAL SAFETY SERIES): Encourages children to solve problems about personal safety through open communication. Informative and non-threatening. Designed for families to watch together. Adult Juror Comments: Though this is a valuable educational tool, adults should definitely watch it with their children or it could be too frightening. Shows good interaction between the kids. Addresses an important topic that leads to discussion after the viewing. Kid Juror Comments: Learned a lot. Appreciated having the kids do the interviews. It's too frightening for five-year-olds to watch without an adult. Age: 5–10; Length: 27 min.; Suggested Retail Price: $14.95, PSI PRODUCTIONS

* LEARNING TO SAVE (THE ADVENTURES OF TWO PIGGY BANKS): Two piggy bank puppets escape from a toy store, are adopted by a school classroom, and teach children the important concepts of saving and sharing. Features original songs as sing-alongs such as "I'm Glad I'm a Piggy Bank." Adult Juror Comments: The first ten minutes are slow and don't engage the audience. Overall, it's a good vehicle to prompt discussion about savings. It offers good tips, is age-appropriate and child-friendly. Kid Juror Comments: The piggy bank characters got a favorable response. One kids' jury was just completing a unit on money, and found this provided good ancillary materials to what they had just learned. It's a good discussion-starter. Age: 4–7; Length: 30 min.; Suggested Retail Price: $19.95, RAINDROP ENTERTAINMENT

** MILK COW, EAT CHEESE (REAL WORLD VIDEO): A multicultural cast learns how to milk a cow and feed a calf. This video visits a dairy farm and a milk-processing plant, showing how milk is tested, processed, and bottled. Adult Juror Comments: Well done. Excellent at showing many aspects of dairy farming—from manure to milk. The kids are realistic, the explanations are thorough, and the music lively. It's informative, fun, and enjoyable. Great diversity. Kid Juror Comments: Cool. Liked watching how ice cream and cheese are made. "They showed how to milk a cow and what milk was made into." "I liked it all." "I didn't know that milk made cheese." "I will never drink milk again." Age: 5–12; Length: 30 min.; Suggested Retail Price: $14.95, REAL WORLD VIDEO

* MORRIS BROTHERS LIVE IN CONCERT, THE: A live performance by the Morris Brothers reinforces positive character traits and teaches better ways to deal with peer pressure and handle conflict. Fosters friendship, encourages cooperation, and promotes unity. Adult Juror Comments: The video addresses accepting others, how to act in school, and believing in yourself. Promotes the idea that you can change the inner you; it's doable. The Morris Brothers' nerd attire and behavior is not appealing to all audiences. Kid Juror Comments: Some thought the Morris Brothers were smart and funny. Others thought it was long and boring. Some would watch it again. Kids liked the phrase "Give yourself a big hand." They liked the part about how to say no to drugs. Age: 5–8; Length: 55 min.; Suggested Retail Price: $14.99, FUNIMATION PRODUCTIONS, INC.

** MY BODY BELONGS TO ME: Good information for preventing sexual abuse and showing how kids can get help. A family therapist acts as a friend and counselor to a puppet. Simple, repetitive safety lessons are presented entertainingly. Adult Juror Comments: Excellent teaching of difficult and delicate material. Information is clearly presented at the intended audience age level. We recommend adult facilitation because of the sensitivity of the subject. Kid Juror Comments: Enjoyed the puppets' humor. The boys were clearly embarrassed. The girls watched closely. "It's good what they talked about." Kids' attention strayed toward the end. Most appropriate for in-school or similar settings. Age: 5–8; Length: 24 min.; Suggested Retail Price: $24.95, DILLINGHAM PRODUCTIONS/CNS

** NO BODY'S PERFECT . . . EVERYBODY'S SPECIAL!: Profiles three kids coping with different disabilities. Olivia has a visual impairment. Tristan is deaf. Emily lost a leg in a farm accident. Encourages viewer to accept differences as essential to growing up. Adult Juror Comments: Very accessible. Features attractive, articulate kids. One gets a sense of their lives and acceptance of their disabilities. Good content, geared toward kids. Studio setting is nicely integrated with visit with kids. Some camera work is poor. Kid Juror Comments: Kids liked seeing children their own age learning to deal with their disabilities. It gave them insight into the feelings that disabled children have about being different and an appreciation for their bravery. Age: 5–10; Length: 21 min.; Suggested Retail Price: $89.00, ATTAINMENT COMPANY

* PEEPERS AND PENNY (TREASURE ATTIC): Filled with lively songs that help develop positive sibling and peer relationships. Penny learns to overcome shyness and fear of rejection. The music drama "A Man, a Boy and a Donkey" teaches character building—do what is right. Adult Juror Comments: Concept of the program is good, but it is not clear what audience level it's aimed at. Did not hold attention of the adults. Needs polishing. Purposeful and offers good lessons (such as teaching how to draw puppets), good ethnicity. Kid Juror Comments: Most children lost interest. Some parts caught the children's attention and enticed them to follow along. "My mom listens to that kind of music." Kids seemed to enjoy the musical part best. Age: 4–7; Length: 25 min.; Suggested Retail Price: $14.95, FAMILY CARE FOUNDATION

*** RAINY DAY MAGIC SHOW, THE: Learning magic tricks builds self-confidence and self-esteem. It's fun too! Children are taught step-by-step how to perform tricks using objects easily found around the home. Adult Juror Comments: Clear, well-explained instructions are easy to follow and fun. Production quality is outstanding: good music, great close-ups, and positive comments. One Juror said, "This is the most interactive video I've seen to date." Kid Juror Comments: Couldn't wait to try the magic tricks. They liked doing magic tricks using common household items. Every child was eager to learn more. "Great for would-be magicians. We tried every one." Age: 5–12; Length: 25 min.; Suggested Retail Price: $14.95, DOLPHIN COMMUNICATIONS

** RICHARD SCARRY'S BEST ABC VIDEO EVER!; see p. 49

*** RICHARD SCARRY'S BEST COUNTING VIDEO EVER!; see p. 49

* SAINTS FOR KIDS, VOLUME 1: Educational and inspiring. Each four-minute animated story shows extraordinary real men and women as outstanding role models. Features Francis of Assisi, Elizabeth, Zechariah, Martin, and others. Includes discussion guide. Adult Juror Comments: Production value is poor and distracting. Sound doesn't always match mouth movement. Stories are accurate, but it is perhaps most appropriate for religious-educational use. Well presented with an excellent study guide. Price high for length. Kid Juror Comments: Good but most appropriate for use at Sunday school. "It taught me things I did not know—to look at life differently." "It was okay." Sometimes it was hard for children to understand the voices. Age: 5–8; Length: 14 min.; Suggested Retail Price: $12.95, PAULINE BOOKS AND MEDIA

* SAINTS FOR KIDS, VOLUME 2: Educational, inspiring. Each four-minute animated story shows extraordinary real men and women as outstanding role models. Features saints including Nicholas, Stephen, Anne, and Joachim. Includes discussion guide. Adult Juror Comments: Respectful and appropriate but slow-paced. Limited audience appeal for a Christian audience, but provides a good teaching tool. Lacks cultural diversity. Promotes helping others, preserving faith, and other excellent general values. Kid Juror Comments: They didn't like the mean people. They did like the pictures and the music. It was short and interesting. "It would be good for church." "I liked learning about St. Nicholas." "It says Stephen was a martyr but doesn't show it." Age: 5–8; Length: 14 min.; Suggested Retail Price: $12.95, PAULINE BOOKS AND MEDIA

** SAVING WITH TOM AND MARTHA (MONEY SMARTZ): Take a trip to the bank to open a savings account. Designed to help parents and kids discuss saving money and enable kids to make smart choices about money. Adult Juror Comments: Adults loved this. A good teaching tool with multicultural representation and great kid participation. Introduces kids to the banking system through well-sequenced, television-advertising techniques. Probably will not be viewed repeatedly. Kid Juror Comments: Slow starting but once the kids got into it they liked it. They even admitted how much they learned. Eight- and nine-year-olds expressed interest in starting their own bank accounts after viewing the tape. Age: 6–12; Length: 24 min.; Suggested Retail Price: $19.95, THE SMARTZ FACTORY, LTD.

** SKILL GAMES; see p. 294

* SMART START GUITAR: Demonstrates a new approach to teaching the guitar to young children. Starts off kids with an open tuning method that enables them to play a chord even before they learn left-hand fingering. Adult Juror Comments: Simple, clear instructions. Best used with motivated students wanting to play the guitar. Audio quality and production values are not great, and it's a little long for this intended audience. Kid Juror Comments: Held the children's interest. Initially, the kids thought the explanations were too complex. Later, they made sense. Kids objected to using baby names for fingers. Age: 5–8; Length: 50 min.; Suggested Retail Price: $19.95, HOMESPUN TAPES

** SPACE CADETS (PROFESSOR IRIS); see p. 50

* STAY SAFE! (VIDEO ADVENTURES OF LOST AND FOUND): Demonstrates safety lessons through an adventure with four children who encounter danger at every turn. Features songs about hot stoves, strangers, and street safety. The message is: "Watch Out! Stay Safe!" Adult Juror Comments: It's an entertaining though corny way to discuss safety and danger. The production quality is good, the characters silly and overacted, detracting from the message. We recommend viewing with an adult and follow-up discussion. Kid Juror Comments: Some kids enjoyed the funny music and sang along. They had a hard time staying with the entire program and found the characters confusing. "'Watch out Willie' looks like a happy face, but tells you there's danger somewhere." Age: 5–8; Length: 25 min.; Suggested Retail Price: $14.95, ATTAINMENT COMPANY

** THAT'S SIGN FOLKS! (SIGN-TOON SERIES): The Sesame Street personality Linda Bove lends a helping hand in signing these cartoon classics for hearing-impaired children. Includes "Rudolph the Red-Nosed Reindeer," "The Wabbit Who Came To Supper," and others. Adult Juror Comments: These classics are wonderfully signed with feeling and respect. Hearing-impaired kids can now enjoy watching them together with those who are able to hear. It could lead to kids learning some sign language. Kid Juror Comments: Liked watching the cartoons and the sign language interpretations simultaneously. "We like the cartoons." "It's neat that they make it so a deaf child can watch and understand them too." Age: 5–8; Length: 30 min.; Suggested Retail Price: $24.95, SIGN ENHANCERS, INC.

*** TRAV'S TRAVELS—GEOGRAPHY FOR KIDS (UNITED STATES OF AMERICA): Teaches the geography, history, culture, and wildlife of the United States, including a range of metropolitan areas, rural towns, and farmlands. Trav, the host, makes learning interesting. Adult Juror Comments: An overview of U.S. cities and farmland with beautiful photography at a fast pace. The vocabulary used is challenging. Good cultural diversity and respect for both people and animals. Could motivate interest and discussion in travel. Kid Juror Comments: Loved it. They enjoyed seeing the volcanoes, appreciated the cultural diversity, and enjoyed learning things even their teachers didn't know. "I wanted to learn more." "We want to visit some of the places." "It made me want to take a vacation." Age: 6–12; Length: 23 min.; Suggested Retail Price: $14.99, IVN ENTERTAINMENT, INC.

*** TRUE FRIENDS (THE ALL NEW CAPTAIN KANGAROO); see p. 50

***VISIT WITH TOMIE DEPAOLA, A: An inside look at the life and art of Tomie dePaola. Follows Tomie through his home and studio, highlighting home movies featuring the young Tomie creating his art. A comprehensive and personal perspective is meant to inform and entertain kids. Adult Juror Comments: What an excellent visit with a successful artist! Viewers will want to explore their own forms of creativity. Excellent production quality; length is just right. Familiarizes kids with a fascinating array of his work. Kid Juror Comments: Enjoyed watching dePaola drawing in his studio and telling stories. "I like his house and all the beautiful things in it." "I want to become an artist too!" Best for seven- to eight-year-olds or those interested in illustration. Age: 6–12; Length: 25 min.; Suggested Retail Price: $39.95, WHITEBIRD INC.

* WE CAN GET ALONG; see p. 89

** WHO IS AN AMERICAN?: Cultivates awareness of America's multiethnic heritage by fostering an appreciation of the contributions of various cultures, exploring the origin of cultural traditions, and learning about the process of becoming a citizen. Adult Juror Comments: Straightforward, accurate information that reinforces the message of inclusion. More appropriate for classroom use and studying diversity. Has little entertainment value. Opens discussion of race and nationality issues. Values contribution by immigrants. Kid Juror Comments: Kids were somewhat bored. It contains good information about constitutional rights, and the quiz section got them involved and searching for answers. Advanced vocabulary was a bit challenging. Kids learned: "There is no one 'type' of American." Good song! Age: 6–10; Length: 26 min.; Suggested Retail Price: $89.00, EDUCATIONAL ACTIVITIES, INC.

* WORD CLUE ADVENTURE (LET'S CLIMB HIGHER): Imaginative phonics approach to teach reading and spelling. Stresses respect for diversity and reminds children and adults that people learn in different ways. Adult Juror Comments: "A wonderfully entertaining way to pique a child's curiosity

about reading and learning." Good educational tool for home use; imaginative plot/characters, high-quality production. Concern over use and speed of phonics songs. Word clues hard to follow. Kid Juror Comments: Okay. It's more educational than entertaining and much too long for most viewers. "It's like going to school." Age: 5–8; Length: 30 min.; Suggested Retail Price: $20.00, ORCHARD HILL PRODUCTIONS

CD-ROMs

** A TO ZAP!; see p. 51

*** ALL DOGS GO TO HEAVEN ACTIVITY CENTER: Teaches language skills, vocabulary, and counting, using the characters from the movie and TV series as guides. Develops critical thinking skills, memory, and hand/eye coordination. Features multiple skill levels. Adult Juror Comments: Well organized, lots of variety, interactive and entertaining things to do and learn. Some educational benefits are well disguised as games. Visually inviting. Nice introduction to art. Very child-appropriate, kids should enjoy this. Kid Juror Comments: Really fun. Kids enjoyed the different activities, particularly the chase game. Easy to install and play. The dog videos were particularly appealing. "It made me really think." "There are so many things to do. It's the best CD-ROM I have ever used." Age: 5–11; Suggested Retail Price: $29.95, METRO-GOLDWYN-MAYER, INC.

** ARIEL'S STORY STUDIO: Children create, learn, and play with characters from *The Little Mermaid* while building skills in reading, vocabulary, and critical thinking. Encourages creativity in music and writing in an enjoyable learning situation. Adult Juror Comments: Program is very entertaining, educational, and not at all didactic. Wholesome and life-affirming. Excellent tool for increasing vocabulary while building general reading skills. Allows children to be creative in an enjoyable manner. Kid Juror Comments: Kids enjoyed making up stories and their own music, the animation, and learning about sea life. They noticed the stereotypical nasty, bad guys and were frustrated because "you have to go through the same story each time you play." Appeals to girls more than boys. Age: 5–8; Suggested Retail Price: $35.00, DISNEY INTERACTIVE

** ARTHUR'S COMPUTER ADVENTURE: Arthur wants to play "Deep Dark Sea" on the computer every chance he gets. When his mom leaves for work and asks him not to touch the computer, Arthur can't resist. Disobedience leads to disaster. Will Arthur be able to fix the computer? Adult Juror Comments: Colorful and child-friendly, though the characters seem stiff compared to those on TV. Offers lots of rewards and treasures. May open discussion about obedience to parents. The game never rises above drill and practice. Kid Juror Comments: Easy to play except that kids had trouble getting out of some parts. Children could use it on their own. Great graphics, color, and special effects. Much variety. "I want to try all the page activities. There are lots of hidden surprises." Age: 4–8; Suggested Retail Price: $29.95, BRODERBUND SOFTWARE, INC.

** ARTHUR'S READING RACE; see p. 52

** BABES IN TOYLAND: AN INTERACTIVE ADVENTURE: Offers an enchanting magical world inspired by animated, musical film. Join Humpty Dumpty, Jack and Jill, and favorite nursery-rhyme characters for action-filled music, games, and puzzles that entertain while teaching valuable early-learning skills. Adult Juror Comments: Child-friendly but not very imaginative. Good variety of animals, music, different cultures. Everything was very clear and colorful. Allows child time to think. Develops coordination skills. Reviews nursery-rhyme characters. Kid Juror Comments: Good graphics but a little too simple. Most kids didn't want to play it again. "The music was putting me to sleep." Children really liked Humpty Dumpty and the puzzles. "I think it's the best CD-ROM for little kids and its okay for me (eleven)." Age: 3–8; Suggested Retail Price: $29.95, METRO-GOLDWYN-MAYER, INC.

*** BABY FELIX CREATIVITY CENTER: Baby Felix helps children learn the basics of art, music, shapes, and colors while being entertained. This three-level program was developed by child educators. Adult Juror Comments: Easy to play. The music and piano section is excellent. Requires auditory memory skills as well as visual. Immediate feedback, nicely tutorial, bright colors. Installs easily and quickly. Kid Juror Comments: Seven-year-olds stayed with it. It took them over an hour to get an entire song complete, but they wanted to play it again. Paint-and-draw portion is engaging and easier than music section. Age: 4–8; Suggested Retail Price: $19.98, TWENTI-ETH CENTURY FOX HOME ENTERTAINMENT

** CAPTAIN KANGAROO: LIFE'S FIRST LESSONS (CAPTAIN KANGAROO): On a treasure hunt with Captain Kangaroo, children find out how much fun helping a friend can be. Discover hidden objects, learn the responsibilities of taking care of pets and plants, and finally be treated to Captain Kangaroo's story. Adult Juror Comments: Great animation and songs. Easy to run. Allows kids to select how the story evolves. Shows positive role models and good rhyming for preschoolers. Printer option had glitches. Only four game choices. Little diversity. Kid Juror Comments: It's cute; it's simple; it's not that varied. Kids sang and bobbed along with the music. Lively enough to keep children's attention while allowing them to control the pace. "I like it a lot. Can I play it again?" Age: 4–8; Suggested Retail Price: $20.00, KNOWLEDGE ADVENTURE

** CHITTY CHITTY BANG BANG: ADVENTURES IN TINKERTOWN: Kids can put the pedal to the metal on a delightful journey in a fantasy world with oversized appliances and household items in need of repair. Refrigerators and telephones magically come to life, as children learn how they work. Adult Juror Comments: There is no apparent logic to this program, which is frustrating and irritating. Promotes concepts about space and time. Enhances memory and counting skills. Good pace, aesthetically pleasing, engages children's interest, but instructions didn't answer kids' questions. Kid Juror Comments: They had a good time with this. "I did well and repaired everyone in Tinkertown." "I liked Louie (screwdriver) best." Program froze at one point. "It was hard at first but I learned the difference between many tools." Age: 5–8; Suggested Retail Price: $19.95, METRO-GOLDWYN-MAYER, INC.

** DANNY AND THE DINOSAUR: This activity center helps children learn beginning reading skills based on the book, *Danny and the Dinosaur*. The five animated games and friendly characters make reading exciting for everyone. Adult Juror Comments: Pace is slow and not very inspiring. Clear and simple games are visually appealing. Focus is on pre-reading "decoding." Offers good reinforcements for word and sound recognition. Three difficulty levels provide a range of options. Kid Juror Comments: Liked the games and were anxious to get to different skill levels. "Danny and the boy are very polite. "The Dinosaur captivated the boys." "They would follow him anywhere." Age: 4–8; Suggested Retail Price: $19.98, TWENTIETH CENTURY FOX HOME ENTERTAINMENT

*** DISNEY'S ACTIVE PLAY, THE LION KING II: Kids join Kiara and Kovu in a jungle filled with playful activities, arts and crafts, sing-alongs, and more. Adult Juror Comments: One of the best CD-ROMs we've seen for young children. Graphics are dazzling and ultra-contemporary. Sing-alongs are ideal for preschool and kindergarten ages. Contains a state-of-the-art paint box with more flexibility than most. Appropriate humor. Kid Juror Comments: Most kids needed help getting started. "Colorful and I can change the pictures." "Animals are funny. I like the music." "I learned how to print the pictures out." It sometimes takes a few clicks to move from place to place. Age: 4–7; Suggested Retail Price: $29.99, DISNEY INTERACTIVE

*** DISNEY'S ANIMATED STORYBOOK, MULAN: A legendary reading adventure packed with games and activities. Mulan's amazing story unfolds as kids play learning games and discover the power of the mind. Adult Juror Comments: Beautifully designed with strong entertainment value and challenging games. Supports girls' independent thinking. Mulan's decisions result in disobedience to family and breaking the law. The outcome justifies these actions, but some may object. Kid Juror Comments: A big hit. Those who saw the movie will enjoy the video. "I liked it but I needed help five times." "If you liked the movie you will like this." Very colorful. Sometimes frustrating. "You don't get bored easily. There are a lot of things to do." Age: 6–10; Suggested Retail Price: $29.99, DISNEY INTERACTIVE

** DISNEY'S MATH QUEST WITH ALADDIN: Children use math skills in a challenging adventure to save Agrabah from Bizarrah, an evil genie. Features eighteen activities designed with leading math educator Marilyn Burns. Addresses standards set by the National Council of Teachers of Mathematics. Adult Juror Comments: Activities are very creative. Most kids do not notice that most of the activities are math. Well done with good music. May require good math and patterning skills. Does not offer a lot of interactivity. Considerable talking. Kid Juror Comments: The games were fun, helpful in learning basic mathematical concepts. Enjoyable and entertaining but "it took almost twenty minutes to get to the first math problem." Advancing in program may be difficult and frustrating for some children. Age: 5–9; Suggested Retail Price: $39.99, DISNEY INTERACTIVE

** DISNEY'S READING QUEST WITH ALADDIN: Teaches essential reading skills including phonics, vocabulary, and reading comprehension with the help of Genie, Jasmine, and Iago. Presents twelve activities in which players help free Aladdin along with three skill-level options. Adult Juror Comments: Easy to use, though pace is too advanced for the audience. Even the lowest level had words too difficult for six- and seven-year-olds. Production quality high, helps initiate and build on reading skills. Excellent use of multiple play levels. Kid Juror Comments: "It was fun." Some words in the program were too difficult for children. Kids didn't like the fact that they had to complete the activity before they could move on. Some directions are difficult for kids to understand, required an adult. Age: 6–9; Suggested Retail Price: $29.99, DISNEY INTERACTIVE

*** DISNEY'S READY FOR MATH WITH POOH; see p. 52

*** DISNEY'S READY TO READ WITH POOH; see p. 52

*** DISNEY/PIXAR'S ACTIVE PLAY, A BUG'S LIFE: Kids discover the world from a bug's-eye view. Explore and create with Flik and the gang through activities, adventures, and printable board games and puppet shows. Adult Juror Comments: Entertaining program that provides occasions for good thinking. Easy for kindergarten to grade-two students to use on their own, though portions will require adult assistance. We experienced some technical problems. Kid Juror Comments: They liked to play this together, taking turns. "Everyone would like this game. It's fun." "The graphics looked cool." "The good thing about this program is that you get to play different things and you learn from them." Age: 5–8; Suggested Retail Price: $29.99, DISNEY INTERACTIVE

*** DR. SEUSS KINDERGARTEN; see p. 53

** FISHER-PRICE READY FOR SCHOOL-TODDLER; see p. 54

** FISHER-PRICE TIME TO PLAY PET SHOP; see p. 54

** FRACTION ATTRACTION: Helps children develop fundamental concepts about fractions, including ordering equivalence, relative size, multiple representations, and locations of fractions on a number line. Adult Juror Comments: Good teaching tool but somewhat boring. Variety of games is limited. Each exercise has depth that extends its use. "Offers a year's worth of fractions that can be reviewed to stretch math skills." The "whacking game" was somewhat violent. Kid Juror Comments: Learned a lot, fast. They liked the pictures and the music. Not as much fun as some games, but it still makes learning fractions a pleasure. Sound effects are great. Adult needed to set skill level. "Better than flash cards by a mile." Age: 6–11; Suggested Retail Price: $19.95, SUNBURST COMMUNICATIONS, INC.

*** FREDDI FISH 3: THE CASE OF THE STOLEN CONCH SHELL (JUNIOR ADVENTURE SERIES): Freddi and Luther follow clues that lead to an adventure: recovering the Great Conch Shell. They make friends, explore ruins, and play games in a tropical paradise. Children piece clues together to solve who's responsible for this underwater caper. Adult Juror Comments: Well produced. Great graphics. Promotes teamwork and models positive behaviors. Helps develop critical thinking and problem-solving skills. Highly entertaining, great music and activities. Characters are likeable and intelligent. Kid Juror Comments: Enjoyed playing and figuring out the mystery. "It's interesting. You get to search for things and find suspects" "I like it because it's fun to play." Children may need some adult instruction. Age: 5–8; Suggested Retail Price: $29.99, HUMONGOUS ENTERTAINMENT

** FROG AND TOAD ARE FRIENDS: Frog and Toad make practicing reading skills more fun and exciting than ever. Based on the best-selling book, this program lets children learn and improve reading essentials with their favorite characters. Adult Juror Comments: Good variety of activities. Pace is a little slow for some adults and children. Excellent graphics, good value for children that are at the reading level. Kid Juror Comments: Enjoyable. More appealing for boys than girls. Children who cannot read yet became frustrated. They could not figure out how to play. Readers loved the characters and the music, especially when Frog wakes up Toad. Age: 6–8; Suggested Retail Price: $19.98, TWENTIETH CENTURY FOX HOME ENTERTAINMENT/FOXTOON

** GRAMMAR ROCK; see p. 296

*** GREEN EGGS AND HAM BY DR. SEUSS: The classic comes to life through cutting-edge animation and silly sound effects. As children explore the story and activities, they learn word recognition, phonic skills, and computer literacy. Adult Juror Comments: High-quality production works well with children learning to read. Encourages confidence in accomplishment. Learning games with multiple levels are engaging. Kid Juror Comments: Children smiled a lot. The games that pop up during the story were fun and helped keep children engaged and on track. They like the voices of the characters. Sometimes kids wanted the program to run faster. Age: 5–7; Suggested Retail Price: $29.95, THE LEARNING COMPANY

** HELLO KITTY CREATIVITY CENTER: Helps children master essential learning skills easily and more enjoyably through lively animation and friendly voice and text prompts. The challenging three-level program was developed with child educators to encourage learning. Adult Juror Comments: Simple but nicely done with good graphics. Adults found it slow-moving. The math section is uninspired, but the "build your own story" book section is great. "Simple drill practice on the computer." "A bit bland." Requires adult assistance to play. Kid Juror Comments: Not very complex or fast-paced. Appealed more to girls than boys. Kids like the music, the vegetable section, and making up their own story. Age: 4–7; Suggested Retail Price: $19.98, TWENTIETH CENTURY FOX HOME ENTERTAINMENT/FOXTOON

*** INTERACTIVE MATH JOURNEY (READER RABBIT'S MATH): Journey through math lands with twenty-five sequenced activities: interactive storybooks, open-ended exploration, challenging games and songs. Makes sense of math by building a child's comprehension. Winner of the 1997 Bologna New Media Prize. Included as a bonus in Reader Rabbit's Math CD-ROM.

Adult Juror Comments: Covers a lot of material. Encourages more than one way to get a correct answer. Presents basic as well as complex math skills. The activity book is a great supplement. Difficult to play with touch pad. Kid Juror Comments: Liked the puzzle style of problem-solving. Their favorite parts were "Measurement Land," the dancing frog, the music and singing. "I like how the characters talk and play." "Gets a little repetitive." Age: 5–8; Suggested Retail Price: $29.95, THE LEARNING COMPANY, INC.

** JUMPSTART KINDERGARTEN; see p. 54

*** JUMPSTART KINDERGARTEN READING; see p. 55

*** JUMPSTART SPANISH; see p. 55

*** JUMPSTART 3RD GRADE; see p. 297

*** JUMPSTART TYPING; see p. 296

*** JUNIOR FIELD TRIPS (LET'S EXPLORE): Kids learn about hundreds of plants, animals, and machines as they explore and create. Packed with games featuring Buzzy the Knowledge Bug and an illustrated tour of farms, airports, and jungles. Adult Juror Comments: Entertaining. Covers spelling, vocabulary, and animal identification. Adapts to child's skill level. Shows women in non-traditional jobs. Contains lots of information. Designed for individual play. Includes workbook, stickers. Kid Juror Comments: Went over well, especially the games, trivia, matching, and paint box. Best used by kids who read, although Buzzy "reads" to you. "I liked all the neat stuff it does. It's very challenging—especially the trivia and spelling sections at the difficult level." Age: 5–8; Suggested Retail Price: $19.95, HUMONGOUS ENTERTAINMENT

** LET'S GO READ! AN ISLAND ADVENTURE; see p. 55

* LENNY'S TIME MACHINE; see p. 297

*LIFT OFF TO THE LIBRARY: Host VIRG, Very Important Robotron Guide, leads children on an interactive, bibliographic journey with games, graphics, video, and audio clips. Introduces different parts and products of a library. Adult Juror Comments: While this had an admirable goal, the program adds little knowledge to most children's understanding of a library. Very limited; games and activities only have one or two versions, so most kids would not spend much time with the program. Kid Juror Comments: Most thought it was too easy. Making their own library was the best part. Kids needed frequent help. "I liked the games with the mazes." Kids enjoyed the graphics and the robot. They were frustrated when the program froze up on them. Age: 5–8; Suggested Retail Price: $40.00, LIBRARY VIDEO NETWORK

*** LION KING, THE — DISNEY'S ACTIVITY CENTER: Explore a king-sized world of games, puzzles, and art activities while building memory, matching, and spelling skills. Paint in the art studio, watch film clips from the hit movie, play with a friend or a favorite Lion King character! Adult Juror Comments: Appealing program young kids can use independently—an important growth step. Material is interesting and age-appropriate but demanding on computer. Appropriate for non-readers and beginning readers, although artwork is coloring-book style only. Kid Juror Comments: Really good. They'd play it again many times. Enjoyed by a wide range of kids, from gifted to challenged. Both loved it and worked together. They like Simba and the puzzle games. Age: 5–8; Suggested Retail Price: $19.98, DISNEY INTERACTIVE

*** MICROSOFT ACTIMATES EARLY LEARNING SYSTEM; see p. 56

** MICROSOFT MY PERSONAL TUTOR; see p. 56

*** MILLIE AND BAILEY KINDERGARTEN; see p. 56

** MULTIPLICATION TOUR WITH MIKE AND SPIKE (LEARNING LADDER): Journey on a concert tour around the world that teaches basic multiplication skills. Twelve lessons take children to twelve cities in eleven countries accompanied by concerts and songs. Games reward success with newly learned skills. Adult Juror Comments: Introduces multiplication and other math concepts. Offers math skill-building practice in an age-appropriate fashion. Adults disliked narrator's voice. Kid Juror Comments: Kept their attention. They liked the music, the characters Mike and Ike, and loved getting the answers right. Challenges kids and encourages continued participation. The speed is frustrating at times. "The stone-hopping taught me a lot." Age: 6–9; Suggested Retail Price: $34.95, PANASONIC INTERACTIVE MEDIA

*** NICK JR. PLAY MATH: Entertaining and curriculum-based, teaches early math skills to preschoolers. Children join a play-group of animated friends in twenty-five activities. Different features track child's progress. Adult Juror Comments: Good blend of tasks and entertainment. Parents can easily check child's progress. Offers polite feedback. Includes manual with follow-up exercises and suggestions for parents. "Our three-year-old adores this and stayed with it for over an hour." Kid Juror Comments: Program can be set to child's level of understanding. "I am becoming really good with the mouse because of my love of this program. I was introduced to patterns that now I look for in other places," commented a three-year-old. Age: 3–8; Suggested Retail Price: $29.95, VIRGIN INTERACTIVE

** PHONICS ADVENTURE WITH SING-ALONG SAM; see p. 57

** POUND PUPPIES INTERACTIVE STORYBOOK AND ACTIVITY CENTER; see p. 57

** READER RABBIT'S INTERACTIVE READING JOURNEY 2: Strengthens reading skills of five- to eight-year-olds while following the adventures of Reader Rabbit, Sam the Lion, and others through fifteen imaginary lands with multilevel activities. Included as a bonus in Reader Rabbit's Reading CD-ROM. Adult Juror Comments: Enjoyable and well designed. Develops reading confidence and language skills. Great sound and animation. Some parts too difficult for pre-readers. Kid Juror Comments: Favorite parts were recording their own voices and reading a story and hearing it played back. Rhyme Time was a hit, as were the fun characters and the sound sorter. Age: 5–8; Suggested Retail Price: $29.95, THE LEARNING COMPANY, INC.

** READING ADVENTURE WITH KENNY KITE (LEARNING LADDER): Learn to read short sentences while attending Kenny Kite's flight school. Increases reading and problem-solving skills. Learners rewarded when they graduate flight school and are listed in the Hall of Fame. Adult Juror Comments: Good scaffold for developing language skills. Progresses at a good pace. Requires basic reading skills. Players must listen carefully to songs to answer the questions. Easy installation. Kid Juror Comments: Five- to seven-year-olds learned the material, liked the pace. Slower readers felt rushed. Kids liked the screen displays, characters, and expressive voices. "Kenny helped me when I needed it." "I liked finding my way home." Age: 5–8; Suggested Retail Price: $34.95, PANASONIC INTERACTIVE MEDIA

** READING MANSION CD-ROM: Reading Mansion teaches reading by having children search through mansions. Activities include letters, phonics, word recognition, sentence skills, and following directions. Features student tracking, tutorials. Customizes for ages three to eight. Adult Juror Comments: Engaging, good coaching for basic reading and phonics skills. Develops critical thinking and problem-solving skills. Educators loved the extensive levels but felt it was somewhat repetitive. Runs poorly on older computers. Content not particularly playful. Kid Juror Comments: Easy to use. Younger kids will need help. Children enjoyed the format and liked how it praised their success. "I got a reward. I'm going to put it on my wall." Most children chose to play it again and challenged themselves by choosing harder levels. Age: 5–8; Suggested Retail Price: $40.00, GREAT WAVE SOFTWARE

* RICHARD SCARRY'S HOW THINGS WORK IN BUSYTOWN (BUSYTOWN): Through hands-on exploration of Busytown's eight interconnecting playgrounds, teaches the importance of working together in a community while gaining valuable early-learning skills. Adult Juror Comments: Shows child how people with different jobs help others. They learn who takes care of certain problems. It's mouse-dependent, which is difficult for a four-year-old. Information lacks depth. Kid Juror Comments: Okay, but had problems with the mechanics of using the mouse. Inspired interest in reading about the book characters. Age: 4–8; Suggested Retail Price: $49.99, VIRGIN INTERACTIVE

*** SCHOLASTIC'S THE MAGIC SCHOOL BUS EXPLORES THE OCEAN: Wacky science teacher Ms. Frizzle and her inquisitive class go on an amazing adventure through the ocean. Join the "Friz" and class as they explore seven distinct ocean zones to discover and solve clues in their search for the sunken treasure. Adult Juror Comments: Wonderful new information. Requires some reading skills. Includes entertaining video sections with a strong environmental awareness. Activity booklet makes a great tool for parent or teacher. Saving is tricky, some games have many levels. Kid Juror Comments: They liked the bus, were confused in some parts, amused in others, and overall, loved playing the program. "This taught me a lot about sea animals." "I learned that sailfish are the fastest fish in the ocean." "The hints were easy to understand." Age: 6–10; Suggested Retail. Price: $44.95, SCHOLASTIC-MICROSOFT

*** SCHOLASTIC'S THE MAGIC SCHOOL BUS EXPLORES THE RAINFOREST: Designed to entertain children while encouraging a sense of adventure and exploration of the fascinating world of science. With the irrepressible science teacher Ms. Frizzle, kids take a field trip to the Costa Rican rainforest. Adult Juror Comments: What every parent wants—a learning tool that's fun as well. Well organized, excellent information about the rainforest. Program maintains consistent enthusiasm. Closed-captioned. Kid Juror Comments: "There's so much to do." Going from the classroom to the environment appeals to kids. They like "going on the bus," the paint box, Ms. Frizzle, and graphics. "This is a fun way to learn new things about the rain-forest." Age: 6–10; Suggested Retail Price: $34.95, SCHOLASTIC/MICROSOFT

** SESAME STREET: GET SET TO LEARN; see p. 57

*** SHEILA RAE THE BRAVE; see p. 58

*** STELLALUNA: Based on the popular children's book by Jane Cannon. Stellaluna, a young fruit bat, is adopted by a family of birds after she becomes separated from her mother. Adult Juror Comments: Kindhearted story demonstrating individual differences. Skills games created from the context of the story are enhanced by the narrative. Gorgeous animated illustrations. Software loads easily and offers a variety of learning benefits. Kid Juror Comments: Captivating. Children liked many of the different activities, such as the Bat Quiz, Bat Game, and the Ice Cream section. Kids learned about trust, love, and self-reliance. Kids interested in animals expressed particularly keen interest. Age: 5–8; Suggested Retail Price: $29.95, THE LEARNING COMPANY

** SPELLING BLASTER AGES 6–9; see p. 301

*** STORYBOOK WEAVER DELUXE, THE: An imaginative writing tool that lets students create their own stories with pictures and words. Features graphics, voice record and playback, text-to-speech capabilities, and the ability to copy and paste scanned images. Bilingual in Spanish and English. Adult Juror Comments: Empowers pre-readers, outstanding for all skill levels. Good team activity. Ideal for budding writers. "One of the best learning programs I've seen to date." Helpful to read "Getting Started" before beginning the story mode. Contains some stereotypes. Kid Juror Comments: "Once kids learned the program, they all loved making up their own stories." Inspired imaginations and developed literacy skills. Their favorites parts were the story starters, the graphics, the music, the pictures, and the objects. Age: 6–13; Suggested Retail Price: $29.95, THE LEARNING COMPANY, INC.

*** SUNBUDDY WRITER: Youngsters learn to write with the lovable Sunbuddies. All the favorite A to Zap! pals—Hopkins, Tiny, Max, Cassie, and Shelby—are back with an easy-to-use writing tool designed especially for young writers. Adult Juror Comments: Great for beginning writers. The teacher's guide outlines activities, collaborative stories, and more. Simple installation, although there are some difficult procedures. Kid Juror Comments: Liked the program at the start of the story. Preferred watching in groups. "No blank-page syndrome." Players enjoyed the "word necklace" and "word finder." Best used by kids who are familiar with the keyboard. Age: 5–8; Suggested Retail Price: $19.95, SUNBURST COMMUNICATIONS, INC.

*** SUPER RADIO ADDITION WITH MIKE AND SPIKE (LEARNING LADDER): Guides children through basic concepts of addition as they play the role of disc jockeys at a radio station. Teaches addition through songs and games. Upon completion, children receive recognition in the "Hall of Fame." Adult Juror Comments: Captivating learning tool. Highly challenging for age group, allows for quick advancement. Requires "fast" action. Encourages kids to keep trying. Even adult jurors liked the music. Kid Juror Comments: As kids improve, the fun increases. Kids liked the humor, the frog named "Mike," the "bubbleloids," and the music. "They really have a hit with this one." Age: 5–8; Suggested Retail Price: $34.95, PANASONIC INTERACTIVE MEDIA

*** THINKING GAMES (MADELINE): Explore Madeline's mansion and uncover challenging and fun games in every room. Kids practice spelling and keyboarding in the classroom, learn French and Spanish vocabulary, decorate Madeline's bedroom, and create music in the studio. Adult Juror Comments: What a great interactive adaptation of this well-loved character! Clever animations, good sequencing, clear sound, and delightful music. A low-key approach and a refreshing change of pace, starring a girl. Kid Juror Comments: Loved seeing one of their favorite book characters, especially girls and those familiar with Madeline. Entertaining, educating, and provokes creative thought. Liked decorating rooms the best. "Better than sliced bread." Age: 4–10; Suggested Retail Price: $39.95, THE LEARNING COMPANY

*** WINNIE THE POOH AND THE HONEY TREE; see p. 58

Family

* ADVENTURES FOR CHILDREN: THRU A DOG'S EYES: Follows a day in the life of a dog as seen from the dog's point of view, about two feet from the ground. The dog takes a car ride, a trip to a farm and visits the zoo, the vet and a pet store. Features original music. Adult Juror Comments: An unusual perspective and the photography is well done, but the unusual camera angle (from a dog's eye-level) disoriented some jurors. Most likely, children will not play more than once. Kid Juror Comments: Interested in seeing things from a dog's perspective. They particularly were fascinated when the dog chased the farm animals. "This is pretty silly." The production is a slow and more appropriate for younger children. Age: 5–8; Length: 25 min.; Suggested Retail Price: $14.95, MADE-FOR-DOG VIDEOS, INC.

* ADVENTURES IN THE SADDLE (REAL-LIFE ADVENTURE SERIES FOR KIDS): Inspires kids and families to be active outdoors. This horse-centered video shows kids in rodeo events, swimming on horseback, galloping in the mountains, and doing riding tricks. Adult Juror Comments: Shows how to train a horse with respect and understanding. The background music is okay, but the singing portions didn't go over well. Encourages self-esteem. Good subject, even though the production is awkward and slightly amateurish. Kid Juror Comments: "I learned stuff that I might want to know when I'm bigger." The humor is a little silly. It's too long and jumps from scene to scene. Kids were bothered by the unsteady camera work. Age: 5–12; Length: 40 min.; Suggested Retail Price: $14.95, FORWARD MOTION PICTURES, INC.

* ALADDIN (ANIMATED CLASSICS): Tells Aladdin's story from his spooky descent into a cave to claim the magic lamp to his marriage to Princess Leila, the Sultan's beautiful daughter. Adult Juror Comments: This is well animated but the story is full of stereotypic characters. Modernizing the language diminishes the classic tale and is not always suitable to the story. Kid Juror Comments: Even though they enjoyed the video, children familiar with the Disney version continually compared stories throughout the screening. They appreciated knowing that different companies produce different versions of the same story. Age: 3–18; Length: 50 min.; Suggested Retail Price: $19.95, GOODTIMES HOME VIDEO

* ALADDIN AND THE KING OF THIEVES: Everyone's third wish comes true in Aladdin's ultimate adventure. Features Robin Williams as the voice of Genie. Adult Juror Comments: Beautifully animated. Contains aggressive language, adult humor, lots of sword fighting, and stereotypical portrayal of Arabs. Glamorizes the knife fight used to gain into entry into "Forty Thieves" gang. Offers a message that "You must fight or else you will be killed." Kid Juror Comments: Big hit. Wanted to watch it again right away. Kids enjoyed the production style and the characters. They did not understand much of the story. The content is more appropriate for older children. It's too scary for children under five. Age: 5–8; Length: 80 min.; Suggested Retail Price: $24.99, WALT DISNEY HOME VIDEO

*** ALL DOGS GO TO HEAVEN: Set in 1939 New Orleans, this colorful, song-filled story features Charles B. Barkin, a roguish German shepherd with the charm of a con man and the heart of a marshmallow. Adult Juror Comments: A lively film that encourages cooperation and honesty. A well-told story with a good mixture of adventure and values. Teaches morality without being pedantic. It's one of the best cartoon movies our jurors have seen.

Kid Juror Comments: Really enjoyed the characters. They reacted strongly to the emotional content, developing empathy for the orphan. They liked how it emphasizes building one's character and learning from mistakes. All said they'd watch this again. Age: 3–12; Length: 85 min.; Suggested Retail Price: $14.95, MGM/UA HOME ENTERTAINMENT

*** ALLEGRA'S CHRISTMAS (ALLEGRA'S WINDOW); see p. 59

*** AMAZING GRACE AND OTHER STORIES (CHILDREN'S CIRCLE): Features three stories adapted from popular children's picture books: "Amazing Grace," "Flossie & the Fox," and "Who's in Rabbit's House?" Adult Juror Comments: Outstanding music and narration. The thematic grouping of beautiful stories is tastefully done and is a great springboard for discussion about history, language, countries, and culture. Shows excellent multicultural mix. "Should be in every library!" Kid Juror Comments: Very attentive and polite while viewing. "We liked all of the stories." The presentation "Amazing Grace" was a little slow. Kids liked the first story best. Age: 5–8; Length: 35 min.; Suggested Retail Price: $14.95, CHILDREN'S CIRCLE HOME VIDEO

*** AMERICAN TAIL, AN: A delightful animated tale of Fievel, the brave little mouse, who journeys from Russia to America with his family seeking a new life free from cat persecution. Fievel's adventure begins after he's lost at sea and washes ashore in New York. Adult Juror Comments: This engaging story is well animated with catchy songs and lovable characters. Viewers are drawn into Fievel's journey. It addresses friendship, death, and separation. Can be scary for younger kids. Motivates discussion about emigration and cultures. Kid Juror Comments: They were rooted to their seats. Loved Fievel's sweetness. Older kids liked the action and the suspense. Kids resonated to the ideas such as: "Never give up, keep trying." "America is a place to find hope." "Not all cats (people) are bad." Age: 5–10; Length: 81 min.; Suggested Retail Price: $19.98, UNIVERSAL STUDIOS HOME VIDEO

** AMERICAN TAIL: FIEVEL GOES WEST, AN: In this adventure, brave little Fievel is lured out West by evil double-dealer Cat R. Waul, who plans to turn the settlers into mouseburgers. With help of his friend Tiger, Fievel joins forces with lawdog Wiley Burp to stop a sinister scheme. Adult Juror Comments: Animation, music, and story are engaging, but it does glamorize gun-shooting scenes. "Story line helps learn about new habitats and adapting to environments." Kid Juror Comments: Swell. Fievel is a likeable, active role model. "The cats were bad when they tried to eat the mice." More

kindness is shown than meanness, though. "I loved when the dog is teaching the tiger." "It made me think about the desert habitat." Age: 4–8; Length: 75 min.; Suggested Retail Price: $19.98, UNIVERSAL STUDIOS HOME VIDEO

* ANASTASIA (ENCHANTED TALES): A young princess finds her life changed forever by the tide of revolution in Czarist Russia. When the evil Rasputin betrays the royal family, Anastasia is forced to flee for her life, aided by the dashing young soldier Alexander. Adult Juror Comments: A charming tale, though the story is too complex for youngest ones and is sometimes scary. This version is more historically accurate than others, though it contains implied violence and has too simplistic a resolution. Kid Juror Comments: Kids four and up liked this, even though they didn't understand the story line. It's hard to know what held kids' attention. "I don't know why Anastasia forgot everything." "I like the little birds." Age: 5–8; Length: 48 min.; Suggested Retail Price: $9.98, SONY WONDER

** AND BABY MAKES FOUR; see p. 58

** AROUND THE WORLD IN A DAZE (WHERE'S WALDO): Join Waldo as he sets out to help a fuddy-duddy explorer. Story combines brain-busters and mazes. Makes use of the pause button on your VCR to increase puzzle-solving time. Adult Juror Comments: This is a good, interactive social studies experience. Faithful to the book, the characters look like what you'd expect. If your VCR is unstable in the "pause" mode, it's difficult to play the games. Sarcastic humor. Kid Juror Comments: Responsive. Kids loved watching the characters move and talk. Enjoyed the puzzles and finding the details in the pictures, although they are difficult to see. Even so, they loved it. "Waldo is good, he can find things, we can too. Woof is adorable." Age: 5–8; Length: 30 min.; Suggested Retail Price: $5.98, TWENTIETH CENTURY FOX HOME ENTERTAINMENT

** AT THE AIRPORT: Explores a busy airport from the ticket counter to the cockpit, baggage handling to jet fueling. Visits to pilots and air traffic controllers. Adult Juror Comments: Shows female pilots and air traffic controllers. An informative production about airports and planes, great for kids taking a field trip to the airport or preparing for a plane ride. Kid Juror Comments: Well-traveled children particularly loved it because they are familiar with the subject. "I liked that they showed different kinds of airplanes!" Older children enjoyed it best. Age: 3–8; Length: 25 min.; Suggested Retail Price: $14.95, PAPILLION PRODUCTIONS

*** BABE: A very special pig turns Hoggett's orderly farm on its ear. A naive newcomer, Babe boldly forges friendships among all the animals and convinces the entire farm that only in the absence of prejudice can one truly be free to soar. Adult Juror Comments: Great! Fabulous. This story respects differences between characters and their abilities. Challenges the notions of solving problems with violence. Babe is a model of goodness. Kid Juror Comments: "I liked how nice the talking animals were." Particularly enjoyed seeing Babe save the sheep. All the animals were adored by the kids, especially the singing mice. They wanted to watch it again. One took it home and watched it five times. Age: 4–12; Length: 92 min.; Suggested Retail Price: $14.98, UNIVERSAL STUDIOS HOME VIDEO

* BABY-SITTERS AND THE BOY SITTERS; see p. 302

** BABY-SITTERS REMEMBER, THE; see p. 303

** BACH AND BROCCOLI (LES PRODUCTIONS LA FETE): Fanny, an eleven-year-old orphan, brings love to her lonely uncle, a middle-aged bachelor whose passion is the music of Bach. Adult Juror Comments: Excellent drama, colorful music. The English dubbing was distracting for some. The main characters were very realistic and dealt with real issues and a range of emotions. Children may not understand the tension between uncle and mother. Kid Juror Comments: Related to the story and the emotional range experienced by the main characters. They enjoyed the scenes with the animals and thought the men were mean and grumpy and the women were kind. Many kids asked to see it again. Age: 4–12; Length: 96 min.; Suggested Retail Price: $14.98, LES PRODUCTIONS LA FETE/LIVE ENTERTAINMENT

*** BALTO: Balto, an outcast sled dog, becomes a hero when he saves the children of Nome, Alaska, from an epidemic. A team of sled dogs, carrying medicine, races 600 miles through a blizzard. Features voices of Kevin Bacon, Bridget Fonda, Bob Hoskins, and Phil Collins. Adult Juror Comments: Excellent, action-packed production. Good adaptation of a true story, demonstrating the idea to "keep trying, don't quit." Children identified with rejection and praise. Encouraged reading the book. More educational than expected. Kid Juror Comments: "Really great." "Exciting." Animal lovers responded particularly well. Kids were curious to know more about the real story. Stimulated discussion afterwards about the role of huskies in everyday life. "Dogs are more than just pets." Age: 5–12; Length: 78 min.; Suggested Retail Price: $14.98, UNIVERSAL STUDIOS HOME VIDEO

*** BARNEY SAFETY; see p. 61

*** BEAUTY & THE BEAST—GOODTIMES (ANIMATED CLASSICS): Beauty's father spends the night at a castle and steals a rose to bring home. The lord of the castle demands a price for the crime: Beauty must live with him forever. Beauty's love finally breaks the evil spell that turned the prince into a beast. Adult Juror Comments: Well-produced classic fairy tale, sound and voices are well done. The characters are typical of this genre, either good or evil. Adults liked the classical music. Kid Juror Comments: Enjoyed this version and compared it to the Disney version. Kids saw through the evil stepsister's plan. "I like the part at the end when the evil fairy was taken away by the ear." Age: 5–12; Length: 50 min.; Suggested Retail Price: $19.95, GOODTIMES HOME VIDEO

** BEING RESPONSIBLE (YOU CAN CHOOSE!): Takes an interesting approach to youth guidance by combining comedy, drama, music, peer-education, and role modeling into a lively format to challenge young viewers. Adult Juror Comments: This kind of program—"have fun with personal change"—is often seen as stupid in the nervous eyes of teens. This one is well done, though the content is best suited for older children and the format best for younger kids. Kid Juror Comments: Appreciated having guidelines on how to behave. They enjoyed the conversation and discussion among the children in the program. Kids had a hard time admitting to one another that they enjoyed the video. Age: 6–11; Length: 28 min.; Suggested Retail Price: $59.95, LIVE WIRE MEDIA

** BERENSTAIN BEARS, VOL. 2; see p. 66

** BIG HARBOR BEDTIME (THEODORE TUGBOAT): Features Theodore, a stouthearted tugboat, and his many friends in the Big Harbor. Anthology includes "Emily and the Sleep Over," "Theodore's Bright Night," and "Foduck and the Shy Ship." Adult Juror Comments: Simple production with characters who are friendly, amusing, and unusual. The content and language are age-appropriate. Encourages respectful behavior. Although long, it can be broken up easily for viewing in four segments. Kid Juror Comments: Liked the short stories and narration, the peer interaction and the showing of emotions. "My seven-year-old watched attentively." "My two-year-olds sang along, pointed at the tugboats, asked questions and imitated words." Age: 4–7; Length: 43 min.; Suggested Retail Price: $12.95, WARNER BROS. FAMILY ENTERTAINMENT

* BIRTHDAY BLOW-OUT, THE (WHERE'S WALDO): Search for the elusive Waldo in Birthday Land. Video includes brain-busters and mazes. Use the pause button on your VCR to give more time for puzzle-solving. Adult Juror Comments: Faithful to the book, artwork, and characters. The puzzles are blurry at times. The suggestion to pause the tape only works on VCRs that pause clearly. Fast-paced. Has good potential for interaction. Kid Juror Comments: "Yes, yes, yes." Most kids loved the humor and the detective work involved. One boy said he preferred reading the book. One said, "I wish I lived in Party Cove." The images are unclear on many VCRs when paused, making it difficult to use. Age: 5–8; Length: 30 min.; Suggested Retail Price: $5.98, TWENTIETH CENTURY FOX HOME ENTERTAINMENT

*** BIRTHDAY STORIES; see p. 67

*** BOY & HIS CAR, A: A young boy finds his heart's desire, a remote-controlled car, loses it, and goes on a quest through the streets and subways of New York to get it back. Features the chorus of St. John the Divine. Adult Juror Comments: A lovely film. Shows good multicultural mix, social themes, and examples of cooperation. Charmingly original, creative, and intriguing, though the ending is awkward. Introduces kids to choir music and religion. Teachers loved it. Kid Juror Comments: Some kids absolutely loved this. The mix of music with an original story are good but a little difficult for kids to follow. Sparks interesting discussion. One boy remembered it from a previous screening where it made a lasting impression. Age: 3–10; Length: 25 min.; Suggested Retail Price: $14.95, ANNE RICHARDSON PRODUCTIONS

* BOY NAMED CHARLIE BROWN, A: The animated Peanuts gang faces the start of the baseball season and a pitcher's mound overgrown with dandelions. Adult Juror Comments: The Peanuts Gang's adventures are imaginative and enjoyable. Explores baseball, friendships, and spelling bees. Children may find the presentation slow. Shows little diversity and stereotypical gender portrayal of characters. Kid Juror Comments: Liked the interactions between Lucy and Charlie Brown. Snoopy of course was a hit. "Poor Charlie Brown, everything always happens to him." "Snoopy and Lucy have all the good luck." "Charlie Brown always keeps trying." Age: 5–8; Length: 85 min.; Suggested Retail Price: $14.98, TWENTIETH CENTURY FOX HOME ENTERTAINMENT

** BOYD'S SHADOW; see p. 304

** **BUDDY:** Rene Russo stars in this family adventure about a woman who opens her home and her heart to a household of creatures including a baby gorilla, Buddy. Based on a true story. Adult Juror Comments: Well produced. Slow-moving, lags in the middle, sad at times, but the resolution redeems it. Good range of emotions with whimsical yet realistic sets and costumes. Kid Juror Comments: Entertaining. Girls liked it; boys were bored. Prompted discussion after about zoos and pets. Kids agreed they would want to have a pet gorilla. "The animals looked healthy and well kept." "I liked when they got into trouble." Age: 5–13; Length: 85 min.; Suggested Retail Price: $14.95, COLUMBIA TRISTAR HOME VIDEO

** **BUGS BUNNY SUPERSTAR:** This classic is narrated by Orson Welles and highlighted by live action and behind-the-scenes interviews with cartoon geniuses Bob Clampett, Tex Avery, and Friz Freling. Adult Juror Comments: Interesting documentary survey of cartoon-making. Shows kids how a character such as Bugs Bunny came to be. Engages kids' awareness of the material on two levels: how animation is made and how characters are created. Kid Juror Comments: Passive reaction at first, but the historical information about cartoon making and character creation caught their interest, and their attention level increased. Interesting as a documentary but not really geared toward children. Age: 6–12; Length: 91 min.; Suggested Retail Price: $14.95, MGM/UA HOME ENTERTAINMENT

** **BUILDING SKYSCRAPERS:** This construction video visits busy building sites with giant jackhammers, flash welders, and excavations. Set among skyscrapers in New York, Chicago, and Hong Kong, viewed from a helicopter. Adult Juror Comments: Informative, well presented, with a good child narrator. Well produced, with good aerial shots. It's very age-appropriate. Parents liked it too. Glamorizes explosives and demolition. Kid Juror Comments: Appealed to boys; girls specifically said they did not like it. The boys liked the explosions particularly well. Several preschoolers and their parents enjoyed this, though they found it too long for younger kids. Age: 4–10; Length: 40 min.; Suggested Retail Price: $19.95, DAVID ALPERT ASSOCIATES, INC.

** **CABBAGE PATCH: THE SCREEN TEST (CABBAGE PATCH KIDS):** The Cabbage Patch Kids decide to team up to make a film for a school project about heroes. They learn that anyone can be a hero. Adult Juror Comments: Cute. Quality production, engaging music, good messages about cooperation, self-worth, and teamwork. Characters are believable and distinct, though it shows some gender stereotypes. Kid Juror Comments: "Loved it, especially the songs and the silly twins." Kids liked seeing a resolution. Even older children enjoyed it. Girls liked it better than boys. Age: 5–8; Length: 30 min.; Suggested Retail Price: $12.98, BMG VIDEO

* CAPTAIN JANUARY (SHIRLEY TEMPLE): A mean truant officer attempts to take Shirley Temple (an orphan) away from a kindly lighthouse keeper. Features the song "The Codfish Ball." Adult Juror Comments: Offers lessons on values, family interactions, and problem solving. But in today's climate, the social generalizations lack sensitivity to cultural and gender diversity, and the characters' argumentative and name-calling behaviors offer poor role models. Kid Juror Comments: Kids were bored and thought it was too long. Most kids thought the sea captain "baby" scene was funny. Younger ones found the story too complex to follow. Age: 5–10; Length: 76 min.; Suggested Retail Price: $14.98, TWENTIETH CENTURY FOX HOME ENTERTAINMENT

*** CARING AND SHARING WITH FRIENDS (RUPERT THE BEAR): Rupert and his friends embark on magical, globe-trotting adventures while offering gentle and humorous lessons about growing up. Adult Juror Comments: Entertaining and well produced. Brings up good issues surrounding responsibility and friendship. Some of the behavior borders on being unsafe. Kid Juror Comments: "Funny. I'd watch more of these programs." Sparked conversations about younger siblings and friendship. One child scooted over and affectionately put her arm around her friend. Age: 5–8; Length: 48 min.; Suggested Retail Price: $9.98, SONY WONDER

** CASE OF THE HOTEL WHO-DONE-IT, THE (THE ADVENTURES OF MARY-KATE AND ASHLEY): A frantic call from a frazzled hotel manager sends the pint-sized Mary-Kate and Ashley to the Hilton Hawaiian Village, a fabulous Honolulu resort hotel that has been plagued by a string of "disappearances." Adult Juror Comments: The twins talk out their reasoning to solve the mystery, which makes audience think. Catchy tunes and visuals. Bike ride to Hawaii is misleading. Wearing helmets a plus. Filled with gender stereotypical behavior and "stupid" portrayal of adults. Kid Juror Comments: Kids liked following the mystery and solving problems with the twins. They asked questions about the Navy ship and said they didn't understand the hotel manager. "The songs and clothes were cool. I would give this video for a birthday present." Age: 5–8; Length: 30 min.; Suggested Retail Price: $12.95, WARNER HOME VIDEO

** CASE OF THE LOGICAL i RANCH, THE (THE ADVENTURES OF MARY-KATE AND ASHLEY): The Olsen and Olsen Mystery Agency is hired to explore the missing cattle at the Logical i Ranch. Adult Juror Comments: Corny but cute and very middle class. Well produced, predictable, but suitable for this age and for kids who like to solve mysteries. Kid Juror Comments: A hit. Afterwards, kids talked about the research the girls did in the library. Much to our surprise, both boys and girls liked it equally, even memorizing some of the songs. This went over best with early elementary-aged kids. Age: 5–9; Length: 30 min.; Suggested Retail Price: $12.95, WARNER HOME VIDEO

** CASE OF THE MYSTERY CRUISE, THE (THE ADVENTURES OF MARY-KATE AND ASHLEY): The pint-sized gumshoes board a cruise ship to soak up some sun, fun, and find themselves engaged in crime-solving on the high seas. Along with their dog, Clue, Mary-Kate and Ashley promise to "solve any crime by dinner time." Adult Juror Comments: This action story kept kids engaged and guessing. The depiction of the parents is rather stereotypical. Mom is frivolous and Dad the worker. Kid Juror Comments: Video motivated kids who came to America by ship to talk about their trip. They tried to figure out the mystery as the story moved along. Kids loved the songs, memorizing the words and singing along. Age: 5–9; Length: 30 min.; Suggested Retail Price: $12.95, WARNER HOME VIDEO

* CASE OF THE SEAWORLD ADVENTURE, THE (THE ADVENTURES OF MARY-KATE AND ASHLEY): Mary-Kate and Ashley, the supersleuths, take the deep plunge to discover a watery mystery. What a truly whale of a tale they find when they discover some of the most remarkable creatures in the sea. Adult Juror Comments: Delightful. The twins talk to each other respectfully, blend good humor and sensitivity to feelings. High-quality content. "Nice to see parents travel with their children while encouraging their creativity." Humor is well suited for this age. Kid Juror Comments: Suspenseful. Inspired kids to solve mysteries on their own. "I want to find a mystery to solve." Prompted a discussion about working at Sea World. Kids liked the Miami song, the costumes and the boat. "I wish my mom and dad talked to dolphins." Age: 5–8; Length: 30 min.; Suggested Retail Price: $12.95, WARNER HOME VIDEO

** CASE OF THE SHARK ENCOUNTER, THE (THE ADVENTURES OF MARY-KATE AND ASHLEY): Mary-Kate and Ashley, the adventurous twosome, take on the undersea case of three pirates who swear that the sharks are actually singing. Adult Juror Comments: Theatrical, goofy, and girlish. Demonstrates problem-solving skills, gives accurate information about sharks, and introduces good vocabulary words. Glorifies pirates as thieves. "I liked that Sharlene Fish, the shark expert, was African-American." Kid Juror Comments: Kids like singing along with the girls. They like the spy stuff and learning about sharks. "Some parts sound like nonsense and some like they're real detectives. I'm not sure how they figured out fishing poles made music." "It's a girls' movie." Age: 5–8; Length: 30 min.; Suggested Retail Price: $12.95, WARNER HOME VIDEO

** CASE OF THORNE MANSION, THE (THE ADVENTURES OF MARY-KATE AND ASHLEY): Mary-Kate and Ashley try to find the ghost in a haunted mansion in Transylvania. With their dog, Clue, they promise to "solve any crime by dinner time." Adult Juror Comments: This mystery is filled with great music and it's well suited for this age. Kids relate to the true-to-life situations the girls get into. It's fun figuring out the mystery from the clues. The treatment of the younger sister is not very good. Kid Juror Comments: Girls loved this and watched it again to learn the songs. Kids objected to the idea that you can cross the ocean on a bike. They learned that there is usually an explanation for everything. It could be scary for those five years of age. Age: 5–9; Length: 30 min.; Suggested Retail Price: $12.95, WARNER HOME VIDEO

** CASE OF THE U.S. NAVY ADVENTURE, THE (THE ADVENTURES OF MARY-KATE AND ASHLEY): Join Mary-Kate and Ashley as they travel to the edge of the world, where a fleet of UFOs has been flying over earth every ninety-three minutes. The twins use all their knowledge, with a little help from the Navy to solve this mystery. Adult Juror Comments: A good transition movie for young girls. Concepts offer opportunity for further discussion about atlases, satellites, UFOs, time, and the armed services. The twins use clear thinking, show respect for adults. Overacting at times is the only drawback. Kid Juror Comments: Kids love being detectives and following clues. They enjoyed the costumes, dancing, singing, and humor. Kids commented on the stereotypical portrayal of science nerds. "The 'kiss me' sign on the dog is funny." Age: 5–8; Length: 30 min.; Suggested Retail Price: $12.95, WARNER HOME VIDEO

** CASE OF THE U.S. SPACE CAMP MISSION, THE (THE ADVENTURES OF MARY-KATE AND ASHLEY): Mary-Kate and Ashley are called in to help the Space Program and Mission Control aided by Alan Bean of Apollo XII, the fourth astronaut on the moon. Unless they solve the mystery of the unknown ticking sounds, the U.S. Shuttle cannot lift off. Adult Juror Comments: Good cinematography. Lacks continuity and jumps from scene to scene. Has good info on space camp and flight training but digresses from the mystery. Good lessons about diction, bravery, critical thinking and asking for help. Not too complex. Kid Juror Comments: Kids liked the footage from outer space and seeing the girls throw meatballs. Opened discussion about how the girls solved the mystery by using their minds to make deductions and conclusions. "Girls can be astronauts too." Age: 5–8; Length: 30 min.; Suggested Retail Price: $12.95, WARNER HOME VIDEO

** CASE OF THE VOLCANO MYSTERY, THE (THE ADVENTURES OF MARY-KATE AND ASHLEY): The case begins with a frantic call from three marshmallow-mining prospectors who have been terrorized by a claim-jumping, snowball-throwing monster. In a wild, volcanic wilderness like Jelly Jungle, what kind of monster can the twins be up against? Adult Juror Comments: Includes many volcano facts and a realistic jungle. The volcanologist adds credibility to the story. The rural minors were obnoxiously stereotyped. Story line is age-appropriate, but adults generally don't care for it. Good-quality production. Kid Juror Comments: Kids like the mystery story. "It was fun and we learned a lot too." Girls enjoy more than boys; they were "genuinely enthralled." They commented that "the girls are real smart and almost as good as superheroes." Some boys refused to watch. Age: 5–8; Length: 30 min.; Suggested Retail Price: $12.95, WARNER HOME VIDEO

* CASPER, A SPIRITED BEGINNING: Casper is on the run from Kibosh, king of spooks. Like his uncles, Casper skips spectral training and finds a friend and teacher in a little boy. Casper discovers his powers, saves a town from the wrecking ball and reunites the boy with his father. Adult Juror Comments: Good final message but poorly acted. Shows poor adult role models, kids playing with knives and food processors, and behaviors by the mean ghosts which are offensive and negative. The "Green Monster" is particularly violent both verbally and physically. Premise of believing in ghosts makes it hard to take seriously. Kid Juror Comments: The ghost train was too scary for youngest kids. The father's behavior, when he ignored his kid, bothered them. They were glad at the end when the father finally realizes his kid needs him. Age: 6–12; Length: 90 min.; Suggested Retail Price: $19.98, TWENTIETH CENTURY FOX HOME ENTERTAINMENT

* CAT'S MEOW, THE; see p. 68

** CHITTY CHITTY BANG BANG: Dick Van Dyke stars as inventor Caractacus Potts, who creates an incredible car that drives, flies, and floats his family into a magical world of pirates and castles. Adult Juror Comments: It's funny, fast-paced, and lively. The simplistic storytelling and the special effects are somewhat dated. Kid Juror Comments: Good story. Kids enjoyed watching with their parents. Many retold the story. Some found it pretty corny. Young kids have trouble with the story line, older kids found it old-fashioned. Appeals to middle range, seven to ten years old. Age: 4–10;

Length: 147 min.; Suggested Retail Price: $14.95, MGM/UA HOME EN-TERTAINMENT

** CIRCUS CHAMPIONS (BARNYARD BUDDIES, THE): The Barnyard Buddies are off on an exciting adventure to the circus. They steal the show when they discover an old barn filled with circus memorabilia. Narration by Sally Struthers. Adult Juror Comments: This is rather an endearing story. Sally Struthers' narration is perfect. Stimulated questions by younger children about the circus. The animation is well done, with original music. Kids really related to the animals. Kid Juror Comments: The characters, music, and story were very good. They wanted to play circus afterwards. The introduction went over children's heads unless they were familiar with the circus. "They liked to see the animals working together." Ages 5–8; Length: 56 min.; Suggested Retail Price: $12.95, THE STARDOM CO. LTD.

** CLAUDIA AND THE MISSING JEWELS (THE BABY-SITTERS CLUB); see p. 305

** CLAUDIA AND THE MYSTERY OF THE SECRET PASSAGE (THE BABY-SITTERS CLUB); see p. 305

*** CLUBHOUSE, THE (CABBAGE PATCH KIDS): The Cabbage Patch dolls come to life. The boys are in for a big surprise when they challenge the girls to a clubhouse-building competition. Adult Juror Comments: Well produced with good message that discourages gender stereotyping. Straightforward, interesting, and thoughtful. Stimulates critical thinking skills. "All the characters have memorable personalities that we enjoy." Kid Juror Comments: Fun to watch. They enjoyed the songs, wanted to see more. Kids liked the good examples of working together. Some kids thought the doll animation was too babyish. Age: 4–8; Length: 30 min.; Suggested Retail Price: $12.98, BMG VIDEO

** COOPERATION (YOU CAN CHOOSE!): When Moose insists on having his own way, it breaks up his singing quartet. He then learns the benefits of co-operation. Features youth advocate Michael Pritchard. Adult Juror Comments: Good for teaching conflict mediation but a little corny and preachy. The format of translating a lecture to video lacks entertainment value. Emphasizes the use of compliments and constructive criticism. "We need to make this information available for ages five to twelve." Kid Juror Comments: The kids responded well to the host. Great discussion starter. Kids enjoyed making a project out of the material. Age: 6–12; Length: 28 min.; Suggested Retail Price: $59.95, LIVE WIRE MEDIA

*** COURAGE OF LASSIE: Loyal Lassie stars in the story of Bill, a pup who becomes separated from his family and is accidentally wounded. Elizabeth Taylor plays Kathie Merrick, the young girl who rescues Bill, nurses him back to health, and helps him prove what an asset he is. Adult Juror Comments: This classic is a great family film. Lassie's experience may be harder for adults to handle than children. It's quite traumatic. "Lassie the collie is a legend and holds up well over time." Scenes of family life are pretty stereotypical of the 1950s. Kid Juror Comments: Appealing. Wanted to watch again. Opening scenes drew them in immediately. Kids truly love Lassie. Some parts may be scary to younger children. Girls enjoyed it most. Even though it's somewhat old-fashioned, it has lasting values. Age: 6–12; Length: 93 min.; Suggested Retail Price: $14.95, MGM/UA HOME ENTERTAINMENT

** CURLY TOP (SHIRLEY TEMPLE): Shirley Temple and Rochelle Hudson are orphans who adore the rich, young, and handsome trustee of their orphanage. When he falls in love with Hudson, Temple plays matchmaker. Adult Juror Comments: By today's standards, the story line is so unrealistic that even the children noticed it. However, Shirley is still adorable to watch, and the sisters' relationship is affectionate. Some empathized with being orphaned. Shows little cultural diversity, and its social interactions are dated. Kid Juror Comments: Younger children were not able to identify with the orphanage setting. They thought Shirley Temple was too perfect, but enjoyed seeing her sing and dance. Girls liked it much more than boys did. They noticed there were no people from different cultures. All the kids wanted to watch this again. It intrigued them. Age: 5–10; Length: 74 min.; Suggested Retail Price: $19.98, TWENTIETH CENTURY FOX HOME ENTERTAINMENT

*** DANCE ALONG WITH THE DAISE FAMILY (GULLAH GULLAH ISLAND): Preschool program features an African-American family, and this episode celebrates the culture and language of Gullah, an island off South Carolina. Kids learn about life issues through interactive singing, dancing, and play. Adult Juror Comments: Great tunes with great ethnic variety—lots of different danceable beats. "I like the focus of the program on an African-American family." Engaging actions stimulated creative movement and encouraged all to "dance their own special way." Kid Juror Comments: Enthusiastic response with singing and dancing. They commented on the variety of interesting ethnic characters. "I danced my feet off!" Kids loved Binyah Binyah Pollywog. "They're awful good at dancing." Age: 3–8; Length: 30 min.; Suggested Retail Price: $9.95, PARAMOUNT HOME VIDEO

** DAWN AND THE HAUNTED HOUSE (THE BABY-SITTERS CLUB); see p. 307

** DAWN SAVES THE TREES (THE BABY-SITTERS CLUB); see p. 307

* DENNIS THE MENACE STRIKES AGAIN: America's favorite menace is back. When Dennis' grandfather moves in, Mr. Wilson feels he must keep up with his rival. Wilson is conned by bogus ways of regaining his youth. Dennis saves the day by getting Mr. Wilson into precarious situations. Adult Juror Comments: Adults had mixed reactions to this title. Contains name-calling, lying, cheating, gender bias, inappropriate language, and bad behavior. Shows characters' concerns for one another, but the slapstick humor often crosses the boundaries of good taste. Kid Juror Comments: Dennis makes a lot of trouble for everyone, and kids commented, "Dennis gave us some fun ideas." They appreciated that Dennis tries to do the right thing and be nice, but commented, "The girls are disrespected and the older people are treated as though they are stupid." Age: 6–12; Length: 75 min.; Suggested Retail Price: $19.94, WARNER BROS. FAMILY ENTERTAINMENT

** DIG HOLE BUILD HOUSE (REAL WORLD VIDEO): Watch earth-moving bull-dozers dig, giant cement trucks pour, and carpenters, framers, roofers, and plumbers saw materials and pound hammers as they turn an empty field and stacks of lumber into a new home. Adult Juror Comments: Simple production that defines and represents visually the technical terms used. Shots of children playing with dump trucks and using tape measures encourages kids to mimic these in their play. Shows good cultural mix. Kid Juror Comments: Some terminology is too advanced for this age. It's too long to hold kids' attention, better viewed in segments. Children were interested in building something of their own after viewing this. Age: 3–10; Length: 30 min.; Suggested Retail Price: $14.95, REAL WORLD VIDEO

** DOING THE RIGHT THING (YOU CAN CHOOSE!): Doing what's right feels better than doing what you can get away with. When a lost wallet is found on the playground, it brings up the question of what is right. Adult Juror Comments: This is a well-produced program, little long-winded at times, with the right amount of moralizing. It's a good catalyst for discussing honesty and respect. Appropriate for the target age group, it's most suited to a school setting. Kid Juror Comments: It took some encouragement from the adult leader to get the children engaged in the program and discuss it afterwards. Some kids laughed and liked the singing and drama. Others did not. Age: 6–12; Length: 28 min.; Suggested Retail Price: $59.95, LIVE WIRE MEDIA

** DOUBLE DOUBLE TOIL AND TROUBLE (MARY-KATE AND ASHLEY): Make way for spells, witches, wizards, and adventure. It's Halloween, the scariest event of fall. For Lynn and Kelly Farmer, something scarier could happen. They could lose their home, unless the spirited twins find a way to save it. Adult Juror Comments: Amusing. Good family film, especially the black and white flashback scenes. Led to discussion about make-believe, safety, and getting along. The girls running off from their parents is not a good role model. Very age-appropriate and appealing. Kid Juror Comments: Kids loved when the twins used a magic word to make a guy spin. Four- and five-year-olds thought it was scary and the witch was mean. The best part is when the twins dress up as mice. Kids responded to the messages about kindness, love, and caring. Age: 5–8; Length: 93 min.; Suggested Retail Price: $14.95, WARNER HOME VIDEO

*** ELMOPALOOZA (SESAME STREET): Elmo, Big Bird, and the rest of Sesame Street Muppets take over Radio City Music Hall for an all-star show. Rosie O'Donnell, Gloria Estefan, Jon Stewart, Chris Rock, and more join the celebration of thirty years of songs and laughs on Sesame Street. Adult Juror Comments: Funny and entertaining. Music makes everyone want to dance. Great humor, superb mix of learning. Kids are exposed to a variety of rhythm and music, plus interesting facts. Kid Juror Comments: Entranced and entertained. "I want to hear more songs." "I can mambo now!" "I liked when the Cookie Monster eats the script." "I like to dance with this." Age: 5–8; Length: 55 min.; Suggested Retail Price: $12.98, SONY WONDER

* EMILY AND HER FRIENDS; see p. 69

** ENCHANTED TALES: THE LEGEND OF SU-LING: A Far East fairy-tale classic springs to life in this richly animated tale of a handsome prince, the peasant girl he is forbidden to love and the tiny nightingale who holds the key to their happiness. Adult Juror Comments: Teaches values of love, work, and family. Shows a strong female character and sensitive male hero. Songs were catchy. The language is too sophisticated for the audience. Discusses happiness, history, culture. Kid Juror Comments: Enjoyed Su-Ling's character but commented, "I think they were making fun of how Chinese people talk." "Chinese people have fairy tales too." "Girls can protect their families too, not just men can be strong." Age: 6–10; Length: 48 min.; Suggested Retail Price: $9.89, SONY WONDER

*** EWOK ADVENTURE, THE: The furry creatures from "Return of the Jedi" crash-land on the planet Endor, befriend a magical Ewok, and search for their missing parents. Adult Juror Comments: Cinematography is beautiful and creative. Entertaining family viewing that truly appeals to both children and adults. Grabs and holds your attention. Separation from parents, possibly permanently, is a difficult subject for younger ones. Kid Juror Comments: "Children always love animals, real or make-believe." It's surprising how preteen boys were spellbound and openly expressed their fondness for Ewok. The kids really enjoyed the Ewok fight with spiders, and when the Ewoks rescued the parents. Age: 4–15; Length: 96 min.; Suggested Retail Price: $14.95, MGM/UA HOME ENTERTAINMENT

*** EWOKS BATTLE FOR ENDOR: When an army of evil marauders attacks the Ewok village and a young Ewok is kidnaped, his friends set out for the castle fortress of the evil King Terak to rescue him. Thrilling adventure. Story by George Lucas. Adult Juror Comments: This classic film of the '80s is visually and technically lavish and compelling. Though it shows violence as a solution, the jurors did not consider it to be gratuitous. Kid Juror Comments: Liked the adventure, found it exciting, and would definitely want to see it again. *Star Wars* fans in particular adore the characters and story. This is enjoyed equally by both girls and boys. Age: 5–15; Length: 98 min.; Suggested Retail Price: $14.95, MGM/UA HOME ENTERTAINMENT

*** FAMILY TALES (MAURICE SENDAK'S LITTLE BEAR); see p. 70

*** FERNGULLY 2: THE MAGICAL RESCUE: Return to the magical forest of Ferngully where Batty, Crystal, Pips, and the Beetle Boys embark on a great adventure to save natural resources. Adult Juror Comments: Appealing. A modern fairy tale that explores environmental issues at a child's level. Very well produced, with good role models. A wonderful discussion starter about the environment and kids' role in conservation. Kid Juror Comments: Big success. Provoked comments about respect for the environment as well as one another. They loved the animals but they thought the "bad men" looked unrealistic. Age: 4–12; Length: 73 min.; Suggested Retail Price: $19.98, TWENTIETH CENTURY FOX HOME ENTERTAINMENT

** FINGERMOUSE, YOFFY, AND FRIENDS: In each sequence, Yoffy the puppeteer sends Fingermouse and some of his finger-puppet friends on various voyages. With each voyage his friends collect different objects and wisdom that are used to tell a story. Adult Juror Comments: This is delightfully simple, yet intriguing. Says a lot about the power of imagination and storytelling. It could motivate creative work or stimulate children's problem-solving skills. Probably appeals to a limited audience. Kid Juror Comments: The stories went over nicely. Wanted to make finger-puppets, discuss the stories, and write stories of their own after viewing. The first part was lengthy, but the rest of it held the kids' attention. They loved the music and watched it again. Age: 3–8; Length: 180 min.; Suggested Retail Price: $19.95, APPLAUSE VIDEO

** FIRE BUSTERS: Explores the world of firefighting, in which helicopters, planes, boats, and trucks are the tools of the trade. Teaches the importance of teamwork and fire safety. Good song and dance. Adult Juror Comments: Simple production that shows examples of cooperation and teamwork. Promotes positive messages about recycling and cleaning up. Firefighting footage provoked a lot of discussion after viewing the tape. The music is catchy; the host is appropriate. Kid Juror Comments: Fascinated. Prompted many questions about safety issues. They asked to see the helicopter and the seaplane section again. Age: 4–7; Length: 30 min.; Suggested Retail Price: $12.95, AZURE BLUES, INC.

*** FLIPPER: The film that brought world awareness to the amazing intelligence of dolphins through a story about a young boy who develops a unique friendship with a wounded dolphin and loves him as a friend. Stars Chuck Connors as the fisherman. Adult Juror Comments: Excellent family film with timely messages and positive role models. Content is great. Story is well presented. Cinematography is beautiful. And it's educational. Requires a good attention span and thinking skills. Parts are completely unrealistic. Kid Juror Comments: Stands the test of time. Older kids enjoyed it most. Younger kids ask lots of questions about the story details. Opening may be a little slow, but after becoming engaged the kids responded well. Most appropriate for six- to ten-year-olds. Age: 3–11; Length: 91 min.; Suggested Retail Price: $14.95, MGM/UA HOME ENTERTAINMENT

** FLIPPER'S NEW ADVENTURE: Sandy and Flipper are threatened by the impending construction of a freeway to be built on their property. To avoid losing Flipper to the local aquarium, Sandy retreats to the sea with him. Adult Juror Comments: While the story is a bit corny, it's sweet. The talents of Flipper are fantastic. It starts out slowly but gains momentum when they get to the island. "Flipper is the hero." Underwater photography is outstanding. Kid Juror Comments: Opening is slow and didn't pull children in. Once they became engaged in the story they enjoyed it. Kids love to watch Flipper's antics. Age: 4–12; Length: 95 min.; Suggested Retail Price: $14.95, MGM/UA HOME ENTERTAINMENT

*** FRANKLIN PLAYS THE GAME: Franklin's soccer team loses every game, but he's still determined to be the best player on the team. Ultimately he learns to put his team ahead of himself as he rallies them for the final game. Also includes the episode "Franklin and the Red Scooter." Adult Juror Comments: Great moral content! Sweet characters. Franklin sorts through situations to find solutions, shows good sportsmanship and cooperation. Insight into familiar problems. Girls and boys play soccer. Kid Juror Comments: Related enthusiastically to the theme of team spirit. Loved the cartoon turtle and friends of all different shapes and sizes. They learned about turning negative feelings into positive ones. "Sharing is nice." Age: 3–8; Length: 25 min.; Suggested Retail Price: $12.95, POLYGRAM VIDEO

** FREEDOM ROCKS; see p. 71

*FRUIT & JINGLES: A LEARNING EXPERIENCE: In true clown fashion, transforms a series of adventures and misadventures into positive learning experiences: fair play, safety, sharing, cooperation, perseverance, and more. Adult Juror Comments: Funny situations are used to teach lessons. Discussion center around safety, making friends, littering, and valuing differences. The pace is slow and the characters are so silly that they are irritating and even condescending. Kid Juror Comments: Funny clowns. "It made me want to find out if there are more fruits and jingle videos." "I learned it's good to share things and that you should wear a bike helmet." Kids said they understood everything and liked the music. Age: 4–7; Length: 30 min.; Suggested Retail Price: $19.95,

** FUN HOUSE MYSTERY (THE ADVENTURES OF MARY-KATE AND ASHLEY): The pint-size twins take a spin on spine-tingling amusement park rides and then team up with some hilarious pirates of the midway to catch the scary monster that lurks inside the freaky Fun House. Adult Juror Comments: Appeals to kids interested in youthful detective stories. Introduces the idea of using reference materials. Alliteration and tongue-twisters abound. Non-violent and entertaining, it teaches about facing our fears. Songs are cute. Kid Juror Comments: Kids enjoyed the twins and their singing. They liked following the mystery, clues, and solving the problem. "It was funny when they screamed at the orangutan. My friends would like the scary monster part." Age: 5–8; Length: 30 min.; Suggested Retail Price: $12.95, WARNER VISION

* GARFIELDS'S FELINE FANTASIES: Garfield's ruminations take him in and out of creative, imaginative daydreams with inventive scenarios. With clever script and characters, Garfield's adventures take him all over the world. Encourages children to use their imagination. Adult Juror Comments: Entertaining but somewhat sexist. Lots of name-calling, like "slobber-job and fatso." Displays positive messages such as "feeling good about yourself."

Shows people drinking and smoking. Animation is appealing and the focus on imagination encouraging. Kid Juror Comments: Pretty silly. They liked watching Garfield in his many adventures. Most would watch it again. Some commented on the smoking and drinking. Age: 5–10; Length: 23 min.; Suggested Retail Price: $5.98, TWENTIETH CENTURY FOX HOME ENTERTAINMENT

** GIANT OF THUNDER MOUNTAIN, THE: Exciting family adventure features Richard Kiel as the giant who must overcome an evil carnival operator, the prejudice of a small town and a 1,500-pound grizzly bear. Adult Juror Comments: Good acting, good story, dealing with differences by showing the damage that prejudice can inflict on society and an individual. Production well-paced for kids. Kid Juror Comments: Exciting. Older kids gave it an all-star. Held everyone's attention straight through until the end. Under-fives were scared when the bear appeared. "The pictures were great." Age: 5–12; Length: 88 min.; Suggested Retail Price: $19.95, AMERICAN HAPPENINGS

*** GOLDILOCKS AND THE THREE BEARS: Goldie, a ten-year-old orphaned city girl, is sent to live with her uncle, deep in a forest, where Goldie discovers three bears who can talk. When the bears realize she is the new protector of their enchanted forest they find their work cut out for them. Adult Juror Comments: Well-made and appealing with good messages. Animals and environment are cute and friendly. Could generate interest and discussion about orphans, the environment, lifestyles, and personal relationships. It's well paced and the perfect length. Kid Juror Comments: "The movie was creative, the acting was good, the forest is important." "I want to know how to stop people from cutting down trees." Kids also pointed out their awareness that "bears can't really talk." Age: 6–12; Length: 85 min.; Suggested Retail Price: $19.95, NEXUS MEDIA INTERNATIONAL

* GREAT LAND OF SMALL, THE (LES PRODUCTIONS LA FETE): When two children from New York spend a weekend with their grandparents, they befriend Fritz, one of the little people, whose gold dust has been stolen. They journey to the Great Land of Small, where they meet some interesting characters before all ends well. Adult Juror Comments: This imaginative fantasy is wonderfully creative but slow-moving and dark. Special effects are well done, the story is executed with care. Appeals to a limited audience. Adult characters are not well developed. Kid Juror Comments: Some scenes seem staged, and the pace is at times tedious. The Land of the Small goes on for too long. The scenes in which the children become immortal and can't return home are not comprehensible by the intended age group. Age: 4–10;

Length: 91 min.; Suggested Retail Price: $29.95, LES PRODUCTIONS LA FETE/ANCHOR BAY

* GRUMPY TREE, THE; see p. 71

* HANSEL AND GRETEL: AN OPERA FANTASY (CHILDREN'S CULTURAL COLLECTION): This version of Engelbert Humperdinck's 1893 opera stars hand-sculpted dolls and lavish sets that create a fantasy land of eerie beauty. The soundtrack received a Grammy nomination. Adult Juror Comments: Although there is background noise, the music is lovely. Animation style is dated and pace seems slow. Hansel and Gretel have a babyish quality. Kid Juror Comments: Younger kids loved it and watched it again. The music and the puppets were a big hit. Some older kids found it too slow. It was difficult for sophisticated music listeners. Age: 6–12; Length: 72 min.; Suggested Retail Price: $19.98, V.I.E.W. VIDEO

** HERMAN AND MARGUERITE (JAY O'CALLAHAN): Herman, a fearful worm, befriends an equally anxious caterpillar, Marguerite. They learn to love and respect each other as they help bring spring to the earth. Adult Juror Comments: Wonderful storytelling, production requires viewers' imagination. Kid Juror Comments: Requires patience and attention. Some did not "get it" or understand the language. Others thought it was just beautiful. Age: 5–12; Length: 28 min.; Suggested Retail Price: $19.95, VINEYARD VIDEO PRODUCTIONS, INC.

** HOW THE WEST WAS FUN (MARY-KATE AND ASHLEY): Mary-Kate and Ashley lead the battle of wits and wills to save the beloved ranch in this feature-length comedy. Adult Juror Comments: Fun, good production quality. Appealing characters, simplistic plot. May create curiosity about mining, camping, nature, and solving problems as they arise. Shows kids working together for their family. Men were shown in a non-traditional light. Kid Juror Comments: Kids liked seeing the girls sing and dance, although they found the storyline to be old. Their favorite parts were the treasure hunt for gold and building a sand castle. "Lots of funny things happened at the ranch. It would be fun to live there." Age: 5–8; Length: 93 min.; Suggested Retail Price: $14.95, WARNER HOME VIDEO

* I CAN FLY—A CHILD'S VIEW OF AIRPLANES AND FLIGHT: This video explores the exciting world of flight, including airplane rides, space exploration and hot-air ballooning. Also joins a pilot in a commercial jet. Adult Juror Comments: Fairly well done, this program holds most kids' interest. Though slow-moving throughout, kids liked the visuals. It may work best with an accompanying discussion about planes, pilots, and space. Not much diversity. Kid Juror Comments: Those with a particular interest or knowledge in airplanes or space found it most enjoyable. Some kids watched it repeatedly. It held the attention for the older kids more than the younger ones. Age: 5–8; Length: 32 min.; Suggested Retail Price: $19.95, MIK VIDEO PRODUCTIONS, INC.

* IMAGINARIA; see p. 310

see p. 310

* IN SEARCH OF THE HAUNTED GOLD MINE (ADVENTURES OF DAVE & BECKY, THE): Dave and Becky are reporters for the hottest children's newspaper in the country, "The Daily Adventure." Their assignment: investigate rumors about a haunted gold mine deep in the woods. The adventure also includes safe camping tips. Adult Juror Comments: The safety tips provide valuable information for potential campers. Segment on caring for animals was well done. Some adults disliked the humor and the gender stereotypes. It portrays a smart woman and a dumb man. Kid Juror Comments: Those who enjoy camping thought it was great, responding well to the hosts and their humor. "Good camping ideas. I learned about hypothermia." One five-year-old found some parts scary. Age: 6–11; Length: 37 min.; Suggested Retail Price: $12.99, THE DAILY ADVENTURE LTD.

** IN SEARCH OF THE WILLIE T (ROUNDABOUT TALES): A pirate who lost his ship heads out to search for it. He boards a schooner, a Coast Guard buoy tender and a submarine. This tongue-in-cheek adventure has laugh potential for kids and adults. Adult Juror Comments: It should be made clear this is a documentary about vessels. Characters were enjoyable. Shows variety of ships, compares old technologies to today's, also covers water safety and other boating subjects. Kid Juror Comments: "This was interesting. I learned a lot about ships." "The captain was a nice pirate." Kids liked the songs. "We did not know how submarines and torpedoes worked." Lots of interesting information is covered. Age: 5–8; Length: 25 min.; Suggested Retail Price: $11.00, SOBO VIDEO PRODUCTIONS, INC

*** INDIAN IN THE CUPBOARD, THE: Based on an award-winning, best-selling children's book, "Indian in the Cupboard" is a touching tale of nine-year-old Omri, who magically brings his three-inch toy Indian to life. Together they embark upon a fabulous adventure. Adult Juror Comments: Very engaging. This is a wonderful extension of the book series. Kids portrayed characters from the program for weeks after viewing. It offers respect for Native American culture and kept the kids' attention. Kid Juror Comments: Fine, in general. Those familiar with the book responded particularly well.

"There was a little bit of fighting between the characters, but good fighting." It motivated the children to further the explore Native American culture. Age: 5–8; Length: 98 min.; Suggested Retail Price: $14.95, COLUMBIA TRISTAR HOME VIDEO

*** IT WAS MY BEST BIRTHDAY EVER, CHARLIE BROWN (PEANUTS): The Peanuts kids get together for their blanket-toting pal's birthday party. Linus wants all his friends to come to his party. Most of all, the birthday boy wants a very special guest to be there. He invites Mimi. Adult Juror Comments: Engages both kids and adults. Good cultural diversity, appropriate humor, and good manners. Sibling and safety issues are handled well. "I like the use of music, foreign language and safety themes." "One of the best videos I've ever seen." Kid Juror Comments: Upbeat, fun, well paced, and very enjoyable! Children love this video. Motivated discussions after about how to celebrate birthdays and the concept of an R.S.V.P. Kids sang along. "I'd like to take it home and share it with my family." Age: 4–9; Length: 25 min.; Suggested Retail Price: $12.95, PARAMOUNT PICTURES

** IT TAKES TWO (MARY-KATE AND ASHLEY): What does it take to bring a single, attractive orphanage case worker and a widowed corporate bazillionaire together? It takes sly maneuvers, crazy mixups and clever switcheroos. Most of all IT TAKES TWO Olsen twins. Adult Juror Comments: Positive story in which the girls resolve problems such as anger and conflict between themselves and the adults. Set in a real world with valid social pressures. Acting is believable and endearing. Stimulates kids and parents to communicate better. Kid Juror Comments: Captured kids' attention for the entire story. Kids cheered the twins' success. They discussed how everyone is capable and worthy of love and how the girls worked together to make their wish come true. Best parts were New York City and summer camp. Age: 5–8; Length: 101 min.; Suggested Retail Price: $19.98, WARNER HOME VIDEO

** IT'S NOT ALWAYS EASY BEING A KID; see p. 310

** IT'S THE PLACE TO BE! (OPRYLAND KIDS CLUB): High-energy music-driven fun. Janet and the kids get a thrill when Crystal Gayle pays a visit to their show. Adult Juror Comments: Humorous, fast, and musical. The songs contain positive self-esteem messages about friendship and positive thinking. Story line is a little weak. Shows limited racial diversity. Kid Juror Comments: "A very happy movie." They got up and danced along with the video. "I liked the songs, but the people look like they're not really saying the words." The children wanted to watch it again. Age: 5–8; Length: 28 min.; Suggested Retail Price: $12.00, PRO KIDS PRODUCTIONS

* JAMES AND THE GIANT PEACH; see p. 311

*** JAZZ TIME TALE: It's 1919 in New York City. Lucinda stops on her way home to hear her neighbor Thomas "Fats" Waller play the piano. In another part of the city, Rose hides in the back of her father's car when he goes to the Lincoln Theater. Narrated by Ruby Dee. Adult Juror Comments: A wonderful, insightful look at one of America's icons, which combines history and fantasy. This story blends divergent lives and shows how similar, in fact, we all are. It's a great film that honors children of color. Kid Juror Comments: African-American children stated that this film made them proud of their heritage. The children didn't want the story to end. "I wish that I could play piano like that." "I like that the two girls became friends forever." Age: 6–12; Length: 27 min.; Suggested Retail Price: $9.98, ARTISAN/FAMILY HOME ENTERTAINMENT

** JESSI & THE MYSTERY OF THE STOLEN SECRETS (THE BABY-SITTERS CLUB); see p. 311

** JET PINK; see p. 311

** JOURNEY BEGINS, THE; see p. 312

*** KRATTS' CREATURES: CHECKIN OUT CHIMPS: Swing around with Chris and Martin Kratts as they explore Africa and discover the wild chimpanzee. You'll see how chimps can be smart, playful, and a whole lot of laughs. Adult Juror Comments: "Yes, yes, yes!" Fascinating, hilarious, educational, and entertaining— full of surprising facts and new vocabulary. Excellent personal interaction and great messages about animal respect. Excellent teaching tool. Kid Juror Comments: Funny, sad and informative. "Those chimps are cute." Kids love exploring with the Kratts brothers. The creatures fascinated them. "Animals are neat." "I didn't know they did all those things." Age: 5–11; Length: 25 min.; Suggested Retail Price: $12.95, POLY-GRAM VIDEO

** KRISTEN'S FAIRY HOUSE: Join Kristen as she vacations on a small island off the New England coast with her Aunt Tracy, an artist. Tracy is creating a picture book about "fairy houses" built in the woods by visiting children. A special relationship develops between them. Adult Juror Comments: Enjoyable, easy to watch, though very low-key. There is no conflict, no character development. There is a natural rapport between adult and child and a link between nature and art, imagination, and life. Further inquiry is possible for make -believe. Kid Juror Comments: They liked how the pictures tell the story. Girls liked it more than boys. Some thought it was too slow. Children were interested in building a fairy house. Age: 5–8; Length: 40 min.; Suggested Retail Price: $19.99, GREAT WHITE DOG PICTURE CO.

** KRISTY AND THE GREAT CAMPAIGN (THE BABY-SITTERS CLUB); see p. 312

*** LAND BEFORE TIME II: THE GREAT VALLEY ADVENTURE, THE: The prehistoric pals Littlefoot, Cera, Spike, Ducky, and Petrie return in this new movie with original songs, colorful animation, and the beloved dinosaurs from "The Land Before Time." Adult Juror Comments: Tells a highly moral story without being preachy. Excellent, high-quality animation. Teaches kids to accept differences as well as how to get along with one another. A little too violent and scary for younger audiences. Kid Juror Comments: Entertaining. Grasped the message: Parents have reasons for the things they do and they're not just trying to keep you from having fun. Two-year-olds found it too scary. Age: 4–10; Length: 74 min.; Suggested Retail Price: $19.98, UNIVERSAL STUDIOS HOME VIDEO

*** LAND BEFORE TIME III: THE TIME OF GREAT GIVING, THE: When a huge meteorite plunges into the Great Valley, it cuts off the water supply to the dinosaurs. Searching for more water, Littlefoot and his friends find a large trapped pool. They learn how they can move mountains by working together. Adult Juror Comments: A morality play that rewards cooperation, delivers environmental messages and rewards good thinking. Shows how diverse groups can co-exist and become friends. "Virtue is rewarded and kids are the heroes." The songs and music are engaging. Kid Juror Comments: The characters are wonderful. Many were familiar with them. "The raptors are cool." Some kids thought the songs were too long, others were mesmerized. "The long necks told the other dinosaurs to share, people should share also." Age: 4–8; Length: 71 min.; Suggested Retail Price: $19.98, UNIVERSAL STUDIOS HOME VIDEO

*** LAND BEFORE TIME IV: JOURNEY THROUGH THE MISTS, THE: Littlefoot, Cera, Spike, Ducky, Petrie, and a shy newcomer, Ali, set off in search of a mysterious, healing flower that grows only in the Land of Mists. A song-filled, animated addition to the continuing story of *The Land Before Time*. Adult Juror Comments: Excellent, well produced. Opportunities to discuss friendships, making new friends, and the impact of moving frequently. The characters are very sweet. Some scenes are scary. Teamwork is emphasized. Appealing songs support messages in story. Kid Juror Comments: Great happy ending. They empathize with Little Foot. "Little Foot is very brave and good to his friends because he can't do everything himself." Children wanted to watch this again and talked about it with one another. Age: 4–7; Length: 74 min.; Suggested Retail Price: $19.98, UNIVERSAL STUDIOS HOME VIDEO

*** LAND BEFORE TIME V: THE MYSTERIOUS ISLAND, THE: Beyond the Great Valley lies an island of beauty and mystery. In this wondrous place, Littlefoot, Cera, Spike, Ducky, and Petrie discover old and new friends, face exciting challenges, and share the adventure of a lifetime. Adult Juror Comments: Good animation, characters, music, and scenery. Teaches children to respect racial differences, emphasizes the importance of friends and family, and promotes the concept of collaboration. The earthquake, sharks, and carnivorous dinosaurs were scary. Kid Juror Comments: Very cute. It held everyone's interest. Kids wanted to watch it again with their friends. They thought some of the characters were frightening and mean. They liked Chomper best. "Good music!" "I like when they got back with their mommy and daddy." Age: 4–10; Length: 74 min.; Suggested Retail Price: $19.98, UNIVERSAL STUDIOS HOME VIDEO

*** LAND BEFORE TIME VI: SECRET OF SAURUS ROCK, THE: On a distant edge of the Great Valley stands mysterious Saurus Rock. The twin baby threehorns, Dianah and Dana, have run away to find it. It's up to Littlefoot, Cera, Spike, Ducky, and Petrie to bring them back. Adult Juror Comments: Enjoyable family entertainment. Presents valuable concepts such as dealing with fears, family members as heroes, helping one another and having faith in oneself. Animation is well done. Provides a basis for a discussion about self-esteem. Kid Juror Comments: Excited to see a new adventure with their dinosaur friends. The songs captured the children's attention. "I want to draw dinosaurs." One juror commented, "My daughter has been reading about dinosaurs for weeks now." Age: 3–7; Length: 77 min.; Suggested Retail Price: $19.98, UNIVERSAL STUDIOS HOME VIDEO

*** LARGER THAN LIFE; see p. 313

*** LASSIE COME HOME: Roddy McDowell stars as Joe, the young boy to whom Lassie is forever loyal. After Joe's father sells Lassie to a wealthy duke, she escapes and travels 100 miles to return to the boy she loves. This was Elizabeth Taylor's magnificent screen debut. Adult Juror Comments: Warm, touching story of human-animal devotion, the rewards of perseverance and loyalty, human kindness. Enormous evergreen appeal as a family film. Kid Juror Comments: Responded to the emotionality and suspense despite the old-fashioned feel. They cheered when Lassie escaped, cried when she was hurt, and thoroughly enjoyed themselves. This belongs in every library of children's classic films. Age: 6–12; Length: 89 min.; Suggested Retail Price: $14.95, MGM/UA HOME ENTERTAINMENT

* LET'S DO IT! (PROFESSOR IRIS); see p. 73

* LIFE WITH LOUIE: THE MASKED CHESS BOY; see p. 313

** LITTLE DRUMMER BOY: A lonely little boy discovers the greatest gift of all on a winter's night in Bethlehem. Narrated by Greer Garson with songs by the Vienna Boy's Choir. Adult Juror Comments: This classic tale represents good values. It's well produced and diverse, though somewhat dated like other Christmas tapes from this era. Kid Juror Comments: Kids enjoyed it. They were sad when the lamb starts to die. Kids liked the creatures and seeing the various cultures. Age: 7–12; Length: 27 min.; Suggested Retail Price: $12.98, ARTISAN/FAMILY HOME ENTERTAINMENT

*** LITTLE MEN: Louisa May Alcott's classic novel comes to life in this film starring Mariel Hemingway as the matriarch of a rural family in the late 1800s. When two troubled boys join the house, one fits in fine but the other can't leave behind his city ways. Adult Juror Comments: This is well produced with beautiful footage and good costumes. Insight into human nature and empathy toward others. Demonstrates powerful moral lessons. Made students curious about other time periods and differences in their lives. Kid Juror Comments: Makes children think about the consequences of their actions. "Gambling, smoking, and lying are stupid." "It was good at explaining what not to do and what it was like growing up in that time period." "I wish I could watch this every day." Age: 6–12; Length: 97 min.; Suggested Retail Price: $19.94, WARNER BROS. FAMILY ENTERTAINMENT

** LITTLE MERMAID, THE (ANIMATED CLASSICS): Princess Lena, a beautiful and adventurous mermaid, has everything she could ever need but longs to travel to the ocean's surface and explore the world of humans. Adult Juror Comments: An engaging, favorite story. Compared to the Disney version, it's weak, with a lot of sexual stereotyping in this version. Kid Juror Comments: Reenacted the story afterwards, touching off a discussion of the likelihood of witches and whether or not one could be mean and still be beautiful. Age: 4–8; Length: 50 min.; Suggested Retail Price: $19.95, GOODTIMES HOME VIDEO

*** LITTLE NEMO COLLECTOR'S SET: Little Nemo journeys to Slumberland, where he encounters the world of Nightmares. He uses the magical royal scepter to free the King of Slumberland and put an end to Nightmare World. Nemo returns to a hero's welcome and flies away into the moonlight. Adult Juror Comments: It's somewhat scary with a basic good-versus-evil story line. The early 20th-century time frame is a little confusing. Kid Juror Comments: Appealing. Some recommended it to others and asked to view it again. Afterward, they used the cassette and drew pictures about the movie. Age: 4–8; Length: 84 min.; Suggested Retail Price: $29.95, PLAZA ENTERTAINMENT

** LITTLE SISTER RABBIT: A whimsical journey through one day in the lives of a boy rabbit and his lovable but stubborn little sister. Adult Juror Comments: Sensitively deals with being an older sibling. There is a difficult scene of the burial of the rabbits' mother. Some negative stereotypes and name-calling. Kid Juror Comments: Likeable story and characters. Prompted a lively discussion about siblings and helping out. Appropriate for ages five and up. Age: 4–8; Length: 25 min.; Suggested Retail Price: $12.98, ARTISAN/FAMILY HOME ENTERTAINMENT

** MAGIC MAP, THE (THE ADVENTURES OF ELMER & FRIENDS): Imagine the thrill of finding an old treasure map, then finding yourself with the man who drew it, who happens to be the author of *Treasure Island*, Robert Louis Stevenson. In the end, "The Magic Map" reveals how easy it is to find a treasure in a book. Adult Juror Comments: Simple production that uses humor, imagination, dance, and song to present ideas about writing stories. Not enough assets to warrant an all-star. The children were disappointed with the ending, which doesn't conclude with finding where the treasure map leads to. Contains Christian overtones. Kid Juror Comments: Lots to like: the humor, the dancing, the songs, and the treasure map. It held their attention. "They treated each other well." "The crow was really silly." "I liked when they went to the beach." Age: 4–7; Length: 30 min.; Suggested Retail Price: $14.95, FEATHERWIND PRODUCTIONS

* MAGICAL WORLD OF TRAINS; see p. 73

*** MAMA DO YOU LOVE ME?; see p. 74

** MARY-KATE AND ASHLEY OLSEN: OUR FIRST VIDEO: From the hit ABC series *Full House*, this program contains seven music videos. The girls introduce each segment with wit and humor, providing a glimpse of life behind the camera. Adult Juror Comments: It's awfully cute, maybe too much so. Fans of the Olsen twins will appreciate it most. Variety of music and good costumes is well selected and appropriate. Kid Juror Comments: The Peanut Butter Band was a favorite. After the screening some children dressed up like Mary-Kate and Ashley had in the video. As expected, the Olsen twins' fans thought this was right up their alley. Age: 5–9; Length: 30 min.; Suggested Retail Price: $12.95, WARNERVISION ENTERTAINMENT

** ME AND MY TUGBOAT; see p. 74

** MRN: CIRCUS FUN; see p. 74

*** MRN: MONSTERS AND DINOSAURS (MISTER ROGERS' NEIGHBORHOOD): Mister Rogers, everybody's trusted neighbor, helps young children understand scary monsters. Visits a dinosaur exhibit and offers reassurances about scary dreams. Adult Juror Comments: Well-paced, not flashy but very solid and child-centered. Encourages listening skills. Kid Juror Comments: An all-time favorite. Because it's long, most adults played it in segments, which worked well. Subject matter held child's attention. Age: 2–7; Length: 64 min.; Suggested Retail Price: $12.95, FAMILY COMMUNICATIONS, INC.

*** MRN: WHAT ABOUT LOVE; see p. 76

** MS. BEAR: A direct-to-video, heartwarming family film featuring Ed Begley Jr., Shaun Johnston, Kaitlyn Burke, and an adorable brown bear. Adult Juror Comments: Story line discusses animal safety, human values, respect, and forgiveness at a child's level. It's age-appropriate, engaging, and well executed. Adults were concerned that portrayal of a female bear doesn't address how dangerous she is. Kid Juror Comments: Ms. Bear was funny and wonderful. "It made me feel happy, sad, and excited." Afterward, it stimulated lots of discussion about forgiveness. Age: 5–12; Length: 95 min.; Suggested Retail Price: $12.00, CABIN FEVER ENTERTAINMENT

** MUMFIE, THE MOVIE: An extra-special little elephant searches for adventure. He joins his friends to recapture the Cloak of Dreams and return to a magical island of happiness. Fourteen sing-along songs move the story along. Adult Juror Comments: This plot weaves magic throughout, touching on loneliness and friendship. Delightful animation, songs, and darling characters. Contains some aggressive language. Visually it appeals to preschoolers, but the plot is geared for children five to eight. Kid Juror Comments: Mesmerized. Even though it was a bit long, kids became very involved in the story, the characters and the outcome. There was never a dull moment. The kids wanted to watch it again. Age: 4–8; Length: 110 min.; Suggested Retail Price: $14.98, BMG VIDEO

** MUPPET TREASURE ISLAND: Robert Louis Stevenson's classic adventure takes a new twist. Jim Hawkins inherits a pirate's treasure map, hires a ship with Captain Smollett (Kermit) and the evil Long John Silver (Tim Curry). Miss Piggy plays Benjamina Gunn, dressed to kill. Adult Juror Comments: The characters, both live and puppets, interact well and appeal to children. The introduction of the crew on-board ship is priceless. The story jumps around and at times it's scary for younger kids. A little slow. Kid Juror Comments: Older kids loved the story and the singing. They stayed for the entire program. Kids were very excited to see Kermit and Miss Piggy, some perennial favorites. It was too scary for the younger ones. Age: 5–12; Length: 100 min.; Suggested Retail Price: $19.99, WALT DISNEY HOME VIDEO

* MYSTERY LIGHTS OF NAVAJO MESA (THE LAST CHANCE DETECTIVES): Four kids escape boredom in a small desert town by forming a detective agency and taking on unwanted and unsolved cases. Mysterious lights in the desert and a local museum heist draw them into a bigger plot than they expect. Adult Juror Comments: A compelling story, technically well produced and good for family viewing. The characters and dialogue seem contrived at times. The story is slow to develop. Contains biblical references. Kid Juror Comments: The story went over the best. Most biblical references went over the heads of the kids, but they found the story exciting and loved the youth detective angle. Age: 5–10; Length: 50 min.; Suggested Retail Price: $19.99, TYNDALE HOUSE PUBLISHERS

** NAMU, MY BEST FRIEND (FAMILY TREASURES): Hank Donner, a naturalist, studies whales in the Pacific Northwest. A dying female killer whale beaches herself, and her heartsick companion refuses to leave her side. Donner tries to help, but the local fishermen are irate since they fear killer whales. Adult Juror Comments: Wonderful movie, stimulated lots of discussion. It is slightly dated and shows smoking by the main character. There is a distinct lack of people of color. Still, most families will enjoy this. Kid Juror Comments: Older kids enjoyed this tremendously. Stimulated lots of discussion about how things change over time, although gets off to a slow start. Younger kids lost the meaning but still found it intriguing. Age: 5–13; Length: 89 min.; Suggested Retail Price: $14.95, MGM/UA HOME ENTERTAINMENT

*** NEW KID, THE (CABBAGE PATCH KIDS): The Cabbage Patch dolls come to life—singing and dancing. Norma Jean, the new kid, shows how everybody is special when she saves the day in the school talent show (animated). Adult Juror Comments: Wonderful, thought-out story. Humorously deals with sensitive issue. Character development is excellent; language is reality-based. Addresses being picked on and working together. Content is suitable for older kids, but presentation is suited to younger ones. Kid Juror Comments: Readily identified with Norma Jean and her situation. They enjoyed the story and thought the music was cute and fit right in. Humor was right at their age level, though the boys thought the dolls were silly. Most would watch it again. Age: 4–8; Length: 30 min.; Suggested Retail Price: $12.98, BMG VIDEO

* NODDY MAKES A NEW FRIEND: Noddy meets a "bunkey," claiming to be half-monkey, half-bunny. Noddy befriends the bunkey, who then causes trouble by taking the possessions of others and giving them to Noddy as thanks for his kindness. Includes two additional episodes. Adult Juror Comments: Noddy's new friend's behavior—theft without consequence—is inappropriate. The production is charming with adorable animation and catchy tunes. Best viewed with an adult in order to discuss the bad behavior. Kid Juror Comments: Bunkey was a hit. Liked Noddy's car and seeing Noddy help Pink Cat find her tail. They discussed Bunkey's lying, disrespect for the police, and stealing other people's belongings. They didn't like animation that failed to move the mouths of the characters. Age: 4–7; Length: 30 min.; Suggested Retail Price: $12.95, POLYGRAM VIDEO

** ONCE UPON A FOREST: Three Furling friends undertake a dangerous journey after a chemical spill destroys Dapplewood and a young friend becomes ill from its toxic fumes. Their wisdom pays off as they restore Dapplewood to its original splendor. Adult Juror Comments: Animals and animation are cute; characters are believable. The story includes a parent's death, which is a difficult issue for a child of this age. Should be viewed with an adult. Kid Juror Comments: The story heightened children's awareness about environmental issues and provoked questions about differences. Some parts were scary. Kids noticed and commented on how all the animals cooperate with one another. Age: 5–8; Length: 71 min.; Suggested Retail Price: $14.98, TWENTIETH CENTURY FOX HOME ENTERTAINMENT

* OPERATION: SECRET BIRTHDAY SURPRISE (THE ADVENTURES OF TIMMY THE TOOTH): Explore Flossmore Valley, where Timmy the Tooth lives with his best buddy Brushbrush and a neighborhood full of lovable characters. Adult Juror Comments: Well produced with creative concepts and songs but tries to cover too many things at once. Conveys a very commercial feeling and lacked adequate useful information about tooth care. Often the terms used related to health have no explanations. Kid Juror Comments: Enjoyed the muppet characters but thought the program was too slow. Their attention wandered. Older kids thought it was too busy and too silly. They did not want to watch it again. Age: 3–8; Length: 30 min.; Suggested Retail Price: $12.98, UNIVERSAL STUDIOS HOME VIDEO

** PAGEMASTER, THE: Richard Tyler enters an empty library and is swept away into the Pagemaster's magical world. Famous literary characters come to life, and young Richard must conquer his fears to return home. Stars Macaulay Culkin, Whoopi Goldberg, and Patrick Stewart. Adult Juror Comments: Well-animated story that provides a glimpse into some classic tales. It could motivate reading or encourage children's interest in libraries. Some parts are scary for younger viewers and depict unsafe behavior. Kid Juror Comments: Related to the child's change from being scared to being brave. Children enjoyed this adventure and the characters from the book. It prompted a discussion about feelings afterwards. Age: 5–12; Length: 76 min.; Suggested Retail Price: $22.98, TWENTIETH CENTURY FOX HOME ENTERTAINMENT

** PAPER BAG PLAYERS ON TOP OF SPAGHETTI, THE; see p. 77

** PEANUT BUTTER SOLUTION, THE; see p. 315

** PET FORGETTERS CURE, THE/NEVER-WANT-TO-GO-TO-BEDDERS CURE (SHELLEY DUVALL PRESENTS MRS. PIGGLE-WIGGLE): Mrs. Piggle-Wiggle has a knack for helping kids and their parents out of the stickiest situations. She's a genius at finding uncommon solutions to the challenges of growing up. Stars Jean Stapleton, Ed Begley Jr., Shelly Duvall, and Phyllis Diller. Adult Juror Comments: Here's a silly fantasy with real people, based on the books by the same title but not quite as entertaining. The individual segments are appealing. Kid Juror Comments: Six years old and up enjoyed this the best. Under, fives had difficulty paying attention. The humor is pretty corny, even for kids and it's way too verbal. It had a hard time holding kids' interest. Age: 3–10; Length: 57 min.; Suggested Retail Price: $12.98, UNIVERSAL STUDIOS HOME VIDEO

** PETER AND THE WOLF: The timeless tale is brought to life with such stars as Kirstie Alley, Lloyd Bridges, Ross Mulinger, and the whole new cast of unforgettable animated characters from the legendary Chuck Jones. Adult Juror Comments: The story is wonderful, with lovely music and beautiful sets. Adults found the animation flat and dull. Little cultural diversity. The story is a little long. Kid Juror Comments: Delightful. The kids loved it and wanted to watch again. They enjoyed the music, the characters, and how they take care of one other. "We liked the part where the duck did a happy dance." Age: 5–8; Length: 60 min.; Suggested Retail Price: $14.98, BMG VIDEO

** PINOCCHIO (ANIMATED CLASSICS): Pinocchio longs to be a real boy. The Blue Fairy watching over Pinocchio helps him escape from danger. When the Blue Fairy becomes ill and Pinocchio assists her, she grants his wish as a reward. Adult Juror Comments: A good story with some modernized narration and some stereotypes. Teaches never to talk to strangers, not to lie, and to care for others. Animation is not equal to Disney's. Production and music are mediocre. Kid Juror Comments: A three-year-old watched it three more times. The length was just right for him. Age: 4–8; Length: 50 min.; Suggested Retail Price: $19.95, GOODTIMES HOME VIDEO

** PIRATE ISLAND (THE ADVENTURES OF ELMER & FRIENDS): How would you like a treasure chest of valuable learning adventures? Benjamin Ouid, the pirate, his parrot, Yappy, and monkey, Mappy, help youngsters discover the rewards of unexpected acts of kindness and the priceless value of good friends. Adult Juror Comments: Corny production with pleasant scenery, songs and respectful characters, but it's a bit slow and sappy and transitions are awkward. Encourages language, singing, and expressive movement. Language is age-appropriate. Christian content. Kid Juror Comments: The girls tended to like the music, the boys liked the pirate. "I wanted to learn the songs." "All the people were nice to each other." "We would love to find a buried treasure." They were captivated by the pirate and bored by the slower songs. Age: 3–7; Length: 30 min.; Suggested Retail Price: $14.95, FEATHERWIND PRODUCTIONS

* PLAY ALONG WITH BINYAH AND FRIENDS (GULLAH GULLAH ISLAND); see p. 78

*RAGGEDY ANN & ANDY: THE MABBIT ADVENTURE: The Mabbits have tried to keep their Book of Spells hidden from the evil wizard, but they are no match for his magic. As a last resort they turn themselves into statues and Raggedy Ann, Raggedy Andy, and Sunny Bunny's magic pen saves the day. Adult Juror Comments: The structure of this story is complicated and seems contrived. It tries to show problem-solving skills. The characters sneak around a lot. It may encourage kids to get a pen pal. Kid Juror Comments: Children ages three to five loved the movie, though some found it difficult to follow. The older kids asked questions while viewing, which helped them understand what's going on. Age: 3–8; Length: 28 min.; Suggested Retail Price: $9.98, TWENTIETH CENTURY FOX HOME ENTERTAINMENT

* RAGGEDY ANN & ANDY: THE PERRIWONK ADVENTURE: Playful Raggedy Andy runs off with Marcella's locket and lets Raggedy Dog bury it in the yard. When he goes to dig it up, it's gone. To find and retrieve the locket the Raggedys must free the Perriwonks from a dragon whom they befriend as well. Adult Juror Comments: Really silly and contrived. The characters and story line are appropriate for this age. Reinforces cooperation in solving problems and conflicts. The long names make it difficult to follow. Some name-calling. Kid Juror Comments: Cute. Children liked this story and wanted to see it again. Parts were scary for the younger kids. The kids found the story line difficult to follow. Age: 5–8; Length: 28 min.; Suggested Retail Price: $9.98, TWENTIETH CENTURY FOX HOME ENTERTAINMENT

* RAGGEDY ANN & ANDY: THE PIXLING ADVENTURE; see p. 79

* RAGGEDY ANN & ANDY: THE RANSOM OF SUNNY BUNNY: Sunny Bunny is doll-napped. The Raggedys play right into the hands of the evil Cracklen, who needs the hair of Raggedy Dog to complete a spell. Raggedy Ann and Andy end up rescuing two of their best friends. Adult Juror Comments: Bright and lively, some cute scenes, a little drama. Contains some aggressive behaviors such as zapping, stealing, and sneaky pie-throwing. "I like the teamwork of the Raggedy team. Loved that the bunny participated in the cooking contest, and won!" Kid Juror Comments: They wanted to make mud pies afterward. The four- and five-year-olds loved it. They learned about caring for friends. There were some scary parts for the younger ones. The kids were concerned about the issue of kidnapping. Age: 4–7; Length: 28 min.; Suggested Retail Price: $9.98, TWENTIETH CENTURY FOX HOME ENTERTAINMENT

* RAGGEDY ANN & ANDY: THE SCARED CAT ADVENTURE: A magic lamp spells adventure for the Raggedys when the genie of the lamp kidnaps Raggedy Cat. Adult Juror Comments: Standard good-versus-evil story line. Egyptian theme is interesting. Has lots of chasing and running from collapsing buildings. Scary parts are good as discussion-starters. Contains some inappropriate language and attitudes. Kid Juror Comments: This title had mixed and limited appeal for children. The Egyptian story line is most suitable for children ages five to eight. Length is appropriate. Age: 5–8; Length: 30 min.; Suggested Retail Price: $9.98, TWENTIETH CENTURY FOX HOME ENTERTAINMENT

* REBECCA OF SUNNYBROOK FARM (SHIRLEY TEMPLE); see p. 316

** RETURN OF THE SAND FAIRY, THE: Four children visit their gruff aunt who doesn't like youngsters. Their lives are changed when they discover a lovable troll who grants all of their wishes. Adult Juror Comments: Charming story but the length was formidable. Good interaction among siblings, accents hard to understand. Some parts seem a little contrived, the sand fairy character not very well developed, lacked cultural diversity. Kid Juror Comments: Enjoyed the time travel and characters becoming invisible, but thought the story was too long. "It was neat to see how people talked and dressed back then." "The troll complained a lot and sometimes he was mean." Age: 6–10; Length: 139 min.; Suggested Retail Price: $29.98, TWENTIETH CENTURY FOX HOME ENTERTAINMENT

*** RIKKI-TIKKI-TAVI (LES PRODUCTIONS LA FETE): Deep in the heart of turn-of-the-century India, a young mongoose hopes to be a house mongoose someday, and indeed, bushy-tailed Rikki-Tikki-Tavi does that and more in this Rudyard Kipling classic. Animated by Chuck Jones. Narrated by Orson Welles. Adult Juror Comments: Well-told story with high-quality music and visual artistry. Adults liked the story as well as the kids. Kid Juror Comments: Kids were drawn into the story and asked to see it again. They were fascinated by what they learned about the mongoose. Age: 4–8; Length: 28 min.; Suggested Retail Price: $9.98, ARTISAN/FAMILY HOME ENTERTAINMENT

*** ROCK DREAMS (PUZZLE PLACE, THE); see p. 79

*RUDY ROO'S TRAINS: LOTS OF TRAINS: Rudy Roo, an animated kangaroo, and two young children learn all about trains as a result of their trip to the library. They ride on a train and a visit a fabulous model train set-up. Adult Juror Comments: Tells a lot about trains, train history, and safety. The connection between books and real life is interesting. The train shots are great. The pace is too slow for older kids while the information is too complex for younger ones. Kid Juror Comments: Six-year-olds enjoyed it most. They followed up by playing train the next day. Boys definitely liked it better than girls. Rudy Roo was too corny for some kids. "I like trains." "I liked the songs." Age: 4–8; Length: 30 min.; Suggested Retail Price: $12.95, MERITAGE PRODUCTIONS, INC.

*** SECRET GARDEN, THE—WARNER BROS.; see p. 318

*** SECRET OF NIMH, THE: A timid mouse becomes a heroine in spite of herself. Clara struggles to save her home from farmer Fitzgibbon's plow and gets help from an awkward crow, a wise owl, and intelligent rats. Adult Juror Comments: A fantastic story! Well presented with beautiful colors, stirring adventure, and good values. Engaged kids empathetically and critically in discussions about courage and progress. Promotes multiculturalism. Kid Juror Comments: Enthusiastic. They loved Clara. The story elicited a lot of discussion afterwards. Age: 3–12; Length: 83 min.; Suggested Retail Price: $14.95, MGM/UA HOME ENTERTAINMENT

** SIMON THE LAMB (PRECIOUS MOMENTS): When Timmy the Angel drops some rainbow paint on Simon the Lamb, he turns from fleecy white to comical blue. The other lambs shun him, but Simon rescues the flock in a blizzard and winds up a hero. Adult Juror Comments: Deals with basic socialization concepts such as differences and helping one another. The teasing segment seems a little drawn-out. The story contains Christian overtones and is not particularly original. Kid Juror Comments: Kids enjoyed it. Girls liked it better than boys. The lost-in-the-woods section and the snowstorm parts were scary. Age: 3–8; Length: 25 min.; Suggested Retail Price: $12.95, WESTERN PUBLISHING CO./GOLDEN BOOK VIDEO

** SINBAD (ANIMATED CLASSICS): Sail through the excitement of a lifetime in this classic tale. Explore the voyages, dangers, and narrow escapes that await the legendary hero. Adult Juror Comments: The story is a winner, though the animation is mediocre and there are no female role models. Some characters seem harsh but they're not, and the overall effect is calming. Very age-appropriate. Kid Juror Comments: Just loved the story, particularly those already familiar with it. Age: 5–8; Length: 50 min.; Suggested Retail Price: $12.95, GOODTIMES HOME VIDEO

* SIX STORIES ABOUT LITTLE HEROES: JAY O'CALLAHAN: Collection of original tales told by Jay O'Callahan, featuring child heroes and heroines. The stories speak about trust, friendship, courage, and common sense. The stories stretch the imagination and inspire children to tell their own tales. Adult Juror Comments: O'Callahan is an engaging storyteller who dramatically acts out this collection of carefully selected stories. Though the stories are well done, the translation to video lacks something that makes the live performances so engaging. Kid Juror Comments: Hard for kids to understand him. They wanted more interaction between the characters as well as more action. The video did not hold their attention and many walked away. Age: 5–12; Length: 38 min.; Suggested Retail Price: $19.95, VINEYARD VIDEO PRODUCTIONS, INC.

*** SKY IS GRAY, THE; see p. 319

*** SMALL IS BEAUTIFUL (ALLEGRA'S WINDOW); see p. 83

*** SNOOPY COME HOME: This animated classic revolves around an incident in which Charlie Brown's beloved beagle turns up missing and the whole Peanuts gang springs into action. Adult Juror Comments: Wonderful family fun with hummable music and a feel-good ending. Shows cooperation between characters. Kid Juror Comments: Always a winner. Definitely held their interest, though they thought Linus and Snoopy were sometimes mean to one another, particularly when they fought over the blanket. Still, they found that funny. They love Woodstock. Age: 4–12; Length: 80 min.; Suggested Retail Price: $14.98, TWENTIETH CENTURY FOX—CBS/FOX VIDEO

** SNOW WHITE CHRISTMAS (HALLMARK HALL OF FAME): Beautiful Snow White and her comical little companions embark on a thrilling quest to thwart the Wicked Queen's malicious magic. Includes new characters, delightful songs and animated fun. Adult Juror Comments: "Content was sort of a jumble of other tales made into a new fairy tale." May be useful for stimulating discussion about good versus evil, caring about others, and doing things for others. The stepparent and older woman are negatively stereotyped. Kid Juror Comments: "This is not the real Snow White!" Thought the wicked queen was cool. It was scary for younger kids. "I liked when her mommy and daddy kissed her to wake her up." "I liked how the giants liked everyone." Age: 5–8; Length: 46 min.; Suggested Retail Price: $9.98, ARTISAN/FAMILY HOME ENTERTAINMENT

*** SOMETIMES I WONDER: A brother and sister run away from home. They think their parents don't care about them because their new baby brother gets all the attention. They gain insight about their family at Grandma's ranch. Stars Colleen Dewhurst. Adult Juror Comments: A wonderful film that addresses sibling rivalry, jealousy, and families. It shows the birth of the colt, which made some adults uncomfortable. We recommend adults view it themselves before showing to kids. A little slow-moving. Kid Juror Comments: Related well to this topic, particularly those with younger siblings. Motivated a discussion about how they felt about younger brother or sisters. The inclusion of the colt's birth is extraordinary and captured the kids' attention. Age: 5–12; Length: 48 min.; Suggested Retail Price: $14.95, MEDIA VENTURES VIDEO, INC.

** SPIN (SECRET ADVENTURES): An imaginative baby sitter runs for class president. After some dirty campaigning, she learns about honesty while taking two of the children on a secret adventure. Adult Juror Comments: The story is realistic and exceptionally creative. The female teacher is a great role model. Contains Christian overtones that are not indicated on the packaging. At times the educational values overwhelm the story. Kid Juror Comments: Some enjoyed it a lot, while others found it to be too slow-moving to stay with. The Christian overtones seemed not to bother them. At least with those who tested this, they weren't affected by it. Age: 4–13; Length: 30 min.; Suggested Retail Price: $19.95, TAWEEL-LOOS & COMPANY

** STACEY TAKES A STAND (THE BABY-SITTERS CLUB); see p. 320

** STACEY'S BIG BREAK (THE BABY-SITTERS CLUB); see p. 320

** STORIES FROM THE JEWISH TRADITION (CHILDREN'S CIRCLE): A wealthy merchant learns the meaning of Hanukkah when he sues a peddler's family for savoring the smell of his wife's pancakes from a window. Adult Juror Comments: This is a terrific collection of Jewish stories, well produced and authentic. Both the live action and the illustrations are also well done. The Hanukkah pictures are particularly beautiful. Whether or not one is Jewish, it has appeal. Kid Juror Comments: Those who were Jewish found it particularly interesting, and even those who weren't were fascinated by learning about the stories. Some parts were too slow. Age: 5–10; Length: 34 min.; Suggested Retail Price: $14.95, CHILDREN'S CIRCLE HOME VIDEO

** STOWAWAY (SHIRLEY TEMPLE): Shirley Temple's Chinese missionary parents are killed, leaving her to fend for herself on the mean streets of Shanghai. Adult Juror Comments: Emphasizes traditional values and questions today's values. Addresses subjects of death, loss, and love. Content is serious but dealt with in a lighthearted manner with simplistic solutions. The colorization makes it more appealing for today's kids. Kid Juror Comments: Children did not identify with characters. Stimulated interest in Chinese culture. "I wish I knew Chinese." Kids liked the way Shirley Temple was dressed. Held children's interest only in spurts. Age: 5–10; Length: 86 min.; Suggested Retail Price: $14.98, TWENTIETH CENTURY FOX HOME ENTERTAINMENT

** SUE'S BIRTHDAY ADVENTURE; see p. 83

* SUMMER OF THE MONKEYS; see p. 321

** THEODORE HELPS A FRIEND; see p. 84

* THIS PRETTY PLANET (TOM CHAPIN): Tom Chapin sings thirteen songs from his award-winning recordings, which are enhanced with spectacular nature footage. Adult Juror Comments: Loved the music. This is better suited for activity than simply viewing. Although the message is important, the presentation is rather slow-moving. Culturally diverse. Kid Juror Comments: Though the kids got up and danced they did not enjoy the music as much as they had hoped. They weren't anxious to see it again. Age: 4–10; Length: 50 min.; Suggested Retail Price: $14.98, SONY WONDER

** THOMAS THE TANK: BETTER LATE THAN NEVER: Thomas misbehaves and gets stuck underground. Find out what happens when Duck doubts Diesel. Enjoy a good laugh as both Gordon and Duck run out of luck and Anne and Clarabel spell double trouble for Thomas. Adult Juror Comments: Good choice of stories and wonderful collection of very different characters. The British accents are somewhat difficult to follow. The three sections are best viewed together, although each one warrants its own discussion. Kid Juror Comments: Threes and fours liked watching this video. However, school-aged kids understand the stories and messages better. Boys were attracted to the trains. Their interest in mechanical things was higher than most of the girls. Many were familiar with the TV show. Age: 3–8; Length: 40 min.; Suggested Retail Price: $12.98, ANCHOR BAY

** THOMAS THE TANK: DAISY AND OTHER STORIES: More escapades of Thomas the Tank Engine and Friends: Daisy, a classy, sassy passenger diesel; Trevor, the very useful tractor engine; and others. Adult Juror Comments: These simple stories are effective and easy for kids to understand. They're well presented and age-appropriate. Though the trains have little action, their humanized faces make very appealing expressions. Kid Juror Comments: Readily identified with the characters. It's surprising how appealing this is to children who often don't enjoy programs with so little movement. Thomas is a hit with both preschoolers and younger school aged children. Age: 3–8; Length: 37 min.; Suggested Retail Price: $12.98, ANCHOR BAY

** THOMAS THE TANK: JAMES GOES BUZZ BUZZ: Still more adventures with Thomas and friends. Meet Bulgy, the devious double-decker bus. Watch Bertie make a mad dash to rescue a tardy Thomas. See James brave a swarm of buzzing bees, and giggle while Percy puffs his way into a sticky predicament. Adult Juror Comments: This is a pleasure. Nicely produced. Helps develop good listening skills. Adults were concerned about lack of attention to safety. They ride over a broken bridge because they're in a hurry. Kid

Juror Comments: Quite appealing and will watch again and again. Kids love learning the identity of each character. They remember them in subsequent viewings. The bee story was a quick favorite. For this age group, it's best viewed in segments. Age: 3–8; Length: 37 min.; Suggested Retail Price: $12.98, ANCHOR BAY

** THOMAS THE TANK: JAMES LEARNS A LESSON: With a peep of his whistle and a puff of steam, Thomas chugs merrily along, pulling the passengers safely behind him. Thomas and friends always learn lessons that get them back on track. Adult Juror Comments: The settings and landscapes are very well done, the narrative is simple. "I'll take your red coat and paint you blue if you don't behave." What makes red better than blue? Could be a good discussion piece about bias. Kid Juror Comments: Captivated by the trains. They would watch it repeatedly, especially when viewed in segments. Kids recognize and relate to Thomas. Prompted discussions afterward about the characters and their individual traits. Age: 3–8; Length: 40 min.; Suggested Retail Price: $12.98, ANCHOR BAY

** THOMAS THE TANK: PERCY'S GHOSTLY TRICK: Percy has Thomas thinking he's just seen a ghost. On their next escapade, the tables turn when Percy puffs away into a giant pile of hay. The seven stories can be watched independently. Adult Juror Comments: Entertaining and imaginative. The content is most appropriate for school-age children, whereas the presentation is more suitable for preschoolers. The narration is appropriately paced and works for both ages. Kid Juror Comments: Liked the narrator's voice and related to the characters, although keeping them separate is a little confusing at first. Boys are particularly responsive; not many female roles. Age: 3–8; Length: 37 min.; Suggested Retail Price: $12.98, ANCHOR BAY

** THOMAS THE TANK: RUSTY TO THE RESCUE & OTHER THOMAS STORIES: Includes six stories and a music video. Thomas meets his new friend Rusty for fun and adventure on the Island of Sodor. Adult Juror Comments: Jurors liked the moral issues in the story but thought it was too complicated for some viewers. Still, it's a great way to introduce new and different vocabulary to preschoolers. Kid Juror Comments: Thomas was particularly attractive. It's surprising how much they respond to him. Too long for the youngest viewers, but the stories can be watched separately. Age: 4–8; Length: 44 min.; Suggested Retail Price: $12.98, ANCHOR BAY

***THOMAS THE TANK: THOMAS AND HIS FRIENDS GET ALONG: This compilation features some of the best Thomas stories on how to get along with one another, work together, and develop trust. Adult Juror Comments: Contains great stories with excellent messages about caring and sharing, friendship, and how to treat one another. Well produced though little diversity is shown. "Children will definitely be engaged in the stories and the trouble Thomas and friends get into." Kid Juror Comments: This was a group favorite that motivated discussion on sharing and caring. "Most kids loved this video." The sets provided strong visual appeal for the youngest kids, and the stories appeal to the four- and five-year-olds. Age: 2–5; Length: 56 min.; Suggested Retail Price: $12.98, ANCHOR BAY

** THOMAS THE TANK: THOMAS BREAKS THE RULES: Adventures abound as James gets into trouble letting off steam. Percy races Harold the Helicopter to a surprise finish, and Thomas gets covered in soot to boot. Adult Juror Comments: This is very British. It requires listening carefully to get all the information in each story. Six- to eight-year-olds can comprehend the moral in each story, as they involve values and discrimination, among others. Best viewed in segments. Kid Juror Comments: Liked Thomas and the different train characters with their varied personality types. The four- and five-year-olds especially enjoyed this. There was lots of train playing afterward. Age: 3–8; Length: 40 min.; Suggested Retail Price: $12.98, ANCHOR BAY

** THOMAS THE TANK: THOMAS GETS BUMPED: Harold thinks he can deliver the mail better than the others. Edward and Trevor prove they are useful despite being older, and a VIP engine visits the yard. The storyteller is George Carlin. Adult Juror Comments: Delightful stories with simple lessons that build interpersonal skills. The short segments are appropriate. A great vehicle to introduce new vocabulary to preschoolers and even early elementary-age children. Kid Juror Comments: Adults wondered whether kids would have difficulty understanding the British accent, but they had no problem with it. High appeal to boys. Age: 3–8; Length: 37 min.; Suggested Retail Price: $12.98, ANCHOR BAY

** THOMAS THE TANK: THOMAS GETS TRICKED & OTHER STORIES: All aboard for a trainload of fun with Thomas and friends. This trip tours the Island of Sodor with Thomas, Gordon, Edward, Percy, Toby, Annie, and Clarabel. Narration is by Ringo Starr. Adult Juror Comments: "One of the best in the series." Great role models for relating with one another and treating people well. Ringo Starr's storytelling is a joy. Some gender stereotyping. Kid Juror Comments: Quietly enjoyed watching. Appropriate for both preschoolers and younger school-age children. Surprisingly, the kids got very attached to the individual train characters. Age: 3–8; Length: 40 min.; Suggested Retail Price: $12.98, ANCHOR BAY

** THOMAS THE TANK: THOMAS' CHRISTMAS PARTY: The Island of Sodor is covered with snow, including Mrs. Kindly's house. Will someone rescue Mrs. Kindly in time for Sir Topham Hatt's Christmas Party? Thomas is missing with the Christmas Tree, and Terence the Tractor helps save the day. Adult Juror Comments: Enjoyable and well produced with creative sets. "Henry's Forest" has great environmental messages. There is some stereotyping of gender portrayed. For example, the more important train cars have male names while lesser ones have female names. Kid Juror Comments: The four- and five-year-olds loved it. Kids recognize Thomas from TV and respond to the characters. They enjoy imitating the characters afterward as they play train. Age: 3–8; Length: 42 min.; Suggested Retail Price: $12.98, ANCHOR BAY

** THOMAS THE TANK: THOMAS, PERCY & THE DRAGON: Watch for miles of smiles from Thomas, Percy, and the gang on the Island of Sodor. Percy meets a dragon. James handles an embarrassing situation. Donald and Douglas rescue Henry, and some silly freight cars cause trouble. Storyteller is George Carlin. Adult Juror Comments: These stories, simply produced, promote positive values and role models. The length of these sweet vignettes is very age-appropriate. The relation of male to female trains seems a bit sexist. Kid Juror Comments: Fixated for the whole program. Children relate well to Thomas as well as the other characters. This tape prompted a discussion about fears afterward. Age: 3–8; Length: 37 min.; Suggested Retail Price: $12.98, ANCHOR BAY

** THOMAS THE TANK: TRUST THOMAS: Mavis, a young diesel engine, puts Toby on the spot. Percy keeps his promise. The engines help Henry rescue the forest. Adult Juror Comments: These stories lead to clarification values and early moral development. The characters have well-defined traits and problems. However, children not fluent in English may find it difficult to understand. It's very language-dependent. Kid Juror Comments: Children responded well to these stories, especially when the engines move. Boys like them better than the girls. The stories are best viewed in segments and discussed afterward. Age: 3–8; Length: 40 min.; Suggested Retail Price: $12.98, ANCHOR BAY

*** THREE MUSKETEERS, THE (ANIMATED CLASSICS): "All for one and one for all" is the motto of this animated tale of royal intrigue and swashbuckling adventure. D'Artagnan and the Three Musketeers battle to save France from the evil Cardinal Richelieu, bringing classic literature to life. Adult Juror Comments: Entertaining presentation of a classic novel. Beware that it does contain rather stereotypical portrayals of women: small voices, secretive, a willingness for sacrifice. Kid Juror Comments: Really enjoyed it. They noticed that the fight scenes were not very graphic. Most asked if they could see the movie again. Children discussed parts of the movie as they watched it. Age: 6–12; Length: 50 min.; Suggested Retail Price: $12.95, GOODTIMES HOME VIDEO

** THUMBELINA (ANIMATED CLASSICS): Based on the story by Hans Christian Andersen which follows the heroine, Thumbelina, in her efforts to save the Little People. Adult Juror Comments: Families will find this ageless tale enjoyable. Animation is mediocre. Shows how uncomfortable situations can be resolved without violence and fear. Could stimulate discussion about cooperation. Kid Juror Comments: Very special. Some wanted to watch it again immediately after it ended; others lost interest. Because of its length, it may be better-suited for younger kids to view in segments. Age: 4–8; Length: 50 min.; Suggested Retail Price: $19.95, GOODTIMES HOME VIDEO

* THUNDERBIRDS ARE GO; see p. 321

*** TOM & JERRY: THE MOVIE: The cat and mouse are at it again in an extravagant full-length musical adventure helping a young girl find her father. Adult Juror Comments: Production is well done, and though the language is sometimes too sophisticated it's still quite humorous. Relationship between Tom and Jerry is charming. The wordplay used in the songs is rich in meanings and rhymes. Kid Juror Comments: A big hit. The familiar characters are appealing and funny. Afterward, kids discussed the nature of the wicked guardian and the cooperation and kindness shown by the rest of the characters. Age: 5–14; Length: 83 min.; Suggested Retail Price: $14.98, ARTISAN/FAMILY HOME ENTERTAINMENT

* TOM AND JERRY'S 50TH BIRTHDAY CLASSICS: From their debut in 1940, almost sixty years later Tom and Jerry are as funny as ever. This collection marks their half-century anniversary with seven classic cat-and-mouse contests. Adult Juror Comments: Like many golden oldies, this brings up issues concerning stereotypical portrayals, such as the African-American housekeeper and the cat-and-mouse behavior. Jurors passed this with some reservation. It provokes discussions about then and now. Kid Juror Comments: A barrel of laughs. The fast action and wildness grabbed their attention. Kids noticed the somewhat violent interaction between the cat and the mouse. "They could hurt someone." Age: 5–12; Length: 57 min.; Suggested Retail Price: $14.95, MGM/UA HOME ENTERTAINMENT

*** TOM SAWYER: This film version of Mark Twain's story is set to music and features a first-rate cast: Johnny Whitaker as Tom; Jodie Foster as Tom's girlfriend, Becky; Celeste Holm as Aunt Polly, and Warren Oates as the boozy Muff Potter. Adult Juror Comments: Good introduction to the work of Mark Twain, this time as a musical, which helps to keep the kids interested. Encourages thinking about people's place within their community and community ethics. Kid Juror Comments: They noticed the dated look of the movie but enjoyed the story anyway and loved the music. Injun Joe was too scary for some. The murder scene is disturbing although it's not graphically depicted. It sparked an interest in reading more Twain. Age: 3–11; Length: 102 min.; Suggested Retail Price: $14.95, MGM/UA HOME ENTERTAINMENT

** TOMMY TRICKER AND THE STAMP TRAVELER (LES PRODUCTIONS LA FETE): Ralph James shares his father's passion for collecting stamps. He makes the mistake of trading one of his father's favorite stamps to Tommy Tricker. A series of adventures follow, as Ralph tries to get his hands on a worthy replacement. Adult Juror Comments: An interesting story that stimulates an interest in geography. Some stereotyping, especially the portrayal of Chinese children. When Tommy steals, cheats, and lies they are all diminished as "tricks." Kid Juror Comments: Learning about the value of stamps intrigued them. They enjoyed the animation and followed up the viewing with a discussion about honesty. Age: 4–12; Length: 105 min.; Suggested Retail Price: $14.98, LES PRODUCTIONS LA FETE/LIVE ENTERTAINMENT

*TOMMY TROUBLES (RUGRATS): Includes four episodes. Tommy attempts to lead his friends away from the confinement of clothing; experiences the supermarket as an amusement park; acts up at the baseball game; anguishes when his favorite stuffed toy is thrown away. Adult Juror Comments: Well produced with subtle learning tucked in. Looks at things from a child's perspective. The inclusion of older people is welcome. Angelica is not the best kid role model. Some sarcasm and stereotyping. Kid Juror Comments: Enjoyable viewing with kids. Funny and easy to follow. Kids relate to it and find it interesting. The comedy is partly about kids in trouble and looks at it from their point of view. Age: 6–9; Length: 63 min.; Suggested Retail Price: $12.95, PARAMOUNT HOME VIDEO

* TRAINS: Explores the history of trains, from the early human-powered pushcart to powerful diesel locomotives of today. Produced in 3-D computer animation. Adult Juror Comments: Entertaining presentation but information lacks depth. An engineer's perspective of tracks, tunnels, and a huge variety of trains. Some concern over kids in apparently unsafe situations. The host is well selected and appealing. Kid Juror Comments: Nice, especially seeing the car wash for trains. They were intrigued by details such as stoking the furnace. Boys liked it better than girls. They would watch it again. It's too long for youngest kids. Age: 5–8; Length: 30 min.; Suggested Retail Price: $19.95, COREY LAKE PICTURES

* TROLLIES MUSICAL ADVENTURE: Exciting action/adventure on the horizon for the Trollies as they thwart the Trouble Trollie Gang's attempt to steal the sun. Adult Juror Comments: Some stories are better than others. At times they are cluttered and confusing. "In a Different Light" is excellent story. Too much emphasis is given to the bad Trollies and their negative behavior. Kid Juror Comments: Good narrative but thought the songs were a too long. Boys liked this better than girls. It was scary for younger kids. Age: 4– 8; Length: 43 min.; Suggested Retail Price: $12.98, PPI ENTERTAINMENT GROUP

*** TUNED IN (THE PUZZLE PLACE): Teaches that there's more to life than what's on TV! Adult Juror Comments: Cheerful, colorful, fast-moving, and humorous. Helps kids examine different perspectives about TV-watching. Provoked discussion about TV-watching rules. The characters' personalities are believable and the children relate to them. Kid Juror Comments: Totally absorbing from the get-go. They danced along while watching. Kids recognized these characters from TV. They talked about how TV shows are made. Animation held children's attention. They loved the puppets. Age: 4–7; Length: 55 min.; Suggested Retail Price: $9.99, SONY WONDER

** URBAN ADVENTURES (HEY ARNOLD!): These five big-city stories follow the adventures of Arnold, a nine-year-old boy, who's as vulnerable to heart-wrenching crushes as he is to head-squeezing bullies. For Arnold and his best friend Gerald, adventure is just a bus stop away. Adult Juror Comments: Excellent animated production. Good friendship role models of a diverse mix of children. Shows life in the big city. Some wisecracks are inappropriate. Kid Juror Comments: Fabulous, especially for those familiar with Arnold. Sparked a curiosity among kids who don't live in urban areas to see people in big cities. One child commented, "Cities are really different from our area." "People were different and all sizes." Age: 6–9; Length: 55 min.; Suggested Retail Price: $12.95, PARAMOUNT HOME VIDEO

*** VEGGIE TALES: ARE YOU MY NEIGHBOR?; see p. 87

*** VEGGIE TALES: DAVE AND THE GIANT PICKLE: Retells the Bible story of David and Goliath. Junior Asparagus plays young David, who takes on a nine-foot pickle. Offers a lesson in self-esteem when Bob the Tomato and Larry the Cucumber teach kids that even little guys can do big things. Adult Juror Comments: Engaging and funny. Not a traditional retelling of the story. The characters are represented by talking vegetables. "It reminded me of something out of Monty Python." Maintains the basic theme of "everyone is special." Appeals to Christian audience. Kid Juror Comments: The message went over well. "It doesn't matter if you are small. You are still great." When asked, "Who would have thought to turn the characters into vegetables?" One eight-year-old responded, "Someone who liked brussel sprouts when they were a kid." Age: 5–8; Length: 30 min.; Suggested Retail Price: $12.99, BIG IDEA PRODUCTIONS

** VEGGIE TALES: GOD WANTS ME TO FORGIVE THEM: Two stories teach children a lesson in forgiveness. In "The Grapes of Wrath," Junior Asparagus leans to forgive the grapes even after they've hurt his feelings. "Larry's Lagoon" is a spoof of *Gilligan's Island* in which passengers learn to forgive. Adult Juror Comments: Negatively stereotypes Appalachian people. Engaging, bright visuals, and clear animation. Great starting point for discussing fairness and forgiveness. Contains Christian overtones and numerous references to God and Jesus. Kid Juror Comments: Terrific. A hoot. They really understood the concepts. "The veggies taught us to forgive." "I think it would be a great movie for preschoolers." Age: 5–8; Length: 30 min.; Suggested Retail Price: $12.99, BIG IDEA PRODUCTIONS

*** VEGGIE TALES: JOSH AND THE BIG WALL: Obedience is taught in this adaptation of a Bible story featuring vegetables. To get to the Promised Land, Larry the Cucumber, Bob the Tomato, and Junior Asparagus must go through Jericho first. It's not easy since Jericho is surrounded by huge wall. Adult Juror Comments: Good animation. Using vegetables as characters is an amusing twist. Delightful music, brilliant colors, and realistic action. Biblical theme is very clear and done in a way that kids can understand. Contains Christian content. Kid Juror Comments: Much appreciated learning about a story they didn't know and discovered what a narrator is. Sang along the second time. Were intrigued with the characters. "I learned that you need to listen to God." "I like how the vegetables talk." Age: 5–8; Length: 30 min.; Suggested Retail Price: $12.99, BIG IDEA PRODUCTIONS

*** VEGGIE TALES: LARRY-BOY AND THE FIB FROM OUTER SPACE!: A little fib turns into a big problem for Junior Asparagus. Junior is advised to cover his tracks with a little white lie. Junior learns that lies have a way of growing and it isn't long before his "little fib" has grown into a 30–foot tall monster. Adult Juror Comments: Entertaining. Good animation with engaging characters, lots of action, well-paced. Promotes discussion about how lies perpetuate themselves. Reinforces the notion that to stop a lie one must confess and tell the truth. Promotes Christian values. Kid Juror Comments: "It's so silly, you have to watch it." Children related well to the characters. Big Fib was a bit scary. Children understood the growing lie. "I learned we shouldn't lie. Lies get bigger and bigger." "I liked it when he decided to tell the truth." Age: 5–8; Length: 30 min.; Suggested Retail Price: $12.99, BIG IDEA PRODUCTIONS

** VEGGIE TALES: RACK, SHACK & BENNY; see p. 88

*** VEGGIE TALES: WHERE'S GOD WHEN I'M S-SCARED?: In "Tales from the Crisper," Junior Asparagus watches a movie that is too scary for him. With help from his friends, his fears are alleviated. In "Daniel and the Lion's Den," Larry the Cucumber finds himself in trouble with the king's conniving men. Adult Juror Comments: Well done. Appealing in sound, sight, and theme. Good example of how to refocus emotions and handle fear. Addresses how to not be afraid of the dark. Biblical story is told in a non-threatening manner. Appeals most to a Christian audience. Kid Juror Comments: Children talked about their fears. Identified with the vegetable. "I would tell my friends to watch this." One child said she wouldn't be afraid of the dark anymore. They liked the song about God being bigger than the monsters. Age: 4–8; Length: 30 min.; Suggested Retail Price: $12.99, BIG IDEA PRODUCTIONS

*** WALLACE AND GROMIT: A GRAND DAY OUT: In this Oscar award-winning claymation, Wallace and Gromit head toward the moon in search of cheese. Adult Juror Comments: Excellent sample of British humor, well produced, colorful, and full of wit. The accents and phrases will be challenging for some children. Very appealing. Material provokes discussion about humor and culture. Kid Juror Comments: Tons of fun. The dog character was a big hit. Kids loved that Gromit the dog is so smart and can read. "How exciting, let's watch it again!" Age: 4–10; Length: 25 min.; Suggested Retail Price: $9.98, TWENTIETH CENTURY FOX HOME ENTERTAINMENT

** YOU CAN RIDE A HORSE (YOU CAN VIDEO SERIES FOR CHILDREN): Explores the world of horses and shows what it's like to work and play with them every day. Full of fascinating facts about horses and exciting stunt-riding scenes. Adult Juror Comments: Informative with clear instructions. Shows that kids can ride a horse and enjoy lessons with other kids. Demonstrates cooperation and teamwork. Little cultural diversity. Pace is a little uneven.

Kid Juror Comments: Girls liked it better than boys. Older kids liked it but found it too simple. Kids appreciated inclusions of a person in a wheelchair and a child with glasses. Age: 4–9; Length: 29 min.; Suggested Retail Price: $12.95, BLACKBOARD ENTERTAINMENT AND RED SKY FILMS

* **YOUNG PEOPLE (SHIRLEY TEMPLE):** Shirley Temple stars in this charming story about a show business couple who retire in a small town to give their daughter a normal life. Features footage from early Shirley Temple films. Adult Juror Comments: Very slow-paced. Old footage of Shirley as a girl singing and dancing has great nostalgic appeal. The story line is sometimes complex and gender stereotypes are rampant. Contains some aggressive language, name-calling, and behavior such as parents slapping children. Kid Juror Comments: Mixed responses. Young children did not understand the story line. The children only sat through part of the program and were not interested in seeing it again. The witches scared them and some kids had bad dreams about them. Led to discussion of different values from that time period. Age: 5–8; Length: 78 min.; Suggested Retail Price: $14.98, TWENTIETH CENTURY FOX HOME ENTERTAINMENT

** **YOU'RE INVITED TO MARY-KATE & ASHLEY'S BALLET PARTY:** What's more exciting than a whirlwind trip to New York City? Mary-Kate and Ashley invite the viewer to join them at the ultimate ballet party at Lincoln Center. Adult Juror Comments: Provokes children's interest in professional ballet. Explains the moves and models the steps. Also addresses instantaneous success and the need to practice to become better. It's a bit disjointed, with no story line to hold it together. Kid Juror Comments: Kids were impressed with the ability and agility of the ballet dancers. Girls were especially enthralled with the actors, the settings, and the music. The focus on the twins was at times distracting. "Ballerinas are beautiful. I love the tutus." Age: 5–8; Length: 30 min.; Suggested Retail Price: $12.95, WARNERVISION

* **YOU'RE INVITED TO MARY-KATE & ASHLEY'S BIRTHDAY PARTY:** Mary-Kate and Ashley plan a birthday party filled with excitement and fun. With five new songs, it's geared up to be the biggest, most fantabulous birthday party in history. Adult Juror Comments: Well produced. Presents many party ideas. Lots of gender stereotypes such as girls' fascination with makeup and clothes, boys causing mischief. Filled with mildly derogatory comments about boys throughout. Attention is overly focused on the twins. Kid Juror Comments: Girls thought it was fun. One boy said dejectedly, "I hate the part when they talk about boys." Sparked an interest in Six Flags' Amusement Park rides. The songs appealed to some. A favorite element was the

outtakes at the end. Age: 5–8; Length: 30 min.; Suggested Retail Price: $12.95, WARNERVISION

* YOU'RE INVITED TO MARY-KATE & ASHLEY'S CAMPOUT PARTY: Hey campers, grab your knapsack, light your lantern, and take along your tent. Get ready for the outrageous antics in the great outdoors with Mary-Kate and Ashley. Adult Juror Comments: Includes several original songs with elaborate choreography. Represents gender stereotypes such as concern about what to wear camping and "creepy crawly" bugs. Some objected to the silliness and the overly materialistic nature of the program. Kid Juror Comments: Children split by gender on its appeal. Girls liked it—the music and the dancing—boys thought it was "dumb." All agreed that boys were poorly depicted. Kids were disappointed not to learn anything about camping. The electric tent was ridiculous. Age: 5–8; Length: 30 min.; Suggested Retail Price: $12.95, WARNERVISION

* YOU'RE INVITED TO MARY-KATE & ASHLEY'S COSTUME PARTY: Mary-Kate and Ashley are dressing up for their costume party. Travel with the girls back in time as they journey through the decades. Adult Juror Comments: Songs and dances are appropriate and tasteful. Demonstrates dances from the '50s through the '80s, including country-western. Female stereotypes prevail— girls focusing on boys and appearance. Lip-syncing by the twins is distracting at times. Kid Juror Comments: The kids responded well to the music and the kids on-screen. They enjoyed the twins and their friends. Prompted discussion about clothes from different eras. "I learned that people used to wear different clothes." "The music was fun to dance to." Age: 5–8; Length: 30 min.; Suggested Retail Price: $12.95, WARNERVISION

** YOU'RE INVITED TO MARY-KATE & ASHLEY'S HAWAIIAN BEACH PARTY: Mary-Kate and Ashley join their friends in Hawaii for swimming, surfing, jet skiing, and singing. They build sand castles, visit a submarine, and dance the day away. Adult Juror Comments: Refreshingly healthy fun. Upbeat, bright, and refreshing—just fun. Beautiful footage introducing the sights of Hawaii. Appropriate language and content for this age range. Includes "surfer" lingo. Kid Juror Comments: Kids enjoyed this. They learned a bit about Hawaii and surfing. "I want to go to the beach now or horseback riding. I want to sing the songs." "The sand castle looked great, but you know they didn't build it." "There's too much singing for me." Age: 5–8; Length: 30 min.; Suggested Retail Price: $12.95, WARNERVISION

** YOU'RE INVITED TO MARY-KATE & ASHLEY'S SLEEPOVER PARTY: Join in the fun as Mary-Kate and Ashley and their friends have pillow fights, dance, and share secrets about friends, school, and sports at their sleepover party. Adult Juror Comments: Engages and entertains. The music, funny situations, and costumes will are appropriate for kids this age. Shows what fun a few friends, stories, and games can be. Kids even clean up after themselves. Stereotypical boy-versus-girl behavior. Kid Juror Comments: Kids thought it was funny that they wanted to sell their brother. They liked watching the girls dress as monsters. All the kids wanted to have a sleepover party with their friends. Some kids sang along. "The fish pizza was disgusting." Age: 5–8; Length: 30 min.; Suggested Retail Price: $12.95, WARNERVISION

** ZEBRA IN THE KITCHEN, A (FAMILY TREASURES): Hilarious chaos reigns when a well-intentioned but misguided twelve-year-old boy lets all the animals out of the zoo and into the backyards, bedrooms, and even bathrooms of the neighborhood. Adult Juror Comments: This is great for family viewing. Both adults and children enjoyed it. A little dated in its portrayal of zoos and how animals are kept. As a result, it prompted discussion about the care of animals and their zoo experiences. Slow-paced. Kid Juror Comments: Very funny though dated. They followed the story and enjoyed watching with the adults. It prompted a discussion about zoos, caring for animals. It's a great introduction for a field trip to a zoo. Age: 5–12; Length: 92 min.; Suggested Retail Price: $14.95, MGM/UA HOME ENTERTAINMENT

CD-ROMs

*** BACKYARD BASEBALL (JUNIOR SPORTS): Sports designed for kids. Features 30 of the funniest boys and girls from the neighborhood, each with a unique personality. Choose your team and pick your players for nonstop thrills and action-packed games. Adult Juror Comments: Entertaining and well produced. Great animation and sound. Teaches a variety of life skills in a variety of ways. Multicultural and special-needs diversity. Can be troublesome to install. Kid Juror Comments: Loved this game. Offers "stealth learning" such as studying statistics for the best pitcher and learning to bat and catch. Fun for all ages, girls and boys, even adults. "I liked choosing my team, then taking our picture. Cool characters." Age: 6–12; Suggested Retail Price: $29.99, HUMONGOUS ENTERTAINMENT

*** DISNEY'S MAGIC ARTIST: Transform your computer into the ultimate art studio. Create works of art with realistic tools like paints that smear, crayons that look waxy. Spray your drawings with special effects. Includes 300 Disney characters, props, and backgrounds. Adult Juror Comments: Sophisticated program. Superior, appealing, excellent production. Entertaining, easy drawing lessons. The Minnie Mouse section is great. Children can produce their own high-quality work. Younger ages may need some help. Kid Juror Comments: Appeals to most, not just game players. Suitable for various ages. Very popular in the classroom. "Easy." "I loved it." "I'm going to ask my Mom for this because it is really fun." "Can I skip recess to do this?" Age: 5–12; Suggested Retail Price: $35.00, DISNEY INTERACTIVE

* GAMEBREAK! TIMON AND PUMBAA'S JUNGLE GAMES: Timon and Pumbaa are the hosts in five arcade-style games of speed, skill, and indigestion. Loaded with hundreds of wacky sound effects and a two-player option. Adult Juror Comments: Challenging, fun to play repeatedly. Kid humor unappealing to adults (belching and gas) but kids love it. Develops eye-hand coordination. Pinball is the best self-explanatory game. Kid Juror Comments: They would play it again. "It's fun and there's lots to do." Age: 6–12; Suggested Retail Price: $29.95, DISNEY INTERACTIVE

** POCAHONTAS (DISNEY'S ANIMATED STORYBOOK): Enter Pocahontas' world and share her adventures as she romps through the woods with Meeko and Flit. Lively storytelling, exciting activities and games, rich animation, and music from the film make interactive magic with the click of the mouse. Adult Juror Comments: Fun, easy to use. Cute games develop eye-hand coordination and matching skills. Shallow and predictable in content area; "Tastes great, but leaves you hungry." Although it's good entertainment the vocabulary is limited. Kid Juror Comments: Fun and challenging. They liked the archery and storytelling. New readers enjoyed the reading skills practice section. Several boys did not want to try it, but once they started playing, couldn't stop. Age: 4–8; Suggested Retail Price: $34.99, DISNEY INTERACTIVE

*** TOY STORY—CD-ROM: Share the adventures of Woody, Buzz, and the rest of the gang from *Toy Story*. You can be a part of their world as toys come to life and the magic begins. Exciting activities, games, rich animation, and lively storytelling. Adult Juror Comments: Familiar family fun. Good characters, challenging, excellent play value, and beautiful graphics. Content is shallow and lacks depth. Slightly difficult to install and set up for younger kids. Kid Juror Comments: Great, especially the escape from Sid's House, seeing the character Buzz Lightyear, and playing the crane game. They got a kick out of bringing the toys to life. Younger kids had a difficult time navigating the program. Age: 4–9; Suggested Retail Price: $34.95, DISNEY INTERACTIVE

Fairy Tales, Literature, and Myths

** ADVENTURES OF CURIOUS GEORGE: Two stories about the world's favorite monkey. One follows the Man with the Yellow Hat to the jungle, where he finds Curious George and brings him to the big city. The other explains how Curious George winds up in the hospital and makes friends. Adult Juror Comments: Nicely produced, good narration. Unlike the book, George takes on human qualities. Good discussion of right versus wrong, good versus bad. Could be used to prepare child for a hospital visit. One adult said, "This was by far my favorite video." Kid Juror Comments: Thoroughly enjoyable. Lots of spontaneous laughter and comments about George's silliness. Kids watched George actively, anticipated events and discussed the consequences of his actions. "I wish I was George." Age: 3–8; Length: 30 min.; Suggested Retail Price: $12.95, SONY WONDER/WESTERN PUBLISHING/GOLDEN BOOK

*** ALADDIN AND THE MAGIC LAMP: From "A Thousand and One Nights," this story is about a young rogue and the genie who helps him win the love of the Sultan's daughter. Musician Mickey Hart weaves the rhythms of the Middle East. Adult Juror Comments: Scored high. This iconographic presentation is faithful to the original story, with excellent narration and music. It is perhaps a little slow-moving for some children, but visually it's beautiful. Kid Juror Comments: Enjoyed the story and the presentation. They were intrigued that it was not the Disney version. Kids liked the narrator but wanted the characters to have motion. "I loved the music and the colors." "I learned to be kind and not selfish." Age: 5–12; Length: 30 min.; Suggested Retail Price: $8.95, RABBIT EARS PRODUCTIONS/ABLESOFT

** ALICE THROUGH THE LOOKING GLASS: A fantasy musical sequel to *Alice In Wonderland* featuring Jimmy Durante, Jack Palance, The Smothers Brothers, and Agnes Moorehead. Nostalgic production values from the '60s. Adult Juror Comments: Surprisingly feminist for its time. Addresses overcoming fears, taking a stand, being wary of strangers, and following one's dream. This is not Lewis Carroll's original tale but it's engaging nonetheless. Lots of humor and a touch of haughtiness. Kid Juror Comments: Kids had mixed reactions to this. "While they loved the slapstick humor and got the general gist of the story, they missed the parts that made it worthwhile." They were not impressed either with acting, costumes, or scenery, and hated the songs. Age: 6–10; Length: 90 min.; Suggested Retail Price: $14.98, TWENTIETH CENTURY FOX HOME ENTERTAINMENT

*** AMAZING BONE & OTHER STORIES, THE (CHILDREN'S CIRCLE): Anthology of four titles: "The Amazing Bone," a Caldecott award–winning story by William Steig of a young girl pig rescued by a talking bone; "John Brown, Rose and the Midnight Cat"; "A Picture for Harold's Room"; and "The Trip." Adult Juror Comments: Four excellent literary titles, good for any child's library. "The Amazing Bone," directed by Michael Sporn, was everyone's favorite. These enduring stories don't go out of fashion. Kid Juror Comments: "The Amazing Bone" is a wonderful story. The other titles, though good stories, are not as well produced or as compelling. Because of the clear division between each story, they're easily watched in segments. Age: 5–12; Length: 33 min.; Suggested Retail Price: $14.95, CHILDREN'S CIRCLE HOME VIDEO

** ANNIE OAKLEY (AMERICAN HEROES AND LEGENDS): Recalls the life and sharpshooting exploits of America's favorite cowgirl, and a star of Buffalo Bill's famous Wild West Show. Narration by Keith Carradine. Music by Los Lobos. Adult Juror Comments: Entertaining biography of a female protagonist. Handles attitudes toward Native Americans delicately, if not accurately. Animation is thoughtfully beautiful though slow. Los Lobos' music is lively and engaging. Kid Juror Comments: Entertaining as well as informative. Kids loved the story, character, narration, and asked to see it again. They loved the music and seeing a girl hero! "We want to keep this one." Age: 5–12; Length: 30 min.; Suggested Retail Price: $19.95, RABBIT EARS PRODUCTIONS/WESTON WOODS

** ARTHUR WRITES A STORY (ARTHUR): Struggling with a school assignment, Arthur decides that with a little imagination he can make his life sound more interesting than it really is. He crosses the line when the story of how he got his puppy starts to involve invisible elephants. Adult Juror Comments: Good story, inspiring, and well produced. Arthur teaches in a gentle yet thorough way. Filled with practical writing tips. Most adults loved Arthur. Kid Juror Comments: They enjoy Arthur as a rule. He's very realistic and deals with issues they relate to. Also, good music and animation. Commented on the negative interaction between the siblings. Age: 4–8; Length: 30 min.; Suggested Retail Price: $12.98, SONY WONDER

*** ARTHUR'S BABY (ARTHUR); see p. 90

** ARTHUR'S EYES (ARTHUR): For some reason, Arthur isn't doing very well in school anymore. Maybe he just needs glasses? The problem is he doesn't want to be seen wearing them. It appears as if Arthur has started a trend. Adult Juror Comments: Good content for discussing differences. It's true to the book, with captivating animation and adorable characters. Realistically shows children responses to attitudes. Shows some negative behaviors. Some segments would benefit from adult explanation. Kid Juror Comments: Great discussion-starter about feelings. Children disliked the name-calling, though it's addressed in a suitable manner. Kids didn't understand all of the concepts involved. They liked best the live segments at the end. Age: 4–8; Length: 30 min.; Suggested Retail Price: $12.98, SONY WONDER

** ARTHUR'S LOST LIBRARY BOOK (ARTHUR): Arthur was the first to take out the new scare-your-pants-off book from the library. A week later, he can't seem to figure out where he put it. Something's weird. It couldn't have just walked off—or could it? Includes two separate stories. Adult Juror Comments: Great story line, age-appropriate. Arthur is an appealing character who deals with issues kids relate to. He teaches social values without being preachy. It does have some inappropriate vocabulary. Kid Juror Comments: "I love Arthur." "Do you have any more Arthur tapes?" This held the children's attention. Kids wanted to see it again. Kids talked about what scares them afterward. Age: 3–8; Length: 30 min.; Suggested Retail Price: $12.98, SONY WONDER

** ARTHUR'S PET BUSINESS (ARTHUR): How can Arthur prove to his parents that he's responsible enough to take care of his very own puppy? "Get a job," suggests D.W. Within two days, Arthur's pet business has its first client. Can Arthur really care for a canine with his own pet? Adult Juror Comments: Beautiful stories, dealing with typical issues in an entertaining way. Arthur is strong, appealing, silly, and age-appropriate. The sibling relationship is negative and doesn't really get resolved. Kid Juror Comments: Cute. Kids love Arthur. They relate to the moral of each story. This one motivated discussion afterwards about responsibility, caring for pets, and helping out in their family. Kids familiar with the TV show were big fans even before the tape played. Age: 4–8; Length: 30 min.; Suggested Retail Price: $12.98, SONY WONDER

** ARTHUR'S TEACHER TROUBLES (ARTHUR); see p. 91

** ARTHUR'S TOOTH (ARTHUR'S HOME VIDEO): Everyone in class has lost a tooth except Arthur, and they keep teasing him about it. Will Arthur have to go through life with a mouthful of baby teeth? Adult Juror Comments: Upbeat, fast-moving, cheerful music and animation. The mystery of the Tooth Fairy is a common topic for children this age. Some name-calling. Arthur's relationship with his sister is realistic but not always positive. Kid Juror Comments: "Arthur is so funny." Kids like all the different things

Arthur does, like soccer, basketball, and swimming, that are fun to watch. "Francine is mean." "I don't like the way D.W. and Arthur fight." "Don't force your teeth out." Age: 5–8; Length: 30 min.; Suggested Retail Price: $12.98, RANDOM HOUSE

*** BABAR RETURNS: Babar shares a tale with a lesson about concentrating on our strengths rather than our weaknesses. Years after the wicked hunter separated Babar from his family, he meets him again, defeats him with his knowledge of man's ways, and is crowned king. Adult Juror Comments: Nicely animated with a good story that's appealing and creative. Delivers positive messages about home, family, and helping others take charge. Kid Juror Comments: Babar is always a favorite. Wanted to watch it repeatedly. Babar's separation from his parents may be frightening for the youngest children. It's best that they view this with their parent present. Age: 3–12; Length: 49 min.; Suggested Retail Price: $12.98, ARTISAN/FAMILY HOME ENTERTAINMENT

** BABAR'S FIRST STEP: Babar tells his son, Alexander, about an event from his childhood: when a hunter terrorized the elephant herd Babar realized that he must face his fears to conquer them. This uplifting adventure explores the meaning of friendship and family. Adult Juror Comments: Good animation and simple, appealing characters. Showing Babar losing his mother could be disturbing for younger viewers. Discussion is required to bring home the point of the story, which is "being yourself." Kid Juror Comments: Big hit. Children laughed at Babar's silliness. Very attentive and curious to see what would happen next. Younger children did not understand why Babar's mom died. This title is more suitable for ages six to eight. Age: 6–8; Length: 49 min.; Suggested Retail Price: $12.98, ARTISAN/FAMILY HOME ENTERTAINMENT

** BABAR'S TRIUMPH: When deadly hunters threaten, Babar helps the animals join forces to protect themselves and their homes. Adult Juror Comments: Colorful video brings a favorite Babar story to life. Great learning potential for discussion of peace and conflict resolution. The story does include the use of guns and provides an ideal opportunity to discuss them. Kid Juror Comments: Several children were disconcerted by segment in which the turtles fought with the hunters. Babar and his family were very appealing to the kids, who wanted to live where Babar lives. "Teaches unity and tolerance." Age: 6–12; Length: 51 min.; Suggested Retail Price: $12.98, ARTISAN/FAMILY HOME ENTERTAINMENT

* BABAR: THE MOVIE: Full-length feature movie based on the charming French classic about Babar, the King of the Elephants. Adult Juror Comments: Well produced with appealing music. It has the standard good-versus-bad scenario with battle scenes. It is violent in parts, though not particularly graphic. Gender roles are fairly rigidly defined and older people are portrayed as slightly senile. Kid Juror Comments: Prompted an animated discussion of the movie and the issues of good versus bad that it raised. Age: 6–12; Length: 79 min.; Suggested Retail Price: $12.98, ARTISAN/FAMILY HOME ENTERTAINMENT

** BEAUTY AND THE BEAST (STORIES TO REMEMBER): Classic enchantment and romance. To save her beloved father, a beautiful young girl agrees to become the companion of a brutish and unhappy beast. As time passes, love works a miraculous change on their lives. Narrated by Mia Farrow. Adult Juror Comments: A beautifully illustrated work of art though not full-range animation. The ending here more accurately reflects the original story than some major studio releases. Kid Juror Comments: Expecting to see the Disney version, kids were surprised with this one. They didn't like that the characters' mouths didn't move. Generated a discussion about how stories can be told differently. Age: 5–12; Length: 27 min.; Suggested Retail Price: $9.95, LIGHTYEAR ENTERTAINMENT

** BEN'S DREAM AND OTHER STORIES (FUN IN A BOX): The lead story is based on the book by Chris Van Allsburg in which a young boy dreams about an imaginary trip around the world. Next, a mile-a-minute train ride on the famous Cannonball Express. Finally, a little girl and three escapades of detection. Adult Juror Comments: The title story, "Ben's Dream," based on a Caldecott award-winning book, is true to the original: delightful and imaginative visits to world-famous landmarks in a geography-induced dream. Kid Juror Comments: Although they enjoyed "Ben's Dream," the other two titles were not as compelling. They talked about the landmarks afterward. Some were familiar with the Eiffel Tower and Mount Rushmore. One asked, "Are these famous places I should know about?" Age: 4–12; Length: 30 min.; Suggested Retail Price: $14.95, MADE TO ORDER PRODUCTIONS/RAINBOW

** BIRTHDAY DRAGON: Every night, Emily is secretly visited by a lovable dragon. Together they play and fly through the skies. Her birthday is coming, and what she wants most is for him to be a part of her celebration, but two dragon hunters stand in her way. Adult Juror Comments: A good birthday choice, entertaining and unusual even though it's simply produced and somewhat slow. Kid Juror Comments: Lots of laughter from attentive audience. The humor is just right for five-year-olds. Kids were confused about how the dragon got out of the net and the bad guys were caught. Age: 5–8; Length: 26 min.; Suggested Retail Price: $9.98, ARTISAN/FAMILY HOME ENTERTAINMENT

* BLUE BIRD, THE (SHIRLEY TEMPLE): Shirley Temple longs to see the world outside her doorstep but soon discovers there's no place like home. Adult Juror Comments: Confusing story and dated special effects. Content is somewhat scary. Despite moral ending, lacks diversity, reflecting its cultural era. Kid Juror Comments: The fairy-tale quality was appealing. They thought the dog and cat were funny. Led to discussions about trustworthiness, luxury, and being happy with what one has. Held kids' attention throughout. Age: 5–8; Length: 83 min.; Suggested Retail Price: $14.98, TWENTIETH CENTURY FOX HOME ENTERTAINMENT

** BRER RABBIT AND BOSS LION (AMERICAN HEROES AND LEGENDS): When mean old Boss Lion threatens the folks of Brer Village, Brer Rabbit teaches him a lesson he'll never forget. Narration is by Danny Glover. Music is by Dr. John's Bayou. Adult Juror Comments: Delightful and amusing, with great music and story line. Excellent addition to any collection of folk tales. Danny Glover's voiceover is perfect. Brer Rabbit is an example of resourcefulness. Kid Juror Comments: Kids loved Brer Rabbit's character. Responded well to Danny Glover's narration and the music. "I like the rabbit because he comes up with good plans." "I wish I could think of things like that." Age: 5–12; Length: 30 min.; Suggested Retail Price: $19.95, RABBIT EARS PRODUCTIONS/WESTON WOODS

* CHILD'S GARDEN OF VERSE, A: This musical special is based on the classic story by Robert Louis Stevenson. Adult Juror Comments: Nicely produced, though the quality of the poetry sometimes gets overshadowed by the music. Loved the animation. The focus on Stevenson's illness as a child is distracting. Viewing with an adult would be helpful in clarifying words and phrases. Kid Juror Comments: Disliked the opening trailers but enjoyed the video. Kids showed concern for Robbie. Too frightening for younger kids, and the language was over their heads at times. Age: 7–9; Length: 26 min.; Suggested Retail Price: $12.98, ARTISAN/FAMILY HOME ENTERTAINMENT

** CHILDREN'S FAVORITES: FIVE FABLES: Animated fables about greedy and quarrelsome birds who learn a lesson, along with well-known fables by Aesop, "Town Mouse and City Mouse," "Lion and the Mouse," "The North Wind," and "The Sun." Adult Juror Comments: Visually interesting with beautiful graphics and music. Requires explanation of background and cultural context. Vocabulary is too sophisticated. Kids will benefit from a little coaching that encourages them to examine the artistry. Kid Juror Comments: Liked it but were bothered by absence of narrative. Related to some characters: County Mouse and City Mouse. "The pictures are nice." "I like the music." Age: 4–7; Length: 26 min.; Suggested Retail Price: $19.95, NATIONAL FILM BOARD OF CANADA

** CHILDREN'S FAVORITES: TALES OF WONDER: Three engrossing tales of magic and love are rendered in colorful animation. Includes "The Boy and the Snow Goose," "The Long Enchantment," and "The Magic Flute." Adult Juror Comments: Good content and aesthetics. "I enjoyed the images and colors." Appeals to imagination, asks audience to interpret the actions and emotions for themselves. As always, high standards from the National Film Board of Canada. Kid Juror Comments: Needed coaching to get beyond the non-narrative nature of the program. Those accustomed to watching standard TV fare didn't "get it." Those that did said, "Great! We really liked the drawings." Lacking diversity. Good discussion about fantasy. Age: 4–8; Length: 30 min.; Suggested Retail Price: $19.95, THE NATIONAL FILM BOARD OF CANADA

** CHILDREN'S STORIES FROM AFRICA — VOL. 1): Charming original songs and delightful African fables entertain and teach youngsters. Enchantingly told by Nandi Nyembe and feature dancers from the Mahlatsi Preschool. Adult Juror Comments: Good storytellers, beautiful sets and music, excellent pace. Excellent story choices recounted with such mirth that it's contagious. Opportunity for cross-cultural learning. Featuring a native speaker was a plus. Kid Juror Comments: "The young dancers, the songs, and the storyteller "were appealing highlights. "The storyteller also was really good; she didn't read from a book." "It told us how to be friends and to not laugh at anyone because they're different." Age: 3–8; Length: 26 min.; Suggested Retail Price: $12.95, MONTEREY HOME VIDEO

** CINDERELLA, CINDERELLA, CINDERELLA: All-time favorite retold three ways—making it three times as entertaining. One is a traditional interpretation illustrated in watercolors, another features animated crayon drawings by fifth-grade students. Adult Juror Comments: Delightful Canadian film demonstrates outstanding artistry. Can be used in the classroom or at home. Presentation demonstrates how styles have changed over the years. Some objected to the portrayal of the prince as a moron in the last title. Kid Juror Comments: Kids enjoyed it, especially the last title. It probably would not be played repeatedly. Kids didn't care for the music. The "penguin" story was everyone's favorite. "Different Cinderellas than the one we know." Age: 5–10; Length: 27 min.; Suggested Retail Price: $19.95, THE NATIONAL FILM BOARD OF CANADA

** CORDUROY AND OTHER BEAR STORIES (CHILDREN'S CIRCLE): Features three stories. Corduroy, the toystore teddy bear who longs for a real home, is dramatized in a live-action performance. "Panama," the crate discovered by Little Bear and "Blueberries for Sal," from the Caldecott award-winning book. Adult Juror Comments: This is a nice thematic presentation of children's favorites. "Corduroy" is excellent; shows good problem-solving skills. Adults liked lead title best, though the security guard appeared threatening. Kid Juror Comments: Held children's interest. They enjoyed seeing books they knew in animated form. Liked the special effects. Encourages reading and literacy. Children who know the books are intrigued by the videos, those who see the videos want to read the books. Age: 3–8; Length: 38 min.; Suggested Retail Price: $14.95, CHILDREN'S CIRCLE HOME VIDEO

*** DAISY HEAD MAYZIE BY DR. SEUSS; see p. 91

*** DAY JIMMY'S BOA ATE THE WASH AND OTHER STORIES, THE (CHILDREN'S CIRCLE): When Jimmy brings his pet on a field trip, one uproarious incident leads to another. Animated by Michael Sporn. Includes three more book-based titles: "Monty," "The Great White Man-Eating Shark," and "Fourteen Rats & The Rat Catcher." Adult Juror Comments: All great stories with good humorous morals, which stimulate an interest in reading the original books. Adults enjoy watching the programs as much as kids. Kid Juror Comments: Loved it! Appealing absurdity. Each story teaches a lesson. Younger kids like the shark story best. They especially liked the colors, the characters' wording, and the shark trick at the beach. Age: 4–9; Length: 35 min.; Suggested Retail Price: $14.95, CHILDREN'S CIRCLE HOME VIDEO

** DR. DESOTO AND OTHER STORIES (CHILDREN'S CIRCLE): Kindhearted Dr. DeSoto, the mouse dentist, outfoxes a fox. Anthology also includes "Curious George Rides a Bike," "Patrick," and "The Hat." Adult Juror Comments: Dr. DeSoto is carried out with glee. The classical music really fits "Patrick." The length is perfect. They are all true to the original. Curious George is iconographic but timeless. Kid Juror Comments: Terrific, especially for kids who are familiar with the programs in book form. Dr. Desoto was their runaway favorite. "Curious George" was second. They were mesmerized by "Patrick." In "The Hat," younger children were upset by the fire in the baby

buggy. Age: 3–9; Length: 35 min.; Suggested Retail Price: $14.95, CHIL-
DREN'S CIRCLE HOME VIDEO

** ELBERT'S BAD WORD/WEIRD PARENTS: "Elbert's Bad Word" is a lesson
about how an inadvertent nasty remark can get out of control. Narrated by
Ringo Starr. "Weird Parents" teaches the values of tolerance and understanding; narrated by Bette Midler. Adult Juror Comments: These are fun
and thought-provoking, though the visuals lack dynamics. Younger kids
didn't understand why the bad word looked like an insect. The commercial
at the beginning was too long and distracting. Kid Juror Comments: Funny.
They laughed out loud. "Weird Parents" provoked a lot of discussion.
"That's just like my parents." Kids accepted this at face value. Age: 5–8;
Length: 30 min.; Suggested Retail Price: $12.98, UNIVERSAL STUDIOS
HOME VIDEO

* EMPEROR'S NIGHTINGALE: Based on the classic tale by Hans Christian Andersen, tells the story of a young boy, the Emperor of China, who is liber-
ated from his palace of rules and rituals by the beauty of a nightingale's
song. Adult Juror Comments: This is a beautiful story though slow-paced
for today's kids. The production quality appears dated. The Chinese characters are stereotypically dressed and portrayed. Kid Juror Comments: Appealing but not all kids stayed with it. Considered slow-moving and "kinda
dark." Age: 6–12; Length: 70 min.; Suggested Retail Price: $24.95, REM-
BRANDT FILMS

** ENOUGH ALREADY! (A BELOVED FOLKTALE ABOUT BEING GRATEFUL): Brings
to life a beloved Jewish tale. "Smooze" is a poor but happy farmer who
brings one after another of his barnyard animals into his crowded house.
The result is a hilarious lesson in togetherness. Adult Juror Comments: Appealing, cute animation, good lessons. Kind and lifelike characters. Good
graphics. Some religious content but it doesn't detract from the story, which
is perhaps a little pedantic and outdated. Kid Juror Comments: Liked the
songs and sang them afterwards. Some kids had trouble understanding the
rabbi. It is slow-moving and long for younger viewers. "It's good because I
love songs." Age: 5–8; Length: 26 min.; Suggested Retail Price: $14.95,
ROSEBERRY ENTERTAINMENT, INC.

*** FACE, THE (STORIES TO REMEMBER): Live-action retelling of a traditional
Zen Buddhist story about a young boy, a dying storyteller, and the boy's desire to have the old man's magical story mask. The new owner must pass a
test of integrity, to grow a plant from a magic seed. Adult Juror Comments:
Led to intense and productive discussion about honesty. Kept children's at-

tention. An example of storytelling invitingly translated to video. "I enjoyed the story myself, but watching with children was even more enjoyable." Nicely paced. Kid Juror Comments: Funny, sad, and scary. "We liked that the face could see things." "This is a good teaching story. It shows the benefits of being honest." "I liked the fish and the face and how the old man taught the kids to be honest and truthful." Age: 5–12; Length: 20 min.; Suggested Retail Price: $19.95, JOSHUA M. GREENE PRODUCTIONS, INC.

** FOLLOW THE DRINKING GOURD (AMERICAN HEROES AND LEGENDS):** Based on the traditional American folk song, the compelling adventures of one family's escape from slavery via the Underground Railroad. Narrated by Morgan Freeman; score by Taj Mahal. Adult Juror Comments: Iconographic presentation. The hardships of the journey to freedom. Follows the story book of the same title and shows strength of people believing in a better life. Uses storytelling and legends to teach history and life's lessons. Kid Juror Comments: Kids said, "Why don't the pictures move?" Prompted discussion of the Underground Railroad. Some kids commented that they liked learning history from cartoons. "I like how the slaves knew they had to be free, even though it was hard and scary to escape. Everybody should be free." Age: 5–12; Length: 30 min.; Suggested Retail Price: $8.95, RABBIT EARS PRODUCTIONS/ ABLESOFT

** FROG AND TOAD ARE FRIENDS (JOHN MATTHEWS COLLECTION):** Frog and Toad star in five claymation short stories of friendship that are faithful to the book in letter, appearance, and wit. Adult Juror Comments: Outstanding claymation and music. Demonstrates cooperation, sharing, and friendship. Deals with relationships suitable for this age. Stimulated one child juror to write a letter as described in story. Slow-paced. Kid Juror Comments: Liked the stories a lot. Enjoyed seeing the book come alive and were fascinated by the technical demonstration on the claymation process. The second segment is more appropriate for older children than the first part. Age: 4–9; Length: 25 min.; Suggested Retail Price: $12.95, SONY WONDER/WESTERN PUBLISHING/GOLDEN BOOK

* GULLIVER'S TRAVELS (ENCHANTED TALES):** This new adaptation of Jonathan Swift's adventure is filled with original songs and kooky characters, and stars Gulliver, the shipwrecked "giant," and the tiny Lilliputians who discover him. Adult Juror Comments: Good introduction to classical music. Singing and humor are suitable. Shows how being "good" brings rewards. May encourage kids to read this classic story. Animation quality is mediocre and the program is front-loaded with commercials. Kid Juror Comments: Gulliver was a hero, especially to the younger ones. They did think it was a

bit wordy and too silly. Older children followed the story best. They liked the music. Age: 6–9; Length: 48 min.; Suggested Retail Price: $9.98, SONY WONDER

*** HAROLD AND THE PURPLE CRAYON (CHILDREN'S CIRCLE): An anthology of adaptations of the books by Crockett Johnson, including: "Harold and the Purple Crayon," "Harold's Fairy Tale," "A Picture for Harold's Room." Adult Juror Comments: The stories have universal appeal and lend themselves to imagination and fantasy on child's part. The adaptations are true to the original books. Kid Juror Comments: Terrific! All ages enjoyed this. Six- to eight-year-olds made sense of Harold's crayon animation. Younger kids enjoyed it but were confused. "My eight-year-old watched it off-and-on all weekend." Age: 3–8; Length: 30 min.; Suggested Retail Price: $14.95, CHILDREN'S CIRCLE HOME VIDEO

* HEIDI (SHIRLEY TEMPLE); see p. 324

* HERCULES (ENCHANTED TALES): Journey back in time to an age of mysteries, superhuman deeds, and mystical adventures. Hercules is a mortal with the strength of a god, destined to become one of the greatest kings ever. But first he must thwart the plots of his enemies. Adult Juror Comments: The dialects and modernizing slightly obscured the story, making it a confusing representation of the myth. Mediocre animation, but the music is engaging. Theme appropriate for this age. Kid Juror Comments: Because of its length, the kids had difficulty staying focused. The story went over the heads of younger children. For older children, it sparked an interest in Greek mythology. Age: 4–8; Length: 48 min.; Suggested Retail Price: $9.98, SONY WONDER

** HERE COMES THE CAT! AND OTHER CAT STORIES (CHILDREN'S CIRCLE): The ominous shadow of a big cat threatens a peaceful settlement of mice in this adaptation of the classic children's picture book, "Here Comes The Cat!" Includes three other stories: "The Cat and the Collector," "The Cat and the Canary," and "Millions of Cats." Adult Juror Comments: These four short stories present simple concepts. Each one stands alone and can be shown separately. "Cat and Collector" may be too intense for little ones. They all supports kids' interest in and exposure to classic literature. Kid Juror Comments: Entertaining. Children were attentive and asked to see it again. All four stories generated conversation afterward. Kids noticed that mice are afraid of cats and talked about that. Age: 3–8; Length: 30 min.; Suggested Retail Price: $14.95, CHILDREN'S CIRCLE HOME VIDEO

** HORTON HATCHES THE EGG — DR. SEUSS (DR. SEUSS VIDEO CLASSICS): Horton the Elephant agrees to help Mayzie the lazy bird. While she takes a "short" vacation, he sits on her egg, enduring terrible snowstorms and jeering friends. Narrated by Billy Crystal. Adult Juror Comments: Good themes, appropriate short-story length. Iconographic presentation lacks dynamics compared to full animation, which many children's titles are available in today. Kid Juror Comments: The rhyming verse went over very well. This makes for a good introduction to the book and to reading for oneself. It's best viewed in two segments. Age: 4–8; Length: 30 min.; Suggested Retail Price: $6.98, SONY WONDER/RANDOM HOUSE

** IRA SLEEPS OVER: Invited to stay at a friend's house, Ira faces a dilemma. "Should he bring the teddy bear he sleeps with?" Based on the best-selling book by Bernard Klaber. Adult Juror Comments: Excellent. Prompted discussion about what others may think of you, including the idea of self-worth. Scenes on bikes started conversation about bicycle safety. A little slow. Kid Juror Comments: Children said that they would recommend it to their friends. Both kids and adults enjoyed the singing. The kids' favorite part was the pillow fight! Age: 5–8; Length: 26 min.; Suggested Retail Price: $12.98, ARTISAN/FAMILY HOME ENTERTAINMENT

** IT ZWIBBLE: EARTHDAY BIRTHDAY: Celebrate Earth Day with a comical clan of modern-day dinosaurs dedicated to protecting the planet. Adult Juror Comments: Somewhat convoluted story for this audience with a weak ending that seems abrupt. Mediocre animation. In the end, though, the characters are excellent role models and make the whole thing engaging. Kid Juror Comments: Good, although they noticed that it seemed somewhat fabricated. Some asked to watch again. Others didn't. Age: 3–10; Length: 30 min.; Suggested Retail Price: $9.98, ARTISAN/FAMILY HOME ENTERTAINMENT

*** IVAN AND HIS MAGIC PONY (MIKHAIL BARYSHNIKOV'S STORIES FROM MY CHILDHOOD): Ivan, a simple country lad, and his magic pony encounter fantastic creatures and adventure in this classic Russian tale with award-winning animation and the voices of Rob Lowe and Hector Elizondo. Adult Juror Comments: Thoughtful, splendid animation with some adult humor. Ivan, the archetypical fool, triumphs in the end because he has good character. Some violence that falls within the context of the tale. Kid Juror Comments: Great! "It was very funny when the king jumped into the milk." "My friend would think it was very good." "This movie was good for kids." "I love seeing the horses." Age: 5–8; Length: 60 min.; Suggested Retail Price: $19.98, VIDEO INFORMATION SOURCE/LIBRARY DVD SOURCE

** JAMES MARSHALL LIBRARY, THE (CHILDREN'S CIRCLE): Contains four fully animated titles: "Wings: A Tale of Two Chickens," "Goldilocks and the Three Bears," "The Three Little Pigs," and "Red Riding Hood." Adult Juror Comments: The animation is charming, the humor appropriate, the pace slow. These three classics are all clever and a delight to watch. Inspired viewers to check the books out from the library. Some values from traditional fairy tales are inappropriate today. Kid Juror Comments: The humor held their attention. Enjoyed the repetition of "I'll huff and I'll puff." Kids made houses afterwards as an art project. Age: 4–8; Length: 43 min.; Suggested Retail Price: $14.95, CHILDREN'S CIRCLE HOME VIDEO

** JOEY RUNS AWAY AND OTHER STORIES (CHILDREN'S CIRCLE): Includes "Joey Runs Away," about a young kangaroo who ventures out of his mother's pouch, "The Cow Who Fell In The Canal," "The Bear and the Fly," and "The Most Wonderful Egg in the World." Adult Juror Comments: These timeless adaptations are charming stories, artfully told. Well paced with wonderful musical accompaniment. The length is fine for this age. Celebrates diversity. Kid Juror Comments: Many stories were new to them, and those familiar with the books loved watching them as videos. Kids not familiar with the books were inspired to read them. Age: 3–8; Length: 28 min.; Suggested Retail Price: $14.95, CHILDREN'S CIRCLE HOME VIDEO

** JOHN HENRY (AMERICAN HEROES AND LEGENDS): Denzel Washington recalls the legend of John Henry, who single-handedly defeated a steam drill in a steel-driving competition. Score is by B.B. King. Adult Juror Comments: Iconographic production, lacks full motion. Inspiring music. The visuals are artistically executed and the narration is poetic. One juror commented, "I felt like I was sitting on a front porch admiring the Spanish moss and wiping the humidity from my face." Kid Juror Comments: Kids asked why the pictures didn't move. This tall tale, new to many of the kids, was great. It prompted discussions about literal exaggerations. They enjoyed Denzel Washington's narration and the music, but found it slow-moving in comparison to what they're accustomed to. Age: 5–12; Length: 30 min.; Suggested Retail Price: $8.95, RABBIT EARS PRODUCTIONS/ABLESOFT

** JOHNNY APPLESEED (AMERICAN HEROES AND LEGENDS): Retelling the story of the benevolent naturalist who roamed the Ohio Valley region in the 1800s, planting apple orchards and spreading good will. Read by Garrison Keillor. Adult Juror Comments: Iconographic presentation limits its appeal. Good introduction to a legendary American figure. Perfect blend of watercolor illustrations, narration, and music. Invites discussion about this complex frontiersman and the riches he brings to settlers and nature. Slow-moving. Kid Juror Comments: An unusual pleasure. Afterwards, they wanted to plant apple trees. They discussed the quality of this production compared to other, more commercial videos they've seen. Conclusion: artistically executed but not always engaging and "a little boring." Age: 6–12; Length: 30 min.; Suggested Retail Price: $8.95, RABBIT EARS PRODUCTIONS/ABLESOFT

** JOURNEY BENEATH THE SEA (OZ KIDS): Jack Pumpkinhead wants to have an adventure in the worst way. The Oz Kids embark on a sea cruise in a leaky boat. Befriended by two mermaids, they explore the underwater world until their tour is cut short by sea devils and the evil Zog. Adult Juror Comments: Contains some good messages, such as "It takes too much time to hate." Too long for this age. The language, animation, and format are fine. "What child doesn't like an adventure with queens, castles, and mermaids?" Kid Juror Comments: First-rate animation and characters. "You could tell the story without sound because the animation was so good." Kids liked how the characters helped each other. Age: 5–8; Length: 66 min.; Suggested Retail Price: $12.95, PARAMOUNT PICTURES

** JOURNEY HOME: THE ANIMALS OF FARTHINGWOOD: Heroic Fox, dutiful Badger, shy Mole, playful Weasel, and their friends are on the move! These are the animals of Farthingwood, looking for a land free of bulldozers and humans—a safe place to call home. From best-selling children's books. Adult Juror Comments: Charming story but a little too long. A little sad in parts, but great voices and enchanting characters. Death of the animals a little too sad for under six. Good humor, great values of how hard it is for animals of different types to work together. Kid Juror Comments: "You can get the feeling it is a very long journey." "The animals are cute. I didn't like that they died." Kids liked the value of the animals of "mutual protection" helping the younger small animals. Younger kids found it too long. Age: 5–10; Length: 120 min.; Suggested Retail Price: $14.98, TWENTIETH CENTURY FOX HOME ENTERTAINMENT

*** LINNEA IN MONET'S GARDEN: Based on the book, blends imagination and education while teaching about the art and life of one of the 20th century's most important painters, Claude Monet. A young girl and an old man, her neighbor, take her on to visit Monet's garden. Adult Juror Comments: Beautifully produced. An inspiring, entertaining, and thoughtful story. A superb mixture of animation, photographs, and live action as well as an effective art education tool. All agreed, "It's one of the best we've seen." Kid Juror Comments: Fantastic! Glued to the screen, especially for the cartoon parts. They enjoyed the friendship between the old man and Linnea. "I loved this video; I want to be Linnea." "I'm an artist like Monet." They wanted to picnic in his garden! Age: 3–10; Length: 30 min.; Suggested Retail Price: $19.95, FIRST RUN FEATURES

** LITTLE ENGINE THAT COULD, THE; see p. 91

*** LITTLE LORD FAUNTLEROY; see p. 325

*** LOST & FOUND (JANE HISSEY'S OLD BEAR STORIES); see p. 92

** MADELINE'S RESCUE (MADELINE): When Madeline tries to balance on a bridge rail, she plunges into the river and is saved by a very special dog. The dog helps with lessons, sings, spells, and even selects her own name, Genevieve. Adult Juror Comments: Delightful adaptation of the book. The high-quality animation and music is charming and entertaining. The "bad man" who got rid of the dog is a sure discussion-prompter. Lacks cultural diversity. A good tie-in to the classic children's book. Kid Juror Comments: Afterwards, the younger ones reenacted the story, humming the music. The songs were a big hit. The accents took some getting used to for the children. Inner-city kids commented that they did not feel represented. Age: 3–9; Length: 25 min.; Suggested Retail Price: $12.95, SONY WONDER/ WESTERN PUBLISHING/GOLDEN BOOK

** MARZIPAN PIG: A story, narrated by Tim Curry, about a candy pig whose sweetness brings the creatures together to dance by the light of the moon. Directed by Michael Sporn. Adult Juror Comments: Beautifully animated with wonderful narration and good music. Thought-provoking and a good discussion-starter on the subjects of death and love. A pleasant, gentle quality to this video. Kid Juror Comments: Not thrilled with this one. Some thought it was "kind of weird." Some responded to its gentle quality. Some children said they would enjoy viewing this with their family. Age: 5–12; Length: 28 min.; Suggested Retail Price: $9.98, ARTISAN/FAMILY HOME ENTERTAINMENT

*** MAURICE SENDAK LIBRARY (CHILDREN'S CIRCLE): Includes the Caldecott Award–winner, "In The Night Kitchen," where bread-dough airplanes fly and everyone dances; "Where the Wild Things Are," the best-selling children's book; and profiles of author Maurice Sendak. Adult Juror Comments: This classic literary anthology features two of Maurice Sendak's best-known stories and stimulates a great discussion about fears of the unknown. The biography of Maurice Sendak is quite fascinating. Kid Juror Comments: Always a winner, in whatever medium. Most are familiar with

Sendak's books, especially "Where the Wild Things Are" and love seeing it come to life. They talked about what scares them afterward. Age: 5–12; Length: 35 min.; Suggested Retail Price: $14.95, CHILDREN'S CIRCLE HOME VIDEO

*** MAX'S CHOCOLATE CHICKEN (CHILDREN'S CIRCLE); see p. 92

*** MERLIN AND THE DRAGONS (STORIES TO REMEMBER): Young Arthur doesn't understand why pulling a sword from a stone qualifies him for kingship. Merlin, the magician, guides him with inspiring stories and prophetic dreams that prepare him to become a magnificent king. Narrated by Kevin Kline. Adult Juror Comments: A wonderful slant on the classic story of King Arthur and his mentor, the incredible magician Merlin. Excellent role models for self-esteem, courage, and trustworthiness. Kid Juror Comments: Compelling and complex. Kids enjoyed the animation, though some scenes were scary for the youngest viewers. The older children were fascinated with it and talked about it later. Age: 5–12; Length: 27 min.; Suggested Retail Price: $9.95, LIGHTYEAR ENTERTAINMENT

* MONKEY BUSINESS (BABAR): Babar runs into trouble guarding the Royal Peanut Patch. Includes "Race to the Moon." Adult Juror Comments: Clear, colorful, but long for younger kids. Characters smoke and drink, and there is some gender stereotyping. The rhino wife is domineering and the husband makes fun of her when she's not around. Kid Juror Comments: A multimedia success, for most. Kids are more fond of some Babar stories than others. They were curious about the king's royal treatment, and discussed it afterward. Age: 5–12; Length: 47 min.; Suggested Retail Price: $12.98, ARTISAN/FAMILY HOME ENTERTAINMENT

* MONKEY PRINCE, THE (OZ KIDS): Dorothy's son, Neddie, programs a computer belonging to the Wizard's son, Frank, to take him and Toto II to China. When the computer is stolen by the Monkey Prince, they will be stranded unless the other Oz Kids can find them. Adult Juror Comments: Amusing story with clearly presented messages about feelings and fears. Well produced. It's very respectful of kids' thinking, feelings, and social skills. The monkey learns from his mistakes. Kid Juror Comments: Younger kids particularly enjoyed it. They loved the animal characters. Good discussion-starter about feelings, emotions, and possible fears. "It teaches you not to be mean to others." Age: 4–7; Length: 65 min.; Suggested Retail Price: $12.95, PARAMOUNT PICTURES

** MOUSE SOUP (JOHN MATTHEWS COLLECTION): A happy-go-lucky field mouse finds himself on the dinner menu of a dim-witted weasel and has to think fast. Adult Juror Comments: Well produced, nicely animated. The attention to detail is exemplary. Addresses positive ways to resolve conflicts. Characters are courteous, kind, and funny. Faithful to the original book. Some stereotyping. Kid Juror Comments: Good fun. Worth repeating. They loved the songs and the characters' voices, and acted out the mouse dance steps afterwards. Age: 4–12; Length: 26 min.; Suggested Retail Price: $12.95, SONY WONDER/WESTERN PUBLISHING/GOLDEN BOOK

*** MOWGLI'S BROTHERS: Follows the adventures of the bear, the panther, and other animals who befriend Mowgli, an orphan. Animated by Chuck Jones, narrated by Roddy McDowall. Adult Juror Comments: Ideas about democracy in a literary style. Encourages reading the original story. Well paced, though images of the tiger are scary for kids under six. Kid Juror Comments: Enthusiastic about seeing this story. Asked many questions about the people represented. Boys liked it more than girls. Kids thought some of the animated scenes were too grim. Age: 5–8; Length: 29 min.; Suggested Retail Price: $9.98, ARTISAN/FAMILY HOME ENTERTAINMENT

** MY NEIGHBOR TOTORO: Japanese children's classic tells of magical creatures who inhabit a tree trunk and the way they touch a child's life. Adult Juror Comments: Truly entertaining. Blends cultural and ethnic characteristics to show the similarities between people, but there is no way the characters look Japanese and there are too many stereotypes: an old hag next door and an imitation Indian war dance. Kid Comments: Prompted discussions about running away and how to handle fear or ghosts. Kids wanted to know who Totoro was. Not a child in the group who didn't like it. "Tell them we just love it." Age: 5–8; Length: 87 min.; Suggested Retail Price: $19.98, TWENTIETH CENTURY FOX HOME ENTERTAINMENT

*** NEW FRIENDS AND OTHER STORIES (FUN IN A BOX): Lead title is adapted from the book *Howard* by James Stevenson. Howard gets lost and ends up in New York City, where he is befriended by a frog and some nice mice. Contains three other shorts. Adult Juror Comments: Great adaptation of the book and true to the original story. For New Yorkers, it has particular appeal, opening up a discussion about friendship and life in the big city. Beautiful animation. Kid Juror Comments: Best story was the first one. Rural kids had questions about the scenes from New York. They liked how Howard's new friends took care of him and how, when he tried to leave them, he was motivated to return. Age: 4–12; Length: 30 min.; Suggested Retail Price: $14.95, MADE TO ORDER PRODUCTIONS/RAINBOW

*** NOAH'S ARK (STORIES TO REMEMBER): A moving drama enacting with heartwarming emotion Noah's heroic mission to rescue all creatures great and small. Based on the book by Peter Spier. Narrated by James Earl Jones. Music is by Stewart Copeland of "The Police." Adult Juror Comments: Great addition any children's video library, well produced and thoroughly engaging. James Earl Jones' narration is perfect for the story and makes it appealing to a contemporary audience. Kid Juror Comments: A big treat. Those familiar with the story were anxious to see if it was accurate to the version they knew. Age: 5–12; Length: 27 min.; Suggested Retail Price: $9.95, LIGHTYEAR ENTERTAINMENT

** NUTCRACKER ON ICE: The Nutcracker, probably the world's most beloved Christmas tale, is performed on ice by Olympic gold medalists, Oksana Baiul and Viktor Petrenko. Adult Juror Comments: an introduction to this classic with music by Tchaikovsky. Those who love figure skating or ballet will particularly enjoy it. The costumes are beautiful, the skating is admirable. Perfect for family viewing or music appreciation. Kid Juror Comments: Spellbound by the talent displayed. Girls enjoyed this more than boys. Act II is more enthralling than Act I. Some kids wandered off but returned for the backstage peek at the end. "The skating is cool." Age: 6–12; Length: 110 min.; Suggested Retail Price: $14.98, TWENTIETH CENTURY FOX HOME ENTERTAINMENT

** ONCE UPON A DINOSAUR: Three tales of "once upon a time" to add to any child's collection of fairy tales: "How Dinosaurs Learned to Fly," "The Emperor's New Clothes," and "The Long Enchantment." Adult Juror Comments: Each story offers a unique style and presentation. Well done with bright animation, intricate sets and costumes. The narrator is at times difficult to understand, and the morals are too advanced for the audience. Kid Juror Comments: On target, though had some problems grasping all the concepts. "I didn't understand it until my Mommy explained it to me." "My daughter watched it three times." All of the programs evoked discussion from the children afterward. Age: 3–7; Length: 26 min.; Suggested Retail Price: $19.95, THE NATIONAL FILM BOARD OF CANADA

*** OWL MOON AND OTHER STORIES (CHILDREN'S CIRCLE): Haunting music and poetic narration underscore the special closeness between father and child as they search for the great horned owl. This book-based program includes three other literary stories. Adult Juror Comments: True to the original though slow-moving at times. Kid Juror Comments: Kids liked the stories though they were disappointed that not all are fully animated. Age: 4–12; Length: 35 min.; Suggested Retail Price: $14.95, CHILDREN'S CIRCLE HOME VIDEO

** PAPER BAG PRINCESS, THE (A BUNCH OF MUNSCH): A clever princess has her kingdom toasted by a fire-breathing dragon that prince-naps Ronald. She finds out that every prince isn't charming, and she can make her own happily-ever-afters. Adult Juror Comments: This charming modern fairy tale has a female heroine. Takes a humorous look at royalty. Some vocabulary was a little over the head of the audience. Deviates from the original book. Some stereotyping. Kid Juror Comments: The story and the music were thoroughly appealing. They laughed at the antics of both the princess and the prince. Most were familiar with the story and the feminist messages. They loved the outcome: the dragon became a better friend in the end. Age: 5–12; Length: 25 min.; Suggested Retail Price: $12.95, SONY WONDER/WESTERN PUBLISHING/GOLDEN BOOK

*** PEGASUS (STORIES TO REMEMBER): Follows the mythological Pegasus from birth to his battle with the multi-headed Chimaera; his appointment by Zeus as thunderbearer and his transformation into the constellation bearing his name. Narrated by Mia Farrow. Adapted by Doris Orgel. Adult Juror Comments: Beautifully animated and an excellent translation of the Greek myth. An engaging way to introduce children to mythology. Kid Juror Comments: After watching, the kids got really jazzed up about mythology in general. Many were familiar with the story of Pegasus and enjoyed watching it on video. It stimulated a search in the library afterward for more myths. Age: 4–12; Length: 25 min.; Suggested Retail Price: $9.95, LIGHTYEAR ENTERTAINMENT

** PIGS PLUS "DAVID'S FATHER" (BUNCH OF MUNSCH, A): Contains two stories. In the first, the pigpen gate is left ajar, opening the way to an adventure. In the second, a young girl who doesn't want to meet her new neighbors changes her mind when an ordinary boy introduces her to his extraordinary father. Adult Juror Comments: Great stories, cute story lines. Some of the music was difficult for kids to follow. The humor is at times odd. David's father was interestingly different. The story brings up the issue of being adopted. At times it makes fun of teachers. Kid Juror Comments: Much appreciated stories and afterward talked about people not being what they seem at first. Age: 4–12; Length: 25 min.; Suggested Retail Price: $12.95, SONY WONDER/WESTERN PUBLISHING/GOLDEN BOOK

*** PIGS' WEDDING AND OTHER STORIES, THE (CHILDREN'S CIRCLE): Porker and Curlytail invite all their favorite friends to their wedding. Everyone comes, along with the rain. Adult Juror Comments: Good literary stories. Not all of the animation is full-range. Some stories are better-produced than others but the content makes up for it. Kid Juror Comments: Stories were fine, but children disappointed when they were not fully animated. They talked about the stories afterward and wanted to watch the video again. Age: 5–12; Length: 39 min.; Suggested Retail Price: $14.95, CHILDREN'S CIRCLE HOME VIDEO

** PINOCCHIO (GLOBALSTAGE 1998 CHILDREN'S THEATRE SERIES); see p. 326

** POCAHONTAS (ENCHANTED TALES): The familiar tale of Pocahontas, a beautiful Indian princess, and the dashing English Virginia settler whose life she saves. Adult Juror Comments: Appropriate humor and well-selected classical music. Several inaccuracies, among them: use of gardening implements not available then, Pocahontas' appearance is not representative of the time. Kid Juror Comments: The animals won over hearts and minds. Many preferred this to the Disney version and thought it was a more complete story. They watched it over and over. Age: 5–12; Length: 48 min.; Suggested Retail Price: $9.98, SONY WONDER

* PRINCE AND THE PAUPER, THE (ENCHANTED TALES): Animated classic about a young prince who swaps identities with a look-alike beggar boy—an adventure tale that has lasted through the ages. Adult Juror Comments: Mediocre animation. The addition of vicarious talking objects who sing and dance is more distracting to the program than beneficial. Kid Juror Comments: Okay but not that funny. "I couldn't tell what those talking things were," commented one child. Age: 5–8; Length: 48 min.; Suggested Retail Price: $14.98, SONY WONDER

** RAILWAY DRAGON: An ancient dragon emerges from beneath a railroad bridge and befriends a young girl. Adult Juror Comments: Adults thought the story was well animated but nothing special. They were concerned about the girl sneaking out at night. It may be understood better if the lesson of the story was explained beforehand. Kid Juror Comments: Appealing. It promoted discussion afterward about imagination. Age: 4–10; Length: 27 min.; Suggested Retail Price: $9.98, ARTISAN/FAMILY HOME ENTERTAINMENT

* RAINBOW FISH; see p. 93

** REAL STORY OF HUMPTY DUMPTY, THE (REAL STORY): One day the misunderstood egg's luck changes. He foils Glitch the Witch's evil plan to poison Princess Allegra and becomes the town hero. Then...crack! Will the power of love save Humpty? Adult Juror Comments: Despite its loose relationship to the original story, it has many merits—a sense of humor, imagination, and fantastic characters. A happy and realistic ending. Some of the language is too aggressive and too advanced for the audience. Kid Juror Comments: The child-centered characters held their attention from beginning to end. The length is perfect. The kids related to the emphasis that "it's okay to be different." Age: 5–8; Length: 25 min.; Suggested Retail Price: $9.95, SONY WONDER/WESTERN PUBLISHING/GOLDEN BOOK

*** RED SHOES, THE: Animated, contemporary version of the Hans Christian Andersen tale, set in Harlem. Instead of the girl dancing to her death, her dance leads her to understanding the importance of friendship. Directed by Michael Sporn. Score by Caleb Sampson. Adult Juror Comments: Exquisite. Fabulous script is well presented and funny. Stimulates discussion about money and greed, theft and the motivation to steal, complicated friendships. Excellent family viewing. Kid Juror Comments: Sensational. Inspired to enthusiastically discuss it further. They laughed out loud, enjoyed everything from the music to the colors used in the production. Girls related to the subject matter more than boys, but both enjoyed it. Age: 5–12; Length: 28 min.; Suggested Retail Price: $9.98, ARTISAN/FAMILY HOME ENTERTAINMENT

* RETURN OF MOMBI, THE (OZ KIDS): Halloween and witchcraft make for another exciting adventure in Oz. Mombi, an evil witch, has returned to Emerald City, kidnapping the Oz adults, good witch Glinda and the Nome King. Now it's up to the Oz kids to save Oz from Mombi's dark powers. Adult Juror Comments: Simply animated story with good narration. The concept is interesting and imaginative. Uses very age-appropriate language. Helpful if the viewer is familiar with the original story. Characters behave respectfully. Too long for some kids. Kid Juror Comments: Interesting characters, though one said, "You have to know the Wizard of Oz to get this." "Some parts are spooky." "It makes me want to learn magic." Most kids liked this video. It may be too slow for some. Age: 5–8; Length: 89 min.; Suggested Retail Price: $12.95, PARAMOUNT PICTURES

* RICHARD SCARRY'S BEST BUSY PEOPLE VIDEO EVER!; see p. 93

** RICHARD SCARRY'S BEST SILLY STORIES AND SONGS VIDEO EVER!: Each hilarious adventure comes to life, as children laugh, learn, and sing along with the Richard Scarry characters Huckle Cat and Lowly Worm. Adult Juror Comments: Entertaining short stories at a good length for this age group. Contains very childlike, silly humor. Shows good gender role models. Kid Juror Comments: Immediate demands for repeat showing. Many recognized the characters and loved the songs. Inspired to visit the library and look for Scarry's books. Excellent teaching video for toddlers to age seven. Age: 3–8; Length: 30 min.; Suggested Retail Price: $9.98, SONY WONDER/RANDOM HOUSE

** RICHARD SCARRY'S BEST SING-ALONG MOTHER GOOSE VIDEO EVER!: While searching for Lowly Worm, Huckle meets lots of new friends. Includes "Mary Had A Little Lamb," "Hey Diddle, Diddle" and other sing-alongs. Adult Juror Comments: Well produced with nice music. The characters are clearly identified, distinct and children relate to them. It's suitable for this age group, especially the four- and five-year-olds. Prompted discussion about the values of classic children's rhymes. Kid Juror Comments: Sang along and repeated rhymes with the tape. Five-year-olds said it was "too silly!" Even the three-year-olds understood "Looking for Lowly" because of the repetition. Age: 3–8; Length: 30 min.; Suggested Retail Price: $9.98, SONY WONDER/RANDOM HOUSE

*** ROSIE'S WALK & OTHER STORIES (CHILDREN'S CIRCLE); see p. 93

** RUMPELSTILTSKIN: Based on the fairy tale about a magical elf who helps the miller's daughter turn straw into gold. Adult Juror Comments: Heroine is bright and articulate. When she talks back to the King, it's done in an appropriate manner. She even reads a book while waiting for the baby. Handles danger well. It's scary enough. Emphasizes the importance of telling the truth. Kid Juror Comments: Enjoyable, although a little long. Experienced a range of emotions while viewing and thought the witch was very mean. They learned that "you shouldn't say things that aren't true." Some wanted to watch it again. Age: 4–10; Length: 27 min.; Suggested Retail Price: $9.98, ARTISAN/FAMILY HOME ENTERTAINMENT

** SAND FAIRY, THE: From the BBC, this story tells the tale of children who discover a troll in the sand who will grant them their wish for a day. Teaches children about appreciating what they have. Adult Juror Comments: Entertaining, but a little too long. Good movie for discussion on choices and their consequences. Costumes, sets, music, and especially the puppet, were wonderful, serving the period feeling very well. Has gender stereotypes, lacks cultural diversity. Kid Juror Comments: "The Sand Fairy was cool." "The kids in the movie were great actors." At times hard to understand what the children were saying because of their accents. "Are Sand Fairies real?" "You have to be careful about wishes." "Can we read the book?" Age: 6–10; Length: 139 min.; Suggested Retail Price: $29.98, TWENTIETH CENTURY FOX HOME ENTERTAINMENT

** SECRET GARDEN, THE — CBS/FOX; see p. 327

** SECRET GARDEN, THE — DISNEY/ABC; see p. 327

** SECRET GARDEN, THE — MGM/UA: Outstanding child actress Margaret O'Brien touches the heart in this classic adventure of a young orphan sent to live at the foreboding English estate of her uncle and his crippled son. Adult Juror Comments: Creates a magical world from a child's point of view. Shows how children can influence and affect events towards a positive outcome. Takes a healthy attitude on bereavement and taking a chance on love. Visually lush and evocative. Invaluable insights. Kid Juror Comments: Good story, but some commented, "Black-and-white is boring." Though took time for them to get into it, provided an opportunity to discuss death, love, and friendship. Age: 6–14; Length: 72 min.; Suggested Retail Price: $14.95, MGM/UA HOME ENTERTAINMENT

*** SNOW QUEEN, THE (STORIES TO REMEMBER): Powerful tale follows a young girl's quest to rescue her playmate from the icy palace of the Snow Queen. Based on the Hans Christian Andersen folk tale. Narrated by Sigourney Weaver. Music by Jason Miles. Adult Juror Comments: Beautifully animated with wonderful character voices and lovely music. Excellent role models. The characters express many emotions that children can relate to, such as caring enough for another to put oneself out for them. Kid Juror Comments: Absorbing. Kids enjoyed the characters' adventures, responded to the story and loved the ending, which reunites the friends. They wanted to watch it again. Age: 5–12; Length: 30 min.; Suggested Retail Price: $9.95, LIGHTYEAR ENTERTAINMENT

** SNOW QUEEN, THE (MIKHAIL BARYSHNIKOV'S STORIES FROM MY CHILDHOOD): A brave young girl defies danger to save a dear friend from a cold but beautiful Snow Queen. Russian animation, with voices of Kathleen Turner, Kristen Dunst, and Mickey Rooney in the classic Andersen tale. Adult Juror Comments: Great model of perseverance and friendship. Somewhat confusing story line, stereotypical female characters. Beautiful illustrations and colors. Lively characters. Works well as an educational tie to folk tales, fairy tales and cultural legends. Some Kid Juror Comments: "Can I get this book?" "The Snow Queen looks mean. I don't want to watch." "The girl is so brave and loves her friend." "I wonder if that is why people get sad in the winter." One group of children were so disturbed they wouldn't watch the whole thing. Age: 5–8; Length: 60 min.; Suggested Retail Price: $19.98, VIDEO INFORMATION SOURCE/ LIBRARY DVD

* SNOW WHITE (ENCHANTED TALES): Classic fairy tale about a princess, a wicked stepmother, seven dwarfs, and a handsome prince. Adult Juror Comments: A twist on the original story, because Snow White knows the prince she falls in love with. Animation quality mediocre, but the appealing, humorous characters and pleasant songs make it worthwhile. Kid Juror Comments: A dwarf by any other name . . . Kids found it entertaining that all the dwarves were named "Joe," and wanted to see it again. Not as scary as the Disney version, and they appreciated that . Good length. Age: 4–9; Length: 48 min.; Suggested Retail Price: $14.98, SONY WONDER

** SPARKY'S MAGIC PIANO: An eight-year-old boy discovers a magic piano which allows him to become a terrific pianist. Trouble ensues when he lets his ability go to his head. Features voices of Mel Blanc and Vincent Price. Adult Juror Comments: A pleasant surprise with a great concept. Emphasizes the ideas to "Believe in yourself," "Don't let other people do everything for you," and "If you have real talent, show it." Fosters music appreciation and might even inspire piano practice. Kid Juror Comments: The messages and the humor were just right. Opened up many opportunities for discussion about believing in yourself but not getting a big head. Older kids didn't enjoy the music as much as the younger ones did. It's a bit too long. Age: 5–10; Length: 50 min.; Suggested Retail Price: $9.98, ARTISAN/FAMILY HOME ENTERTAINMENT

*** STORIES FROM THE BLACK TRADITION (CHILDREN'S CIRCLE): Contains four wonderful stories: "A Story, A Story" by Gail E. Haley, "Mufaro's Beautiful Daughters" by John Steptoe, "In the Village of the Round and Square Houses" by Ann Grifalconi, and "Goggles" by Ezra Jack Keats. Adult Juror Comments: Rich texture, warm feelings. The short stores, ten minutes each, can be shown in segments. Sensitive to fathers' relationship with daughters. All themes are centered around the community. Kid Juror Comments: "Magical, wonderful, and different." Kids enjoyed hearing the African accents. "Showed how African men and women appreciate one another." Referring to the story about mosquitoes, "I will never look at a mosquito the same way again." Age: 5–12; Length: 52 min.; Suggested Retail Price: $14.95, CHILDREN'S CIRCLE HOME VIDEO

* STORY OF JONAH AND THE WHALE, THE (THE BEGINNER'S BIBLE): Jonah tries to escape God's command, runs away on a ship, and gets swallowed by a gigantic but friendly whale. Inside the whale's stomach, Jonah learns an astonishing lesson about God's love and forgiveness, even for those who disobey Him. Adult Juror Comments: Entertaining, with good role models. However, the concepts and language are more suitable for ages five and up. Better-suited to a Christian audience. Borders on talking down to kids. Kid Juror Comments: A lot of information that fives and up can relate to and understand. Stimulated discussion afterward. Some kids thought it was too preachy. The language used was too difficult for the younger kids. Age: 4–8; Length: 30 min.; Suggested Retail Price: $12.98, SONY WONDER

** STORY OF JOSEPH AND HIS BROTHERS, THE; see p. 94

** STORY OF THE DANCING FROG: Amanda Plummer narrates the animated, musical tale of George, the many-talented frog whose leaps and bounds bring him fame and fortune. Directed by Michael Sporn. Adult Juror Comments: Lovely. An excellent example of a mother telling her child a story and their discussions afterward. Narrator has a refreshing and soothing voice quality, though the pace is slow. Kid Juror Comments: Not too enthusiastic. The story better suited to older kids, yet the animation appeals to younger ones. Age: 5–12; Length: 28 min.; Suggested Retail Price: $9.98, ARTISAN/FAMILY HOME ENTERTAINMENT

* STORY OF THE PRODIGAL SON, THE (THE BEGINNER'S BIBLE): To teach repentance, forgiveness, and love, Jesus tells about a son who refused to work on the family farm. He goes off to see the world where he encounters the glittering temptations of the city. When he returns, his fathers welcomes him in love. Adult Juror Comments: Good storybook quality and visually appealing. Teaches lessons by showing how to handle different behaviors. The vignettes lack continuity, and most characters are white. Best for Christian viewers. Kid Juror Comments: "That was a good cartoon." "It's better than church, where they just tell about it," commented one six-year-old. Some children didn't understand the meaning of the story. Others talked about their relationship with their parents. Age: 4–8; Length: 30 min.; Suggested Retail Price: $12.98, SONY WONDER

** STREGA NONNA AND OTHER STORIES (CHILDREN'S CIRCLE): Includes "Strega Nonna," the Chinese "Tikki Tikki Tembo," an African folk tale "A Story, A Story," and "Foolish Frog," a folk song by Pete Seeger. Adult Juror Comments: Interesting flavor promotes multicultural understanding. Beautifully done with great music. "Foolish Frog" is a fun sing-along song.

The stories can be viewed individually with discussion and activities in between. Kid Juror Comments: Older kids loved the stories, especially "Tikki Tikki Tembo" and "A Story, A Story." Younger kids paid more attention to the stories with songs. They liked the representation of many different cultures and asked questions afterwards. Age: 4–9; Length: 35 min.; Suggested Retail Price: $14.95, CHILDREN'S CIRCLE HOME VIDEO

** SWAN PRINCESS, THE: From the director of "The Fox and the Hound," this animated feature-length film stars John Cleese as Jean-Bob the Frog, Jack Palance as Rothbart, Sandy Duncan as the Queen, and Steven Wright as Speed the Turtle. Adult Juror Comments: Animation is excellent, with colorful characters and uplifting music. A simplistic version of the classic fairy tale and best suited for four- to ten-year-olds. Kid Juror Comments: Okay but not great. "It's a fairy tale that turns out good." Age: 4–10; Length: 90 min.; Suggested Retail Price: $19.98, WARNER HOME VIDEO

*** TAILOR OF GLOUCESTER, THE (THE WORLD OF PETER RABBIT AND FRIENDS): The Tailor of Gloucester is exhausted and ill with fever. Yet he still hasn't finished making the elaborate silk coat for the Mayor's wedding on Christmas day. Adult Juror Comments: This beautiful production has exquisite animation and captivating artistry, faithful to the original story. The music is soothing yet lighthearted. It may encourage reading the original book. A jurors' favorite. Kid Juror Comments: Charmed with the story and the production even though it's somewhat slow. They knew the accents were English but stayed with it and didn't have a difficult time understanding. All the kids wanted to watch this again. Age: 3–12; Length: 30 min.; Suggested Retail Price: $14.95, GOODTIMES HOME VIDEO

*** TALE OF MRS. TIGGY-WINKLE AND MR. JEREMY FISHER, THE (THE WORLD OF PETER RABBIT AND FRIENDS): Contains two stories. When Lucie loses her handkerchiefs, yet again, she never imagines that her search will end with a kindly washerwoman, Mrs. Tiggy-Winkle. Adult Juror Comments: A wonderful production with excellent animation and soothing music. True to the original classic story and a little slow-moving, but it may promote an interest in reading the story. Kid Juror Comments: Girls liked it more than boys. Both were a little confused to find the two stories don't relate to each other. Age: 3–12; Length: 30 min.; Suggested Retail Price: $14.95, GOODTIMES HOME VIDEO

*** TALE OF PETER RABBIT AND BENJAMIN BUNNY, THE (THE WORLD OF PETER RABBIT AND FRIENDS): Peter was very lucky to escape from Mr. MacGregor's garden without getting caught. When his cousin, Benjamin, suggests that they visit the garden again, Peter is more than a little nervous. Adult Juror Comments: Charming production retains the spirit of the original art while making the stories accessible to contemporary audiences. May promote an interest in reading. Kid Juror Comments: English accents were no big problem. Kids stayed with it and could understand without too much trouble. Age: 3–12; Length: 30 min.; Suggested Retail Price: $14.95, GOODTIMES HOME VIDEO

** TALE OF PETER RABBIT, THE: Beatrix Potter's classic comes to musical life through animation and the voice of Carol Burnett. Adult Juror Comments: Good story. The father's death is dealt with more than in the original story. Some stereotyping: Girls are good and expected to "obey"; boys are naughty and it's okay for them to "explore" and be forgiven. Kid Juror Comments: A grand show, especially the funny parts. Afterward, they asked to read the books. It's most appropriate for ages four and up. Age: 3–10; Length: 28 min.; Suggested Retail Price: $12.98, ARTISAN/FAMILY HOME ENTERTAINMENT

** TALE OF PIGLING BLAND, THE (THE WORLD OF PETER RABBIT AND FRIENDS); see p. 328

*** TALE OF SAMUEL WHISKERS, THE (THE WORLD OF PETER RABBIT AND FRIENDS): Samuel Whiskers the rat thinks that Tom Kitten could be made into an excellent roly-poly pudding for dinner. Adult Juror Comments: Excellent production with beautiful animation. Faithful to the book, with a compelling live-action opening sequence. May promote an interest in children's literature. Kid Juror Comments: Loved the kittens, the rat, and the mice. The English accents were occasionally difficult to understand. Age: 3–12; Length: 30 min.; Suggested Retail Price: $14.95, GOODTIMES HOME VIDEO

*** TALE OF TOM KITTEN AND JEMIMA PUDDLEDUCK, THE (THE WORLD OF PETER RABBIT AND FRIENDS: The farmyard garden is not the place for Tom Kitten and his sisters to play if they are going to keep their clothes clean for their mother's tea party. Adult Juror Comments: Superior production and animation retains spirit of original stories. Could stimulate interest in the books. Kid Juror Comments: Some kids went overboard for it. One child was ready to trade a "Barney" movie for this video. Age: 3–12; Length: 30 min.; Suggested Retail Price: $14.95, GOODTIMES HOME VIDEO

** TALES FROM THE CRIB (RUGRATS): Not yet two years old, Tommy Pickles is as mischievous and talkative as someone twice his age. Tommy and

Chuckie find all kinds of trouble in a spooky toy store. Adult Juror Comments: The individual stories are clever. Appropriate humor for this age group. Animation has a clear contemporary feeling. Little cultural diversity. Kid Juror Comments: Laughed throughout, enjoying the fantasy. Boys liked it better than girls. "In cartoons, they can do anything, because it's not for real." Some kids thought this was too "loud." Age: 4–10; Length: 40 min.; Suggested Retail Price: $9.95, PARAMOUNT HOME VIDEO

** TALES OF BEATRIX POTTER: Six classic stories, including "The Tale of Peter Rabbit," "The Story of Miss Moppet," and "The Tale of Two Bad Mice." Adult Juror Comments: Good stories, separated by nursery rhymes. Includes activity book for parents. Faithful to original artwork. Kid Juror Comments: Okay but a little long. Sound wasn't always clear. Too sophisticated for younger children. Age: 4–10; Length: 44 min.; Suggested Retail Price: $12.98, ARTISAN/FAMILY HOME ENTERTAINMENT

* TALES OF BEATRIX POTTER VOLUME 2: Beatrix Potter's illustrations come vividly to life in this second volume of her classic fairy tales. Narrated by storyteller Sydney Walker, who guides the viewer on a journey into the world of Ms. Potter's beloved animal friends. Adult Juror Comments: Nicely animated with lively music and good narration. Use of a gun to chase the rabbit is objectionable. Addresses conflict resolution, friendship, and cooperation. The "Tale of Fierce Bad Rabbit" is too scary for younger ones. Kid Juror Comments: Children under five found the "real-life" experiences too scary. They liked the poems at the end, which helped them to read along. The slow pacing made kids a little drowsy. Best viewed in segments. Age: 5–10; Length: 46 min.; Suggested Retail Price: $12.98, ARTISAN/ FAMILY HOME ENTERTAINMENT

** TEDDY BEARS' PICNIC, THE: For one magical day every year, the teddy bears of the world come alive to gather in the forest for food, fun, and games. Adult Juror Comments: This charming, lovely fantasy provides lots of opportunities to stop and ask questions. The characters are good role models. Opens the way to discuss emotions and cooperation. Kid Juror Comments: The bear fantasy was great. Age: 3–12; Length: 26 min.; Suggested Retail Price: $9.98, ARTISAN/FAMILY HOME ENTERTAINMENT

** TOM THUMB: The classic adventures of a tiny boy in the Big World. Adult Juror Comments: Purists will be disappointed because it does not closely follow the original story. It's still a good story, simply produced. Jurors were disturbed that Tom's size was not consistent. Kid Juror Comments: Funny and cute. Best-suited to younger children, though it may have some frightening aspects. Age: 3–18; Length: 26 min.; Suggested Retail Price: $9.98, ARTISAN/FAMILY HOME ENTERTAINMENT

* TREASURE ISLAND (ENCHANTED TALES): Set course for the grandest pirate yarn ever, in this animated, song-and-laughter-filled version of Robert Louis Stevenson's swashbuckling classic. Adult Juror Comments: Entertaining and well produced but portrayal of characters is stereotypical. Shows disrespect of others as funny. Not true to original story, adding silly elements for the sake of humor, which don't help at all. Kid Juror Comments: Catchy songs, even if some kids were bothered that the mouths didn't match the animated characters. Boys liked it better than girls. Age: 5–8; Length: 48 min.; Suggested Retail Price: $9.99, SONY WONDER

*** UNCLE ELEPHANT (JOHN MATTHEWS COLLECTION): The parents of nine-year-old Arnie the elephant vanish, and his life abruptly changes. Arnie's Uncle Elephant tries to lift his spirits. Their new friendship tickles everyone. Arnie's parents are rescued and return to a rousing welcome. Adult Juror Comments: Has a wonderful story line and fantastic animation. A sensitive exploration of emotion shows there can be laughter even during difficult times. A good connection between youth and the elderly. Some sequences quite surrealistic. Kid Juror Comments: Made some kids sad and needed to talk it through. When the parents are rescued, the resolution is comforting. The production values were appreciated. Age: 4–12; Length: 26 min.; Suggested Retail Price: $12.95, SONY WONDER/WESTERN PUBLISHING/ GOLDEN BOOK

* UNDERGROUND ADVENTURE (OZ KIDS); see p. 328

*** VINCENT AND ME; see p. 329

** WHEN NINO FLEW; see p. 94

*** WHITE SEAL: Roddy McDowall narrates this classic story from Rudyard Kipling's "Jungle Book." Follows the adventures of a very special baby seal who grows up to save his tribe from the men who slaughter seals. Animated by Chuck Jones. Adult Juror Comments: Good story line. Encourages children to think for themselves, find solutions, and make an effort to care for their community. Starts discussion about endangered species. Some objected to the violence even though it furthers the story. Kid Juror Comments: Though kids enjoyed the video they asked, "Why are the daddy seals so mean?" They also commented, "I never knew seals had to learn to swim."

"Are there really white seals?" Age: 3–12; Length: 29 min.; Suggested Retail Price: $9.98, ARTISAN/FAMILY HOME ENTERTAINMENT

*** WILD SWANS, THE (STORIES TO REMEMBER): Princess Elise is exiled and her brothers are transformed into wild swans by an envious Queen. Elise searches for her brothers. Although faced with a daunting task, she succeeds. Narrated by Sigourney Weaver from a tale by Hans Christian Andersen. Adult Juror Comments: This well-told, imaginatively animated classic makes a great addition to any child's video collection. The sibling relationship is an exemplary role model. Some aspects of the story may be frightening for younger kids. Kid Juror Comments: Completely focused on it and interacted with each other throughout the screening. "I loved this movie." "It was very entertaining." They noticed that "the mouths don't move when they talk." Age: 4–12; Length: 25 min.; Suggested Retail Price: $9.95, LIGHTYEAR ENTERTAINMENT

* WILLIAM WEGMAN'S MOTHER GOOSE (SESAME STREET): How will Mother Goose ever teach her son, Simon Goose, the art of rhyming? Who will carry on the great goose tradition of rhyming rhymes? Favorite children's rhymes are infused with Wegman's wry sense of humor and charm. Adult Juror Comments: Perfect subject for this age. The language is difficult for under fives. Presumes kids know the nursery rhymes and understand sarcasm and wit. Though Wegman's work is skillful, the dogs dressed in clothes is strange. Kid Juror Comments: Not a grabber. Kids wandered in and out during viewing. They liked the costumes and the visuals. Preschoolers didn't understand the sophisticated sense of humor, but the adults did. Age: 4–8; Length: 30 min.; Suggested Retail Price: $12.98, SONY WONDER

*** WINTER TALES (MAURICE SENDAK'S LITTLE BEAR); see p. 95

*** YEH-SHEN: A CINDERELLA STORY FROM CHINA; see p. 332

** YOUNG MAGICIAN, THE; see p. 332

CD-ROMs

*** FREDDI FISH 2: THE CASE OF THE HAUNTED SCHOOLHOUSE: A ghost has invaded the schoolhouse and is stealing all the guppies' toys. Freddi and Luther's job is to build a trap to capture the ghost and reclaim the toys. Adult Juror Comments: Excellent for building critical thinking and memory skills. Engaging graphics, sound effects, and music. Great for school readiness. Encourages teamwork for children at different levels. Colorful graphics are realistic and pleasing. Kid Juror Comments: Chasing a ghost is very interesting. Children enjoyed helping each other remember where things were. The game changes to keep children's interest. They liked the fact that the program talks to them while playing. Kids wanted to play this again. Age: 4–8; Suggested Retail Price: $39.95, HUMONGOUS ENTERTAINMENT

*** FREDDI FISH AND THE CASE OF THE MISSING KELP SEEDS: Players help Freddi Fish and her friend Luther search for Grandma Grouper's missing kelp seeds. An underwater adventure rich in discovery, laughter, and learning, with exciting surprises, enchanting characters, and rich animation. Adult Juror Comments: In addition to cooperative learning and problem solving, teaches spatial relationships, geography, logic, and reasoning. Demands memory skills and concentration. The math section has multiple skill levels that start with counting. Kid Juror Comments: Loved the challenges, songs, and their ability to make things happen with the program. Kids learned what the bottom of the sea looks like. Has limited repeat play value. Age: 5–8; Suggested Retail Price: $39.95, HUMONGOUS ENTERTAINMENT

** LITTLE WIZARD, THE: Join the Little Wizard on his quest to find a special friend. But he must journey beyond his home deep into the Eartail Forest to strange and mystical lands. Teaches reading, math, and decision-making skills. Helps improve memory recognition and keyboard skills. Adult Juror Comments: Programming is excellent but they need to hire an early-childhood professional to consult on story line, which is insipid. The games, special effects, and interactivity are well done. Child needs to be able to read well to participate. Kid Juror Comments: The games, especially the number game, were terrific, but kids were bored with the story. Easy to use. Great graphics. Kids liked clicking the same object to get different action. "I liked making the trees sing." Age: 5–8;   min.; Suggested Retail Price: $29.95, GIZMO GYPSIES

*** PAJAMA SAM IN NO NEED TO HIDE WHEN IT'S DARK OUTSIDE: Pajama Sam is afraid of the dark until he turns into the world's youngest Super Hero and sets out to confront fear. Kids must help Pajama Sam find his way through adventures in a fantastic world of talking trees, dancing furniture, and more. Adult Juror Comments: Good problem-solving exercises. Colorful and fun, comic-book style animation. Suitable for many different skill levels. Kids intuitively know how to play this game and enjoyed the variety of sound effects. Non-readers can play along with readers. Kid Juror Comments: Loved the surprise ending and the "darkness" character. Deals sensitively with a common fear. Six- to eight-year-olds adored the "Calvin and Hobbes"-type humor. Age: 5–8; Suggested Retail Price: $39.95, HUMON-GOUS ENTERTAINMENT

*** PUTT-PUTT SAVES THE ZOO: When the baby animals are missing from the Zoo, it's up to Putt-Putt to save them. Kids develop problem-solving and critical-thinking skills while seeing how their decisions change the world around them. Adult Juror Comments: Game is challenging but the same solutions work every time except once. Variety of interactive diversions offers a break from problem-solving—ice hockey, tag, and making monkey rhymes. Kid Juror Comments: Happily spent at least two hours in the first session trying to save the baby animals. They loved this Putt-Putt program the best. The little kids needed help from adults or older kids. Once solved, the games are easy to replay. Age: 5–8; Suggested Retail Price: $39.95, HU-MONGOUS ENTERTAINMENT

*** PUTT-PUTT TRAVELS THROUGH TIME: Mr. Firebird's experimental time machine has gone haywire, and Putt-Putt needs help to find Pep and recover his lost school supplies. Silverado Sam, Tyrannosaurus Rex, and King Chariot are there to help Putt-Putt. Adult Juror Comments: Content is diverse and entertaining. With so much to do, children forget what they are out to find. Develops basic skills of math, counting, matching, eye-hand coordination, and memory. Gracefully free of gender stereotypes. Kid Juror Comments: The future setting and the pet-food maker were among the highlights. The Dinosaur Age was also a hit. Funny and entertaining. They thought Putt-Putt was a great role model who takes pride in school performance. Enjoyed the different levels of play. Age: 4–8; Suggested Retail Price: $39.95, HUMONGOUS ENTERTAINMENT

*** VELVETEEN RABBIT: The Velveteen Rabbit sits alone in a little boy's nursery, wanting nothing more than to be real. One day the little boy picks up the rabbit and never puts him down. Christopher Plummer narrates this children's classic about love and imagination. Adult Juror Comments: Good story, comfortable pace. Charming, beautifully produced, classic story. This should be in every children's video library along with the book. Some stereotypical dress. Kid Juror Comments: Kids liked this. They related to the story. They began to clap when the rabbit came to life, and were very happy when he was able to play and be among the other rabbits. Age: 5–8; Length: 27 min.; Suggested Retail Price: $12.98, ARTISAN/FAMILY HOME ENTERTAINMENT

Foreign Language

** BONJOUR LES AMIS VOLUME ONE: What, you don't speak French? Moustache teaches how to speak French while introducing his friends, singing songs, and visiting a magic show. Adult Juror Comments: Very slow-paced. Clever, innovative approach to teaching French. The lessons are short, challenging, and require concentration. Sufficient repetition without becoming insulting. The cats were great. "Good, not great, not all-star, pretty static." Kid Juror Comments: Kids had trouble reading the French words on-screen. Using songs makes it much easier to learn another language than using straight vocabulary. Introduces kids to the intricacies of learning another language. Age: 4–10; Length: 48 min.; Suggested Retail Price: $19.95, MONTEREY HOME VIDEO

** EL BARCO MAGICO (JUANA LA IGUANA): A beach day becomes a fantastic experience for Pablo and Ana when they sail in a magic ship with Juana the Iguana. Through music and exploration, it conveys a message that learning can be a magical adventure. In Spanish, for Spanish-speaking kids. Adult Juror Comments: Nice mix of songs, good blend of eye-catching live action and puppetry, engaging child performers. Imaginative and creative, it stimulates a positive response. Good for bilingual language enrichment. Poor sound-quality background noise overshadows characters' narrative. Kid Juror Comments: Kids go for make-believe. They sang along while learning new vocabulary words. Some four-year-olds found the pirate section scary. Older kids responded best. "This made all of us feel special," commented some Spanish-speaking kids. Age: 3–8; Length: 30 min.; Suggested Retail Price: $14.95, IGUANA PRODUCTIONS

*** ERES TU MI MAMA? (ARE YOU MY MOTHER?); see p. 95

* HOLA AMIGOS VOLUME 1: Teaches the basics of Spanish, with Paco and his friends from Veracruz as hosts. The songs and action that fill their trips help kids recognize and recall numbers, letters, colors, and everyday words. Adult Juror Comments: A little academic but appealing, particularly to children interested in foreign languages. Its strength is the choice of words and phrases. Portrayal of the Hispanic family is stereotypical, as are the gender roles. Animation is simple. Kid Juror Comments: Excited about learning Spanish, though they found this a little slow-moving. Age: 5–8; Length: 55 min.; Suggested Retail Price: $19.95, MONTEREY HOME VIDEO

** MORE SPANISH (LYRIC LANGUAGE): Learning a foreign language is fun when it's combined with music and live-action adventures. Teaches Spanish through songs and images. Can be used to teach Spanish-speaking kids English as well. Adult Juror Comments: Songs were catchy and repetitive. The on-screen lyrics are useful, but the pace is so fast it's difficult to follow along. It's a good supplemental tool for learning either Spanish or English. Photography is creative and interesting. Contains some stereotyping. Kid Juror Comments: Children who already speak Spanish respond to it best and are most motivated to stick with the tape. Nice songs—too fast to pick up easily. Everyone had a different favorite song or part. They also enjoyed the food and the clowns. Age: 4–12; Length: 35 min.; Suggested Retail Price: $14.95, PENTON OVERSEAS, INC.

** SPANISH (LYRIC LANGUAGE): Learning a new language is fun when children listen and sing along to catchy tunes, easily learning new words and phrases. Lyrics are clearly subtitled on the screen in English and in Spanish. Animation features Family Circus characters. Adult Juror Comments: Colorful, engaging, and active with sing-along tunes. A good tool for teaching English to Spanish-speaking children or vice versa. The music and images work well together, reinforcing the lessons. Each song may be viewed individually. Kid Juror Comments: Good reception. The visual aspect helped them to remember many things. Age: 4–8; Length: 35 min.; Suggested Retail Price: $14.95, PENTON OVERSEAS, INC.

CD-ROMs

*** KIDS! SPANISH: Interactive fun with wacky monsters hosting over thirty-five activities at five progressive levels. Teaches more than 400 Spanish words and phrases for sports, animals, food, time, colors, and family members. Covers letters, numbers, and everyday expressions. Adult Juror Comments: Good resource. Teaches nouns, alphabet, and numbers. Good educational tool. An adult needs to install program and interpret feedback. Reinforces memory skills. Contains varied levels for different abilities. Kid Juror Comments: Though some words were hard, kids learned a lot and found this entertaining. "I can teach my friends when we play school." Kids missed seeing written words on screen. They loved the playback feature and learning new words in Spanish. Age: 6–10; Suggested Retail Price: $30.00, SYRACUSE LANGUAGE

Holiday

*** ALL DOGS CHRISTMAS CAROL, AN (FAMILY ENTERTAINMENT): Charlie, Itchy, and Sasha star in a canine version of the Charles Dickens Christmas tale. When Carface the bulldog devises a corrupt plan to ruin Christmas, Charlie and his pals visit him as the ghosts of Christmas past, present, and future. Adult Juror Comments: Promotes Christmas spirit; good things come if we hold fast; good will toward others. Also gives a spin to the classic story. Characters inspire compassion for animals. Adults objected to a zombie scene in which a spell is cast on the dogs. Kid Juror Comments: Great heroes, funny adventure. Charlie dances in the yellow suit and listens to the other dogs sing. "It's relaxing. I like the magical things they do with cartoons." "Most characters behaved, some needed to learn to be nice." Age: 5–8; Length: 76 min.; Suggested Retail Price: $14.95, MGM HOME ENTERTAINMENT

*** BABAR AND FATHER CHRISTMAS: Babar, that most regal of elephants, searches for the legendary Father Christmas, eager to make this Christmas a holiday his children will remember. He persuades Santa to take a holiday in the Land of Elephants and proves himself a worthy king. Adult Juror Comments: True to the spirit of the characters, and made a familiar book come alive. A great story with redeeming values. Animation and production is excellent. Kid Juror Comments: What's better than a happy ending and everyone gets what they want? Better-suited to those who have read the books. Age: 5–11; Length: 33 min.; Suggested Retail Price: $12.98, ARTISAN/FAMILY HOME ENTERTAINMENT

** BEAR WHO SLEPT THROUGH CHRISTMAS, THE (CHRISTMAS CLASSICS): While the rest of the world is getting ready for Christmas, all the bears in Bearbank are getting ready to go to sleep. That is, except Ted E. Bear, who wants to find out just what Christmas is all about. Adult Juror Comments: Very good story overall, with few multicultural aspects. Prompted discussion after viewing about bears and hibernation. Kid Juror Comments: A very different approach to the traditional Christmas holiday story and very appealing. Age: 3–9; Length: 27 min.; Suggested Retail Price: $12.98, ARTISAN/FAMILY HOME ENTERTAINMENT

** CASPER'S FIRST CHRISTMAS: On Christmas Eve, Casper and Hairy Scarey are house-hunting because Hairy's haunt has been condemned. Caught in a snowstorm, Yogi Bear, Boo-boo, and Huckleberry Hound take refuge in the haunted house. New friends are made in the spirit of the season. Adult

Juror Comments: This is goofy yet engaging, with pleasant old-fashioned animation and nice music. Good entertainment value while teaching a lesson about selfishness. "What's the point of marketing these old cartoons?" Kid Juror Comments: Kids couldn't follow the plot and wandered off after five minutes. Some got into the spirit of the video, laughing and booing along the way. Kids recognized the familiar television-based characters. One child said, "It's too babyish." Plot is too complicated for the younger kids to get. Age: 5–9; Length: 25 min.; Suggested Retail Price: $9.98, WARNER HOME VIDEO

** CHANUKA AT BUBBE'S (BUBBE'S BOARDING HOUSE): While this colorful group of puppet characters prepares for the holiday feast, the past comes alive as Bubbe relates the story of Chanuka—the fight between the Greeks and Maccabees and the miracle of the burning oil. Adult Juror Comments: Provides an excellent introduction to the story of Chanuka. Promotes cultural awareness for non-Jewish and Jewish children alike. Well written and well produced. Kid Juror Comments: Both Jewish and non-Jewish children enjoyed the puppets and learning about Chanuka. The kids were able to follow the story line. Age: 3–11; Length: 30 min.; Suggested Retail Price: $19.95, MONTEREY HOME VIDEO

** CHRISTMAS ADVENTURE, THE; see p. 96

** CHRISTMAS CAROL, A: Holiday story with a musical twist. An animated version featuring the voices of Whoopi Goldberg, Ed Asner, Michael York, Tim Curry, and Jodi Benson. Adult Juror Comments: Age-appropriate introduction to this classic. The vocabulary is right on target. Delivers positive messages about caring, being kind, and giving. Some great songs. Animated characters are very realistic, attracting the viewer. Kid Juror Comments: Imaginative animation; liked the singing and the story, too. "I liked the singing and the ghosts best." Received high points from younger kids. They enjoyed the lessons about kindness and how to act toward other people. Age: 6–12; Length: 72 min.; Suggested Retail Price: $19.98, TWENTIETH CENTURY FOX HOME ENTERTAINMENT

** CHRISTMAS STORY, A (DOUG): Doug's dog is mistakenly accused of biting his friend Beebe during an ice-skating outing. Adult Juror Comments: Though the story resolves positively, it has little rewatching value. Kid Juror Comments: Kids liked this a lot. Some wanted to see it again, others said, "No, thank you." Age: 4–11; Length: 30 min.; Suggested Retail Price: $9.98, PARAMOUNT HOME VIDEO/NICKELODEON

** CHRISTMAS TREE STORY, THE: From seedling to recycling, a magical, musical, and adventuresome journey to discover where Christmas trees come from. Plants a seed of hope for the future of this Christmas tradition. Adult Juror Comments: Subject matter is interesting, and this makes a good learning tool. The host was very natural and fun to watch. It's good to hear something good can be done with old Christmas trees. It's appropriate for a library collection. Production value is mediocre. Kid Juror Comments: Interest in the life cycle of Christmas trees. Even those who do not celebrate Christmas thought it was informative and enjoyed watching. Has limited repeat play value. "Now that I know where Christmas trees come from and why they cost so much, I'll never watch it again." Age: 5–8; Length: 25 min.; Suggested Retail Price: $14.95, YOUNGHEART MUSIC

* CHRISTMAS TREE TRAIN, THE (CHUCKLEWOOD CRITTERS); see p. 97

* CINCO DE MAYO (THE HOLIDAYS FOR CHILDREN VIDEO SERIES): The history of Cinco de Mayo, Mexico's independence celebration. Includes traditional Mexican folk songs and discusses the Mayan myth of creation. Adult Juror Comments: A simple production, short but well done. The focus on traditional music is quite engaging. Good background on Mexico culture and history. The pace is just about right. The plot jumps around a bit. Kid Juror Comments: Highest score with children from Mexico and Central America, who liked the mural made by the children and the way the kids help to tell the story. Five- through seven-year-olds loved it. Age: 5–12; Length: 25 min.; Suggested Retail Price: $29.95, SCHLESSINGER MEDIA

*** COUNTRY MOUSE AND THE CITY MOUSE: A CHRISTMAS STORY, THE; see p. 97

** FROSTY RETURNS: In this delightful sequel to the original, it's up to Frosty and his friend Holly to convince the people of Beansboro that snow is good for them. Voices are by Jonathan Winters, Andrea Martin, and Brian Doyle Murray. Adult Juror Comments: This remake brings Frosty into the '90s. The humor will appeal to both adults and children. Has excellent narration, story and values. Kid Juror Comments: Helped children to remember how much fun it is to have snow and snowball fights. Said one group of children, "We need snow for the earth." Age: 5–8; Length: 25 min.; Suggested Retail Price: $12.98, ARTISAN/FAMILY HOME ENTERTAINMENT

** FROSTY THE SNOWMAN: Follows the charming and musical adventures of a snowman accidentally brought to life. He must endure many adventures before he can find safety and happiness at the North Pole. Features the voice of Jimmy Durante. Adult Juror Comments: Good messages about friendship. While the animation seems simplistic and the story does not reflect any cultural diversity by today's standards, the story is charming. This perennial favorite will be enjoyed by families for years to come. Kid Juror Comments: Good story, although children noticed that it was outdated. They related to the messages about friendship. Age: 5–8; Length: 30 min.; Suggested Retail Price: $12.98, ARTISAN/FAMILY HOME ENTERTAINMENT

** FUN IN A BOX 3: THE BIRTHDAY MOVIE (FUN IN A BOX): Hosted by the Birthday Spirit, who knows all there is to know about birthday fun, and explores a multicultural melange of birthday lore from Hispanic piñatas to Japanese rice cakes. Adult Juror Comments: Good production, though it moves around a lot. The inclusion of birthday traditions from other cultures is interesting. Some jurors objected to a scene of birthday spanking. Kid Juror Comments: Learning about other cultural traditions was interesting. Age: 6–12; Length: 30 min.; Suggested Retail Price: $14.95, MADE TO ORDER PRODUCTIONS/RAINBOW

* HALLOWEEN TREE, THE: An adventure that reveals the magical secrets of past and present Halloweens. Adult Juror Comments: Encourages exploration into Halloween practices around the world. Might be too scary for younger children. Asks age-appropriate questions. Kid Juror Comments: Really enjoyed the subject, although the production didn't hold their attention as well as they had anticipated. May motivate kids to read. Age: 5–8; Length: 70 min.; Suggested Retail Price: $14.95, WARNER HOME VIDEO

* HE AIN'T SCARY, HE'S OUR BROTHER (CASPER); see p. 98

** HERE COMES PETER COTTONTAIL: Peter and his friend Seymour S. Sassafrass race to distribute the most eggs on Easter Sunday. This original holiday classic features songs by Danny Kaye. Adult Juror Comments: Artistically appealing animation and narration makes this a rich presentation. The main characters are great, especially the French Pilot. Format is a little complex and confusing for younger viewers. Music is appealing. Kid Juror Comments: Prompted much discussion about different holidays and accompanying activities, as well as "good versus bad." They laughed at the mixed-up holidays. Age: 4–8; Length: 53 min.; Suggested Retail Price: $12.98, ARTISAN/FAMILY HOME ENTERTAINMENT

*** HOW THE GRINCH STOLE CHRISTMAS: A Dr. Seuss tongue-twisting verse with lighthearted music. What holiday is complete without this timeless tale of the mean-spirited Grinch and his feeble attempt to steal the yuletide celebration of Whoville? Adult Juror Comments: Recommended for every child's library. The music, the characters, and the rhymes are imaginative and engaging. Presents good message about love and giving. "Giving is more important than getting." Kid Juror Comments: Dr. Seuss? "He's the best." Kids liked the message and wanted to watch again, right away. It's a winner—well produced with a meaningful lesson. Age: 3–12; Length: 26 min.; Suggested Retail Price: $12.95, MGM/UA HOME ENTERTAINMENT

* LET'S CREATE FOR THANKSGIVING (LET'S CREATE): Looking at this American holiday, children are guided in creating art projects that relate to their heritage and are fun to make. Adult Juror Comments: A good range of craft techniques but lacks dialogue between the instructor and kids. Tells the Thanksgiving story from the Pilgrims' perspective, which may be objectionable to Native Americans. Projects are instructional rather than creative. Kid Juror Comments: Songs were fine, but some thought it was too long. Age: 5–12; length: 50 min.; Suggested Retail Price: $24.95, LET'S CREATE, INC.

* MOUSE ON THE MAYFLOWER: Set sail with the tiniest Pilgrim for a music-filled voyage to the land of the free in a Rankin-Bass animated Thanksgiving holiday treat. Features the voices of Tennessee Ernie Ford and Eddie Albert. Some religious overtones. Adult Juror Comments: While the music and animation are fine, the historical information contains inaccurate references to Native Americans that may be close to offensive and lack sensitivity. Kid Juror Comments: Younger kids did not understand the concepts, which are best for eight- to ten-years-olds. Age: 6–12; Length: 46 min.; Suggested Retail Price: $12.98, ARTISAN/FAMILY HOME ENTERTAINMENT

* NIGHT BEFORE CHRISTMAS, THE; see p. 98

** NOEL: Poignant tale of a magical Christmas-tree ornament that comes to life. As it is passed down from one generation to another, we see the wonder, joy, and spirit of Christmas. Adult Juror Comments: This touching Christmas holiday makes a colorful family movie with classic appeal. Tugs at the heart while subtly teaching the meaning of Christmas. Deals with separation, loss, and death. Noel clearly has pathos. Contains Christian overtones. Kid Juror Comments: Considerable empathy for Noel, whose happiness and sadness were felt deeply by the audience. They fell in love with Noel, and cried when the ornaments were put away. Age: 4–7; Length: 25 min.; Suggested Retail Price: $9.95, POLYGRAM VIDEO

** PASSOVER AT BUBBE'S: Spring is here, and it's time to celebrate "Passover at Bubbe's." From the creators of the award-winning "Chanuka at Bubbe's" comes this puppet cast once again. Adult Juror Comments: Attempts to cover too many concepts, and becomes confusing despite strong family values. Stimulates discussion about religions, language, culture. Addresses the history and traditions of Passover. Older kids will understand content best. Kid Juror Comments: Some kids wanted to learn more about Passover and start preparing to celebrate. Hebrew-speaking audience liked hearing the prayers they've learned. They wanted to watch it again, but non-Jewish kids had a difficult time understanding the subject matter. Age: 4–8; Length: 30 min.; Suggested Retail Price: $19.95, MONTEREY MOVIE COMPANY

** PEE WEE'S PLAYHOUSE CHRISTMAS SPECIAL: This wild holiday has many visiting celebrities stopping by to wish Pee Wee a merry Christmas. They include Annette Funicello, Frankie Avalon, Magic Johnson, Cher, Joan Rivers, Oprah Winfrey, Whoopi Goldberg, Little Richard, k.d. lang, and Zsa Zsa Gabor. Adult Juror Comments: Pee Wee's very clever, and his original approach teaches kids good social behaviors. May be a little dated now, but it's still very clever. Lots of gags, though some humor may be above children's understanding. Kid Juror Comments: Great, especially for those at the younger end of the recommended age range. Age: 5–8; Length: 48 min.; Suggested Retail Price: $12.95, MGM/UA HOME ENTERTAINMENT

* PRANCER; see p. 334 see p. 334

** RUDOLPH THE RED-NOSED REINDEER (CHRISTMAS CLASSICS): Remember how the North Pole's favorite reindeer saves Christmas? Puppetmation with narration and singing by Burl Ives. Adult Juror Comments: Still a good story with entertaining, colorful presentation. Addresses questions of fitting in, peer acceptance, and differences. An appealing non-Christian tale for Christmastime. Kid Juror Comments: Who's the greatest? Santa and Rudolph, who's very childlike. Younger kids were afraid of the snowmonster. Age: 4–8; Length: 53 min.; Suggested Retail Price: $12.98, ARTISAN/FAMILY HOME ENTERTAINMENT

** SANTA CLAUS IS COMING TO TOWN (CHRISTMAS CLASSICS): Holiday favorite told and sung by Fred Astaire, with the voices of Mickey Rooney as Kris, and Keenan Wynn as Winter. Features the Westminster Children's Choir. Adult Juror Comments: Good story, good values. It still holds up. "As an adult, I remember what a lasting impression it made on me as a child." Lacks continuity. Kid Juror Comments: Loved the songs and sang them afterward. "The part where the big guy (warlock) was bad. It could really happen." Age: 4–8; Length: 53 min.; Suggested Retail Price: $12.98, ARTI-SAN/FAMILY HOME ENTERTAINMENT

* SANTA EXPERIENCE, THE (RUGRATS): The talkative toddlers and their families share Christmas in a mountain cabin and plot to trap Santa. Adult Juror Comments: This funky story has Santa coming to a family, telling them to be good. The jokes are more suitable for adults than children. Camera work is creative. The characters are rather one-dimensional and sometimes obnoxious. "I cringed throughout." Kid Juror Comments: For these children, the children in the video were most interesting. Some wanted to watch it again. Age: 5–10; Length: 25 min.; Suggested Retail Price: $9.98, PARA-MOUNT HOME VIDEO

* SANTA'S FIRST CHRISTMAS: Santa himself recalls his first bumbling attempt to deliver toys to every child in the world, and what he's done to create one of the smoothest-running operations today. Adult Juror Comments: This story is definitely weird. Good music but the language is difficult for the audience. Lacks cultural diversity, has poor role models, and the production value is mediocre. "It's too smart-alecky." Kid Juror Comments: Shifting between past and present complicated the narrative and made it difficult to understand. The plot is best understood by older kids. Age: 5–8; Length: 25 min.; Suggested Retail Price: $9.98, BMG VIDEO

*** SHARON, LOIS & BRAM: CANDLES, SNOW & MISTLETOE; see p. 99

* SILENT MOUSE: Live-action film reveals the true story behind the creation of the beloved carol "Silent Night." Narrated by Lynn Redgrave, the video features remarkable photography and splendid music performed by Europe's acclaimed choirs and orchestras. Adult Juror Comments: Nicely produced. Creatively teaches how to turn a bad situation into a good one, with a little luck and the help of friends. Little diversity. Humorous, cute holiday video, but the narration is sometimes distracting. The mouse is adorable. Kid Juror Comments: The mouse as the main character and storyteller was wonderful. "It kind of changed my thinking about 'Silent Night.' They did not like how the priest was represented. Age: 5–10; Length: 50 min.; Suggested Retail Price: $19.95, INTERAMA INC.

** SQUANTO AND THE FIRST THANKSGIVING (AMERICAN HEROES AND LEGENDS): True story about a Native American from colonial Massachusetts who was sold into slavery in Spain. Years later, he returns to America and teaches the Pilgrims how to survive the difficult years at the Plymouth colony. Narrated by Graham Greene. Music by Paul McCandless. Adult

Juror Comments: Excellent. Makes a wonderful addition to any child's collection. Somewhat slow-moving, but the information is compelling. "This will become a holiday regular for our classroom." Kid Juror Comments: Learned a lot about Thanksgiving that they did not know before. They enjoyed the production even though they thought it was slow. Age: 5–12; Length: 30 min.; Suggested Retail Price: $8.95, RABBIT EARS PRODUCTIONS/ABLESOFT

* TALES & TUNES: CHRISTMAS TALES & TUNES; see p. 99

** TALES & TUNES: HANUKKAH TALES & TUNES; see p. 99

** THUMPKIN & THE EASTER BUNNIES; see p. 99

* TROLLIES CHRISTMAS SING-ALONG, THE: The Trollies celebrate Christmas in this delightful sing-along. The Trouble Trollies try to ruin Christmas by attempting to steal the Christmas tree, but the Trollies thwart them again. Adult Juror Comments: Recommend viewing with an adult. The bad behavior of the Trouble Trollies needs a filter for discussion. One character hits another. More focus on the "bad Trollies" than the positive characters. Kid Juror Comments: Kids watched this only intermittently. Age: 4–8; Length: 30 min.; Suggested Retail Price: $12.98, PPI ENTERTAINMENT GROUP

* TURKEY CAPER, THE (CHUCKLEWOOD CRITTERS): In celebrating Thanksgiving, the Chucklewood Critters learn about the Pilgrims, the Indians, and how friendships develop. The cubs, unsure of two strangers who enter the forest, face some touchy moments while making friends with the newcomers. Adult Juror Comments: Demonstrates cooperation and care for wildlife. Animals are all respectful toward each other. Language is age-appropriate. Sometimes-choppy story. Portrayals of Native Americans are stereotypical. Production value is mediocre. Kid Juror Comments: Liked the talking animals and learning about Thanksgiving, but did not maintain their interest. Probably little repeat viewing value. Age: 3–8; Length: 25 min.; Suggested Retail Price: $9.98, UNAPIX/MIRAMAR

* 'TWAS THE DAY BEFORE CHRISTMAS; see p. 100

** 'TWAS THE NIGHT BEFORE CHRISTMAS (CHRISTMAS CLASSICS): A gentle retelling of the all-time favorite Christmas tale. Adult Juror Comments: This rather mediocre production has attractive outdoor scenes. Portions were omitted, which may be disconcerting to children familiar with the poem. Background music is repetitive, pace is slow, no cultural diversity. Kid Juror

Comments: Didn't like the reindeers arguing, although it provided an opportunity to discuss conflict resolution. Age: 4–8; Length: 27 min.; Suggested Retail Price: $12.98, ARTISAN/FAMILY HOME ENTERTAINMENT

*** TWELVE DAYS OF CHRISTMAS, THE (ANIMATED CLASSICS): Ever wonder how that silly Christmas carol "The Twelve Days of Christmas," got started? When Sir Carolboomer sends his bumbling squire to steal the Christmas list of Princess Silverbelle he grabs the answers to the king's crossword puzzle instead. Adult Juror Comments: Good story line, silly adaptation of the "story behind the song." Makes for good family viewing. Kid Juror Comments: Exceptional animation and offbeat plot. Captured and held their attention throughout. Age: 5–8; Length: 30 min.; Suggested Retail Price: $14.95, GOODTIMES HOME VIDEO

*** UGLY DUCKLING'S CHRISTMAS WISH, THE: This animated adaptation of Grimm's fairy tale features an outcast duckling who wishes to find a place it can belong. Adult Juror Comments: Good story for a child expecting a new sibling. Has a happy ending and it's full of sad, joyful, and angry emotions. Raises issues of homelessness, loneliness, friendship, difference, and family. Encourages one to be nice to all people and animals. Kid Juror Comments: Everyone watched this twice. They loved the happy ending. Kids empathized with the ugly duckling and the girl with the same wish. "You shouldn't run away from home." "It teaches you not to be mean." "It was sad in parts." Age: 4–8; Length: 70 min.; Suggested Retail Price: $9.99, ANCHOR BAY ENTERTAINMENT

** VEGGIE TALES: THE TOY THAT SAVED CHRISTMAS; see p. 100

* VISIT WITH SANTA, A: A group of children visit Santa at the North Pole and discuss the holiday traditions and sing Christmas songs. In the process, they discover a wonderful secret: Santa will visit as long as children believe in him. Adult Juror Comments: Entertaining, cheerful, and colorful. Addresses Christmas traditions worldwide. Interview style lacks child appeal. Little diversity. Good motivation for discussion about materialism. Promotes idea that "Christmas is about giving." Kid Juror Comments: The always-popular Santa and enjoyable sing-along. The interview style did not engage them. Prompted discussion about the meaning of Christmas. Age: 4–8; Length: 30 min.; Suggested Retail Price: $12.00, THURSTON JAMES

** WHITE CHRISTMAS: Dorothy, whose only wish is to have a white Christmas, is whisked off to the magical world of Weatherland by Santa, who is touched by Dorothy's unselfish plea. Includes Bing Crosby's classic song, "White Christmas." Adult Juror Comments: This entertaining, different twist to the classic story has lots of action and stimulates the imagination. The female lead is strong, but other characters are gender-stereotyped. Kid Juror Comments: Enchanted. Enjoyed the animation. Encouraged them to use their imaginations. "It was the best. I always wanted to know what was coming next." Kids wanted to watch again. Age: 5–8; Length: 26 min.; Suggested Retail Price: $12.98, SONY WONDER

How-To

** BREADTIME TALES: How does bread become bread? Follows three young bakers and shows how to bake bread. Adult Juror Comments: The written instructions (included) are useful in extending the lesson into an activity. It was interesting to watch the baking process. Good for teaching life skills. Kid Juror Comments: Eager to bake their own bread afterwards. Youngest members of the audience wandered. Moves a little slowly. Age: 3–8; Length: 30 min.; Suggested Retail Price: $12.95, KAROL MEDIA, INC.

** I CAN BUILD!; see p. 101

** JUGGLE TIME: Learn confidence while learning to juggle in slow-motion by using scarves. Three colorful scarves are included in package. Adult Juror Comments: Good instructional program. Age-appropriate with clear directions. The singing can become a little annoying and very silly. Nice pace. Kid Juror Comments: The rhyming and music was very annoying. Content was for older kids but the format was for younger one. A few parts were hard to follow. Age: 5–12; Length: 30 min.; Suggested Retail Price: $15.95, JUGGLEBUG

** KARATE FOR KIDS II: INTERMEDIATE: The second video in an award-winning three-part series. The upbeat music keeps the workout fast and fun. Adult Juror Comments: Best-suited for children who already have a basic knowledge of karate, since the moves are a little fast. Karate instructors did not encourage use unless accompanied by professional instruction. Kid Juror Comments: Boys participated aggressively. Age: 5–12; Length: 30 min.; Suggested Retail Price: $9.95, BRIGHT IDEAS PRODUCTIONS

** KIDS GET COOKING: THE EGG: Celebration of food and cooking teaches about recipes, experiments, crafts, and more. Adult Juror Comments: Good for teaching kids how to find their way around the kitchen. Instructions clear and child-centered. The food itself is nothing extraordinary but will appeal to most. Kid Juror Comments: "This is cool." Liked the idea of cooking for themselves and learning new items. Didn't like the puppets that kept interrupting the show. "I learned how to tell the difference between a hard-boiled egg and fresh one." Age: 4–10; Length: 30 min.; Suggested Retail Price: $14.95, KIDVIDZ

* KIDS' GUITAR 1: Three easy guitar lessons introduce children to the guitar and to basic music theory. Teaches basic techniques, strumming, and eight popular songs. Adult Juror Comments: Good instructional program. Meets a need for inexpensive guitar lessons and is well paced. Appropriate for a music class or on your own. Even adults interested in learning the guitar enjoyed this. Kid Juror Comments: Those who already had expressed an interest in learning how to play the guitar enjoyed this the most. They thought the directions were clear and the language suitable for them. Age: 6–12; Length: 90 min.; Suggested Retail Price: $24.95, HOMESPUN TAPES

** LET'S CREATE ART ACTIVITIES: Teacher Ann Felice motivates kids while doing imaginative projects. Fosters respect for nature, the environment, and peers. Adult Juror Comments: Presents clear ideas that encourage creativity. Best used in a setting where children can follow along with their own project or with teachers inspired to do the projects. Presentation somewhat patronizing. Kid Juror Comments: The projects were so exciting that children did not want to sit through the demonstration before starting the experiments. A little too long. Age: 5–10; Length: 51 min.; Suggested Retail Price: $24.95, LET'S CREATE, INC.

** LET'S CREATE FOR HALLOWEEN: How to create seven Halloween projects. Adult Juror Comments: Good ideas and illustrations for arts and crafts projects, ideal for holiday programs with teachers or parents as group leaders. Well produced. Catchy music. Kid Juror Comments: Variety of projects. A lot of things they'd like to make throughout the year. Age: 5–12; Length: 65 min.; Suggested Retail Price: $24.95, LET'S CREATE, INC.

* LET'S CREATE FUN JEWELRY FOR BOYS & GIRLS: Create rings, medallions, and pins from everyday items for yourself or as a gift for someone else. Adult Juror Comments: Good crafts instruction. Clear directions with interesting history included. Some projects require adult supervision and a list of needed materials. Stopping the tape in order to catch up with the instruction is useful. Kid Juror Comments: Some were anxious to try some of the ideas, others were not interested at all. Boys were more interested than they thought they would be. Age: 6–14; Length: 60 min.; Suggested Retail Price: $24.95, LET'S CREATE, INC.

** LOOK WHAT I FOUND: MAKING CODES AND SOLVING MYSTERIES: Explores the scientific secrets of being a detective. Be a super-sleuth with your own spy gadgets. Includes making a periscope out of recycled materials, making a tin-can telephone, secret codes, fingerprint identification, and disguises. Adult Juror Comments: Projects are well selected and child-appropriate. Benefits from some adult supervision. Better-suited for adults with no background in art. Use of language is sometimes inaccurate. Kid Juror Comments: Interested in the subject, but some kids thought it dragged a bit. Not interested in watching again. Age: 5–10; Length: 45 min.; Suggested Retail Price: $14.95, GILBERT PAGE ASSOCIATES

*** LOOK WHAT I GREW: WINDOWSILL GARDENS; see p. 336

** LOOK WHAT I MADE: PAPER PLAYTHINGS AND GIFTS: A variety of things to make and enjoy. Get out the scissors, paper, and tape. Imagine your kids' pleasure when they make a bouquet of flowers, a party piñata, and hats or even a newspaper hammock from watching this video. Adult Juror Comments: Excellent for teaching crafts. Better-suited to adults with no background in art. Kid Juror Comments: Ingenious activities. Wanted to see it over and over. Age: 6–12; Length: 45 min.; Suggested Retail Price: $14.95, GILBERT PAGE ASSOCIATES

* MY FIRST PARTY VIDEO: How to create a party, based on the book series. Adult Juror Comments: Presents good party ideas. Requires adult supervision for younger kids. Safety orientation is age-appropriate. Parents will appreciate the quality instruction. The cooking segment shows only girls participating, no boys. Sometimes patronizing. Kid Juror Comments: Liked the suggestions and wanted to try the activities. They did, however, want to see more kid interaction in the video. "Some of the food looked yucky." Age: 5–12; Length: 45 min.; Suggested Retail Price: $12.98, SONY WONDER

** PAWS, CLAWS, FEATHERS & FINS (A KID'S GUIDE TO PETS): Generally, kids receive little preparation for living with and caring for pets. This program helps families make appropriate choices in pet selection, and emphasizes both the joys and the responsibilities of living with a pet. Adult Juror Comments: Practical information about every aspect of having a pet. Shows children speaking about and working gently with animals. Can be broken into segments to absorb the material. Teaches gentleness and responsibility. Could be useful for families. Kid Juror Comments: Eager to discuss their pets. "We talked about being gentle, kind, and caring for our pets." It's very age-appropriate, and the children appreciated the new information. Age: 5–12; Length: 30 min.; Suggested Retail Price: $14.95, KIDVIDZ

** PIGGY BANKS TO MONEY MARKETS (A KID'S GUIDE TO DOLLARS AND SENSE): American children spend over $6 billion annually but have a limited understanding of money and how it works. Presents the ins and outs of earning, saving, and spending. Adult Juror Comments: Clear, informative, lively, and believable presentation of some complex topics. Shows how some children make mistakes and try again. Should stir an interest in saving, investing, keeping records, and business enterprise. Good diversity. Kid Juror Comments: Prompted a lot of discussion about personal experiences with allowances, garage sales, savings, and money in general. "It would be great to earn my own money." Kids were fascinated and wanted to watch it again. Age: 5–12; Length: 30 min.; Suggested Retail Price: $14.95, KIDVIDZ

*** SQUIGGLES, DOTS AND LINES: Ed Emberly presents his drawing alphabet as a tool for kids to unlock their creativity. The on-camera kids share stories, make cards and books, create a giant mural, and get ready for a party. Adult Juror Comments: Simple production with good ideas and an excellent introduction to drawing. Kid Juror Comments: Wanted to try their hand at drawing right away. Age: 5–12; Length: 25 min.; Suggested Retail Price: $14.95, KIDVIDZ

* UKULELE FOR KIDS PART ONE AND TWO: Child-friendly lessons give kids an early start on music-making. Ginger, a lovable dog puppet, helps Marcy teach ten basic chords, plus ear training, music theory, strumming techniques, and several popular songs, including "Skip To My Lou." Adult Juror Comments: Good production that appeals to a special audience. Some jurors felt that the dog puppet was too babyish. Kid Juror Comments: Not surprisingly, those more interested in music were most interested. "The ukelele is difficult to play." Age: 6–10; Length: 100 min.; Suggested Retail Price: $39.90, HOMESPUN TAPES

Music

* ANASTASIA SING ALONG: Features sing-along songs from the movies "Anastasia," "FernGully: The Last Rainforest," and "On the Riviera." Invites kids to follow along with the words on the screen and join in the chorus with familiar characters. Adult Juror Comments: Having "Anastasia" on the cover is a bit misleading. Different clips vary in production quality. Requires being able to read quickly. Some of the older clips were not very appealing. Kid Juror Comments: Loved the chance to sing along, especially when they learned new songs. Girls liked this better than boys. Popo the Puppet was a big hit, as was Shirley Temple and the dog from "Anastasia." Age: 5–8; Length: 25 min.; Suggested Retail Price: $14.98, TWENTIETH CENTURY FOX HOME ENTERTAINMENT

** BEETHOVEN LIVES UPSTAIRS (CLASSICAL KIDS): A young boy develops a special friendship with Beethoven, watches as he creates and rehearses the Ninth Symphony, and is invited to its premiere performance. Adult Juror Comments: Demanding story respects and challenges its audience. Adults expressed a need for more stories like this. Beautifully told. Promotes lessons in kindness, friendship, and differences. Kid Juror Comments: Attractive story and related to the boy who befriended Beethoven. "More, more." "I could watch it again." They liked the costumes and the period setting. Age: 6–12; Length: 52 min.; Suggested Retail Price: $21.98, THE CHILDREN'S GROUP

*** CONCERT IN ANGEL-LAND; see p. 102

** DR. SEUSS'S MY MANY COLORED DAYS (NOTES ALIVE!): Engaging story features colorful 3–D animation of a child and dog experiencing their feelings through color and music. Narrated by Holly Hunter; music score by Richard Einhorn; performed by the Minnesota Symphony Orchestra. Adult Juror Comments: Too slow, too long, style is stiff. Enhances pride in individuality and self-expression. Teaches communication skills using emotions. Beautiful music, but cuts to the orchestra distract from the story. Kid Juror Comments: Good production, though some parts lost their attention. Some students clapped, swayed, and danced along. Others found it boring and confusing. "The music people are not fun." "Made us think about how our hearts feel." Age: 5–8; Length: 45 min.; Suggested Retail Price: $19.95, MINNESOTA ORCHESTRA VISUAL ENTERTAINMENT

* EARTH TUNES FOR KIDS: A musical celebration of our planet as a collection of nine fast-paced segments with strong messages unequivocally rendered in song and aerial photography. Adult Juror Comments: Entertaining and educational qualities, but lacks continuity. Promotes respect and care for people and the environment in a lively, musical presentation. Combines live-action clips, animation, and live performances. Kid Juror Comments: The songs and the music hit the mark. Stimulated discussions about endangered species, animal rights, and the rain forest. Kids said the "Garbage

Man" gave them a good feeling. Pace is slow at times. Age: 5–8; Length: 30 min.; Suggested Retail Price: $14.95, THE KIDS SHOP

** FRED PENNER: WHAT A DAY!: Fred Penner discovers a magic photo booth with songs about fun, friendship, and life. Adult Juror Comments: Jurors liked using music and songs to stimulate happiness in a concert format. The story line didn't hold together. Kid Juror Comments: Fun and engaging, but younger children lost interest. It's better-suited for school-age viewers than preschool. Age: 3–13; Length: 28 min.; Suggested Retail Price: $10.98, OAK STREET MUSIC

* FRIENDS; see p. 102

** I DIG DIRT: Highlights a fascinating display of really big earth-movers in action. Winner of a CINE golden eagle. Catchy music by Grammy-winning Jeff Tyzik. Adult Juror Comments: The first part is quite good. Honesty in presenting fascinating machinery in action, but the trickery at the end contradicts that. The kids' narration and hosting is well done, especially the interview with female driver. Kid Juror Comments: Fascinated by variety of machinery, the size comparison, and ways to play in the dirt. Enjoyed the kids' narration. Kid scores were high across the board. It's a little long and sophisticated for younger ones. Age: 3–8; Length: 30 min.; Suggested Retail Price: $14.95, DREAMS COME TRUE PRODUCTIONS

** IS NOT, IS TOO! (CATHY AND MARCY'S SONG SHOP): Cathy and Marcy lead children and adults in singing, signing, dancing, and yodeling. While children listen to a variety of instruments including the hammer dulcimer, mandolin, and banjo, they're invited to play along at home on their air guitars. Adult Juror Comments: Active, well-selected songs stimulate creative interaction. The production is simple and pleasing. Kudos for including sign language. Although this is directed at children, it's useful for adults too. Kid Juror Comments: Enjoyed the interaction and caught on quickly. They learned some new songs which they soon sang, especially the younger ones. Age: 4–8; Length: 30 min.; Suggested Retail Price: $14.95, COMMUNITY MUSIC, INC.

*** JOE SCRUGGS IN CONCERT: Upbeat tunes, unbeatable lyrics, lively puppets, and larger-than-life props and characters make this show a non-stop family frolic. Adult Juror Comments: Joe's songs are wonderfully imaginative, visuals are fun and attractive. Kid Juror Comments: Very singable. Asked to watch it often. Age: 3–8; Length: 51 min.; Suggested Retail Price: $14.95, SHADOWPLAY RECORDS & VIDEO

** JOE'S FIRST VIDEO: Combines animation, live action, and irresistibly enchanting songs that create a musical masterpiece in a class by itself. Features Joe Scruggs. Adult Juror Comments: Wonderful music video for kids. Very age-appropriate. Kid Juror Comments: Wanted to watch again. Age: 3–8; Length: 31 min.; Suggested Retail Price: $14.95, SHADOWPLAY RECORDS & VIDEO

* LET'S KEEP SINGING (SING ALONG WITH JOHN LANGSTAFF): Draws children into the wonderful world of music-making with master music educator and Pied Piper John Langstaff. Designed for children watching alone or in groups. Adult Juror Comments: Song selection is good. Adults wanted more explanation and movement instructions. Better-suited to classroom than home use. Kid Juror Comments: Not very attractive and only sporadically held their attention. Age: 5–8; Length: 45 min.; Suggested Retail Price: $19.95, LANGSTAFF VIDEO PROJECT

** MADELINE AND THE DOG SHOW (MADELINE): Scrubbed and perfumed, Genevieve, Madeline, the girls, and Miss Clavel line up to register for the show. Genevieve cannot enter. She has no pedigree! Delightfully animated and filled with music, fun, and adventure. Adult Juror Comments: Excellent adaptation of the classic book with colorful, entertaining characters. Strong female characters. Kid Juror Comments: Infectious. Girls enjoyed it more than boys. They sang and hummed afterwards, stimulated their interest in the books. Age: 4–12; Length: 26 min.; Suggested Retail Price: $12.95, SONY WONDER/WESTERN PUBLISHING/GOLDEN BOOK

** MONKEY MOVES: Walk like a woo woo. Roll like a baboon. Based on the work of Moshe Feldenkrais, designed to help children develop balance, coordination, and motor skills while moving to music. Music by Paul McCandless. Adult Juror Comments: Applause for the concept of teaching different ways to exercise and making goofy animal sounds. Thought the speaker was awkward. Kid Juror Comments: Enjoyed exercising with this video. Liked the imaginative approach. "I'm building muscles by doing this." Three-year-olds may have trouble watching the video and doing the exercises at the same time. Age: 3–9; Length: 26 min.; Suggested Retail Price: $19.95, ROSEWOOD PUBLICATIONS, INC.

** MOVE LIKE THE ANIMALS: Roll like a cat. Crawl like an alligator. Based on the work of Moshe Feldenkrais, it helps children develop balance, coordination, and motor skills while moving to original music. Adult Juror Comments: Clever and thoughtful production. The information about animal movement is as appealing as the performances themselves. Instrumentation is excellent and well paced. Adults appreciated that the kids can be understood when they're speaking. Kid Juror Comments: The originality—participating with the musical performances—was quite successful. They thought the performers were energetic and appealing, and wanted to share this video with friends so they could do it again. Age: 3–8; Length: 24 min.; Suggested Retail Price: $19.95, ROSEWOOD PUBLICATIONS, INC.

* MRN: MUSIC AND FEELINGS (MISTER ROGERS); see p. 75

** MUSIC AND MAGIC (POSITIVE MUSIC VIDEOS FOR TODAY'S KIDS): Contains seven original songs set to video in a fast-paced style. Kevin Anthony sings "Positive Music Videos for Today's Kids." Strong, upbeat music with messages that promote self-esteem. Adult Juror Comments: Capitalizes on kids interest in fast-paced programming. Some songs are better than others, and sometimes the messages get lost in the snazzy presentation. Good diversity but too much emphasis is on the adult singers. Kid Juror Comments: Enjoyable, especially the bubbles. "My two-year-old daughter loved it." Age: 5–11; Length: 30 min.; Suggested Retail Price: $12.95, BRIGHT IDEAS PRODUCTIONS

** MUSIC MANIA (PROFESSOR IRIS); see p. 105

** MUSICAL MAX AND OTHER MUSICAL STORIES (CHILDREN'S CIRCLE): Animated stories include the antics of a lively fiddle, a woman who would rather play trombone than clean her house, and a girl who travels to Africa to play her spirited violin. Adult Juror Comments: Stories true to the original book and have wonderful voices, music. Well selected, show equal gender balance. Kid Juror Comments: The female characters particularly attractive. Seems more suited to ages three to seven. Age: 5–8; Length: 37 min.; Suggested Retail Price: $14.95, CHILDREN'S CIRCLE HOME VIDEO

*** MRN: MUSICAL STORIES (MISTER ROGERS); see p. 105

* NURSERY SONGS & RHYMES; see p. 105

* ON THE DAY YOU WERE BORN (NOTES ALIVE!): Debra Frasier's award-winning book comes alive with bold three-dimensional animation and sights and sounds of the world-class Minnesota Symphony Orchestra. Features Steve Heitzeg. Adult Juror Comments: Stunning, gentle production combines music and animation in an intriguing combination of creative writing and fine art. The interviews and deconstruction of the tape are fascinating. Special appeals to new-age philosophy. Moves slowly. Kid

Juror Comments: Excellent artist interviews. Enjoyed learning how the video was made and, for the most part, loved the music. "I wanted to hear what the writer had to say." Some little ones were put to sleep. Age: 5–8; Length: 30 min.; Suggested Retail Price: $19.95, MINNESOTA ORCHESTRA VISUAL ENTERTAINMENT

*** RICHARD SCARRY'S BEST LEARNING SONGS VIDEO EVER; see p. 106

*** SHARON, LOIS & BRAUM: ONE ELEPHANT WENT OUT TO PLAY; see p. 106

*** SING ALONG WITH BINYAH BINYAH (GULLAH GULLAH ISLAND); see p. 106

*** SING ALONG, THE (CABBAGE PATCH KIDS): All the songs from the Cabbage Patch series with on-screen lyrics. Adult Juror Comments: Helps kids realize that their thoughts, dreams, and feelings are okay, and encourages self-esteem. The characters accurately depict children's attitudes. The doll figures are cleverly manipulated to show movement and expression. Kid Juror Comments: How do the Cabbage Patch Kids work together, maintain their friendships, and have fun? A good discussion on that. The child jurors sang along with the song selections. Everyone's favorite part was the clubhouse. Age: 5–8; Length: 30 min.; Suggested Retail Price: $12.98, BMG VIDEO

** SING ME A STORY: RABBI JOE BLACK IN CONCERT; see p. 107

*** SING 'N SIGN FOR FUN: Gaia and a group of hearing and deaf children perform seven upbeat songs with American Sign Language, teach signs for greetings and the manual alphabet. Signed, voiced, and open-captioned for total communication. Adult Juror Comments: Thoughtful production introduces sign language through singing. Songs are hip and portray a sense of hope. Shows good friendship-making skills and concern about global issues. Requires repeat viewing to learn signing. Good diversity. Kid Juror Comments: Wonderful music, singing, and finger spelling. Asked many questions about being deaf. Prompted discussion about believing in one's self, respecting others, differences, and making friends. Girls enjoyed Gaia. Age: 5–8; Length: 42 min.; Suggested Retail Price: $14.95, HEARTSONG COMMUNICATIONS

*** SINGING FOR FREEDOM (A CONCERT FOR THE CHILD IN EACH OF US): A gathering of people from all walks of life sing and dance as they become a powerfully united congregation at a "Sweet Honey in the Rock" concert at Glide Memorial Church in San Francisco. Adult Juror Comments: A marvelous family concert, truly inspirational. Aptly captures the group's charisma and musicality. Elementary music teachers thought this was a wonderful introduction to music. Everyone noted how it motivated them to want to get up and dance! Kid Juror Comments: Didn't take long for children to get up and sing and dance to this tape. "This is a lot of fun, watching people of all races sing together." Age: 5–12; Length: 59 min.; Suggested Retail Price: $14.98, MUSIC FOR LITTLE PEOPLE

*** SOMETHING SPECIAL; see p. 108

*** STEPPING OUT WITH HAP PALMER; see p. 108

** TALES & TUNES: ORIGINAL TALES & TUNES; see p. 109

** TALES & TUNES: SILLY TALES & TUNES; see p. 109

* TALES & TUNES: SPOOKY TALES & TUNES: Haunting new collection of stories and songs from the creators of the award-winning Baby Songs. Great assortment of cartoons, live-action, and sing-along songs for ages two to eight. Adult Juror Comments: Surely not appropriate for the age group indicated by the supplier, because it's too scary for kids under five. The resolution of fears in "Spooky Dreams" is well done. "Monsters in the Morning" is clever. Kid Juror Comments: Reaction varied widely. Some children under five were uncomfortable, while others liked it. Older kids enjoyed it and found it wasn't as scary as they thought it was going to be. They related to the events as similar to their everyday life and found them funny. Age: 3–8; Length: 30 min.; Suggested Retail Price: $12.98, ANCHOR BAY ENTERTAINMENT

* TALES & TUNES: SPORTS TALES & TUNES: Cartoons, live-action antics, and songs bring out the "good sport" in everyone. Includes "Follow That Baseball," "Yes You Can," "Let's Play Ball," and "Teamwork." Adult Juror Comments: Humor is very appropriate for this age. The material varies in quality, though. One storylike section, although predictable, has an emotional appeal. Others are somewhat repetitive, and approach is superficial. Kid Juror Comments: Related to the subject. Some children joined in singing along with it. Age: 4–8; Length: 30 min.; Suggested Retail Price: $12.98, ANCHOR BAY

** TEDDY BEARS' JAMBOREE: Music pioneers Gary Rosen and Bill Shontz (the award-winning duo, Rosenshontz) perform live for 10,000 fans and their teddy bears. Filled with zany humor, superb harmonies, instrumental versatility, and inventive lyrics. Invites audience to sing along. Adult Juror Comments: Live family concert features delightful music by accomplished musicians whose music is filled with positive lyrics. Content and performers are engaging. Lyrics and melodies are simple to remember. Kid Juror Comments: Easy to sing along. Because it's long, might be best used in segments. Liked watching the kids dance together with their teddy bears. Age: 4–9; Length: 62 min.; Suggested Retail Price: $9.95, LIGHTYEAR ENTERTAINMENT

** TICKLE TUNE TYPHOON: LET'S BE FRIENDS: Twelve joyful songs from the Typhoon's three award-winning albums come alive with dance and colorful costumed characters. Includes "Let's Be Friends," "My Body Belongs To Me," and "Hug Bug." Adult Juror Comments: Songs are compelling and fun, but it's too slow. It's a videotaped production of a live concert that loses its energy in the translation. Great diversity and skill at playing instruments. Kid Juror Comments: Sang and danced along. Characters very appealing, especially the dancing veggies and the Tooth Fairy. Some thought the music was too loud and it was hard to hear the words. "The Hokey Pokey was my favorite." "That man played the drums with his feet!" Age: 3–9; Length: 58 min.; Suggested Retail Price: $14.95, JUST FOR KIDS/CELEBRITY HOME VIDEO

* TUBBY THE TUBA; see p. 110

** VEGGIE TALES: A VERY SILLY SING-ALONG!: Sing yourself silly with Bob the Tomato, Larry the Cucumber, and all their veggie buddies in this silly collection of favorite tunes from the Veggie Tales series. Adult Juror Comments: amusing as well as interesting. Excellent colors and sound quality. Songs in Spanish make it more challenging. Helps teach rhythm and musical scale. "Hairbrush song was like Gilbert and Sullivan for vegetables." Contains Christian-based content. Kid Juror Comments: Music was fun and catchy. Imaginative production. "I liked the Spanish." But overall, it did not hold the children's attention as well as the Veggie Tales with stories. Age: 4–8; Length: 30 min.; Suggested Retail Price: $12.99, BIG IDEA PRODUCTIONS

** VEGGIE TALES: SILLY SING-ALONG 2: THE END OF SILLINESS?; see p. 110

* WE'RE ALL AMERICANS: Celebrate diversity with songs about connections, community, growing up with love and trust, understanding differences, and healing social wounds. Adult Juror Comments: Interesting and unusual. A little preachy and long. Technically well done, but the excitement of a real concert is not conveyed. "Makes one think of issues of race and

work ethics. Teaches good values—do your best, be kind, love one another. Kid Juror Comments: "I liked listening and singing to the music." Not a lot of action. Presentation gets boring for kids after a few songs. Sometimes kids couldn't hear the performers voices. Multicultural cast is appealing. Age: 5–8; Length: 51 min.; Suggested Retail Price: $19.99, CHARLES R. ROTHSCHILD PROD.

** WEE SING: CLASSIC SONGS FOR KIDS; see p. 112

** WEE SING FAVORITES: ANIMAL SONGS; see p. 110

** WEE SING: GRANDPA'S MAGICAL TOYS; see p. 112

** WEE SING IN SILLYVILLE; see p. 110

** WEE SING IN THE BIG ROCK CANDY MOUNTAINS; see p. 111

** WEE SING IN THE MARVELOUS MUSICAL MANSION; see p. 111

** WEE SING: KING COLE'S PARTY; see p. 113

*** WEE SING THE BEST CHRISTMAS EVER!; see p. 111

** WEE SING TOGETHER; see p. 111

*** WEE SING TRAIN, THE see p. 112

** WEE SING UNDER THE SEA; see p. 112

*** WEESINGDOM-THE LAND OF MUSIC AND FUN see p. 113

*** ZIN! ZIN! ZIN! A VIOLIN (READING RAINBOW): LeVar finds out how orchestra members combine their sounds and work as a team. Demonstrates creativity, expression, rhythm, dance, and self-expression as a joint effort. Explores rhyming, melodies, math, and their interrelationship. Adult Juror Comments: Great introduction to music. Frank discussion of the hours of practice, pressure, and hard work. Balances a variety of musical information and stimulates interest in music while informing children. A delight. Kid Juror Comments: Great, great, great. Discussed strings, brass, and horns. "I want to be a musician." "I like the flute and the French horns." "The 'Stomp' part was cool." After watching, kids got out instruments and made their own orchestra. Age: 5–8; Length: 28 min.; Suggested Retail Price: $23.95, GPN/READING RAINBOW

CD-ROM

** BEETHOVEN LIVES UPSTAIRS; see p. 252

Nature

*** ADVENTURES IN ASIA (REALLY WILD ANIMALS): A wild magic carpet ride around Asia—cuddly giant pandas in Southern China, hairy orangutans in Borneo, huge manta rays in the Red Sea, and close-knit elephant families in India. Adult Juror Comments: Packed with information from the various locations. The music captured kids' attention. The jokes sometime detract from the information the program is trying to convey. Some explanations are not particularly clear. Kid Juror Comments: Likeable host, good show with fine mix of animation and live action. Children got a kick out of the animals' humor. Even the three-year-olds loved it. Girls were more attentive than boys. Age: 3–12; Length: 40 min.; Suggested Retail Price: $14.95, NATIONAL GEOGRAPHIC/WARNER HOME VIDEO

*** AMAZING NORTH AMERICA (REALLY WILD ANIMALS): From the frozen Arctic to the Florida Everglades, the animals of North America are on parade: alligators patrolling the swampy waters of the Okefenokee , ground squirrels battling rattlesnakes in the Wild West, and many other encounters. Adult Juror Comments: Visually interesting, entertaining, and well paced. Scored high with jurors. Humor sometimes gets in the way of information. Organization is a little confusing. Suitable for home or school use. Kid Juror Comments: Scored high. Music helped capture their interest. Fills a much-needed gap of nature videos designed specifically for kids. Prompted discussions about animals in different regions. Age: 5–12; Length: 47 min.; Suggested Retail Price: $14.95, NATIONAL GEOGRAPHIC/WARNER HOME VIDEO

* AMERICA'S NATIONAL PARKS (WHERE IN THE WORLD): Explores Yellowstone, the Grand Canyon, the Everglades, and other American parks. Features wildlife, caves, and waterfalls from the rain forests of the Olympic Peninsula to the giant sequoias of Yosemite. Adult Juror Comments: Glorious footage, good historical and reference source. Fictional portion lacks believability. Opening section seems contrived. Good multicultural represen-

tation. Kid Juror Comments: Motivated to learn more. Found the opening a little hokey but enjoyed the rest. Age: 4–11; Length: 40 min.; Suggested Retail Price: $9.95, IVN ENTERTAINMENT, INC.

** ANIMAL QUEST; see p. 114

*** ANIMALS & ME: EATING AT THE ZOO: Satisfies children's curiosity about wildlife. Entertaining and educational. Narrated by children. Features chimpanzees, bears, and elephants, along with exotic sounds and music. Adult Juror Comments: Excellent, realistic photography, content and presentation. Stands out for polish and high standards. Narration effective and natural. Kid Juror Comments: "I liked the elephants eating." "It's fun watching the bears catch fish." "This movie gets all happies" (happy faces on the evaluation tool). Age: 3–8; Length: 30 min.; Suggested Retail Price: $14.95, SMALL WORLD PRODUCTIONS

** ANTLERS BIG AND SMALL (MOTHER NATURE): Examines nearly a dozen different cousins of the deer family in their forest habitats of the great North American Wilderness. Adult Juror Comments: Lots of information. Uses real-life footage (somewhat dated) of animals in their natural habitat. Appeals to older kids as well. Great learning tool. Some adults objected to the reference to the animals' mating practices. Kid Juror Comments: Fascinating and humorous. Those who like animals were most attentive. The footage looked slightly faded. Age: 6–12; Length: 25 min.; Suggested Retail Price: $12.95, DISCOVERY COMMUNICATIONS

** AT THE ZOO: 2; see p. 114

** BABES IN THE WOODS (MOTHER NATURE): Baby animals in nursery habitats ranging from pouches to telephone poles, and from around the world as they learn and grow. Includes newborn koalas, kangaroos, and cranes, small key deer, noisy woodpeckers, and a Canadian gosling. Adult Juror Comments: Good footage though slightly faded. Interesting choice of animals. Informative and engaging without being didactic, although language is more suitable for older kids. Wonderful prelude for a trip to the zoo. Kid Juror Comments: Held their attention and was the right length, with the right selection of animals. Dated, slow-moving and not upbeat when compared to other current nature titles. Age: 5–8; Length: 25 min.; Suggested Retail Price: $12.95, DISCOVERY COMMUNICATIONS

*** BEAR CUBS, BABY DUCKS, AND KOOKY KOOKABURRAS (GEOKIDS): Uncle Balzac guides Sunny and Bobby into the world of baby animals—baby turtles, bear cubs, penguin chicks, a lost zebra, and even a peek at stingrays. Adult Juror Comments: Respect for nature and the environment. Music is terrific. The mix of live action, graphics, and animation enhances literacy. Kid Juror Comments: "This is the best video we saw." Children sang along, clapped, asked questions, and jumped out of their seat with excitement. They loved the animal pictures drawn by the children. Great pace. Works best with younger audience. Age: 1–10; Length: 33 min.; Suggested Retail Price: $14.95, NATIONAL GEOGRAPHIC/WARNER HOME VIDEO

* BEARS EVERYWHERE; see p. 114

* BIG HORSE: Loving and respectful survey of the role big horses have played in human history—on farms, in industry, and even in wartime. Features Percherons, Belgians, and Clydesdales. Adult Juror Comments: Appealed most to kids who love horses. Stimulated further inquiry. A good learning tool with simple production values, though a little slow-paced. Narrator annoyed some children. Kid Juror Comments: Didn't like seeing the animals roughed up. Liked the foals and seeing people taking good care of the animals. Age: 5–8; Length: 30 min.; Suggested Retail Price: $19.95, BIG HORSE PRODUCTIONS

** BIGGEST BEARS!, THE: Stunningly photographed in Alaska, with a young narrator. Explores myths about grizzlies, the biggest bears. Adult Juror Comments: Outstanding nature film for educational value. Excellent child narrator, wonderful photography. Environmental values emphasized. Kid Juror Comments: Children enjoyed learning about different types of bears. "I liked watching the bears catch the fish. They must be very fast." Age: 4–9; Length: 30 min.; Suggested Retail Price: $14.95, BULLFROG FILMS

** BORN TO BE WILD (OWL/TV VIDEO): Many, many funny, furry, fuzzy animals—monkeys, bears, and chimps. Follows a mother koala and her baby who is tracked by a radio implant, and observes Quing Quing and Quan Quan, the endangered giant pandas, at lunch. Adult Juror Comments: Excellent use of animation to provide information that would be difficult to show live. Also enjoyable are the children who interview researchers about working at the zoo. Some concern about the safety of being around wild animals. Kid Juror Comments: Fascinated by the information about animal behavior. Enjoyed seeing how the animals care for their young. The pandas were everyone's favorite. Age: 4–13; Length: 28 min.; Suggested Retail Price: $12.95, THE CHILDREN'S GROUP

** **BRINGING UP BABY (MOTHER NATURE):** Visits wildlife nurseries and the proud parents and babies there. A lost sea lion finds its mother, and a mama coyote rescues her pups when she senses a cougar nearby. Adult Juror Comments: Excellent photography and well-chosen background music. Good variety of birds and mammals. Alliteration in narration is overdone. Kid Juror Comments: Stimulated discussion about how many birds used regurgitation methods of feeding their young. "Cute cubs. I liked finding out how babies live." Age: 5–8; Length: 25 min.; Suggested Retail Price: $12.95, DISCOVERY COMMUNICATIONS

** **BUSINESS OF BEAVERS, THE (MOTHER NATURE):** Visits a beaver lodge and the family. Also explains the importance of beavers to the forest habitat. Adult Juror Comments: Interesting close-up of habitat, habits, and the lives of beavers. Exceptional learning potential to expand vocabulary. A little slow-moving for those not fascinated by beavers. Kid Juror Comments: Sat through the entire video but weren't interested in seeing it again. Age: 5–8; Length: 25 min.; Suggested Retail Price: $12.95, DISCOVERY COMMUNICATIONS

** **CAMOUFLAGE, CUTTLEFISH, AND CHAMELEONS CHANGING COLOR (GEOKIDS);** see p. 115

** **CASTAWAYS OF GALAPAGOS (MOTHER NATURE):** Who occupies the remote Galapagos Islands? The legendary 500-pound Galapagos tortoise, amazing marine iguanas, graceful flamingos, awkward blue-footed booby birds, and the albatross. Stunning wildlife scenes. Adult Juror Comments: Informative and beautiful, helps link past and present in a true island adventure of the most natural kind. At times, the vocabulary is far too advanced. Kid Juror Comments: Educational. Remembered the animal names. One six-year-old said, "These are the animals I like the best. The kind we don't have in Wisconsin." Some wanted to watch it again immediately. Age: 5–8; Length: 25 min.; Suggested Retail Price: $12.95, DISCOVERY COMMUNICATIONS

*** **CHOMPING ON BUGS, SWIMMING SEA SLUGS AND STUFF THAT MAKES ANIMALS SPECIAL (GEOKIDS);** see p. 115

** **COOL CATS, RAINDROPS, AND THINGS THAT LIVE IN HOLES (GEOKIDS):** Sunny is shocked that bushbabies sleep in hollow trees. Uncle Balzac explains that many animals make their homes in holes. This episode features "Cool Cats," a rhythm-and-blues tribute to the feline family. Created by Hank Saroyan. Adult Juror Comments: Great cinematography, fine characters, and clever songs. But tries to do too much, for example, by squeezing in a phonics lesson. Kid Juror Comments: Enjoyed seeing animals they don't usually see. Humor is inappropriate and over their head at times. Age: 4–7; Length: 33 min.; Suggested Retail Price: $14.95, NATIONAL GEOGRAPHIC/WARNER HOME VIDEO

*** CREEPY CREATURES & SLIMY STUFF (OWL/TV VIDEO): A curious look at slugs, snakes, and other slimy stuff. From the rain forest to the desert, explores the weird and wonderful world of scorpions, frogs, eels, and bats. Adult Juror Comments: Informative, with clever animation and excellent cinematography. Narration and dialogue easy to follow. Songs have excellent audio quality. Low-key presentation. Kid Juror Comments: Ready to watch it again. "My six-year-old girl loved it!" Age: 4–13; Length: 30 min.; Suggested Retail Price: $9.98, THE CHILDREN'S GROUP

** CREEPY CRITTERS (PROFESSOR IRIS); see p. 116

** CURIOUS COUGAR KITTENS (MOTHER NATURE): Birth of two cougar kittens in the high country of Utah. Mom protects and teaches her playful, adventurous kittens. Dated, washed-out footage, slow narration, not upbeat enough. Adult Juror Comments: Much information in an educational format. Intimate view of the daily life of cougar kittens. Kid Juror Comments: Enjoyed the cougar antics, particularly when they tried to get the turtle out of its shell. Asked to see it a second time. Asked good questions and wanted books about cougars. Age: 5–8; Length: 25 min.; Suggested Retail Price: $12.95, DISCOVERY COMMUNICATIONS

*** DEEP SEA DIVE (REALLY WILD ANIMALS): Explores the last great frontier on earth, the magnificent oceans, from surface to sea floor. Great whales, friendly dolphins, scary sharks. Features award-winning cinematography by National Geographic Magazine. Narrated by Dudley Moore. Adult Juror Comments: Fabulous footage. Informative yet entertaining. Songs are smarmy and predictable, but also meaningful. Worthy message: "Keep waters clear." Kid Juror Comments: A pleasure. Liked the fast pace, new information, the humor, and the music. Laughed and screamed with delight. Afterward, discussed their knowledge about some of the animals. Age: 5–12; Length: 40 min.; Suggested Retail Price: $14.95, NATIONAL GEOGRAPHIC/WARNER HOME VIDEO

** DESERT ANIMALS (SEE HOW THEY GROW): The desert is home to a tiny tarantula, gerbil, tortoise, and gecko, and gives them a sunny start on their life adventures. Narrated by the baby animals, so to speak. Adult Juror

Comments: Most of the photography is staged—not in the natural habitat. Good introduction to a variety of desert animals. Slow-moving but thorough and includes little-known facts. Kid Juror Comments: It was fun to hear the animals talk about themselves. Liked the animal voices and the tarantula's jokes. "I liked the animation that shows how each animal grows and changes." Not interested in viewing it again. Age: 4–7; Length: 30 min.; Suggested Retail Price: $12.00, SONY WONDER

** DR. ZED'S BRILLIANT SCIENCE ACTIVITIES (OWL/TV VIDEO): Dr. Zed's hands-on introduction to the magic of science through simple tricks and activities. Test the principles of flying, create colorful molecular art, discover the power of a finger, and take a close-up look at optical illusions. Adult Juror Comments: Lively suggestions for projects that kids can do with adults as an introduction to scientific concepts. Somewhat dated and slow-paced. Good diversity. Production quality lacks clarity at times. Kid Juror Comments: Wanted to watch it again. Learned a lot, even though a few didn't understand Dr. Zed's explanations. Age: 4–12; Length: 30 min.; Suggested Retail Price: $9.98, THE CHILDREN'S GROUP

** EXPLORING THE RAIN FOREST (REDBOOK LEARNING ADVENTURES): Delightful songs and film clips of the rain forest, featuring Fluffy Duffy and friends who explain why the rain forest is worth protecting. Adult Juror Comments: Conveys important information clearly. Songs are repetitive and at times long, although the repetition helps learning. Some also thought that the mix of fantasy and reality didn't work well. Kid Juror Comments: Danced along and liked the songs. Reenacted the spaceship blastoff. Definitely watch this again. It's most suitable for four-to seven-year-olds. Age: 4–7; Length: 30 min.; Suggested Retail Price: $12.98, ANCHOR BAY

** FLYING, TRYING, AND HONKING AROUND (GEOKIDS): With help from Uncle Balzac, Sunny and Bobby learn about different birds and find out why most birds fly and why other animals can't. Wacky Francisco Flamingo flaps by with Flamingo Facts and introduces counting, phonics and rock 'n' roll. Adult Juror Comments: Incredible animal footage and facts, but overall it's not clear who the audience is. Individual segments suitable for different ages. Video jumps from offering fairly complex animal facts to teaching the alphabet. Why? Kid Juror Comments: Really excited about the topic but found the presentation confusing. Lost their interest when the information wasn't suitable for their age and ability. Age: 3–8; Length: 33 min.; Suggested Retail Price: $14.95, NATIONAL GEOGRAPHIC/WARNER HOME VIDEO

* GOOD NEIGHBOR GROUND SQUIRREL (MOTHER NATURE): Visit to a den where a mother squirrel has pups. Explains the amazing alarm system of squirrels when they're threatened by a badger, a coyote, and a hawk. Adult Juror Comments: Interesting information about different species and habitats. Jurors enjoyed the female narrator, since most nature programs have male voices. Some footage appears washed-out. Kid Juror Comments: Appreciated the educational information, such as learning there are more species of squirrels than the backyard variety they're familiar with. Too long for this audience. Age: 5–8; Length: 25 min.; Suggested Retail Price: $12.95, DISCOVERY COMMUNICATIONS

** IF WE COULD TALK TO THE ANIMALS (KIDSONGS); see p. 116

** IN THE COMPANY OF WHALES: Observe whales, the largest animals to ever live on earth, powerful creatures of extraordinary grace and intelligence, masters of their realm for more than 30 million years. Adult Juror Comments: High scores. Great visuals, an excellent introduction to the subject, even though some parts were very slow and too technical for kids. Kid Juror Comments: Those interested in animals and nature really enjoyed this. Others found it too long and some words hard to understand. "I would love to swim with them." Age: 5–12; Length: 55 min.; Suggested Retail Price: $19.95, DISCOVERY COMMUNICATIONS

** JUNGLE ANIMALS (SEE HOW THEY GROW): Illustrates how the lush jungle offers a perfect place to grow up for a little scorpion, alligator, snail, and two tiny tigers. Adult Juror Comments: Good combination of animation and live action, with excellent photography and music. "Makes learning fun." Humor is more appropriate for adults than children, and it's slow-moving. Kid Juror Comments: Enjoyable, appealing most to those interested in nature. Age: 3–8; Length: 30 min.; Suggested Retail Price: $12.98, SONY WONDER

** LET'S CREATE A BETTER WORLD: How to create environmentally sensitive art projects with recyclable materials that are usually thrown away. Adult Juror Comments: Jurors liked the focus on reduce-reuse-recycle-respect. Children need to be attentive while watching the demonstrations. For classroom setting or at home with an adult helping. Focus does not encourage independent creativity. Kid Juror Comments: Interest in the activities, especially paper-making. A good tool for children who need a little nudge in the creative area. Age: 5–12; Length: 70 min.; Suggested Retail Price: $24.95, LET'S CREATE, INC.

** LET'S EXPLORE . . . FURRY, FISHY, FEATHERY FRIENDS; see p. 117

*** LITTLE DUCK TALE, A: This tender, heartwarming story portrays the true-life adventures of "Chibi" and his duckling brothers and sisters as they struggle for survival in downtown Tokyo. Children will find joy in this tale of determination and triumph. Adult Juror Comments: Absolutely fabulous story, perhaps a wee bit too long. Shows a great role model for the mother, engaging an international community of support for her. Kid Juror Comments: Kids loved this. Much to our surprise, even the boys did. They stayed with it even though it's long. They were anxious to retell the story to their parents. Age: 5–12; Length: 55 min.; Suggested Retail Price: $14.95, DISCOVERY COMMUNICATIONS

* MOMMY GIMME A DRINKA WATER; see p. 117

* MORE ZOOFARI; see p. 117

* NEW WORLD OF THE GNOMES, THE: Produced in cooperation with the World Wide Fund for Nature, emphasizes respect for the planet while enjoying the amazing adventures of the gnomes. Adult Juror Comments: Well produced, simply animated but colorful. Creates an awareness for endangered species and environment. Conveys some anti-human sentiment and shows some stereotyping. Language is sometimes too advanced for kids. Kid Juror Comments: Appealing fantasy story about little people in a happy society with animal friends where everyone helps and promotes goodness. They didn't always understand what was happening. Age: 5–8; Length: 26 min.; Suggested Retail Price: $19.95, B.R.B. INTERNACIONAL, S.A.

** ORCA WHALES & MERMAID TALES (MOTHER NATURE): An intimate look at huge orca whales and mysterious manatees, once thought to be mermaids. Explains the orca's fascinating blowhole and watches a manatee calf swimming just hours after it's born. Adult Juror Comments: Well produced. Respectful and inspiring story with beautiful cinematography. Contains lots of information, well paced, with interesting narration. It's a little dense with information. Kid Juror Comments: "The kids really sat and watched this video." The entire program kept their attention, and they wanted to watch again. Some language and terminology were way over their heads. Age: 4–12; Length: 25 min.; Suggested Retail Price: $12.95, DISCOVERY COMMUNICATIONS

** PENGUINS IN PARADISE (MOTHER NATURE): Penguins in their coastal paradise of Patagonia, waddling on land and gliding underwater. Introduces their neighbors, cormorants and sea lions. Adult Juror Comments: Well-produced nature video. "If you enjoy nature documentaries, you'll enjoy this one." Informative with a good ecology message. Some graphic images are below average. Kid Juror Comments: Liked learning about the penguins. What kept their attention was how funny they seemed. Generated a lot of discussion about animals and the environment. "People should help penguins by not polluting." Age: 5–8; Length: 25 min.; Suggested Retail Price: $12.95, DISCOVERY COMMUNICATIONS

** **SEA ANIMALS (SEE HOW THEY GROW):** An underwater wonderland becomes the cradle of life for the fast-growing little ray, pipefish, cuttlefish, and the hermit crab. Adult Juror Comments: Opportunity to learn about new animals and their habitat. Suitable for classroom or for learning at home. Narration is lively, though some language is too advanced for preschoolers. Tends to be a little preachy and moves slowly. Kid Juror Comments: Those interested in animals enjoyed this the most. It held the attention of the older children best. Prompted discussion afterward about sea creatures and their environment. Age: 3–8; Length: 30 min.; Suggested Retail Price: $12.98, SONY WONDER

** **SPRINGTIME TODDLER TALES (MOTHER NATURE):** From mountaintops to treetops, proud parents nurture their springtime toddlers: bison calves, elephant seal pups, black bear cubs, pelicans, and more. They all explore, grow, and learn. Adult Juror Comments: Lovely footage of animal young. Only occasionally does the narration become cloying and anthropomorphic. Otherwise, it's inviting and informative. And a good teaching tool for classroom or home. Kid Juror Comments: Okay, but they thought the birth scenes were "sort of gross." They learned a lot of new things. Age: 5–8; Length: 25 min.; Suggested Retail Price: $12.95, DISCOVERY COMMUNICATIONS

** **SWINGING SAFARI (REALLY WILD ANIMALS):** Leads young viewers deep into wildest Africa. Spin, National Geographic's animated globe-on-the-go host, is the safari guide. He shows what it's like to live with animals in the wild. Adult Juror Comments: Captivating, entertaining, and educational, with disappointing photography that looks several generations old. Good pace, songs range from corny to sappy. Introduces concepts about the food chain and endangered animals. Lion segment occurs twice. Kid Juror Comments: Children generally respond well to animal videos, and this was no exception. They liked Spin, the scenes from old movies, the pace and the humor. Age: 4–10; Length: 40 min.; Suggested Retail Price: $14.95, NATIONAL GEOGRAPHIC/WARNER HOME VIDEO

*** TADPOLES, DRAGONFLIES, AND THE CATERPILLAR'S BIG CHANGE (GEOKIDS); see p. 118

*** TOTALLY TROPICAL RAIN FOREST (REALLY WILD ANIMALS): Explores the rain forests of Central and South America with the greatest variety of plants and animals than anywhere else on earth , including spotted jaguars and poison-arrow frogs. Filmed by National Geographic's filmmakers. Narrated by Dudley Moore. Adult Juror Comments: Informative and lighthearted. Nice musical accompaniment. Well-executed, well-organized introduction to the rain forest. "Gives you all the information you ever wanted to know." Kid Juror Comments: Got a kick out of all the bugs and weird animals, and enjoyed learning how animals survive. It made them want to study bats. The humor tends toward the sarcastic, but the kids respond well to that. It's more entertaining than they expected. Age: 5–12; Length: 40 min.; Suggested Retail Price: $14.95, NATIONAL GEOGRAPHIC/WARNER HOME VIDEO

** TRAILSIGNS NORTH: POOP, PAW & HOOF PRINTS: Teaches how to read trail signs that animals leave in the wilderness. Trail guide Eric, his friend Max, and the animated Mambo Moose transport the viewer to the spectacular Alaskan wilderness. Contains rare footage of animals in their habitats. Adult Juror Comments: Print material about identifying animals by their poop is hard to find. The innovative approach here teaches a lot about animals and their habitats. Provides a new approach to identifying animals in the wild. Eric and Maxwell are good role models. Kid Juror Comments: Appealed most to kids with a special interest in animals and trail signs. The title was distracting to some. It held their interest once they got into it. There was the occasional "gross" remark. Age: 4–8; Length: 25 min.; Suggested Retail Price: $14.95, PARAGON MEDIA

** TREE ANIMALS (SEE HOW THEY GROW): Shows how a baby chameleon, stick insect, fruit bat, and buzzard take to the trees to climb, crawl, and fly their way into young adulthood. Adult Juror Comments: Encourages appreciation for nature and environmental awareness. Having the animals speak is unrealistic and not believable. Makes a good prelude to field trips to the library, zoo, or wilderness. "I like its simplicity. Even I learned something." Kid Juror Comments: Most enjoyable: the part about the chameleons. They were intrigued by how and what they ate. Good length. Shows variety of animals that interested the kids. They especially liked learning how animals grow to adulthood. Kept their interest. Age: 4–9; Length: 30 min.; Suggested Retail Price: $12.98, SONY WONDER

** WET AND WILD (OWL/TV VIDEO): Explores the coral reef off the coast of Kenya, swimming alongside dolphins, getting close to penguins, visiting a trawler, and observing the effects of pollution on sea otters. An educational and entertaining journey. Adult Juror Comments: Shows wonderful variety of sea life and people. Refreshing to have an elderly expert on-camera. Well produced with excellent cinematography. Kid Juror Comments: It was cool to have child narrators. They liked learning about survival and wanted to see it again. Provoked an interest in aquariums and sea life. "It's great when the kids interview the adults." "I liked the starfish facts." Age: 5–12; Length: 30 min.; Suggested Retail Price: $9.98, THE CHILDREN'S GROUP

** WHEN GOATS GO CLIMBING (MOTHER NATURE): Mountain goats cavort on craggy peaks and endure a harsh snowstorm. Young goats climb and play on the day they're born. Points out their amazing vision. Adult Juror Comments: Makes a good teaching tool for classroom or home. Well produced, informative, and appropriately paced. The scenery is stunning. Engaging and educational for a child motivated to learn. Vignettes are particularly well done. Kid Juror Comments: Favorites, among many: the baby goats. They laughed and said they learned something about how animals survive. Appealed most to kids interested in animals. Age: 5–8; Length: 25 min.; Suggested Retail Price: $12.95, DISCOVERY COMMUNICATIONS

*** WILDLIFE SYMPHONY (READER'S DIGEST): Combines classic symphonies with stunning footage of animals as they frolic, prance, and dance in their own inimitable way. Shows lions at play, insects at work, wildlife in the rain forest, and dolphins in the sea. Adult Juror Comments: Has beautiful cinematography, and it's funny but long. It's great to listen to as well as watch. Sparks an interest in nature, insect world. Kid Juror Comments: Images of animal usually touch children. Some were mesmerized when viewing. Some were surprised to find there was no narration. Kids related different animal traits to themselves. They said it was "relaxing." Age: 6–12; Length: 48 min.; Suggested Retail Price: $29.95, IVN ENTERTAINMENT, INC.

*** WONDERS DOWN UNDER (REALLY WILD ANIMALS): Travels to the land "down under" to learn about Australia's unusual animals. Leaping kangaroos, paddling platypuses, and cuddly koalas make this immense island-continent their home. Dudley Moore is the voice of Spin, National Geographic Magazine's animated host. Adult Juror Comments: Entertaining and informative. Moore's cheerful narration is superb. Fascinating footage is enhanced by helpful commentary that sometimes can be corny.

Confusing when some animals are shown but not discussed. Kid Juror Comments: Children enjoyed the humorous comments and the fast pacing. A good tool for further discussion. Kids wrote volumes afterwards about what they learned. They wanted to watch it again immediately. Age: 4–10; Length: 40 min.; Suggested Retail Price: $14.95, NATIONAL GEOGRAPHIC/WARNER HOME VIDEO

*** WORLD ALIVE, A: Profiles the myriad creatures of the planet, their activities and interactions. Has a dramatic musical score. Narrated by James Earl Jones. Adult Juror Comments: Well produced shows an excellent selection of wildlife. Footage of animals in their habitats is extraordinary. Kid Juror Comments: The colors and pictures were very attractive. They called out the animals when they saw them. "This was great because we saw animals all around the world, even some we didn't know about!" "Animals were eating each other, but they had to because of the food chain." Age: 5–12; Length: 25 min.; Suggested Retail Price: $14.95, SEA STUDIOS

*** WORLDS BELOW, THE: Herds of sea lions, snowstorms of plankton, starfish in motion, and majestic underwater forests. A newborn seal swims among wave-swept rocks. Vast submerged plains in the mysterious depths. Adult Juror Comments: Beautifully produced with excellent cinematography. Well constructed. Kid Juror Comments: Captivating for kids interested in animals and the sea. Age: 5–12; Length: 48 min.; Suggested Retail Price: $19.95, SEA STUDIOS

** ZOO FOOD WITH GRANDPA NATURE (GRANDPA NATURE'S KIDS COLLECTION): Grandpa Nature and his kids lead a behind-the-scenes tour of the zoo. Comedian Jonathan Winters is the voice of Grandpa Nature. Many original songs. Adult Juror Comments: Well produced with interesting music and photography. Opportunities to introduce concepts about life cycles. Science portrayed in an original manner suitable for home and school. Kid Juror Comments: Fascinating. Used by some parents and teachers as a preview to a field trip to the zoo. Kids were eager for their visit afterwards. "I wanted to see more magic." Age: 5–8; Length: 32 min.; Suggested Retail Price: $12.95, MILESTONE MEDIA

* ZOOFARI!: Have you ever wanted to go on a safari? To discover and marvel at the splendid variety of animals? Join Sir Arthur Blowhard and his assistant Smythe on a zoofari, as they explore the wonders of nature's creatures, big and small, up-close and personal. Adult Juror Comments: Contains lots of good information. Children are always interested in seeing real animals. The music is too loud at times. An inside look at animals in

captivity. Hosts reflect old colonial stereotypes, and the presentation is a bit shallow. Kid Juror Comments: Okay, although they thought sequences were too long for younger kids. "Too bad they're all in a zoo." "The lions seem so sad." Age: 3–8; Length: 32 min.; Suggested Retail Price: $14.95, WHITE TREE PICTURES, INC.

Special Interest

*** ACCENTUATE THE POSITIVE (THE PUZZLE PLACE): Kids reprogram a robot's rude manners and take a journey into space, discovering that friendship is the best thing on earth. Adult Juror Comments: Well produced. Addresses social problems, such as name-calling, that are very real for kids. Shows good ways of dealing with conflict resolution. The characters interact realistically and are believable. "If only the world was really this way." Kid Juror Comments: "I love this movie!" "I like Sky and the rest of them too," one child's response. They loved the robots, the rockers, the tongue twisters, the cat and dog, the music, and puppets. Provides impetus to talk about friendship, self-esteem, and feelings. Age: 4–8; Length: 60 min.; Suggested Retail Price: $9.98, SONY WONDER

** ALASKA (WHERE IN THE WORLD): Kids explore "the land of the midnight sun" as they pan for gold, race a dog sled team, carve a totem pole, and explore the artistry of Coastal Indians. Adult Juror Comments: Provides a good overview of the Coastal Indians, with a suitable pace, interesting visuals, and appropriate cultural and historical information. Makes learning this information interesting and fun. Kid Juror Comments: "Alaska is beautiful." Kids really liked it. "I want to travel all around the world. I'll start in Alaska!" "We learned about the Eskimo people and about the oil spill and what Alaskan kids do for fun." "I liked learning the history of Alaska." Age: 6–12; Length: 30 min.; Suggested Retail Price: $9.95, IVN ENTERTAINMENT, INC.

** ASHOK BY ANY OTHER NAME: Ashok wants to change his ethnic-sounding name to something more American. Addressing ethnic pride, this speaks to those with unusual names, and to anyone who feels a need to change in order to fit in. Adult Juror Comments: Good topic, suitable for this age. Good script, mediocre production values. Storytelling format is not what children are accustomed to, but it works. Supports tolerance and ethnic diversity. It would be helpful for an adult to help facilitate. Kid Juror Comments: Appreciated the lesson and were somewhat uncomfortable with the topic. They enjoyed the history lesson at the end and the "meet the authors" section. Age: 6–12; Length: 45 min.; Suggested Retail Price: $29.95, AIMS MULTIMEDIA

** ASTRONOMY 101: A FAMILY ADVENTURE: For those who have looked at the night sky and wondered what is really up there, join Michelle and her mother as they explore the night sky together. Adult Juror Comments: Use of mother-and-daughter team was refreshing. Showing women in science is an intelligent move. Effectively combines information and entertainment in a visually compelling format. Kid Juror Comments: Enjoyed the pictures of the night sky and the stars. Some of information was much too complicated and technical for the children. Students who are star watchers enjoyed it the most. Age: 6–14; Length: 25 min.; Suggested Retail Price: $14.95, MAZON PRODUCTIONS, INC.

*** BARRY'S SCRAPBOOK: A WINDOW INTO ART: Barry Louis Polisar hosts a visual and musical tour through the world of art. Features hands-on art projects using recycled materials and interviews with artists and songs. Adult Juror Comments: Has high learning potential that engages children's thinking skills, teaches collage-making, deals with textures, and relates instruction to art seen in museums. Polisar and the museum narrator were effective speakers. Shows minority artists. Kid Juror Comments: Learned some important things about art. Participated eagerly, answering questions and anxiously wanting to try the projects. They enjoyed seeing the artists at work. Age: 5–14; Length: 40 min.; Suggested Retail Price: $19.95, ALA/LIBRARY VIDEO NETWORK

** BIG AIRCRAFT CARRIER, THE (REAL LIFE ADVENTURES): Offers a behind-the-scenes look at flight operations and life on board a floating city of six thousand crew members. Music, child narration, and voice-over of pilots enhance the tour. Adult Juror Comments: Good production, clearly presented, and shows cooperation. It's well paced and informative but has no female role models. Good child narrator. "Kids should love this." Kid Juror Comments: Impressed by the size of the aircraft carrier and how it functions. Kids enjoyed seeing different pilots, planes, and how they take off. Age: 5–8; Length: 40 min.; Suggested Retail Price: $14.95, LITTLE MAMMOTH MEDIA

*** BIG AQUARIUM, THE (THE BIG ADVENTURE SERIES): Visit the largest freshwater aquarium in the world in Chattanooga, TN. Shows hundreds of fish and animals from various habitats, divers feeding fish, and a look behind-the-scenes at the control center, the veterinarian, and the research lab. Adult Juror Comments: Wonderful footage of a wide variety of aquatic plants, animals, and fish. Eye-catching and informative. This would be a great tool for ocean studies. Fosters an appreciation for aquatic life as well as interest in unique species. Kid Juror Comments: Colorful, scientific, cool. Great animals. "I loved the colors of the fish." Showed people working with the animals. "I'd like to work there." Age: 5–8; Length: 48 min.; Suggested Retail Price: $14.95, LITTLE MAMMOTH MEDIA

* BIG BOATS, LI'L BOATS (ADVENTURES WITH MY UNCLE BILL): Josh, his friends, and Uncle Bill explore all kinds of boats and ships. Introduces the captain, shows the engine room, and visits the wheel house. Adult Juror Comments: Interesting and varied boat footage. Informative, well paced, and well produced. Though they go a little overboard with talking in unison. Kid Juror Comments: It's a little long for this age group. Kids didn't understand the connection to "Uncle Bill." His character was unnecessary and detracted slightly from the general message. Age: 3–8; Length: 29 min.; Suggested Retail Price: $14.95, PARAGON MEDIA

*** BIG PARK, THE (THE BIG ADVENTURE SERIES): Explores Yellowstone National Park, its wildlife, and the people who preserve it. Explains how animals are monitored, how the wolf program safeguards an endangered species. Shows firefighters and rescue helicopters and discusses geothermal systems. Adult Juror Comments: Educational but needs supplementary explanation. Teaches a lot about parks. Good explanations that are educationally sound and authentically depicted. Beautiful scenery. Pace is a little slow. Kid Juror Comments: Mixed reaction. Kids said they wouldn't want to sit at home and watch it, but they would in school. They thought the narrator spoke too fast and was difficult to understand. It made them want to visit a park. They loved the images of the bubbling water. Age: 6–11; Length: 48 min.; Suggested Retail Price: $14.95, LITTLE MAMMOTH MEDIA

** BIG PLANE TRIP, THE (REAL LIFE ADVENTURES): Offers a behind-the-scenes look at the operations of an international flight from a child's point of view, with a child narrator, lively music, and graphics. Adult Juror Comments: Informative. Shows all the jobs on airlines. Child narrator, asking questions, works well in the format. Lots of technical information and detail. A little long for audience to watch all in one sitting. Kid Juror Comments: Narration helped the children understand the presentation. Younger children lost interest when the information became too technical. They enjoyed the scenes in Switzerland. Age: 5–10; Length: 45 min.; Suggested Retail Price: $14.95, LITTLE MAMMOTH MEDIA

** BIG RENOVATION, THE (THE BIG ADVENTURE SERIES): Shows a home renovation from the ground up, including demolition, framing, plumbing, electrical wiring, and heating, ventilating, and air-conditioning. Visits the architect, builder, an entomologist, a tile factory, and a sawmill. Adult Juror Comments: While the explanations are good, it moves too slowly. Content is straightforward, easily understood, presented in a safe and wholesome setting. Young people learn safety and proper procedures around construction sites. Kid Juror Comments: "I learned how it takes a lot of people and materials to build a house." Too long, but they liked seeing the finished house and the steps it took to get there. Uses technical terms beyond kids' comprehension. Age: 6–10; Length: 48 min.; Suggested Retail Price: $14.95, LITTLE MAMMOTH MEDIA

*** BIG SPACE SHUTTLE, THE (THE BIG ADVENTURE SERIES): Explores the behind-the-scenes action at the space shuttle program, including the astronaut training, the crew roles, shuttle maintenance, and orbital gravity experiments. Adult Juror Comments: A big hit. Everyone liked the narrator, the backstage look, and seeing real astronauts. A topic kids relate to. "It was great to watch with my child, interesting, no violence and a great learning tool," one mom said. Kid Juror Comments: Captured kids' interest and motivated further inquiry into the subject. Kids liked it because it was real. They particularly enjoyed the launch. "Everything in it is great." "I liked seeing the girl scientists." Age: 6–10; Length: 50 min.; Suggested Retail Price: $14.95, LITTLE MAMMOTH MEDIA

*** BIG SUBMARINE, THE; see p. 341

** BIG TRAINS, LITTLE TRAINS; see p. 118

** BIG ZOO, THE (REAL LIFE ADVENTURES): Learn why zebras have stripes and flamingos are pink. Shows feeding day at the reptile house at the zoo––and much more. Adult Juror Comments: Offers a guided tour of the zoo, from out front and behind the scenes. "The people working in the zoo were shown to be such caring people." A good resource tool for classroom or home. Jurors objected to all the commercials at the start. Kid Juror Comments: Impressed by seeing what the different animals eat and how zookeepers take care of everything. They wanted to go to the zoo afterward. "I like the real pictures, they made me want to go to the zoo." Age: 5–8; Length: 45 min.; Suggested Retail Price: $14.95, LITTLE MAMMOTH MEDIA

* BUILT FOR SPEED: Follows a stock car driver and her two young friends in an action-packed day at the stock car races. Explains how a race car differs from a regular car. Adult Juror Comments: Those interested in stock cars may find this appealing. It's simply produced but has poor sound quality. Includes female drivers but makes light of car crashes despite discussion of safety. Kid Juror Comments: The racing segments were exciting, and why not? "Girls can drive fast and get paid for it?" asked one child. Age: 5–10; Length: 30 min.; Suggested Retail Price: $14.95, WHITE TREE PICTURES, INC.

** CLASSIC NURSERY RHYMES; see p. 119

* COME FLY WITH US: This sing-along musical has on-camera kids that fly on barnstormers, seaplanes, and with the famous Blue Angels demonstration daredevil team. Tours a flight museum and visits a Boeing 747 cockpit. Adult Juror Comments: Good music and scenery, but material is redundant and the production quality is mediocre. Lacks cultural diversity. Kid Juror Comments: General enthusiasm, although a few left during the screening. Those interested in planes were engaged. Age: 5–8; Length: 30 min.; Suggested Retail Price: $14.95, PARAGON MEDIA

* DR. BIP'S NEW BABY TIPS; see p. 120

** EVERYTHING YOU EVER WANTED TO KNOW ABOUT PLANES, BUT DIDN'T KNOW WHO TO ASK: Many interesting facts about planes, from landing gear to flaps, from de-icing to the speed of sound. Shows painted planes with designs from the Simpsons, Disney characters, creatures of the sea, and wild animals. Adult Juror Comments: Production is age-appropriate and interesting. Kids will enjoy learning about the variety of planes and how they fly. Kid Juror Comments: Appealed most to kids who are fascinated about planes or travel. Others could take it or leave it. Boys enjoyed this more than girls. Age: 4–8; Length: 20 min.; Suggested Retail Price: $9.95, JUST PLANES VIDEOS

** FIREMAN JIM'S AMAZING RESCUE RIGS: Entertaining, educational video about fire trucks and other rescue vehicles. Includes six safety messages including 9–1–1; fire prevention; stop, drop, roll; fire drills at home; etc. Lessons are taught by firefighters and kids. Adult Juror Comments: A nice blend of action and instruction. Lots of lights, sirens, and smoke. Jim is a friendly and informative role model. Overall, gives viewer a sense of confidence. Useful in the home, classroom and community. Kid Juror Comments: Kids love watching the rescue vehicles "on the move," the sights and sounds captivated them. Children relate to the straight facts. They like Fireman Jim and the kids commentaries. "I want to know more about fires, so I can be safe." Age: 5–8; Length: 30 min.; Suggested Retail Price: $14.95, THE MULTIMEDIA GROUP, INC.

** GOOD ENOUGH TO EAT (BECAUSE NATURAL IS FUN): So you want to make organic chicken soup? Visit the warehouse, kitchen, the produce aisle, the butcher, and meet people working at the market. Adult Juror Comments: Good presentation of interesting information and concepts about the food industry. Production quality is mediocre, making it difficult to watch. Kid Juror Comments: After viewing this, when children went to the grocery store, they spoke about the behind-the-scenes activities. Age: 4–8; Length: 30 min.; Suggested Retail Price: $12.95, KAROL MEDIA INC.

** GRANDPA WORKED ON THE RAILROAD; see p. 120

** HEAVY EQUIPMENT OPERATOR; see p. 120

** HEY WHAT ABOUT ME; see p. 121

** HOUSE CONSTRUCTION AHEAD; see p. 122

** HOW A CAR IS BUILT, WITH I.Q. PARROT: Follows the nine-mile Ford Mustang assembly line and observes how workers and high-tech machines transform giant rolls of steel into gleaming new cars. Adult Juror Comments: Simply produced but clear. Presentation is long and sometimes technical. Comparing a mustang horse with the Mustang car was well done. Safety demonstrations were convincing. "I learned a lot and enjoyed the old assembly-line footage." Kid Juror Comments: They liked the idea of comparing an assembly line to a river. Commented on how the people work together and on the many people needed to build a car. "It takes a long time to build a car, and teamwork to get the job done." Age: 5–12; Length: 30 min.; Suggested Retail Price: $14.95, THINK MEDIA

** HOW A TUGBOAT WORKS, WITH IQ PARROT: Kids board a tugboat and watch it dock the Queen Elizabeth II, using hand signals, whistles and ropes. Includes rare footage of early tugboats. Demonstrates teamwork and the success of tiny tugs pulling off Herculean tasks. Adult Juror Comments: Well presented with interesting camera angles and editing. Contains lots of little-known information in great detail. Most suitable for special-interest groups. Encouraged searching out more information in books. Kid Juror Comments: Repeat viewing strongly supported. Boys and girls liked it equally and wanted to go for a ride on a tugboat. "I liked seeing a boat that's longer than three football fields." It's too long for younger kids. Age: 5–8; Length: 28 min.; Suggested Retail Price: $14.95, THINK MEDIA

* HOW IT'S DONE — EPISODE #1 — FROM ROLLER COASTERS TO ICE CREAM: Discover fascinating facts about making everyday things in factories and farms. Detective Howie Dunn undertakes a behind-the-scenes investigation to solve the mystery of "how it's done." Adult Juror Comments: Presents good information in an interesting way. A useful educational tool, although too fast-paced and lacking in serious detail. Jurors did not care for the puppet character. Kid Juror Comments: Sought more information about the subjects that the program just begins to cover. Brought up more questions than answers. "I liked the part about baseballs best." Age: 5–10; Length: 32 min.; Suggested Retail Price: $9.99, ANCHOR BAY

* HOW IT'S DONE — EPISODE #2 — FROM BASEBALL BATS TO POTATO CHIPS: Investigates "The mystery of the missing oranges" and squeezes out some juicy facts. Visits a baseball bat factory for a look at how a piece of wood is turned into a real slugger. Adult Juror Comments: Begins to answer a lot of "why and how" questions. The live action sections are fine but the puppetry is awkward. Adults thought that the presentation was mediocre and slow. The packaging cover is somewhat misleading. Kid Juror Comments: Favorite segment: how the yo-yo works. They wanted to learn more. Howie Dunn's humor was just right for them. They learned some new things and some wanted to take home the video and share with their parents. First graders enjoyed the puppet. Age: 5–10; Length: 34 min.; Suggested Retail Price: $9.99, ANCHOR BAY

** HOW TO BE A BALLERINA; see p. 122

*** I DIG FOSSILS: A family learning adventure uncovers 300-million-year-old fossils close to home. As nine-year-old Scott and his dad embark on a real-life adventure, Scott explains how fossils are formed as their hunt for treasures. Adult Juror Comments: Fascinating topic with excellent material. Informal science education, as well as good father and son role models. Safety and legal issues are well addressed. Scott is energetic, involved, and believable. Provokes an interest in history. Kid Juror Comments: Appealing child narrator. Made them curious about hunting for fossils. Some were disappointed when they didn't immediately find any in their backyard. Age: 5–12; Length: 24 min.; Suggested Retail Price: $14.95, MAZON PRODUCTIONS, INC.

* IT'S SLEEPY TIME; see p. 122

* IT'S TOOL TIME FOR KIDS; see p. 122

*** JANEY JUNKFOOD'S FRESH ADVENTURE!: This Emmy award-winning video features rap music, juggling, and splashy graphics. Guides kids through the confusing food marketplace and gets them off the junk food track. Adult Juror Comments: Informative, thoughtful, and entertaining. The children were realistic and the adults funny. Quality nutrition information is offered. Well produced, though the audio falters throughout. Using original ideas for delivering complex concepts. Kid Juror Comments: Enjoyed the rap music, the on-camera kids, and the comedic parts. They understood the information presented about healthy eating and talked about it afterward. Age: 5–12; Length: 28 min.; Suggested Retail Price: $24.95, FOODPLAY PRODUCTIONS

** JAZZ (MISS CHRISTY'S DANCIN): Incorporating ballet, tap, and modern dance, Christy introduces children to the basics of jazz dancing. Adult Juror Comments: Has good descriptions and good warm-up exercises. Teaches dance vocabulary in a simple way. Uses contemporary music and encourages group performances. Recommended by dance professionals as an adjunct to regular classes. Kid Juror Comments: Girls responded best. A favorite for those with an existing interest in dance. The kids liked watching the students dancing in the ending. Age: 6–12; Length: 30 min.; Suggested Retail Price: $12.98, PPI ENTERTAINMENT GROUP

* KENYA (WHERE IN THE WORLD): Take a pretend safari and discover secrets of the African nation of Kenya. Kids herd cattle with nomad tribes, unearth ancient artifacts and experience tribal customs and traditional family life. Adult Juror Comments: Offers an unusual approach to geography study. Creatively combines elements and resources of one's own community. Archival footage is disappointing. Kid Juror Comments: Captured kids' interest. They thought it educational but the acting was not believable. They were bothered that "they didn't really go to Kenya." Age: 5–12; Length: 30 min.; Suggested Retail Price: $9.95, IVN ENTERTAINMENT, INC.

** KIDS LOVE THE CIRCUS; see p. 123

** KIDS LOVE TRAINS (KIDS LOVE): Travel on steam trains, freight trains, big and small trains, fast and slow trains, an orange train, a snowplow train, and even a Santa train. A look at what it takes to make the trains run on time. Includes songs by Red Wagon Music. Adult Juror Comments: Well produced with catchy songs, good visuals that reinforce the information. Child narrators enhanced the production, though some of the dialogue was too fast. Kid Juror Comments: Liked the songs, some of which were familiar. Kids with a passion for trains got their fill. It inspired the kids to play with trains afterward. Age: 3–8; Length: 30 min.; Suggested Retail Price: $14.95, ACORN MEDIA PUBLISHING, INC.

*** KIDS' KITCHEN: MAKING GOOD EATING GREAT FUN!: A child's cookbook comes to life as a juggling nutrition magician and her kitchen crew of multiethnic schoolchildren create kids' favorite nutritious and delicious snacks without cooking. Includes an animated depiction of the food pyramid. Adult Juror Comments: Offers creative, original ideas for presenting complex nutrition information to children. Important information that can be pretty boring is well presented. It's well paced for discussion during and after. Can easily be broken into segments. Kid Juror Comments: Enjoyed watching the kids on-screen make snacks they could relate to. It's sort of corny, but they still wanted to watch it again. Age: 5–10; Length: 45 min.; Suggested Retail Price: $34.95, FOODPLAY PRODUCTIONS

*** LEARNING BASIC SKILLS: MUSIC BY HAP PALMER: Teaches color, letter, and number recognition to Hap Palmer's best-loved songs. Includes "All the Colors in the Rainbow," "Marching Around the Alphabet," "A Pocketful of B's," and "30–Second Challenge." Adult Juror Comments: Hap Palmer's music is fun, funny, and intelligent, entertaining and realistic. He knows how to reach kids. Shows great respect for cultural diversity. Kid Juror Comments: They were excited to hear the first letter of their name sung in the alphabet song. Age: 4–8; Length: 24 min.; Suggested Retail Price: $19.95, EDUCATIONAL ACTIVITIES, INC.

** LET'S GET A MOVE ON: Millions of families move each year. Teaches how to survive the impact of changing places, saying goodbye, and adjusting to new people, new situations, and new spaces. Adult Juror Comments: Great video for kids who are anxious about moving. Kids in video are realistic and talk about the concerns of most kids: Will I make new friends, will I like my house, will I learn my way around the new town? Great diversity. Kid Juror Comments: Reassuring. Kids learned that moving is not a scary event. "I liked how it told you it might be different in your new home, but you can make new friends and it might take a while." "I don't want to move." "What happens if you don't like the new place?" Age: 4–10; Length: 30 min.; Suggested Retail Price: $14.95, KIDVIDZ

* LOOK WHAT HAPPENS . . . AT THE CAR WASH; see p. 124

* LOTS AND LOTS OF TRAINS VOLUME I: Shows a great variety of live-action trains—big trains, little trains, steam, diesel, freight, and passenger trains—new trains, fast trains, slow trains, city, country, and mountain trains, toy trains, even trains that blow through snow. Adult Juror Comments: Not particularly stimulating. Great shots of trains but a little too long and repetitive except for avid train fans. No insights into types of trains, railroad history or which country trains are from. Music sound track fits the mood. Kid Juror Comments: Wanted more information about trains. It was a little boring. "I didn't like it because it didn't tell me anything about the trains." "I wanted to know where the trains were going." Age: 5–10; Length: 30 min.; Suggested Retail Price: $14.95, SUPERIOR HOME VIDEO

*** MAGIC SCHOOL BUS FOR LUNCH, THE (THE MAGIC SCHOOL BUS): Arnold doesn't go on a field trip. He accidentally swallows his miniaturized classmates and becomes the field trip! Better than an amusement park, Arnold's digestive system is full of surprises. Adult Juror Comments: An outstanding tool for teaching complicated concepts in science. Factual but fun, clever, lively, and entertaining. Children gain an understanding of the digestive system in an imaginative manner. Kid Juror Comments: Girls and boys alike of varying ages enjoyed this. Kept their attention throughout and encouraged questions during and afterward. Age: 4–12; Length: 27 min.; Suggested Retail Price: $12.95, WARNERVISON ENTERTAINMENT

*** MAGIC SCHOOL BUS GETS LOST IN SPACE, THE (THE MAGIC SCHOOL BUS): Janet drives the whole class crazy when she joins Ms. Frizzle's class on a field trip and gets them lost in outer space. When the navigational system breaks down, Janet is the only one with the knowledge to save them. Adult Juror Comments: A wonderful adaptation of the book. Well produced. Most kids are fascinated with the Magic School Bus book series. Kid Juror Comments: Laughter and smiles throughout. Asked to watch it again. Kept their attention, and they felt they learned something about space. Age: 5–12; Length: 30 min.; Suggested Retail Price: $12.95, WARNERVISION ENTERTAINMENT

* MAX AND FELIX: Max applies his talents as a skateboard daredevil, master carpenter, spellbinding storyteller, and champion fisherman. Felix photographs the disastrous and hilarious results. Adult Juror Comments: Theme of friendship is well represented throughout the story. Price is considered too high for most home use, and the video is only eleven minutes long. Designed to suit a narrow age bracket. Kid Juror Comments: "It's funny and easy to figure out." "I really like the story about the porch."

"It's interesting and silly too." Age: 3–8; Length: 11 min.; Suggested Retail Price: $29.95, AIMS MULTIMEDIA

* MEXICO (WHERE IN THE WORLD): Viewers investigate Aztec and Mayan ruins, share a meal with a Mexican family, join guitar players and flamenco dancers at a festival, and discover maps and Mexican treasures. Adult Juror Comments: Good content and music, with realistic acting. Some footage looks outdated and makes broad generalizations. The last fifteen minutes explore Mexico's geography, history, and culture. The opening segment, promoting tourism, was inappropriate. Kid Juror Comments: Interesting to learn about the nation's clothing and foods. They objected to the footage that looked dated, and did not find the on-screen kids believable or an accurate portrayal of the Mexican people. Age: 5–12; Length: 28 min.; Suggested Retail Price: $9.95, IVN ENTERTAINMENT, INC.

** MIGHTY CONSTRUCTION MACHINES; see p. 124

* MR. TIBBS & THE GREAT PET SEARCH; see p. 125

*** MRN: WHEN PARENTS ARE AWAY (MISTER ROGERS); see p. 125

* NATHALIE'S FIRST FLIGHT (JUST PLANES FOR KIDS): Before the plane takes off Nathalie tours a maintenance facility where planes are repaired. During the flight, she explores the cabin, cockpit, and galley. Includes tips on preparing for a plane trip. Adult Juror Comments: Provides a good introduction to planes and flying , spectacular views. Leisurely paced. Vocabulary is too technical and beyond the understanding of the audience. The on-camera talent lacks zest. Kid Juror Comments: Those who like airplanes enjoyed this most. Some others lost interest, but it's a great introduction for a child who's never flown before. Age: 4–8; Length: 32 min.; Suggested Retail Price: $14.95, JUST PLANES VIDEOS

* NEW SOCCER FOR FUN AND SKILLS (NEW GAMES VIDEO): These games encourage players to improve and develop soccer skills and team building. Adult Juror Comments: Offers some excellent game strategies, although advanced and experienced soccer players will find it too basic. Suggestions for safe, noncompetitive play. Kid Juror Comments: Good ideas presented well enough. Age: 6–12; Length: 24 min.; Suggested Retail Price: $29.95, NEW GAMES

** OPEN YOUR HEART AMERICA (LEARN TO SING AND SIGN WITH GAIA): Gaia introduces American Sign Language with an inspiring song for children that also features a homeless woman. Encourages activism and a renewed spirit in America. Part two teaches how to sign the song. Adult Juror Comments: This is a little corny but appealing. At times it talks down to kids. The songs are well selected and not overbearing in delivering uplifting message. Length is right for this audience. Kid Juror Comments: Enjoyed learning sign language, and most kids wanted to see it again right after the first screening. Most imitated signing and remembered a few signs. "It's different and may help someone." Age: 6–12; Length: 20 min.; Suggested Retail Price: $12.95, HEARTSONG COMMUNICATIONS

* RAILROADERS; see p. 126

*** SAMMY AND OTHER SONGS FROM GETTING TO KNOW MYSELF: Nice examples of children stretching, jumping and discovering the joy of moving. Good awareness of body image and the body's position in space and body movements. Adult Juror Comments: Well produced. Gives pleasant, clear demonstrations of movement concepts and body parts. Insights for a child that enhances their self-image. Good cultural diversity. Song lyrics are shown on-screen, encouraging readers to sing along. Kid Juror Comments: Much fun. They sang along when they could. Age: 3–9; Length: 30 min.; Suggested Retail Price: $19.95, EDUCATIONAL ACTIVITIES, INC.

** SHEEP CROSSING: Using equal doses of fact and fun, program explores the world of sheep and wool. Features real people, especially children who work with sheep, enhanced with graphics and music. Adult Juror Comments: Has a limited audience, but would be very good for research or if a child had a special interest in sheep. Focus on wool became a bit boring. Music is distracting. Initially, it is not clear who is being referred to—a person or a sheep. Kid Juror Comments: The level of interest was surprising. "My friends and I would like to see more about sheep." Seeing the sheep being sheared upset them until they learned it doesn't hurt. They enjoyed the new baby sheep. "I'm going to work on a sheep farm when I grow up." Age: 5–8; Length: 27 min.; Suggested Retail Price: $14.95, GREAT WHITE DOG PICTURE CO.

** SIGN SONGS (SIGN LANGUAGE FOR KIDS): Learning sign language offers benefits for hearing kids even if they never use it. Improves reading and motor skills and appreciation of different cultures. Hosted by Ken Lonnquist, from the National Theater of the Deaf. Adult Juror Comments: This is a good idea but the signing is too fast for young children to track. Some songs are simply wonderful and can be used to build enthusiasm for learning to sign. Animation lacks appeal. It's probably best used in segments. Kid

Juror Comments: The music and the signing were interesting. Younger ones lost attention quickly. "This is a grown-up movie." Age: 3–10; Length: 29 min.; Suggested Retail Price: $19.98, AYLMER PRESS

*** SIGN AND ABC'S (SIGN LANGUAGE FOR KIDS): Focus on the alphabet—the most important tool developed by humans. Video teaches the written, spoken, and American Sign Language (ASL) alphabets, introduces spelling and teaching the signs for eighty-eight words. Adult Juror Comments: Nice pacing allows for review, but still challenging. Very well executed. Wonderful exposure to sign language. This can be used in the classroom or at home. "It demonstrated that everyone can learn to sign." Kid Juror Comments: "It was funny." "It taught me a lot of signs. I would like to learn more." Kids tried to converse in sign after the video. They were intrigued by the skits and the gestures. Age: 5–10; Length: 50 min.; Suggested Retail Price: $14.98, AYLMER PRESS

** SIGN-ME-A-STORY: Linda Bove, from *Sesame Street,* introduces children to American sign language, teaching simple signs and acting out familiar tales. Adult Juror Comments: well-conceived production. Provides an introduction to sign language, with a short lesson before each story. Well sequenced. Linda Bove is excellent. Offers opportunity for discussion on being hearing-impaired. Slow-paced. Kid Juror Comments: Liked the music and wanted to watch it again. Many recognized Linda Bove from *Sesame Street.* They are inherently interested in learning sign language and wanted to try it afterward. Age: 3–8; Length: 30 min.; Suggested Retail Price: $14.98, SONY WONDER/RANDOM HOUSE

** TAP (MISS CHRISTY'S DANCIN): Introduction to tap dancing, an American-originated form of dance noted for developing coordination, balance, rhythm, and speed. Adult Juror Comments: Music and pace are appropriate for kids. Has good warm-up exercises and a good introduction to basic tap steps. Instruction is clear but dance professionals suggested using the video as supplement to regular instruction, not instead of. Kid Juror Comments: Discovered that it was far more difficult to learn the steps than they thought. Those familiar with tap said it lacked depth of instruction. Yet, "It's more fun than ballet." Age: 6–12; Length: 30 min.; Suggested Retail Price: $12.98, PPI ENTERTAINMENT GROUP

* THERE GOES A BOAT (LIVE ACTION VIDEO FOR KIDS): What child isn't thrilled to see jet planes landing on an aircraft carrier? Join a visit to a variety of ships, from passenger ships to submarines. Adult Juror Comments: Good information with an emphasis on safety. Subject is appealing to kids but this is too technical. Presenting military ships and missiles as toys was disturbing. Kid Juror Comments: Okay, particularly the boys. Age: 5–8; Length: 35 min.; Suggested Retail Price: $10.95, WARNERVISION ENTERTAINMENT

** THERE GOES A BULLDOZER (LIVE ACTION VIDEO FOR KIDS): Construction foreman explains machines associated with heavy construction—jackhammers to bulldozers—with close-ups of sights and sounds surrounding a construction crew at work. Adult Juror Comments: Good information with good demonstrations. Good opportunity to examine different careers in construction. Shows little diversity. Kid Juror Comments: The slapstick humor really went over. They related the information in the video to their own experiences. Some wanted to see it again. Boys enjoyed it more than girls did. Age: 3–8; Length: 35 min.; Suggested Retail Price: $10.95, WARNERVISION ENTERTAINMENT

** THERE GOES A FIRE TRUCK (LIVE ACTION VIDEO FOR KIDS): Features fire equipment operated by professionals. Fireman Dave shows kids what it's like to be a firefighter and demonstrates how the equipment works. Adult Juror Comments: Colorful visually, but there's a great deal of information to absorb all at once. May stimulate further inquiry. Shows little ethnic cultural diversity and hardly any women are practicing firefighters. Kid Juror Comments: Stimulated play imitating fire trucks. They were fascinated by the yellow fire trucks at the airport and wanted to go to a fire station after viewing this. Age: 3–8; Length: 35 min.; Suggested Retail Price: $10.95, WARNERVISION ENTERTAINMENT

* THERE GOES A POLICE CAR (LIVE ACTION VIDEO FOR KIDS): Behind-the-scenes look at police officers and their equipment from horses to motorcycles, helicopters to special radios. Adult Juror Comments: Contains good information. Most felt the slapstick approach to the encouragement of respect for police officers was inappropriate. Officer's gear was captivating, but using "bad guys" was inappropriate. Lacks cultural and gender diversity. Kid Juror Comments: The live-action section scored high. They wanted to watch it again. One boy noticed the use of the word "policemen" and said, "I told you girls can't be police." Age: 5–8; Length: 35 min.; Suggested Retail Price: $10.95, WARNERVISION ENTERTAINMENT

* THERE GOES A RACE CAR (LIVE ACTION VIDEO FOR KIDS): Shows race cars and the people behind them, from behind-the-scenes pre-race preparation to crossing the finish line. Examines unusual types of racing. Adult Juror Comments: Fast-paced and interesting. The accident scenes tend to glamorize danger. Points out the importance of safety. Toyota endorsement is prominent. Some parts are too technical for this audience. Hosts are pretty silly. Kid Juror Comments: "My eight-year-old son loved it." (As did most of the boys.) It's most suitable for a special-interest audience. Age: 5–8; Length: 35 min.; Suggested Retail Price: $10.95, WARNERVISION ENTERTAINMENT

* THERE GOES A SPACESHIP (LIVE ACTION VIDEO FOR KIDS): Visits the Kennedy Space Center and Space Camp and explores the challenges of living in space. Looks at what it takes to be a NASA astronaut. Adult Juror Comments: Good introduction to the study of space and space travel. However, the promotional advertising is objectionable. Kid Juror Comments: Kept their attention. Most suitable for kids interested in subject. Age: 5–8; Length: 35 min.; Suggested Retail Price: $10.95, WARNERVISION ENTERTAINMENT

** THERE GOES A TRAIN (LIVE ACTION VIDEO FOR KIDS): Offers a close-up look at the world of trains, from steam engines to locomotives. Explores the many functions of today's trains, including the caboose. Adult Juror Comments: Well produced. Use of real people is a plus. Filled with information, though it starts out slowly. Good safety messages. Kid Juror Comments: Enjoyable, though a little long. Age: 5–8; Length: 35 min.; Suggested Retail Price: $10.95, WARNERVISION ENTERTAINMENT

** THERE GOES A TRUCK (LIVE ACTION VIDEO FOR KIDS): Take a ride through the exciting world of trucks. Safe inside the cab, kids feel the exhilaration of operating everything from sanitation trucks to the super truck that transports the NASA space shuttle. Adult Juror Comments: Tends to be rather silly, a little too long, and too technical. Featuring both female and male drivers brought kudos from jurors. The recycling message is good. Shows some unsafe behavior. Kid Juror Comments: Kids definitely enjoyed this more than the adults. They liked the realistic sounds and the silly humor. "Be careful around a truck!" Real footage and sounds are a plus. Age: 5–8; Length: 35 min.; Suggested Retail Price: $10.95, WARNERVISION ENTERTAINMENT

* THERE GOES AN AIRPLANE (LIVE ACTION VIDEO FOR KIDS): Shows how airplanes are used for many different purposes, from passenger planes to "the fastest planes of all"—fighter jets. Visits the deck of an aircraft carrier and watches jet fighters take off and land at high speed. Adult Juror Comments: Appealing for those interested in planes. Shows little gender or ethnic diversity. Fast-paced action is just right for young children. Shows a good variety of planes. Kid Juror Comments: "Boys were glued to the screen." The humor went over some children's heads. Descriptions were too difficult for this age range and delivered too fast. Age: 5–8; Length: 35 min.; Suggested Retail Price: $10.95, WARNERVISION ENTERTAINMENT

* THOSE DOGGONE DOGS AND PUPPIES; see p. 128

*** TOOL POWER; see p. 128

** VRRROOOMMM — FARMING FOR KIDS; see p. 128

** WACKY DOGS; see p. 129

* WALK, RIDE, FLY; see p. 129

* WHEN I GROW UP I WANTA BE . . . AN ASTRONAUT: Twelve children train for and conduct a space shuttle mission with astronaut Bob Springer as their mentor at U.S. Space Camp. Gives an overview of the history of space exploration. Adult Juror Comments: Well produced, it answers a lot of questions. Shows good cultural mix and girls play important roles. It is best suited for kids who have an interest in this subject. Tends to be too long. Kid Juror Comments: "This is good for people who want to be astronauts." "I like that girls get training." Some kids thought it was too long. "It shows kids of all colors." A good starting point for talking about career in space. Age: 5–10; Length: 45 min.; Suggested Retail Price: $19.95, FIVE POINTS SOUTH PRODUCTIONS

** WHEN I GROW UP I WANTA BE . . . VOL. 1: Seven children perform in real-life settings as a jockey, zoo veterinarian, fire and rescue worker, auto racer, and jet fighter pilot. Special appearance is made by the Blue Angels. Adult Juror Comments: This is appealing and educational. Stimulated kids thinking about their particular talents, interests, and career aspirations. Shows little diversity. Kid Juror Comments: Kids liked this. "I enjoyed it because it shows that you can be anything you would like to be." "It made me think about what I want to do." "I am too little to think about it right now!" Afterward, kids talked about what they wanted to be when they grew up. Age: 5–10; Length: 44 min.; Suggested Retail Price: $19.95, FIVE POINTS SOUTH PRODUCTIONS

** WHERE THE GARBAGE GOES; see p. 129

** WHISTLEPUNKS & SLIVERPICKERS (I CAN DO IT! VIDEO FIELD TRIPS): Puts girls and boys in the driver's seat while they explore forests by planting trees, operating enormous machines, driving big trucks, milling lumber, and building a house. Shows skilled women and men working together. Adult Juror Comments: Provides good information on forestry and logging. Creative presentation with interesting photography. Unfortunately, the packaging is somewhat misleading. Useful for classroom study about trees or home. Kid Juror Comments: One class had just completed studying machines and related to the subject particularly well. Shows good gender role models. Age: 3–9; Length: 30 min.; Suggested Retail Price: $18.95, I CAN DO IT! PRODUCTIONS

*** YOGA KIDS; see p. 130

** YOU CAN FLY A KITE (YOU CAN VIDEO SERIES FOR CHILDREN): Demonstrates teamwork while playing in the magical world of kites. Teaches how to build and fly a kite, kite history, and introduces young champion kite flyers. Adult Juror Comments: Kids on-screen are very natural. Well paced. Photography of kite-flying competition is compelling. Not much cultural diversity. Kid Juror Comments: "Cool. I especially liked the team flying." Wanted to build a kite immediately. A little long for younger kids. Age: 5–8; Length: 30 min.; Suggested Retail Price: $12.95, BLACKBOARD ENTERTAINMENT AND RED SKY FILMS

8

Middle School

(Ages 8–12)

Introduction: Irene Wood

High-quality videos are seldom available for children between the ages of eight and twelve. When the first blush of innocence and credulity begin to fade and the world-weary sophistication of adolescence has yet to bloom, videos and CD-ROMs designed to capture the interest of this age group are noticeably absent.

The plethora of productions for younger children—visits to see farm animals, learning about the world beyond their own home—are now disdainfully dismissed by these middle-school children as "too babyish." This age group is often captivated by a weekly television series or, in their rush to grow up, lured to the pounding immediacy of MTV. At the same time, their intellects are being challenged (we hope) by the demands of schoolwork. Kids at this age are also becoming more interested in the surrounding adult world and the emotional experiences they're exposed to as they grapple for a better understanding of life. They are forming close friendships (gaggles of giggling girls) and gaining more independence (gangs of after-school sports enthusiasts), especially in this society of more and more working- and single-parent households in which children are increasingly left on their own. That is why this chapter presents the perfect opportunity to introduce some high-quality viewing that can meet both educational and personal needs.

IRENE WOOD is the editor of Media Reviews for *Booklist*, a publication of the American Library Association. She holds an M.L.S. from the University of Washington.

The best videos and CD-ROMs are characterized by accurate, up-to-date, and well-developed content, well-written scripts, and sharp production values. Moreover, children's media should convey to its audience a respect for their intelligence and imagination. Since children like to watch others their age, or older, in both familiar and unusual situations, they appreciate captivating dramas or stories in which problems are solved through perseverance and consideration for others, and portrayals of times, places, and events from which they can learn about the larger world beyond their own environment.

Viewing titles such as *Bully Smart* and *Stranger Smart* gives older children valuable, concrete guidance for dealing with common social issues they may encounter. These programs also give parents and kids a chance to talk about people or incidents that might trouble children in their daily life. Students looking for better ways to survive in school will appreciate tips in programs such as *How to Study for Better Grades* or *Geometry World.* Personal interests are addressed by *Nancy Drew: Secrets Can Kill* and *Stories and Other Legends from Other Lands,* among others. The middle years often include music lessons and that bane of many kids' existence, practicing. The *Marsalis on Music* series brings perspective to the perplexities of learning an instrument and engages the student's interest in the larger context of music appreciation. The *Beethoven Lives Upstairs* CD-ROM offers a wonderful introduction to Beethoven and an imaginary hero. The baby-sitting instructional tape and the *Baby-Sitters Club* series are perfectly suited to girls between the ages eight and twelve; the first title prepares them to handle their first paying job and increases their sense of accomplishment, while the others are appealing entertainment that explores friendships and problem-solving in the familiar milieu of girlfriends.

Family-oriented feature films, from the tried-and-true *Please Don't Eat the Daisies* to the more recent *Summer of the Monkeys,* let children experience human relationships in unfamiliar and unusual family situations. *Cyrano* and *Black Beauty,* with sensitivity, acquaint children with some stalwart works of literature in fine productions. *Bizet's Dream,* a multidimensional work, introduces both the music of this nineteenth-century composer and the creative process, and portrays a young girl's evolving relationships in a creative, spectacularly produced drama.

Just as the world of eight- to twelve-year-olds is expanding, so too are the opportunities to offer imaginative, eye-opening, mind-stretching media for these children. The following videos and CD-ROMs represent an excellent array of productions that touch on the interests and needs of "middle-age" children.

Educational/Instructional

*** ANCIENT EGYPT (ANCIENT CIVILIZATIONS FOR CHILDREN): Travel back in time to ancient Egypt, a civilization that began along the Nile River over five thousand years ago. These early people advanced civilization by building pyramids and temples, establishing a vast trading system, and developing hieroglyphics. Adult Juror Comments: Holds your interest from beginning to end. Flows well from one subject to the next. Topic appealing, very informative, good videography and format. "Provides accurate and factual information in an age-appropriate fashion." Aesthetically pleasing. Kid Juror Comments: "It was gross when they talked about taking the brains out. It was cool seeing inside the tombs." Kids complained about the captions but learned a lot from them. Got them thinking about Egyptians and other cultures." Age: 8–12; Length: 23 min.; Suggested Retail Price: $29.95, SCHLESSINGER MEDIA

** BABY-SITTING: THE BASICS & BEYOND (KIDS 101): The fairy good-sitter teaches new baby-sitters about feeding, diapering, avoiding accidents, and entertaining children. Includes a question-and-answer session on preventing and handling emergencies. Ideal for new parents or future baby-sitters. Adult Juror Comments: Teaches good baby-sitting practices in an appealing way. Contains safety information that few programs offer. Good pace, sparkling special effects, and true stories. Important information and high-quality presentation. Great discussion-starter. Kid Juror Comments: Much better than taking a baby-sitting class. Kids liked the "fairy good-sitter." It's great for an older sibling." "I liked that there were examples of good things to do." "Makes sense." Age: 8–12; Length: 30 min.; Suggested Retail Price: $14.95, CAR POOL PRODUCTIONS

* BULLY SMART (STREET SMART): Teaches a four-step personal safety system to deal with bullies. The children represented go to school fearing a bully and are instructed on how to deal with them. Adult Juror Comments: Good advice for kids. Emphasizes self-esteem and personal safety. Best watched with parent or adult. Offers a lot of material for discussion. Lacks cultural diversity. Kid Juror Comments: Kids recognized the incidents from the video in their daily lives and thought the advice was good. "Maybe bullies shouldn't watch it or they might get some new ideas and techniques to attack others." Age: 8–12; Length: 32 min.; Suggested Retail Price: $19.95, PFS STREET SMART

* CHICKEN FAT AND THE YOUTH FITNESS VIDEO; see p. 134

** COOPERATIVE GROUP GAMES (NEW GAMES): A useful video for teachers and group leaders. The twelve games teach and reinforce basic skills in math, English, creativity, teamwork, listening, and other things. Useful for children of various ages. These games are also for coed P.E. programs. Twelve games. Adult Juror Comments: Kids are obviously having a lot of fun. Offers teachers and group leaders of elementary age kids a simple, clear presentation of new ideas for interactive physical activities. Sound and video quality are not great. Great diversity. Kid Juror Comments: "It's hard to hear what leader is saying." Kids learned new games they've not seen before. "Can we go out and play these games?" "Good to watch when you're bored." Age: 7–11; Length: 30 min.; Suggested Retail Price: $29.95, NEW GAMES

* DIGGING FOR DINOSAURS; see p. 134

*** FAMILIES OF JAPAN; see p. 135

*** FAMILIES OF SWEDEN; see p. 135

* FIT FOR A KING: THE SMART KID'S GUIDE TO FOOD & FUN; see pp. 135–36

** GIRL'S WORLD, A (A GIRL'S WORLD): This real-life adventure takes girls on an exciting day of fun, friendship, and discovery as they explore the worlds of Annie, a horse vet; Karen, an artist; and Suzanne, a jet pilot. Adult Juror Comments: This video shows great role models for young girls. Unfortunately, the sound level is so low at times you can't hear what's being said. Highly motivating. It offers a clever look at occupations that will inspire any young girl. Kid Juror Comments: Boys and girls alike enjoyed learning more about various careers, especially the pilot and the glass-blower. They were inspired. "It's good to see girls with strong careers." It's too bad the sound is so poor at times. Age: 8–12; Length: 45 min.; Suggested Retail Price: $14.95, LAURIE HEPBURN PRODUCTIONS

** HOW MUCH IS A MILLION? (READING RAINBOW): LeVar explores ways of counting large numbers as he talks to people who share grouping and estimating techniques. This episode helps viewers visualize how much are a million, a billion, and a trillion. Adult Juror Comments: Good presentation of intangibles. Beginning moves slowly and is hard to follow, but matters soon improve. High quality with interesting camera work. Format is wonderful for parent-child interaction. Very informative and understandable. Kid Juror Comments: Discussion and illustrations helped to understand numbers. Not bright enough, no music. "Children didn't become interested until the production at the crayon factory." "I liked the different locations." Age: 7–10; Length: 28 min.; Suggested Retail Price: $23.95, GPN/READING RAINBOW

** HURRICANES AND TORNADOES (WEATHER FUNDAMENTALS): The awesome force of hurricanes and tornadoes, the most destructive storms on earth, are fascinating. Students study both phenomena from their early formation to the full-blown maturity that wreaks havoc on land. Adult Juror Comments: Live clips of storm are very dramatic. Narration makes concept easy to understand. Good multicultural cast, but not all are skilled. "Fascinating facts and experiments kept the subject lingering in your mind." "Makes a lasting impression." Kid Juror Comments: Kids liked the fast pace and the visual excitement. They liked the live-action footage of real storms. "I learned a lot about the weather." Age: 8–12; Length: 23 min.; Suggested Retail Price: $29.95, SCHLESSINGER MEDIA

* IMPORTANCE OF TREES; see p. 137

*** JET PILOT: Solid examination of what it takes to be a jet pilot—from pilot training to cockpit controls, from hand signals to communicate between ground crew and pilot to the importance of maintenance operations. Adult Juror Comments: Informative and well written. Doesn't talk down to children. Explains the process of flying a jet. "The aerial photography made me feel I was in the cockpit flying my own jet." Kid Juror Comments: Engaging. Kids learned that they need to go to college to become a pilot. Motivated discussion about female pilots and those of varied ethnic backgrounds. Appealed to girls as well as boys. "Do pilots make money having so much fun?" Age: 6–12; Length: 30 min.; Suggested Retail Price: $12.95, BC ENTERTAINMENT

* KEEPING KIDS SAFE!: A GUIDE FOR KIDS AND THEIR FAMILIES; see p. 137

** MASTERING ASTHMA: A FAMILY'S GUIDE TO UNDERSTANDING; see p. 345

** NOBODY'S PERFECT . . . EVERYBODY'S SPECIAL!; see p. 139

* OUR DISAPPEARING WORLD FORESTS (THINK ABOUT IT): Features a talking computer who leads children to look at the complex issues surrounding our vanishing forests. In interviews, experts assesses research data. Adult Juror Comments: Encourages critical thinking. Information provided is very instructive without being overly technical. Exemplifies cooperative learning. The talking computer was not well received, and the acting scored particu-

larly low. Kid Juror Comments: Just okay. They liked the ecosystem poster. Could be useful for further research about forests. Age: 8–12; Length: 27 min.; Suggested Retail Price: $19.95, PARAGON MEDIA

** SKILL GAMES (NEW GAMES): Teaches developmental skills that promote learning and social skills. Included are physical skills like throwing, catching, running, plus social experiences like cooperation, teamwork, inclusion, and fun. Adult Juror Comments: Not particularly entertaining but offers good instruction for non-competitive games. Mediocre production values. Producer is respectful of children's questions and takes time to really listen. Encourages teamwork and good sportsmanship. Lacks diversity. Kid Juror Comments: Kids learned new games, but need to watch it again to learn how to play them. They were not motivated to watch it at first. "Good directions given on how to play." "We need to show our gym coach this." Age: 7–12; Length: 30 min.; Suggested Retail Price: $29.95, NEW GAMES

** STRANGER SMART (STREET SMART): Features a fouteen-year police veteran with experience in the dangers children face. Teaches skills and principles of a four-step personal safety system designed to protect kids from would-be abductors and molesters. Adult Juror Comments: Excellent advice. Jurors liked the inclusion of Internet safety tips. Should be watched with parent or adult, since some information is directed at parents. Lacks cultural diversity. Kid Juror Comments: Kids thought it gave them good advice. They too felt that it was best viewed with an adult and thought it might be scary for younger kids. Age: 8–12; Length: 32 min.; Suggested Retail Price: $19.95, PFS STREET SMART

** WHO IS AN AMERICAN?; see p. 142

** WORKING IT OUT, A SURVIVAL GUIDE FOR KIDS; see p. 370

CD-ROMs

*** ASTRO ALGEBRA; see pp. 344, 347

** DEVILS CANYON: A DINAMATION ADVENTURE (TIME BLAZERS): Cyberaptor, a mechanical creature that interfaces with a time-travel device malfunctions and strands its creator, Dr. Cope, in a prehistoric jungle. Your mission is to rescue Dr. Cope from the past after you take a training program. Adult Juror Comments: Interesting approach that is engaging, entertaining, and educational. Supplementary materials include membership card and Web site information. Requires patience on the part of the player. Kid Juror Comments: Challenging. Kids enjoyed it, particularly activities similar to "real-life" undertakings, such as the time and the patience needed to pick out a fossil. Some children were frustrated initially but went back to play the game later. Age: 8–12; Suggested Retail Price: $39.95, PARAGON MEDIA

*** DIGITAL FIELD TRIP TO THE RAIN FOREST, THE; see pp. 344, 347

*** DIGITAL FIELD TRIP TO THE WETLANDS, THE; see p. 348

** DISNEY'S ADVENTURES IN TYPING WITH TIMON & PUMBAA: Kids build essential typing skills, including finger placement, speed, and letter recognition, while getting plenty of laughs from Timon and Pumbaa in this wild and wacky adventure. Adult Juror Comments: Wonderful and entertaining way to introduce keyboard and typing skills. "What better way than through this amusing yet educational method?" One parent asked to take it home so she could learn to type herself. Kid Juror Comments: Some kids liked the characters but not the typing. If they stick with it, they can learn a lot. "It taught me where to put my fingers." "It's dumb, it says 'let's work on posture.' " Kids loved getting the certificates. Some thought it was boring. Age: 8–12; Suggested Retail Price: $29.99, DISNEY INTERACTIVE

*** DISNEY'S ANIMATED STORYBOOK, MULAN; see pp. 132, 146

*** ENCARTA ENCYCLOPEDIA 98 DELUXE; see p. 348

*** ENCARTA ENCYCLOPEDIA DELUXE 99; see pp. 344, 348

*** ENCARTA VIRTUAL GLOBE; see pp. 348–49

** FRACTION ATTRACTION; see p. 147

** GEOMETRY WORLD: Interactively explores geometric principles. Creates tessellating patterns, tangram designs, and symmetric figures. Uses a Geoboard and geometric programming tool to create and explore plane figures. Two great adventures. Adult Juror Comments: Easy to install, difficult to operate, interesting variety. Good visual quality. Excellent tool for use in conjunction with classroom instruction or for motivated kids, on their own. Stimulating and diverse. Good review for older kids. Kid Juror Comments: Kids needed help with difficult parts. Some areas were very difficult—formula for area of triangles, obtuse angles. Good visuals, graphics. Some parts were particularly fun: tangrams, drawing with symmetry. Kids liked the adventure. Age: 10–18; Suggested Retail Price: $39.95, COGNITIVE TECHNOLOGIES CORPORATION

** GRAMMAR ROCK (SCHOOLHOUSE ROCK): Imagine . . . children mastering the building blocks of language through rock music. Kids rock out to the Emmy Award–winning rock video grammar lessons from ABC's Saturday morning lineup. Includes over twenty grammar activities at three skill levels. Adult Juror Comments: Very engaging and rewarding. Excellent learning tool. Involves children creatively. Great for home learning. The videos are a bit dated. Program had some glitches and locked up on slower computers. Kid Juror Comments: Scored high with kids. A "lifesaver." "It makes learning boring stuff fun." The music videos were the high point of the program. Kids liked printing out their own silly stories. Students familiar with the cartoons had an advantage. Age: 7–12; Suggested Retail Price: $39.95, THE LEARNING COMPANY

** HOT DOG STAND: THE WORKS: Players are challenged to successfully manage their own small business with this simulation program. Creates a stimulating learning environment that practices critical math, problem-solving, and communications skills. Adult Juror Comments: Offers a unique perspective on learning. Good graphics and support materials. Easy to install. Explores challenging and new business concepts for kids, such as backward planning and market values. Repetition of setting up business becomes boring over time. Kid Juror Comments: Funny animation. Kids liked seeing how well they could forecast sales. Boys seemed to be more interested in content than girls. They realized how much planning was involved and still enjoyed the game. Setting up each business is repetitious. Age: 10–16; Suggested Retail Price: $14.95, SUNBURST COMMUNICATIONS, INC.

*** INDIAN IN THE CUPBOARD, THE: Based on the book and the critically acclaimed movie. Explores the Iroquois culture, crafts, and adventures in a beautifully rendered woodlands environment. Adult Juror Comments: Treats the Native American culture with respect, although in a Hollywood fashion. Installation instructions were inadequate for some. Kid Juror Comments: Kids liked this. "My twelve-year-old, who normally does not play computer games, spent an entire evening enthralled with this game." Age: 8–12; Suggested Retail Price: $22.95, VIRGIN INTERACTIVE

*** JUMPSTART TYPING: Using an Olympic metaphor, this program helps kids build important keyboarding skills that prepare them for the computer-dominated world. Contains more than thirty "extreme key-boarding" techniques such as rock-climbing and snowboarding. Adult Juror Comments: Great format, age-appropriate. Different levels offer adaptability. It was surprising how much children learned during the evaluation session. It makes you want to type. Helps develop motor skills. Does not offer the opportunity to correct work. Kid Juror Comments: Overall, kids enjoyed it. Children couldn't wait to play this. "It's just plain fun and I'm learning to type." "It's really fun, I like the snowboarding game." "The games were my favorite and I liked winning gold medals without help." Kids had technical problems with this one. Age: 7–11; Suggested Retail Price: $30.00, KNOWLEDGE ADVENTURE

*** JUMPSTART 3RD GRADE: ANOTHER STAR LOST IN THE BLACK HOLE: An activity-filled curriculum-based program blending the core subjects for third grade, including language arts, math, science, history, music, and art. Offers an adventure in an educational game format. Adult Juror Comments: Enormously successful at integrating facts, skills, learning, and problem-solving. The story is absorbing, the robots are fun, and each puzzle gives a reward. Clear instructions, helpful hints. Adult assistance is helpful to get started. Kid Juror Comments: Kids enjoyed the variety of activities, the graphics, and the songs. They were engaged and challenged to build upon skills they have already. Might test a child's attention span. Their favorite parts were robot, different rooms, going back in time. Age: 7–10; Suggested Retail Price: $40.00, KNOWLEDGE ADVENTURE

** JUMPSTART ADVENTURES 6TH GRADE: Launches media-savvy tweens into a brain-building mission with console-style games and over 4,000 curriculum challenges. Builds knowledge of language arts, math, ancient history, geography, and science. Adult Juror Comments: Easy to install. Content is really good but actual play is poorly explained. Instructions not very clear. Sometimes skips or repeats words. Challenging. Far above the level of sixth grade. Kid Juror Comments: Good but difficult. Kids got frustrated. "The program was very hard." Kids found it difficult to move around but thought it contained interesting information. Enjoyed the "Save the Rain Forest" section. Age: 10–14; Suggested Retail Price: $20.00, KNOWLEDGE ADVENTURE

* LENNY'S TIME MACHINE: All about people and culture in challenging multilevel games, puzzles, creative activities, and facts. Players create scenes while learning about music, science, art, and leisure. Adult Juror Comments: Arcade-style game. The historical selections seem trite, offering only one screen of "facts" for each time period. Adults experienced some technical difficulties. Even the company's technical support agreed the instructions are poor. Kid Juror Comments: Some kids loved it. Others were intrigued at first but didn't stay with it. Others found it challenging once they got the hang of it. Held the interest of kids well over eight years old. Age: 7–12; Suggested Retail Price: $49.99, VIRGIN INTERACTIVE

** MAKE A MAP (LEARNING LADDER): Creates maps that turn into 3-D cities that you can "get into your car and drive through." Teaches geography, map-making, and basic orienteering. Develops map reading, critical thinking, problem-solving, spatial relationships, and community awareness. Adult Juror Comments: Fun game that helps to develop a sense of direction and geography. Driving the car was difficult at first. Sarcasm is used throughout. It could be frustrating for younger children. Kid Juror Comments: Kids enjoyed making their own maps and driving. "I liked learning geography." The crashing aspect of the car was initially very frustrating, because it was hard to control. Age: 8–12; Suggested Retail Price: $39.95, PANASONIC INTERACTIVE MEDIA

*** MATH BLASTER 4TH GRADE: Good story, superior graphics and sound, interesting characters, and a wide range of play at various levels of difficulty. Includes addition and subtraction, multiplication and division, fractions, decimals, and complex numbers. Adult Juror Comments: Very user-friendly and appealing to kids. Excellent developmental program for audience. Develops cognitive and problem-solving skills. Well organized. Program adapts to child's abilities. Offers good rewards. Too fast for first-time users. Juror Comments: They loved the "mental math" section and the problem-solving. "Awesome." "This is a fun way to practice. Can we keep it?" "I had screams of delight and students jumping for joy when they got answers correct." "Great special effects." Age: 8–12; Suggested Retail Price: $20.00, KNOWLEDGE ADVENTURE

*** MATH FOR THE REAL WORLD: Kids try out their math skills in a "real" context. They join a band and travel on a ten-city road tour across the United States while solving practical math problems such as purchasing music equipment, food, and gas. Adult Juror Comments: An offbeat, challenging way to learn math. Teaches logic, fractions, time, money, charts, maps, volume, weight, measurement, patterns, and more. Wow! Easy to install and operate. Kid Juror Comments: Kids loved making music videos and getting chased by the press. The math games are challenging as well as age-appropriate. Also, kids worked together. Their other favorite parts were building roads and getting food. Age: 10–14; Suggested Retail Price: $20.00, KNOWLEDGE ADVENTURE

*** NANCY DREW: SECRETS CAN KILL: An interactive mystery game that challenges girls to solve a murder as they become the famous teenage girl detective, Nancy Drew. Players must find hidden clues, solve brain-teasing puzzles, collect inventory items, and interrogate suspects. Adult Juror Comments: Installation difficult. Impressive production makes it very challenging. Great content, wonderful music, excellent graphics. Presents a problem, gives tools to solve it, stimulates curiosity and creativity. Kid Juror Comments: "We had fun and it was easy to use." "All of our friends are asking us about this and want to play." Girls love company motto, "For girls who aren't afraid of a mouse." "Cool." Age: 8–14; ; Suggested Retail Price: $39.95, HER INTERACTIVE

** PHONICS GAME, THE: A systematic teaching tool disguised as a game. Interactive technique teaches sounds and rules of phonics and spelling while students engage in competitive play. Learning reinforced by CD-ROM games and audio tapes. Adult Juror Comments: Appropriate, accurate, and fun. Personalizing the phonics rules makes them easier to remember. Video was a little stilted. Little diversity. Can be used in classroom or home, but needs adult guidance. Kid Juror Comments: "I learned a lot." "It's easy to learn when you don't realize you're being taught." Children were delighted to be able to read words more easily after the first time. They commented on how "old" it looked. "They all liked being called 'Mega Stars.'" Age: 8–12; Suggested Retail Price: $284.90, A BETTER WAY OF LEARNING, INC.

** PRE-ALGEBRA WORLD: A highly interactive program to develops math skills. Master fractions in the stock market, a pizza parlor, and an art gallery. Learn estimation and rounding in a basketball court. Uncover prime numbers in an archaeological dig. Adult Juror Comments: The program consists of good drill and practice activities. Great for students in fifth and sixth grade before pre-algebra. Simple. Easy to install, but difficult to move around to different games. Kid Juror Comments: Well-produced program that some kids found easy and colorful. They liked practicing skills they learned in math. "It was fun to shoot basketball." "We liked the pizza parlor." "My mom would like me to have it." Age: 10–13; Suggested Retail Price: $39.95, COGNITIVE TECHNOLOGIES CORPORATION

** RAMAGON INTERACTIVE CONSTRUCTION KIT; see pp. 350–51

** READING BLASTER 4TH GRADE: Six villains vanish in Dr. Dabble's spooky mansion. Join a daring hunt while mastering reading comprehension. Contains seventy-five stories at three levels of difficulty. Includes parent tips by the Director of the National Reading Diagnostics Institute. Adult Juror Comments: Fun, colorful, user-friendly, and age-appropriate program. Covers wide range of curriculum. Well-thought-out for reading skills practice. No problems or glitches detected. Offers a fun way to learn. Kid Juror Comments: Makes learning fun for kids. "This software has great graphics." "I liked the castles, monsters, and mysteries." "I learned some new words." "This is a very creative program." Age: 8–12; Suggested Retail Price: $20.00, KNOWLEDGE ADVENTURE

*** READING BLASTER 5TH GRADE: Offers challenging game play within a mystery environment. A large selection of vocabulary words accompanied with talking word lists ensures a unique experience each time a child plays. Contains an easy-to-use editor. Adult Juror Comments: Builds and reinforces vocabulary in a challenging way. Good visuals, cute characters, positive feedback. Has a variety of increasing difficulty levels. Easy operation. Requires active thinking. "This will get kids' brains working." Kid Juror Comments: Kids liked being the detective and solving the mystery. Most enjoyed the anagram game, which required thinking of new words before their opponent did. "Great list of words." "I like the funny characters. They made learning fun." Age: 9–12; Suggested Retail Price: $20.00, KNOWLEDGE ADVENTURE

*** READING BLASTER: VOCABULARY (BLASTER LEARNING SYSTEM): Challenging game within a mystery environment. A large selection of vocabulary words accompanied by talking word lists ensures a unique experience each time. Contains an easy-to-use editor. Adult Juror Comments: Builds and reinforces vocabulary in a challenging way. Good visuals, cute characters, positive feedback. A variety of increasing difficulty levels with easy operation. Requires active thinking. "This will get kids' brains working." Kid Juror Comments: Kids liked being the detective and solving the mystery. Most enjoyed the anagram game, which required thinking of new words before their opponent did. "Great list of words." "I like the funny characters. They made learning fun." Age: 9–12; Suggested Retail Price: $20.00, KNOWLEDGE ADVENTURE

** SCHOLASTIC'S MAGIC SCHOOL BUS EXPLORES THE OCEAN; see p. 152

*** SCHOLASTIC'S MAGIC SCHOOL BUS EXPLORES THE RAINFOREST; see p. 152

*** SPACE STATION ALPHA: THE ENCOUNTER; see p. 351

*** SKY ISLAND MYSTERIES (THINKIN' THINGS): Teaches vital skills like giving priorities to different tasks, draws conclusions based on observation and logic. Communicates through a mix of words and pictures. Allows opportunities to solve fourteen mysteries on four different islands. Adult Juror Comments: Great games using problem-solving skills. Difficult at times but excellent. Beautiful graphics, challenging and fun, good quality. Offers educational problem-solving using games. Somewhat slow-starting. takes time to install but it's easy. Kid Juror Comments: Kids found it challenging and difficult. They really liked the graphics and the opening music. They liked the "worm" character and enjoyed all the game levels which challenged their different skills. The airplane game was a favorite Age: 8–12; Suggested Retail Price: $29.95, EDMARK

** SPELLING BLASTER AGES 6–9 (BLASTER LEARNING SYSTEM): A tropical island, an ice island, and a dark island are the settings where children are asked to solve the mystery of ancient books that have disappeared. As they play, children build important spelling skills. Adult Juror Comments: Easy to use. Entertaining way to learn spelling. Word list and puzzles can be printed. Lacks interpersonal and positive role models. User is praised but with limited number of phrases. Kid Juror Comments: Kids enjoyed the mix of arcade-type and skill-based games. They found solving and completing a mission an exciting challenge. Some parts were frustrating or tedious. Good graphics. "I liked the mountain climbing. You have to think fast." Age: 7–10; Suggested Retail Price: $20.00, KNOWLEDGE ADVENTURE

*** THINKING GAMES (MADELINE); see p. 154

** TYPE TO LEARN: Program has taught over 15 million people to master keyboarding and has undergone a major overhaul. Remains educationally sound with new games, voice prompts, graphics, and other features. Adult Juror Comments: Format makes a great tutorial, except the drill section is boring and the graphics are out-of-date. Best for beginners on the keyboard. Follows the child's progress and gives constant feedback. Kid Juror Comments: Instructions are easy to follow but kids found this extremely boring. They enjoyed the sound effects. "Helped me learn typing skills." "Told me when I made a mistake and kept track of how I was doing." "I'm telling my friends about this program." Age: 8–14; Suggested Retail Price: $24.95, SUNBURST COMMUNICATIONS, INC.

** WEB WORKSHOP: Create World Wide Web pages using familiar drawing tools without learning HTML or other programming. Select backgrounds, add text, place pictures, and you're set to go. Includes free online publishing to the Sunburst Server. Adult Juror Comments: Great tool for novices. Easy to use. Users may feel limited by graphics and background, but it sure beats learning HTML programming. Develops creativity and skills. Difficult to get going at first. Kid Juror Comments: "Awesome, cool, really fun." Makes a popular but difficult task accessible to kids and adults. Comes with excellent collection of clip art. Kids liked learning more about the Internet. Age: 8–12; Suggested Retail Price: $19.95, SUNBURST COMMUNICATIONS, INC.

*** WORLD BOOK 1998 MULTIMEDIA ENCYCLOPEDIA; see p. 351

Family

*** AN AMERICAN TAIL; see p. 156

** ARNOLD'S CHRISTMAS (HEY ARNOLD!): During Arnold's hip, urban Christmas, tough Helga has the holiday all figured out—cash, presents, and getting what you wish no matter what. But Christmas Eve finds Arnold searching for ways to help a man reunite with his daughter. Adult Juror Comments: Entertaining. Some inappropriate wisecracking. Promotes good social values such as sacrifice, selflessness, charity, and the positive results that come from helping others. Shows good cultural diversity. Kid Juror Comments: Children identified with many parts of the story. Both boys and girls liked Arnold as well as the other characters. It motivated a discussion about the benefit of giving and what leads to greed. Kids' favorite part is when he got his daughter back. Age: 8–12; Length: 37 min.; Suggested Retail Price: $12.95, PARAMOUNT HOME VIDEO

* BABY-SITTERS AND THE BOY-SITTERS, THE (THE BABY-SITTERS CLUB): Mishaps and mayhem ensue when the boys decide to start their own baby-sitting club. Is there room for two clubs in one town? Adult Juror Comments: This is perhaps a little middle-class idealistic but does address appropriate issues for children of this age. Well produced and fun. Shows little diversity. Kid Juror Comments: Kids enjoyed this, particularly the girls. Well produced, well acted. Boys and girls interacting shows positive gender awareness and role models. "There was no meanness, everyone gets along." "It was a little too much like a TV sitcom." Age: 7–14; Length: 30 min.; Suggested Retail Price: $14.95, WARNERVISION ENTERTAINMENT

** BABY-SITTERS REMEMBER, THE (THE BABY-SITTERS CLUB): In this episode, the Baby-Sitters share their funniest and fondest memories and celebrate their unique friendship. Adult Juror Comments: Funny. Lightly presents issues of contemporary life, offers positive role models that take responsibility, earn money, and cooperate with one another. Will appeal most to young girls. Kid Juror Comments: Kids related to this story, particularly the girls. Not very appealing to the boys. Addresses issues that concern girls at this age such as how to establish lasting friendships. Age: 7–14; Length: 30 min.; Suggested Retail Price: $14.95, WARNERVISION ENTERTAINMENT

*** BACH'S FIGHT FOR FREEDOM (THE COMPOSERS' SPECIALS): This fictional story shows Johann Sebastian Bach struggling for the freedom to compose music. Bach argues passionately that the only master you can serve faithfully is your own heart, and he recognizes a kindred soul in a ten-year-old assistant. Adult Juror Comments: Great story. Gives an impression of what 18th-century life is like. Characters are exaggerated to adult eyes but appealing to children. Well produced. Bach's compositions made wonderful background music. Kid Juror Comments: Kids loved everything about it, from the costumes to the sets to the story. Pleasantly presented insights into Bach's music. A little long for younger kids. Age: 8–12; Length: 53 min.; Suggested Retail Price: $19.95, DEVINE ENTERTAINMENT CORPORATION

** BEING RESPONSIBLE (YOU CAN CHOOSE!); see p. 159

*** BIZET'S DREAM (THE COMPOSERS' SPECIALS): Fictional story of the friendship between composer Georges Bizet and his twelve-year-old piano student, Michelle, who is captivated by the story of the gypsy Carmen (heroine of Bizet's opera). Adult Juror Comments: Exquisite production, a wonderful introduction to Bizet's music, the creative process and the relationship between art and life. Great family viewing. Kid Juror Comments: Good story. Held children's attention. Kids enjoyed discovering a story line based on real life or parallels to life. They liked the music, dancing, and costumes. Girls particularly enjoyed it. Age: 8–12; Length: 53 min.; Suggested Retail Price: $19.95, DEVINE ENTERTAINMENT CORPORATION

*** BLACK BEAUTY: Classic tale about the friendship between a young boy and his colt, based on Anna Sewell's novel. The pair are parted, and before they reunite, Beauty passes from owner to owner. A passionate argument for the humane treatment of animals. Adult Juror Comments: Well produced. Shows the beautiful English countryside and costumes. Captures children's love for horses and evokes deep empathy. Motivates respect for animals. Some scenes of animal cruelty, violence, and corpses are too intense for young viewers. Kid Juror Comments: Kids loved the scenes when Beauty is young. Prompted discussion about animal cruelty. "It got weird in the middle. I liked the beginning and the end best." Favorite parts were the circus, training, grooming, and riding Black Beauty. Age: 8–12; Length: 105 min.; Suggested Retail Price: $14.95, PARAMOUNT HOME VIDEO

*** BLACK STALLION, THE; see p. 352

*** BLACK STALLION RETURNS, THE; see p. 352

*** BOOKER: Set in the 1860s south, Booker is the impassioned story of the boy who struggled through slavery to found the Tuskegee Institute. Through the eyes of nine-year-old Booker T. Washington. Stars LeVar Burton, Shelly Duvall, Judge Reinhold. Adult Juror Comments: Well acted and produced; a realistic depiction of the institution of slavery and its dehumanizing process. Values education as a precious commodity. Shows how through education one achieves true freedom. Also shows not all white people were evil. Kid Juror Comments: Kids enjoyed it. When Booker reads to his class, they commented, "I couldn't believe slaves were not allowed to read." Realistic, kids couldn't believe how the children had to work. "Black people were treated badly, both as slaves and when freed." Age: 8–12; Length: 60 min.; Suggested Retail Price: $14.95, BONNEVILLE ENTERTAINMENT

** BOYD'S SHADOW: This story tells of a lonely boy and his invisible friend, Shadow, who coaxes Boyd into confronting a scary hermit. Boyd learns valuable lessons about the healing quality of friendship and the power of a smile. Adult Juror Comments: Simple story, moderately paced. Good message with a happy ending. The acting falls short. Shows some poor role models such as spanking. The sister's behavior is atrocious in the beginning but she makes a turnaround, somewhat unbelievable, at the end. Kid Juror Comments: Kids identified with the prejudice shown toward the hermit. When he turns out to be nothing but a misunderstood old man, they were relieved. They enjoyed the messages about friendship. Age: 7–11; Length: 45 min.; Suggested Retail Price: $19.95, HORIZON FILM AND VIDEO

*** BRIDGE TO TERABITHIA: Jesse Aarons, a shy fifth-grader, learns about love when he strikes up a friendship with the new girl in town. Together they create a fantasy world they call "Terabithia" in a pine forest near their farms. Adult Juror Comments: Thoughtful and intriguing. Well produced. True to the original book. Deals realistically with problems. A great story about differing values and finding common ground. Addresses friendship, moving away, and death. Somewhat dated presentation. Kid Juror Comments: Great story, sad ending. Slow at the beginning but it held the kids' interest. Story looks "real," not like Hollywood-perfect. "It is good to be nice to a new kid." "It showed that girls can do a lot." "Some characters were disrespectful." Age: 8–12; Length: 60 min.; Suggested Retail Price: $14.95, BONNEVILLE ENTERTAINMENT

** BUILDING SKYSCRAPERS; see p. 161

* CAPTAIN JANUARY (SHIRLEY TEMPLE); see p. 162

** CHITTY CHITTY BANG BANG; see pp. 165–66

* CHRISTMAS REUNION: After being orphaned, Jimmy moves in with his callous grandfather, who because of his own grief cannot accept Jimmy into his heart. Feeling unwanted and isolated, Jimmy sets off on a mystical journey with a very special guide, Santa. Adult Juror Comments: Good story, well produced. Deals with difficult issues—prejudice, gypsy culture, class struggles, abandonment, acceptance. Stresses independent thinking. Pace is awkward for this complex story line. Kid Juror Comments: Kids liked the story and the period costumes and sets. They didn't like the negative portrait of gypsies and the presentation seemed too muddled for complete understanding. Age: 10–16; Length: 88 min.; Suggested Retail Price: $12.95, SABAN HOME ENTERTAINMENT

** CITY BOY; see pp. 344, 353

** CLAUDIA AND THE MISSING JEWELS (THE BABY-SITTERS CLUB): Claudia's jewelry designs are a huge hit at the Stoneybrook Crafts Fair, and she's on the road to fame and fortune. When her jewelry vanishes, the Baby-Sitters set off to solve the mystery. Adult Juror Comments: Good story, promotes values about friendship but the presentation is very middle-class and promotes stereotypes. Kid Juror Comments: Very popular with middle-school girls. They thought that it was realistic and that making jewelry was "cool." Age: 7–14; Length: 30 min.; Suggested Retail Price: $12.95, WARNERVISION ENTERTAINMENT

** CLAUDIA AND THE MYSTERY OF THE SECRET PASSAGE (THE BABY-SITTERS CLUB): A note found in the secret passage at Mary Anne and Dawn's house leads Claudia and her friends on an adventure. Will they be able to settle an ancient feud, or does only danger await them? Adult Juror Comments: Acting good, music lively. Successfully translates the popularity of the "Baby-Sitters" book series and portrays the characters well. Advertisements at the beginning of the tape are objectionable. Kid Juror Comments: Girls loved this. Boys did not want to watch. Children liked how this promoted being nice to siblings. Age: 7–14; Length: 30 min.; Suggested Retail Price: $14.95, WARNERVISION ENTERTAINMENT

*** COURAGE MOUNTAIN: Fifteen-year-old Heidi leaves her beloved grandfather, her childhood sweetheart, and her cherished Swiss mountains to attend boarding school in Italy. When World War I breaks out, the girls escape and embark on a daring trek across the frozen Alps. Adult Juror Comments: Everyone enjoyed this. Great role models—caring, brave, and intelligent. Conveys a can-do attitude. Stimulates curiosity and creativity. Girls liked it better than boys. Kid Juror Comments: Great. Learned a lot about the war and life in an orphanage. "A little scary, but exciting." "The people looked old-fashioned, this must have been long ago." Kids learned not to judge people by how they look. Age: 8–12; Length: 105 min.; Suggested Retail Price: $14.95, MGM HOME ENTERTAINMENT

*** COURT JESTER; see p. 353

** CURLY TOP (SHIRLEY TEMPLE); see p. 167

** CYRANO (GLOBALSTAGE 1998 CHILDREN'S THEATRE SERIES): This adaptation of Edmond Rostand's classic story is performed by Antwerp's Blauw Vier Theatre. Cyrano, thinking his nose is too large, and Christian, thinking he's not intelligent enough, combine efforts to woo Roxanne with the written word. Adult Juror Comments: This filming of a stage production makes a slow-moving video by most standards. Good acting, costumes, sets. Addresses love, duty, and self-esteem The backstage section was interesting. Kid Juror Comments: Kids found it extremely slow-moving and noted the lack of diversity. They enjoyed learning about technical aspects. "I liked the poetry in the letters. The ending is very sad, Cyrano should have told Roxanne he loved her." Age: 8–15; Length: 101 min.; Suggested Retail Price: $27.00, GLOBALSTAGE

** DAWN AND THE DREAM BOY (THE BABY-SITTERS CLUB): It's love at first sight when Dawn meets Jamie Anderson. She's sure that Jamie would be a "dream date" for the Sweetheart Dance. Does Jamie feel the same way? Adult Juror Comments: Entertaining and appealing for pre-teen girls. Realistically portrays girls' interests. Smooth but unrealistic conflict resolution. Only affluent suburban families are represented. Some jurors objected to the story and the gender stereotyping. Kid Juror Comments: Most all of the girls ages nine through twelve liked it and would watch it again. Some kids were visibly embarrassed by the referrals to boy/girl crushes. Age: 9–12; Length: 30 min.; Suggested Retail Price: $12.95, WARNERVISION ENTERTAINMENT

** DAWN AND THE HAUNTED HOUSE (THE BABY-SITTERS CLUB): Dawn is convinced that Claudia's strange behavior has something to do with the haunted house on the hill and the spooky woman who lives there. Can the Baby-Sitters Club help solve the mystery? Adult Juror Comments: Promotes friendship and caring. Offers positive messages in the dialogue between mother and daughter about the need for tutoring. Discusses reluctance to admit to having learning problems. Contains gender stereotypes. Kid Juror Comments: Kids familiar with the book series liked the story most. They especially liked the haunted house but thought it unfair to tell stories about the old lady to scare people. Age: 7–14; Length: 30 min.; Suggested Retail Price: $14.95, WARNERVISION ENTERTAINMENT

** DAWN SAVES THE TREES (THE BABY-SITTERS CLUB): When the city plans to build a road through the local park, Dawn leads the Baby-Sitters in a fight to save the trees. The group is ready to do anything, but has Dawn gone too far? Adult Juror Comments: Enjoyable. Encourages reading and activism in a way that bridges generations. The Baby-Sitters are clever and intelligent. They don't just turn on the TV. Offers good humor for girls and boys. Kid Juror Comments: Girls enjoyed this more than the boys. They liked the actresses selected to portray the characters they're familiar with from the books. Realistically portrayed issues they deal with. Age: 7–14; Length: 30 min.; Suggested Retail Price: $14.95, WARNERVISION ENTERTAINMENT

*** DEGAS AND THE DANCER (THE ARTISTS' SPECIAL): The 19th-century French painter Edgar Degas paints to survive. Initially, he is scornful of painting dancers but gets caught up in a ballerina's life and becomes interested in a ballerina named Marie. They reveal their hopes and fears to one another. Adult Juror Comments: Worthwhile story, beautifully produced. Degas is shown as a self-centered old man whose art is more important than people. Marie's influence changes his behavior for the better. Begs the question, "Does being a genius give you license to treat others badly?" Kid Juror Comments: "I learned about what it takes to be an artist." "I liked the way they all taught each other something. The painter taught her that if you don't make a mistake you'll never learn. She taught him not to be so grouchy and have respect for others." Age: 8–12; Length: 55 min.; Suggested Retail Price: $19.95, DEVINE ENTERTAINMENT

*** EDISON: THE WIZARD OF LIGHT (THE INVENTORS' SPECIALS): Thomas Edison's research in moving images is disrupted by a scruffy lad, Jack. Edison recognizes something of himself in the boy and takes him in. Together Edison and Jack pursue the dream of the motion picture. Adult Juror Comments: Inspiring. Excellent balance between history, science, and imagination. Time-period clips enhanced visual and cognitive understanding. Promotes a healthy respect for intelligence and inquiry. It's a great way to introduce inventors and science. Kid Juror Comments: Children were riveted, entertained, and informed. They loved the set of Edison's shop. "I liked how it told how the inventions were made." "I didn't know that the first movies didn't have sound." Age: 8–12; Length: 54 min.; Suggested Retail Price: $19.95, DEVINE ENTERTAINMENT CORPORATION

*** EINSTEIN: LIGHT TO THE POWER OF 2; see p. 354

* ENCHANTED TALES: A TALE OF EGYPT (ENCHANTED TALES): Plucked from the Nile by the daughter of Pharaoh, Moses grows up as the favored friend of Pharaoh's son Ramses. After witnessing the cruel treatment of the Israelites, Moses discovers his true identity and his destiny. Adult Juror Comments: Interesting dialogue and musical interpretations will captivate students' attention. Religious overtones. Animation not synchronized with audio, and transitions between scenes are difficult. Violent scenes are pertinent to the story but are somewhat excessive. Kid Juror Comments: Best viewed with an adult. "There is a lot of fighting." "After the first miracle, I saw that God was trying to get the Pharaoh to change his mind." Age: 8–12; Length: 48 min.; Suggested Retail Price: $9.98, SONY WONDER

** ENCHANTED TALES: THE LEGEND OF SU-LING; see p. 169

** FAR FROM HOME: THE ADVENTURES OF YELLOW DOG: A boy and his dog, lost in the wilderness, fight for survival in an emotional tale of friendship and courage. Adult Juror Comments: Appealing animal story, visually driven. Good family interaction and respect for nature, with examples of survival skills. Depicts the outdoors as both gentle and rugged. Children are never underestimated. Contains some strong language. Kid Juror Comments: Kids clapped when the dog returned. Lots of things going on make this story a little complicated to follow. Led to discussion of literature-related themes and realism of the adventure, and to "practice what you are." Some kids thought it was slow. Age: 8–12; Length: 81 min.; Suggested

Retail Price: $19.98, TWENTIETH CENTURY FOX HOME ENTERTAIN-
MENT

*** FLY AWAY HOME; see pp. 354–55

** FRANKENSTEIN (GLOBALSTAGE 1998 CHILDREN'S THEATRE SERIES): Mas-
terful stage production combined with vivid costumes and sets in Stage
One's live performance and adaptation of Mary Shelley's "Frankenstein."
Filmed and edited by the BBC. Adult Juror Comments: High-quality production with excellent sound, sets, lighting, acting. Starts slow. True to the
book. The story, by definition, is scary and creepy. Stimulated a discussion
about lightning and energy. Kid Juror Comments: Kids varied in their response to this. The genre, filming a stage production, is not engaging for all.
Most enjoyed learning about the technical aspects of the production and
enjoyed learning that "a lady wrote it." They liked the monster. Age: 8–15;
Length: 96 min.; Suggested Retail Price: $27.00, GLOBALSTAGE

*** GALILEO: ON THE SHOULDERS OF GIANTS; see p. 355

* GARFIELD'S FELINE FANTASIES; see pp. 172–73

** GETTING EVEN WITH DAD: A small-time crook thinks the only way he can
go straight is with money from one last heist. But son catches on, and concocts a plan to make him do time—as a Dad. Stars Ted Danson and
Macaulay Culkin. Adult Juror Comments: Reinforces the idea that "the
clever, ethical child can reform his wayward parent"—placing a lot of questionable responsibility on children. Laudable for addressing parental negli-
gence but offers little challenge. Reinforces gender stereotypes. Kid Juror
Comments: The kids related to Timmy. Some discussed their similar experiences. Kids liked the action, the smart boy, and the funny parts of the story
line. Age: 8–14; Length: 108 min.; Suggested Retail Price: $14.95,
MGM/UA HOME ENTERTAINMENT

*** GIRL OF THE LIMBERLOST: Elnora Comstock is determined to attend high
school. Although her widowed mother thinks it's a "foolish dream," Elnora
is comforted by free-spirited naturalist Mrs. Porter. Based on the book by
Gene Stratton Porter. Stars Joanna Cassidy and Annette O'Toole. Adult
Juror Comments: Excellent. Great example of showing rather than telling
a story. Characters demonstrate perseverance, dedication, forgiveness, and
striving for acceptance. Views a turn-of-the-century farming community
and environmental concerns from that time period. Kid Juror Comments:
Kids liked Elnora's tenacity and curiosity. "The people were so real." "I

think Elnora did a good job of helping her mom and growing up." "I liked the way Elnora wasn't afraid to touch things like snakes and bugs." Appeals to both boys and girls. Age: 8–12; Length: 111 min.; Suggested Retail Price: $19.95, BONNEVILLE ENTERTAINMENT

*** GOOD MORNING, MISS TOLIVER; see p. 345

* GREAT LAND OF SMALL, THE; see pp. 173–74

*** HANDEL'S LAST CHANCE (THE COMPOSERS' SPECIALS): James, a Dublin street kid, is enrolled in an upper-crust school where he is treated like an outsider. He is befriended by Handel and chosen as a principal choirboy for the "Messiah." Jamie is rescued by Handel. The "Messiah" is a huge success. Adult Juror Comments: Beautifully produced. Provides an excellent introduction to the "Messiah," with a wide range of humor, music, values, and historical commentary. Shows how new friends support one another. Somewhat harsh and scary at times and moves rather slowly. Kid Juror Comments: They thought it was amusing and that it looked realistic. "I enjoyed the boy's singing." Kids enjoyed conflict with bullies. "I liked when Handel tells Jamie, 'Listen to the voice deep inside your heart.'" Age: 8–12; Length: 51 min.; Suggested Retail Price: $19.95, DEVINE ENTERTAINMENT CORPORATION

* IMAGINARIA: A computer animation odyssey for kids with colorful, playful imagery and music by award-winning composer Gary Powell. Upbeat, playful, interactive, it requires kids to use their imaginations. Adult Juror Comments: Fantastic and sophisticated program. Exquisitely matched sound and computer graphics. Jurors voiced concern over some violent imagery and the extra-fast pace. Kid Juror Comments: Kids thought this was "weird." They weren't interested in watching it again. Age: 7–12; Length: 40 min.; Suggested Retail Price: $9.98, UNAPIX/MIRAMAR

* IN SEARCH OF THE HAUNTED GOLD MINE; see p. 175

** IT'S NOT ALWAYS EASY BEING A KID: Young Charlie struggles to regain his self-esteem after failures at school. He's encouraged to aim at real accomplishment instead of trying to "be cool" by smoking. Adult Juror Comments: Production is heavy-handed in delivering messages about not smoking. Tends to rely heavily on narration. Audio is difficult to understand. Uses puppets as positive role models, but they tend to be fairly preachy. Kid Juror Comments: Children enjoyed the puppets. This is suitable for early adolescents who are dealing with peer pressure. However, using the Tortoise and Hare fable as a smoking metaphor is confusing way to deliver the message. Age: 7–10; Length: 15 min.; Suggested Retail Price: $19.95, JUDY THEATRE, THE

** JACOB HAVE I LOVED: A sixteen-year-old girl (Bridget Fonda) wishes she can leave her isolated Chesapeake Bay community and escape the shadow of her beautiful and talented twin (Jenny Robertson). A turn of events moves her from jealousy to self-realization. Adult Juror Comments: Beautiful production, great scenery. Helps audience focus inward and think about their own interactions with others and why they behave the way they do. Respectful of children's abilities; speaks openly about the destruction of hate and jealousy. Kid Juror Comments: Very appealing title on a subject not often talked about—twins not liking each other. Parts are sad; the girl kept getting ignored and left alone. "I liked when the girl was with her dad." "I like movies about kids having adventures." Age: 8–12; Length: 60 min.; Suggested Retail Price: $14.95, BWE VIDEO

* JAMES AND THE GIANT PEACH: A literary, imaginative tale about a little boy who journeys to a wondrous city "where dreams come true." Adult Juror Comments: A frightening representation of the book, with nightmarish imagery, extreme cruelty from adults, and violent fights between insects. Beautiful production that combines live actors and animation. Intense and not suitable for all kids. Parents should be careful. Kid Juror Comments: Kids liked this even though they found it scary. One child had nightmares afterward. Some were inspired to read the book. Kids enjoyed the vibrant characters. Age: 7–12; Length: 79 min.; Suggested Retail Price: $19.99, WALT DISNEY HOME VIDEO

** JESSI AND THE MYSTERY OF THE STOLEN SECRETS (THE BABY-SITTERS CLUB): When club secrets are mysteriously leaked to outsiders, the Baby-Sitters go undercover to find the culprit. Bumbling detective work makes things worse. Can the girls solve the mystery or is it the end of the Baby-Sitters Club? Adult Juror Comments: Good plot and entertaining production. It deals with issues such as privacy that children this age can relate to. Good discussion-starter. Kid Juror Comments: Kids loved this. Captures this age group's attention. Kids enjoy the story and the characters. Boys enjoyed it as well as girls. Age: 7–14; Length: 30 min.; Suggested Retail Price: $14.95, WARNERVISION ENTERTAINMENT

** JET PINK (THE PINK PANTHER CARTOON COLLECTION): Clear the funway. It's an all-out "air-farce" as the Pink Panther tries to earn his military wings and go from top cat to Top Gun. Buckle up for a close encounter with an alarming clock, a hapless house painter, and a gang of gunslingers. Adult Juror Comments: Well produced. Clever, entertaining even though it's predictable. The best value of cartoons is their zaniness. Action-packed. Does feature variety of cartoon violence and unsafe behavior. There is hitting, falling, and lots of sight gags. Kid Juror Comments: Kids thought it was extremely funny. They got a kick out of the creative problem-solving, brainstorming, and imagination. "I want to watch it again." They loved when the Pink Panther was painting everything pink while the painter was painting it blue. Age: 7–12; Length: 51 min.; Suggested Retail Price: $12.95, MGM/UA HOME ENTERTAINMENT

** JOURNEY BEGINS, THE (TELL ME WHO I AM): Contains original stories, captivating music, and positive messages for the entire family. Traces the time-travel adventures of Nia, an African princess and her magical pet, Funzi the Fuzzwuzz, as they learn about famous African-American heroes. Adult Juror Comments: Appealing, cute characters, good story, great music. Presents positive African-American historical figures. Good preparation for learning science, history, language, and black history. "Best part is when they tell what's real and what's not." Kid Juror Comments: The music was a hit. The story confused them when it jumps between past and present. Kids like the ending that explains what was real and what wasn't. Most kids liked the game "Tell Me Who I Am" and the music even if they couldn't understand all of it. Age: 7–12; Length: 35 min.; Suggested Retail Price: $19.90, POSITIVE COMMUNICATIONS, INC.

*** KRATTS' CREATURES: CHECKIN OUT CHIMPS; see p. 177

** KRISTY AND THE GREAT CAMPAIGN (THE BABY-SITTERS CLUB): Kristy and the Baby-Sitters hit the campaign trail for a new girl who they think is terrific, but a little shy. When they offer to manage her campaign, the question is "Does Kristy really want Courtney to win or her opponent to lose?" Adult Juror Comments: Good story line but predictable. Appeals to girls more than boys. Interactions are gender-stereotyped. Kid Juror Comments: Kids familiar with the books liked it although they thought parts were corny. Age: 7–10; Length: 30 min.; Suggested Retail Price: $12.95, WARNERVISION ENTERTAINMENT

*** LAND BEFORE TIME II, THE: THE GREAT VALLEY ADVENTURE; see p. 178

*** LAND BEFORE TIME IV, THE: THE MYSTERIOUS ISLAND; see p. 179

*** LARGER THAN LIFE: They say an elephant never forgets, but this is an elephant you'll never forget. Vera, a four-ton bundle of fun, brings a trunk full of love, laughter, and excitement to this adventure. Stars Bill Murray and Janeane Garofalo. Adult Juror Comments: Humorous, enjoyable story that is visually appealing and a little offbeat. Offers insights into humane animal treatment, training, and transporting an elephant. Scenes with Hispanics and Indians were poorly done. Some sexual innuendo and exaggeration. Kid Juror Comments: "It was fun, slow at times." "We liked when Bill Murray started being nice to the elephant." Kids appreciated the creative camera angles, and made note that all the main characters were white. Good script, age-appropriate. Age: 7–12; Length: 93 min.; Suggested Retail Price: $14.95, MGM/UA HOME ENTERTAINMENT

* LAST WINTER, THE: A ten-year-old country boy learns to accept change and his family's decision to move to the city. Adult Juror Comments: Contains mature themes on moving, death, and young love. Contains some profanity, nudity, a sub-plot of marriage between cousins, and a mother who shoots a deer to show her glee with a new shotgun. We recommend it be shown with adult supervision. Kid Juror Comments: Kids had mixed reactions to this. Some thought it was "weird" and did not like it. Children thought the story was sad but it made them talk about loss, grief, and fear of change afterward. Kids' response varied according to their maturity. Age: 8–12; Length: 103 min.; Suggested Retail Price: $92.98, TWENTIETH CENTURY FOX HOME ENTERTAINMENT

*** LEONARDO: A DREAM OF FLIGHT (INVENTOR'S SPECIALS): Family drama stars Brent Carveras as Leonardo da Vinci, the 15th-century genius obsessed with flying, and David Felton as Roberto, the young boy he takes under his wing. Adult Juror Comments: Interesting story, quality production with visual appeal. Historically accurate. Good introduction to the concept of flight. Presents the reality of what it's like to be a genius. Suitable for use in a classroom or for home viewing. Kid Juror Comments: Terrific. Kids wanted to learn more about Leonardo da Vinci. Several did independent research on da Vinci after watching this. "I learned a lot." "This was better than the books I have read about Leonardo." Age: 9–14; Length: 48 min.; Suggested Retail Price: $19.95, DEVINE ENTERTAINMENT CORPORATION

* LIFE WITH LOUIE: THE MASKED CHESS BOY (LIFE WITH LOUIE): Louie discovers he's got a knack for chess, but hides his identity at the all-school tournament. Share the fun as Louie inspires his pals to reach for their dreams without worrying what other kids say. Adult Juror Comments: Although the characters are stereotyped and sarcastic, it addresses an issue that almost all children face—peer pressure. It's almost too exaggerated, bordering on being demeaning. It stereotypes "smart" kids. Kid Juror Comments: Children liked the cartoon and enjoyed how Louie and his father came together in the end. May provoke an interest in learning to play chess. Boys liked Louie in a mask. Some voices were hard to understand. Age: 7–11; Length: 21 min.; Suggested Retail Price: $5.98, TWENTIETH CENTURY FOX HOME ENTERTAINMENT

** LISZT'S RHAPSODY (THE COMPOSERS' SPECIALS): Set in Budapest in 1846, the video celebrates the inextinguishable flame of genuine talent shown by a free-spirited eleven-year-old gypsy boy who inspires a frustrated Franz Liszt to reach his own potential. Adult Juror Comments: Introduces classical music through a biographical sketch of a composer's life with a fictional side involving a child co-star thrown in. Quality production, beautiful costumes and sets. Historical characters are well presented. A little slow-moving. Kid Juror Comments: Kids had mixed reactions to this. Some thought it was boring, had an uninteresting plot, and that only kids interested in music would like it. Those interested in piano or violin music enjoyed learning about Liszt. They enjoyed the child character. Age: 8–12; Length: 49 min.; Suggested Retail Price: $19.95, DEVINE ENTERTAINMENT CORPORATION

*** LITTLE HORSE THAT COULD, THE; see p. 356

** LITTLE PRINCESS, THE (SHIRLEY TEMPLE); see p. 356

*** MARIE CURIE: MORE THAN MEETS THE EYE (THE INVENTORS' SPECIALS): The Boudreau sisters are determined to aid the war effort by catching German spies. Madame Curie is a prime suspect. She is in fact helping save lives through her research, and the sisters learn that curiosity is essential to science and life. Adult Juror Comments: Excellent use of historical fiction as a teaching tool. Made kids think, debate and form their own opinions. Nice web of humor, mystery, and facts that catch the imagination. Brings scientific discovery to children's level. Kid Juror Comments: Kids enjoyed learning how X-rays were discovered, about important women in science, and World War I in France. "I liked figuring out all the pieces of the story." "It looked scary but it ended up to be a good thing. It made science fun." Age: 8–12; Length: 54 min.; Suggested Retail Price: $19.95, DEVINE ENTERTAINMENT CORPORATION

** MARY ANNE AND THE BRUNETTES (THE BABY-SITTERS CLUB): Mary Anne likes Logan Bruno. So does Marci, the most popular girl in the eighth grade.

Will Mary Anne lose Logan because she's too shy? Adult Juror Comments: Addresses teenagers' dating behavior. Story line is rather trite, predictable, and shows gender stereotyped "boy-crazed" characters. Jurors objected to the commercials at the beginning of the tape. Kid Juror Comments: Kids enjoy the Baby-Sitters, regardless of the stereotyped behaviors. It addresses issues they relate to and they find it funny. Some objected to the reference to the "beautiful blond hair" and said, "Boo, talks down to us." Age: 8–14; Length: 30 min.; Suggested Retail Price: $14.95, WARNERVISION ENTERTAINMENT

* MOZART'S THE MAGIC FLUTE STORY; see p. 366

* MYSTERY LIGHTS OF NAVAJO MESA; see p. 183

*** NATIONAL VELVET; see p. 357

*** NEWTON: A TALE OF TWO ISAACS (INVENTORS' SPECIALS): Isaac Newton's original theories on celestial movement and gravity jolted the Royal Academy in 1683. His young scribe finds even that even the greatest men must overcome personal tragedies to achieve success. Adult Juror Comments: Engaging. An example of how mathematics, curiosity, and problem-solving mesh as science. Demonstration of Newton's laws of motion is wonderfully well done. A pleasant mix of science and historical fiction. Kid Juror Comments: Kids enjoyed problem-solving and solutions that relate to their own perspective. Liked the proverbial apple falling on Newton's head, which gave him the idea of gravity. "The science scenes were neat." "I liked the costumes and the sets. I'd watch it again." Age: 8–12; Length: 51 min.; Suggested Retail Price: $19.95, DEVINE ENTERTAINMENT CORPORATION

*** OUR FRIEND MARTIN; see pp. 357–58

** PEANUT BUTTER SOLUTION, THE (LES PRODUCTIONS LA FETE): An eleven-year-old hero investigates a haunted house and gets so frightened that all his hair falls out. A magic recipe to make his hair grow back produces astonishing results. Adult Juror Comments: Challenging and imaginative tape with an interesting and creative plot. Challenges children's critical thinking skills. Technical qualities are low, uses the word God as an expletive throughout. Kidnapping scene could scare young children. Kid Juror Comments: Kids laughed and talked about the program. The children thought that the plot developed slowly but the excitement at the end was enjoyed by all. Kids said they would recommend it to friends. Some may have difficulty with the French-Canadian accent. Age: 7–12; Length: 90 min.; Suggested Retail Price: $29.95, LES PRODUCTIONS LA FETE/ANCHOR BAY

*** **PEOPLE:** Cara and her lovable grandfather embark on a journey of imagination that brings them face to face with the wonderful variety of people in the world. Based on Peter Spier's book. Music by Al Jarreau, Chaka Kan, Grover Washington Jr., Vanessa Williams. Adult Juror Comments: Original. Deals with the difficult topic of divorce. The content is rendered sensitively, yet makes its point about celebrating diversity and cultural differences with positive stereotyping. Varied animation styles. "Flashes of brilliance." Kid Juror Comments: Great music. Kids loved it. Fast-paced animation style appeals to kids more than adults. Kids liked the rap music section with Heavy D a lot. Kids relate to characters, dialogue, and the topics discussed. "Cara was goody-goody." Age: 8–12; Length: 54 min.; Suggested Retail Price: $12.95, LIGHTYEAR ENTERTAINMENT

* **PLEASE DON'T EAT THE DAISIES (FAMILY TREASURES):** When sudden fame goes to a drama critic's head, it's up to his family to get his feet back on the ground in this light and frothy comedy that generates laughs for all. Adult Juror Comments: This old-fashioned story has many elements and wholesome values but is somewhat dated. The four brothers are mischievous characters. Kid Juror Comments: Kids didn't get some of the social interactions. They liked the part with the kids the best. Age: 8–12; Length: 111 min.; Suggested Retail Price: $14.95, MGM/UA HOME ENTERTAINMENT

* **PREHISTORIC PINK;** see p. 358

** **QUICK AND THE FED, THE (REBOOT):** Dot is partially erased by a magnet. Bob races against time to return her to normal, a difficult task made worse by the hostile dragons, knights, and skeletons of a descended Game Cube. Adult Juror Comments: Filled with sophisticated humor, good computer-generated animation, and suspense. Contains scary images and characters, lots of sword-fighting, combat, and destruction. Filled with computer-related jokes. Kid Juror Comments: Kids enjoyed this. They liked the jokes. Kept their attention. Kids were eager to discuss what went on afterward. Age: 8–12; Length: 25 min.; Suggested Retail Price: $12.95, POLYGRAM-ALLIANCE

* **REBECCA OF SUNNYBROOK FARM (SHIRLEY TEMPLE):** Shirley Temple sings, dances, and charms her way through this classic. Orphan Rebecca auditions for a radio show and doesn't get hired, so her stepfather sends her off to live with relatives while the show's talent agent searches frantically for

her. Adult Juror Comments: Excellent opportunity to introduce kids to the book by Kate Douglas Wiggin. Discussion about the time period helps understand portrayal of minorities. Kid Juror Comments: Kids enjoyed the movie, especially Shirley Temple. Girls liked it best, though most of the kids enjoyed it. They thought Shirley was funny. Age: 6–12; Length: 81 min.; Suggested Retail Price: $14.98, TWENTIETH CENTURY FOX HOME ENTERTAINMENT

** RETURN OF THE SAND FAIRY, THE; see p. 188

** ROBIN OF LOCKSLEY (HALLMARK HALL OF FAME): After his parents win the lottery, archery and computer whiz Robin McCallister is put in Locksley, a private boys school. Disgusted by the rich bullies there, he concocts a brilliant, daring plan to help a poor classmate. Stars Sarah Chalke. Adult Juror Comments: Clever version of Robin Hood story with good use of characters. Excellent production quality. Addresses ethics in a high-tech world. Shows compassion. Kid Juror Comments: Appeals to action-oriented children. They found it interesting placing an old story in a contemporary setting. It piqued their interest in the Internet and archery. Age: 10–16; Length: 97 min.; Suggested Retail Price: $9.98, ARTISAN/FAMILY HOME ENTERTAINMENT

** ROOKIE OF THE YEAR: When a young boy's broken arm heals, he finds he can throw a baseball with awesome speed. Soon he's in the major leagues on his way to the World Series. Adult Juror Comments: Fun fantasy. Contains some socially inappropriate actions, such as insults from the coach in opening scene, the mother punching her boyfriend and saying, "I should have killed him." Overall, enjoyable, nicely paced, girls and boys both like this. Kid Juror Comments: Children liked this very much. One girl in the group said, "I liked the characters even though it's a 'boy' story." Age: 8–12; Length: 103 min.; Suggested Retail Price: $14.98, TWENTIETH CENTURY FOX HOME ENTERTAINMENT

** ROSSINI'S GHOST (THE COMPOSERS' SPECIALS): Reliana is transported back in time to a theater in which 19th-century composer Gioacchino Rossini is about to launch "The Barber of Seville." Invisible to everyone but Rossini, Reliana watches her grandmother and a friend fight over the composer, and the opera's disastrous premiere. Adult Juror Comments: Beautifully done, lovely costumes and sets. Filled with facts and information. The story depends a lot on the background narration and is sometimes confusing. Somewhat didactic in presenting history and meaning of the opera. Good friendship models. Kid Juror Comments: Stimulated children's interest in the opera and William Tell. "I like the line 'Friends are like money—hard to get and easy to throw away.' " Girls liked it more than boys, especially the romantic climax. Age: 8–12; Length: 52 min.; Suggested Retail Price: $19.95, DEVINE ENTERTAINMENT CORPORATION

*** SALT WATER MOOSE: A young boy's lonely summer becomes the adventure of a lifetime when he comes to the aid of a moose stranded on a nearby island. Timothy Dalton and Lolita Davidovich star in this courageous and heartwarming tale set along the northeastern coast. Adult Juror Comments: Good story. Lots of appeal. Supports children's sense of adventure and need for accomplishment. Deals with issues of divorce and equality in sports. Conflicts are handled well. Female character is strong, athletic, smart, and willful. Kid Juror Comments: Kids liked this, both the boy and the girl and the girl's relationship with her father. Some boys wanted to buy it. Said one child juror, "Dreams do come true." Age: 8–14; Length: 90 min.; Suggested Retail Price: $14.95, ARTISAN/FAMILY HOME ENTERTAINMENT

** SANDLOT, THE: Kids spend a summer during the '60s playing baseball, noticing girls, and finding out what's really behind that fence. Adult Juror Comments: Nice male-bonding story. Fails to include girls in sports. However, girls and boys enjoyed it equally. Talks about some real-life teen issues with harsh realities—feelings, hopes, and dreams. The characters work out their problems without violence. Kid Juror Comments: The kids laughed, squealed, tittered, and watched in stunned silence throughout the entire movie. They loved that the story provided thinking opportunities. Age: 8–12; Length: 101 min.; Suggested Retail Price: $14.98, TWENTIETH CENTURY FOX HOME ENTERTAINMENT

*** SECRET GARDEN, THE—WARNER BROS.: One of the best-loved of all children's tales blooms anew in this enchanting version of Frances Hodgson Burnett's turn-of-the-century classic. Brought together at a country house, Mary, Colin, and Dickson discover a locked garden and bring it to life. Adult Juror Comments: Kids identify with characters on many levels—losing parents, being part of a family, and learning to understand feelings. Wonderful, universal story. Content is appropriate to this audience. Stimulates students' creativity. Kid Juror Comments: Kids are inspired and moved by the emotions present in each of the characters. "No matter what your problems are, you can overcome them." "It must have been taped in a big garden. It was neat." "Awesome, it was the best video ever." Age: 7–12; Length: 102 min.; Suggested Retail Price: $19.98, WARNER BROS. FAMILY ENTERTAINMENT

*** SINGING FOR FREEDOM; see pp. 256–57

*** SKY IS GRAY, THE (THE AMERICAN SHORT STORY COLLECTION): From Ernest J. Gaines, author of "The Autobiography of Miss Jane Pittman," comes a deceptively simple yet emotionally complex tale of what it is like to be black in Louisiana during the 1940s. Adult Juror Comments: A wonderful opportunity for discussion of some very enormous issues—racism, respect, tolerance. Very realistic—music and setting are great. Excellent teaching tool. Kid Juror Comments: "Kind of slow but real good." "No one moved a muscle during the entire video." "Really good movie." Age: 6–12; Length: 46 min.; Suggested Retail Price: $24.95, MONTEREY MOVIE COMPANY

*** SOUNDER; see pp. 363–64

*** SPORTS ILLUSTRATED FOR KIDS VOL. 1 (SPORTS ILLUSTRATED FOR KIDS): The approach here—"sports as a metaphor for life"—teaches children about responsibility, self-control, and the importance of teamwork. Volume 1 features Grant Hill, Brett Favre, and Mia Hamm. Adult Juror Comments: A great motivational tool. Presents idea that "hard work equals positive results" and "learn from your mistakes." The "ask-the-athlete" format makes it seem real. Provokes an interest in athletic careers for both genders. Fast, entertaining pace. Kid Juror Comments: Students were hooked from the beginning—no wiggles, chatting, or inappropriate behavior. They truly enjoyed the program. "It's neat that the kids talked to pros about their games and other things like food and hobbies." It's fun to watch. Age: 8–12; Length: 50 min.; Suggested Retail Price: $14.98, TWENTIETH CENTURY FOX HOME ENTERTAINMENT

*** SPORTS ILLUSTRATED FOR KIDS VOL. 2 (SPORTS ILLUSTRATED FOR KIDS): The "sports as a metaphor for life" approach teaches kids about responsibility, self-control, and the importance of teamwork. Volume 2 features Derek Jeter, Venus Williams, and Steve Young. Adult Juror Comments: Practice makes perfect. Shows excellent attitudes from positive role models. The athletes' personal lives led to a discussion about hobbies, ability, and endurance. Presents the idea "Take pride in what you do." Excellent production quality. Kid Juror Comments: Presents a variety of sports, such as karate and snowboarding. Kids appreciate the honesty of athletes having hard times. "It's nice to know about women in sports." Offers good advice about practicing, teamwork, and working hard to be your best. Age: 8–12; Length: 50 min.; Suggested Retail Price: $14.98, TWENTIETH CENTURY FOX HOME ENTERTAINMENT

** STACEY TAKES A STAND (THE BABY-SITTERS CLUB): Stacey is tired of juggling life between two cities. The Baby-Sitters rescue Stacey, reminding her that home is where the heart is. Adult Juror Comments: Presents an issue that is significant for many children—pulls of divorced parents and living part-time with both parents. Lively, appealing. Shows children talking things out, offering emotional support, enjoying differences and problem-solving. Kid Juror Comments: Kids liked this, especially the girls. They thought the program could help diffuse the stress of divorced parents. They wanted to see it again. Some felt it was a little corny. Age: 7–14; Length: 30 min.; Suggested Retail Price: $14.95, WARNERVISION ENTERTAINMENT

** STACEY'S BIG BREAK (THE BABY-SITTERS CLUB): Stacey's new career as a fashion model means endless fittings and photo shoots and no time for her friends. Will Stacey choose modeling or her life as one of Stoneybrook's favorite Baby-Sitters? Adult Juror Comments: Simplistic story but addresses issues relevant to this age group. Girls' values are rather superficial. Contains a lot of gender stereotypes. Some objected to Stacey's pursuit of a modeling career. Kid Juror Comments: Kids thought this was okay but noted that "nobody talks like that." Age: 7–14; Length: 30 min.; Suggested Retail Price: $14.95, WARNERVISION ENTERTAINMENT

** STAY OUT OF THE BASEMENT (GOOSEBUMPS): Margaret's dad starts acting weirdly, spending all his time in the basement. Strange sounds leads to explore their father's spooky secret. Adult Juror Comments: Sharing a scary experience with another helps children address their fears. In this program, siblings related well to each other by resolving conflicts together. It's full of scary scenes, and the father's behavior is strange. Kid Juror Comments: Kids jumped at the chance to watch Goosebumps. It held their attention, especially the eight-year-olds. They liked the plant food that the dad created and seeing the kids help each other. Age: 8–12; Length: 44 min.; Suggested Retail Price: $14.98, TWENTIETH CENTURY FOX HOME ENTERTAINMENT

** STORIES FROM THE JEWISH TRADITION (CHILDREN'S CIRCLE); see p. 191

** STOWAWAY (SHIRLEY TEMPLE); see p. 191

** SUMMER OF THE COLT (LES PRODUCTIONS LA FETE): On a magnificent ranch in Argentina three children from Buenos Aires visit their grandfather. Explores the sorrows and joys of growing older. Adult Juror Comments: Addresses its message with sensitivity while keeping the audience's attention. Shows a beautiful and touching story with some slower moments that allow for reflection. Some jurors objected to the breast-feeding scene. Kid Juror Comments: One child watched several times over one weekend. Some kids were bothered by a lip-sync problem. The breast-feeding scene was uncomfortable for some kids. The toilet scene brought about uncomfortable laughter. Age: 8–14; Length: 96 min.; Suggested Retail Price: $19.95, LES PRODUCTIONS LA FETE/HEMDALE HOME VIDEO

* SUMMER OF THE MONKEYS: Based on the award-winning novel by Wilson Rawls. A twelve-year-old boy, Jay Berry Lee, encounters four runaway circus monkeys who prove to be clever troublemakers. Adult Juror Comments: This coming-of-age story deals with a boy's misbehavior and selfishness and his transformation, bringing his family closer together. Insight into a rural family, their community, and their values. The grandfather plays an inspiring role. Kid Juror Comments: Learned about the importance of goals, family, and sacrifice. Enjoyed the monkeys' antics and showed some concern about the aggressive behavior of the boy and his peers, and the treatment of the boy's dog. Age: 7–11; Length: 90 min.; Suggested Retail Price: $19.99, BUENA VISTA HOME ENTERTAINMENT

** TAKE MY BROTHER PLEASE! (CLARISSA EXPLAINS IT ALL): Contains two episodes, "Darling Wars" and "Brain Drain," featuring Clarissa and her brother Ferguson at their bickering best. Includes a "Sibling Survival Guide" video. Adult Juror Comments: Clarissa is a positive girl role model. The content is believable and cute. The negative behavior between siblings does not find solutions but might lead to discussion. Demonstrates realistic family issues about intelligence and responsibility. Kid Juror Comments: Kids liked this. They thought the actors behaved as it they were really brother and sister. Age: 8–12; Length: 60 min.; Suggested Retail Price: $14.98, PARAMOUNT HOME VIDEO

* THIS PRETTY PLANET; see p. 192

* THUNDERBIRDS ARE GO: Zerox, a 21st-century spacecraft, is leaving Earth's atmosphere, bound for Mars with five men aboard. But the craft disappears and the Tracy team launches an exciting rescue mission in space. Adult Juror Comments: Dated, a bit primitive for some audiences. Opening sequence is slow-moving. The women's roles appear superficial. Appeals most to boys with special interests. Kid Juror Comments: Girls said "This is boys' stuff, they like these kinds of movies with rockets and fights." Favorite parts: jet-docking the shuttle, puppets. Age: 7–12; Length: 94 min.; Suggested Retail Price: $19.98, MGM/UA HOME ENTERTAINMENT

** TIFF, THE (REBOOT): After an argument, Bob and Dot become insufferable. One scheme after another to rekindle their friendship fails, until a dangerous encounter forces the two to work together and they learn to respect each other's point of view. Adult Juror Comments: A computer-generated update of the Jetsons, complete with updated means of resolving conflict that includes the use of guns. Family seems almost human. Kid Juror Comments: Kids liked this a lot. They liked the characters and the way it looks. "The video shows how friends can like each other better and how it's important not to take sides and be mad at one another." Age: 8–14; Length: 25 min.; Suggested Retail Price: $12.95, ALLIANCE

* TOY STORY: Newcomer Buzz Lightyear crash-lands in Woody's world, igniting a rivalry that lands them in the hands of Sid, the toy-torturing boy next door. By working together and recognizing their friendship they manage to survive. Adult Juror Comments: Includes some bizarre behaviors by the neighbor boy, such as blowing up toys. Additionally, Sid's behavior goes unnoticed by his parent, exemplifying bad parenting as well. His resolved behavior change is not credible. Nostalgic in other ways. Kid Juror Comments: Kids enjoyed the screening. Parts were scary for some who asked, "Turn it to a different part. This is naughty." Most children would never consider abusing their toys, but this could influence them to do so. Age: 8–12; Length: 81 min.; Suggested Retail Price: $26.99, WALT DISNEY HOME VIDEO

* TWEETY AND SYLVESTER; see p. 359

** TWO SOLDIERS; see pp. 344, 359

*** WALLACE AND GROMIT: A CLOSE SHAVE; see p. 359

*** WALLACE AND GROMIT: A GRAND DAY OUT; see p. 200

*** WALLACE AND GROMIT: WRONG TROUSERS, THE; see p. 360

** WELCOME TO THE DEAD HOUSE (GOOSEBUMPS): Josh and Amanda reluctantly move to a new town where there are strange things goings on. Is it a chemical spill that is the cause, or something more sinister? Based on the first Goosebumps book. Adult Juror Comments: Chilling scary stuff. Formulaic, but good quality. Fun to watch because it doesn't take itself too seriously. Appropriate content for audience, and well produced. Unique catch at the end. May provoke an interest in kids to read the books. Kid Juror Comments: "Scary, spooky, creepy." Captured kids' attention. Kept them in suspense. Audience couldn't believe that the family stayed together. They liked this better than the book. "It just really scared me." Age: 8–12; Length: 42 min.; Suggested Retail Price: $14.98, TWENTIETH CENTURY FOX HOME ENTERTAINMENT

** WEREWOLF OF FEVER SWAMP, THE (GOOSEBUMPS): A young boy sets out to discover the mystery behind the werewolf legend in his new town of Fever Swamp. Adult Juror Comments: Creates opportunity to discuss fears, fact versus fiction, and werewolves. Content is tasteful yet scary. Has some stereotypes but shows them as flawed. Kid Juror Comments: Good and scary without being "real." Great effects such as the use of fog. "I like spooky videos." "I liked the book better." "The ending is great because you don't really know what's going to happen." Age: 8–12; Length: 46 min.; Suggested Retail Price: $14.98, TWENTIETH CENTURY FOX HOME ENTERTAINMENT

* WITH SIX YOU GET EGGROLL: Doris Day and Brian Keith star in this romantic comedy about coping with kids, marriage, and a newly created family. Adult Juror Comments: Lively and entertaining. It demonstrates individual family members' viewpoints and how they reach a resolution to create a healthy family unit. Some funny moments from adult perspective, and still sensitive to youth. Predictable and silly. Kid Juror Comments: Kids enjoyed the '60s aspects. They learned lessons about being nice to others, especially parents and siblings. Kids found the story unrealistic and the characters irrational. "Most families aren't that way now." Age: 12–15; Length: 95 min.; Suggested Retail Price: $98.98, 20TH CENTURY FOX HOME ENTERTAINMENT

*** WIZARD OF OZ, THE; see p. 360

*** YOURS, MINE AND OURS; see p. 360

CD-ROMs

*** EASY BOOK DELUXE: Draws children into the world of creative storytelling by printing out double-sided books in four sizes—from mini to poster size. Includes spell-checker, thesaurus, text-to-speech, and sound. Adult Juror Comments: Installs easily. Straightforward and simple to operate, fun and creative. Content is determined by the child. Motivated kid jurors to write a book and gain design experience. Best for kids comfortable with the computer. Kid Juror Comments: Kids thought it was a lot of fun. Several kids made a book of their own using this. "This is awesome." Their favorite part was making a finished book. Some parts were hard to access. Kids liked the science fiction, fairy tale, and comic book format. Age: 8–12; Suggested Retail Price: $14.95, SUNBURST COMMUNICATIONS, INC.

Fairy Tales, Literature, Myths

** ALICE THROUGH THE LOOKING GLASS; see p. 205

** ANASTASIA: Spectacular animated story about a lost Russian princess and her quest to find her true identity. Features celebrity voices and spellbinding music, including "Once Upon a December." Adult Juror Comments: This production combines adventure, sensitivity, history, music appreciation, and a strong female role model. Some Rasputin scenes are graphic and extremely frightening. Kid Juror Comments: Boys and girls alike loved this. Boys loved the revolution. Girls loved the relationship issues. Kids liked the glimpses of history. They asked, "Which parts are real and which aren't?" Kids thought Rasputin was too "monsterish." Age: 8–12; Length: 94 min.; Suggested Retail Price: $26.95, TWENTIETH CENTURY FOX HOME ENTERTAINMENT

** ASHPET: AN AMERICAN CINDERELLA; see p. 361

** CINDERELLA, CINDERELLA, CINDERELLA; see pp. 211–12

* HAUNTED MASK (GOOSEBUMPS): Shy, quiet Carly Beth is a target for everyone's teasing and practical jokes. One Halloween, she finds a wonderfully spooky mask that has her tormentors scared and running. When she refuses to take her mask off, strange things happen. Adult Juror Comments: The message is positive: developing self-awareness and the value of friends and family. But the moral is almost lost in the frightening scenario. Jurors objected to manipulating the viewers' emotions. Kid Juror Comments: Kids like the thrill quotient, the pace, and the visuals. "The talk is mean and ugly, but the effects were awesome." Kids liked the transforming mask. More sophisticated kids were bored, younger kids were scared. Age: 8–12; Length: 44 min.; Suggested Retail Price: $14.98, TWENTIETH CENTURY FOX HOME ENTERTAINMENT

* HEIDI (SHIRLEY TEMPLE): Shirley Temple plays the spirited young heroine in the classic novel on which the movie is based. Although the orphan is forced to live with her gruff grandfather, he eventually comes to adore her. Adult Juror Comments: Cute and charming. Offers examples of honesty, an assertive role model, strong characters and families. Contains some re-ligious content—prayer, singing, and schooling. Has some unfavorable stereotypes. Kid Juror Comments: Enjoyed by girls more than boys. Dated; some kids saw the nuns dressed in traditional habits from the back and thought they were some kind of "bad guy." Could be a springboard for read-ing the book. Age: 7–11; Length: 88 min.; Suggested Retail Price: $14.98, TWENTIETH CENTURY FOX HOME ENTERTAINMENT

* HUCKLEBERRY FINN: Ron Howard is Huck in this classic Mark Twain story of life on the Mississippi. Adult Juror Comments: Sophisticated content contains some aggressive language and physical interactions. Issues of slav-ery, abuse, name-calling, and theft are big topics for this age. It's too fright-ening for younger viewers though the content has considerable historical value. Kid Juror Comments: Children who lack information on this period in history were confused about issues like slavery-versus-freedom concepts that are key to this film. Kids discussed how the father and son treated each other. Age: 9–13; Length: 77 min.; Suggested Retail Price: $14.98, TWEN-TIETH CENTURY FOX HOME ENTERTAINMENT

** JOURNEY HOME: THE ANIMALS OF FARTHINGWOOD; see p. 218

** LES MISERABLES (ANIMATED CLASSICS COLLECTION): Against a vivid backdrop spanning forty of the most exciting years in French history, Vic-tor Hugo's timeless novel springs to life. A tale of love and sacrifice, sin and redemption, and one man's struggle to make a place for himself. Adult Juror Comments: Well produced, however story is confusing and difficult to follow. Understanding causes of conflicts in French society after the French Revolution is required to understanding the story line. May en-courage further study. Kid Juror Comments: Led to history discussion and possible desire to read the orginal text. Kids asked clarification questions. "These are famous stories we should know." "Showed how to treat others." Age: 8–14; Length: 60 min.; Suggested Retail Price: $19.95, JUST FOR KIDS/CELEBRITY HOME VIDEO

*** LITTLE LORD FAUNTLEROY: A poor boy discovers he is heir to a vast for-tune. He goes to live with his miserly grandfather and brings joy to all who know him. Eventually, he softens even the old man's heart. Based on the classic novel by Frances Hodgson Burnett. Adult Juror Comments: A heart-wrenching story for boys. The compassion and kindness of the main char-acter is refreshing. Plot is clear and moves along smoothly. Contains historically accurate costumes with updated language. Exemplifies enter-tainment with a message. Kid Juror Comments: Held kids' attention. They enjoyed learning a few things about this time period and setting. "They showed how being a kind, good, and friendly person pays off. And they did it in a fun way." "I liked it and can't wait to watch it again." Age: 7–12; Length: 100 min.; Suggested Retail Price: $14.98, TWENTIETH CENTURY FOX HOME ENTERTAINMENT

*** LITTLE MATCH GIRL: Recast in the future, this classic story sensitively recounts the trials of a poor, homeless little girl. Narrated by F. Murray Abraham, animated and directed by Michael Sporn. Adult Juror Comments: Good story line, illustrates the trials of being homeless, though not accurately reflecting conditions of homeless people today. Offers simplistic solutions. Has its light moments and good repeat viewing value. It's too scary for children under six. Kid Juror Comments: Kids liked the movie, although some misinterpreted the plot. They thought it was a happy movie even though it had its sad parts. Afterwards, they discussed ways they could help the homeless in their own community. Age: 8–12; Length: 28 min.; Suggested Retail Price: $9.98, ARTISAN/FAMILY HOME ENTERTAINMENT

** PHANTOM OF THE OPERA (ANIMATED CLASSICS COLLECTION): For generations, this story of love, music, and madness has inspired countless retellings on the stage and on film. Gaston Leroux's immortal novel leaps from the page to the screen in this animated adaptation. Adult Juror Comments: Rather simplistic production. Plot is confusing in parts. Introduces children to opera. The phantom captured children's interest; full of drama, excitement, and the triumph of good over evil. Kid Juror Comments: "Exciting, scary, and fun to watch." Kids familiar with story liked the production. It did not appeal to all the children. The killing of the cat was unnecessary and disturbing. Discussion about phantom followed. Age: 8–14; Length: 60 min.; Suggested Retail Price: $19.95, JUST FOR KIDS/CELEBRITY HOME VIDEO

** PINOCCHIO (GLOBALSTAGE 1998 CHILDREN'S THEATRE SERIES): This is an adaptation of a stage production of the classic tale of Pinocchio, the wooden puppet. Performed in the style of commedia dell'arte, Professor McNamer and sidekick Preston host the play with behind-the-scenes commentary. Adult Juror Comments: True to the original, it addresses the story's place in Italian history. However, this genre—videotaping stage productions—does not have high appeal to children. Appears to be too schoolish. Shows good diversity. Kid Juror Comments: Some children liked the production but found the story line confusing. Some found it boring. It led to a discussion about responsibility. "I like the colorful artwork, costumes, music, and humor." "I didn't like the masks on the characters." Age: 7–12; Length: 94 min.; Suggested Retail Price: $27.00, GLOBALSTAGE

** **RAILWAY DRAGON;** see p. 224

** **RUMPELSTILTSKIN;** see p. 226

** **SECRET GARDEN, THE—CBS/FOX:** Mary Lennox, a recently orphaned little girl, is sent to live with her uncle in his oppressive house on the Yorkshire moors. Through the companionship of new friends, they bring life back to the estate and find new strength in themselves. Adult Juror Comments: Well produced, unusual plot. Looks at different cultures, handles universal themes of neglect, boredom, loneliness, friends, and overcoming adversity. Kid Juror Comments: Kids thought the pace was too slow. The overall setting is somber, and they thought the girl character was rude. Girls, ages four to five, enjoyed it best. The British accent was difficult for some. "Looks like a play, not a movie." Age: 7–12; Length: 107 min.; Suggested Retail Price: $14.98, TWENTIETH CENTURY FOX—CBS/FOX VIDEO

** **SECRET GARDEN, THE—DISNEY/ABC:** "The Secret Garden" comes alive in this full-length animated version with sing-along songs. Adult Juror Comments: Beautiful story, excellent animation. Extremely well done. Good discussion-starter. Screaming and ridicule are a bit much at times. Kid Juror Comments: Kids really enjoy this classic. They pick up on the songs quickly and had strong opinions about the actors. It evoked questions about cholera and epidemics. Age: 5–12; Length: 72 min.; Suggested Retail Price: $16.95, DISNEY/CAPITAL CITIES/ABC

*** **SOLDIER JACK;** see p. 363

** **SPARKY'S MAGIC PIANO;** see p. 228

** **STORIES AND OTHER LEGENDS FROM OTHER LANDS:** Folklore beautifully illustrated in styles of the country of origin: Germany, Ireland, Israel, and Yugoslavia. Adult Juror Comments: Amusing. Great for studying folk tales. Exposes viewer to different myths. Illustrations beautifully represent each story, as does the ethnic music. Contains some nudity and inappropriate behavior (e.g., killing the neighbor's cow). Kid Juror Comments: Provoked discussions about wealth and animal rights. Introduced kids to some new stories. Kids were bothered by the name-calling and stealing. "People are not always nice to each other." Age: 8–12; Length: 23 min.; Suggested Retail Price: $19.95, NATIONAL FILM BOARD OF CANADA

** SWAN LAKE STORY, THE: A DANCE FANTASY (CHILDREN'S CULTURAL COL-LECTION): This classic ballet, performed by the State Ballet of Oregon in a spectacular outdoor setting, tells the romantic story of a young maiden who is turned into a swan by an evil spell, which can only be broken through a pledge of eternal love. Adult Juror Comments: Introduces children to the music of Tchaikovsky and dance. Beautifully produced with breathtaking outdoor scenes. The orchestra sounds good, but the performers are not polished. Can lead to a discussion about fairy tales. Kid Juror Comments: Girls liked this ballerina and prince tale better than boys. All the kids liked the music. The younger children will benefit from adult guidance. Kids familiar with dance enjoyed this best. Age: 8–12; Length: 38 min.; Suggested Retail Price: $19.98, V.I.E.W. VIDEO

** SWAN PRINCESS, THE; see p. 230

** TALE OF PIGLING BLAND, THE (THE WORLD OF PETER RABBIT AND FRIENDS): Pigling Bland is off to find a job in the market. Getting there is not as easy as he anticipates. Adult Juror Comments: Good production, excellent animation. Retains charm and spirit of original artwork while making it accessible to a contemporary audience in terms of pace, mood, and captivating characters. Elements of this story are very confusing. Kid Juror Comments: Kids liked this. They discussed the issue of the license needed for a pig to be on the road afterward. Kids wanted to read the book afterward. "That was a nice story." Age: 7–12; Length: 30 min.; Suggested Retail Price: $14.95, GOODTIMES HOME VIDEO

** TALES FROM THE CRIB (RUGRATS); see pp. 231-32

** TALES OF BEATRIX POTTER; see p. 232

* TALES OF BEATRIX POTTER VOLUME 2; see p. 232

* UNDERGROUND ADVENTURE (OZ KIDS): What begins as an innocent bus trip for Frank, the Wizard's son, turns into a wild underground ride for all the kids as they encounter dragonettes, merry-go-round mountains, an enormous teddy bear, and more. Adult Juror Comments: Addresses fear and feelings. Offers lessons in grammar, science, and geography. Displays some negative and disrespectful attitudes and stereotypes. Language and thinking skills vary in age-appropriateness; difficult to determine proper age audience. Kid Juror Comments: A bit long. Sometimes weird or doesn't make sense. One character calls her brother a dummy several times. "I liked the vegetables when they ran." "I liked when the little boy saved the other chil-

dren and then returned home safely." Age: 7–12; Length: 64 min.; Suggested Retail Price: $12.95, PARAMOUNT PICTURES

*** VINCENT AND ME (LES PRODUCTIONS LA FETE): Jo hopes to learn to paint like Vincent van Gogh. A mysterious European art dealer buys a few of her drawings and tries to sell them as original van Goghs. Adult Juror Comments: Excellent production, funny, and with an engaging approach to art and children. Sensitive portrayal of a character who is deaf. Vincent is perfectly cast. The detective is good, too. Resourcefulness is valued. Kid Juror Comments: Attentive audience explained scenes to each other while watching. Kids said they'd watch it again. They enjoyed the drawing and learning about Vincent van Gogh. Girls thought the character Jo was a "show-off." Age: 7–13; Length: 100 min.; Suggested Retail Price: $19.95, LES PRODUCTIONS LA FETE/HEMDALE HOME VIDEO

* VOYAGE TO THE BOTTOM OF THE SEA: A routine scientific expedition to the North Pole turns into a race to save mankind when a polar ice cap is on fire and threatens the world. A submarine is sent to the rescue. Cast includes Peter Lorre, Barbara Eden, and Frankie Avalon. Adult Juror Comments: Though dated, the story is exciting. Underwater photography is excellent. Sparks an interest in science, modern submarines. Contains some aggressive language and behaviors, and characters that smoke. Kid Juror Comments: Kids really liked the story line and special effects, especially boys. "I was really nervous and excited to see what happened at the end." "The submarine was cool but the squid looked fake." Age: 8–12; Length: 106 min.; Suggested Retail Price: $14.98, TWENTIETH CENTURY FOX HOME ENTERTAINMENT

** WISHBONE: A TAIL IN TWAIN: Kids have an end-of-summer adventure and learn about the power of stories. Wishbone, as Tom Sawyer, has an adventure with Huck Finn in this tale based on Mark Twain's "The Adventures of Tom Sawyer." Adult Juror Comments: Interesting and creative. Well produced with excellent sets. Good way to introduce classic books to kids today. However, some of the scenes between present time and Tom Sawyer's are questionable and confusing. Kid Juror Comments: Kids related to the characters seeking adventure in this story. "Makes me want to go out and read the story by Mark Twain." They objected to the scene with the knife. Age: 8–12; Length: 60 min.; Suggested Retail Price: $19.95, LYRICK STUDIOS

***WISHBONE: A TERRIFIED TERRIER: Joe's loyalty is tested when he is invited to hang out with older and more popular kids. War tests the character of

Wishbone, as Henry Fleming, in a story based on Stephen Crane's "The Red Badge of Courage." Adult Juror Comments: Tension of new friends versus old friends is handled well. Resolution works for audience. Contains explosions and killings, though not gratuitously. Civil War enactment provides authenticity, Excellent handling of a difficult subject. Kid Juror Comments: Kids love how the dog conveys emotion. They especially liked the behind-the-scenes section showing how "Wishbone tries to solve the problem but it's really up to the kids to fix things." Age: 8–12; Length: 25 min.; Suggested Retail Price: $12.95, LYRICK STUDIOS

*** WISHBONE: A TWISTED TAIL: A crime wave hits the Oakdale neighborhood, making kids more careful about choosing new friends. Wishbone, as the orphan Oliver Twist, is trapped by a Web of Crime in London. Adult Juror Comments: Well-developed plot and character development. Good blend of past and present, of literature and values. Suitable humor for this age group. Somewhat confusing. Kid Juror Comments: Kids enjoyed this, especially those familiar with the Charles Dickens novel. A favorite segment: the trial of the dog. Good discussion followed the video. Age: 8–12; Length: 30 min.; Suggested Retail Price: $12.95, LYRICK STUDIOS

** WISHBONE: BONE OF ARC: Contains two parallel stories. One shows Samantha as the heroine of the boys soccer team, with Wishbone as her ally. In the other, Joan of Arc leads the French army against the English in Mark Twain's "Joan of Arc" with Wishbone as Louis de Conte. Adult Juror Comments: Two stories with parallel themes are somewhat confusing to viewers. They're still entertaining and stimulate an interest in the classic tale. Slow-paced. Kid Juror Comments: "It was a good movie and I recommend it." "Now I'd like to read the book," quotes one child juror. Some kids thought the language was "dorky." Age: 8–11; Length: 30 min.; Suggested Retail Price: $12.95, LYRICK STUDIOS

**WISHBONE: FRANKENBONE: David's got trouble on his hands when he adds a little spark to his science fair project. Meanwhile, Wishbone, as Dr. Frankenstein, unleashes a monster in this version of Mary Shelley's "Frankenstein." Adult Juror Comments: This is quite an imaginative adaptation of the classic story. It switches between a contemporary story and the classic tale, which is a little confusing. Still, it's appealing. Kid Juror Comments: Just scary enough. At times, the vocabulary is a little difficult for the target audience. "Encouraged me to find a book about the lady who wrote the book." Age: 8–11; Length: 20 min.; Suggested Retail Price: $12.95, LYRICK STUDIOS

* WISHBONE: HOMER SWEET HOMER: Based loosely on the ancient Greek tale "The Odyssey." The kids refuse to give up when developers come to destroy Jackson Park and their favorite tree. Wishbone, as Odysseus, never gives up the heroic quest to save his home. Adult Juror Comments: Wishbone is sensitive to environmental issues. Both kids and adults are portrayed as smart and caring. Transition between today and ancient Greece is confusing. Adults objected to this version of the classic story because they felt it was demeaning. Kid Juror Comments: Kids like the dog's imagination and cute clothes. The ecological message was confusing. Even so, both boys and girls laughed most of the time. The vocabulary and ancient Greece history was way over their heads. Age: 8–12; Length: 30 min.; Suggested Retail Price: $12.95, LYRICK STUDIOS

** WISHBONE: THE PRINCE AND THE POOCH: Based on the Prince and the Pauper. Joe coaches Emily's T-ball team and Wishbone plays both parts in this adaptation of a Mark Twain novel, ending up in major trouble. Adult Juror Comments: Although he's a dog, Wishbone has a fanciful imagination. His literary adventures also include a moral theme. The costumes are great but the bumbling girls baseball team is overdone. Some objected to this interpretation of the classic story. Kid Juror Comments: Kids laughed a lot. They loved the animals and thought the dog was appealing. Many were familiar with the "Prince and the Pauper" but the adult leader had to point out the connection. This assumes familiarity with the original story. Age: 8–12; Length: 30 min.; Suggested Retail Price: $12.95, LYRICK STUDIOS

** WISHBONE: SALTY DOG: Samantha leads Joe and David into a dangerous adventure while searching for gold. Based on Robert Louis Stevenson's "Treasure Island." Adult Juror Comments: Well produced, unique concept. The idea of adventure and danger is well presented. Children love the explanation of how special effects are achieved. Kid Juror Comments: Kids thought it was exciting. They especially liked the ending that showed how the special effects were created. They absolutely loved the dog, Wishbone. Inspired kids to read the original story. Age: 8–12; Length: 25 min.; Suggested Retail Price: $12.95, LYRICK STUDIOS

** WISHBONE: THE SLOBBERY HOUND: Based on Sir Arthur Conan Doyle's "The Hound of the Baskervilles." After Wishbone is falsely accused, he and the kids team up as detectives to prove his innocence. Wishbone, as Sherlock Holmes, investigates an alleged canine criminal. Adult Juror Comments: The simultaneous stories, contemporary and original, meld literature with current events. "It's wild." The combination of classic stories with present-day characters is sometimes confusing. Wishbone's imagination, voice, and wit are fantastic. Kid Juror Comments: Kids like this, especially the dog as a detective hero. It's funny and weird at the same time. They liked the computer a lot. Some viewers had trouble following the plot. It was confusing to go back and forth between the simultaneous stories. Age: 8–12; Length: 30 min.; Suggested Retail Price: $12.95, LYRICK STUDIOS

*** YEH-SHEN: A CINDERELLA STORY FROM CHINA: This is the original Cinderella, a thousand years older than the European version we all know and love. Won the Children's Book of the Year award from the Library of Congress. Adult Juror Comments: Mystical, marvelous, creative, and thrilling twist to a classic story. Characters present positive images, and it gives insight into another culture. Artistic elements are excellent overall. Teaching ideas are endless from folk tales to cultural study. Kid Juror Comments: Kids were enamored by the characters and the story. They wanted to see it again. Good discussion-starter. One viewer, an adopted child, took offense at the orphan being called "worthless and good-for-nothing." Age: 7–12; Length: 25 min.; Suggested Retail Price: $9.98, TWENTIETH CENTURY FOX—CBS/FOX VIDEO

** YOUNG MAGICIAN, THE (LES PRODUCTIONS LA FETE): Pierrot, a twelve-year-old boy who is passionate about magic, discovers that he has powers of telekinesis—he can make objects move without touching them—he can't control. While learning how to harness his powers, he is called on to save an entire city from a huge bomb blast. Adult Juror Comments: Wonderful, creative entertainment. Witty production with good character development and relationships. Adult role models are not so good. "All kids wish they had magic powers." Adults objected to lack of attention given to safety issues. Kid Juror Comments: Kids like the story. Dubbing was distracting at first but viewers get caught up in the story and it soon became a non-issue. Age: 7–12; Length: 99 min.; Suggested Retail Price: $14.98, LES PRODUCTIONS LA FETE/LIVE ENTERTAINMENT

CD-ROMs

* CROC: LEGEND OF THE GOBBOS: Invites the player to help Croc, the crocodile, rescue his peace-loving friends from the grasp of the evil magician, Baron Dante. Features five different 3-D worlds, including volcanoes, forests, ice glaciers, and underwater caves. Adult Juror Comments: Excellent graphics, nice activities, easy to use. Fairly straightforward and amusing with a cute, animated character. Low levels of interactivity. Objects on screen were much the same. "This program offers plain old good fun." Kid Juror Comments: Kids liked the characters and the graphics. Easy for kids to install. Movement is sometimes hard to control. "Cool game if you like adventure and fantasy." "The Gobos are cute." "Croc can jump really far." Age: 8–12; Suggested Retail Price: $49.98, TWENTIETH CENTURY FOX HOME ENTERTAINMENT

* EDWARD LEAR'S BOOK OF NONSENSE: In celebration of the 150th anniversary of Edward Lear's first "Book of Nonsense," this title is packaged with a book of fifty of his limericks, illustrations, and an audio compact disk. Adult Juror Comments: Based on an old book, contains some gender stereotypes but not negatively so. Silly, classy, original verse. Clever graphics, although repeat play would be limited. Provides an introduction to Lear and his style of writing. Kid Juror Comments: Some kids absolutely loved this while others were less enthusiastic. Easy to use. Kids incorporated a writing exercise after playing with it. Age: 8–12; Suggested Retail Price: $18.95, MAXIMA NEW MEDIA

** TALE OF ORPHEO'S CURSE, THE (ARE YOU AFRAID OF THE DARK?): Encourages kids to use their wits to explore Orpheo's haunted theater and unravel the mystery ghost tale. Distinguished by its sophisticated storytelling design, it features a variety of rich graphic styles and the cast of the TV show. Adult Juror Comments: Multiple layers of engagement. A little scary but intriguing. Allows children to explore on their own and finish the story. "Essentially a non-violent video game." High quality graphics. Kid Juror Comments: Interesting, interactive, and fun. Younger kids needed help from adults or older kids to play. One eleven-year-old said, "Absolutely thumbs up." Age: 8–12; Suggested Retail Price: $59.99, VIACOM NEW MEDIA

Foreign Language

Video

** BONJOUR, LES AMIS VOLUME ONE; see p. 237

* YOU CAN SIGN VOLUME ONE; see pp. 365–66

CD-ROM

* KIDS! SPANISH; see p. 238

Holiday

* BABAR AND FATHER CHRISTMAS; see p. 239

* CHRISTMAS STORY, A (DOUG); see p. 240

* CHRISTMAS STORY, A; see p. 364

** EASTER STORYKEEPERS THE (STORYKEEPERS): In the dark days of Roman persecution, a Christian story keeper, Ben the Baker, and his friends spread the tale of Easter and of Jesus' death and resurrection. This action-packed story teaches faith, family values, and the history of Easter. Adult Juror Comments: Raises good philosophical questions and moral dilemmas. Usefulness as history depends on the viewer's religious beliefs. Includes an oddly accented African family. Contains some violence, such as scenes of Rome burning, attacks on people, crucifixion. Kid Juror Comments: Kids were enthralled and full of questions about the Romans and the Christians. Provides a discussion-starter for moral issues without being preachy. "It showed us how to be good." Their favorite part was Jesus rising from the dead. Age: 8–12; Length: 70 min.; Suggested Retail Price: $14.98, TWENTIETH CENTURY FOX HOME ENTERTAINMENT

* JINGLE ALL THE WAY; see p. 364

* MIRACLE ON 34TH STREET; see p. 365

* PINK CHRISTMAS, A; see p. 365

* PRANCER: A wounded reindeer and a precocious eight-year-old girl form an everlasting bond in this tender holiday drama about true devotion and friendship. Enchanting, filled with heart and gumption. Adult Juror Comments: A unique holiday story with real-life issues. Shows a lack of concern for safety when the girl hangs onto the side of a moving car, climbing onto the roof, wrestles a gun away from her dad. The father's behavior is awful. His change, unbelievable. Kid Juror Comments: Kids related to the girl and her problems with her dad. They commented that she had a lot of freedom and did things "they certainly would get in trouble for." Their favorite part was the ending, when Prancer flew away with Santa. Age: 7–10; Length: 103 min.; Suggested Retail Price: $14.95, MGM/UA HOME ENTERTAINMENT

* SANTA EXPERIENCE, THE (RUGRATS); see p. 245

** SCROOGE: Albert Finney plays Ebenezer Scrooge, who is persuaded by ghosts to change his penny-pinching ways. Great musical score by Leslie Bricusse. Adult Juror Comments: Potentially scary ghost scenes are handled well. Great score and cast, beautiful production design. This classic tale has classic appeal. Some language is too difficult to understand. Kid Juror Comments: Dated. Some children found the movie to be a bit slow. However, the high drama and ghosts held their interest. Most kids lost interest during the musical sections. Age: 8–12; Length: 113 min.; Suggested Retail Price: $14.98, TWENTIETH CENTURY FOX HOME ENTERTAINMENT— CBS/FOX

* SILENT MOUSE; see p. 245

How-To

* HOW TO PLAY THE SPOONS: MUSIC FROM THE KITCHEN: Takes you through the basics of the age-old art of playing the spoons. "Spoon Man" demonstrates two methods of playing—thumbs and pointer—and correct wrist technique. Adult Juror Comments: Presentation is rather dry, narration not compelling. Instructions are pretty good and address ten styles of music. Sets not interesting. Historical background on spoons shows diversity and encourages hands-on learning. Kid Juror Comments: Limited appeal. Boring to some. Others were interested enough to try playing the spoons. "Spoon Man talks too much." "I never knew you could do that with spoons." "I would like to see other people play the spoons." Age: 8–12; Length: 30 min.; Suggested Retail Price: $19.95, SPOON MAN INC

* HOW TO STUDY FOR BETTER GRADES: From the editors of World Book Encyclopedia, contains concise and easily understood strategies for building successful study skills. Produced in a hip, easy-to-follow style. Adult Juror Comments: Helpful for kids having trouble in school. Somewhat dated approach, though. No mention of the Internet or computers. Many ideas are presented. Sequences are long. May be more effective if the child doesn't try to process the information all at once. Kid Juror Comments: Well organized. Covers many curriculum-based concepts. Encourages kids to think, reason, and question. Kids liked the music but thought it was too long. They did not remember all of the study techniques afterwards. Age: 10–13; Length: 45 min.; Suggested Retail Price: $24.95, CREATIVE STREET, INC.

** KIDS GET COOKING: THE EGG; see pp. 248–49

** LET'S CREATE ART ACTIVITIES; see p. 249

** LOOK WHAT I FOUND: MAKING CODES AND SOLVING MYSTERIES; see p. 250

*** LOOK WHAT I GREW: WINDOWSILL GARDENS (ON MY OWN ADVENTURE): Shows kids how to make nature come alive anywhere, anytime. Gives clear demonstrations that lead to "growing your own supper." Includes making a terrarium, growing your personal indoor salad garden, and writing a garden journal. Adult Juror Comments: Instructions are clear and child-oriented. Can stimulate learning about the subject. Because many projects require a sharp knife, adult supervision recommended. "So many ideas, it's hard to remember them all." Kid Juror Comments: Kids were eager to participate in the activities. Their curiosity level was high. Age: 7–12; Length: 45 min.; Suggested Retail Price: $14.95, GILBERT PAGE ASSOCIATES

* MY FIRST MAGIC VIDEO (MY FIRST): Teaches how to create a magic show. Based on the popular "My First Book" series. Adult Juror Comments: Well produced, child-oriented. Safety is emphasized. Interactivity is not encouraged, however, and the focus is more on crafts than magic. It requires a lot of cutting and gluing. The adult instruction is dry and often dull. Kid Juror Comments: Kids liked it but said that it moved too fast to learn the tricks. One older child said she would have preferred seeing kids do the activities. Age: 8–12; Length: 45 min.; Suggested Retail Price: $12.98, SONY WONDER

** SECRETS OF MAGIC WITH DIKKI ELLIS: Dikki Ellis shares his special blend of comedy and magic as well as the actual secrets of how to do magic tricks. Presents basic performing tips to build skills and confidence, followed by step-by-step instructions. Adult Juror Comments: Great potential for involvement and fun. Helps to have the materials ready beforehand so kids can learn along with video. "Ellis offers some valuable and fairly sophisticated hints on presentation." Kid Juror Comments: This video includes a lot of information. Some students took notes in order to remember everything. "Let's do that trick." Kids wanted to learn more original magic tricks in addition to those shown in the video. Age: 8–12; Length: 30 min.; Suggested Retail Price: $14.95, VIDEO VACATIONS

* UKULELE FOR KIDS PART ONE AND TWO; see p. 251

Music

*** LISTENING FOR CLUES (MARSALIS ON MUSIC): Wynton says, "Learn structure and form, and music unfolds like a story." He shows how to identify different forms, moving effortlessly from Prokofiev to Gershwin, Ellington to Ives. Once form is recognized, we can start swinging to it. Adult Juror Comments: Contains lots of technical information. It's a crash course on music. Kids like Wynton very much. They enjoyed the relationship of music to literature and the structure of school day. Has good culturally diversity. Kid Juror Comments: Kids who had an interest in music responded to this with great enthusiasm. Those in band were enthralled. Others were not as interested. Age: 8–12; Length: 54 min.; Suggested Retail Price: $19.98, SONY CLASSICAL

** MUSIC AND MAGIC; see p. 255

* NUTCRACKER: THE UNTOLD STORY (NOTES ALIVE!): Based on the original E.T.A. Hoffman tale, this Tchaikovsky classic is told in rhyme combined with 3-D animation of Maurice Sendak's illustrations, a live ballet performance and music by the Minnesota Symphony Orchestra. Adult Juror Comments: Lovely production, bright, lively images—captivating. The format, changing from live action to animation, makes the story confusing. Shots of the orchestra are somewhat disembodied from the action scenes. Language is too complex for the audience. Kid Juror Comments: Kids loved Sendak's animation, particularly the mice. Children under eight found it hard to follow. Some vocabulary was too advanced for them to understand. "Pretty to look at." Kids loved the battle scenes. Age: 8–12; Length: 50 min.; Suggested Retail Price: $19.95, MINNESOTA ORCHESTRA VISUAL ENTERTAINMENT

*** SOUSA TO SATCHMO (MARSALIS ON MUSIC): Wynton shows how John Phillip Sousa's European-style orchestra was transformed by an American band. Once ragtime and raggin' changed its beat, collective improvisation turned it into New Orleans jazz. Includes rousing performances of Sousa, Scott Joplin, and Louis Armstrong. Adult Juror Comments: Top-notch production, full of information. Music is great. History is interesting, showing relationship of past to present. Blends visuals and content well. Involves kids throughout. Kid Juror Comments: Kids enjoyed this, especially those interested in music. They liked learning the history of bands and orchestras. Age: 8–12; Length: 54 min.; Suggested Retail Price: $19.98, SONY CLASSICAL

*** TACKLING THE MONSTER (MARSALIS ON MUSIC): Wynton refers to practicing music as "the large monster" and has a strategy for slaying this monster. With cellist Yo-Yo Ma, he shows young musicians how to practice new or difficult pieces. Together they play a thrilling jazz improvisation. Adult Juror Comments: Excellent material that is practical information for kids. Has great ethnic representation. Relates the benefits of practice and its effects to everyday life. Shows good intergenerational and ethnic mix. Kid Juror Comments: Kids liked the interaction between Yo-Yo Ma and Marsalis, especially those interested in music. Kids liked watching other kids practice. Age: 8–12; Length: 54 min.; Suggested Retail Price: $19.98, SONY CLASSICAL

*** WHY TOES TAP (MARSALIS ON MUSIC): Using Tchaikovsky's original and Ellington's jazz arrangement of "The Nutcracker," Wynton demonstrates how composers use rhythm to express a wide variety of emotions. With simple instruction Wynton teaches how to swing with the music. Adult Juror Comments: Marsalis is excellent. He interacts well with children and makes use of excellent sports' analogies. Shows good multicultural diversity. "I enjoyed it immensely." Kid Juror Comments: Kids enjoyed it, held their interest, especially those with a music background. Too much verbalization for some children. Age: 8–12; Length: 54 min.; Suggested Retail Price: $19.98, SONY CLASSICAL

CD-ROMs

** BEETHOVEN LIVES UPSTAIRS (CLASSICAL KIDS): Journey through a magical world of music, games, and artistic inspiration with Ludwig van Beethoven as the musical guide. Through a wide range of goal-oriented games and creative activities, children learn all aspects of music. Adult Juror Comments: Wonderful for musical play and training. Extremely creative and well presented. Difficult to install; freeze-ups and crashes were common. Interesting variety of content. Kid Juror Comments: "This was cool." "There was so much to do." Age: 6–12; ; Suggested Retail Price: $29.98, THE CHILDREN'S GROUP (CD-ROM)

Nature

* AMERICA'S NATIONAL PARKS; see pp. 260–61

** ANIMALS OF THE AMAZON RIVER BASIN: Stained like tea from the forest's fallen leaves, the Rio Negro is one of the world's great rivers. Program explores the Amazon River basin in Brazil's rain forest and the extraordinary wildlife in the area. Adult Juror Comments: A beautiful documentary with great educational value, sophisticated narrative, and great camera work. Quality and depth in an accurate and sensitive presentation. Shows how quiet the world is in the animal kingdom. Kid Juror Comments: Referring to the KIDS FIRST! happy-sad face evaluation tool, kids said, "This movie only gets happies from us, no frowns or angries." Kids loved the weird frog and other animals they hadn't seen before. They wanted to see it again. Age: 8–12; Length: 29 min.; Suggested Retail Price: $29.95, AIMS MULTI-MEDIA

** CORAL REEF, THE: A LIVING WONDER (NATURE'S WAY): Coral reefs are living animal colonies, very important to the tropical ocean ecosystem and an integral part of the cycle of life as home to thousands of fish and invertebrates. Adult Juror Comments: Young viewers will find the pace a bit slow. Contains gorgeous visuals, though the narration is not as compelling. New words on the screen help kids learn new concepts. Excellent education value for learning about oceans. Kid Juror Comments: Kid felt this was a little academic and had limited repeat play value. They all thought the information was interesting and well presented. The word prompts were helpful. Age: 9–16; Length: 16 min.; Suggested Retail Price: $29.95, AIMS MULTIMEDIA

** DANCES WITH HUMMINGBIRDS; see p. 366

*** LITTLE CREATURES WHO RUN THE WORLD (NOVA: ADVENTURES IN SCIENCE); see pp. 366–67

** MY FIRST NATURE VIDEO; see p. 367

*** PEOPLE OF THE FOREST: THE CHIMPS OF GOMBE; see p. 367

** SECRET PATHS IN THE FOREST (SECRET PATHS): BLACK HOLE: A friendship adventure for girls, where characters need help to explore feelings and friendship. Girls help the characters by going on a quest through the wilderness, solving puzzles that reveal secret stones with hidden messages that offer help. Adult Juror Comments: Well designed, easy to use. Beautiful graphics. Looks at typical real-life problems and social interactions. Good diversity. Moves pretty fast at times. Challenging adventure with beautiful graphics and sound effects. Kid Juror Comments: Easy to use, directions could be better. Girls thought it was cool because it was humorous and difficult. "I liked their stories. When I got something right, my heart bounced." "I thought it was very cool." Age: 8–12; Suggested Retail Price: $29.95, PURPLE MOON

** SWINGING SAFARI (REALLY WILD ANIMALS); see p. 268

*** WIDE WORLD OF ANIMALS (ABC WORLD REFERENCE): Comprehensive geographical approach to more than six hundred animals. Combines breathtaking imagery with fascinating information and statistics on mammals, birds, reptiles, amphibians, and fish from around the world. Panoramic views of animals' habitats. Adult Juror Comments: Ingenious, delightful learning tool. High-quality production captures children's love of animals while teaching geography, geology, and botany. Amazing soundtrack. Kid Juror Comments: Kids loved it. They found it full of information and fun to play. Best suited for the upper end of recommended age range. "Terrific for the home with many-aged siblings." Age: 8–12; Suggested Retail Price: $39.95, THE LEARNING COMPANY

*** WONDERS DOWN UNDER (REALLY WILD ANIMALS); see pp. 270–71

Special Interest

* ALICE IN WONDERLAND/A DANCE FANTASY (CHILDREN'S CULTURAL COLLECTION): Alice, the Mad Hatter, the Cheshire Cat, and the Queen are brought to life by the Prague Chamber Ballet. Creatively interprets timeless children's stories and tales through a medley of dance, music, and theater. Adult Juror Comments: This is a beautiful and abstract production with excellent sets and costumes. Very sophisticated content and musical score. Extremely scary for younger kids. The teacher is stiff and hard-edged. Offers stereotypes of good and evil. Kid Juror Comments: Appeals most to children who appreciate and relate to dance or to those who are intrigued by the Alice in Wonderland story. Age: 8–12; Length: 27 min.; Suggested Retail Price: $19.98, V.I.E.W. VIDEO

*** BIG PARK, THE; see pp. 132, 274

** BIG PLANE TRIP, THE; see p. 274

** BIG RENOVATION, THE; see p. 275

*** BIG SPACE SHUTTLE, THE; see p. 275

** BIG SUBMARINE, THE (THE BIG ADVENTURE SERIES): Voyage under the sea with the crew of a giant Trident submarine. See what it's like to live underwater for months at a time. Discover how submarines work. Visits to the bridge, kitchens, and more. Adult Juror Comments: Good presentation, easy to understand. Child narrators enhance appeal. Limited information about nuclear technology. Little diversity of race or gender. Kid Juror Comments: Presentation is a little long. Kids enjoyed seeing the behind-the-scenes shots of a real submarine. They commented about the teamwork that was represented. Age: 7–12; Length: 40 min.; Suggested Retail Price: $14.95, LITTLE MAMMOTH MEDIA

* BUILT FOR SPEED; see p. 276

*** DARE TO DANCE: Chronicles three young girls' passion for ballet. Explores the joys and challenges of class and performance. Interviews with instructors, parents, and professional dancers are informative and inspirational. Adult Juror Comments: Beautifully presented, displays the dedication required. An unusually sensitive, honest, and appealing introduction to the dance world. Profiles some talented youngsters. Provides accurate information for kids interested in pursuing dance as a career. Kid Juror Comments: Girls who have studied danced loved it. They felt it was a true picture of what it is like to study dance and why dancers work so hard. "They're just like us and they can do all those beautiful steps." Age: 8–16; Length: 40 min.; Suggested Retail Price: $19.95, PARAGON MEDIA

* HOW IT'S DONE — EPISODE #1 — FROM ROLLER COASTERS TO ICE CREAM; see p. 278

* HOW IT'S DONE — EPISODE #2 — FROM BASEBALL BATS TO POTATO CHIPS; see p. 278

*** KIDS' KITCHEN: MAKING GOOD EATING GREAT FUN!; see p. 280

** LET'S GET A MOVE ON; see p. 280

* LOTS AND LOTS OF TRAINS VOLUME I; see p. 281

*** SIGN AND ABC'S; see p. 284

*** THIS OLD PYRAMID (NOVA: ADVENTURES IN SCIENCE): Egyptologist Mark Lehner and stonemason Roger Hopkins test clever and bizarre theories about pyramids by building one. Tours hidden tombs and passageways of the Great Pyramid of Giza and shows computer re-creations of sites. Adult Juror Comments: Well presented with good narration. Provides an excellent exercise in problem-solving, critical thinking, and a fascinating contemporary look at the question "How were the pyramids of Egypt built?" Kid Juror Comments: Excellent. Kids learned a lot about building methods. They liked learning about the pyramids. It has great educational value, more so than its entertainment value. A bit long. Age: 10–14; Length: 90 min.; Suggested Retail Price: $19.95, WGBH/BOSTON

* WHEN I GROW UP I WANTA BE . . . AN ASTRONAUT; see p. 287

** WHEN I GROW UP I WANTA BE . . . VOL. 1; see p. 287

** WHERE'S THE TV REMOTE?: AMERICAN SIGN LANGUAGE VIDEO COURSE; see pp. 369–70

9

Junior and Senior High School

(Ages 12–18)

Introduction: Allan J. Brenman and Adelaide Vinneau

Although today's teens are far less controlled by their parents than were their parents' generation at the same age, they also have more responsibility. Teens today have more financial obligations, are entrusted with the care of younger siblings, and shop and prepare meals for their families. Eighty percent of teenage girls do their family's laundry! Nevertheless, they remain adolescents and filter information through the mind of a teenager. They are romantic, idealistic, and naive as well as cynical, rebellious, jaded, and overmarketed.

A teen's world revolves around the issues of acceptance, self-image, popularity, relating to the opposite sex, defying authority, and developing a sense of identity. As they make the journey toward maturity, their friends become the center of their lives and their families take a backseat. A desire for independence and autonomy develops as adolescents question, challenge, and frequently reject their parents' lifestyles and values. Teens struggle with questions about themselves: Who am I? What kind of per-

ALLAN J. BRENMAN is a staff psychologist at Bradley Hospital in Providence, Rhode Island. He has both a Doctorate and a Masters of Education with a concentration in interactive media from Harvard University. Adelaide Vinneau is the director of the Nashville, Tennessee, YWCA's Domestic Violence Program.

son should I be? How do I make and keep friends? How do I get along with the other sex? What do I really believe in? You will find programs in this chapter that expand their experiences, introduce them to new ideas and attitudes, and give them insight into unknown territories, such as those portrayed in *City Boy, Journey, Two Soldiers,* or *The Great Dictator.*

Teens are primary targets for the marketers of many products, from entertainment to clothes, sports equipment, computers, and soft drinks. Businesses recognize the financial clout of the teenage population and target them relentlessly. Teenage girls spent more then $80 billion in 1998. In the process of shopping and spending, teens are learning to make informed choices and become discriminating consumers. On a different level, they also are learning to use logical and sophisticated reasoning skills, and are absorbing new ideas as they develop a wider view of the world. They need guidance, encouragement, and the resources to do that. Among such resources are some titles found in this chapter: *The Digital Field Trip to the Rain Forest, In Search of Human Origins: The Story of Lucy,* and *How the West Was Lost.*

Television that addresses common adolescent issues helps them learn new ways of handling their problems and to feel less awkward, alone, and different. Typically, adolescents function like an adult one moment and like a child the next. Teens crave guidance from adults even while they are verbally rejecting it. Videos and CD-ROMs that address relationships, the struggle for independence, insecurities, fitting into a peer group, substance abuse, and sexuality help them deal with their own dilemmas. Programs such as *Self-Esteem and Drugs, The Boyhood of John Muir, Working It Out: A Survival Guide for Kids,* and *Life Begins* help develop healthy attitudes and opinions.

We also know that teens have access to more information more readily than ever before. They are more computer-savvy than most of their parents and teachers will ever be. Teenage girls use computers and the Internet as much as boys do. Both genders respond positively to music, humor, positive attitudes, and integrity. Many CD-ROMs teach skills in such a way that it's hard to separate the fun from the learning. Among them are *New Millennium World Atlas Deluxe, Mission to Planet X: Internet Coach, Encarta Encyclopedia Deluxe 99,* and *Astro Algebra.* These excellent educational programs are both compelling and entertaining. Dozens of others like them are summarized and evaluated in this chapter. And in Chapter Eleven are five hundred films chosen by Peter Nichols for quality, showmanship, and a rich variety of themes represented in the category known as family entertainment.

Educational/Instructional

*** GOOD MORNING, MISS TOLIVER: A captivating look at Presidential Award-winner Kay Toliver, who combines math and communication–arts skills to inspire and motivate her East Harlem Tech students. Adult Juror Comments: An upbeat and inspiring portrait of a dedicated and creative teacher. Miss Toliver is a role model for students and teachers, offering excellent ideas for teaching math to all students. "This is a must-see for teacher training." Kid Juror Comments: Everyone wished they had a teacher with Miss Toliver's qualities. They enjoyed seeing how math can be interesting, relevant, and not just scary. Led to a discussion about inner-city schools and their students. Age: 10–18; Length: 27 min. ; Suggested Retail Price: $24.95, FASE PRODUCTIONS

*** INVENTION/3 VOLUMES: Celebrates great inventions that have altered our world, including the marvels of simple gadgets such as the mousetrap. Looks behind the scenes at enterprising people whose tenacity and ingenuity stimulate creativity in everyone. Adult Juror Comments: Stimulating program for teens, with excellent graphics. Motivates an intergenerational discussion. Occasionally contains some dated material. Shows women as positive role models. Kid Juror Comments: Among the favorite segments: "Popular Science" segments from the 1940s, the timed dog-food dispenser, and the interviews with inventors. Section on carbon dating interested them the most. A big hit with boys! Age: 12–18; Length: 300 min.; Suggested Retail Price: $59.95, DISCOVERY COMMUNICATIONS

** MASTERING ASTHMA: A FAMILY'S GUIDE TO UNDERSTANDING: Follows the diagnosis and treatment of asthma in the daily lives of three children of different ages, addressing common questions and teaching mastering skills. Teaches parents to become active partners by offering practical, everyday tips. Adult Juror Comments: Good overview of asthma that blends factual information and dramatic delivery of information. Suitable for family viewing as well as for school groups to understand their friends who have asthma. Comforting for parents as well as children. Kid Juror Comments: Very informative. "I want my mom to see it." "What about grown-ups, do they have it too?" Helps to reduce fear of asthma. "I'd like to learn more about medicine and science." Age: 7–ADULT; Length: 20 min.; Suggested Retail Price: $34.95, AMERICAN ACADEMY OF PEDIATRICS

*** MATH . . . WHO NEEDS IT?: Stars Jaime Escalante, the math teacher who inspired the movie nominated for an Academy Award, "Stand and Deliver," and his students at Garfield High in West Los Angeles. Bill Cosby and Dizzy Gillespie make guest appearances. Adult Juror Comments: Inspiring, humorous, and enlightening, with stimulating narrative. Suitable for high school students or family viewing. Kid Juror Comments: Admired Jaime Escalante. Skeptical at first because it was about math, but most actually liked it. Everyone felt it was best-suited for older students. Age: 8–18; Length: 58 min.; Suggested Retail Price: $19.95, FASE PRODUCTIONS

*** WITNESS: VOICES FROM THE HOLOCAUST: Some of the earliest recorded testimonies and rare archival footage provide school-age viewers with a uniquely personal introduction to the Holocaust. Jews, resistance fighters, American POWs, children survivors tell stories in their own words. Adult Juror Comments: An intensive and chilling reminder of the catastrophe. Very interesting and challenging, excellent document for teachers of history. Powerful and touching. Marvelous editing job. Stimulates inquiry and thought. Humanizes history. Kid Juror Comments: "I think it presented touchy material in a positive and informative way." Actual stories "helped give a better understanding of the Holocaust." "Was interesting but too long." "This seems to be happening again in Kosovo." Age: 12–18; Length: 86 min.; Suggested Retail Price: $24.95, STORIES TO REMEMBER

CD-ROMs

*** ALGEBRA WORLD: Highly interactive math-building tools covering equations, ratios, percentages, variables, geometry, and negative numbers. Kids solve a mystery while exploring these math challenges. Has three skill levels and a user-tracking feature. Adult Juror Comments: Good teaching tool for difficult concepts. Program offers activities covering skills such as problem-solving and introduces algebraic concepts. Puzzles are difficult. Excellent 3-D graphics, great music. Kid Juror Comments: Challenging and fun on different levels. Made kids think and come up with solutions. Kids enjoyed the graphics. "I like building my own shapes." "I didn't know algebra was fun." The different levels are really useful. Age: 12–18; Suggested Retail Price: $39.95, COGNITIVE TECHNOLOGIES CORPORATION

** ASL SIGN LANGUAGE, VOLUME ONE: VOCABULARY, GRAMMAR AND SENTENCES: Designed to teach American Sign Language skills, this program is simple to use and has all the features of state-of-the-art multimedia software. Adult Juror Comments: Impressive. A superior instructional program, exceptionally informative. Adults thought children would need to have some motivation to learn sign language in order to enjoy this. Responsive, gives constant positive feedback. Installation difficult. Kid Juror

Comments: Children were intrigued and kept going back to this. The video section can be slowed down to see the hand movements clearly. A great tool that could be used in conjunction with live instruction. Age: 12–18; Suggested Retail Price: $95.00, SIGN ENHANCERS, INC.

*** ASTRO ALGEBRA (MIGHTY MATH): Covers major algebraic topics in a game format. Includes negative integers, equivalent expressions, ratio and proportions, exponential notation, and inverse operations. Adult Juror Comments: Awesome. Outer space setting is very imaginative and visually stimulating. Great graphics and sound. Presents algebra painlessly, with positive reinforcement. Challenging content. Excellent teaching tool. Particularly helpful for slow learners. Kid Juror Comments: Much fun with this program. They were challenged, motivated, and thought it was fantastic! "I liked solving the problems at the space station." "If you like math, you'll love this." "It was cool, fun, and taught me stuff." Age: 10–18; Suggested Retail Price: $29.95, EDMARK

** DIGITAL FROG 2, THE: Teaches frog dissection, anatomy, and ecology with full-color photographs, full-motion video, narration, and detailed animations—including 3-D. Interactive map, context-sensitive help, and definitions make it easy to use. Adult Juror Comments: Interesting alternative to a real dissection, with good graphics. "It helped me understand what we were doing in my biology class." It doesn't tell what the user did wrong. Kid Juror Comments: Very easy. "It was great." "I could go up to the menus at any time to change areas." "I liked the display of a heart and then a smaller section and a smaller section and then the pumps for the heart." "Helped me understand my biology class." Age: 12–18: Suggested Retail Price: $85.00, DIGITAL FROG INTERNATIONAL, INC.(CD-ROM)

*** DIGITAL FIELD TRIP TO THE RAINFOREST, THE: Explore the Blue Creek Rain Forest Reserve in Belize, Central America, with hundreds of photos, videos, and interactive activities. Learn about the world's rain forests, the diversity of plants and animals, and the importance of vital ecosystems. Adult Juror Comments: Excellent learning tool, kid-friendly, easy to use. Contains good reference material that is educational and entertaining. Information on vegetation, strata, and water cycles, using diagrams, charts, and graphs. A superior program. Kid Juror Comments: Lots of good information. Kids enjoyed learning the geography lessons, especially when video was used. They liked the monkeys and the other animals, but eating bugs was their favorite part. "The more games the better, because they make me think." Age: 11–18; Suggested Retail Price: $49.00, DIGITAL FROG INTERNATIONAL, INC.

*** DIGITAL FIELD TRIP TO THE WETLANDS, THE: Virtual reality technology allows users to visit the wetlands in Algonquin Park, Canada. Hundreds of photos, videos, animations, and engaging interactivities make it perfect for nature enthusiasts, students, or anyone interested in nature. Adult Juror Comments: Easy to use, no glitches, covers many disciplines. Well produced with excellent learning and reference tools. Useful information through reading, visuals, and memorization. Kid Juror Comments: Enjoyed the web game, field trip, and vacation. "I liked finding animals in the bog, looking around at the scenery and playing the game." A resourceful, informative program with good graphics, video and audio. "Makes learning fun." Age: 10–18; Suggested Retail Price: $49.00, DIGITAL FROG INTERNATIONAL, INC.

*** ENCARTA ENCYCLOPEDIA 98 DELUXE: State-of-the-art multimedia encyclopedia provides top-quality information with current and authoritative content, dynamic multimedia features, and links to the Internet. Adult Juror Comments: A wealth of information. Excellent tool for researchers. Easy to use. Cross-referencing makes it appropriate for older kids. Excellent resource with great graphics. Includes Web site links. Lightning-fast. Kid Juror Comments: Marvelous virtual tours of ruins and hieroglyphics, collages, time lines, and the links to the Internet. Highlights included the maze game and the interactive world languages. Perfect tool for junior researchers. Age: 8–A; Suggested Retail Price: $69.95, MICROSOFT

*** ENCARTA ENCYCLOPEDIA 99 DELUXE: A powerful learning resource that helps users find more information through an interface to the Internet. Engaging multimedia features and content. Comes with a research organizer that's useful for research, writing and homework. Adult Juror Comments: Very good. Extremely easy to use. Excellent reference resource. "A lot more fun than looking it up in the library." Great maps, graphics, and sound. Ability to go on-line provides cutting-edge opportunities for student research. Kid Juror Comments: Unbelievable, awesome. Kids were clamoring to use it. Makes research painless and fun. Very few topics they could not find. Information is clear and concise. "Unbelievable, how could we live without it?" Age: 8–18; Suggested Retail Price: $69.00, MICROSOFT

*** ENCARTA VIRTUAL GLOBE: Comprehensive world atlas offers an excellent geographic reference guide for home or school use. Delivers the highest-quality detailed maps, up-to-date statistical data, and the richest cultural information of any atlas in any medium. Adult Juror Comments: Outstanding atlas/encyclopedia with fantastic links to the Internet. Great for social studies use. The "name that place" game increases map skills. Fabulous geography resource. Kid Juror Comments: Loved the animal sounds, the "flying views" music, and the videos. Biggest drawback: lacks sound with geographical descriptions. Kids under ten needed help to play. Age: 10–18; Suggested Retail Price: $54.95, MICROSOFT

** **GEOMETRY WORLD;** see pp. 290, 295–96

** **HOT DOG STAND: THE WORKS;** see p. 296

* **IMPACT: GROUND ZERO:** Examines the massive impact of an asteroid that many scientists believe collided with Earth and wiped out the dinosaurs 65 million years ago. Also introduces the astronomers who scan the skies for dangerous objects heading our way. Adult Juror Comments: Factual but dry presentation. Quality varies. Jurors had difficulty installing and experienced audio difficulties. Content is interesting but narration too long-winded. Classic example of turning a theory into a fact. Kid Juror Comments: The images were fine, but problems hearing the scientists. Found it boring and difficult at times. "I liked the picture of the meteors and asteroids and the link to the Internet." Kids enjoyed the quiz about asteroid impact. Age: 12–18; Suggested Retail Price: $24.95, BAMBOOLE, INC.

* **INTERNET COACH FOR NETSCAPE NAVIGATOR:** Multimedia tutorial and on-line reference tool walks the user step-by-step through the Internet. A one-click menu makes navigation a snap. All Netscape features are simply explained and demonstrated. Adult Juror Comments: Direct and straightforward learning tool. Useful to Internet newcomers. Simple language is used in a rather dry format with cute characters. Doesn't necessarily make the Internet look interesting. Best for real beginners. Kid Juror Comments: Useful learning about the Internet but not interesting for those with previous Internet experience. Kids enjoyed the cartoon demonstration. Age: 12–18; Suggested Retail Price: $28.95, APTE, INC.

** **JUMPSTART ADVENTURES 6TH GRADE;** see p. 297

*** **LIFE BEGINS:** Provides parents with a new way to teach human conception through birth. Lockout program allows parents to customize material to the age of their child. Adult Juror Comments: Effective, well organized, and indexed. Tastefully done, good visuals. Good teaching and resource tool. Blocking of inappropriate material works well. Delivers strong message about responsible sexual behavior. We experienced technical problems. Kid Juror Comments: Some kids were embarrassed. Elicited interesting comments and questions, such as, "I wish we had this when I was in eighth grade." "I liked seeing the baby grow." Discussion of motherhood followed viewing. Error screen came up too often. Age: 12–18; Suggested Retail Price: $69.95, QUALITY INTERACTIVE MEDIA

*** MATH FOR THE REAL WORLD; see p. 298

* MISSION TO PLANET X: INTERNET COACH: Simulates the Internet, with the latest multimedia technology. Using a game format, players are challenged to reach the mysterious planet X as they learn to surf the Web. Adult Juror Comments: Great idea but hard to follow their method of searching the Internet. Kids loved the puzzles. At times frustrating, the icons and text are hard to read, and the instructions are difficult to follow. Kid Juror Comments: Great puzzles and visual effects, especially the pictures of planets. Boys stayed interested the longest. This complex puzzle had mixed success holding children's interest. The kids found it too slow and it skipped around too much. Age: 12–18; Suggested Retail Price: $38.95, APTE, INC.

*** NEW MILLENNIUM WORLD ATLAS DELUXE: Create your own global journey with in-depth geographical information and a sophisticated 3-D map that helps define the constantly changing world. Tools supplied for creating maps and organizing information. Adult Juror Comments: Filled with interesting articles. Detailed coverage about cultures, history, physical geography, even selecting a college. Visual representation of the world is well done. Easy to operate. Kid Juror Comments: Best segments: mapmaking, travel information and notebook guide. "Really colorful. Makes an excellent educational resource and reference tool." Easy to use. Atlas contains new informational facts that are perfect for school reports. Age: 12–18; Suggested Retail Price: $44.95, RAND McNALLY NEW MEDIA

** PRE-ALGEBRA WORLD; see p. 299

** RAMAGON INTERACTIVE CONSTRUCTION KIT: Makes use of animated building pieces. Kit allows children of all ages to use their imagination to formulate and build their own creations. Their work comes alive with movement and sound. Adult Juror Comments: Content is interesting, challenging, creative. Exceptionally confusing and difficult to install. After watching instruction videos, adults still couldn't get it to do what they wanted. Made the children want to play with real Tinkertoys afterward. Kid Juror Comments: Every single kid needed help to install. Experienced users had to reset computer to use it. Boys responded to it better than girls. "We liked the way the shapes moved around the screen, and choosing our own colors." "I liked adding my own things." Age: 8–18; Suggested Retail Price: $24.95, EL-KO INTERACTIVE, INC.

*** SPACE STATION ALPHA: THE ENCOUNTER (TIME BLAZER): You are a mission specialist on Space Station Alpha. Your top-secret mission is to board and investigate an alien spacecraft to determine its origin and mission. A prototype spacesuit aids you as mission control guides you through the spaceship. Adult Juror Comments: Excellent graphics. Slow at beginning. "One of the most interesting approaches to acquiring and using information." Good repeat-use value. Includes supplementary materials such as a membership card and Web site information. Kid Juror Comments: "Fun stuff." Kids liked the images, the sounds, and the movement. Challenging, but required patience. Kids tended to speed through it until they got hooked. Kids had more success and enjoyment when playing in small groups. Age: 10–18; Suggested Retail Price: $54.95, PARAGON MEDIA

** TYPE TO LEARN; see p. 301

*** WORLD BOOK 1998 MULTIMEDIA ENCYCLOPEDIA: Learn, achieve, and succeed. Two CDs contain all the articles from the print World Book Encyclopedia and features 360-degree views, interactive simulations, videos, animation, photographs, illustrations, and audio. Allows access to the Internet. Adult Juror Comments: Easy to install. Clear and concise. An excellent resource with solid, current content. Well designed to answer questions, encourage browsing, or exploring new topics. Switching CDs is a slight nuisance. It's a complete multimedia encyclopedia. Kid Juror Comments: Tremendous way to use the computer. "This program would help me do my homework." Kids love the facts, images, monthly events, and going to the Internet. "I learned all about bears, even the football team." Program kept kids interested. Age: 8–18; Suggested Retail Price: $69.95, IBM MULTIMEDIA

Family

* ALL CREATURES GREAT AND SMALL: James Herriot left World War II a shaken man, but the country veterinarian learned peace through his remarkable ability to heal animals. Based on a true story. Stars Christopher Timothy, Robert Hardy, Peter Davison, and Carol Drinkwater. Adult Juror Comments: Lovely story with solutions to problems returning veterans face, such as family tensions and dealing with difficult people. Set in rural

England in 1946. Slightly unsafe behavior. Kid Juror Comments: Story okay but the pace too slow. They had difficulty relating to the setting and WW II period. Some scenes evoked giggles. There is little repeat viewing value for this age. Age: 12–18; Length: 94 min.; Suggested Retail Price: $19.98, TWENTIETH CENTURY FOX HOME ENTERTAINMENT

* AUTHOR, AUTHOR!: Al Pacino plays a playwright living in New York with five children and stepchildren. Parental role reversal occurs when the mother leaves the household and the father's commitment to the children pulls together an unlikely new family structure. Adult Juror Comments: The father and children relate to each other in extraordinary ways. Addresses separation and divorce. Contains some profanity, gender stereotypes, and sexual overtones. "Wild and crazy family but still charming." Dated approach to topic. Kid Juror Comments: Deals with family crisis in a way children can understand. The child characters appealed most to children experiencing similar situations. Kids enjoyed seeing Al Pacino as a young actor. Age: 12–18; Length: 109 min.; Suggested Retail Price: $14.98, TWENTIETH CENTURY FOX HOME ENTERTAINMENT

*** BLACK STALLION, THE: A shipwreck leaves Alec and a wild Arabian stallion stranded on a desolate island. Their survival forges a lasting bond of friendship. Adult Juror Comments: An uplifting and spirited story with strong humanistic appeal. Every turn of events leads to a positive outcome. Vivid settings. Kid Juror Comments: Children adored this film. They loved the horse and the adventure. Opening segment is great. They were spellbound. Exciting story held their attention longer than common for audience. Age: 4–18; Length: 117 min.; Suggested Retail Price: $14.95, MGM/UA HOME ENTERTAINMENT

*** BLACK STALLION RETURNS, THE: Alec pursues his beloved horse, Black, who's been kidnapped by his original owner. Alec's mystical bond with Black makes him "the one fated rider" for the film's big race. Adult Juror Comments: Lots of action, backed with excellent photography. A wonderful portrait of a boy and the emotional ties with his horse. Sensitive and respectful treatment of other cultures. The death scene may bother some children. Kid Juror Comments: Terrific. Age: 6–18; Length: 125 min.; Suggested Retail Price: $14.95, MGM/UA HOME ENTERTAINMENT

** BOYHOOD OF JOHN MUIR, THE: Dramatic feature tells the early story of Scottish emigrant John Muir, known today as the founder of the Sierra Club, and Yosemite National Park, and as America's first great spokesman for the wilderness. Adult Juror Comments: Teaches about early conservation efforts. Portrays a strongly patriarchal society and religious narrow-mindedness. Addresses family relationships and perseverence. Scenery is awe-inspiring. Kid Juror Comments: Most boys knew who Muir was. "History brought to life—Bravo!" Shows how different cultures meet and clash. Strictness of Muir's father prompted discussion about parental behavior. Age: 12–18; Length: 78 min.; Suggested Retail Price: $29.95, BULLFROG FILMS

* CHRISTMAS REUNION; see p. 305

** CITY BOY: Nick, a 17-year-old orphan, leaves Chicago in search of his identity, and unexpectedly finds romance and a home in a majestic forest. He soon finds himself torn between his love for Angelica and loyalty to his boss. Adult Juror Comments: Appealing teen portrayal. Nick is an orphan with emotional problems related to his past. He overcomes many difficulties, a dishonest friend, a handicapped hand, fear of fire, and ignorance about nature, and helps save the day. Some mild violence. Kid Juror Comments: Kids enjoyed the story. Stimulated discussions about loyalty, environment and tenacity. Audio and video are poor at times. Kids discussed importance of choices they make and the friends they choose. They related to Simon being a phony and a "jerk." Age: 10–16; Length: 110 min.; Suggested Retail Price: $19.95, BONNEVILLE ENTERTAINMENT

*** COURT JESTER: Framed by the pageantry of 12th-century England, Danny Kaye sings, dances, and clowns, yet still finds time for dangerous duels with swordsmen and rescuing damsels in distress. A delightful comedy. Adult Juror Comments: Contains some questionable language. Appeals to entire family. Presents a rather nasty view of the English upper class in another time period. Wit and humor throughout. "Kids enjoyed, so did I, we all laughed out loud." Kid Juror Comments: Great humor but kids definitely thought it was too dated. "I liked the sword fighting." Characters think their way through problems. "I liked when the witch hypnotized the jester. That was funny." Age: 8–18; Length: 101 min.; Suggested Retail Price: $14.95, PARAMOUNT HOME VIDEO

** CREATURE COMFORTS: Four short films from Nick Park, creator of "Wallace and Gromit." Features the Academy Award–winning "Creature Comforts" about zoo life. Adult Juror Comments: Delightful, creative, challenging. Connection between hell and non-payment of contracts is illogical. Wonderfully produced in claymation format. Shows anatomically correct clay man. English accent is difficult. "Handbag" is unsuitable for anyone. Kid Juror Comments: Sophisticated humor was above the level of many kids. Non-English-speaking kids didn't get it at all. Most loved the claymation. Some watched it several times. Anatomically correct clay guy brought snickers. "Best clay-animation I've seen" Age: 12–18; Length: 33 min.; Suggested Retail Price: $14.98, TWENTIETH CENTURY FOX HOME ENTERTAINMENT

** CYRANO (GLOBAL STAGE THEATRE SERIES); see pp. 290, 306

* D.P. (THE SHORT STORY COLLECTION II): On the barren German landscape after World War II a lonely black orphan boy discovers the only other black he has ever seen—an American Army soldier. Adult Juror Comments: Very slow-moving and difficult to follow. Did not engage children despite excellent historical information and acting. Pictures some racist behavior. Story line is hard to follow. "You really feel for the little boy in this movie." Despite the awards this show has won, it had almost no appeal to our child jurors. Kids Juror Comments: Dull and depressing. Showed people of different races making fun of each other. Film looks dated as well. Age: 13–18; Length: 55 min.; Suggested Retail Price: $24.95, MONTEREY MOVIE COMPANY

*** EINSTEIN: LIGHT TO THE POWER OF 2 (INVENTORS' SPECIALS): A fictional friendship between an African-American girl and the renowned physicist, who encourages her to fulfill her potential and defend her rights. Adult Juror Comments: Intergenerational story motivates, stimulates, even inspires. School problems such as grades, peer pressure, and race relations are treated in an intriguing format. Offers potential for further discussion. Exceptionally executed. Kid Juror Comments: Enthusiastic. "I like what Einstein tells the girl about being a minority." Einstein is portrayed as a champion, mentor, teacher. Provoked inquiry into his life and work. Eye-opener for kids regarding race relations in the 1950s. Age: 8–18; Length: 55 min.; Suggested Retail Price: $19.95, DEVINE ENTERTAINMENT CORPORATION

*** FLY AWAY HOME: Wonderful adventure of a thirteen-year-old girl and her estranged father who discover what families are all about when they adopt orphaned geese and teach them to fly. Adult Juror Comments: Charming, wholesome movie with powerful acting by likeable characters. Without being overly sentimental, shows how parent and child can reconcile differences. Inspiring insights into flight, migration, death, and self-strength. Kid Juror Comments: Students were moved and touched by the family's commitment to the geese. "It was a wonderful movie, beautifully filmed." Kids thought some parts were unrealistic, such as the game warden and army guys." Good discussion followed the viewing. Age: 7–18; Length: 107 min.; Suggested Retail Price: $14.95, COLUMBIA TRISTAR HOME VIDEO

** FRANKENSTEIN (GLOBALSTAGE THEATRE SERIES); see p. 309

*** GALILEO: ON THE SHOULDERS OF GIANTS (INVENTORS' SPECIALS): The 17th-century astronomer Galileo uncovers mysteries of the universe while dealing with financial problems, an unemployed brother, and a jealous rival. He finds unlikely support from a Medici son. The pair struggles together for intellectual freedom while they pursue the invention of the first telescope. Adult Juror Comments: Very informative and stimulating. Opens further inquiry into Galileo's theories about planetary motion. Excellent production quality, great settings, good acting. Offers insight on social conditions and issues. Kid Juror Comments: Kids enjoyed learning about Galileo's experiments to track the movement of stars and planets. Appreciated the realistic sets and costumes. "It showed us how everybody can think alike and still be wrong, as well as how society punishes creative ideas." Age: 8–18; Length: 57 min.; Suggested Retail Price: $19.95, DEVINE ENTERTAINMENT CORPORATION

** GETTING EVEN WITH DAD; see p. 309

*** GREAT DICTATOR, THE: Chaplin's brilliant lampoon of the Third Reich features Charlie in a dual role as a Jewish barber and the Hitlerian dictator. Adult Juror Comments: This classic lacks the production quality and special effects kids are accustomed to today. Yet it addresses important concepts—Nazism, oppression of Jews, and military aggression. Demands critical-thinking skills and requires advance preparation. Kid Juror Comments: Young adults with some understanding of World War II benefitted most from this story. Kids felt that much preparation was needed to really understand this film, although some liked the comedy as fair value on its own. Age: 12–18; Length: 126 min.; Suggested Retail Price: $19.98, TWENTIETH CENTURY FOX HOME ENTERTAINMENT

** HELLO, DOLLY! Barbra Streisand stars as the famous matchmaker Dolly Levi, who sets out to get Walter Matthau for herself. Lavish musical production features great songs by Jerry Herman. Adult Juror Comments: Good family entertainment. This classic Broadway musical with elaborate sets and choreography also exemplifies the predictable humor of the genre. Loaded with subtle sexual innuendos and gender-stereotyped behavior. Kid Juror Comments: Appealing costumes and fashions, but thought the story did not apply to their lives. Girls enjoyed this more than boys. Age:

12–18; Length: 146 min.; Suggested Retail Price: $14.98, TWENTIETH CENTURY FOX HOME ENTERTAINMENT

** JOURNEY (HALLMARK HALL OF FAME): Devoted grandparents pick up the pieces that their restless daughter leaves behind, teaching how family is all about the people who love you. Stars Jason Robards, Brenda Fricker, and Meg Tilly. Adult Juror Comments: Inspirational and attractive production. Contemporary subject matter deals with difficult emotional issues about abandonment. Slow-moving, serious, and thoughtful. Kid Juror Comments: Favorite sections: the grandfather's picture-taking and the grandmother's handling of the children. Age: 12–18; Length: 99 min.; Suggested Retail Price: $14.00, ARTISAN/FAMILY HOME ENTERTAINMENT

*** LEONARDO: A DREAM OF FLIGHT; see p. 313

*** LITTLE HORSE THAT COULD, THE: This real-life story tells about a little horse with a big heart and the young woman, Carol Kozlowski, who trains and competes with him. Carol takes you behind the scenes to see all that is involved in the caring for and training of a champion. Adult Juror Comments: Beautifully filmed, slow-moving, yet interesting. Provides insight about horse competition. Horse's point of view is an unusual touch. Teaches a valuable lesson about not giving up and working toward personal goals. Kid Juror Comments: Horse lovers were totally captivated. They learned respect and delight for these amazing animals. As the story unfolded, their enthusiasm grew. "I liked learning how to take care of horses." Age: 8–18; Length: 60 min.; Suggested Retail Price: $12.95, DREAMS COME TRUE PRODUCTIONS

** LITTLE PRINCESS, THE (SHIRLEY TEMPLE): In Shirley Temple's first Technicolor musical, she goes from a snooty prep-schooler to a servant when her rich father dies. Based on the novel by Frances Hodgson Burnett. Song-and-dance routines with Arthur Treacher. Adult Juror Comments: Adults enjoyed this for nostalgic reasons—it is familiar. Offers complex messages regarding death, poverty, and hope. Some children will have difficulty relating to the historical time period. Its fairy-tale appeal is timeless. Kid Juror Comments: Children politely watched but said they would not have selected it on their own. It was difficult to follow, and many got very restless. They liked the happy ending, compared the movie version to the book, and asked questions about boarding schools. Age: 7–18; Length: 93 min.; Suggested Retail Price: $14.98, TWENTIETH CENTURY FOX HOME ENTERTAINMENT

** MARY ANNE AND THE BRUNETTES (BABY-SITTERS CLUB, THE); see pp. 314-15

*** NATIONAL VELVET (FAMILY ENTERTAINMENT): With excellent performances and exhilarating footage of horse racing, this cherished story of a small girl who realizes her big dream—first prize in England's National Steeplechase—remains enchanting. Stars Elizabeth Taylor, Mickey Rooney. Adult Juror Comments: Classic film shows healthy family interactions and excellent female role models. Mickey Rooney plays a weak character who grows stronger with the family's trust in him. The horse and race scenes are stunning. Kid Juror Comments: Gripping. The older ones were particularly interested in following the specifics of the plot. Horse-lovers were thrilled. Age: 5–18; Length: 124 min.; Suggested Retail Price: $14.90, MGM/UA HOME ENTERTAINMENT

** OKLAHOMA!: Rodgers and Hammerstein's landmark musical is brought to the screen with all the spirit and energy of the Broadway production. Oscar-winning score. Adult Juror Comments: Classic with adult themes about marriage, sex, love, death, suicide, and politics. Very dated approach, with great music, costumes, and phony sets. Contains potential theme of sexual assault. Shows women as vain and simple. Kid Juror Comments: Corny and hokey. Limited action and a "lame" love story. Some liked the songs and dancing. Others couldn't get into it. Led to a discussion about western settlements as well as traditional theater. Age: 12–18; Length: 145 min.; Suggested Retail Price: $19.98, TWENTIETH CENTURY FOX HOME ENTERTAINMENT

** OPUS & BILL: A WISH FOR WINGS: Based on the well-known comic strip characters. Opus the Penguin wants to fly like a real bird. In pursuing his desire, he learns to value his natural attributes. Adult Juror Comments: Attractive animation, sophisticated comedy with fairly hip attitudes. Contains some adult language. Subject matter is appropriate for older kids or family viewing. Kid Juror Comments: Lots of laughs. Parts of the story are confusing, but one thing is clear: the penguin wants to fly. "It talks about how it's okay to be who you are and how we all have something that makes us special." Age: 15–18; Length: 30 min.; Suggested Retail Price: $12.98, UNIVERSAL STUDIOS HOME VIDEO

*** OUR FRIEND MARTIN: The remarkable life of Dr. Martin Luther King, Jr., using modern animated characters who travel back in time and meet Dr. King at various points in his career. Approved by the King family. Adult Juror Comments: Excellent use of live-action historical footage mixed with animation. Traces his influence on American history. Graphic images depicting racist behavior is best viewed with adults. Stellar cast includes voices of Oprah Winfrey, John Travolta, and others. Kid Juror Comments: Impressive. Many were not aware of the content. "This video taught us to respect other people, not hate each other because of color." "It taught me a lot of history, and it was sad." "I liked when they time-traveled." Age: 8–18; Length: 60 min.; Suggested Retail Price: $14.98, TWENTIETH CENTURY FOX HOME ENTERTAINMENT

** PHAR LAP: Based on the true story of a New Zealand race horse who becomes the legendary winner of thirty-seven races. Adult Juror Comments: Interesting historical plot with great horse racing scenes. Addressed anti-Semitism and class struggles in Australia. Also portrays the grim aspects of the sport. Foreign accents difficult to understand. Kid Juror Comments: "Loved the show; it made me cry." Kids were intrigued when they discovered it was based on a real story, and went on to look up information about horses in Australia and New Zealand. Age: 12–18; Length: 107 min.; Suggested Retail Price: $14.98, TWENTIETH CENTURY FOX HOME ENTERTAINMENT

* PREHISTORIC PINK (THE PINK PANTHER CARTOON COLLECTION): Pink Panther goes primeval, helping a dull-witted caveman invent the wheel. He dukes it out with persistent pests, vexing vampires, stubborn stallions, and an annoying astronomer who sends him around the moon in eight out-of-this-world escapades. Adult Juror Comments: Contains slapstick violence, but message cautions that such behavior is not okay. Best viewed by kids who understand absurdity and sophisticated humor. Contains some sexual innuendo. The sight gags appeal to all ages. Kid Juror Comments: Wonderful. Pink Panther character and the music were great. They pointed out that "duking it out" was inappropriate behavior. Age: 8–18; Length: 51 min.; Suggested Retail Price: $12.95, MGM/UA HOME ENTERTAINMENT

** ROBIN OF LOCKSLEY; see p. 317

** SABRINA THE TEENAGE WITCH (HALLMARK HALL OF FAME): Based on the Archie cartoon series, relays the story of a young woman who receives a very unusual present for her sixteenth birthday—magical powers. Stars Melissa Joan Hart from "Clarissa Explains It All." Adult Juror Comments: Well produced with good cinematography. Kids shown are very wealthy. Provides insight into growing up, interpersonal relationships, making decisions. Kid Juror Comments: All the kids responded positively to the script. They enjoyed the romance and the plot. Especially for kids who enjoy high school dramas. Girls related to it better than boys. Age: 12–18; Length: 91 min.; Suggested Retail Price: $14.95, ARTISAN/FAMILY HOME ENTERTAINMENT

*** SALT WATER MOOSE; see p. 318

** SUMMER OF THE COLT; see pp. 320–21

** TIFF, THE; see p. 322

* TWEETY AND SYLVESTER: Sufferin' Succotash! A match made in heaven teams up the lisping pussycat Sylvester and the not-so-innocent little canary named Tweety. Adult Juror Comments: Tiny canary outsmarts voracious but not-too-bright cat, sometimes by clever ruses but usually by violent means. Although the violence is of the broad, slapstick variety, it is the constant means of resolving conflict, get what you want, etc. Kid Juror Comments: Compared to the superheroes of today, this violence is pretty mild stuff. Kids laughed at the silliness and commented, "We would never do stuff like that." Redeeming virtue—little, weak, smart Tweety always wins. Repetitive. Age: 4–18; Length: 60 min.; Suggested Retail Price: $12.95, MGM/UA HOME ENTERTAINMENT

** TWO SOLDIERS (THE SHORT STORY COLLECTION II): Charming tale of a Southern small farm boy who runs away in search of his older brother who had joined the Army in World War II. Adult Juror Comments: Good story and actors. Sad ending. Shows lying and knifing. Beautiful footage accurately portrays rural community in the South. Creates an appetite for more of William Faulkner's novels. Kid Juror Comments: Retained attention. "The little boy had a lot of freedom for his age." "I liked seeing how people lived in another part of the country." "I'm glad I didn't live there." Best viewed with an adult who can help explain difficult parts. Age: 8–18; Length: 30 min.; Suggested Retail Price: $24.95, MONTEREY MOVIE COMPANY

*** WALLACE AND GROMIT: A CLOSE SHAVE: Academy Award-winner for Best Animated Short Film. Animator Nick Park's cool claymation couple, Wallace and Gromit, get wrapped up in a sheep-napping yarn. Adult Juror Comments: Wonderful family viewing, clever, and artistic. The "Britishisms" are odd and a pleasure to watch. Excellent quality will spark interest in claymation. Adults loved this, perhaps even more than children. Kid Juror Comments: Good sense of mystery. British humor did not escape the kids. They thought it was clever that the dog never speaks, but relies on facial expressions and physical antics. They loved Gromit, as well as the inventions and gadgetry. Age: 8–18; Length: 30 min.; Suggested Retail Price: $9.98, TWENTIETH CENTURY FOX HOME ENTERTAINMENT

*** WALLACE AND GROMIT: THE WRONG TROUSERS: Wallace, an eccentric inventor, and Gromit, his ingenious canine, match wits against a mysterious penguin and a sinister pair of trousers in this Oscar-winning animated title. Adult Juror Comments: Excellent claymation. Superior mystery story wrapped in a perfectly detailed, miniature set and performed by endearing clay characters. Good for repeat viewing by many age groups. "Wow! I haven't been this impressed in a long time." Kid Juror Comments: Perfect entertainment—the story, the characters, the attention to detail, and the wide range of emotions. They were enthralled even in the third viewing. "It's great." They loved Gromit. Age: 5–18; Length: 29 min.; Suggested Retail Price: $14.98, TWENTIETH CENTURY FOX HOME ENTERTAINMENT

*** WIZARD OF OZ, THE: Swooped away from her Kansas farm by a mighty twister, Dorothy and her dog Toto end up in a world of witches and wizards. Dorothy's only hope of returning home is to find the Wizard of Oz. Stars Judy Garland, Ray Bolger, Jack Haley, Bert Lahr. Adult Juror Comments: What a delight to watch this timeless classic about courage, love, brains, family, and adventure. Could lead to discussion about society, make-believe versus reality, and idea of "home." Has value for repeat viewing. Great for entire family. Kid Juror Comments: Kids loved the flying monkeys, the scarecrow, the tin man, and Toto. Most have seen it before, but still wanted to watch again and again. Some parts are scary for younger kids. Age: 5–18; Length: 103 min.; Suggested Retail Price: $19.98, MGM/UA HOME ENTERTAINMENT

*** YOURS, MINE AND OURS (FAMILY TREASURES): When a widow and a widower tie the knot, they share eighteen children, four bathrooms, and endless domestic hilarity in this "affectionate investigation of American family life at its fallible best." (The Hollywood Reporter) Stars Lucille Ball and Henry Fonda. Adult Juror Comments: Very funny. Sheds light on the importance of family and the struggles they endure. Wonderful problem-solving skills and sensitive values are demonstrated. Addresses adult ideas more than child's perspective, and uses a sophisticated vocabulary. Kid Juror Comments: Appealing. They recognized Lucy. "It's about friendship and love and a big family that learns to get along." Age: 8–18; Length: 107 min.; Suggested Retail Price: $14.95, MGM/UA HOME ENTERTAINMENT

CD-ROMs

** KUBA, THE CLASSIC PUSH TO PLAY CD-ROM GAME: Based on the European hit board game that uses marbles, the object is to push seven neutral marbles or all of your opponent's marbles off the playing board. Offers play options over a local area network, modem, or anywhere through the Internet. Adult Juror Comments: Can improve eye-hand coordination, attention span, and memory. Teaches teamwork. Shows ways to view a problem as a challenge and opportunity. Similar to playing checkers. Can be played with a friend or on the Internet. Kid Juror Comments: Great family game. Ranges from easy to hard. Strategy takes a while to figure out. "I liked winning." "The computer played really well. It beat me a lot." Kids liked the music and the special effects with the realistic graphics. Age: 10–18; Suggested Retail Price: $30.00, PATCH PRODUCTS, INC.

*** NANCY DREW: SECRETS CAN KILL; see pp. 290, 299

*** NICKELODEON DIRECTOR'S LAB: Turns kids' computers into a complete "production studio," allowing them to draw, compose music, create animation, and record their own voice. Create from scratch or adapt familiar elements from the Nickelodeon Network. Adult Juror Comments: Good content, would have been fabulously successful if not for technical problems. Does very complex functions that require prior knowledge of video editing. Must have a sound card for certain functions, helps to have a microphone. Kid Juror Comments: Some kids adored it, thought it was absolutely great. Their reaction depends on their interest in the subject. "Wonderful for budding producers." It allows kids to create their own short videos. Age: 8–18; Suggested Retail Price: $54.95, VIACOM NEW MEDIA

Fairy Tales, Literature, and Myths

** ASHPET: AN AMERICAN CINDERELLA (FROM THE BROTHERS GRIMM): This humorous version of Cinderella, set in American South, provides a way for children and adults to explore values, self-esteem, and sibling rivalry. Adult Juror Comments: Many opportunities to compare this with other versions of the classic tale. Jurors responded favorably to the Southern setting and the period costumes. They thought the ending was not as powerful as other versions. Kid Juror Comments: Girls enjoyed this best. The World War II setting was somewhat confusing. Several kids thought it ended too abruptly with little explanation. Ten- to twelve-year-olds loved it. "The African-American lady told a good story." Age: 8–18; Length: 25 min.; Suggested Retail Price: $29.95, DAVENPORT FILMS

** CHILDREN'S FAVORITES: LEGENDS: Five classic legends come to life with colorful, spirited animation. The lyrical story of Syrinx, Daedalus the artful craftsman of Greek mythology, plus three stories: "The Sufi Tale," "The Flying Canoe," and "Paradise." Adult Juror Comments: Beautiful, sensitively rendered. The first four stories contain no language, only music. Some nudity and abstraction. May need explanation of background and cultural context. Kid Juror Comments: Most suitable for older children or children with more sophisticated tastes in art and animation. The abstract presentation was hard for some to follow, but others found it "neat," "cool." "I loved the music." Age: 13–18; Length: 44 min.; Suggested Retail Price: $19.95, NATIONAL FILM BOARD OF CANADA, THE

* CURSE OF THE LOST GOLD MINE: Adventure and greed in the mountains of British Columbia, Canada. Recounts the legend of the Indian named Slumach and the search for his lost gold mine. Adult Juror Comments: Good mystery. Part of the legend includes repeated scenes of hanging a convicted murderer and shootings. As much a tale of justice as a tale of an expedition to find gold, though the reenactment is hokey. Can provoke a discussion about values. Kid Juror Comments: Enjoyed the spooky mystery, though portrayal of the Indians was inappropriate. Kids found the story line confusing. Initially it sparked their interest, but didn't deliver. Age: 12–18; Length: 50 min.; Suggested Retail Price: $19.95, SUPERIOR PROMOTIONS, INC.

* EBENEZER: A Wild West setting for Charles Dickens' classic, "A Christmas Carol," featuring Jack Palance as Scrooge, the most greedy and mean-spirited crook in the West. Ghosts of Christmas past, present, and future open Scrooge's eyes to love and friendship. Adult Juror Comments: Staging of this Christmas classic takes place in the "Old West," complete with bar scenes, brothels, smoking, cussing, fighting, etc. Ebenezer comes around in the end, but the process of getting there presents lots of negative and adult images. Kid Juror Comments: Almost all children knew the story and preferred the more familiar version. Half liked this, half did not. "I liked seeing people happy at the end." "My favorite part is seeing Ebenezer with the past, present, and future ghosts." Age: 14–18; Length: 94 min.; Suggested Retail Price: $14.95, PLAZA ENTERTAINMENT

*** GREAT BOOKS: FRANKENSTEIN, THE MAKING OF THE MONSTER (GREAT BOOKS): Entering the dark, mysterious world of Mary Shelley, this video helps to understand why her brooding masterpiece continues to fascinate and frighten. "Great Books" series shows how classic literature has not only shaped our lives, but continues to influence our thinking. Adult Juror Comments: Well produced and intellectually stimulating. Best-suited for older children with sophisticated critical thinking skills. Kid Juror Comments: Very interesting, informative and easy to understand. "It kept me intrigued." Age: 14–18; Length: 50 min.; Suggested Retail Price: $19.95, DISCOVERY COMMUNICATIONS

*** GREAT BOOKS: LE MORTE D'ARTHUR (GREAT BOOKS): Visit the possible site of Camelot and learn the connection between Sir Thomas Mallory's 15th-century masterpiece and George Lucas' "Star Wars" trilogy. Adult Juror Comments: Excellent production, with clear narration appropriately paced. Offers insight for high school students who are familiar with the history and legend of King Arthur. Presentation is a bit wordy. Kid Juror Comments: "It's not acting, it's history." Eighteen-year-olds were fascinated with use of different time periods to relate a story to our own era. Explanation of armor and "Star Wars" segments were particularly well done. Age: 14–18; Length: 50 min.; Suggested Retail Price: $19.95, DISCOVERY COMMUNICATIONS

** LES MISERABLES; see p. 325

** PHANTOM OF THE OPERA; see p. 326

*** SOLDIER JACK (FROM THE BROTHERS GRIMM): Set in rural America after World War II, Jack returns from the war and receives two gifts: a sack that can catch anything, and a jar that tells whether a person will live or die. Jack eliminates death from the world, until he realizes what a mistake that is. Adult Juror Comments: Excellent production. Scene with devils is too frightening for younger kids. Offer insight about life and death that is suitable for older kids, or younger ones when accompanied by an adult. Provokes interest in Appalachian folk tales. Kid Juror Comments: Well-received lesson about how to treat others. Some were familiar with this story. They enjoyed the wartime setting. Age: 7–18; Length: 40 min.; Suggested Retail Price: $29.95, DAVENPORT FILMS

*** SOUNDER: An Academy Award-nominated story about a sharecropper during the Depression. Paul Winfield plays the desperate father who steals for his family. Cicely Tyson plays his wife, Ken Hooks his oldest son. They love, laugh, struggle, and endure. Adult Juror Comments: Accurately represents the original book. Has great learning potential and is very respectful of children. Shows that dignity is possible even under oppression. This is a difficult subject that is handled extremely well. Kid Juror Comments: Educational and enjoyable. "It made me want to find out more about black sharecroppers." Not all kids were aware of discrimination, and some were taken aback by what they saw. "It was sad, but I learned a lot." Age: 8–18;

Length: 105 min.; Suggested Retail Price: $14.95, PARAMOUNT HOME VIDEO

Holiday

*** CHRISTMAS CAROL, A: A new version of the holiday classic tale about Ebenezer Scrooge, the Victorian misanthrope, whose life is radically changed on Christmas Eve by the visits of three spirits—the ghosts of Christmas Past, Christmas Present, and Christmas Yet to Come. Adult Juror Comments: Wonderful, classic story—not too scary. Beautifully produced, wonderful message. Provides thoughtful family holiday entertainment for Christmastime. Kid Juror Comments: Engaging, timeless tale tells a good story. Kids enjoyed watching it together with adults during the holiday season. Age: 12–18; Length: 100 min.; Suggested Retail Price: $14.98, TWEN-TIETH CENTURY FOX HOME ENTERTAINMENT

* CHRISTMAS STORY, A: More than anything, nine-year-old Ralphie Parker wants a "Genuine Red Ryder Carbine Action Two Hundred Shot Lightning Loader Range Model Air Rifle." Standing between him and the gift of his dreams are two parents opposed to his acquiring a rifle. Adult Juror Comments: Situation is timeless. Narrative delivery is well done. Contains strong language, aggression. Appropriateness of promoting a gun as a gift may be troubling. Raises issues of peer pressure and deep, deep emotions. Kid Juror Comments: Provocative, especially among boys. Many felt their parents would act the same if they asked for a gun. The 1940s setting evoked discussion about different values and points of view. Long, inappropriate for younger kids. Age: 10–18; Length: 95 min.; Suggested Retail Price: $14.95, MGM/UA HOME ENTERTAINMENT

* JINGLE ALL THE WAY: A father is desperate to buy his son that "must-have" holiday toy. In a frantic last-minute shopping spree he is pitted against a stressed-out postal carrier, a sleazy Santa, and lots of other parents. Stars Arnold Schwarzenegger as dad. Adult Juror Comments: Very thin, many negative messages and stereotypical behavior. The children behaved better than the adults. Kid Juror Comments: "There's too much fighting." "Some pictures were too fake." "Little kids shouldn't see the drinking part." "The adults didn't treat each other well." Middle-class kids related best, at-risk kids didn't relate to this at all. Age: 10–18; Length: 90 min.; Suggested Retail Price: $19.98, TWENTIETH CENTURY FOX HOME ENTERTAINMENT

*** MIRACLE ON 34TH STREET (FAMILY FEATURE): Six-year-old Susan has doubts about childhood's most enduring miracle—Santa Claus. Although she doesn't expect anything from Santa this year she gets instead the most precious gift of all: something to believe in. Based on the 1947 classic. Adult Juror Comments: Charming, well acted, and well produced. The child star is excellent. While some items are unreal, the story is so strong that it suspends reality. Opens avenues for discussing human relationships and adult interactions. Kid Juror Comments: The best. Entirely held kids' attention. Made them feel sad and then happy. "Pretty cool even though it is old." Age: 6–18; Length: 113 min.; Suggested Retail Price: $14.98, TWENTIETH CENTURY FOX HOME ENTERTAINMENT

** PINK CHRISTMAS, A: A blue Christmas appears to be in store for the Pink Panther, alone, cold, and hungry on a Central Park bench in New York City. He sets out in search of a meal, concocting a wild array of hare-brained ploys and disguises along the way. Adult Juror Comments: Pink Panther a perennial favorite that's light and entertaining with good music. His antics don't make him the best role model all the time, but in the end, he does show how cooperation helps. Little diversity. Kid Juror Comments: The Pink Panther is fun, wholesome, and entertaining. They asked to watch this program again. Age: 5–18; Length: 27 min.; Suggested Retail Price: $9.95, MGM/UA HOME ENTERTAINMENT

How-To

Video

* HOW TO STUDY FOR BETTER GRADES; see pp. 290, 335

Foreign Language

**YOU CAN SIGN: VOLUME ONE (AMERICAN SIGN LANGUAGE FOR BEGINNERS): A user-friendly program designed for anyone who wants to learn American Sign Language. Lessons focus on common topics applicable to daily life. Viewers are entertained by the Bravo family and guided by deaf instructor Billy Seago. Adult Juror Comments: Uses effective teaching strategies—signs are given in advance, then demonstrated in a realistic environment. Production quality is quite good. Instruction offers a useful resource for any ASL class. Repetition is suitable for beginners. Kid Juror Comments: Kids tried to figure out the parts that were only given in sign language, and enjoyed understanding new communication skills. They were fascinated watching family members speak in ASL. Kids wishing to learn sign language will enjoy this most. Age: 12–18; Length: 82 min.; Suggested Retail Price: $29.95, SIGN ENHANCERS, INC.

Music

* MOZART'S THE MAGIC FLUTE STORY (CHILDREN'S CULTURAL COLLECTION): Mozart's great opera "The Magic Flute," narrated in English and sung in its original German. Performed by the famous Gewandhaus Orchestra of Holland. Adult Juror Comments: Good narration, costumes, staging, and cinematography. Offers children a suitable introduction to opera. The story is difficult to follow. Kid Juror Comments: Enjoyable, especially for those interested in music. Even teenage boys responded reasonably well. Music teachers thought performance was mediocre. Age: 10–18; Length: 42 min.; Suggested Retail Price: $19.98, V.I.E.W. VIDEO

Nature

** CORAL REEF, THE: A LIVING WONDER; see p. 339

** DANCES WITH HUMMINGBIRDS: Get close to the lightning-fast hummingbirds in their dance of life, accompanied by traditional American, Flamenco and Andean musical compositions. Naturalist Michael Godfrey describes the feeding, nesting, and courtship behavior of hummingbirds. Adult Juror Comments: The visual music program is separated from the informational portion, which was a wonderful way to present this program. Bird enthusiasts will drool over this title. Kid Juror Comments: "It was cool." Kids liked it, although they found it a bit overwhelming. Some were mesmerized. Kids decided that they wanted a hummingbird feeder afterwards. Age: 8–18; Length: 31 min.; Suggested Retail Price: $19.95, ARK MEDIA GROUP, LTD./NEW ERA MEDIA

*** LITTLE CREATURES WHO RUN THE WORLD (NOVA: ADVENTURES IN SCIENCE): Travel to rain forests and deserts with naturalist Edward O. Wilson to observe the world of ants. Close-up photography shows ordinary ants and their unusual cousins. Wilson teaches the benefits of cooperation by observing these creatures. Adult Juror Comments: Excellent production, interesting and informative. Good music, outstanding photography and content. Presents the message that "working together builds strength." "Offers more science than I can teach in five days." Kid Juror Comments: Wonderful and informative. Kids never dreamed there was so much to know about ants. It made them want to study ants. "Bugs are cool!" Age: 8–18; Length: 60 min.; Suggested Retail Price: $19.95, WGBH/BOSTON

** **MY FIRST NATURE VIDEO (MY FIRST):** Answers nature questions. Kids discover how much fun nature can be by planting seeds, making creepy-crawly traps, and growing a miniature garden in a bottle. Adult Juror Comments: Inspires young minds to explore nature. Asks questions, presents problems, and challenges each child at his or her own level and ability. Some projects require equipment, assembling materials, and tasks that need adult assistance. Kid Juror Comments: Children eager to do the activities at home. They enjoyed learning new things and wanted to share with their classmates or friends. "My sister would like this too." Age: 6–18; Length: 40 min.; Suggested Retail Price: $12.98, SONY WONDER

*** **PEOPLE OF THE FOREST: THE CHIMPS OF GOMBE (THE DISCOVERY VIDEO LIBRARY):** Trace twenty years of love and rivalry by a tribe of chimpanzees from the forests surrounding Lake Tanganyika, based on the research of naturalist Jane Goodall. Intricate tapestry of emotion and drama, narrated by Donald Sutherland. Adult Juror Comments: Great program. Well produced, excellent cinematography. Kid Juror Comments: Enthusiastic, especially those who love animals. Stimulates a lot of discussion about the subject. Age: 5–18; Length: 90 min.; Suggested Retail Price: $19.95, DISCOVERY COMMUNICATIONS

* **SPIRITS OF THE RAINFOREST (THE DISCOVERY VIDEO LIBRARY):** Discover a pristine environment containing more species of animals than any other part of the world. Encounter six-foot river otters. Boat down uncharted rivers. Share the myths and magic of the Machiguenga Indians, whose tribal lifestyle has changed little since the time of the Incas. Adult Juror Comments: Gorgeous nature documentary and lush footage offers excellent geography lessons. Stimulated interest in the spiritual link between people and their environment. The hunting section was bothersome to some. Native dialogue seems contrived. Kid Juror Comments: A top favorite among children interested in rain forests and the environment. Age: 13–18; Length: 90 min.; Suggested Retail Price: $19.95, DISCOVERY COMMUNICATIONS

*** **WILD INDIA (THE DISCOVERY VIDEO LIBRARY):** The culture of India once enjoyed a mutually respectful relationship with nature. But the British Raj introduced hunting parties, and a growing population threatened India's animals. Traces efforts to preserve the nation's environment and wildlife. Adult Juror Comments: Beautiful documentary. Stimulating, thoughtful, and interesting. Background music is lively, and the terminology is quite sophisticated. This is a marvelous resource. Kid Juror Comments: Peaceful, rich, and revealing. Older children enjoyed the classical music accompaniment. Suitable for both classroom and home use. Age: 13–18; Length: 90 min.; Suggested Retail Price: $19.95, DISCOVERY COMMUNICATIONS

Special Interest

*** DARE TO DANCE; see p. 473

*** DAREDEVILS OF THE SKY (NOVA: ADVENTURES IN SCIENCE): Ever wanted to fly like a bird and soar in the wind? Stunning photography of dizzying aerobatic stunts puts the viewer in the pilot's seat for snap rolls, loops, humpty bumps, and hammerheads. It's fantastic fun at two hundred miles an hour. Adult Juror Comments: Interesting presentation, with applications that apply to math and physics. Covers the history of aviation and aerobatics, and features two female flyers. Kid Juror Comments: "My eleven-year-old son loved this." Kids who are interested in flying got a real kick out of this. They were surprised how much they learned. Lengthy for this age. Age: 12–18; Length: 60 min.; Suggested Retail Price: $19.95, WGBH/BOSTON

*** HOW THE WEST WAS LOST/3 TAPES: Documentary about the struggle for the American West and the tragic decimation of five Native American nations—the Navajo, Nez Perce, Apache, Cheyenne, and Lakota. They didn't just fight for territory. They fought to preserve a way of life. Adult Juror Comments: A wonderful and moving story. Slow-moving but worth every moment. Suitable for adults as well as older children, particularly those whose history lessons have not offered accurate information about Native Americans. Kid Juror Comments: Children appreciated the archival photography and were in awe of the landscape. Led to discussions about the injustice done to Native Americans. Kids thought the interviews and music became repetitive, Age: 12–18; Length: 300 min.; Suggested Retail Price: $79.95, DISCOVERY COMMUNICATIONS

*** IN SEARCH OF HUMAN ORIGINS, EPISODE 1: THE STORY OF LUCY (NOVA: ADVENTURES IN SCIENCE): Anthropologist Don Johanson may have solved the mystery of the missing link between man and ape in finding the remains of a tiny female, named Lucy, who is over 3 million years old. Travel back in time through re-creations about Lucy and her world. Adult Juror Comments: Excellent introduction to anthropology and human evolution. Invitingly framed as a mystery or thriller, captures the excitement through its portrayal of life long ago. Kid Juror Comments: Informative, exciting reenactments held kids' attention. Suitable for kids curious about anthropology, evolution, and the history of mankind. Age: 14–18; Length: 60 min.; Suggested Retail Price: $19.95, WGBH/BOSTON

*** LIVING AND WORKING IN SPACE: THE COUNTDOWN HAS BEGUN: Interviews today's space professionals—a space doctor, the "lunar lettuce man," and designers of space clothing and Mars vehicles. Adult Juror Comments: Excellent informal science education, captivating concept, well developed. Executed with polish, verve, and imagination. Gender representation is non-traditional. Vocabulary is somewhat technical and advanced. Kid Juror Comments: Captured kids' interest in space, and life's new directions and possibilities. Strong gender and ethnic role models were a plus for kids. "Space" enthusiasts were thrilled with this.. Age: 12–18; Length: 60 min.; Suggested Retail Price: $29.95, FASE PRODUCTIONS

* SELF-ESTEEM AND DRUGS (VOICES FROM THE FRONT): Frank testimonials from teens with chemical-dependency problems and discussion of the impact on their self-esteem. Fast-moving, MTV-style, designed to be hard-hitting but teen-friendly. Adult Juror Comments: Very realistic on the challenges and peer pressure experienced by teens. Positive role models are represented. Recommend using with adult intervention. "I'd love to see all the programs in this series." Kid Juror Comments: Well received, though they said it's not something they would choose to watch on their own. Age: 13–18; Length: 30 min.; Suggested Retail Price: $39.00, ATTAINMENT COMPANY, INC.

** TOTAL TEEN FITNESS WITH DOCTOR A: Total Teen Fitness offers an entertaining exercise video for teens, which is a complete workout accompanied with nutritional messages, anti-drug and alcohol tags, and self-esteem-boosting lyrics. Features a culturally diverse group of kids. Adult Juror Comments: Graphics are well done. Carries a strong message regarding the need for a healthy lifestyle. Accompanied by an excellent poster for holistic health. Has appropriate messages about nutrition. Kid Juror Comments: Motivating. Enjoyed the graphics but found the humor a little corny. The material is repetitive. Age: 12–18; Length: 30 min.; Suggested Retail Price: $19.95, ARCHER, SEARFOSS & ASSOC., INC.

** WHERE'S THE TV REMOTE? AMERICAN SIGN LANGUAGE VIDEO COURSE: Have you ever lost your TV remote? Join the amusing search while learning household signs, as the Bravo family looks for theirs. The remote may be lost but Billy Seago makes sure that you aren't. Adult Juror Comments: Makes learning sign language easy and pleasant. Connecting the signing to a real-life story is a fabulous way to teach sign language. Best viewed with adult guidance. An adequate but not particularly imaginative production. Kid Juror Comments: Learning sign language is interesting. They liked the story and new concepts. After viewing, they used sign language throughout the day. Age: 5–18; Length: 30 min.; Suggested Retail Price: $49.95, SIGN ENHANCERS, INC.

** WORKING IT OUT, A SURVIVAL GUIDE FOR KIDS (THE PERSONAL SAFETY SERIES): Every day, children are faced with issues involving peers that directly affect their personal safety. This program takes a no-nonsense look at peer-related issues. Adult Juror Comments: A serious and practical approach to real issues faced by kids. Addresses difficult concepts with role-playing sections that answer important questions. Implied issues are scary. "Not particularly enjoyable, but contains excellent information." Kid Juror Comments: "Now I know what to say to that jerk at school." Kids related to many of the situations. Adult intervention to help discuss the heavy material is useful. Some thought the acting was stilted and not very realistic. Age: 10–18; Length: 30 min.; Suggested Retail Price: $19.95, PSI PRODUCTIONS

10

Parenting

(Adults)

Introduction: Karen Kurz-Riemer

What do dog kennels, Tae Bo, and parenting have in common? They are the subjects of instructional videos and CD-ROMs. Whether for training a puppy, doing an aerobic workout, or caring for a newborn, videos and CD-ROMs are now available to make our task easier. Most parents would acknowledge there is probably no task more challenging than raising children, and an ever-expanding number of videos and CD-ROMs are available to help. Yet perhaps no endeavor is as emotionally charged, culturally influenced, and intensely personal as parenting. Those who take on the challenge of instructing parents must, in their teaching, reflect current research on child and parent development, convey their message in an accessible and engaging format, and allow for cultural and religious differences in parenting styles. That's a tall order. Videos such as *About Us: The Dignity of Children*, hosted by Oprah Winfrey, offer insight into a child's world and excellent diversity.

Public awareness of how research can inform parenting has been heightened by media coverage of neuroscientific findings that the structure of the human brain is affected by the quality and range of life experiences,

KAREN KURZ-RIEMER is a family education writer, consultant, and trainer based in Minneapolis. She has over twenty years of experience working with Minnesota's Statewide Early Childhood Family Education (ECFE) program, the oldest and largest program of its kind in the country. She is co-author with Martha Farrell Erickson of "Infants, Toddlers, and Families: A Framework for Support and Intervention" (Guilford Press, October 1999).

most dramatically from birth to age three. Although it doesn't always reflect the latest in child development research, the "correct" advice to parents has changed dramatically over the years. During the 1950s, parents
were told to feed their babies on a four-hour schedule, to formula-feed
rather than breast-feed because formula was more "modern" and nutritious, and not to hold their babies too much or respond too promptly to
their cries for fear of spoiling them. No longer.

We now turn to videos such as *A Baby's World, The First Years Last Forever,* and *Ten Things Every Child Needs,* which reinforce current thought
about how widely individual babies can differ, that feeding infants when
they are hungry is a more reliable way to ensure their healthy growth,
that breast milk is generally the most nourishing food for babies, and that
babies whose dependent needs are met are not "spoiled" but are actually
more likely to be emotionally secure and eager to learn.

In addition to communicating current theory and "best practice" to parents, it is important that parenting programs speak and write in plain English, without professional jargon, which conveys respect for parents' intelligence and experience. Parents and children featured in such programs
should be diverse by education, income, race, and age. Fathers and grandparents should be as visible as mothers. Useful messages should be offered
as suggestions or strategies, not prescriptions. They ought to reflect practical knowledge and awareness of the difficulties in raising children in two-
parent as well as single-parent families. *A New Idea for Special Education* and
Exercise With Daddy and Me are two examples of videos that promote
thoughtful parenting. It helps if programs explain the rationale for their
proposed techniques.

"Talking heads" are among the least-interesting formats for instructional
purposes. Parenting programs that use action shots of parents and children, interspersed with occasional featured experts, are more appealing to
most audiences. *The Touchpoint Boxed Set,* by Dr. T. Berry Brazelton, exemplifies how graphics and print add to clarity and aesthetic appeal. In recognition of the serious and challenging work of parenting, "cutesy" approaches that patronize or minimize the dignity of children or parents
should be avoided. At the same time, a sense of humor and a creative approach to the presentation strengthens the impact of the message. Since
parenting is as much an emotional experience as it is intellectual, programs
that address both means of perception are more powerful than programs
that focus on one level at the expense of the other.

Just as there is no single "right way" to raise children, there is no parenting video that appeals to all parents. *Finding Quality Child Care* supports
the idea that parenting practices vary by cultural and individual belief systems. Our interactions with children echo the conscious or unconscious

memories of our own childhood experiences and the positive and negative behavior of our own parents and caregivers. If a program can help us focus on our hopes and dreams for our children and give us information about the potential impact of various parenting practices, it will help us make more informed parenting choices. Effective parenting programs take into account the perspectives of diverse parents and diverse children, while conveying their research-based and practical messages clearly, creatively, and respectfully.

Educational/Instructional

* ABC'S OF TEACHING ABC'S, THE: How to teach the alphabet while going about daily activities. Puts parents back into the picture by encouraging them to act as their child's first teacher. Adult Juror Comments: Supports concept of "parents as children's first teachers," showing how kids learn through everyday activities. Adults felt there was too much pressure placed on kids to learn without having fun. Some phonics information is inaccurate. Length: 14 min.; Suggested Retail Price: $24.95, SOS VIDEOS, INC.

*** ABOUT US: THE DIGNITY OF CHILDREN: Oprah Winfrey offers a refreshing and insightful look into the world of children through their own words. Intimate portrait of what it's like to be a child and the very experience of childhood itself. Adult Juror Comments: A "must-see movie." Extremely insightful and an excellent parenting tool. Excellent diversity of children, including children of different abilities. Beautifully choreographed, scripted, and edited. Opens your eyes and your heart. Length: 94 min.; Suggested Retail Price: $19.98, STEEPLECHASE ENTERTAINMENT/ZIA FILM

*** BABY'S WORLD, A: Examines early child development and processes that transform infant capabilities into walking, talking human beings. Each episode looks at different human characteristics, tracing development through the first years of life. Adult Juror Comments: An extraordinary series rich with information. "Wonderful survey on cognitive and motor development in the first three years of life." Beautiful photography. Features diverse group of children and families. Adults had some safety concerns. Length: 180 min.; Suggested Retail Price: $39.95, DISCOVERY COMMUNICATIONS

** DAY ONE A POSITIVE BEGINNING: Practical tips for parents and caregivers to create positive environments, from birth, to promote children's fullest mental, physical, and emotional development. Used by hospitals, birthing centers, and parenting education programs. Adult Juror Comments: Well organized. Text is sophisticated, clearly presented, and articulated. Good sound, excellent visuals, good diversity but too wordy. Parenting advice is appropriate and suggestions easy to implement. Delivery lacks impact and appeal. Length: 30 min.; Suggested Retail Price: $125.00, NEW HORIZONS FOR LEARNING

* DISCIPLINE MAKES THE DIFFERENCE (SUCCESSFUL PARENTING): No one method of discipline works with all children, and no one method works every time. This video presents a range of alternatives that teach responsible behavior and self-control without damaging a child's self-esteem. Adult Juror Comments: Good examples of each disciplinary technique, with ways to proceed in a positive manner. Some thought portions were disrespectful, such as using the "time-out" chair. Low production and audio quality. Length: 17 min.; Suggested Retail Price: $49.95, ACTIVE PARENTING PUBLISHERS

** FIRST YEARS LAST FOREVER, THE: Hosted by actor Rob Reiner. New research in brain development reports vital importance of the relationship between caregiver and child in the critical first years of life. Discusses bonding and development, communication, health, and nutrition. Adult Juror Comments: Cohesive, informative, with good balance between narration and visual presentation. Sophisticated but not highbrow. Good for new parents. "Makes me want to have another baby." Length: 30 min.; Suggested Retail Price: $5.00, I AM YOUR CHILD

* MAKE WAY FOR BABY!: Focuses on the prenatal stimulation research done by Dr. Beatriz Manrique. Teaches pregnancy care, fetal development, calisthenics, and stimulation before birth that helps form a closer bond between parents and baby. Adult Juror Comments: Good message about connecting emotionally and physically with fetus early in pregnancy. Well organized, contains useful prenatal health information though some claimed benefits are highly speculative. Background music is at times intrusive. Length: 55 min.; Suggested Retail Price: $19.95, AMPHION COMMUNICATIONS

*** TEN THINGS EVERY CHILD NEEDS: Three leading authorities—Drs. T. Berry Brazelton, Bruce Perry, and Barbara Bowman—explain recent discoveries about how the brain develops and outline ten simple ways to build a better foundation for learning. Adult Juror Comments: Very well presented. Comments by experts are interspersed with shots of parents and children illustrating or demonstrating the statement made by the experts. Thought-provoking for parents. Should reinforce the importance of early learning. Length: 57 min.; Suggested Retail Price: $29.95, DREAMING BIG PUBLISHING, INC.

*** TOUCHPOINT BOXED SET, THE: Dr. T. Berry Brazelton, a leading pediatrician, guides new parents through every stage of parenting from pregnancy through toddlerhood. He helps parents understand and advance their child's development. Adult Juror Comments: Excellent video for new parents. Deals with major concerns. Shows great diversity. Brazelton points out the behaviors parents can identify as cues to their child's continuous changes. Fathers were delighted to hear the explanations and reassurances. Length: 45 min.; Suggested Retail Price: $39.95, PIPHER FILMS

CD-ROMs

* ACTIVE PARENTING TODAY: Develop courage, responsibility, and self-esteem in your child, using Active Parenting principles. Contains an hour of video illustrating styles of parenting, effective non-violent discipline skills, and logical consequences. Adult Juror Comments: Content is very good with realistic lessons that are valuable to any parent. The presentation lacks appeal. The video clips are only a few inches in diameter, the narrator is dull, and it lacks flexibility, forcing constant review of some segments. Age: ADULT; Suggested Retail Price: $39.95, ACTIVE PARENTING PUBLISHERS

How-To

*** CARING FOR YOUR NEWBORN (HEALTH ANSWERS FOR PARENTS): This educational, entertaining video answers the most frequently asked questions for new parents. Uses lighthearted vignettes to present situations all parents encounter. Four pediatricians discuss each topic. Adult Juror Comments: Comprehensive information in a clearly presented format, addresses primary concerns. Shows involvement of both parents in infant care. Organized so viewer can easily return to specific area in the future. "Though not high-tech, it works well." Humor suitable. Length: 40 min.; Suggested Retail Price: $19.95, AMERICAN ACADEMY OF PEDIATRICS

** EXERCISE WITH DADDY & ME: An amusing program for dads looking for a way to relate to their new babies. Offers ways for father and baby to interact through movement, music, and massage. Features a group discussion on fatherhood. Instructors are a registered nurse and a pediatrician. Adult Juror Comments: Well done, visually appealing, good pace. Useful if adults will interact with baby in the ways shown in video. Little cultural diversity. Great idea for engaging fathers. Instructions on how to hold baby properly are not very clear. Length: 50 min.; Suggested Retail Price: $14.95, MY BABY AND ME EXERCISE, INC.

* PARTY GAMES (ACTION GAMES): Teachers, parents, and caregivers can utilize these games for an entertaining, noncompetitive experience. All children are winners. Adult Juror Comments: Delightful ideas for easy, inexpensive games. Information about the skills these activities help cultivate. Simply produced with captions that emphasize certain points. Little diversity. Useful for both parents or providers. Length: 25 min.; Suggested Retail Price: $14.95, ACTION GAMES

Music

** MAKING MUSIC WITH CHILDREN: AGES 3 – 7: John Langstaff demonstrates ways to introduce children to music. Includes singing games, rhythm and movement activities, and music from different cultures. Suitable for teacher training or parent education. Adult Juror Comments: Explanations are clear and understandable. Respect for children is evident. Shows diverse group of children. Useful for a nonmusical adult who is interested in singing with kids. Length: 59 min.; Suggested Retail Price: $24.95, LANGSTAFF VIDEO PROJECT

** MAKING MUSIC WITH CHILDREN: AGES 7 – 11: John Langstaff demonstrates easy, effective ways to engage children in music. Includes rhythm and movement games for building orchestras out of household objects. Lyrics and music are included. Adult Juror Comments: Quite useful for music teachers preparing to teach new songs to a class. Best when viewed and used a few songs at a time. Excellent information but the speaker lost the audience's interest quickly. Length: 59 min.; Suggested Retail Price: $24.95, LANGSTAFF VIDEO PROJECT

* SONGS AND FINGERPLAYS FOR LITTLE ONES: Teaches hand and body movements to accompany seventeen songs. A day-care provider engages and entertains children at the same time. Adult Juror Comments: Delightful selection of songs and fingerplays, in appropriate sequencing from easy to difficult. Best used as a teaching aid. Adult caregiver is an excellent role model, showing understanding for child reluctant to participate. Length: 30 min.; Suggested Retail Price: $14.95, CLEVER PRODUCTIONS

Special Interest

** BREAKTHROUGH: HOW TO REACH STUDENTS WITH AUTISM: A hands-on, how-to program for teachers and parents, featuring "Teacher of the Year" Karen Sewell. Sewell demonstrates the rigorous but compassionate program she has developed over her career, making significant progress with a four-year-old student. Adult Juror Comments: Excellent, helpful information on living with an autistic child. Shows the benefits of early intervention and what the future holds. Quality production offers specific techniques showing problems, progress, and completion. Length: 26 min.; Suggested Retail Price: $59.00, ATTAINMENT COMPANY

** FINDING QUALITY CHILDCARE (THE PARENTS' SURVIVAL VIDEO SERIES): Easy-to-follow tips with solid guidelines for assessing the quality of any child care program. Recommends what to look for and which questions to ask. Experts address health, curriculum, safety, and more. Includes quality checklist. Adult Juror Comments: Comprehensive observations and descriptions of different types of child care. Providers, consultants, center directors, and parents provide information and sound advice. Well produced, easy to follow. Length: 45 min.; Suggested Retail Price: $19.95, QUARTET CREATIVE SERIES

** NEW IDEA FOR SPECIAL EDUCATION, A: Designed for parents, educators, and other professionals working with children with special needs. Sensitively produced, offers guidance and valuable resources. Includes information about the new regulations governing placement, discipline, and referral for Individual Education Programs. Adult Juror Comments: Good basic guide. Stresses importance of finding a teacher or administrator to help guide parents through the process. Respectful. Presents the law clearly. "Professional content is excellent." Length: 45 min.; Suggested Retail Price: $49.95, EDVANTAGE MEDIA, INC.

* PARENTING THE GIFTED CHILD, PART I AND II: Is your child gifted? Video explains the characteristics of gifted children and offers parenting tips. Adult Juror Comments: Covers the current knowledge on gifted children. Presentation is basically a videotaped lecture. Defines giftedness as based on child's test scores. Could be beneficial to parents, teachers, and administrators. Length: 96 min.; Suggested Retail Price: $39.95, NICHOLS-GALVIN

** STRAIGHT TALK ABOUT AUTISM WITH PARENTS AND KIDS: Features interviews with autistic children and their parents. The first video looks at early childhood, the second investigates adolescent issues. Areas covered include communication difficulties, social skills, transition, and difficulty of diagnosis. Adult Juror Comments: Emotional insight and encouragement to those working with autistic children and teens, stresses potential of the individual. Creative and resourceful ideas on how to develop socialization situations. Reverberates with experience of daily life. Not a kid title, although may be used with teenagers who have autistic siblings or for sensitivity training. Length: 79 min.; Suggested Retail Price: $129.00, ATTAINMENT COMPANY

** THREE R'S FOR SPECIAL EDUCATION, THE: Practical guide designed for parents of children with special needs. Professionals and experienced parents explain how to advocate on behalf of such children. Discusses parental rights, legal underpinnings, and processes of special education. Adult Juror Comments: Empowering, helpful, and reassuring. Offers an excellent resource targeted for parents of children with special needs. Discusses financial issues. Thorough and careful presentation for parents of children with special needs. Length: 60 min. Suggested Retail Price: $50.00, EDVANTAGE MEDIA, INC.

** TAMING THE STRONG-WILLED CHILD: Family psychologist John Rosemond shares six reliable tips for taming the strong-willed child. Various scenes demonstrate both appropriate and inappropriate methods of interacting with such children. Adult Juror Comments: Simple production with content that is respectful of children. Ideas are consistent with current theory, translated into action. Appropriate for group use. Includes follow-up activities. Jurors had trouble using the words "taming" and "obey." Length: 24 min.; Suggested Retail Price: $19.95, PARENT POWER PRODUCTIONS, INC

** WHAT CHILDREN NEED IN ORDER TO READ: Provides research-based information on the skills needed by children for success in reading, including knowledge of the alphabet, sound structure of language, and the pleasure of books. Resource for anyone working with young children. Adult Juror Comments: This is not really a teaching video but contains a discussion about reading. Presentation is rather dry. Combines commentary with singing and reading by children. Suitable for teachers, librarians, or parents interested in helping their child read. Kid Juror Comments: Age: ADULT; Length: 30min.; Suggested Retail Price: $35.00, DEBECK EDUCATIONAL VIDEO

PART III

Family Films
for
Teenagers

11

Family Films for Teenagers

Peter M. Nichols

Introduction

A few general guidelines prevailed in the compilation of this list. First, teenagers aren't that drawn to older films, though there are many they would enjoy if they gave them a chance. For this reason, there is some segregation according to year. Action films, comedies, and dramas released prior to 1980 (an arbitrary date) are put into a separate category called Oldies. Older animated films, documentaries, musicals, and westerns are not separated and are listed with newer entries.

Many films in all categories have sequels, which in most cases (but not all) are inferior to the original. If a sequel is worthy in its own right, it is listed separately. Otherwise sequels are usually mentioned in the description of the first film.

A word about ratings. The vast majority of these five hundred films are rated PG or PG-13, but certain movies with an R rating are also included if they have proved popular with teenagers and are generally regarded as having elements of value and artistic merit. In these cases, the R is noted at the end of the entry.

Finally, the studios and companies listed with each title are the distributors of the film on video. In some cases, a movie may be out of current video distribution, but, of course, it may appear on cable.

PETER M. NICHOLS writes the Home Video column for *The Times*.

Action and Adventure

The Abyss. Ed Harris, Mary Elizabeth Mastrantonio, Todd Graff, Michael Biehn. Divers descend to a crippled nuclear submarine and discover a mysterious and all-powerful watery force. 1989. Directed by James Cameron. Fox.

The Adventures of Baron Munchausen. John Neville, Eric Idle, Sarah Polley, Valentina Cortese. On his exotic travels, the Baron encounters Venus and the King of the Moon and nothing is quite as it seems. 1989. Directed by Terry Gilliam. Columbia Tri-Star.

The Adventures of Milo & Otis. A Japanese chidren's film tells the story of a farm dog and cat and their adventures after the cat is swept away on a river. Sorry, but no humans allowed and none appear. 1989. Directed by Masanori Hata. Columbia Tri-Star.

Air Force One. Harrison Ford, Gary Oldman, Glenn Close. The plane carrying the American President (an honorable, courageous fellow) is hijacked by a group of Kazakhstan terrorists who want the release of their own President (a mass murderer), who's been snatched by the Americans. 1997. Columbia Tri-Star. R.

Anaconda. Ice Cube, Jon Voight, Jennifer Lopez, Eric Stoltz. Once upon a time in the Amazon there was this forty-foot-long snake that tore down houses and swallowed people. 1996. Directed by Luis Llosa. Columbia Tri-Star.

Arachnophobia. Jeff Daniels, John Goodman. A doctor who's terrified of spiders (arachnophobic) joins forces with an ace exterminator to battle a deadly super specimen that migrates from South America and attacks a small town. 1990. Directed by Frank Marshall. Out of video distribution.

Backdraft. Robert De Niro, Kurt Russell, William Baldwin, Donald Sutherland. Chicago firemen battle spectacular blazes set by an arsonist in a film weak on plot but strong on special effects. 1991. Directed by Ron Howard. Universal. R.

Back to the Future. Michael J. Fox, Christopher Lloyd. A mad scientist customizes a DeLorean automobile to transport a young man back to 1955, where he must accomplish a set of heroics and get back to the future just in the knick of time. 1985. Directed by Robert Zemeckis. Universal.

Batman. Michael Keaton, Jack Nicholson, Kim Basinger. The Caped Crusader takes on the Joker in the first and by far the best of the Batman films. 1989. Directed by Tim Burton. Fox.

Blade Runner. Harrison Ford, Rutger Hauer. Millennium anyone? In 21st-century Los Angeles, a police officer tracks down a rogue band of "replicants" on the prowl for ways to extend their lifetimes, which only lasts days. 1982. Directed by Ridley Scott. Columbia Tri-Star. R.

The Bodyguard. Kevin Costner, Whitney Houston. A plain vanilla former Secret Service man takes up security duties for a pop star. 1992. Directed by Mick Jackson. Warner. R.

Buffy the Vampire Slayer. Kristy Swanson, Luke Perry, Donald Sutherland. A campy spoof turns an L.A. mall girl loose for some no-nonsense retaliation against an army of vampires. 1992. Directed by Fran Rubel Kazui. Fox.

Chain Reaction. Keanu Reeves, Morgan Freeman. A young lab assistant battles unknown agents for control of a pollution-free source of energy. 1996. Directed by Andrew Davis. Fox.

Congo. Dylan Walsh, Laura Linney, Ernie Hudson. A mission into the bush runs into skulduggery as it tries to return a baby gorilla named Amy to her natural habitat and find a lost city. 1995. Directed by Frank Marshall. Paramount.

Crocodile Dundee. Paul Hogan, Linda Kozlowski. Taken with a colorful local she finds in the Outback, a New York reporter brings him home and turns him loose in the big city. 1986. Directed by Peter Faiman. Paramount.

Days of Thunder. Tom Cruise, Robert Duvall, Randy Quaid, Nicole Kidman. In the first race film that strapped a camera to a car, a hot young driver has to learn to develop his talent, keep the girl, and dodge the bad guy at 200 m.p.h. 1990. Directed by Tony Scott. Paramount.

Deep Impact. Morgan Freeman, Robert Duvall, Lea Leoni, Elijah Wood. Americans from all walks try to make the best of it as an incoming meteorite kicks up a mile-high tidal wave and obliterates about everything else. 1998. Directed by Mimi Leder. Paramount.

Dick Tracy. Warren Beatty, Madonna, Charlie Korsmo, Glenne Headly, Al Pacino. A stylistically colorful telling of the comic strip detective's tale with great music to boot. 1990. Directed by Warren Beatty. Touchstone.

The Empire Strikes Back. Mark Hamill, Carrie Fisher, Harrison Ford, Billy Dee Williams, Alec Guinness. In the second film of the "Star Wars" trilogy, Luke Skywalker trains to become a Jedi knight and battle Darth Vader. 1980. Directed by Irvin Kershner. Fox.

Flipper. Elijah Wood, Paul Hogan. A tough city kid and his crusty uncle take up the cause of an orphaned dolphin, which leads them to an evil environmental polluter. 1996. Directed by Alan Shapiro. Universal.

Godzilla. Matthew Broderick, Jean Reno, Hank Azaria. It's not the greatest movie, but he's big and loud and hatches 200 babies (have you ever seen a lizard punch a hole in the old Pan Am building?) 1998. Directed by Roland Emmerich. Columbia Tri-Star.

Goldeneye. Pierce Brosnan, Famke Janssen. With the Cold War over, Bond takes on the Russian Mafia, which wants to sabotage a satellite and wreck global financial markets. 1995. Directed by Martin Campbell. MGM.

The Hunt for Red October. Sean Connery, Alec Baldwin, Richard Jordan, Scott Glenn. A rogue Soviet submarine heads for United States waters with hunter-killer subs from both countries in hot pursuit. Leave it to Tom Clancy, on whose novel this film is based. 1990. Directed by John Mc-Tiernan. Paramount.

The Incredible Hulk. Bill Bixby, Susan Sullivan, Lou Ferrigno. A scientist achieves super size and strength after taking on too many gamma rays, but forget the social life. 1977. Directed by Kenneth Johnson. Universal.

Independence Day. Bill Pullman, Will Smith, Jeff Goldblum, Judd Hirsch. Confronted with a gigantic alien spacecraft carrying creatures intent on appropriating the planet, the American President rallies mankind and jumps into a jet fighter himself. 1996. Directed by Roland Emmerich. Fox.

Indiana Jones and the Last Crusade. Harrison Ford, Sean Connery, Denholm Elliott. Indie and his dad, a renowned archeologist, race the Nazis for the Holy Grail. 1989. Directed by Steven Spielberg. Paramount.

Indiana Jones and the Temple of Doom. Harrison Ford, Kate Capshaw. In Indie's second outing (after "Raiders of the Lost Arc"), he's off to retrieve the Ankara Stone and break up a cult that has enslaved scores of children. 1984. Directed by Steven Spielberg. Paramount.

Jackie Chan's First Strike. Jackie Chan. One is never sure exactly what is going on in a zany plot, but a weapons ring challenges the Chinese detective with the lightning hands and feet. 1996. Directed by Stanley Tong. New Line.

The Jewel of the Nile. Michael Douglas, Kathleen Turner, Danny DeVito. In the sequel to "Romancing the Stone," Jack the adventurer seeks to rescue Joan the romance novelist from the hands of a North African no-goodnick. 1985. Directed by Lewis Teague. Fox.

Jumanji. Robin Williams, Kirsten Dunst, Bonnie Hunt, Bradley Michael Pierce. A board game with a jungle theme draws in two youngsters, who unwittingly release a horde of wild animals into the real world. 1995. Directed by Joe Johnston. Columbia Tri-Star.

Jurassic Park. Sam Neill, Laura Dern, Jeff Goldblum. Genetically reproduced from DNA, dinosaurs and other prehistoric creatures get loose and go on a tear on a remote island. 1993. Directed by Steven Spielberg. Universal.

The Karate Kid. Ralph Macchio, Noriyuki Morita, Elisabeth Shue. A young boy learns all the moves, and their meaning, from an old master. 1984. Directed by John G. Avildsen. Columbia Tri-Star.

Lethal Weapon. Mel Gibson, Danny Glover, Gary Busey. In the original and best film of the series, a pair of freestyle Miami detectives, one of whom is totally crazy and the other long-suffering, take on a heroin ring. 1987. Directed by Richard Donner. Warner.

Lost in Space. William Hurt, Mimi Rogers, Gary Oldman, Heather Graham. With Earth almost uninhabitable in 2058, a Swiss Family Robinson is sent off to colonize another planet. But where is it? 1998. Directed by Stephen Hopkins. New Line.

The Lost World: Jurassic Park. Jeff Goldblum, Julianne Moore, Vince Vaughn. Don't look now, but those prehistoric critters are still bopping around that island off Costa Rica. 1997. Directed by Steven Spielberg. Universal.

Mad Max. Mel Gibson, Joanne Samuel, Hugh Keays-Byrne. In a post-apocalyptic world, a lone biker pits himself against a gang that killed his family. 1980. Directed by George Miller. Artisan. R.

The Mask of Zorro. Antonio Banderas, Anthony Hopkins, Catherine Zeta-Jones. The aging first Zorro passes on all the old tricks to his younger replacement, the better to foil a mortal enemy. 1998. Directed by Martin Campbell. Columbia Tri-Star.

Memphis Belle. Matthew Modine, John Lithgow, Eric Stoltz. A feature film based on a documentary tells the story of a young B-17 crew, the first to complete 25 missions. 1990. Directed by Michael Caton-Jones. Warner.

Men in Black. Tommy Lee Jones, Will Smith, Linda Fiorentino, Rip Torn, Vincent D'Onofrio. Action mixes with comedy as Government agents assigned to keep track of aliens zero in on an extraterrestrial bad boy who would destroy us. 1997. Directed by Barry Sonnenfeld. Columbia Tri-Star.

Mission: Impossible. Tom Cruise, Jon Voight, Emmanuelle Beart, Ving Rhames. Based on the television show, a very big action film pits a young and suspicious agent against a constantly shifting background of double-dealing treachery. 1996. Directed by Brian DePalma. Paramount.

The Net. Sandra Bullock, Jeremy North. The going gets perilous for a reclusive computer analyst as she begins to learn too much about a plot to crack top-secret databases. 1995. Directed by Irwin Winkler. Columbia Tri-Star.

The Newton Boys. Matthew McConaughey, Skeet Ulrich, Ethan Hawke, Vincent D'Onofrio. A band of roistering Texas brothers bank rob their way from Texas to Toronto in the 20's and 30's. 1997. Directed by Richard Linklater. Fox.

Pink Cadillac. Clint Eastwood, Bernadette Peters, Timothy Carhart. A bail bondsman helps a mother and baby flee some bad guys. 1989. Directed by Buddy Van Horn. Warner.

The Pelican Brief. Julia Roberts, Denzel Washington, John Heard. A law student lands too close to the truth for her own health and welfare after she writes a fictional brief that conjectures about the murder of two Supreme Court Justices. 1993. Directed by Alan J. Pakula, based on the John Grisham thriller. Warner.

Raiders of the Lost Ark. Harrison Ford, Karen Allen, Wolf Kahler. In the first of the Indie adventures, Indiana Jones vies with Nazis for the Ark of the Covenant. 1981. Directed by Steven Spielberg. Paramount.

The River Wild. Meryl Streep, Kevin Bacon, John C. Reilly, David Strathairn, Joseph Mazzello. The scenery is spectacular but the company could be improved upon as two escaped killers force themselves on a family on a white-water rafting trip. 1994. Directed by Curtis Hanson. Universal.

Robocop. The brain of a Detroit cop becomes the nerve center for a crime-busting robot in a desolate but entertaining view of the future. 1987. Directed by Paul Verhoeven. Orion. R.

Romancing the Stone. Michael Douglas, Kathleen Turner, Danny DeVito. In the first of the "Stone" movies, a romance novelist and a soldier of fortune get into adventurous difficulties over a mysterious map leading to hidden treasure. 1984. Directed by Robert Zemeckis. Fox.

The Rocketeer. Bill Campbell, Jennifer Connelly. Alan Arkin, Timothy Dalton. Wonderful special effects also star as a 1930's stunt pilot develops a jet backpack coveted by the Nazis. 1991. Directed by Joe Johnston. Disney.

Runaway Train. Jon Voight, Eric Roberts, Rebecca DeMornay. Two escaped convicts find themselves on a train without a crew and running out of control through northwestern Canada. 1985. Directed by Andrei Konchalovsky. MGM. R.

Rush Hour. Jackie Chan, Chris Tucker. In one of many virtually interchangeable Jackie Chan flicks, a motor-mouthed Chicago cop is assigned to help a nimble Chinese detective out of a jam with a Hong Kong drug lord. 1998. Directed by Brett Ratner. New Line.

Sneakers. Robert Redford, Sidney Poitier, River Phoenix, Dan Aykroyd, Ben Kingsley. Five computer hackers get together on a project to steal a black box of security code. 1992. Directed by Phil Alden Robinson. Universal.

Speed. Sandra Bullock, Keanu Reeves, Dennis Hopper. A bus rigged with a bomb will explode if the vehicle slows to under 50 miles per hour—and good luck in that Los Angeles traffic! 1994. Directed by Jan De Bont. Fox. R.

Stargate. Kurt Russell, James Spader, Jaye Davidson. A military swat team leaps through a huge ring dating to ancient Egyptian times and finds itself in a strange civilization on another planet. 1994. Directed by Roland Emmerich. Artisan.

Star Trek 2: The Wrath of Khan. William Shatner, Leonard Nimoy, Ricardo Montalban. Everybody has favorites among the 10 big-screen "Star Trek" films, but the second one, in which Kirk and the *Enterprise* encounter an old enemy, is preferred by many. 1982. Directed by Nicholas Meyer. Paramount.

Star Trek: First Contact. Patrick Stuart, Jonathon Frakes, Brent Spiner, LeVar Burton. In the eighth adventure, Captain Picard is at the controls of the *Enterprise,* now threatened by a force called the Borg, whose evil designs go all the way back to 2063. 1996. Directed by Jonathon Frakes. Paramount.

Terminator 2: Judgment Day. Arnold Schwarzenegger, Linda Hamilton, Edward Furlong. A super cyborg returns to Earth to save a young boy destined to lead civilization in a post-nuclear world, but they both have to survive the gelatinous killing machine known as T-1000. 1991. Directed by James Cameron. Artisan. R.

Top Gun. Tom Cruise, Kelly McGillis, Val Kilmer. Tom Skerritt, Anthony Edwards. It's a fantasy tale (and one of the most popular videos of all time), but hotshot Navy pilots put on quite a show in the wild blue yonder. 1986. Directed by Tony Scott. Paramount.

Turner and Hooch. Tom Hanks, Mare Winningham. On a murder investigation, a fastidious cop gets paired with a huge slobbering hound who witnessed the crime. 1989. Directed by Roger Spottiswoode. Touchstone.

Twister. Bill Paxton. Helen Hunt, Gary Elwes. A crew of tornado chasers catch up to some huge winds in central Oklahoma. 1996. Directed by Jan De Bont. Warner.

The Untouchables. Kevin Costner, Sean Connery, Robert De Niro. The T-man Eliot Ness emerges from the TV series to battle Al Capone and the rest of organized crime in the 1920's. 1987. Directed by Brian DePalma. Paramount. R.

Waterworld. Kevin Costner, Dennis Hopper, Jeanne Tripplehorn. A mutant man-fish roams a post-apocalyptic world comprised entirely of water and terrorized by a mob of renegades called the Smokers. 1995. Directed by Kevin Reynolds. Universal.

Animated

Aladdin. Voices of Robin Williams and many others. Teen-agers will be amused by Williams's antics as the big blue genie in the story of boy courts the princess. 1992. Directed by Ron Clements and John Musker. Disney.

Antz. Voices of Woodie Allen, Gene Hackman, Sharon Stone, Sylvester Stallone, others. In another recent ant adventure, an upstart worker with a genius for one-liners (Allen) helps about a billion of his comrades from the genocidal plans of General Mandible (Hackman). 1998. Directed by Eric Darnell and Tim Johnson. Dreamworks.

Bambi. The great old classic that so affected baby-boomers is still worth a look today. 1942. Directed by David Hand. Disney.

Beauty and the Beast. With music by Alan Menken and Howard Ashman, this is the first animated film to be nominated for an Oscar as best picture. 1991. Directed by Kirk Wise and Gary Trousdale. Disney.

Beavis and Butt-Head Do America. Hired by a man named Muddy to kill a redhead named Dallas, the boys wreak havoc from coast to coast, destroying Hoover Dam and alienating everybody from Government agents to Chelsea Clinton. 1996. Directed by Mike Judge. Paramount.

A Bug's Life. Voices of Dave Foley, Kevin Spacey, Julia Louis-Dreyfus, Phyllis Diller, others. A bumbling but determined ant enlists a troupe of road show performers to help save his people from some domineering grasshoppers. 1998. Directed by John Lasseter. Disney.

Fantastic Planet. A race of humanoids gets together to fight giant oppressors in the animated French sci-fi tale. 1973. Directed by René Laloux. Various distributors.

Heavy Traffic. A long way from Disney, Ralph Bashki's film checks out the underside of the urban world. 1973. Directed by Ralph Bakshi. Warner.

The Lion King. Voices of Matthew Broderick, Jeremy Irons, James Earl Jones. If he's ever to be king, Simba the lion cub must overcome the designs of his treacherous Uncle Scar. Is this the best of the major Disney animated films? 1994. Directed by Rob Minkoff and Roger Allers.

Pocahontas. Voices of Mel Gibson, Irene Bedard, Judy Kuhn. The Indian maiden and the Englishman, Captain John Smith, are caught in a clash of cultures. 1995. Directed by Mike Gabriel and Eric Goldberg. Disney.

Small Soldiers. Kirsten Dunst, Gregory Edward Smith, with the voices of Jay Mohr, Denis Leary, David Cross, Kirsten Dunst, Tommy Lee Jones, others. Outfitted with a microchip intended for weaponry, some G.I.-Joe-type toys turn even more warlike and challenge two teen-agers to quell the miniature menace. Joe Dante's film mixes computer animation and live action. 1998. Dreamworks.

Space Jam. Michael Jordan, Bill Murray, Wayne Knight. In another combined animated-live action tale, Jordan must play some roundball against space invaders who'd like to abscond with Bugs Bunny. 1996. Directed by Joe Pytka. Warner.

Toy Story. Voices of Tom Hanks, Tim Allen, Annie Potts, others. In the first completely computer-animated film, a child's pull-string cowboy named Woody and a rival play space ranger named Buzz Lightyear must join forces to survive in the outside world. 1995. Directed by John Lasseter. Touchstone.

Wallace and Gromit: The Wrong Trousers. In one of several clay-animation tales by Nick Park (this one won an Academy Award), Wallace and his canine sidekick encounter stolen diamonds, nasty penguins, and a pair of "techno trousers." 1993. Fox.

Who Framed Roger Rabbit. Bob Hoskins, Christopher Lloyd. Cartoon and live action come together as a detective who hates cartoons discovers a conspiracy to wipe them all out. 1988. Directed by Robert Zemeckis. Touchstone.

Yellow Submarine. In a phantasmagorical fantasy of animation and imagery filled with their songs, the Beatles rescue Dr. Pepper, Strawberry Fields, and Pepperland from the Blue Meanies. 1968. Directed by George Duning and Dick Emery. Not in distribution.

Documentary

Fast, Cheap and Out of Control. A topiary gardener, a lion tamer, a scientist who creates robotic insects, and a lover of mole rats are unlikely subjects of the same movie in Eroll Morris's keenly observed and intriguingly shot film. 1997. Columbia Tri-Star.

Gimme Shelter. At the end of the 60's, 300,000 people get close to out of control at the infamous Rolling Stones concert in Altamount, CA. 1970. Directed by David Maysles. Columbia Tri-Star.

A Hard Day's Night. The Beatles trot through a typical daily routine, as if there ever was such a thing. Directed by Richard Lester. 1964. MPI.

Hoop Dreams. Two Chicago inner-city kids, Arthur Agee and William Gates, feed themselves to the basketball mill at St. Joseph, a mostly white Catholic high school, in the hopes of landing scholarships to play big-time college ball. 1994. Directed by Steve James. New Line.

Microcosmos. You're right in there with them, and they're right out there with you, in this intense, graphic exploration of the world of insects. 1996. Directed by Claude Nuridsany and Marie Perennou. Touchstone.

Soul in the Hole. A driving playground basketball coach bullies and babies Kenny's Kings, his team of Brooklyn street kids, toward a city title. 1998. Directed by Danielle Gardner. Crocus.

The Thin Blue Line. Randall Adams is wrongfully convicted of shooting a Dallas cop in 1977. 1988. Directed by Eroll Morris. HBO.

When We Were Kings. George Plimpton, Spike Lee and Norman Mailer all appear in Leon Gast's chronicle of the Muhammad Ali–George Foreman fight in Zaire, the rumble in the jungle, which won the Oscar as best documentary in 1996. Polygram.

Woodstock. Youngsters will see where a lot of their parents' generation were headed more than 400,000 strong on that summer weekend in 1969. Directed by Michael Wadleigh. Warner.

Comedy

Ace Ventura: Pet Detective. Jim Carrey. Ace locates those missing pets, large or small, saving a dolphin in time for the Super Bowl. 1993 . Directed by Tom Shadyac. Warner.

Addams Family Values. Raul Julia, Anjelica Huston, Christina Ricci, Joan Cusack, Christopher Lloyd. A new arrival touches off sibling rivalry and prompts the Addams parents to hire a serial killer as nanny to watch over the brood. 1993. Directed by Barry Sonnenfeld. Paramount.

Airplane! Robert Hays, Julie Hagerty, Lloyd Bridges. In the silly but riotous mother of all movie lampoons, a former pilot with a fear of flying takes over an airliner after the crew comes down with food poisoning. 1980. Directed by Jerry Zucker, Jim Abrahams and David Zucker. Paramount.

Annie Hall. Woodie Allen, Diane Keaton, Tony Roberts. Leaving no neurosis unturned, Allen's classic dissects the relationship between a Jewish comic and a WASP named Annie. 1977. MGM.

Austin Powers: International Man of Mystery. Mike Myers, Elizabeth Hurley. A 60's spy (Mr. Myers) and his enemy, Dr. Evil (Mr. Myers), freeze themselves for 30 years and awaken to renew the rivalry in a wild new world in which they are totally out of date. 1997. Directed by Jay Roach. New Line.

Beetlejuice. Michael Keaton, Alec Baldwin, Geena Davis. In a highly inventive scenario, a ghost is hired to evict the new owners of a house belonging to a deceased couple. 1988. Directed by Tim Burton. Warner.

Beverly Hills Cop. Eddie Murphy, Judge Reinhold, John Ashton, Lisa Eilbacher. When a friend is murdered in Los Angeles, a fast-talking Detroit cop barges in on the West Coast upper crust and uncovers a stolen art ring. 1984. Directed by Martin Brest. Paramount.

Bill & Ted's Excellent Adventure. Keanu Reeves, Alex Winter, George Carlin. In a make-or-break situation on their history final, two teen-agers get into a special phone booth and go time traveling to actually meet some of those dudes they're being tested on. 1989. Directed by Stephen Herek. Columbia Tri-Star.

Billy Madison. Adam Sandler, Darren McGavin. A 20-something idiot is promised he can take over his father's hotel chain if he prepares by repeating grades 1 to 12. 1994. Directed by Tamra Davis. Universal.

Blazing Saddles. Cleavon Little, Harvey Korman, Madeline Kahn, Gene Wilder, Mel Brooks. The notorious convict Black Bart gets to go free if he pins on a sheriff's badge and cleans up a down-and-dirty frontier town. 1974. Directed by Mel Brooks. Warner. R.

The Blues Brothers. John Belushi, Dan Aykroyd, James Brown. Jake and Elwood Blues run riot in Chicago as they try to put their band back together and earn $5,000 for the orphanage where they grew up. 1980. Directed by John Landis. Universal.

Caddyshack. Chevy Chase, Rodney Dangerfield, Ted Knight, Bill Murray, Michael O'Keefe. Silliness scores a hole in one at a country club beset by a crass developer and a lunatic greenskeeper who chases gophers. 1980. Directed by Harold Ramis. Warner.

City Slickers. Billy Crystal, Jack Palance. A group of saddle-sore New York tenderfeet get some rough-and-ready Western religion during a sojourn at a cattle ranch. 1991. Directed by Ron Underwood. Columbia Tri-Star.

Clueless. Alicia Silverstone. Like, hello? A spoiled rich kid throws her trust fund and very considerable social weight around as she arranges the affairs of her high school circle. 1995. Directed by Amy Heckerling. Paramount.

Coming to America. Eddie Murphy, Arsenio Hall, James Earl Jones. To avoid an arranged marriage back home, an African prince takes on disguises to better court the beautiful alternative whom he finds in New York. 1988. Directed by John Landis. Paramount.

Dirty Rotten Scoundrels. Michael Caine, Steve Martin, Glenne Headly, Barbara Harris. A crude American con man cuts in on the turf of his suave European counterpart, inspiring a bet over which of them can seduce and swindle a rich heiress. 1988. Directed by Frank Oz. Orion.

Dr. Dolittle. Eddie Murphy, Oliver Platt, Peter Boyle, and the voices of Albert Brooks, Chris Rock, John Leguizamo, Garry Shandling, others. In a remake of the 1967 film, the good doctor rediscovers his talent for talking to animals, who with this kind of voice talent talk right back. 1998. Directed by Betty Thomas. Fox.

Dumb and Dumber. Jim Carrey, Jeff Daniels, Lauren Holly. To return a bag of money to a beautiful woman, an idiotic limo driver and a moronic dog groomer head cross country in a van disguised as a sheepdog. 1994. Directed by Peter Farrelly. Turner.

Fast Times at Ridgemont High. Sean Penn, Jennifer Jason Leigh, Judge Reinhold. Experimenting with about everything they can get hold of, California teen-agers come of age and then some. 1982. Directed by Amy Heckerling. Universal.

Ferris Bueller's Day Off. Matthew Broderick, Mia Sara, Alan Ruck. A slick teen-ager feigns illness to skip school and take off in his friend's dad's antique Ferrari. 1986. Directed by John Hughes. Paramount.

Fletch. Chevy Chase, Dana Wheeler-Nicholson, Tim Matheson, Joe Don Baker. A rich man who says he is dying hires an investigative reporter to murder him for the life insurance. But then the reporter uncovers a drug-smuggling ring and things start to get complicated. 1985. Directed by Michael Ritchie. Universal.

Flubber. Robin Williams, Marcia Gay Harden. In a remake of "The Absent Minded Professor," a mad scientist invents some flying green gunk that cures many ills and attracts the most ruthless of business people. 1997. Directed by Les Mayfield. Touchstone.

George of the Jungle. Brendan Fraser, Leslie Mann, Thomas Haden Church. In a live-action version of the 60's cartoon, a rich girl takes a shine to a jungle boy named George and, ditching her loathesome fiancé, takes him back to San Francisco. But George hears that an ape he calls brother has been kidnapped and returns to the bush. 1997. Directed by Sam Weisman. Touchstone.

Ghostbusters. Bill Murray, Dan Aykroyd, Harold Ramis, Sigourney Weaver, Annie Potts. A group of investigators specializing in what they call the paranormal get to work ridding Manhattan of its infestation of ghosts. 1984. Directed by Ivan Reitman. Columbia Tri-Star.

The Gods Must Be Crazy. Marius Weyers, Sandra Prinsloo, Louw Verwey. Slapstick adventures ensue when a Coke bottle falls out of a plane and lands among jungle people who regard it as a gift from the gods. 1984. Directed by Jamie Uys. Fox.

Gregory's Girl. Gordon John Sinclair, Dee Hepburn, Chic Murray. In Scotland a gawky teen-ager falls for his high school's female soccer goalie. 1982. Directed by Bill Forsyth. HBO.

Groundhog Day. Bill Murray, Andie MacDowell, Chris Elliott. An odious weatherman goes to cover groundhog day in Punxatawney, PA, where he gets trapped by a blizzard he didn't know was coming and is forced to stay there living the same day over and over. 1993. Directed by Harold Ramis. Columbia Tri-Star.

Happy Gilmore. Adam Sandler. Sure, it's a terrible movie, but it's high Sandler. A total idiot transfers his hockey skills, or lack of them, to the golf course, where he revolutionizes the game while lowering its level of decorum. 1996. Directed by Dennis Dugan. Universal.

House Party. Christopher Reid, Robin Harris, Martin Lawrence, Christopher Martin. Black youngsters throw a 50's party hip-hop style, with a kid called the Kid breaking out of the house and getting into all kinds of scrapes with thugs and cops before he gets to the big bash. Lots of rap and hot dancing. 1990. Directed by Reginald Hudlin. New Line.

Jerry Maguire. Tom Cruise, Cuba Gooding Jr., Renee Zellweger, Kelly Preston, Bonnie Hunt. Show me the money. A sports agent finds religion of a kind and actually starts caring about the athletes he represents. 1996. Directed by Cameron Crowe. Columbia Tri-Star. R.

Jumpin' Jack Flash. Whoopi Goldberg, Stephen Collins, Carol Kane, Annie Potts. A bank clerk gets into the humorous reaches of international intrigue when her computer terminal flashes a call for help from a British spy in the Soviet Union. 1986. Directed by Penny Marshall. Fox.

Kindergarten Cop. Arnold Schwarzenegger, Penelope Ann Miller, Pamela Reed, Linda Hunt. In pursuit of a drug lord, a large lunk of a cop goes undercover as a substitute teacher. 1990. Directed by Ivan Reitman. Universal.

Kingpin. Woody Harrelson, Randy Quaid, Vanessa Angel, Bill Murray. A rundown ex-bowling star with a rubber hand finds rejuvenation in the form of a young Amish ten-pin phenom, whom he takes to a Reno tournament in hopes of cashing in big. 1996. Directed by Peter Farrelly and Bobby Farrelly. MGM.

King Ralph. John Goodman, Peter O'Toole, Camille Coduri. Under the tutelage of an imperious butler who knows the royal ropes, a shiftless lout ramps up, as it were, to become his country's monarch after more suitable heirs are accidentally wiped out. 1991. Directed by David S. Ward. Universal.

Living in Oblivion. Steve Buscemi, Catherine Keener, James LeGros. Everything that could go wrong does on the set of a B movie (bring on the overly sensitive dwarf). 1994. Directed by Tom DiCillo. Columbia Tri-Star. R.

Major League. Charlie Sheen, Tom Berenger. A very bad ball club has a slugger on voodoo, a pitcher who can't hit the backstop let alone the strike zone, and an owner who wants the team to lose so she can relocate it to Miami. 1989. Directed by David S. Ward. Paramount. R.

Mars Attacks! Jack Nicholson, Glenn Close, Martin Short. A huge spoof of a sci-fi epic deliberately stays tacky as slimy green invaders have their nasty way with all manner of bumbling humans. 1996. Directed by Tim Burton. Warner.

The Mask. Jim Carrey, Cameron Diaz, Peter Greene, Peter Riegert. An ancient mask with magical powers turns an ordinary guy into a wildly gyrating physical marvel with both good inclinations and bad. 1994. Directed by Chuck Russell. New Line.

Mouse Hunt. Nathan Lane, Lee Evans, Christopher Walken. Trying to fix up a mansion they've inherited so they can sell it for a fortune, the Smuntz brothers are foiled by an army of 65 mice, who are determined to hang on in the old place. 1997. Directed by Gore Verbinski. Universal.

The Naked Gun: From the Files of the Police Squad. Leslie Nielsen, Ricardo Montalban, Priscilla Presley, George Kennedy. The gags just keep coming as Lt. Durbin of the L.A.P.D. deals with a plot to kill Queen Elizabeth on her visit to Los Angeles. 1988. Directed by David Zucker. Paramount.

The Nutty Professor. Eddie Murphy, Jada Pinkett Smith, James Coburn. Jerry Lewis did it first in 1953, but this time Murphy is the rotund but nice Professor Sherman Klump, who gulps a potion to lose weight and make himself more attractive to women. 1996. Directed by Tom Shadyac. Universal.

Overboard. Goldie Hawn, Kurt Russell. A spoiled rich woman falls off a boat and washes ashore with amnesia. There she is rescued by a carpenter who convinces her she is his wife and the mother of his four bratty kids. 1987. Directed by Garry Marshall. MGM.

Paulie. Jay Mohr, Gena Rowlands, Tony Shaloub. A talkative parrot goes through a succession of owners and crazy situations on a cross-country quest to find the little girl who owned him originally. 1998. Directed by John Roberts. Dreamworks.

Planes, Trains and Automobiles. Steve Martin, John Candy, Edie Mc-Clurg, Kevin Bacon. When their flight is delayed, a proper businessman trying to get home for Thanksgiving reluctantly joins forces with a boorish and totally crazy shower-curtain-ring salesman. 1987. Directed by John Hughes. Paramount.

Police Academy. Steve Guttenberg, Kim Cattrall, George Gaynes. A failed parking lot attendant makes a crackerjack recruit on a force that has let its admissions standard down to the point where there are none at all. Yes, it's dumb all right, but wildly popular and the precursor of five even dumber more sequels. 1984. Directed by Hugh Wilson. Warner.

Private Benjamin. Goldie Hawn, Eileen Brennan, Albert Brooks. When her husband expires on their wedding night, a Jewish princess enlists in the Army and experiences all the indignities that go along with a very rude awakening. 1980. Directed by Howard Zieff. Warner.

Raising Arizona. Holly Hunter, Nicolas Cage, Trey Wislon, John Goodman. A childless couple—he's a con man and she's a police photographer—kidnap a quintuplet and get into all kinds of problems with escaped convicts, a murderous biker, and assorted others. 1987. Directed by Joel Coen. Fox.

Robin Hood: Men in Tights. Cary Elwes, Richard Lewis, Roger Rees. A take-off on the legendary tale misses on some cylinders, but there's always a laugh or two to be had in a Mel Brooks movie. 1993. Fox.

Roxanne. Steve Martin, Daryl Hannah, Rick Rossovich, Shelley Duvall. In a reprise of "Cyrano de Bergerac," a big-nosed fire chief pines for the astronomer he loves. 1987. Directed by Fred Schepisi. Columbia Tri-Star.

Sgt. Bilko. Steve Martin, Dan Aykroyd, Phil Hartman, Glenne Headly. The 50's sitcom gets an update, with the sarge trying to preserve his base for a few more good scams. 1995. Directed by Jonathan Lynn. Universal.

Risky Business. Tom Cruise, Rebecca DeMornay. With his parents out of town, a sex-starved teen-ager sets up a bordello for a night. 1983. Directed by Paul Brickman Warner. R.

Slums of Beverly Hills. Alan Arkin, Marisa Tomei, Natasha Lyonne, Kevin Corrigan. To keep his kids in the Beverly Hills school district, a hard-pressed dad keeps hopping them from one low-rent apartment to the next, which isn't the best thing for teen-age angst. 1998. Directed by Tamara Jenkins. Fox. R.

Soapdish. Sally Field, Kevin Kline, Robert Downey, Jr. She may be a household word, but the star of the soap opera "The Sun Also Sets" is only as safe as the show's latest ratings. 1991. Directed by Michael Hoffman. Paramount.

There's Something About Mary. Cameron Diaz, Ben Stiller, Matt Dillon, Chris Elliott. Still in love with Mary years after their disastrous prom night date, a poor guy finds her in Florida with the help of a private detective, who falls in love with her himself. 1998. Directed by Peter Farrelly and Bobby Farrelly. Fox. R.

This Is Spinal Tap. Michael McKean, Christopher Guest, Harry Shearer, Tony Hendra. A heavy metal band goes on tour in a scathing and riotous satire of the rock music scene. 1984. Directed by Rob Reiner. New Line. R.

Tootsie. Dustin Hoffman, Jessica Lange, Teri Garr, Dabney Coleman. To land a part, an unemployed actor cross-dresses as a woman to get himself a part in a soap opera. Can stardom be far behind? 1982. Directed by Sydney Pollack. Columbia Tri-Star.

Uncle Buck. John Candy, Amy Madigan, Jean Kelly, Macaulay Culkin. With no other babysitter available for their small son and teen-age daughter, the parents must turn to a lazy and surprising cigar-puffing uncle. 1989. Directed by John Hughes. Universal.

The Waterboy. Adam Sandler, Kathy Bates, Henry Winkler. A dork who lives only to serve the football team, H_2O is transformed into bone-crushing linebacker. 1998. Directed by Frank Coraci. Touchstone.

Wayne's World. Mike Myers, Dana Carvey, Rob Lowe. A slippery producer has big-time plans for two zany characters and their little basement public-access TV show. 1992. Directed by Penelope Spheeris. Paramount.

The Wedding Singer. Adam Sandler, Drew Barrymore. Jilted at the altar himself, a crooner carries on singing for a living at other people's receptions. 1997. Directed by Frank Coraci. New Line.

What About Bob? Richard Dreyfuss, Bill Murray, Julie Hagerty. Fraught with separation anxiety, a radically neurotic patient follows his psychiatrist on his summer vacation, inserting himself into the family with hilarious and touching results. 1991. Directed by Frank Oz. Touchstone.

Zebrahead. Michael Rapaport, N'Bushe Wright, Ray Sharkey, DeShonn Castle. Two high school kids fall in love, which creates some problems because one is white and the other is black. 1992. Directed by Tony Drazan. Columbia Tri-Star. R.

Drama

The Age of Innocence. Daniel Day-Lewis, Michelle Pfeiffer, Winona Ryder. A stunning-looking adaptation of Edith Wharton's novel recreates machinations and passions among the New York upper crust of the 1850's. 1993. Directed by Martin Scorsese. Columbia Tri-Star.

Anne of Green Gables. Megan Follows, Colleen Dewhurst, Richard Farnsworth. In a fine adaptation drawn from the L.M. Montgomery novel, a young orphan comes of age under stern tutelage on Prince Edward Island. 1985. Directed by Kevin Sullivan. Disney.

Apollo 13. Tom Hanks, Kevin Bacon, Bill Paxton, Gary Sinisie, Ed Harris. And that problem, Houston, is that an explosion on the moon mission may mean that the astronauts won't make it back alive. 1995. Directed by Ron Howard. Universal.

As Good as It Gets. Jack Nicholson, Helen Hunt, Greg Kinnear, Cuba Gooding Jr. Try as he might to avoid the situation, a crotchety, monumentally self-centered writer finds himself cottoning up to a spirited waitress who might or might not have the patience to put up with him. 1997. Directed by James L. Brooks. Columbia Tri-Star.

Awakenings. Robert De Niro, Robin Williams. In a story by Dr. Oliver Sacks, the drug L-dopa temporarily revives a number of patients who have been "asleep" for decades. 1990. Directed by Penny Marshall. Columbia Tri-Star.

Babe. James Cromwell, Magna Szubanski. A sweet pig helps Farmer Hoggett save the farm by displaying unusual skills and winning a contest for sheep dogs. 1995. Directed by Chris Noonan. Universal.

Betsy's Wedding. Alan Alda, Molly Ringwald, Joey Bishop, Madeline Kahn. She wants it simple, but Dad wants a major occasion—now all he has to do is pay for it. 1990. Directed by Alan Alda. Touchstone. R.

Big. Tom Hanks, Elizabeth Perkins, John Heard, Robert Loggia. A 13-year-old-boy who wants to be an adult suddenly gets his wish and must confront life as a child in a man's body. 1988. Directed by Penny Marshall. Fox.

Biloxi Blues. Matthew Broderick, Christopher Walken. A New York kid gets drafted and goes to boot camp in Biloxi, Mississippi. 1988. Directed by Mike Nichols. Universal.

Black Beauty. Andrew Knott, Sean Bean, David Thewlis, Jim Carter. The famed quarterhorse named Justin takes life as it comes in a fine adaptation of Anna Sewell's novel. 1994. Directed by Caroline Thompson. Warner.

Born on the Fourth of July. Tom Cruise, Kyra Sedgwick, Raymond J. Barry. In a story based on the real-life experiences of Ron Kovic, a paraplegic wounded in Vietnam protests the war from his wheelchair. 1989. Directed by Oliver Stone. Universal. R.

The Borrowers. John Goodman, Hugh Laurie, Jim Broadbent, Mark. Williams. The picture might be a trifle on the young side for teens, but there's good fun involved when some very little people who live under the floorboards get out and about and "borrowing" items from the large Lenders who own the house. 1997. Directed by Peter Hewitt. Polygram.

Boyz N the Hood. Laurence Fishburne, Ice Cube, Cuba Gooding Jr., Nia Long. Four Los Angeles street kids try to survive the gangs and racism long enough to grow up. 1991. Directed by John Singleton. Columbia Tri-Star. R.

Breaker Morant. Edward Woodward, Jack Thompson, John Waters, Bryan Brown. In 1901, three Australian soldiers are court martialed in a trumped-up case in South Africa. 1980. Directed by Bruce Beresford. Artisan.

Broadcast News. William Hurt, Albert Brooks, Holly Hunter. An up-and-coming young woman reporter gets professionally enmeshed in network news politics and personally caught between the nice guy newsman and the slick anchorman. 1987. Directed by James L. Brooks. Fox.

Bull Durham. Kevin Costner, Susan Sarandon, Tim Robbins. Tired veterans and rookies mix as another season of very minor league ball plays out in colorful and entertaining fashion. 1988. Directed by Ron Shelton. Orion. R.

Chaplin. Robert Downey Jr., Dan Aykroyd, Geraldine Chaplin (who plays her own grandmother), Kevin Dunn, Anthony Hopkins. Downey is brilliant as Chaplin in a life story that travels from the London slums to fame and fortune. 1992. Directed by Richard Attenborough. Artisan.

Chariots of Fire. Ben Cross, Ian Charleson, Nigel Havers, Ian Holm. Two English runners driven by strong but different inspirations compete in the Paris Olympics of 1924. 1981. Directed by Hugh Hudson. Warner.

Coal Miner's Daughter. Sissy Spacek, Tommy Lee Jones, Levon Helm, Beverly D'Angelo. Growing up dirt poor in Appalachia, the country singer Loretta Lynn climbs the charts with the help her husband, Mooney. 1980. Directed by Michael Apted. Universal.

Cocoon. Don Ameche, Wilford Brimley, Hume Cronyn, Jessica Tandy, Steve Guttenberg. Slowly deteriorating at the nursing home, an elderly group suddenly finds renewed vigor in the swimming pool and a brighter tomorrow with benevolent aliens. 1985. Directed by Ron Howard. Fox.

Cold Comfort Farm. Kate Beckinsale, Eileen Atkins, Ian McKellen. An orphaned London girl moves to the family farm and takes charge of her inept country cousins. 1994. Directed by John Schlesinger. Universal.

Crooklyn. Alfre Woodard, Delroy Lindo, Zelda Harris, David Patrick Kelly. The only girl in a family of five children grows up in Brooklyn during the 70's. 1994. Directed by Spike Lee. Universal.

Crossing Delancey. Amy Irving, Reizl Bozyk, Peter Riegert, Jeroen Krabbe. A young woman manages a bookstore and has a rent-controlled apartment, but much to the distress of her grandmother, she has no husband. 1988. Directed by Joan Micklin Silver. Warner.

The Crucible. Daniel Day-Lewis, Winona Ryder, Paul Scofield, Joan Allen, Bruce Davison. Riled into a frenzy by one of their number, a group of hysterical teen-age girls ignite the 17th-century Salem witch trials. 1996. Directed by Nicholas Hytner, adapted from the play by Arthur Miller. Fox.

The Cutting Edge. D. B. Sweeney, Moira Kelly. A frosty ice princess has to make do with a hockey player as a doubles partner in a figure-skating competition. 1992. Directed by Paul Michael Glaser. MGM.

Dances With Wolves. Kevin Costner, Mary McDonnell, Graham Greene Rodney Grant. A Civil War soldier goes to live with the Lakota Sioux, becoming one of them. 1990. Directed by Kevin Costner. Orion.

Dave. Kevin Kline, Sigourney Weaver, Frank Langella, Kevin Dunn, Ving Rhames. An ordinary guy who happens to look exactly like the President is surreptitiously substituted for the duly elected occupant of the Oval Office, who has suffered a paralyzing stroke during an illicit sexual encounter. 1993. Directed by Ivan Reitman. Warner.

Dazed and Confused. Jason London, Rory Cochrane, Sasha Jensen, Wiley Wiggins. Eight recent high school graduates with empty time on their hands haze incoming students and try to get a bead on what comes next in their none-too-promising futures. 1993. Directed by Richard Linklater. Universal. R.

Dead Poets Society. Robin Williams, Ethan Hawke, Robert Sean Leonard, Josh Charles, Gale Hansen. A visionary English teacher plants the seeds of literary creation in students at a stuffy Vermont prep school. 1989. Directed by Peter Weir. Touchstone.

Diner. Steve Guttenberg, Daniel Stern, Mickey Rourke, Kevin Bacon, Ellen Barkin. In Baltimore in 1959, a group of buddies hang around the diner and ponder life after high school. 1982. Directed by Barry Levinson. MGM.

Dirty Dancing. Patrick Swayze, Jennifer Grey, Jerry Orbach. A 16-year-old in the Catskills for the summer gets swept away by her sexy dance instructor. 1987. Directed by Emile Ardolino. Artisan.

Dominick and Eugene. Tom Hulce, Ray Liotta, Jamie Lee Curtis. One brother is in medical school, the other is a slightly retarded garbage man who is helping with the tuition. And if that isn't delicate enough, the student is considering transferring to a school in California. 1988. Directed by Robert M. Young. Orion.

Don Juan Demarco. Marlon Brando, Johnny Depp, Faye Dunaway. A burned out psychiatrist gets a new lease on life from a young man who is convinced he is Don Juan. 1994. Directed by Jeremy Leven. Turner.

Do the Right Thing. Danny Aiello, Ossie Davis, Ruby Dee, Richard Edson, Giancarlo Esposito, Spike Lee. A white pizza store owner fights to keep up his good relations with his black clientele in Brooklyn. 1989. Directed by Spike Lee. Universal. R.

Down in the Delta. Alfre Woodard, Al Freeman Jr., Wesley Snipes, Mary Alice. Threatened by drugs and crime in Chicago, a mother and her two children travel to the family farm in Mississippi, where they learn about their roots and get to try another way of life. 1999. Directed by Maya Angelou. Miramax.

Driving Miss Daisy. Jessica Tandy, Morgan Freeman, Dan Aykroyd, Esther Rolle. In Atlanta in the 40's a feisty Jewish grandmother gradually becomes close to her black chauffeur. 1989. Directed by Bruce Beresford. Warner.

Edward Scissorhands. Johnny Depp, Winona Ryder, Diane Wiest, Vincent Price. Created by a mad scientist, a bionic teen-ager has to make do with gardening sheers for hands, which makes him odd kid out in pastel suburbia. 1990. Directed by Tim Burton. Fox.

Ed Wood. Johnny Depp, Sarah Jessica Parker, Martin Landau, Bill Murray. Depp stars as the eccentric but well-meaning visionary (of a kind) whom many regard as the worst filmmaker ever. 1994. Directed by Tim Burton. Touchstone. R.

Eight Men Out. John Cusack, D. B. Sweeney, Perry Lang, Jace Alexander. In 1919, Shoeless Joe Jackson and the rest of the Black Sox sell out the national pastime for $80,000. 1988. Directed by John Sayles. Orion.

The Elephant Man. Anthony Hopkins, John Hurt, Anne Bancroft, John Gielgud. With a doctor's help, a severely deformed man escapes a life sentence as a sideshow freak. 1980. Directed by David Lynch. Paramount.

The Emerald Forest. Powers Boothe, Meg Foster, Charley Boorman, Dira Pass. In the Amazon, a father searches 10 years for a son kidnapped by tribesmen during a family vacation in the Brazilian jungle. 1985. Directed by John Boorman. Not in distribution.

Emma. Kate Beckinsale, Mark Strong, Samantha Bond, Prunella Scales, Bernard Hepton. With romances to arrange, Emma of the Jane Austen novel meddles where she has no business. 1997. Directed by Diarmuid Lawrence. A&E.

Empire of the Sun. Christian Bale, John Malkovich, Miranda Richardson, Nigel Havers. A privileged 11-year-old British boy living in Shanghai has his world uprooted when he is separated from his parents and thrown into a Japanese prison camp. 1987. Directed by Steven Spielberg. Warner.

Eve's Bayou. Samuel L. Jackson, Lynn Whitfield, Debbi Morgan, Diahann Carroll. A young girl from an upper-middle-class black family in the South comes to grips with the fact that her father, a doctor, is unfaithful to her mother, which in turn taints her relationships with all her relatives. 1997. Directed by Kasi Lemmons. Turner.

Fat Man and Little Boy. Paul Newman, Dwight Schultz, Bonnie Bedelia, John Cusack, Laura Dern. As they develop the first atomic bomb, the physicist J. Robert Oppenheimer has problems with the project director, General Leslie Groves. 1989. Directed by Roland Joffe. Paramount.

A Few Good Men. Jack Nicholson, Tom Cruise, Demi Moore. Assigned to defend two marines accused of killing a colleague, a Navy lawyer smells a cover-up by a dictatorial base commander. 1992. Directed by Rob Reiner. Columbia Tri-Star. R.

Field of Dreams. Kevin Costner, Amy Madigan, James Earl Jones, Burt Lancaster, Ray Liotta. An Iowa farmer becomes convinced that if he builds a ballpark in his cornfield, he will be visited by the ghosts of the 1919 Chicago Black Sox. 1989. Directed by Phil Alden Robinson. Universal.

The Fisher King. Robin Williams, Jeff Bridges, Amanda Plummer, Mercedes Ruehl. In Manhattan a down-and-out disk jockey befriends a quite mad derelict with visions of medieval intrigue and a passion to retrieve the Holy Grail. 1991. Directed by Terry Gilliam. Columbia Tri-Star.

Fitzcarraldo. Klaus Kinski, Claudia Cardinale, Jose Lewgoy. An Irish dreamer acts on his determination to build an opera house in the middle of the Amazon jungle, going so far as to drag a large boat over a mountain. 1982. Directed by Werner Herzog. Warner.

The Flamingo Kid. Matt Dillon, Hector Elizondo, Molly McCarthy. A Brooklyn lad of modest means gets big ideas about living in high style while working at a fancy beach club. 1984. Directed by Garry Marshall. Paramount.

Forrest Gump. Tom Hanks, Robin Wright Penn, Sally Field, Gary Sinise. A good-hearted simpleton survives Vietnam and all his other misfortunes to help inspire the lives of people around him. 1994. Directed by Robert Zemeckis. Paramount.

Four Weddings and a Funeral. Hugh Grant, Andie MacDowell, Simon Callow, Kristin Scott Thomas. An engaging British bachelor floats among the weddings of his friends, managing never to get led to the altar himself. 1994. Directed by Mike Newell. Polygram. R.

Free Willy. Jason James Richter, Lou Petty. A tough runaway kid befriends and takes up the cause of a whale he is determined to set free. 1993. Directed by Simon Wincer. Warner.

The Freshman. Marlon Brando, Matthew Broderick. A naive college lad goes to work for a Mafia don (Brando in an amazing parody of his "Godfather" role) without any real idea of what the fellow does for a living. 1990. Directed by Andrew Bergman. Columbia Tri-Star.

Fried Green Tomatoes. Kathy Bates, Jessica Tandy, Mary Stuart Masterson, Mary-Louise Parker, Cicely Tyson. Fueled by Ninny Threadgoode's reminiscences about life during the Depression in Whistle Stop, AL, four women share experiences and spread their Southern charm. 1991. Directed by Jon Avnet. Universal.

Gandhi. Ben Kingsley, Candice Bergen, Edward Fox, John Gielgud, John Mills. A sweeping biography takes Gandhi from his days as an attorney in South Africa to his passive leadership of India to independence and his assassination. 1982. Directed by Richard Attenborough. Columbia Tri-Star.

Gas Food Lodging. Brooke Adams, Ione Skye, Fairuza Balk, James Brolin. A waitress works hard to raise her two restless daughters in Laramie, New Mexico. 1992. Directed by Allison Anders. Columbia Tri-Star. R.

Ghost. Patrick Swayze, Demi Moore, Whoopi Goldberg. With the help of a medium who to her surprise discovers that her powers are real, a man murdered in a botched hit attempt returns from the dead to protect his lover. 1990. Directed by Jerry Zucker. Paramount.

Glory. Matthew Broderick, Morgan Freeman, Denzel Washington. The white commander Robert Gould Shaw leads the black 54th Massachusetts into battle during the Civil War. 1989. Directed by Edward Zwick. Columbia Tri-Star.

Good Will Hunting. Matt Damon, Ben Affleck, Robin Williams. A janitor finds that he's a mathematical genius and a potential celebrity, but that's only part of the problem for a kid with a chip on his shoulder and a big fear of living with his talent. 1997. Directed by Gus Van Sant. Touchstone.

Gorillas in the Mist. Sigourney Weaver, Bryan Brown, Julie Harris. This is the life of Dian Fossey, the naturalist and gorilla expert who was killed by poachers. 1988. Directed by Michael Apted. Universal.

The Great Santini. Robert Duvall, Blythe Danner, Michael O'Keefe. A frustrated marine takes his career disappointments out on his family, but making life tough is the only way he can show affection. 1980. Directed by Lewis John Carlino. Warner.

Greystoke: The Legend of Tarzan, Lord of the Apes. Christopher Lambert, Ralph Richardson, Ian Holm, James Fox, Andie MacDowell. Tarzan takes a breather and goes back to his old ancestral seat in Scotland, where he makes a bumpy adjustment but seems lost without his jungle brio. 1984. Directed by Hugh Hudson. Warner.

Hamlet. Mel Gibson, Glenn Close, Alan Bates, Paul Scofield, Ian Holm, Helena Bonham Carter. Young people should take to this colorful and accessible production, but the Kenneth Branagh version of 1996 is excellent, too. 1990. Directed by Franco Zeffirelli. Warner.

Heathers. Winona Ryder, Christian Slater. Kim Walker, Shannen Doherty, Lisanne Falk, Penelope Milford. Two teenage outcasts exact darkly humorous revenge on officiously "in" kids at school. 1989. Directed by Michael Lehmann. Various distributors. R.

He Got Game. Denzel Washington, Ray Allen, Lonette McKee, Bill Nunn. A top high school basketball star copes with college recruiters and the sudden presence of his father, who has been given a special leave from prison to convince his son to attend the governor's alma mater. 1998. Directed by Spike Lee. Touchstone.

Hook. Dustin Hoffman, Robin Williams, Julia Roberts, Bob Hoskins. Peter Pan goes to the rescue of children kidnapped by Captain Hook. 1991. Directed by Steven Spielberg. Columbia Tri-Star.

Hoosiers. Gene Hackman, Barbara Hershey, Dennis Hopper. An inspirational coach makes winners of some small-town Indiana kids. 1986. Directed by David Anspaugh. Artisan.

The Horse Whisperer. Robert Redford, Kristin Scott Thomas, Scarlett Johansson. A young girl and her badly injured horse are taken in hand by a gently wise cowboy with a healing touch. 1998. Directed by Robert Redford. Touchstone.

How to Make an American Quilt. Winona Ryder, Ellen Burstyn, Anne Bancroft, Lois Smith, Jean Simmons. A young woman weighing a marriage proposal gets advice from a nurturing group of older women who make her a quilt and relate their own experiences. 1995. Directed by Jocelyn Moorhouse. Universal.

The Hudsucker Proxy. Tim Robbins, Paul Newman, Jennifer Jason Leigh, Charles Durning. As part of a scheme to drive off investors, a crafty old robber baron installs a mailroom boy as president of the company. 1993. Directed by Joel Coen. Warner.

I.Q. Tim Robbins, Walter Matthau, Meg Ryan. Albert Einstein figures his niece could use a little romance, so he hooks her up with a very bright auto mechanic. 1994. Directed by Fred Schepisi. Paramount.

Jane Eyre. William Hurt, Anna Paquin, Charlotte Gainsbourg, Joan Plowright. This is the fourth film adaptation of Charlotte Brontë's classic about the governess and her mysterious employer. Youngsters may take to this more modern version, but the 1944 movie with Joan Fontaine and Orson Welles is the best (also there is a fine 1997 television production with Samantha Morton and Ciaran Hinds). The Hurt-Paquin film was released in 1996. Directed by Franco Zeffirelli. Touchstone.

Joe Versus the Volcano. Tom Hanks, Meg Ryan, Lloyd Bridges, Robert Stack. There some symbolism to ponder as a young man with not long to live contracts with a millionaire to jump into a live volcano. 1990. Directed by John Patrick Shanley. Warner.

The Joy Luck Club. Tsai Chin, Kieu Chinh, France Nuyen, Rosalind Chao. The tumultuous lives of four Chinese women are revealed and woven into their relationships with their own daughters. 1993. Directed by Wayne Wang, adapted from the novel by Amy Tan. Touchstone.

Jungle 2 Jungle. Tim Allen, Sam Huntington, Martin Short, JoBeth Williams. A doctor seeking a divorce discovers he has a 13-year-old son living in the Amazon and so he brings him back to Manhattan. 1996. Directed by John Pasquin. Disney.

Kundun. Tanzin Thuthob Tsarong, Robert Lin. The 14th Dalai Lama grows to manhood in Tibet before being forced to flee into exile in 1959. 1997. Directed by Martin Scorsese. Touchstone.

La Bamba. Lou Diamond Phillips, Esai Morales, Danielle von Zemeck. This is the life story of the 50's pop singer Ritchie Valens, who went down on the same plane with Buddy Holly. 1987. Directed by Luis Valdez. Columbia Tri-Star.

A League of Their Own. Tom Hanks, Geena Davis, Madonna, Lori Petty. Meet the Rockford Peaches, the class of the All American Girls Professional Baseball League, formed in the 40's while the men were off at war. 1992. Directed by Penny Marshall. Columbia Tri-Star.

Lean on Me. Morgan Freeman, Robert Guillaume. A tough principal named Joe Clark turns around an equally tough New Jersey school. 1989. Directed by John G. Avildsen. Warner.

Legends of the Fall. Brad Pitt, Aidan Quinn, Julia Ormond, Anthony Hopkins. In Montana a retired Army colonel raises sons of very different natures but with a hankering for the same woman. 1994. Directed by Edward Zwick. Columbia Tri-Star.

Little Man Tate. Jodie Foster, Dianne Wiest, Harry Connick Jr., Adam Hann-Byrd. A boy genius is the object of a tug-of-war between his mother, who wants him left alone to lead a normal life, and a school director who wants to see his intellect fully developed. 1991. Directed by Jodie Foster. Orion.

Little Women. Winona Ryder, Susan Sarandon, Gabriel Byrne, Trini Alvarado, Samantha Mathis, Kirsten Dunst. The four March sisters grow up in the Civil War era. Gillian Armstrong's film rivals George Cukor's with Katharine Hepburn (1933) as the best of the adaptations of Louisa May Alcott's classic. 1994. Columbia Tri-Star.

Local Hero. Peter Riegert, Denis Lawson, Burt Lancaster, Fulton Mackay. A yuppie sent to buy a Scottish village for an American oil company falls in love with the place and its formidable locals. 1983. Directed by Bill Forsyth. Warner.

Looking for Richard. Al Pacino, Alec Baldwin, Winona Ryder, Kevin Spacey, Aidan Quinn, F. Murray Abraham, Kenneth Branagh. Al Pacino endeavors to make Shakespeare's "Richard III" understandable to one and all. 1996. Fox.

Lost in America. Albert Brooks, Julie Hagerty, Michael Greene, Tom Tarpey. An ad executive with identity problems chucks it all and with his wife sets out across the country in a Winnebago. 1985. Directed by Albert Brooks. Warner. R.

The Madness of King George. Nigel Hawthorne, Helen Mirren, Ian Holm, Rupert Everett, Amanda Donohoe. George III not only loses the colonies but his mind as well, going absolutely crackers for extended periods. 1994. Directed by Nicholas Hytner. Hallmark. R.

Malcolm X. Denzel Washington, Angela Bassett, Albert Hall, Al Freeman Jr., Delroy Lindo. The black leader's career moves from prison in the 50's to the leadership of the Nation of Islam and assassination in 1965. Directed by Spike Lee. Warner.

Matilda. Mara Wilson, Danny DeVito, Rhea Perlman. With rotters for parents and only a first-grade teacher for a supporter, a little girl takes dead aim on those who mistreat her. 1996. Directed by Danny DeVito. Columbia Tri-Star.

Melvin and Howard. Paul LeMat, Jason Robards Jr., Mary Steenburgen.

Melvin Dummar gives a lift to Howard Hughes and later claims part of his estate. 1980. Directed by Jonathan Demme. Universal.

Mermaids. Cher, Winona Ryder, Bob Hoskins, Christina Ricci. Trying to stay out of a serious relationship, a town-hopping single mom with long-suffering daughters, one 15 and the other 8, finally runs into a town and a man she can't run away from. 1990. Directed by Richard Benjamin. Orion.

The Mighty Ducks. Emilio Estevez, Joss Ackland, Lane Smith. An inner city hockey team finds purpose and victory under the tutelage of a yuppie lawyer. 1992. Directed by Stephen Herek. Touchstone.

Miss Firecracker. Holly Hunter, Scott Glenn, Mary Steenburgen, Tim Robbins, Alfre Woodard. Down South a girl with a loose reputation strives to improve her image by entering the local beauty pageant. 1989. Directed by Thomas Schlamme. HBO.

Missing. Jack Lemmon, Sissy Spacek, John Shea. A wrought father tries to find his son, who has been taken political prisoner during a coup in Chile. 1982. Directed by Constantin Costa-Gavras. Universal.

The Mission. Robert DeNiro, Jeremy Irons. During the 18th century, Jesuit missionaries battle the Portuguese slave trade and other obstacles in the Brazilian jungle. 1986. Directed by Roland Joffe. Warner.

Moonstruck. Cher, Nicolas Cage, Olympia Dukakis. In Brooklyn a widow engaged to an older man falls in love with his younger brother. 1987. Directed by Norman Jewison. MGM.

Mrs. Doubtfire. Robin Williams, Sally Field, Pierce Brosnan. When his former wife gets custody of his children, a father disguises himself as a woman and becomes the kids' nanny. 1993. Directed by Chris Columbus. Fox.

Much Ado About Nothing. Kenneth Branagh, Emma Thompson, Robert Sean Leonard, Kate Beckinsale, Michael Keaton. Love takes many twists in Shakespeare's rollicking tale, which is made wonderfully accessible. 1993. Directed by Kenneth Branagh. Columbia Tri-Star.

My Best Friend's Wedding. Julia Roberts, Cameron Diaz, Dermot Mulroney, Rupert Everett. With her best old boyfriend about to marry another woman, Julianne realizes she is in love with him and does all she can to break up the nuptials. 1997. Directed by P.J. Hogan. Columbia Tri-Star.

My Girl. Macaulay Culkin, Dan Aykroyd, Jamie Lee Curtis. Helped by her understanding boyfriend, an 11-year-old girl and her mortician father wrestle with her mother's death. 1991. Directed by Howard Zieff. Columbia Tri-Star.

Mystic Pizza. Julia Roberts, Annabeth Gish, Lili Taylor, Vincent

D'Onofrio. With attendant romantic and personal trials, two sisters and their best friend pass bumpily into young womanhood in Mystic, CT. 1988. Directed by Donald Petrie. Virgin Vision. R.

An Officer and a Gentleman. Richard Gere, Debra Winger, Louis Gossett Jr. A young man at a dead end finds direction in the Navy's Officer Candidate School, where he is pushed to the brink by a tough instructor and builds a romantic relationship with a cannery worker. 1982. Directed by Taylor Hackford. Paramount. R.

Ordinary People. Mary Tyler Moore, Donald Sutherland, Timothy Hutton, Judd Hirsch. A family struggles to overcome the accidental death of one son and the attempted suicide of another. 1980. Dircted by Robert Redford. Paramount.

Out of Africa. Meryl Streep, Robert Redford, Klaus Maria Brandauer. There's epic sweep to the African life and adventures of the Danish writer Isak Dinesen. 1985. Directed by Sydney Pollack. Universal.

Pecker. Christina Ricci, Edward Furlong, Lili Taylor. A light-eating (thus the name Pecker) photographer from Baltimore becomes a celebrity in New York before he and his family decide it's a lot of nonsense and go back home. 1998. Directed by John Waters. New Line.

Persuasion. Amanda Root, Ciaran Hinds, Susan Fleetwood. Interfering relatives stand in the way of Anne Elliot and the handsome Frederick Wentworth, not once but twice. 1995. Directed by Roger Mitchell. Columbia Tri-Star.

The Piano. Holly Hunter, Harvey Keitel, Anna Paquin, Sam Neill. A mute widow from Scotland migrates with her young daughter and her piano to New Zealand, where she marries an insensitive landowner but falls for a rough, vital settler. 1993. Directed by Jane Campion. Artisan. R.

Places in the Heart. Sally Field, John Malkovich, Danny Glover, Ed Harris, Lindsay Crouse. During the Depression a young widow endures every kind of hardship trying to make a go of it on a small farm in Texas. 1984. Directed by Robert Benton. Fox.

Pleasantville. Tobey Maguire, Reese Witherspoon, Joan Allen, William H. Macy, J.T. Walsh, Don Knotts. Sucked into their television set and transported back to the 50's, two very 90's youngsters have to get in step with an earlier era. 1998. Directed by Gary Ross. New Line.

Prefontaine. Jared Leto, R. Lee Ermey, Ed O'Neill, Amy Locane. The brash runner Steve Prefontaine sets many records and champions a few causes before he's killed in auto accident at age 24. 1998. Directed by Steve James. Touchstone.

Raging Bull. Robert De Niro, Cathy Moriarty, Joe Pesci. One of the best American films ever tells the story of the boxer Jake LaMotta. 1980. Directed by Martin Scorsese. MGM.

Rain Man. Dustin Hoffman, Tom Cruise. A smooth operator angling for his family's money re-establishes connections with his autistic brother and together they go on a cross-country journey. 1988. Directed by Barry Levinson. MGM. R.

Red Dawn. Patrick Swayze, C. Thomas Howell, Harry Dean Stanton, Powers Boothe. High school kids take to the hills to fight the Russians, who have invaded the U.S.A. 1984. Directed by John Milius. MGM.

Regarding Henry. Harrison Ford, Annette Bening, Bill Nunn, Mikki Allen, Elizabeth Wilson. A crass lawyer loses his memory after suffering a head injury during a holdup, but on recovery he turns out to be a much nicer guy than he was before. 1991. Directed by Mike Nichols. Paramount.

Reality Bites. Winona Ryder, Ethan Hawke, Ben Stiller, Janeane Garofalo. In Houston four recent college grads set up their lives and do the 20-something thing. 1994. Directed by Ben Stiller. Universal.

Return of the Jedi. Mark Hamill, Carrie Fisher, Harrison Ford. Luke Skywalker and Darth Vader battle on in the third film of the "Star Wars" series. 1983. Directed by Richard Marquand. Fox.

Richie Rich. Macaulay Culkin, John Larroquette, Edward Hermann. When his flighty parents disappear, the world's richest boy takes over the family's business. 1994. Directed by Donald Petrie. Warner.

The Right Stuff. Ed Harris, Dennis Quaid, Sam Shepard, Scott Glenn, Fred Ward. The test pilot Chuck Yeager and the Mercury astronauts blast off. 1983. Directed by Philip Kaufman, adapted from Tom Wolf's book. Warner.

A River Runs Through It. Craig Sheffer, Brad Pitt, Tom Skerritt, Brenda Blethyn. Raising two young sons in Montana, a Presbyterian minister connects life's lessons and fly fishing. 1992. Directed by Robert Redford. Columbia Tri-Star.

Robin Hood: Prince of Thieves. Kevin Costner, Morgan Freeman, Mary Elizabeth Mastrantonio. As always a gallant, idealistic fellow, Robin Hood gets kicked around a little more than usual in a thinking-man's version of the tale. 1991. Directed by Kevin Reynolds. Warner.

A Room With a View. Helena Bonham Carter, Julian Sands, Denholm Elliott, Maggie Smith, Daniel Day-Lewis. In 1907 a proper young Englishwoman is whisked away from the wrong type of man and placed with the right type. But then the first fellow reappears and passion reignites. 1986. Directed by James Ivory, adapted from the novel by E.M. Forster. Fox.

Rushmore. Bill Murray, Jason Schwartzman, Olivia Williams. A 15-year-old wheeler-dealer at Rushmore Academy forms an unlikely alliance with an eccentric steel baron. 1998. Directed by Wes Anderson. Touchstone.

Sabrina. Harrison Ford, Julia Ormond, Greg Kinnear. In a remake of the Billy Wilder film of 1954, two brothers, one a dour business type and the other an irresponsible rogue, wind up competing for the gorgeous daughter of the family chauffeur (by way of some schooling in Europe). 1995. Directed by Sydney Pollack. Paramount.

Sarafina! Leleti Khumalo, Whoopi Goldberg, Miriam Makeba, John Kani. In a quasi-musical, a young girl grows amid strife in Soweto, South Africa. 1992. Directed by Darrell Roodt. Touchstone.

Sarah Plain and Tall. Glenn Close, Christopher Walken, Lexi Randall, Margaret Sophie Stein. In about 1910, a New England schoolteacher answers an advertisement and goes to Kansas to marry a widowed farmer. 1991. Directed by Glenn Jordan. Republic.

Saving Private Ryan. Tom Hanks, Tom Sizemore Edward Burns, Barry Pepper. Surviving the slaughterhouse on Omaha Beach, a detail moves inland to find the paratrooper James Ryan, the sole surviving son in a family of four boys. 1998. Directed by Steven Spielberg. Paramount.

Schindler's List. Liam Neeson, Ben Kingsley, Ralph Fiennes. An industrialist uses his connections with the Nazis to save the lives of hundreds of Jews by employing them in his factories in Poland. 1993. Directed by Steven Spielberg. Universal. R.

School Daze. Spike Lee, Laurence Fishburne, Giancarlo Esposito. Racial identity questions swirl around the fraternity scene at a black college in the South. 1988. Directed by Spike Lee. Columbia Tri-Star. R.

School Ties. Brendan Fraser, Matt Damon, Chris O'Donnell. In the 1950's, a star quarterback lands a scholarship to an elite prep school by hiding the fact that he is Jewish. But then the truth is discovered, leading to his resolve to confront an ugly situation. 1992. Directed by Robert Mandel. Paramount.

Searching for Bobby Fisher. Joe Mantegna, Joan Allen, Max Pomeranc, Ben Kingsley, Laurence Fishburne. A 7-year-old's talent for chess threatens any chance he has at a normal childhood. 1993. Directed by Steven Zaillian. Paramount.

The Secret of Roan Innish. Jeni Courtney, Michael Lally, Eileen Colgan. An Irish child explores family and place through stories of her ancestors on the island of Roan Innish. 1994. Directed by John Sayles. Columbia Tri-Star.

Sense and Sensibility. Emma Thompson, Kate Winslet, Hugh Grant, Alan Rickman. Romantic complications abound as the capable Elinor Dashwood takes over the family fortunes after her father dies and the Dashwoods are forced to move to a country cottage. 1995. Directed by Ang Lee. Columbia Tri-Star.

The Shawshank Redemption. Tim Robbins, Morgan Freeman. A bank executive in prison for murder learns to get some good out of the experience with the help of a sage old inmate named Red. 1994. Directed by Frank Darabont. Columbia Tri-Star.

Shine. Geoffrey Rush, Noah Taylor, Armin Mueller-Stahl, Lynn Redgrave. An Australian piano prodigy cracks up under the strain of trying to live by the stifling dictates of his obsessively possessive father. 1995. Directed by Scott Hicks. New Line.

Silkwood. Meryl Streep, Kurt Russell, Cher. This is the true story of Karen Silkwood, a nuclear plant worker and activist who dies under mysterious circumstances after protesting unsafe conditions at the Kerr-McGee plant in Oklahoma. 1983. Directed by Mike Nichols. Paramount.

Singles. Matt Dillon, Bridget Fonda, Campbell Scott, Kyra Sedgewick, Sheila Kelly. Twenty-somethings survive a 90's Seattle scene set to a great soundtrack featuring Pearl Jam as the fictional alternative band Citizen Dick. 1992. Directed by Cameron Crowe. Warner.

Sleepless in Seattle. Tom Hanks, Meg Ryan. A lonely widower in Seattle goes on talk radio to express his feelings. That attracts a lonely woman on the opposite coast and she heads west in search of destiny. 1993. Directed by Nora Ephron. Columbia Tri-Star.

Stand and Deliver. Edward James Olmos, Lou Diamond Phillips, Rosana De Soto. A Los Angeles teacher whips barrio students into shape for the big calculus exam. 1988. Directed by Ramon Menendez. Warner.

Stand by Me. Richard Dreyfuss, River Phoenix, Wil Wheaton, Jerry O'-Connell, Corey Feldman, Kiefer Sutherland. Four 12-year-olds learn a lot about life when they hike into the wilderness to find the body of a boy hit by a train. 1986. Directed by Rob Reiner. Columbia Tri-Star.

Stealing Home. Mark Harmon, Jodie Foster, William McNamara. An over-the-hill ball player relives his relationship with his old babysitter and first love, who has committed suicide. 1988. Directed by Steven Kampmann and Will Aldis. Warner.

Steel Magnolias. Sally Field, Dolly Parton, Shirley MacLaine, Julia Roberts, Daryl Hannah, Olympia Dukakis. Five spirited, offbeat Southern women carry on with their lives, aided and abetted by camaraderie around the beauty shop. 1989. Directed by Herbert Ross. Columbia Tri-Star.

Stepmom. Julia Roberts, Susan Sarandon, Ed Harris, Jena Malone, Liam Aiken. A mother who is dying of cancer gradually comes to terms with her ex-husband's young fiancee, who will be caring for the children after she's gone. 1998. Directed by Chris Columbus. Columbia Tri-Star.

Tender Mercies. Robert Duvall, Tess Harper, Betty Buckley, Ellen Barkin. A country singer on his uppers tries to get it back together helped by the love of a woman. 1983. Directed by Bruce Beresford. Republic.

Terms of Endearment. Shirley MacLaine, Jack Nicholson, Debra Winger,

John Lithgow, Jeff Daniels, Danny DeVito. The relationship between a mother and daughter evolves over the years, with a nice assist from the astronaut (Nicholson) who lives next door. 1983. Directed by James L. Brooks. Paramount.

Thelma and Louise. Geena Davis, Susan Sarandon, Harvey Keitel, Christopher McDonald, Michael Madsen, Brad Pitt. Two women who are best friends break away from repressive lives and relationships and take to the road as a pair of wandering renegades. 1991. Directed by Ridley Scott. MGM. R.

Titanic. Leonardo DiCaprio, Kate Winslet. The big craft goes to the bottom of the ocean and to the top of the all-time box-office chart. 1997. Directed by James Cameron. Paramount.

The Trip to Bountiful. Geraldine Page, Rebecca DeMornay, John Heard. An elderly widow gets tired of living with younger relatives and boards a bus for a visit to her old hometown. 1985. Directed by Peter Masterson, adapted from the play by Horton Foote. Columbia Tri-Star.

The Truman Show. Jim Carrey, Ed Harris, Laura Linney, Noah Emmerich, Natascha McElhone. Truman Burbank comes to the realization that his entire life is actually a television show. 1998. Directed by Peter Weir. Paramount.

The Truth About Cats and Dogs. Janeane Garofalo, Uma Thurman, Ben Chaplin, Jamie Foxx. In a female variation of the Cyrano de Bergerac story, a young woman who considers herself unattractive enlists the help of her gorgeous but dim friend to woo the handsome owner of a Great Dane. 1996. Directed by Michael Lehmann. Fox.

Welcome to the Dollhouse. Heather Matarazzo, Brendan Sexton III. An 11-year-old middle child from New Jersey has an awful time fitting in anywhere. 1995. Directed by Todd Solondz. Columbia Tri-Star. R.

What's Eating Gilbert Grape? Johnny Depp, Leonardo DiCaprio, Juliette Lewis, Mary Steenburgen. In an Iowa town young Gilbert tries to manage his large mom (she weighs over 500 pounds) and his squabbling, dysfunctional family. 1993. Directed by Lasse Hallstrom. Paramount.

White Squall. Jeff Bridges, Scott Wolf, Caroline Goodall. A square-rigger with a crew of young people is sunk in a storm with loss of life and a subsequent trial for the captain. 1996. Directed by Ridley Scott. Touchstone.

William Shakespeare's Romeo and Juliet. Leonardo DiCaprio, Claire Danes, John Leguizamo, Paul Sorvino. They still talk like it's the 16th century, but the lovers are now in a modern fantasyland called Verona Beach. 1996. Directed by Baz Luhrmann. Fox.

The Wind in the Willows. Terry Jones, Steve Coogan, Eric Idle, Anthony Sher, Nicol Williamson. In a Monty Pythonesque treatment of Kenneth Grahame's 1908 children's book, weasels try to take over Toad Hall while

Toad, infatuated with cars, just keeps buying more vehicles. 1996. Directed by Terry Jones. Not in distribution.

Without Limits. Billy Crudup, Donald Sutherland, Monica Potter, Jeremy Sisto. The late miler Steve Prefontaine gets his second movie within a year (see "Prefontaine"). This one tells about his relationship with his coach, Bill Bowerman, the founder of Nike. 1997. Directed by Robert Towne. Warner.

Ulee's Gold. Peter Fonda, Tom Wood, Vanessa Zima. Although he'd rather not, a middle-aged beekeeper and Vietnam War veteran is forced by circumstances to care for his troubled granddaughters. 1997. Directed by Victor Nunez. Orion.

Vanya on 42d Street. Wallace Shawn, Julianne Moore, Brooke Smith, Larry Pine. Checkhov's "Uncle Vanya" gets wonderful treatment staged in the run-down New Amsterdam Theater. 1994. Directed by Louis Malle. Columbia Tri-Star.

Victor/Victoria. Julie Andrews, James Garner, Robert Preston, Lesley Ann Warren. During the Depression in Paris an unemployed actress impersonates a man impersonating a woman. 1982. Directed by Blake Edwards. MGM.

White Men Can't Jump. Woody Harrelson, Wesley Snipes, Rosie Perez. An overgrown white kid tries to prove he can be competitive at playground basketball. 1992. Directed by Ron Shelton. Fox. R.

Year of Living Dangerously. Mel Gibson, Sigourney Weaver, Linda Hunt. An Australian journalist covers the political scene in Indonesia at the time of the coup against General Sukarno in 1965. 1982. Directed by Peter Weir. MGM.

You've Got Mail. Meg Ryan, Tom Hanks. Reprising the types of roles they played in "Sleepless in Seattle," Ryan and Hanks swap e-mail without knowing each other's identity and then finally fall for each other after they do meet. 1998. Directed by Nora Ephron. Warner.

Oldies

The Adventures of Robin Hood. Action adventure. Errol Flynn, Olivia de Havilland, Basil Rathbone. Flynn makes the most dashing Robin in a rollicking contest of wits with the Sheriff of Nottingham. 1938. Directed by Michael Curtiz. MGM.

The African Queen. Drama. Humphrey Bogart, Katharine Hepburn. A grizzled steamer captain takes a spinster missionary for a wild ride down river. 1951. Directed by John Huston. Fox.

Alice's Restaurant. Comedy. Arlo Guthrie, James Broderick, Pat Quinn.

Guthrie plays himself (it's his song, after all) in a 60's period piece about hippies, draft dodging, dropping out of college, and defying the pigs. 1969. Directed by Arthur Penn. MGM.

All the President's Men. Drama. Dustin Hoffman, Robert Redford, Jason Robards Jr., Martin Balsam. The Watergate case gets broken wide open in the newsroom of the *Washington Post.* 1976. Directed by Alan J. Pakula. Warner.

American Graffiti. Drama. Richard Dreyfuss, Ron Howard, Cindy Williams, MacKenzie Phillips. A bunch of new high school grads cruise around listening to Wolfman Jack and wondering what life will bring in an era before the Vietnam War. 1973. Directed by George Lucas. Universal.

The Americanization of Emily. Comedy drama. James Garner, Julie Andrews. A pacifistic Navy officer tries to get out of being the first casualty during the Normandy invasion and, while he's at it, seduce an attractive jeep driver who thinks he's a coward. 1964. Directed by Arthur Hiller. MGM.

Anatomy of a Murder. Mystery/crime. James Stewart, George C. Scott, Ben Gazzara, Lee Remick. In perhaps the best courtroom drama ever, an army officer stands trial for murder. 1959. Directed by Otto Preminger. Columbia Tri-Star.

Apocalypse Now. Drama. Marlon Brando, Martin Sheen, Robert Duvall. A mission into the Cambodian jungle to kill a renegade colonel is a chronicle of all that went wrong with the war in Vietnam. 1979. Directed by Francis Ford Coppola. Paramount. R.

Bad Day at Black Rock. Drama. Spencer Tracy, Robert Ryan, Anne Francis, Dean Jagger. A one-armed stranger comes into a small western town looking for a Japanese farmer and stays to uncover a dark conspiracy. 1955. Directed by John Sturges. MGM.

Bang the Drum Slowly. Drama. Robert De Niro, Michael Moriarty, Vincent Gardenia. A baseball player dying of Hodgkins disease tries to make it through one more season. 1973. Directed by John Hancock. Paramount.

Barry Lyndon. Drama. Ryan O'Neal, Marisa Berenson, Patrick Magee. Set in the 18th century, a colorful adaptation of the Thackeray novel depicts the adventures and downfall of an arrogant young Irish gambler. 1975. Directed by Stanley Kubrick. Warner.

Being There. Drama. Peter Sellers, Shirley MacLaine, Melvyn Douglas. A retarded gardener whose entire knowledge comes from watching television goes into politics and is hailed as an icon. 1979. Directed by Hal Ashby. Fox.

The Birds. Mystery horror. Tippi Hedren, Rod Taylor, Jessica Tandy,

Suzanne Pleshette. Crows and seagulls are the main bad actors as birds attack humans in a classic tale of horror. 1963. Directed by Alfred Hitchcock. Universal.

Ben-Hur. Drama. Charlton Heston, Jack Hawkins, Stephen Boyd, Haya Harareet. A Palestinian Jew takes on the Roman Empire and don't miss that chariot race! 1959. Directed by William Wyler. MGM.

Breakfast at Tiffany's. Comedy. Audrey Hepburn, George Peppard, Patricia Neal. In Truman Capote's romance, a New York playgirl tries romance with a writer. 1961. Directed by Blake Edwards. Paramount.

Breaking Away. Drama. Dennis Christopher, Dennis Quaid, Daniel Stern. An Indiana high school graduate gets addicted to bicycle racing. 1979. Directed by Peter Yates. Fox.

Brewster McCloud. Drama. Bud Cort, Sally Kellerman, Shelley Duvall. Watched over by a guardian angel, a whimsical young fellow with dreams of flying takes up residence in the rafters of the Houston Astrodome. 1970. Directed by Robert Altman. MGM.

The Bridge on the River Kwai. Drama. Alec Guinness, William Holden, Jack Hawkins, Sessue Hayakawa. A British commander in a Japanese prison camp is forced to use his men to build a railroad bridge by his captors. Proud of his accomplishment at first, he later realizes it must be destroyed. 1957. Directed by David Lean. Columbia Tri-Star.

The Buddy Holly Story. Drama. Gary Busey, Don Stroud, Charles Martin Smith. Here is the life story of the 50's pop singer from his Texas boyhood to the fatal plane crash. 1978. Directed by Steve Rash. Columbia Tri-Star.

Bullitt. Action. Steve McQueen, Robert Vaughn, Jacqueline Bisset. A detective is assigned to guard a key witness, who is murdered. And the car chase up and down San Francisco hills is among the movies' best. 1968. Directed by Peter Yates. Warner.

Casablanca. Drama. Humphrey Bogart, Ingrid Bergman, Paul Henreid, Claude Rains, Peter Lorre, Sydney Greenstreet. Here's looking at you, kids. Nazi-occupied Morocco is a tough place to mix romance and politics in a film, considered by many to be best ever made, that everybody should see at least a couple of times. 1942. Directed by Michael Curtiz. MGM.

Catch-22. Drama. Alan Arkin, Martin Balsam, Art Garfunkel, Jon Voight, Richard Benjamin. In an adaptation of Joseph Heller's classic antiwar novel, a group of flyers go crazy in the Mediterranean during World War II. 1970. Directed by Mike Nichols. Paramount. R.

The China Syndrome. Drama. Michael Douglas, Jane Fonda, Jack Lemmon. A California news crew uncovers a nuclear power plant that is about to blow. 1979. Directed by James Bridges. Columbia Tri-Star.

Chinatown. Drama. Jack Nicholson, Faye Dunaway, John Huston, Diane

Ladd. In a superb mystery, intrigue over Los Angeles water rights entangles the lives of the protagonists. 1974. Directed by Roman Polanski. Paramount. R.

Citizen Kane. Drama. Orson Welles, Joseph Cotten, Everett Sloane. In the greatest rise and fall in American film, a newspaper magnate (modeled after William Randolph Hearst) goes from power to eclipse. 1941. Directed by Orson Welles. Fox.

The Conversation. Drama. Gene Hackman, John Cazale, Frederic Forrest. A surveillance expert gradually goes crazy after discovering that he may be implicated in a murder. 1974. Directed by Francis Ford Coppola. Paramount.

Cooley High. Drama. Motown hits flavor the scene as black high school seniors approach graduation in Chicago. 1975. Directed by Michael A. Schultz. Orion.

Cool Hand Luke. Drama. Paul Newman, George Kennedy, Strother Martin, J.D. Cannon, Jo Van Fleet. A petty thief refuses to knuckle under to brutal regimen on a prison chain gang. 1967. Directed by Stuart Rosenberg. Warner.

David Copperfield. Lionel Barrymore, W.C. Fields, Maureen O' Sullivan, Freddie Bartholomew, Basil Rathbone. With all manner of help and hindrance, Dickens's famed orphan grows to manhood. 1935. Directed by George Cukor. MGM.

The Diary of Anne Frank. Drama. Millie Perkins, Joseph Schildkraut, Shelley Winters. The famous 13-year-old reflects on her life in the diary she kept while her family hid from the Nazis in Amsterdam. 1959. Directed by George Stevens. Fox.

The Dirty Dozen. Action drama. Lee Marvin, Ernest Borgnine, Charles Bronson, Jim Brown, George Kennedy, John Cassavetes. Dangling their freedom as the carrot, an Army major whips 12 tough convicts into shape for a suicide mission into Nazi Germany. 1967. Directed by Robert Aldrich. MGM.

Doctor Zhivago. Drama. Omar Sharif, Julie Christie, Geraldine Chaplin, Rod Steiger, Alec Guinness. Boris Pasternak's tale of dislocated lovers spills across Russia in the years after the Bolshevik Revolution. 1965. Directed by David Lean. MGM.

Dr. Jekyll and Mr. Hyde. Drama. Fredric March, Miriam Hopkins, Halliwell Hobbes. In the best of many movie tellings of Robert Louis Stevenson's story, the doctor's monster takes up with a prostitute and turns to murder. 1932. Directed by Rouben Mamoulian. MGM.

Dr. Strangelove or: How I Learned to Stop Worrying and Love the Bomb. Drama. Peter Sellers, Sterling Hayden, George C. Scott, Keenan Wynn. Out of his mind and acting on his own, the loose canon General Jack D. Ripper sends his bombers toward the Soviet Union, leaving the befuddled President and his Communist counterpart struggling to prevent the holocaust. 1962. Directed by Stanley Kubrick. Columbia Tri-Star.

Duck Soup. Comedy. The Marx brothers. Groucho takes over Freedonia and signs on Chico and Harpo as spies. 1933. Directed by Leo McCarey. Universal.

East of Eden. Drama. James Dean, Julie Harris, Raymond Massey, Jo Van Fleet. The movie adapts John Steinbeck's Cain-and-Abel story about a young man's painful struggle to find love and the truth about his mother. 1954. Directed by Elia Kazan. Warner.

Easy Rider. Drama. Peter Fonda, Dennis Hopper, Jack Nicholson. High on their big Harley's (and a few other things), a pair of road-struck wanderers cruise a Southwest full of hippies, red necks, hookers, and violence. 1969. Directed by Dennis Hopper. Columbia Tri-Star.

Father of the Bride. Comedy. Spencer Tracy, Elizabeth Taylor, Joan Bennett. By turns proud and threatened, Dad has a tough time with the notion of giving away his little girl (Taylor at her most astonishingly beautiful). 1950. Directed by Vincente Minnelli. MGM.

Frankenstein. Horror. Boris Karloff, Colin Clive, Mae Clarke. Mary Shelley's monster runs amok in what still plays as one of the best horror flicks of all time. 1931. Directed by James Whale. Universal.

The French Connection. Action. Gene Hackman, Roy Scheider, Fernando Rey. The relentless New York detective Popeye Doyle closes in on one of the biggest drug busts ever. 1971. Directed by William Friedkin. Fox.

From Russia With Love. Action adventure. Sean Connery, Daniela Bianchi, Lotte Lenya, Robert Shaw. In what may be the best of the James Bond films, 007 is in Istanbul and in a contest with both the Russians and the organization called Spectre. 1963. Directed by Terence Young. MGM.

Giant. Drama. Rock Hudson, James Dean, Elizabeth Taylor, Carroll Baker. From jealous relatives to amorous cow punchers, a young bride from the east faces myriad challenges on her husband's Texas ranch. 1956. Directed by George Stevens. Warner.

The Godfather. Drama. Marlon Brando, Al Pacino, Robert Duvall, James Caan, Diane Keaton. In one of the truly great American films, the mob ebbs and flows during the 40's. Directed by Francis Ford Coppola, adapted from the novel by Mario Puzo. 1972. Paramount.

The Godfather, Part 2. Drama. Al Pacino, Robert De Niro, Diane Keaton, Robert Duvall. The Corleone family saga is continued with a circling back to its founding in New York's Little Italy 60 years earlier. 1974. Directed by Francis Ford Coppola. Paramount.

Gone With the Wind. Drama. Vivien Leigh, Clark Gable, Olivia de Havilland, Leslie Howard. The south falls in classic fashion, not to mention Rhett and Scarlett, in Victor Fleming's film adapted from Margaret Mitchell's novel. 1939. MGM.

Goldfinger. Action adventure. Sean Connery, Honor Blackman, Gert Frobe. In a surpassingly good early Bond, 007 stalks the tycoon who would rob Fort Knox. 1964. Directed by Guy Hamilton. MGM.

Goodbye, Columbus. Comedy drama. Richard Benjamin, Ali MacGraw, Jack Klugman. In an adaptation of Philip Roth's novel, a poor Jewish librarian falls for a Jewish-American princess who goads him to be more ambitious and then drops him to head off to college. 1969. Directed by Larry Peerce. Paramount.

The Graduate. Drama. Dustin Hoffman, Anne Bancroft, Katharine Ross. Trying to get his feet under him after college, the shy Benjamin Braddock is pulled this way and that in a world that little understands him and could care less. 1967. Directed by Mike Nichols. New Line.

The Grapes of Wrath. Drama. Henry Fonda, Jane Darwell, John Carradine. The poverty-stricken Joad family heads west from the Oklahoma dust bowl to the orange groves of California. 1940. Directed by John Ford, adapted from the novel by John Steinbeck. Fox.

The Great Escape. Action adventure. Steve McQueen, James Garner, Richard Attenborough, James Coburn. In what is considered one of the best war movies ever, a group of allied prisoners make a break from a supposedly escape-proof German prison camp. 1963. Directed by John Sturges. MGM.

The Great Train Robbery. Action. Sean Connery, Donald Sutherland, Lesley-Anne Down. In 1855 a dashing thief makes off with the Folkstone bullion express. 1979. Directed by Michael Crichton. MGM.

The Great Waldo Pepper. Action adventure. Robert Redford, Susan Sarandon, Margot Kidder. Acrobatics in vintage aircraft are the main attraction as a World War I flying ace and barnstormer becomes a stunt pilot for the movies. 1975. Directed by George Roy Hill. Universal.

Guess Who's Coming to Dinner. Comedy. Spencer Tracy, Katharine Hepburn, Sidney Poitier, Katharine Houghton. Dad and Mom, upper-middle-class and white, meet their daughter's choice for a husband, who is brilliant and black. 1967. Directed by Stanley Kramer. Columbia Tri-Star.

Gunga Din. Action adventure. Cary Grant, Victor McLaglen, Douglas Fairbanks Jr., Sam Jaffe. A rambunctious trio of British sergeants stands tall in colonial India. 1939. Directed by George Stevens, adapted from the poem by Rudyard Kipling. Turner.

The Guns of Navarone. Action adventure. Gregory Peck, David Niven, Anthony Quinn, Richard Harris. A commando team takes out a pair of huge German guns guarding a strategic passage in the Aegean. 1961. Directed by J. Lee Thompson. Columbia Tri-Star.

Heaven Can Wait. Comedy drama. Warren Beatty, Julie Christie, Charles Grodin. A football star mistakenly sent to heaven before his time is allowed to go back to living, only now he's a corrupt businessman about to be murdered by his wife. 1978. Directed by Buck Henry. Paramount.

Heaven Knows, Mr. Allison. Action drama. Robert Mitchum, Deborah Kerr. A Marine sergeant is stranded with, and falls for, an Irish nun on a Pacific island occupied by the Japanese. 1957. Directed by John Huston. Fox.

The Hustler. Drama. Paul Newman, Jackie Gleason, Piper Laurie, George C. Scott. With a pile riding at the pool table, young Fast Eddie Felson takes on Minnesota Fats. 1961. Directed by Robert Rossen. Fox.

I'm All Right, Jack. Comedy. Peter Sellers, Ian Carmichael, Terry-Thomas. In a hilarious satire, a young English worker improves plant-working conditions, prompting his union to go on strike and disrupt the nation. 1959. Directed by John Boulting. Facets.

It Happened One Night. Comedy. Clark Gable, Claudette Colbert. An heiress runs away from home and encounters a tough newspaper reporter who pretends he doesn't recognize her so he can get a good story. Naturally they fall in love but not before he teaches her a thing or two about real people. 1934. Directed by Frank Capra. Columbia Tri-Star.

It's a Wonderful Life. Drama. James Stewart, Donna Reed, Henry Travers, Thomas Mitchell, Lionel Barrymore. In the All-American classic, a man contemplating suicide is saved by an angel who convinces him of his worth to his loved ones. 1946. Directed by Frank Capra. Republic.

The Jackie Robinson Story. Drama. Jackie Robinson, Ruby Dee, Minor Watson. Jackie plays himself in a film that might be a little corny but still tells the famous story. 1950. Directed by Alfred E. Green. MGM.

Jaws. Action drama. Roy Scheider, Richard Dreyfuss, Robert Shaw. The classic about the man-eating great white shark is the first of the modern blockbuster action films. 1975. Directed by Steven Spielberg. Universal.

Kind Hearts and Coronets. Drama. Alec Guinness, Valerie Hobson. An ambitious rogue schemes to do away with eight relatives (all played by Guinness) and walk away with the family fortune. 1949. Directed by Robert Hamer. Republic.

King Kong. Action drama. Fay Wray, Bruce Cabot, Robert Armstrong, Frank Reicher. The big guy still sets New York on its ear. 1933. Directed by Ernest B. Schoedsack and Merian Cooper. Paramount.

Kramer vs. Kramer. Drama. Dustin Hoffman, Meryl Streep, Justin Henry, Jane Alexander. A father and his young son are whipped around when his former wife leaves them to do other things with her life and then returns wanting the boy back. 1979. Directed by Robert Benton. Columbia Tri-Star.

The Lady Vanishes. Mystery suspense. Margaret Lockwood, Paul Lukas, Michael Redgrave. An old woman disappears from a speeding train, leaving an imposter in her place and a mystery to be solved. 1938. Directed by Alfred Hitchcock. Home Vision.

The Last Picture Show. Drama. Jeff Bridges, Timothy Bottoms, Ben Johnson, Cloris Leachman, Cybill Shepherd, Ellen Burstyn. Lives twine and tangle in a dusty Texas town about to lose its movie theater. 1971. Directed by Peter Bogdanovich. Columbia Tri-Star.

Laura. Mystery suspense. Gene Tierney, Dana Andrews, Clifton Webb. A detective assigned to investigate the murder of a beautiful woman falls in love with her portrait. 1944. Directed by Otto Preminger. Fox.

The Lavender Hill Mob. Comedy. Alec Guinness, Stanley Holloway, Sidney James, Alfie Bass. One way to dispose of stolen gold is to melt it down and turn it into miniature Eiffel Towers. 1951. Directed by Charles Crichton. Republic.

Lawrence of Arabia. Drama. Peter O'Toole, Omar Sharif, Anthony Quinn, Alec Guinness, Jack Hawkins. Rebelling against his English traditions, T.E. Lawrence takes to the desert to aid the Bedouins against the Turks during World War I. 1962. Directed by David Lean. Columbia Tri-Star.

The Lion in Winter. Drama. Peter O'Toole, Katharine Hepburn. The aging Henry II and his wife, Eleanor of Aquitaine, clash over which of their heirs should assume the throne. 1968. Directed by Anthony Harvey. Columbia Tri-Star.

Little Fugitive. Drama. Richie Andrusco, Ricky Brewster, Winnifred Cushing. When pranksters convince him that he's murdered his brother, a 7-year-old runs away to Coney Island. 1953. Directed by Morris Engel and Ruth Orkin. Kino.

Little Murders. Comedy (but black). Ellott Gould, Vincent Gardenia. Mugging, murder, and other crimes are somehow horrifyingly funny in Jules Feiffer's story about a beleaguered photographer's travails in New York City. 1971. Directed by Alan Arkin. Fox. R.

The Longest Day. Drama. John Wayne, Robert Mitchum, Henry Fonda, Robert Ryan, Rod Steiger. An epic recreates almost every detail of the Normandy invasion. 1962. Directed by Ken Annakin. Time-Life.

Love and Death. Comedy. Woody Allen, Diane Keaton, Frank Adu. In Allen's hilarious spoof of "War and Peace," a Slav is caught trying to assassinate Napoleon and given two hours to muse over his misspent life. 1975. MGM.

Lust for Life. Drama. Kirk Douglas, Anthony Quinn. Vincent van Gogh has a very rough time being a genius (and why can't he sell a painting?). 1956. Directed by Vincente Minnelli. MGM.

The Maltese Falcon. Crime. Humphrey Bogart, Mary Astor, Peter Lorre, Sydney Greenstreet. The detective Sam Spade chases a rare bird. 1941. Directed by John Huston. MGM.

A Man for All Seasons. Drama. Paul Scofield, Robert Shaw, Orson Welles, Wendy Hiller. Thomas More, Chancellor of England, goes head-to-head (and eventually headless) with his king, Henry VIII, who seeks More's acquiescence to his plan to divorce Catherine of Aragon and marry Anne Boleyn. 1966. Directed by Fred Zinnemann. Columbia Tri-Star.

The Manchurian Candidate. Drama. Frank Sinatra, Laurence Harvey, Angela Lansbury, Janet Leigh. A Korean War veteran suspects that he and his men have been brainwashed when they were prisoners of war and that his friend has been programmed as an assassin. 1962. Directed by John Frankenheimer. MGM.

The Man Who Would Be King. Sean Connery, Michael Caine, Christopher Plummer. Two mercernary soldiers trek to Karifstan with a notion to take over the country and set themselves up as kings. 1975. Directed by John Huston. Fox.

Marty. Drama. Ernest Borgnine, Betsy Blair, Esther Minciotti, Joe De Santis. What do you want to do tonight? After long, bleak nights hanging out with his pals, a lonely bachelor finally finds love. 1955. Directed by Delbert Mann. MGM.

M.A.S.H. Comedy. Donald Sutherland, Elliott Gould, Tom Skerritt, Sally Kellerman. Surgeon and nurses like it madcap at an army surgical hospital during the Korean War. 1970. Directed by Robert Altman. Fox.

Mister Roberts. Comedy drama. Henry Fonda, James Cagney, Jack Lemmon, William Powell. The crew of a freighter floating around the Pacific during World War II battles boredom by making life miserable for its eccentric captain, who then returns the favor. 1955. Directed by John Ford and Mervyn LeRoy. Warner.

Mr. Smith Goes to Washington. Drama. James Stewart, Jean Arthur, Edward Arnold, Claude Rains, Thomas Mitchell. Taking over for an incapacitated Senator, an idealistic young fellow finds that everything isn't all that above board in the nation's Capitol. 1939. Directed by Frank Capra. Columbia Tri-Star.

Murder on the Orient Express. Mystery suspense. Albert Finney, Martin Balsam, Ingrid Bergman, Lauren Bacall, Sean Connery. Looking for a killer, Hercule Poirot sifts through a trainload of suspects on the famed run from Istanbul to Calais. Directed by Sidney Lumet, adapted from the story by Agatha Christie. 1974. Paramount.

Mutiny on the Bounty. Drama. Clark Gable, Franchot Tone, Charles Laughton. In 1788, Fletcher Christian and mates decide they've had it up to here with the sadistic Captain Bligh. 1935. Directed by Frank Lloyd. MGM.

My Brilliant Career. Drama. Judy Davis, Sam Neill, Wendy Hughes. A headstrong young Australian woman takes her life into her own hands, a gutsy thing to do at the turn of the century. 1979. Directed by Gillian Armstrong. Not in distribution.

Nashville. Drama. Keith Carradine, Lily Tomlin, Henry Gibson, Ronee Blakley, Keenan Wynn, Geraldine Chaplin. A roiling slice of American life is revealed through 24 characters attending a Nashville political convention. 1975. Directed by Robert Altman. Paramount. R.

National Lampoon's Animal House. Comedy. John Belushi, Tim Matheson, John Vernon, Donald Sutherland. From fraternity rush week to homecoming, every college ritual is given a thoroughly disgusting and perfectly hilarious going over in a classic satire. 1978. Directed by John Landis. Universal.

Network. Drama. Faye Dunaway, Peter Finch, William Holden, Robert Duvall. They're selling out on network television and an old anchorman is fed up and not going to take it anymore. 1976. Directed by Sidney Lumet. MGM.

A Night at the Opera. Comedy. The Marx Brothers. "Cosi Cosa" is but one of the arias as the brothers go wild in a large-scale spoof that at one point ends up in a very crowded closet. 1935. Directed by Sam Wood. MGM.

Norma Rae. Drama. Sally Field, Ron Leibman, Beau Bridges. A lowly textile worker gets her dander up and becomes a rousing labor organizer. 1979. Directed by Martin Ritt. Fox.

North by Northwest. Mystery suspense. Cary Grant, Eva Marie Saint, James Mason. Landing in some international intrigue, a smug advertising executive dangles from Mount Rushmore and, in one of the movie's most famous scenes, ducks a plane chasing him across a farm field. 1959. Directed by Alfred Hitchcock. MGM.

Nosferatu. Drama. Klaus Kinski, Isabelle Adjani, Bruno Ganz. It's a gentler, more reflective Count Dracula who seeks Lucy's neck in this highly stylized and beautifully scenic version of the vampire tale. 1979. Directed by Werner Herzog. Anchor Bay.

On the Waterfront. Drama. Marlon Brando, Lee J. Cobb, Rod Steiger, Eva Marie Saint, Karl Malden. An ex-fighter (yes, he should have been a contender) turned stevedore gets mixed up with gangsters on the New York docks. 1954. Directed by Elia Kazan. Columbia Tri-Star.

One Flew Over the Cuckoo's Nest. Drama. Jack Nicholson, Brad Dourif, Louise Fletcher, Will Sampson. A convict transferred to a mental hospital tries to rally the patients against a dominating nurse. 1975. Directed by Milos Forman, adapted from the novel by Ken Kesey. Republic.

Paper Moon. Drama. Ryan O'Neal, Tatum O'Neal, Madeline Kahn. A Bible-belt con man hooks up with a 9-year-old who turns out to be a sharper swindler than he is. 1973. Directed by Peter Bogdanovich. Paramount.

Papillon. Action drama. Steve McQueen, Dustin Hoffman. Prisoners check in but they don't check out of Devil's Island, the notorious French penal colony. Still, a wily convict and his swindler pal give escape a try. 1973. Directed by Franklin J. Schaffner. Fox.

The Philadelphia Story. Comedy. Katharine Hepburn, Cary Grant, James Stewart, Ruth Hussey. A woman's plans to remarry are thrown severely off-kilter with the reappearance of her former husband. 1940. Directed by George Cukor. MGM.

Picnic at Hanging Rock. Mystery suspense. Margaret Neslon, Rachel Roberts, Anne Lambert, Dominic Guard. In 1900 three Australian schoolgirls vanish from a picnic, never to be heard from again. 1975. Directed by Peter Weir. Home Vision.

The Pink Panther. Comedy. Peter Sellers, David Niven, Capucine, Robert Wagner, Claudia Cardinale. Sellers is a monumentally incompetent Inspector Clouseau, who can never quite catch up to an international jewel thief (and Clouseau's wife's lover). 1964. Directed by Blake Edwards. MGM.

Planet of the Apes. Action drama. Charlton Heston, Roddy McDowall, Kim Hunter, Maurice Evans. Astronauts crash on a planet in the first and best of a series in which humans play second fiddle to a supposedly superior breed. 1968. Directed by Franklin J. Schaffner. Fox.

The Pride of the Yankees. Drama. Cary Cooper, Teresa Wright, Babe Ruth, Walter Brennan. Lou Gehrig's career starts in 1923 and, including that 2,130 consecutive game streak, runs through his farewell statement in 1939. 1942. Directed by Sam Wood. Fox.

Rear Window. Mystery suspense. James Stewart, Grace Kelly, Thelma Ritter. Certain that he has detected a murder in his neighbor's apartment, a newspaper photographer endeavors to solve the crime himself. 1954. Directed by Alfred Hitchcock. Universal.

Rebecca. Mystery suspense. Joan Fontaine, Laurence Olivier, Judith Anderson, George Sanders. A young woman marries a man obsessed with the memory of his first wife. 1940. Directed by Alfred Hitchcock. Fox.

Rebel Without a Cause. Drama. James Dean, Natalie Wood, Sal Mineo. An alienated teenager who refuses to conform gets baited into a contest that ends in tragedy. 1955. Directed by Nicholas Ray. Warner.

The Red Shoes. Drama. Moira Shearer, Anton Walbrook, Marius Goring. When her company director disapproves of her relationship with a composer, a brilliant ballerina is torn between love and career. 1948. Directed by Michael Powell and Emeric Pressburger. Paramount.

The Road to Morocco. Comedy. Bob Hope, Bing Crosby, Dorothy Lamour, Anthony Quinn. In the third of the Hope-Crosby road movies (and the best), the boys vie for Lamour, continually having to rescue her from each other and finally a third suitor. 1942. Directed by David Butler. Universal.

Rocky. Action drama. Sylvester Stallone, Burgess Meredith, Talia Shire. Yes, it's that classic underdog, the kid from the slums of Philadelphia, slugging his way to the heavyweight crown in the first and by far the best film of the series. 1976. Directed by John G. Avildsen. MGM.

Romeo and Juliet. Drama. Olivia Hussey, Leonard Whiting. Of all the film versions of Shakespeare's tale, this one is still popular with young people. 1968. Directed by Franco Zeffirelli. Paramount.

Rosemary's Baby. Mystery suspense. Mia Farrow, John Cassavetes, Ruth Gordon. A pregnant woman discovers that she has fallen among witches and warlocks who claim her baby as the antichrist. 1968. Directed by Roman Polanski. Paramount. R.

Slap Shot. Action drama. Paul Newman, Michael Ontkean, Jennifer Warren, Lindsay Crouse. A grizzled old hockey coach gets the most out of a team of misfits by encouraging violence on the ice. Directed by George Roy Hill. Universal.

Sleeper. Comedy. Woody Allen, Diane Keaton. A nerd awakens to a whole new ball game after being frozen for 200 years. Smoking is now good for you (but the Volkswagen still starts). 1973. Directed by Woody Allen. MGM.

Smokey and the Bandit. Comedy. Burt Reynolds, Sally Field, Jackie Gleason. For fans of the car chase, here is one that lasts all movie long as a trucker bets he can take a cargo of beer from Texas to Atlanta in 28 hours. 1977. Directed by Hal Needham. Universal.

Some Like It Hot. Comedy. Jack Lemmon, Tony Curtis, Marilyn Monroe. Having witnessed the St. Valentine's Day massacre, two musicians flee by dressing in drag and joining an all-female band on a train bound for Florida. Then comes the good news: the band's gorgeous ukulele player (Monroe). Directed by Billy Wilder. MGM.

Spellbound. Mystery suspense. Gregory Peck, Ingrid Bergman, Leo G. Carroll. An amnesia victim accused of murder benefits from a little Freudian analysis. 1945. Directed by Alfred Hitchcock. Fox.

Stalag 17. Drama. William Holden, Don Taylor, Peter Graves. An arrogant, self-serving American in a German prisoner-of-war camp is suspected of informing on his fellows. 1953. Directed by Billy Wilder. Paramount.

Star Wars. Mark Hamill, Carrie Fisher, Harrison Ford, Alec Guinness. The first of the trilogy, and the sci-fi action film that changed special effects forever, pits rebel forces against Darth Vader and the galactic empire. 1977. Directed by George Lucas. Fox.

The Sting. Action drama. Paul Newman, Robert Redford, Robert Shaw. A couple of con artists spring a scam on a big-time racketeer. 1973. Directed by George Roy Hill. Universal.

A Streetcar Named Desire. Drama. Marlon Brando, Vivien Leigh, Kim Hunter, Karl Malden, Rudy Bond. Blanche Dubois has a problem cozying up to her sister's brutal husband, Stanley Kowalski, in a superb adaptation of Tennessee Williams's play. 1951. Directed by Elia Kazan. Fox.

The Sugarland Express. Drama. Goldie Hawn, Ben Johnson. When the authorities threaten to take away her baby, a young woman helps her husband break out of prison and the two of them take flight in a police cruiser with a cop as hostage. 1974. Directed by Steven Spielberg (his first film). Universal.

Sullivan's Travels. Comedy. Joel McRea, Veronica Lake, William Demarest, Robert Warwick. Tired of superficiality, a director of Hollywood comedies disguises himself as a hobo and, together with an unemployed actress, heads cross country in search of the real stuff for his next movie. 1941. Directed by Preston Sturges. Universal.

Superman: The Movie. Action adventure. Christopher Reeve, Margot Kidder, Marlon Brando, Gene Hackman. A baby from the doomed planet of Krypton becomes the man of steel in the first and best of four films based on the DC Comics hero. 1978. Directed by Richard Donner. Warner.

The Thin Man. Comedy. William Powell, Myrna Loy, Maureen O'Sullivan. In their first case, the gadfly detectives Nick and Nora Charles are hired to find an heiress's father. 1934. Directed by W.S. Van Dyke II. MGM.

The Third Man. Mystery suspense. Joseph Cotten, Orson Welles. A writer of pulp westerns goes to Vienna to work for an old friend only to find he has been murdered. Or so it would appear. 1949. Directed by Carol Reed. Various distributors.

The 39 Steps. Drama. Robert Donat, Madeleine Carroll, Godfrey Tearle. A Canadian in London is given a map of Scotland by a dying agent and then is pursued by the police, who want him for the agent's murder, and by foreign agents, who want the map. 1939. Directed by Alfred Hitchcock. Various distributors.

Tom Jones. Comedy. Albert Finney, Susannah York, Hugh Griffith, Edith Evans. In a wonderful adaptation of Henry Fielding's novel, a playful young rake makes his way through 18th-century England on his way to discovering his true ancestral connections. 1963. Directed by Tony Richardson. HBO.

To Kill a Mockingbird. Drama. Gregory Peck, Mary Badham, Brock Peters, Phillip Alford. During the 30's in Alabama, a widowed lawyer defends a black man accused of raping a white woman. 1962. Directed by Robert Mulligan. Universal.

Topkapi. Comedy. Melina Mercouri, Maxmillian Schell, Peter Ustinov, Robert Morley. Inept thieves go after the trove of jewels in Topkapi Palace. 1964. Directed by Jules Dassin, based on the novel by Eric Ambler. Fox.

The Treasure of the Sierra Madre. Drama. Humphrey Bogart, Walter Huston, Tim Holt. There's gold in them thar Mexican Hills, and a slew of murderous bandits, too. 1948. Directed by John Huston. MGM.

A Tree Grows in Brooklyn. Drama. Peggy Ann Garner, James Dunn, Dorothy McGuire, Joan Blondell. A bright young dreamer tries to outgrow her upbringing in the tenements. 1945. Directed by Elia Kazan. Various distributors.

Twelve Angry Men. Drama. Henry Fonda, Martin Balsam, Lee J. Cobb, E.G. Marshall, Jack Klugman. Only one of 12 jurors holds out for acquittal in a murder trial, but he has strong powers of persuasion. 1957. Directed by Sidney Lumet. Orion.

Twelve O'Clock High. Drama. Gregory Peck, Hugh Marlowe, Gary Merrill, Dean Jagger. The strain of commanding a bomber squadron takes its toll on its commanding officer, who begins to soften his stance as disciplinarian and identify with his men. 1949. Directed by Henry King. Fox.

Vertigo. Mystery suspense. James Stewart, Kim Novak. On the trail of an unstable woman, a detective's fear of heights takes him to the edge. 1958. Directed by Alfred Hitchcock. Universal.

Wuthering Heights. Drama. Laurence Olivier, Merle Oberon, David Niven, Geraldine Fitzgerald. An orphaned stable boy falls in love with the daughter of a Yorkshire family. She marries another, but their involvement carries on in perhaps the movies' greatest romance. 1939. Directed by William Wyler. HBO.

Young Frankenstein. Comedy. Gene Wilder, Peter Boyle, Marty Feldman, Madeline Kahn, Cloris Leachman, Teri Garr. Now the proprietor of the old family digs in Transylvania, a brain surgeon schemes to create his own monster. 1974. Directed by Mel Brooks. Fox.

Foreign (all films are subtitled)

Amarcord. Magali Noel, Bruno Zanin, Pupella Maggio, Armando Brancia. In Federico Fellini's autobiographical film, life burbles in an Italian town of about 1930. 1974. Italian. Home Vision.

Au Revoir Les Enfants. Gaspard Manesse, Raphael Fejto, Francine Racette. At a French boarding school a catholic boy befriends a Jewish student using an assumed name to hide from the Nazis. 1988. Directed by Louis Malle. French. Orion.

The Bicycle Thief. Lamberto Maggiorani, Enzo Staiola. When the bike he needs for his livelihood is stolen, a poor worker and his small son wander through Rome looking for the thief. 1949. Directed by Vittorio De Sica. Italian. Various distributors.

Big Deal on Madonna Street. Marcello Mastroianni, Vittorio Gassman, Claudia Cardinale. A gang of bumblers hilariously botch a jewel heist. 1958. Directed by Mario Monicelli. Italian. Various distributors.

Cinema Paradiso. Philippe Noiret, Jacques Perrin, Salavatore Cascio. In Italy during World War II, a small boy develops a love of film through a close friendship with the projectionist in the local movie house. 1988. Directed by Giuseppe Tornatore. Italian. HBO.

Das Boot. Juergen Prochnow, Herbert Gronemeyer, Klaus Wennemann. Life gets tense for a German U-boat crew far under the surface of the Atlantic in World War II. 1981. Directed by Wolfgang Petersen. German. Columbia Tri-Star.

Diva. Wilhelmenia Wiggins Fernandez, Frederic Andrei, Richard Bohringer. A messenger gets into trouble fit for an action movie after he surreptitiously tapes a famous opera singer. 1982. Directed by Jean-Jacques Beineix. French. MGM.

Eat Drink Man Woman. Sihung Lung, Kuei-Mei Yang, Yu-Wen Wang, Chien-Lien Wu. In a wry film with a comic touch, a widowed master chef who has lost his sense of taste copes with three quarrelsome daughters beset with their own personal problems. 1994. Directed by Ang Lee. Chinese. Hallmark.

Les Enfants du Paradis (Children of Paradise). Jean-Louis Barrault, Arletty, Pierre Brasseur, Maria Casares. In what many people consider the greatest film ever made (and made during the Nazi occupation of Paris), a mime falls in love with an actress and the mistress of a count. 1945. Directed by Marcel Carne. French. Home Vision.

Europa, Europa. Marco Hofschneider, Klaus Abramowsky, Michele Gleizer. A gutsy Jewish teenager escapes the Nazis by passing himself off as one and attending an elite Nazi academy. 1991. Directed by Agnieszka Holland. German and Russian. Orion.

Fanny and Alexander. Pernilla Allwin, Bertil Guve, Ewa Froling. A Swedish brother and sister flourish in a warm family setting but then must adjust when their father dies and their mother marries a dour clergyman. 1983. Directed by Ingmar Bergman. Swedish. Columbia Tri-Star.

The 400 Blows. Francois Truffaut, Jean-Pierre Leaud, Claire Maurier, Albert Remy. In a classic of French film, a 12-year-old has a terrible time growing up. 1959. Directed by Francois Truffaut. Home Vision.

Il Postino (The Postman). Massimo Troisi, Philippe Noiret, Maria Grazia Cucinotta, Linda Moretti. A postal clerk befriends the worldly exiled Chilean poet Pablo Neruda, who has been given asylum on tiny Isla Negra. 1994. Directed by Michael Radford. Italian. Touchstone.

Like Water for Chocolate. Lumi Cavazos, Marco Leonardi, Regina Torne. Using her mystical powers of cooking, the youngest of three Mexican daughters infects all who partake of her food with her own feelings of longing and passion. 1993. Directed by Alfonso Arau. Spanish. Touchstone. R.

My Life as a Dog. Anton Glanzelius, Tomas von Bromssen, Anki Liden. A difficult young boy fights to find acceptance and understand love when he is sent to live with relatives. 1985. Directed by Lasse Hallstrom. Swedish. Fox Lorber.

Tampopo. Tsutomu Yamakazi, Nobuko Miyamoto, Koji Yakusho. A mysterious stranger helps a widow develop a scrumptious recipe for her noodle shop. 1986. Directed by Juzo Itami. Japan. Republic.

The Tin Drum. David Bennent, Angela Winkler, Mario Adorf. A small boy survives the Nazis by never growing bigger and entertaining them with his shattering scream. 1979. Directed by Volker Schlöndorff, adapted from the novel by Gunter Grass. German. Kino. R.

The Wild Child. Jean-Pierre Cargol, François Truffaut, Jean Daste. A French doctor attempts to raise a boy found in the wilderness who has no knowledge of human life. 1970. Directed by François Truffaut. French. MGM.

Wings of Desire. Bruno Ganz, Solveig Dommartin, Otto Sander. As he watches over the citizens of war-torn Berlin, a guardian angel has a desire to live life as humans do. 1988. Directed by Wim Wenders. German. Orion.

Musicals

Bugsy Malone. Jodie Foster, Scott Baio, Florrie Augger. Shooting whipped cream instead of bullets, an all-kids cast spoofs 30's gangster movies. 1976. Directed by Alan Parker. Paramount.

Damn Yankees. Gwen Verdon, Tab Hunter, Ray Walston. An older guy contracts with the devil to become a baseball star. 1958. Directed by George Abbott and Stanley Donen. Warner.

Grease. John Travolta, Olivia Newton-John, Stockard Channing. A wholesome girl falls for a greaser, but where there's love there's a way. 1978. Directed by Randal Kleiser. Paramount.

Hair. Treat Williams, John Savage, Beverly D'Angelo. "Aquarius" and other 60's favorites blast out as flower children chafe under the threat of the Vietnam War. 1979. Directed by Milos Forman. MGM.

The King and I. Deborah Kerr, Yul Brynner, Rita Moreno. An English governess works her gentle, strong way on a dictatorial Siamese monarch and his children. 1956. Directed by Walter Lang. Fox.

My Fair Lady. Audrey Hepburn, Rex Harrison, Stanley Holloway. Professor Henry Higgins performs some remodeling on that scruffy flower girl. 1964. Directed by George Cukor. Fox.

Saturday Night Fever. John Travolta, Karen Gorney, Barry Miller. The film is very dated by now, but there are some great disco numbers as well as a good look at the early Travolta. 1977. Directed by John Badham. Paramount. R.

Singin' in the Rain. Gene Kelly, Donald O'Connor, Debbie Reynolds, Jean Hagen, Cyd Charisse, Rita Moreno. A 20's movie star adjusts to the talkies and romances a young actress, angering his co-star, who wants her for himself. 1953. Directed by Gene Kelly and Stanley Donen. MGM.

The Sound of Music. Julie Andrews, Christopher Plummer, Eleanor Parker, Peggy Wood, Angela Cartwright, Richard Haydn. The hills are alive as the Austrian von Trapp family, led by a singing nun turned governess, escape the Nazis and flee to Switzerland. 1965. Directed by Robert Wise. Fox.

That Thing You Do! Tom Hanks, Tom Everett Scott, Jonathon Schaech, Liv Tyler. After a substitute drummer adds some punch to a new song, a small-town group called The Wonders gets hot and climbs the charts. 1996. Directed by Tom Hanks. Fox.

West Side Story. Natalie Wood, Richard Beymer, Russ Tamblyn, Rita Moreno. Set to music by Leonard Bernstein, ethnic gang strife 50's style on New York's West Side feeds a love story loosely modeled after Romeo and Juliet. 1961. Directed by Robert Wise and Jerome Robbins. MGM.

Sci-Fi

The Adventures of Buckaroo Banzai. Peter Weller, Ellen Barkin, Jeff Goldblum, Christopher Lloyd, John Lithgow. Buckaroo rides a rocket-propelled Ford Fiesta through the eighth dimension to Planet 10, where he gets to use his vast intellectual powers against an evil ruler. 1984. Directed by W. D. Richter. Artisan.

Close Encounters of the Third Kind. Richard Dreyfuss, Teri Garr, Melinda Dillon. A power company employee comes across UFO's and tries to get at the truth behind the official cover-up. 1977. Directed by Steven Spielberg. Columbia Tri-Star.

Contact. Jodie Foster, Matthew McConaughey, James Woods, Tom Skerritt. A young scientist fights to be the first to go when signals from space turn out to be the plans for a ship that will carry Earthlings to a meeting with aliens. 1997. Directed by Robert Zemeckis. Warner.

E.T.: the Extra-Terrestrial. Henry Thomas, Dee Wallace Stone, Drew Barrymore. In one of the most popular films ever, a young boy bonds with a little space visitor. 1982. Directed by Steven Spielberg. Universal.

2001: A Space Odyssey. Keir Dullea, Gary Lockwood, William Sylvester, Dan Richter. A computer called Hal eventually runs the show on the famous space probe to Jupiter. 1968. Directed by Stanley Kubrick. MGM.

Westerns

Butch Cassidy and the Sundance Kid. Paul Newman, Robert Redford, Katharine Ross. The outlaws Butch and Sundance go on the run, eventually to Boliva, accompanied by the school marm who loves them both. 1969. Directed by George Roy Hill. Fox.

High Noon. Gary Cooper, Grace Kelly, Lloyd Bridges. A marshall stands tall—and alone—against gunmen who have come to kill him. 1952. Directed by Fred Zinnemann. Republic.

Little Big Man. Dustin Hoffman, Faye Dunaway, Chief Dan George. A 121-year-old scout recounts his life as a gunslinger, fake Indian, and the one white man to survive the Little Big Horn. 1970. Directed by Arthur Penn. Fox.

Maverick. Mel Gibson, Jodie Foster, James Garner. In a big-screen tribute to the old TV series, Bret Maverick goes gambling once again. 1994. Directed by Richard Donner. Warner.

McCabe and Mrs. Miller. Warren Beatty, Julie Christie, William Devane, Keith Carradine. The evasive McCabe runs a brothel with the help of Mrs. Miller until gunmen arrive on the scene to threaten the operation and make him take a stand. 1971. Directed by Robert Altman. Warner. R.

Red River. John Wayne, Montgomery Clift, Walter Brennan, Joanne Dru, John Ireland. In a classic of the genre, a two-fisted father wars with his son during and after a brutal cattle drive. 1948. Directed by Howard Hawks. MGM.

The Searchers. John Wayne, Natalie Wood, Jeffrey Hunter, Vera Miles, Ward Bond. A grizzled frontiersman spends seven years searching for his niece, who was kidnapped by Indians. 1956. Directed by John Ford. Warner.

Stagecoach. John Wayne, Claire Trevor, Thomas Mitchell, John Carradine, George Bancroft. The Ringo Kid takes over a stagecoach full of strangers besieged by Indians and bandits. 1939. Directed by John Ford. Warner.

Unforgiven. Clint Eastwood, Gene Hackman, Morgan Freeman, Richard Harris. An old gunfighter would just as soon be left alone to raise his pigs and his stepchildren, but the Schofield Kid lures him along on one last bounty hunt. 1992. Directed by Clint Eastwood. Warner. R.

The Wild Bunch. William Holden, Ernest Borgnine, Robert Ryan, Warren Oates. Facing obsolescence, a band of outlaws saddles up for a last hurrah. 1969. Directed by Sam Peckinpah. Warner.

Titles that Suit Special Interests

MULTICULTURAL / DIVERSITY

Age: 2–5

Age: 8–12

Age: 12–18

Adult/Parents

TITLES BEST FOR GIRLS

Age 2–5:

Age: 12–18

TITLES BEST FOR BOYS

Age: 2–5

Age: 5–8

Age: 8–12

Age: 12–18

DEALING WITH PROBLEMS, CONFLICT RESOLUTION

Age: 0–2

Age: 2–5

Age: 5–8

Age: 8–12

Age: 12–18

Producers, Addresses and Telephone Numbers

A BETTER WAY OF LEARNING, INC.
150 PAULARINO, STE. 120
COSTA MESA, CA 92626
www.abwol.com

A KID AT HEART PRODUCTIONS, INC.
4903 CRYSTAL LAKE DR.
GREENSBORO, NC 27410
800-70-KIDDY

ACORN MEDIA PUBLISHING INC.
7910 WOODMONT AVE., STE. 350
BETHESDA, MD 20814-3015
www.acornmedia.com

ACTION GAMES
6647 N. RIVER ROAD
GLENDALE, WI 53217

ACTIVE PARENTING PUBLISHERS
810-B FRANKLIN CT.
MARIETTA, GA 30067
800-625-0565
www.activeparenting.com

AIMS MULTIMEDIA
9710 DeSOTO AVE.
CHATSWORTH, CA 91311-4409
800-367-2467
http://www.aims-multimedia.com

ALA VIDEO/LIBRARY VIDEO NETWORK
320 YORK RD.
TOWSON, MD 21204-5179
800-441-TAPE

AMERICAN ACADEMY OF PEDIATRICS
141 NORTHWEST POINT BLVD.
ELK GROVE VILLAGE, IL 60007-1281
www.aap.org

AMERICAN HAPPENINGS
P.O. BOX 3636
LAGUNA HILLS, CA 92654

AMPHION COMMUNICATIONS
4701 NORTH FEDERAL HWY., STE
   301-C1
POMPANO BEACH, FL 33064
www.amphion-comm.com/baby/

ANCHOR BAY ENTERTAINMENT
500 KIRTS BLVD.;
TROY, MI 48084
800-745-1145
www.anchorbay.com

ANNE RICHARDSON PRODUC-
   TIONS
509 WEST 110TH ST., #6D
NEW YORK, NY 10025

APPLAUSE VIDEO
85 LONGVIEW RD.
PORT WASHINGTON, NY 11050-
   3099

APTE, INC.
1840 OAK AVE.
EVANSTON, IL 60201-3686
800-494-1112
www.apte.com

ARDEN MEDIA RESOURCES
1105 N. FRANKLIN
WILMINGTON, DE 19806
800-656-1338
www.familiesoftheworld.com

ARK MEDIA GROUP, LTD./NEW
   ERA MEDIA
425 ALABAMA ST.
SAN FRANCISCO, CA 94110
800-727-0009
sales@arkmedia.com

ARTISAN ENTERTAINMENT
2700 COLORADO AVE., 2ND
   FLOOR
SANTA MONICA, CA 90404
800-650-7099

ATTAINMENT COMPANY, INC.
504 COMMERCE PKWY.
VERONA, WI 53593-0160
800-327-4269
www.attainment-inc.com

AYLMER PRESS
1016 E. DAYTON ST., #2
MADISON, WI 53703
888-SIGN-IT2
www.signit2.com

AZURE BLUES, INC.
31900 FOXFIELD DR.
WESTLAKE VILLAGE, CA 91361
800-263-3737

B & D ENTERPRISES
1910 ZIPPER ST.
GARDEN CITY, KS 67846
888-283-6602
www.playalong.com

B.R.B. INTERNACIONAL,
S.A. AUT. GUENCARRAL-AL
MADRID, SPAIN 28049

BAMBOOLE
1702-H MERIDIAN, STE. 102
SAN JOSE, CA 95125

BANG ZOOM! ENTERTAINMENT
1800 RICHARD ST.
BURBANK, CA 91504

BARRY SIMON PRODUCTIONS
12229 HILLSLOPE ST.
STUDIO CITY, CA 91604

BC ENTERTAINMENT
6 ARROW RD., STE. 205
RAMSEY, NJ 07446

BIG HORSE PRODUCTIONS
124 LONGRIDGE RD.
WEST REDDING, CT 06896

BIG IDEA PRODUCTIONS
168 N. CLINTON ST., 6TH FLOOR
CHICAGO, IL 60661
www.bigidea.com

BIG KIDS PRODUCTIONS, INC.
1606 DWYER AVE.
AUSTIN, TX 78704
800-477-7811
www.awardvids.com

BLACKBOARD ENTERTAINMENT
2647 INTERNATIONAL BLVD.,
   STE. 853
OAKLAND, CA 94601
800-968-2261
www.blackboardkids.com

BLUE BYTE SOFTWARE
870 E. HIGGINS RD., STE. 143
SCHAUMBERG, IL 60173
www.bluebyte.com

BMG HOME VIDEO
1540 BROADWAY, 26TH FL.
NEW YORK, NY 10036

BO PEEP PRODUCTIONS, INC.
321 BEACH AVE.
INGLEWOOD, CA 90302

800-532-0420
www.bopeepproductions.com

BOHEM INTERACTIVE
2226 EASTLAKE AVE. EAST,
   STE. 61
SEATTLE, WA 98102

BONNEVILLE ENTERTAINMENT
55 NORTH 300 WEST, STE. 315
SALT LAKE CITY, UT 84110-1160
www.bwwe.com

BRAUN FILM AND VIDEO, INC.
46444 SPRINGWOOD CT.
STERLING, VA 20165

BRENTWOOD HOME VIDEO
31344 VIA COLINAS, STE. 106
WESTLAKE VILLAGE, CA 91362

BRENTWOOD MUSIC
1801 WEST END AVE., STE. 1100
NASHVILLE, TN 37203

BRIGHT IDEAS PRODUCTIONS
31220 LA BAYA DR., STE. 110
WESTLAKE VILLAGE, CA 91362
800-458-5887
www.brightideasproductions.com

BRODERBUND SOFTWARE
500 REDWOOD BLVD.
NOVATO, CA 94948-6125
800-521-6263
www.broder.com

BUENA VISTA HOME ENTER-
   TAINMENT
350 S. BUENA VISTA ST.
BURBANK, CA 91521-6556

BULLFROG FILMS
P.O. BOX 149
OLEY, PA 19547
800-543-3764
www.bullfrogfilms.com

CABIN FEVER ENTERTAINMENT
100 WEST PUTNAM AVE.
GREENWICH, CT 06830

CAN TOO! TAPES/BELLMAN
  GIRLS, L.L.C.
P.O. BOX 488
SCOTTSDALE, AZ 85252-0488
800-945-1002

CARPOOL PRODUCTIONS
145 VAN WINKLE DR.
SAN ANSELMO, CA 94960
800-998-7101

CARTER PRODUCTIONS
P.O. BOX 3537
BOULDER, CO 80307

CHARLES R. ROTHSCHILD
330 E. 48 ST.
NEW YORK, NY 10017
413-637-4210

CHICKEN FAT ENTERPRISES
P.O. BOX 687
ABERDEEN, NJ 07747
800-433-6769

CHILDREN'S CIRCLE
265 POST RD. WEST
WESTPORT, CT 06880
800-243-5020

CLEVER PRODUCTIONS
13 SUFFIELD CIRCLE
SALINAS, CA 93906

CLOVERNOOK COMMUNICA-
  TIONS
220 E. CLOVERNOOK LN.
FOX POINT, WI 53217

CNS COMMUNICATIONS
525 CAMINO MILITAR
SANTA FE, NM 87501

COGNITIVE TECHNOLOGIES
  CORP.
5009 CLOISTER DR.
ROCKVILLE, MD 20852
800-335-0781
www.cogtech.com

COLUMBIA TRI-STAR HOME
  VIDEO
10202 W. WASHINGTON BLVD.
CULVER CITY, CA 90232-3195

COMMUNITY MUSIC, INC.
7008 WESTMORELAND AVE.,
  STE. E-5
TAKOMA PARK, MD 20912
800-669-3942
www.folkmusic.com/cathymarcy

CONCEPT ASSOCIATES
4809 MORGAN DR.
CHEVY CHASE, MD 20815
800-333-8252

COOKOO PRODUCTION
11 LITTLE'S POINT
SWAMPSCOTT, MA 01907
800-720-4973

COREY LAKE PICTURES, INC.
30 WEST 21ST ST.
NEW YORK, NY 10010

CREATIVE STREET
3719 WASHINGTON BLVD.
INDIANAPOLIS, IN 46205
800-733-8273

CREATIVE WONDERS
595 PENOBSCOT DR.
REDWOOD CITY, CA 94063
800-543-9778

DANCE ADVENTURE ENTER-
TAINMENT
230 MASON ST.
GREENWICH, CT 06830
800-341-1620

DAVENPORT FILMS
11324 PEARLSTONE LN.
DELAPLANE, VA 20144

DAVID ALPERT ASSOCIATES,
INC.
611 WEST 111TH ST., #35
NEW YORK, NY 10025
800-265-7744

DEBECK EDUCATIONAL VIDEO
3873 AIRPORT WAY, BOX 9754
BELLINGHAM, WA 98227-9754

DEVINE ENTERTAINMENT CORP.
2 BERKELEY ST., STE. 504
TORONTO, ON M5A 2W3
CANADA
www.devine-ent.com

DIGITAL FROG INTERNATIONAL,
INC.
7377 CALFASS RD., RR#2
PUSLINCH, ON N0B2J0
CANADA
www.digitalfrog.com

DIGITAL GENERATION ENTER-
TAINMENT
1000 N. HALSTEAD
CHICAGO, IL 60622

DISCOVERY COMMUNICATIONS
7700 WISCONSIN AVE.
BETHESDA, MD 20814-3579

DISNEY INTERACTIVE
500 S. BUENA VISTA ST.
BURBANK, CA 91521-8096
www.disneyinteractive.com

DOLPHIN COMMUNICATIONS
18 BROADWAY
NIANTIC, CT 06357

DREAMING BIG PUBLISHING,
INC.
880 LEE ST., STE. 206-A
DES PLAINES, IL 60016
www.dreamingbig.com

DREAMS COME TRUE PRODUC-
TIONS
80 NORTH UNION ST.
ROCHESTER, NY 14607
800-297-8787

EARTHWALKER ENTERTAIN-
MENT
36726 NORTON CREEK RD.
P.O. BOX 505
BLODGETT, OR 97326

EDMARK
6727 185 AVE., NE
REDMOND, WA 98073-9721
800-426-0856
www.edmark.com

EDUCATIONAL ACTIVITIES, INC.
1937 GRAND AVE.
BALDWIN, NY 11510
800-645-3739
www.edact.com

EDVANTAGE MEDIA, INC.
12 FORREST AVE.
FAIR HAVEN, NJ 07704
800-375-5100
www.edvantagemedia.com

EL-KO INTERACTIVE, INC.
1341 N. DELAWARE AVE., #502
PHILADELPHIA, PA 15124
www.el-ko.com

ELBEE PRODUCTIONS
766 LANINA PL.
KIHEI, HI 96753

ELC PRODUCTIONS, LLC
2647 INTERNATIONAL BLVD.,
    STE. 853
OAKLAND, CA 94601
800-968-2261
www.blackboardkids.com

FAMILY CARE FOUNDATION
27636 YNEZ RD., BLDG. L7,
    STE. 220
TEMECULA, CA 92591
www.familycare.org

FAMILY COMMUNICATIONS,
    INC.
4802 FIFTH AVE.
PITTSBURGH, PA 15213
www.fci.org

FARMER SMALL PRODUCTIONS
415 CONCORD RD.
WESTON, MA 02493

FASE PRODUCTIONS
4801 WILSHIRE BLVD., STE. 215
LOS ANGELES, CA 90254
800-888-0600

FEATHERWIND PRODUCTIONS
5401 AUTUMN SPRINGS CT.
MUNCIE, IN 47304
800-288-5555
www.elmer.com

FIRST RUN FEATURES
153 WAVERLY PL.
NEW YORK, NY 10014

FIVE POINTS SOUTH PRODUC-
    TIONS
3108 MEMORY BROOK CIRCLE
BIRMINGHAM, AL 35242
800-714-4769

FOODPLAY PRODUCTIONS
221 PINE ST.
NORTHAMPTON, MA 01060
800-366-3752

FORWARD MOTION PICTURES,
    INC.
7090 UTICA LN.
CHANHASSEN, MN 55317

FRED LEVINE PRODUCTIONS, INC.
64 MAIN ST., STE. 26
MONTPELIER, VT 05602
800-843-3686

FUNIMATION PRODUCTIONS, INC.
6851 NE LOOP 820, STE. 247
FT. WORTH, TX 76180
www.FUNimation.net

GILBERT PAGE ASSOCIATES
174 LAKEVIEW AVE,
CAMBRIDGE, MA 02138

GIZMO GYPSIES
990 LINDEN DR.
SANTA CLARA, CA 95050
www.gizmogypsies.com

GLOBALSTAGE
465 CALIFORNIA, STE. 525
SAN FRANCISCO, CA 94104
888-324-5623

GOLDHIL HOME MEDIA
137 E. THOUSAND OAKS BLVD., STE. 207
THOUSAND OAKS, CA 91360

GOLDSHOLL: LEARNING VIDEOS
420 FRONTAGE RD.
NORTHFIELD, IL 60093
www.modelmasters.com

GOODTIMES HOME VIDEO
16 E. 40TH ST.
NEW YORK, NY 10016

GPN/READING RAINBOW
601 W. 50TH, 6TH FLOOR
NEW YORK, NY 10019
800-228-4630
gpn.unl.edu/rainbow.htm

GRANT-JACOBY
737 N. MICHIGAN AVE., 22ND FLOOR
CHICAGO, IL 60611
800-426-9400
www.grantjacoby.com

GREAT WAVE SOFTWARE
5353 SCOTTS VALLEY DR.
SCOTTS VALLEY, CA 95066
800-423-1144

GREAT WHITE DOG PICTURE CO.
10 TOON LN.
LEE, NH 03284

HEARTSONG COMMUNICA-TIONS
P.O. BOX 2455
GLENVIEW, IL 60025

HER INTERACTIVE
11808 NORTHUP WAY, STE. 350
BELLEVUE, WA 98005
www.herinteractive.com

HIGH PROFILES
BOX 161
CEDARBURG, WI 53012

HOMESPUN TAPES
P.O. BOX 694
WOODSTOCK, NY 12498
800-338-2737
www.homespuntapes.com

HORIZON FILM AND VIDEO
6200 LA CALMA, STE. 100
AUSTIN, TX 78752
800-540-2785
www.horizonvideo.com

HUGGABUG PRODUCTIONS, INC.
4048 LAS PALMAS WAY
SARASOTA, FL 34238

HUMONGOUS ENTERTAINMENT
3855 MONTE BELLA PKWY.
BOTHELL, WA 98021
www.humongous.com

I AM YOUR CHILD
335 N. MAPLE DR.
BEVERLY HILLS, CA 90210
www.iamyourchild.com

I CAN DO IT! PRODUCTIONS
3301A NE CORNELL RD.
HILLSBORO, OR 75204

IBM MULTIMEDIA
590 MADISON AVE.
NEW YORK, NY 10022
800-426-7235
www.ibm.com/pc/multimedia

IGUANA PRODUCTIONS
10101 COLLINS AVE., #10F
W. MIAMI BEACH, FL 33102
www.juanalaiguana.com

INFORMEDIA, INC.
26324 HUMBER
HUNTINGTON WOODS, MI 48070

INTERAMA, INC.
301 WEST 53RD ST., STE. 19E
NEW YORK, NY 10019-5774

IVN ENTERTAINMENT, INC.
1390 WILLOW PASS RD., STE. 900
CONCORD, CA 94520
www.ivn.com

IVY VIDEO
9 SW PACK SQUARE
ASHEVILLE, NC 28801

JIM HENSON HOME VIDEO
350 S. BUENA VISTA ST.
BURBANK, CA 91521-7141

JSK ENTERPRISES
6165 ZUMIREZ DR.
MALIBU, CA 90265

JUGGLEBUG
ONE SPORTIME WAY
ATLANTA, GA 30340

JUMPING FISH PRODUCTIONS
644 BROADWAY, LOFT 5E
NEW YORK, NY 10012

JUST FISH IT, INC.
108-A 20TH AVE. NORTH
INDIAN ROCKS BEACH, FL 33785

JUST FOR KIDS/CELEBRITY
  HOME VIDEO
22025 VENTURA BLVD., STE. 200
WOODLAND HILLS, CA 91364

JUST OUR SIZE VIDEOS
14010 FALLS RD.
COCKEYSVILLE, MD 21030

JUST PLANES VIDEOS
P.O. BOX 285214
BOSTON, MA 02128-5214
800-PLANES6
justplanes.com

KAROL MEDIA, INC.
P.O. BOX 7600
WILKES-BARRE, PA 18773
800-526-4773

KIDEO PRODUCTIONS, INC.
611 BROADWAY, STE. 523
NEW YORK, NY 10012
www.kideo.com

KIDQUEST
11886 GREENVILLE AVE., #112
DALLAS, TX 75243
800-687-2177
www.jayjay.com or www.wonder-wings.com

KIDS TREK PRODUCTIONS
5319 W. 120TH ST.
DEL AIRE, CA 90304
800-505-0303

KIDVIDZ
618 CENTRE ST.
NEWTON, MA 02158
800-840-8004
www.kidvidz.com

KIDZ-MED, INC.
P.O. BOX 490862
MIAMI, FL 33149-0862
www.kidzmed.com

KNOWLEDGE ADVENTURE
19840 PIONEER AVE.
TORRANCE, CA 90503
800-545-7677

LANGSTAFF VIDEO PROJECT
3421 N. 30TH ST.
TACOMA, WA 98407
510-453-9334

LANITUNES
4911 GUADALUPE TRAIL
ALBUQUERQUE, NM 87107

LAURIE HEPBURN PRODUC-
TIONS
449 MAIN ST.
RIDGEFIELD, CT 06877
800-275-9101

LEARNING THROUGH ENTER-
TAINMENT, INC.
3303 SOUTH NEW HOPE RD.
GASTONIA, NC 28052

LES PRODUCTIONS LA FETE/AN-
CHOR BAY
387 ST. PAUL WEST
MONTREAL, QUEBEC
CANADA, H2Y 287
info@lafet.com

LET'S CREATE, INC.
50 CHERRY HILL RD.
PARSIPPANY, NJ 07054
973-299-0633
www.letscreate.com

LIBRARY VIDEO NETWORK
7 E. WYNNEWOOD RD./P.O. BOX
580
WYNNEWOOD, PA 19096

LIFESTYLE VIDEO PRODUCTIONS
1298 SOUTHWEST 15TH ST.
BOCA RATON, FL 33486

LIGHTBRIDGE PRODUCTIONS
160 FUNSTON AVE.
SAN FRANCISCO, CA 94118

LIGHTYEAR ENTERTAINMENT
350 FIFTH AVE., STE. 5101
NEW YORK, NY 10118

LITTLE MAMMOTH MEDIA
750 RALPH McGILL BLVD. NE
ATLANTA, GA 30312
800-543-8433
www.littlemammoth.com

LITTLE ONE'S PRODUCTIONS
40 W. EASY ST., #4
SIMI VALLEY, CA 93065
888-566-BABY

LIVE WIRE MEDIA
3450 SACRAMENTO ST.
SAN FRANCISCO, CA 94118

LIVINGARTS
2434 MAIN ST.
SANTA MONICA, CA 90405

LYRICK STUDIOS
2435 NORTH CENTRAL EXPRESS-
   WAY, #1600
RICHARDSON, TX 75080-2722

M3D, INC.
15820 ARMINTA ST.
VAN NUYS, CA 91406
800-886-7763

MADE TO ORDER PRODUC-
   TIONS/RAINBOW
636 DEMING PL.
CHICAGO, IL 60614
www.mcs.net/~rainbow

MADE-FOR-DOG VIDEOS, INC.
2325 GIRARD AVE. S.
MINNEAPOLIS, MN 55405

MAXIMA NEW MEDIA
2472 BROADWAY, BOX 195
NEW YORK, NY 10025

MAZON PRODUCTIONS, INC.
3821 MEDFORD CIRCLE
NORTHBROOK, IL 60062
800-332-4344

MEDIA VENTURES VIDEO, INC.
1728 KENWOOD PKWY.
MINNEAPOLIS, MN 55405

MERITAGE PRODUCTIONS, INC.
100 LOCKERBIE LN.
WEST CHESTER, PA 19832

MGM/UA HOME ENTERTAIN-
   MENT
2500 BROADWAY
SANTA MONICA, CA 90404

MICROSOFT
MICROSOFT WAY
REDMOND, WA 98052

MIK PRODUCTIONS
6904 CONFEDERATE RIDGE LN.
CENTREVILLE, VA 22020
800-441-IFLY

MILESTONE MEDIA, INC.
4425 VILLA ESPERANZA
SANTA BARBARA, CA 93110

MINNESOTA ORCHESTRA VI-
SUAL ENTERTAINMENT
1111 NICOLET MALL
MINNEAPOLIS, MN 55403
888-MN-NOTES
wwww. mnorch.org

MONTEREY HOME VIDEO
566 ST. CHARLES DR.
THOUSAND OAKS, CA 91360-
3901
800-934-4336

MOTHER'S HELPER, INC.
3004 S. 9TH AVE.
SIOUX FALLS, SD 57105
www.iw.net/motrhelp

MUSIC FOR LITTLE PEOPLE
P.O. BOX 1460
REDWAY, CA 95560
800-346-4445

MUSIC RHAPSODY
1524 GATES AVE.
MANHATTAN BEACH, CA 90266
888-TRYMUSIC

MVP HOME ENTERTAINMENT,
INC.
9030 ETON AVE.
CANOGA PARK, CA 91304
888-325-0049
www.mvphomevideo.com

MY BABY AND ME EXERCISE,
INC.
1689 N. HIATUS RD., STE. 173

PEMBROKE PINES, FL 33026
888-741-BABY
www.mybabyandme.com

MYSTIC FIRE VIDEO
524 BROADWAY, STE. 604
NEW YORK, NY 10012
www.mysticfire.com

NATIONAL FILM BOARD OF
CANADA
350 FIFTH AVE., STE. 4820
NEW YORK, NY 10118
800-542-2164

NATIONAL GEOGRAPHIC/
WARNER HOME VIDEO
1145 17TH ST. NW
WASHINGTON, DC 20036-4688

NATIVE AMERICAN PUBLIC
TELECOMMUNICATIONS, INC
P.O. BOX 83111
LINCOLN, NB 68501

NEW DISCOVERIES, INC.
15717 OAKLAND AVE.
OAKLAND, FL 34760

NEW GAMES
P.O. BOX 1641 K
MENDOCINO, CA 95460
www.mcn.org/a/newgames/

NEW HORIZONS FOR LEARNING
2128 38TH AVE. EAST
SEATTLE, WA 98112

NEXUS MEDIA INTERNATIONAL
3025 W. OLYMPIC BLVD.
SANTA MONICA, CA 90404
www.nexusstudios.com

NICHOLS GALVIN PRODUCTIONS
110 WOOD ST.
BATAVIA, OH 45103

ORCHARD HILL PRODUCTIONS
2195 NW JACKSON CREEK DR.
CORVALLIS, OR 97330
800-811-5372

PANASONIC INTERACTIVE MEDIA
4701 PATRICK HENRY DR.
SANTA CLARA, CA 95054

PAPILLION PRODUCTIONS
553 HEADLANDS CT.
SAUSALITO, CA 94965

PARAGON MEDIA
55 S. ATLANTIC ST., STE. 200
SEATTLE, WA 98134
800-874-5547
www.paragongroup.com

PARAMOUNT HOME VIDEO
5555 MELROSE AVE.
HOLLYWOOD, CA 90038

PARENT POWER PRODUCTIONS,
  INC.
1493 FREEDOM CT.
GASTONIA, NC 28056

PATCH PRODUCTS, INC.
1400 E. INMAN PKWY.
BELOIT, WI 53511
800-524-4263

PAULINE BOOKS AND MEDIA
50 ST. PAUL'S AVENUE
BOSTON, MA 02130-3491
800-876-4463
www.pauline.org

PENTON OVERSEAS, INC.
2470 IMPALA DR.
CARLSBAD, CA 92008-7226

PFS STREETSMART
8 E. BROADWAY, STE. 200
SALT LAKE CITY, UT 84111

PHOENIX MEDIA
280 UTAH ST.
SAN FRANCISCO, CA 94103
800-700-3153

PIPHER FILMS, INC.
12 TOMAC AVE.
OLD GREENWICH, CT 06870

PLAZA ENTERTAINMENT
304 N. EDINBURGH
LOS ANGELES, CA 90048

POLYGRAM VIDEO
825 EIGHTH AVE.
NEW YORK, NY 10019

POSITIVE COMMUNICATIONS,
  INC.
9315 LARGO DR. WEST, STE.275
LARGO, MD 20774
www.poscomm.com

PPI ENTERTAINMENT GROUP
88 ST. FRANCIS ST.
NEWARK, NJ 07105
800-272-4214
www.peterpan.com

PRIMALUX VIDEO
30 W. 26TH ST.
NEW YORK, NY 10010

PRO KIDS PRODUCTIONS
1838 ELM HILL PIKE, STE. 127
NASHVILLE, TN 37201

PSI PRODUCTIONS
22 BRIGHAM HILL RD.
ESSEX JUNCTION, VT 05452

QUALITY MULTIMEDIA, LC.
2255 N. UNIVERSITY PKWY.,
  STE. 15-112
PROVO, UT 84604

QUARTET CREATIVE SERVICES
P.O. BOX 410835
SAN FRANCISCO, CA 94141-0835
800-859-5105

RABBIT EARS
  PRODUCTIONS/ABLESOFT
8550 REMINGTON AVE.
PENNSANKEN, NJ 08110
ablesoft@inc.com

RAINBOW COMMUNICATIONS
1276 SCHOOL RD.
VICTOR, NY 14564
www.farmkid.com

RAINDROP ENTERTAINMENT
111 N. RENGSTORFF, #26
MOUNTAIN VIEW, CA 94043

RAND MCNALLY NEW MEDIA
8255 N. CENTRAL PARK
SKOKIE, IL 60076

RANDOM HOUSE HOME VIDEO
201 EAST 50TH ST.
NEW YORK, NY 10022

REAL WORLD VIDEO
P.O. BOX 2465
GIG HARBOR, WA 98335

REMBRANDT FILMS
BALLYHOCK ROAD
BREWSTER, NY 10509

RMC INTERACTIVE
1753 NORTHGATE BLVD.
SARASOTA, FL 34234

ROSEBERRY ENTERTAINMENT
4452 ABBOTT AVE. S.
MINNEAPOLIS, MN 55410

ROSEWOOD PRODUCTIONS
712 CROSSWAY RD.
BURLINGAME, CA 94403

SABAN ENTERAINMENT
10960 WILSHIRE BLVD.
LOS ANGELES, CA 90024

SANDBOX HOME VIDEOS
4178 STURGEON CT.
SAN DIEGO, CA 92130

SCHLESSINGER MEDIA
7 E. WYNNEWOOD RD.
WYNNEWOOD, PA 19096-0580
800-843-3620
www.libraryvideo.com

SCHOLASTIC/MICROSOFT
524 BROADWAY, 5TH FLOOR
NEW YORK, NY 10012

SEA STUDIOS
810 CANNERY ROW
MONTEREY, CA 93940

SEGMENTS OF KNOWLEDGE,
  INC.
424 NORTH CALHOUN ST.
TALLAHASSEE, FL 32301
800-816-6463

SHADOWPLAY RECORDS &
  VIDEO
4412 SPICEWOOD SPRINGS RD.,
  STE. 200
AUSTIN, TX 78759
800-274-8804

SHORT STUFF ENTERTAINMENT
5520 14TH AVE. SOUTH
MINNEAPOLIS, MN 55417

SIDEWALK PRODUCTIONS
P.O. BOX 25154
PORTLAND, OR 97298
www.sidewalkfun.com

SIGN ENHANCERS, INC
P.O. BOX 12687
SALEM, OR 97309
800-767-4461
www.teleport.com/~sign

SMALL FRY PRODUCTIONS
1200 ALPHA DR., STE. B
ALPHARETTA, GA 30004
800-521-5311
www.ftsbn.com/~smallfry

SMALL WORLD PRODUCTIONS
21 HOLDEN RD.
BELMONT, MA 02478-2221

SOBO VIDEO PRODUCTIONS,
  INC.
7002F GOLDEN RING RD.
BALTIMORE, MD 21237-3076
www.sobovideo.com

SONY CLASSICAL
550 MADISON AVE., 16TH FLOOR
NEW YORK, NY 10022-3211

SONY WONDER
2100 COLORADO AVE.
SANTA MONICA, CA 90404

SOS VIDEOS, INC.
1000 N. LAKE SHORE PLAZA,
  #53B
CHICAGO, IL 60611

SOUND BEGINNINGS
123 WORLD TRADE CENTER
  P.O. BOX 420726
DALLAS, TX 75342

SPOON MAN, INC.
P.O. BOX 53
JENISON, MI 49429
www.getspooned.com

STEEPLECHASE ENTERTAIN-
  MENT
4872 TOPANGA CANYON BLVD.,
  STE. 347
WOODLAND HILLS, CA 91364
www.brainplay.com

STORIES TO
  REMEMBER/JOSHUA M.
  GREENE PRODUCTIONS
P.O. BOX 311
OLD WESTBURY, NY 11568
www.hanuman.org

SUNBURST COMMUNICA-
TIONS/HOUGHTON MIFFLIN
101 CASTLETON ST.
PLEASANTVILLE, NY 10570

SUPERIOR PROMOTIONS/HOME
VIDEO, INC.
22159 N. PEPPER RD., STE. 9
BARRINGTON, IL 60010
www.superiorvideo.com

SYRACUSE LANGUAGE
5790 WIDEWATERS PKWY.
SYRACUSE, NY 13214
www.languageconnect.com

TAWELL-LOOS & CO.
4024 RADFORD AVE.
STUDIO CITY, CA 91604-2101

THE BABY EINSTEIN COMPANY
10840 BOBCAT TERRACE
LITTLETON, CO 80124
800-793-1454
www.babyeinstein.com

THE BABY SCHOOL COMPANY
P.O. BOX 330341
COCONUT GROVE, FL 33233-
0341
800-663-2741
www.sosmart.com

THE CHILDREN'S GROUP
7-1400 BAYLY ST.
PICKERING, ONTARIO L1W 3R2
CANADA
www.childrengroup.com

THE IDEA BANK
1139 APS
SANTA BARBARA, CA 93103
800-621-1136
www.theideabank.com

THE ITSY BITSY ENTERTAIN-
MENT CO.
156 FIFTH AVE.
NEW YORK, NY 10010
www.tibeco.com

THE JUDY THEATRE
37 FOUNTAIN ST.
SAN FRANCISCO, CA 94114

THE LEARNING CO.
6493 KAISER DR.
FREMONT, CA 94555
800-227-5609
www.learningco.com

THE MULTIMEDIA GROUP, INC.
2425 GOLF LAKE CIRCLE, #5221
MELBOURNE, FL 32935
800-338-7855

THE PAPER BAG PLAYERS
50 RIVERSIDE DR.
NEW YORK, NY 10024

THE RICHARDS GROUP
8750 N. CENTRAL EXPRESSWAY,
13TH FLOOR
DALLAS, TX 75231

THE SMARTZ FACTORY, LTD.
401 BEDFORD ST.
RICHARDSON, TX 75080

THE STARDOM COMPANY, LTD.
4626 W. DEER RUN DR., #103
BROWN DEER, WI 53223
800-368-2278
www.execpc.com/-byb

THINK MEDIA
ONE LEXINGTON AVE.
  1ST FLOOR
NEW YORK, NY 10010

THURSTON JAMES
15136 HARTSOOK ST.
SHERMAN OAKS, CA 91403
www.webaccess.com/santa

TIME-LIFE KIDS
2000 DUKE ST.
ALEXANDRIA, VA 22314
800-TIME-VID

TODDLER TALES
15030 VENTURA BLVD.,
  STE 22-854
SHERMAN OAKS, CA 91403
www.toddlertales.com

TONY ARTZ SUPREME VIDEO
  WORKS
230 LONETOWN RD.
REDDING, CT 06896

TOP SHELF PRODUCTIONS
62 UNION AVE.
NEPTUNE CITY, NJ 07753

TOW TRUCK PRODUCTIONS
P.O. BOX 1165
CONCORD, MA 01742

TWENTIETH CENTURY FOX
  HOME ENTERTAINMENT
2121 AVE. OF THE STARS, 25TH
  FLOOR
LOS ANGELES, CA 90067

TYCO TOYS, INC.
6000 MIDLANTIC DR.
MT. LAUREL, NJ 08054

TYNDALE HOUSE PUBLISHERS
351 EXECUTIVE DR., BOX 80
WHEATON, IL 60189-0080

UBI SOFT ENTERTAINMENT
5505 ST. LAURENT BLVD., STE.
  4204
MONTREAL, PQ
CANADA H2T 1S6
www.ubisoft.com

UNAPIX/MIRAMAX
200 2ND AVE. W.
SEATTLE, WA 98119

UNIVERSAL STUDIOS HOME
  VIDEO
70 UNIVERSAL CITY PLAZA, #435
UNIVERSAL CITY, CA 91608-4912

V.I.E.W. VIDEO
34 EAST 23RD ST.
NEW YORK, NY 10010
800-843-9843
www.view.com

VERMONT STORY WORKS
1606 DYWER AVE.
AUSTIN, TX 78704
800-206-8383

VIACOM NEW MEDIA
1515 BROADWAY
NEW YORK, NY 10036

VIDEO INFORMATION SOURCE
3395 SOUTH JONES BLVD., #212
LAS VEGAS, NV 89146
800 557 3772

VIDEO TREASURES, INC.
500 KIRTS BLVD.
TROY, MI 48084
800-362-9660

VIDEO VACATIONS
306 WEST AVE.
LOCKPORT, NY 14094

VINEYARD VIDEO PRODUC-
   TIONS
BOX 370 8 ELIAS LN.
WEST TISBURY, MA 02575
800-664-6119

VIRGIN INTERACTIVE
18061 FITCH AVE.
IRVINE, CA 92614

WABU-TV 68
1660 SOLDIERS FIELD
BOSTON, MA 02135

WALT DISNEY PICTURES
350 S. BUENA VISTA ST.
BURBANK, CA 91521

WARNER BROS. FAMILY ENTER-
   TAINMENT
3903 OLIVE AVE., ROOM. 3148
BURBANK, CA 91505
www.warnerbros.com

WATERFORD INSTITUTE
1590 E. 9400 S.
SANDY, UT 84093

WESTERN PUBLISHING
   CO/GOLDEN BOOKS VIDEO
5945 ERIE ST.
RACINE, WI 53404

WESTHILL PRESS INC.
FISCHER HILL
FITZWILLIAM, NH 03447

WGBH/BOSTON
125 WESTERN AVE.
BOSTON, MA 02134
www.wgbh.org

WHITE STAR VIDEO
195 HIGHWAY #36
WEST LONG BEACH, NJ 07764

WHITE TREE PICTURES, INC.
P.O. BOX 55113
SHERMAN OAKS, CA 91413
800-981-7813
http://www.venture818.com

WHITEBIRD, INC.
300 COUNTY RD.
NEW LONDON, NH 03251

XENON ENTERTAINMENT
   GROUP
1440 NINTH ST.
SANTA MONICA, CA 90401
800-829-1913

ZEEZEL PIXS
1524 PORTIA ST.
LOS ANGELES, CA 90026
800-200-3688

Index